Lecture Notes in Computer Sci

Commenced Publication in 1973
Founding and Former Series Editors:
Gerhard Goos, Juris Hartmanis, and Jan van Leeuwen

Jin Kwak   Robert H. Deng   Yoojae Won
Guilin Wang (Eds.)

Information Security
Practice
and Experience

6th International Conference, ISPEC 2010
Seoul, Korea, May 12-13, 2010
Proceedings

 Springer

Volume Editors

Jin Kwak
Soonchunhyang University
Department of Information Security Engineering
646 Eupnae-ri, Shinchang-myun, Asan-si, Chungcheongnam-do, 336-745, Korea
E-mail: jkwak@sch.ac.kr

Robert H. Deng
Singapore Management University
School of Information Systems
469 Bukit Timah Road, 259756, Singapore
E-mail: robertdeng@smu.edu.sg

Yoojae Won
Korea Internet and Security Agency
Internet and Security Policy Division
Daedong B/D, Garak-dong 79-3, Songpa-gu, Seoul, 138-950, Korea
E-mail: yjwon@kisa.or.kr

Guilin Wang
University of Birmingham
School of Computer Science
Birmingham, B15 2TT, UK
E-mail: g.wang@cs.bham.ac.uk

Library of Congress Control Number: 2010925440

CR Subject Classification (1998): E.3, K.6.5, D.4.6, C.2, J.1, K.4.4

LNCS Sublibrary: SL 4 – Security and Cryptology

ISSN   0302-9743
ISBN-10   3-642-12826-2 Springer Berlin Heidelberg New York
ISBN-13   978-3-642-12826-4 Springer Berlin Heidelberg New York

springer.com

© Springer-Verlag Berlin Heidelberg 2010
Printed in Germany

Typesetting: Camera-ready by author, data conversion by Scientific Publishing Services, Chennai, India
Printed on acid-free paper   06/3180

Preface

The 6th International Conference on Information Security Practice and Experience (ISPEC 2010) was held in Seoul, Korea, May 12–13, 2010.

The ISPEC conference series is an established forum that brings together researchers and practitioners to provide a confluence of new information security technologies, including their applications and their integration with IT systems in various vertical sectors. In previous years, ISPEC has taken place in Singapore (2005), Hangzhou, China (2006), Hong Kong, China (2007), Sydney, Australia (2008), and Xi'an, China (2009). For all sessions, as this one, the conference proceedings were published by Springer in the *Lecture Notes in Computer Science* series.

In total, 91 papers from 18 countries were submitted to ISPEC 2010, and 28 were selected for inclusion in the proceedings (acceptance rate 30%). The accepted papers cover multiple topics of information security and applied cryptography. Each submission was anonymously reviewed by at least three reviewers. We are grateful to the Program Committee, which was composed of more than 56 well-known security experts from 16 countries; we heartily thank them as well as all external reviewers for their time and valued contributions to the tough and time-consuming reviewing process.

The conference was hosted by Soonchunhyang University, Korea, supported by Korea Internet & Security Agency (KISA), Korea; Electronics and Telecommunications Research Institute (ETRI), Korea, in Corporation with Korea Institute of Information Security & Cryptography (KIISC), Korea, and sponsored by Korea Communications Commission (KCC), Korea. We sincerely thank the Honorary Chair and the General Chairs of ISPEC 2010 for their strong support. We also thank the System Management Chair for managing the conference website, and the Organizing Chair and Committee for dealing with local issues.

There are many people who contributed to the success of ISPEC 2010. We would like to thank all authors from around the world for submitting and presenting their papers. We are deeply grateful to the Program Committee members for their fair review. It would have been impossible to organize ISPEC 2010 without the hard work of all our Chairs and Committees. Finally, we would like to thank all the participants for their contribution to ISPEC 2010.

May 2010

Jin Kwak
Robert H. Deng
Yoojae Won
Guilin Wang

ISPEC 2010

6th International Conference
on Information Security Practice and Experience

Seoul, Korea
May 12–13, 2010

Hosted by

Soonchunhyang University, Korea

Supported by

Korea Internet & Security Agency (KISA), Korea
Electronics and Telecommunications Research Institute (ETRI), Korea

In Corporation with

Korea Institute of Information Security & Cryptography (KIISC), Korea

Sponsored by

Korea Communications Commission (KCC), Korea

Honorary Chair

Heejung Kim — Korea Internet & Security Agency (KISA), Korea

General Chairs

Heung Youl Youm — Soonchunhyang University, Korea
Jong in Im — Korea University, Korea
Feng Bao — Institute for Infocomm Research (I^2R), Singapore

Program Chairs

Jin Kwak — Soonchunhyang University, Korea
Robert H. Deng — Singapore Management University, Singapore
Yoojae Won — Korea Internet & Security Agency (KISA), Korea

Program Committee

Joonsang Baek — Institute for Infocomm Research (I^2R), Singapore
Kefei Chen — Shanghai Jiaotong University, China
Liqun Chen — Hewlett-Packard Laboratories, UK

Hyoung-Kee Choi	Sungkyunkwan University, Korea
Debbie Cook	Telcordia, USA
Xuhua Ding	Singapore Management University, Singapore
Clemente Galdi	Università di Napoli "Federico II", Italy
David Galindo	University of Luxembourg, Luxembourg
Dong-Guk Han	Kookmin University, Korea
N. Jaisankar	VIT University, India
Stefan Katzenbeisser	Technical University of Darmstadt, Germany
Hyong-Shik Kim	Chungnam National University, Korea
Jeasung Kim	Korea Internet & Security Agency (KISA), Korea
Rack-Hyun Kim	Soonchunhyang University, Korea
Xuejia Lai	Shanghai Jiao Tong University, China
Deok Gyu Lee	ETRI, Korea
Sunyoung Lee	Soonchunhyang University, Korea
Yunho Lee	Sungkyunkwan University, Korea
Tieyan Li	Institute for Infocomm Research (I^2R), Singapore
Yingjiu Li	Singapore Management University, Singapore
Benoît Libert	Universite Catholique de Louvain, Belgium
Chae Hoon Lim	Sejong University, Korea
Dongdai Lin	SKLOIS, Chinese Academy of Sciences, China
Masahiro Mambo	University of Tsukuba, Japan
Atsuko Miyaji	JAIST, Japan
Yi Mu	University of Wollongong, Australia
Nhut Nguyen	Samsung Telecommunications America, USA
SooHyun Oh	Hoseo University, Korea
Daniel Page	University of Bristol, UK
Namje Park	UCLA, USA
Raphael C.-W. Phan	Loughborough University, UK
C. Pandu Rangan	Indian Institute of Technology Madras, India
Mark Ryan	University of Birmingham, UK
Jorge Villar Santos	UPC, Spain
Hee Suk Seo	Korea University of Technology and Education, Korea
SeongHan Shin	AIST, Japan
Alice Silverberg	University of California, Irvine, USA
Kyungho Son	Korea Internet & Security Agency (KISA), Korea
Willy Susilo	University of Wollongong, Australia
Tsuyoshi Takagi	Future University Hakodate, Japan
Toshiaki Tanaka	KDDI R&D Laboratories Inc., Japan
Zhiguo Wan	Tsinghua University, China
Huaxiong Wang	Nanyang Technological University, Singapore
Lina Wang	Wuhan University, China

Duncan Wong	City University of Hong Kong, Hong Kong
Yongdong Wu	Institute for Infocomm Research (I^2R), Singapore
Chaoping Xing	Nanyang Technological University, Singapore
Wei Yan	Trendmicro, USA
Chung-Huang Yang	National Kaohsiung Normal University, Taiwan
Wansuck Yi	Korea Internet & Security Agency (KISA), Korea
Yunlei Zhao	Fudan University, China
Fangguo Zhang	Sun Yat-Sen University, China
Rui Zhang	AIST, Japan
Jianying Zhou	Institute for Infocomm Research (I^2R), Singapore
Bo Zhu	Concordia University, Canada
Huafei Zhu	Institute for Infocomm Research (I^2R), Singapore

Publication Chair

Guilin Wang	University of Birmingham, UK

Organizing Committee Chair

Ji Hong Kim	Semyung University, Korea

Organizing Committee

JaeCheol Ha	Hoseo University, Korea
Jongsoo Jang	ETRI, Korea
Hyuncheol Jeong	KISA, Korea
DaeHun Nyang	Inha University, Korea
Dong Gue Park	Soonchunhyang University, Korea
Gwangsoo Rhee	Sookmyung Women's University, Korea
Jeong-Mo Yang	Joongbu University, Korea
Kangbin Yim	Soonchunhyang University, Korea

System Management Chairs

Min Hong	Soonchunhyang University, Korea
Sang-Soo Yeo	Mokwon Univeristy, Korea

External Reviewers

Jianhong Chen
Xiaofeng Chen
Donghyun Choi
Hyunwoo Choi
Sherman Chow
C. Clough
Ton van Deursen
Oriol Farras
Ge Fu
Woong Go
Zheng Gong
Hui-Ting Hsieh
Qiong Huang
JoungYoun Hwang
Moonyoung Hwang
Jaehoon Jang
Heasuk Jo
HeeSeok Kim
Jongsung Kim
Junsub Kim
Woo Kwon Koo
Noboru Kunihiro
Hidenori Kuwakado
Taekyoung Kwon
Fabien Laguillaumie
Junzuo Lai
Byunghee Lee

Dongbum Lee
Jesang Lee
Kwangwoo Lee
Youngsook Lee
Yan Li
Joseph Liu
Yiyuan Luo
Xianping Mao
Takahiro Matsuda
Chihiro Ohyama
Daesick Park
Mathieu Renauld
Francesco Sica
Chunhua Su
Koutarou Suzuki
Qiang Tang
Isamu Teranishi
Jie Wang
Yongtao Wang
Baodian Wei
Jian Weng
Kuo-Hui Yeh
Dongu Yeo
TaeYoung Youn
Mingwu Zhang
Benwen Zhu
Bo Zhu

Table of Contents

Cryptanalysis

Algorithms and Implementations (I)

Algorithms and Implementations (II)

Network Security

Access Control

Identity Management

Trust Management

Public Key Cryptography

Security Applications

Improved Related-Key Boomerang Attacks on Round-Reduced Threefish-512*

Jiazhe Chen and Keting Jia

Key Laboratory of Cryptologic Technology and Information Security, Ministry of
Education, Shandong University, Jinan 250100, China
{jiazhechen,ketingjia}@mail.sdu.edu.cn

Abstract. Hash function Skein is one of the 14 NIST SHA-3 second
round candidates. Threefish is a tweakable block cipher as the core of
Skein, defined with a 256-, 512-, and 1024-bit block size. The 512-bit
block size is the primary proposal of the authors. Skein had been updated after it entered the second round; the only difference between
the original and the new version is the rotation constants. In this paper we construct related-key boomerang distinguishers on round-reduced
Threefish-512 based on the new rotation constants using the method of
modular differential. With these distinguishers, we mount related-key
boomerang key recovery attacks on Threefish-512 reduced to 32, 33 and
34 rounds. The attack on 32-round Threefish-512 has time complexity
2^{195} with memory of 2^{12} bytes. The attacks on Threefish-512 reduced to
33 and 34 rounds have time complexity of $2^{324.6}$ and $2^{474.4}$ encryptions
respectively, and both with negligible memory. The best key recovery
attack known before is proposed by Aumasson et al. Their attack, which
bases on the old rotation constants, is also a related-key boomerang attack. For 32-round Threefish-512, their attack requires 2^{312} encryptions
and 2^{71} bytes of memory.

Keywords: Threefish-512, related-key boomerang attack, modular
differential.

1 Introduction

Cryptographic hash functions play a very important role in cryptology. With the
break of MD5 and SHA-1 [14][15], the situation of the hash functions becomes
alarming. Although no flaws of SHA-2 have been found, SHA-2 still has the same
structure and design principle as MD5 and SHA-1. To deal with the undesirable
situation, NIST held a hash competition for a new hash standard(SHA-3). At
this time, 56 out of 64 submissions to the SHA-3 competition are publicly known
and available. There are 51 submissions in the first round and 14 submissions
have entered the second round. Skein [10] is one of the second-round candidates,
bases on the tweakable block cipher Threefish, which is defined with a 256-, 512-,

---

* Supported by 973 Program of China (Grant No.2007CB807902) and National Outstanding Young Scientist fund of China (Grant No. 60525201).

J. Kwak et al. (Eds.): ISPEC 2010, LNCS 6047, pp. 1–18, 2010.

Table 1. Existing Key Recovery Attacks on Round Reduced Threefish-512

Attack	#rounds	#keys	time	memory	source
related-key key recovery*	25	2	$2^{416.6}$	–	[1]
related-key key recovery*	26	2	$2^{507.8}$	–	[1]
related-key boomerang key recovery*	32	4	2^{312}	2^{71}	[1]
related-key boomerang key recovery	32	4	2^{195}	2^{12}	Section 4
related-key boomerang key recovery	33	4	$2^{324.6}$	–	Section 5
related-key boomerang key recovery	34	4	$2^{474.4}$	–	Section 5

* results based on the old rotation constants

1024-bit block size and 72, 72, 80 rounds respectively. After getting into the second round, the authors changed the rotation constants [11]. In this paper, we will focus on Threefish-512 with the new rotation constants.

In paper [1], Aumasson et al. presented several results on Skein-512 and Threefish-512, all the results are based on the original constants. They gave a known-related-key 35-round boomerang distinguisher on threefish-512, but they had only given a key recovery attack of 32 rounds. The difference they used is the XOR difference and they used the algorithms in [9] to find the differentials of their attacks. Their attacks can be applied for the new rotations as well, with new differential trails and different probabilities.

We use another kind of difference, i.e. modular differential and use the method of Wang et al. [13,14] to construct modular differential paths. Then we use the modular differential to construct the boomerang distinguishers based on the new rotation constants. The use of modular differential is essential as the modular differential has advantages against the XOR differential for attacking Threefish. With the modular differential, we can get differential trails with much higher probability. Furthermore, we can get many trails with the same probability, so we can get boomerang distinguishers with much higher probability. The results are summarized in Table 1.

This paper is organized as follows. In Section 2.2, we give a brief description of Threefish. The related-key boomerang attack is described in section 3. Section 4 and Section 5 give our main attacks. Finally, we give the conclusion in Section 6.

2   Preliminaries and Notations

In this section, we first list some notations used in this paper, then give brief descriptions of Threefish.

2.1   Notations

- $\Delta x = x' - x$: the word difference
- $\Delta x_{j-1} = x'_{j-1} - x_{j-1} = \pm 1$: the signed bit-wise difference that is produced by changing the j-th bit of x (for $j = 1, \ldots, 64$). $x[j]$, $x[-j]$ are the resulting values by only changing the j-th bit of the word x. $x[j]$ is obtained by changing the j-th bit of x from 0 to 1, and $x[-j]$ is obtained by changing the j-th bit of x from 1 to 0.

- $x[\pm j_1, \pm j_2, \ldots, \pm j_l]$: the value by changing j_1-th, j_2-th, $\ldots$, j_l-th bits of x. The sign "+" (usually is omitted) means that the bit is changed from 0 to 1, and the sign "−" means that the bit is changed from 1 to 0. We use it to represent the signed bit-wise difference of Δx.
- $\mathcal{K}_1, \mathcal{K}_2, \mathcal{K}_3, \mathcal{K}_4$: four related keys, all of them are 512 bits and composed of eight 64-bit words
- Δ_k^1, Δ_k^2: word-wise differences of the keys
- T_1, T_2, T_3, T_4: four related tweak values, all of them are 128 bits and composed of two 64-bit words
- Δ_t^1, Δ_t^2: word-wise differences of the tweaks
- $\alpha, \beta, \gamma, \zeta, \eta$: 512-bit differences, composed by eight 64-bit words
- k_d: the $(d+1)$-th word of a subkey $(0 \le d \le 7)$
- $k_{s,d}$: the $(d+1)$-th word of the $(s+1)$-th subkey$(0 \le s \le 18, 0 \le d \le 7)$
- $k_{s,d,j}$: the $(j+1)$-th bit of the $(d+1)$-th word of the $(s+1)$-th subkey $(0 \le s \le 18, 0 \le d \le 7, 0 \le j \le 63)$
- P_i: $(i = 1, 2, 3, 4)$ 512-bit plaintext, composed by eight 64-bit words
- C_i: $(i = 1, 2, 3, 4)$ 512-bit ciphertext, composed by eight 64-bit words
- $p_{i,j}$: the $(j+1)$-th word of P_i $(j = 0, \ldots, 7)$
- $c_{i,j}$: the $(j+1)$-th word of C_i $(j = 0, \ldots, 7)$
- MSB: the most significant bit.

2.2   Brief Description of Threefish

The following notions are the same as those in [11]. The word size which Threefish operates on is 64 bits. Let N_w denotes the number of words in the key and the plaintext, N_r be the number of rounds. For Threefish-512, $N_w = 8$ and $N_r = 72$. Let $v_{d,i}$ be the value of the ith word of the encryption state after d rounds. The procedure of encryption is:

$$v_{0,i} = p_i \text{ for } i = 0, \ldots, N_w - 1,$$

where p_i is a 64-bit word and $(p_0, \ldots, p_{N_w-1})$ is the 512-bit plaintext.

For each round, we have:

$$e_{d,i} = \begin{cases} (v_{d,i} + k_{d/4,i}) \bmod 2^{64} & \text{if } d \bmod 4 = 0, \\ v_{d,i} & \text{otherwise.} \end{cases}$$

Where $k_{d/4,i}$ is the i-th word of the subkey added to the d-th round. For $i = 0, \ldots, N_w - 1$, $d = 0, \ldots, N_r - 1$. Then mixing and word permutations followed:

$$(f_{d,2j}, f_{d,2j+1}) := \text{MIX}_{d,j}(e_{d,2j}, e_{d,2j+1}) \text{ for } j = 0, \ldots, N_w/2 - 1,$$
$$v_{d+1,i} := f_{d,\pi(i)} \text{ for } i = 0, \ldots, N_w - 1.$$

Where $\text{MIX}_{d,j}(x_0, x_1) = (x_0 + x_1, (x_1 \lll R_{d,j}) \oplus (x_0 + x_1))$, with $R_{d,j}$ a rotation constant depending on d and j. The permutation $\pi(\cdot)$ can be found in Table 3 of [11], and the rotation constant $R_{d,j}$ can be referred to Table 4 of [11]. The original rotation constants can be found in [10].

After N_r rounds, the ciphertext is given as follows:

$$c_i := (v_{N_r,i} + k_{N_r/4,i}) \bmod 2^{64} \quad \text{for } i = 0, \ldots, N_w - 1,$$

where $(c_0, \ldots, c_{N_w-1})$ is the 512-bit ciphertext.

The key schedule starts with the key $K_0, \ldots, K_{N_w-1}$ and the tweak t_0, t_1. First we compute:

$$K_{N_w} := \lfloor 2^{64}/3 \rfloor \oplus \bigoplus_{i=0}^{N_w-1} K_i \quad \text{and} \quad t_2 := t_0 \oplus t_1.$$

Then the subkeys are derived:

$$\begin{aligned}
k_{s,i} &:= K_{(s+i) \bmod (N_w+1)} & \text{for } i = 0, \ldots, N_w - 4 \\
k_{s,i} &:= K_{(s+i) \bmod (N_w+1)} + t_{s \bmod 3} & \text{for } i = N_w - 3 \\
k_{s,i} &:= K_{(s+i) \bmod (N_w+1)} + t_{(s+1) \bmod 3} & \text{for } i = N_w - 2 \\
k_{s,i} &:= K_{(s+i) \bmod (N_w+1)} + s & \text{for } i = N_w - 1
\end{aligned}$$

3   Related-Key Boomerang Attack

The boomerang attack was first introduced by Wagner[12]. It is an adaptive chosen plaintext and ciphertext attack. And it was further developed by Kelsey et al. [8] into a chosen plaintext attack called the amplified boomerang attack, then Biham et al. further developed it into the rectangle attack [3]. The related-key boomerang attack was first published in [4]. Both of the attacks in this paper and in [1] are related-key boomerang ones. One can extend the attacks to amplified boomerang attacks, with more data and time complexity. In the following, we only introduce the 4-related-key, adaptive chosen plaintext and ciphertext scenario. We use the modular differential, in the rest of the paper the addition and subtraction are modular addition and subtraction.

The boomerang attack bases on the differential attack [2], the idea is joining two short differential characteristics with high probabilities in a quartet instead of a long differential to get a distinguisher with more rounds and higher probability. Let E be a block cipher with block size of n, it is considered as a cascade of two sub-ciphers: $E = E^1 \circ E^0$. For the sub-cipher E^0 there is a related-key differential trail $\alpha \to \beta$ with probability p, and for E^1 there is a related-key differential trail $\gamma \to \zeta$ with probability q. $E^{-1}, E^{0^{-1}}, E^{1^{-1}}$ stand for the inverse of E, E^0, E^1 respectively. The related-key boomerang distinguisher can be constructed as follows:

- Randomly choose a pair of plaintexts (P_1, P_2) such that $P_2 - P_1 = \alpha$.
- Encrypt P_1, P_2 with two related keys $\mathcal{K}_1$ and $\mathcal{K}_2$ respectively to get $C_1 = E_{\mathcal{K}_1}(P_1)$, $C_2 = E_{\mathcal{K}_2}(P_2)$.
- Compute $C_3 = C_1 + \zeta$, $C_4 = C_2 + \zeta$. Decrypt C_3, C_4 with $\mathcal{K}_3$ and $\mathcal{K}_4$ respectively to get $P_3 = E_{\mathcal{K}_3}^{-1}(C_3)$, $P_4 = E_{\mathcal{K}_4}^{-1}(C_4)$.
- Check whether $P_4 - P_3 = \alpha$.

We call a quartet (P_1, P_2, P_3, P_4), whose corresponding ciphertexts (C_1, C_2, C_3, C_4), which passes the boomerang distinguisher a right quartet if it satisfies the following conditions besides $P_2 - P_1 = \alpha$ and $P_4 - P_3 = \alpha$,

$$E_{\mathcal{K}_2}^0(P_2) - E_{\mathcal{K}_1}^0(P_1) = \beta \tag{1}$$

$$E_{\mathcal{K}_3}^{1}{}^{-1}(C_3) - E_{\mathcal{K}_1}^{1}{}^{-1}(C_1) = E_{\mathcal{K}_4}^{1}{}^{-1}(C_4) - E_{\mathcal{K}_2}^{1}{}^{-1}(C_2) = \gamma \tag{2}$$

If a quartet satisfies the two equations above, we have $E_{\mathcal{K}_4}^{1}{}^{-1}(C_4) - E_{\mathcal{K}_3}^{1}{}^{-1}(C_3) = \beta$. Since we have a differential $\alpha \to \beta$ in E^0 and $P_2 - P_1 = \alpha$, the probability of equation 1 is p. Similarly, the probability of equation 2 is q^2, as the probabilities of $\gamma \to \zeta$ and $\gamma \leftarrow \zeta$ are the same. Finally, there is another probability of p to get $P_4 - P_3 = \alpha$ from $E_{\mathcal{K}_4}^{1}{}^{-1}(C_4) - E_{\mathcal{K}_3}^{1}{}^{-1}(C_3)$. As a result, the probability to get a right quartet is $p^2 q^2$. The quartets that pass the distinguisher but don't satisfy equations (1) (2) are called false quartets. It's known that for a random permutation, $P_4 - P_3 = \alpha$ with probability 2^{-n}. Therefore, $pq > 2^{-n/2}$ must hold for the boomerang distinguisher to work.

Furthermore, the attack can be mounted for all possible β's and γ's simultaneously, so a right quartet can be gotten with probability $(\hat{p}\hat{q})^2$, where:

$$\hat{p} = \sqrt{\sum_\beta \Pr^2(\alpha \to \beta)} \quad \text{and} \quad \hat{q} = \sqrt{\sum_\gamma \Pr^2(\gamma \to \zeta)}$$

In our attacks, we get boomerang distinguishers with many possible β's and γ's. More details about boomerang attack can be found in [12,3].

4   Improved Related-Key Boomerang Key Recovery Attack on 32-Round Threefish-512

In this section, we describe the related-key boomerang distinguisher on Threefish-512 reduced to 32 rounds, which can be used to recovery the key of 32-round Threefish-512. In the rest of this paper, the least significant bit is the 1-st bit, and the most significant bit is the 64-th bit.

4.1   The Modular Differential

Wang et al. [13,14] introduced the technique of modular differential, which can be used to to find efficiently collisions on the main hash functions from the MD4 family. They considered the relationship among the modular differences, XOR differences and the signed bit-wise differences. With the technique, we find a good differential characteristic for 16-round Threesfish-512.

Here we introduce two theorems from [7] that are useful in our attack,

Theorem 1. *(from [7]) If $x[\pm j_1, \pm j_2, \dots, \pm j]$ is fixed, then the difference Δx and the XOR-difference are uniquely determined.*

Theorem 2. *(from [7])* $x \in \mathbb{Z}_{2^n}$ *chosen uniformly at random. If* $\Delta x = 2^k$, $0 \leq l \leq n-k-1$, *then* $Pr(x[k+l, -(k+l-1), \ldots, -k]) = 2^{-(l+1)}$, $Pr(x[-(n-1), \ldots, -(k)]) = 2^{-(n-k)}$. *If* $\Delta x = -2^k$, $0 \leq l \leq n-k-1$, *then* $Pr(x[-(k+l), k+l-1, \ldots, k]) = 2^{-(l+1)}$, $Pr(x[n-1, \ldots, k]) = 2^{-(n-k)}$.

The proofs of the two theorems are refered to [7]. The two theorems play an important role in our attacks. As we know, there are only three operations in Threefish: modular addition, XOR, and rotational shift. The operation between the subkeys and intermediate states is modular addition. So we choose modular subtraction as the measure of difference in the plaintext and the ciphertext. Among the differential path, we fix the signed bit-wise differences of the two operators before the XOR operation by means of Theorem 2. Then we can get a signed bit-wise difference after the XOR operation with certain probability.

For example, in the MIX function, suppose we have $y_0[-11, 16]$ and $x_1[2, 4, 7]$. After left shift of, say, 9 bits, x_1 becomes $(x_1 \lll 9)[11, 13, 16]$. So for $y_1 = (x_1 \lll 9) \oplus y_0$, the bit differences in bit 11 and 16 disappear with probability 1. $y_1[13]$ if the 13-th bit of y_0 is 0 and $y_1[-13]$ if the 13-th bit of y_0 is 1, both of them appear with probability 1/2. We call it that there is a bit condition on the 13-th bit of y_0.

4.2   The 32-Round Boomerang Distinguisher with 4 Related Keys

The four related keys have the relationship below.

$$\mathcal{K}_2 = \mathcal{K}_1 + \Delta_k^1, \mathcal{K}_3 = \mathcal{K}_1 + \Delta_k^2, \mathcal{K}_4 = \mathcal{K}_1 + \Delta_k^1 + \Delta_k^2.$$

The four related tweaks have the similar relationship:

$$T_2 = T_1 + \Delta_t^1, T_3 = T_1 + \Delta_t^2, T_4 = T_1 + \Delta_t^1 + \Delta_t^2.$$

Then one can deduce

$$\mathcal{K}_4 = \mathcal{K}_2 + \Delta_k^2, \mathcal{K}_4 = \mathcal{K}_3 + \Delta_k^1, T_4 = T_2 + \Delta_t^2, T_4 = T_3 + \Delta_t^1.$$

In this attack, we make use of two 16-round differential trails, each one of them is extended from a 8-round local collision by adding four addition rounds on the top and the bottom. Set $\delta = 2^{63}$, $\Delta_k^1 = (0,0,0,0,0,0,0,\delta)$, $\Delta_k^2 = (0,0,\delta,\delta,0,0,0,0)$, $\Delta_t^1 = (\delta, 0)$, $\Delta_t^2 = (\delta, \delta)$.

According to the key schedule algorithm, we can get two subkey differential trails $Trail^1$ and $Trail^2$. The differential trails are given in Table 2.

It is obvious that the probabilities of $Trail^1$ and $Trail^2$ are both 1.

We decompose the 32-round Threefish-512 into: $E = E^1 \circ E^0$, where E^0 contains the fisrt 16 rounds(including the subkey adding of 16-th round) and E_1 contains round 17-32(excluding the subkey adding of the 16-th round, including the subkey adding of the 32-th round).

Using the related-key boomerang distinguisher in Section 3, we first find related-key differential trails $\alpha \rightarrow \beta$ and $\gamma \rightarrow \zeta$. Subkey differential $Trail^1$ is compatible with $\alpha \rightarrow \beta$, and subkey differential $Trail^2$ is compatible with $\gamma \rightarrow \zeta$.

Table 2. Subkey Differential Trails for 32-round Distinguisher

s	$Trail^1$								$Trail^2$							
	k_0	k_1	k_2	k_3	k_4	k_5	k_6	k_7	k_0	k_1	k_2	k_3	k_4	k_5	k_6	k_7
0	0	0	0	0	0	δ	0	δ	0	0	δ	δ	0	δ	δ	0
1	0	0	0	0	0	0	0	δ	0	δ	δ	0	0	δ	0	0
2	0	0	0	0	0	0	0	0	δ	δ	0	0	0	0	δ	0
3	0	0	0	0	δ	0	0	0	δ	0	0	0	0	δ	δ	0
4	0	0	0	δ	δ	0	δ	0	0	0	0	0	0	δ	0	δ
5	0	0	δ	δ	0	δ	δ	0	0	0	0	0	0	0	0	δ
6	0	δ	δ	0	0	δ	0	0	0	0	0	0	0	0	0	0
7	δ	δ	0	0	0	0	δ	0	0	0	0	0	δ	0	0	0
8	δ	0	0	0	0	δ	δ	0	0	0	0	δ	δ	0	δ	0
9	0	0	0	0	0	δ	0	δ	0	0	δ	δ	0	δ	δ	0

We set $\alpha = (1+2^8+2^{12}+2^{18}+2^{30}+2^{36}+2^{40}+2^{54}+2^{58}, -1-2^8-2^{30}-2^{36}-2^{58}, 2^4+2^{10}+2^{15}+2^{40}+2^{43}+2^{46}, -2^4-2^{10}-2^{40}-2^{43}, 2^{33}+2^{49}+2^{52}, -2^{33}-2^{49}+2^{63}, 2^4+2^{15}+2^{31}, -2^{15}-2^{31}+2^{63})$,
$\zeta = (2^9+2^{42}, 2^7, 2^9+2^{38}+2^{48}, 2^{21}+2^{63}, 2^{63}, 2+2^9+2^{30}+2^{38}+2^{40}+2^{48}+2^{55}, 2^{63}, 2^9+2^{13}+2^{34}+2^{42})$.

For β and γ, we have many choices as we can choose the sign of difference.

One of the differential trails $\alpha \to \beta$ is shown in Table 4 in the Appendix, and the first column is the intermediate values. We make $v_{i,j}$, $e_{i,j}$, $f_{i,j}$ be the same meaning as in Section 2.2. $v_{i,j,k}$, $e_{i,j,k}$, $f_{i,j,k}$ are the $(k+1)$-th bits of $v_{i,j}$, $e_{i,j}$, $f_{i,j}$ ($k = 0,\ldots,63$). The second column gives the differences of column one. The third column means the signed bit-wise differences of column two. It means that any signed bit-wise difference with the difference in the second column is OK if we don't give a value in the third column. The sufficient conditions to make the third column hold are given in Table 7.

We can get many other β's by flipping certain bit differences of $e_{14,5}$, $e_{15,3}$, $e_{15,5}$, $e_{15,7}$, $v_{16,1}$, $v_{16,3}$, $v_{16,5}$ and $v_{16,7}$. For example, in Table 4, we choose the difference of $e_{14,5}$ to be -2^9+2^{63} instead of 2^9+2^{63} by changing the bit condition of $e_{14,5,9}$ into 1. Then the difference of $e_{15,2}$ becomes $-2^9 + 2^{63}$. We keep the other differences of e_{15} unchanged, then the difference of $v_{16,0}$ and $e_{16,0}$ becomes -2^9+2^{42}. So we get a different β with the same probability. By similar methods, we can get 2^{18} β's. The β's can be formulated as:
$\beta\text{'s} = (\pm2^9 \pm 2^{42}, \pm2^7, \pm2^9 \pm 2^{38} \pm 2^{48}, \pm2^{21} + 2^{63}, 2^{63}, \pm2 \pm 2^9 \pm 2^{30} \pm 2^{38} \pm 2^{40} \pm 2^{48} \pm 2^{55}, 2^{63}, \pm2^9 \pm 2^{13} \pm 2^{34} \pm 2^{42})$,

and all the differential trails $\alpha \to \beta$ have the same probability.

Similarly, there are many γ's by flipping the differences of $e_{16,0}$, $e_{16,2}$, $e_{16,4}$ and $e_{16,6}$. According to the signs of differences of $e_{16,0}$, $e_{16,2}$, $e_{16,4}$ and $e_{16,6}$, the signs of differences of $e_{i,j}$'s ($i = 16, 17, 18, 19; j = 1, 3, 5, 7$) should be decided to get the local collision after the 20-th round. So the γ's can be formulated as:
$\gamma = (\pm1 \pm 2^8 \pm 2^{12} \pm 2^{18} \pm 2^{30} \pm 2^{36} \pm 2^{40} \pm 2^{54} \pm 2^{58}, \mp1 \pm 2^8 \mp 2^{30} \mp 2^{36} \mp 2^{58}, \pm2^4 \pm 2^{10} \pm 2^{15} \pm 2^{40} \pm 2^{43} \pm 2^{46}, \mp2^4 \mp 2^{10} \mp 2^{40} \mp 2^{43}, \pm2^{33} \pm 2^{49} \pm 2^{52}, \mp2^{33} \mp 2^{49} + 2^{63}, \pm2^4 \pm 2^{15} \pm 2^{31}, \mp2^{15} \mp 2^{31} + 2^{63})$.

Once the differences of $e_{16,0}$, $e_{16,2}$, $e_{16,4}$ and $e_{16,6}$ are chosen, the differences of $e_{16,1}$, $e_{16,3}$, $e_{16,5}$ and $e_{16,7}$ are determined. So we can get 2^{21} differential trails $\gamma \rightarrow \zeta$. All the trails have the same probability. One of the differential trails $\gamma \rightarrow \zeta$ starts from the second row of Table 4, it has the same probability as the differential $\alpha \rightarrow \beta$.

Notice that in the trail of Table 4, there is no conditions on the MSB. But it will add one bit condition in the next round if the MSB shifts to anther position and XORs with a bit that has no difference. The probabilities of the resulting bit difference to be 1 or -1 are both $1/2$ no matter what the sign of MSB is.

From Table 7 we know that $Pr(\alpha \rightarrow \beta) = Pr(\gamma \rightarrow \zeta) = 2^{-57}$. So $\hat{p}\hat{q} = \sqrt{2^{18} \times 2^{2\times(-57)}} \sqrt{2^{21} \times 2^{2\times(-57)}} = 2^{94.5}$. Therefore, the probability of our related-key boomerang distinguisher is 2^{-189}.

4.3 The Key Recovery Attack on 32-Round Threefish-512

We give the key recover attack on 32-round Threefish-512 exploiting the 32-round boomerang distinguisher above.

1. For $i = 1, ..., 2^{193}$
   (a) Randomly choose plaintexts P_1^i, compute $P_2^i = P_1^i + \alpha$.
   (b) Encrypt plaintext pair (P_1^i, P_2^i) with $\mathcal{K}_1, \mathcal{K}_2$ resp. to get (C_1^i, C_2^i). Compute $C_3^i = C_1^i + \zeta$, $C_4^i = C_2^i + \zeta$. Then decrypt (C_3^i, C_4^i) with $\mathcal{K}_3, \mathcal{K}_4$ resp. to get (P_3^i, P_4^i).
   (c) Check whether $P_3^i - P_4^i = \alpha$, if so, store the quartet $(C_1^i, C_2^i, C_3^i, C_4^i)$.
2. (a) Guess 192 bits of the final subkey words $k_{8,0}, k_{8,2}, k_{8,7}$ and subtract them from the corresponding words of every elements of quartets stored in Step 1. If there are at least 13 quartets, whose resulting words satisfy the signed bit-wise differential, we store this 192-bit subkey triple $(k_{8,0}, k_{8,2}, k_{8,7})$.
   (b) Then guess 192 bits of the final subkey words $k_{8,1}, k_{8,3}, k_{8,5}$ and subtract them from the corresponding words of every elements of quartets stored in Step 1. If there are at least 13 quartets, whose resulting words satisfy the signed bit-wise differential, we store this 192-bit subkey triple $(k_{8,1}, k_{8,3}, k_{8,5})$.
3. Search the remaining 128 bits of the final subkey by brute force.

Once we recover the subkey, the main key is known too.

Analysis of the Attack. In Step 1, we need 2^{194} encryptions and 2^{194} decryptions.

Since the probability of the related-key boomerang distinguisher is 2^{-189}, there will be $2^{193} \times 2^{-189} = 2^4$ right quartets and $2^{193} \times 2^{-512} = 2^{-319}$ false quartets left. The complexity of Step 2 is 2^{197} one round encryptions, which equivalent to 2^{192} 32-round encryptions. So the complexity is dominated by Step 1.

In Step 2, (a) and (b) are executed independently. For (a), the probability for a ciphertext pair to satisfy the signed bit-wise differential after subtracting the round key is 2^{-9}. Therefore, the probability for a quartet to satisfy the conditions is 2^{-18}. So the probability for a false subkey triple to be stored is $2^{-18\times13} = 2^{-234}$, and a right subkey triple will be stored with probability 1. The number of false subkey triples to be stored is $2^{192} \times 2^{-234} = 2^{-42}$. For (b), the situation is the same as (a).

The expected number of quartets passed Step 2 for a false key is $2^4 \times 2^{-18} = 2^{-14}$. Let Y be the number of the quartets passed Step 2 for a false key, using the Poisson distribution, we have $Pr(Y \geq 13) \approx 0$. The expected quartets passed Step 2 for the right key is 16. Let Z be the number of the quartets passed Step 2 for the right key, $Pr(Z \geq 13) \approx 0.81$.

From the analysis above, the only memory needed is to store the 16 quartets, about 2^{12} bytes. The time complexity is 2^{195}, the success rate is 0.81.

5   Related-Key Boomerang Key Recovery Attack on Threefish-512 Reduced to 33 and 34 Rounds

Obviously, to extend the attack to 33 and 34 rounds, we have to construct 33- and 34-round related-key boomerang distinguishers. We decompose the 33-round Threefish-512 into: $E' = E'^1 \circ E'^0$. E'^0 is the same as E^0 in Section 4. E'^1 is extended from E^1 by adding one more round to the bottom. After the last round, a final subkey is added. The 34-round distinguisher adds two rounds in stead of one round to the bottom of E^1, and it has different subkey differential trails. There is a main obstacle that if we want to extend the distinguisher to more than 32 rounds we have to fix four words' signed bit-wise differences before and after the 32-th round's subkey adding. But for a given unknown key it is unclear what the probability for fixing both the differences actually is.

To solve this problem, we first assume that the key is chosen uniformly at random and compute the probability for 33- and 34-round distinguishers, then use the distinguishers to recover the keys using method different from that in Section 4.

Note that we still have many β's and γ's to construct distinguishers of 33 and 34 rounds. Moreover, our differential trails from round 1 to round 16 for 33-round and 34-round distinguishers are both the same as those in the 32-round distinguisher. And differential trails from round 16 to round 31 for 33-round distinguisher are the same as those in the 32-round distinguisher. In the 34-round distinguisher, as we have different subkey differential trails, we have different trails from round 16 to round 34. The subkey differential trail for 34-round distinguisher are given in Table 3. We give the differential trail of round 32 and 33 for 33-round distinguisher in Table 5, one of the differential trails from round 16 to round 34 for 34-round distinguisher is given in Table 6. The columns in Table 5,6 have the same meaning as those in Table 4. The sufficient conditions for the differential in Table 5 are given in Table 8. Table 5, 6, 8 are given in the Appendix. For the reason of page limitation, we omit the sufficient conditions of Table 6 in this paper.

Table 3. Subkey Differential Trails for 34-round Distinguisher

s	Trail'1 k_0	k_1	k_2	k_3	k_4	k_5	k_6	k_7	Trail'2 k_0	k_1	k_2	k_3	k_4	k_5	k_6	k_7
0	0	0	0	0	0	δ	0	δ	0	0	0	δ	0	δ	δ	0
1	0	0	0	0	0	0	0	δ	0	0	δ	0	δ	δ	δ	0
2	0	0	0	0	0	0	0	0	0	δ	0	δ	0	δ	0	0
3	0	0	0	0	δ	0	0	0	δ	0	δ	0	0	0	δ	0
4	0	0	0	δ	δ	0	δ	0	0	δ	0	0	0	δ	δ	0
5	0	0	δ	δ	0	δ	δ	0	δ	0	0	0	0	δ	0	δ
6	0	δ	δ	0	0	δ	0	0	0	0	0	0	0	0	0	0
7	δ	δ	0	0	0	0	δ	0	0	0	0	0	0	0	δ	δ
8	δ	0	0	0	0	δ	δ	0	0	0	0	0	δ	δ	δ	0
9	0	0	0	0	0	δ	0	δ	0	0	0	δ	0	δ	δ	0

5.1 Related-Key Boomerang Key Recovery Attack on 33-Round Threefish-512

We can know from Table 7 8 that the probability of the differential trails from round 16 to round 33 is 2^{-118}. So the probability of the 33-round distinguisher is $(2^{18} \times 2^{2 \times (-57)}) \times (2^{21} \times 2^{2 \times (-118)}) = 2^{-311}$.

We will use a method similar to that used in [5] [6] to recover the subkey bits.

When recovering keys of 33-round Threefish-512, we will use the inverse direction of the distinguisher, say we choose ciphertext pairs, decrypt them, add differences of the first round to the plaintexts then encrypt them to test whether there are quartets passing the boomerang distinguisher.

It is obvious that if the differences of a ciphertext pair after subtracting the last subkey don't satisfy the conditions of the boomerang distinguisher, then this pair can't follow the differential trails of the distinguisher. Therefore, we can control some bits of the ciphertext pair to make certain one bit condition of the last round difference depends completely on a corresponding last subkey bit. In this way, we can recover 192 last subkey bits one by one. We will recover the least significant 10 bits of $k_{9,0}$, $k_{9,1}$ and $k_{9,6}$; the least significant 35 bits of $k_{9,3}$ and $k_{9,4}$; the least significant 31 bits of $k_{9,2}$; the least significant 39 bits of $k_{9,5}$; and the least significant 22 bits of $k_{9,7}$.

We will depict how to recover the least significant 10 bits of $k_{9,6}$ as an example to illustrate the method. We make use of two of the bit conditions in $v_{33,6}$, i.e. $v_{33,6}[8, 10]$. Instead of using randomly chosen ciphertexts (C_1, C_2) only with $C_2 - C_1$ matching the desired difference, we also fix the least significant 7 bits of $c_{1,6}, c_{2,6}$ to be zero, the 8-th bit of $c_{1,6}, c_{2,6}$ to be 0, 1 resp. and the other bits of C_1, C_2 are chosen randomly. Now there is no carry in the 8-th bit, so only when $k_{9,6,7} = 0$ can $v_{33,6}$ satisfy the bit condition of $v_{33,6}[8]$.

Then we choose sufficiently many such cipherext pairs and make them go through the boomerang distinguisher. If there are quartets passed, we know that $k_{9,6,7} = 0$. Otherwise, we conclude that $k_{9,6,7} = 1$.

Now we are leaving to estimate the probability of making a mistake that wrongly assuming $k_{9,6,7} = 1$ while in fact $k_{9,6,7} = 0$. Since our related-key boomerang distinguisher has a probability of 2^{-311}, if we make our decision after $t2^{311}$ tries, the error probability can be approximated by

$$(1 - 2^{-311})^{t2^{311}} = ((1 - 2^{-311})^{2^{311}})^t \approx (1/e)^t$$

After recovering $k_{9,6,7}$, we modify the choice of ciphertext pairs and recover key bit $k_{9,6,6}$.

- If $k_{9,6,7} = 0$, then we generate ciphertext pairs where the least significant 7 bits are 1000000. The 8-th bit of $c_{1,6}$ is set to 0, the 8-th bit of $c_{2,6}$ is set to 1. It must be $k_{9,6,6} = 0$ to satisfy the bit condition. So after $t2^{311}$ tries, if there are quartets passed, we conclude $k_{9,6,6} = 0$. Otherwise, $k_{9,6,6} = 1$.
- If $k_{9,6,7} = 1$, we generate ciphertext pairs where the the least significant 7 bits are 1000000. The 8-th bit of $c_{1,6}$ is set to 0, the 8-th bit of $c_{2,6}$ is set to 1. But in this case, we demand for a carry in the 8-th bit, so when $k_{9,6,6} = 1$ can the difference satisfy the bit condition.

Apply this procedure recursively to recover the least significant 8 bits of $k_{9,6}$. After that, a similar argument allows to recover $k_{9,6,8}$ and $k_{9,6,9}$. We use the already known key bits, choose ciphertext pairs to control the bit differences and carries. And then we make the decision. In some cases, one might have to fix several bits in the ciphertext pair in order to get one bit difference, but the idea is the same.

For the other subkey words we recover the bits with a very similar procedure. In our attack, we choose $t = 16$.

Analysis of the Attack. For each bit to be recovered, we need at most $2t2^{311} = 2^{316}$ decryptions and the same number of encryptions. So the most complexity for recovering one bit is 2^{317} encryptions. As we want to recover 192 bits, we need $192 \cdot 2^{317} \approx 2^{324.6}$ encryptions. After recovering the 192 bits, we search the rest 320 bits by brute force. So the time complexity is about $2^{324.6}$, memory complexity is negligible.

The success rate of one bit is $1 - (1/e)^{16}$, so the total success rate is $(1 - (1/e)^{16})^{192} \approx 0.99998$.

5.2 Related-Key Boomerang Key Recovery Attack on 34-Round Threefish-512

From Table 6 we know that one of the differential trails from round 16 to round 34 has probability 2^{-200}, and we have 2^{33} such differential trails with the same probability.

As the differential trails from round 1 to round 16 are the same as those in the 32-round distinguisher, the probability of the 34-round distinguisher is $(2^{18} \times 2^{2 \times (-57)}) \times (2^{33} \times 2^{2 \times (-200)})) = 2^{-463}$.

The method to attack the 34-round Threefish-512 is similar to that in Section 5.1. And this time we can use either forward or backward direction of the boomerang distinguisher, here we use the forward direction. Then we recover 42 bits of the first subkey by the means of Section 5.1. The attack needs about $2^{474.4}$ encryptions and negligible memory.

6   Conclusion

We use the modular differential instead of the XOR differential to construct boomerang distinguishers of Threefish-512. We fixed the signed bit-wise differences to get our differential trails and mount an attack on 32-round Threefish-512 with complexity that is far lower than that in [1].

Then we extend the attack to 33 and 34 rounds with 33- and 34-round related-key boomerang distinguishers, but with a different method. We fix some bits in the ciphertext(plaintext) pairs and run the distinguisher sufficiently many times to recover one key bit at a time.

Further work on the key recovery attack of Threefish-512 up to 35 rounds or more comes with unaffordable cost by means of the methods above. One may have to find some other ways to make further improvement.

Acknowledgement

We are grateful to the anonymous reviewers for their valuable comments.

References

1. Aumasson, J.-P., Calik, C., Meier, W., Ozen, O., Phan, R.C.W., Varici, K.: Improved Cryptanalysis of Skein. In: Matsui, M. (ed.) ASIACRYPT 2009. LNCS, vol. 5912, pp. 542–559. Springer, Heidelberg (2009)
2. Biham, E., Shamir, A.: Differential Cryptanalysis of The Data Encryption Standard. Springer, London (1993)
3. Biham, E., Dunkelman, O., Keller, N.: The Rectangle Attack - Rectangling the Serpent. In: Pfitzmann, B. (ed.) EUROCRYPT 2001. LNCS, vol. 2045, pp. 340–357. Springer, Heidelberg (2001)
4. Biham, E., Dunkelman, O., Keller, N.: Related-Key Boomerang and Rectangle Attacks. In: Cramer, R. (ed.) EUROCRYPT 2005. LNCS, vol. 3494, pp. 507–525. Springer, Heidelberg (2005)
5. Borghoff, J., Knudsen, L.R., Leander, G., Matusiewicz, K.: Cryptanalysis of C2. In: Halevi, S. (ed.) CRYPTO 2009. LNCS, vol. 5677, pp. 250–266. Springer, Heidelberg (2009)
6. Contini, S., Yin, Y.L.: Forgery and Partial Key-Recovery Attacks on HMAC and NMAC Using Hash Collisions. In: Lai, X., Chen, K. (eds.) ASIACRYPT 2006. LNCS, vol. 4284, pp. 37–53. Springer, Heidelberg (2006)
7. Daum, M.: Cryptanalysis of Hash Fucntions of the MD4 Family, http://www.cits.rub.de/imperia/md/content/magnus/idissmd4.pdf
8. Kelsey, J., Khono, T., Schneier, B.: Amplified Boomerang Attacks Against Reduced-Round MARS and Serpent. In: Schneier, B. (ed.) FSE 2000. LNCS, vol. 1978, pp. 75–93. Springer, Heidelberg (2001)

9. Lipmaa, H., Moriai, S.: Efficient Algorithms for Computing Differential Properties of Addition. In: Matsui, M. (ed.) FSE 2001. LNCS, vol. 2355, pp. 336–350. Springer, Heidelberg (2002)
10. Ferguson, N., Lucks, S., Schneier, B., Whiting, D., Bellare, M., Kohno, T., Callas, J., Walker, J.: The Skein Hash Function Family, http://csrc.nist.gov/groups/ST/hash/sha-3/Round1/documents/Skein.zip
11. Ferguson, N., Lucks, S., Schneier, B., Whiting, D., Bellare, M., Kohno, T., Callas, J., Walker, J.: The Skein Hash Function Family, http://www.schneier.com/skein.pdf
12. Wagner, D.: The boomerang attack. In: Knudsen, L.R. (ed.) FSE 1999. LNCS, vol. 1636, pp. 156–170. Springer, Heidelberg (1999)
13. Wang, X.Y., Lai, X.J., Feng, D.G., Chen, H., Yu, X.Y.: Cryptanalysis of the Hash Functions MD4 and RIPEMD. In: Cramer, R. (ed.) EUROCRYPT 2005. LNCS, vol. 3494, pp. 1–18. Springer, Heidelberg (2005)
14. Wang, X.Y., Yu, H.B.: How to Break MD5 and Other Hash Functions. In: Cramer, R. (ed.) EUROCRYPT 2005. LNCS, vol. 3494, pp. 19–35. Springer, Heidelberg (2005)
15. Wang, X.Y., Yin, Y.L., Yu, H.B.: Finding Collisions in the Full SHA-1. In: Shoup, V. (ed.) CRYPTO 2005. LNCS, vol. 3621, pp. 1–16. Springer, Heidelberg (2005)

A   Appendix

Table 4. One of the Differential Trails $\alpha \to \beta$

Intermediate values	Differences	Signed Bit-wise Differences
$v_{0,0}$	$1 + 2^8 + 2^{12} + 2^{18} + 2^{30} + 2^{36} + 2^{40}$ $+2^{54} + 2^{58}$	
$v_{0,1}$	$-1 - 2^8 - 2^{30} - 2^{36} - 2^{58}$	
$v_{0,2}$	$2^4 + 2^{10} + 2^{15} + 2^{40} + 2^{43} + 2^{46}$	
$v_{0,3}$	$-2^4 - 2^{10} - 2^{40} - 2^{43}$	
$v_{0,4}$	$2^{33} + 2^{49} + 2^{52}$	
$v_{0,5}$	$-2^{33} - 2^{49} + 2^{63}$	
$v_{0,6}$	$2^4 + 2^{15} + 2^{31}$	
$v_{0,7}$	$-2^{15} - 2^{31} + 2^{63}$	
$e_{0,0}$	$1 + 2^8 + 2^{12} + 2^{18} + 2^{30} + 2^{36} + 2^{40}$ $+2^{54} + 2^{58}$	
$e_{0,1}$	$-1 - 2^8 - 2^{30} - 2^{36} - 2^{58}$	$e_{0,1}[-1, -9, -31, -37, -59]$
$e_{0,2}$	$2^4 + 2^{10} + 2^{15} + 2^{40} + 2^{43} + 2^{46}$	
$e_{0,3}$	$-2^4 - 2^{10} - 2^{40} - 2^{43}$	$e_{0,3}[-5, -11, -41, -44]$
$e_{0,4}$	$2^{33} + 2^{49} + 2^{52}$	
$e_{0,5}$	$-2^{33} - 2^{49}$	$e_{0,5}[-34, -50]$
$e_{0,6}$	$2^4 + 2^{15} + 2^{31}$	
$e_{0,7}$	$-2^{15} - 2^{31}$	$e_{0,7}[-16, -32]$
$e_{1,0}, e_{1,1}$	$2^{15} + 2^{46}, \qquad -2^{46}$	$e_{1,0}[16, 47], e_{1,1}[-47]$
$e_{1,2}, e_{1,3}$	$2^{52}, \qquad -2^{52}$	$e_{1,2}[53], e_{1,3}[-53]$
$e_{1,4}, e_{1,5}$	$2^4, \qquad -2^4$	$e_{1,4}[5], e_{1,5}[-5]$
$e_{1,6}, e_{1,7}$	$2^{12} + 2^{18} + 2^{40} + 2^{54}, \qquad -2^{12} - 2^{40}$	$e_{1,6}[13, 19, 41, 55], e_{1,7}[-13, -41]$
$e_{2,4}, e_{2,5}$	$2^{18} + 2^{54}, \qquad -2^{18}$	$e_{2,4}[19, 55], e_{2,5}[-19]$
$e_{2,6}, e_{2,7}$	$2^{15}, \qquad -2^{15}$	$e_{2,6}[16], e_{2,7}[-16]$
$e_{3,2}, e_{3,3}$	$2^{54}, \qquad -2^{54}$	$e_{3,2}[55], e_{3,3}[-55]$
$v_{4,7}$	2^{63}	$v_{4,7}[*64]$
$e_4 \sim v_{12}$	0	
$e_{12,4}$	2^{63}	$e_{12,4}[*64]$
$e_{13,2}, e_{13,5}$	$2^{63}, \qquad 2^{63}$	$e_{13,2}[*64], e_{13,5}[*64]$
$e_{14,0}, e_{14,2}$	$2^{63}, \qquad 2^{63}$	$e_{14,0}[*64], e_{14,2}[*64]$
$e_{14,5}, e_{14,7}$	$2^9 + 2^{63}, \qquad 2^{63}$	$e_{14,5}[10, *64], e_{14,7}[*64]$
$e_{15,0}, e_{15,1}$	$2^{63}, \qquad 2^{63}$	$e_{15,0}[*64], e_{15,1}[*64]$
$e_{15,2}, e_{15,3}$	$2^9 + 2^{63}, \qquad 2^{42} + 2^{63}$	$e_{15,2}[10, *64], e_{15,3}[43, *64]$
$e_{15,4}, e_{15,5}$	$2^{63}, \quad 2^9 + 2^{38} + 2^{48} + 2^{63}$	$e_{15,4}[*64], e_{15,5}[10, 39, 49, *64]$
$e_{15,6}, e_{15,7}$	$2^{63}, \qquad 2^{63}$	$e_{15,6}[*64], e_{15,7}[*64]$
$v_{16,0}, v_{16,1}$	$2^9 + 2^{42}, \qquad 2^7$	$v_{16,0}[10, 43], v_{16,1}[8]$
$v_{16,2}, v_{16,3}$	$2^9 + 2^{38} + 2^{48}, \qquad 2^{21}$	$v_{16,2}[10, 39, 49], v_{16,3}[22]$
$v_{16,4}, v_{16,5}$	$0, \ 2 + 2^9 + 2^{30} + 2^{38} + 2^{40} + 2^{48} + 2^{55}$	$v_{16,5}[2, 10, 31, 39, 41, 49, 56]$
$v_{16,6}, v_{16,7}$	$0, \ 2^9 + 2^{13} + 2^{34} + 2^{42}$	$v_{16,7}[10, 14, 35, 43]$
$e_{16,0}, e_{16,1}$	$2^9 + 2^{42}, \qquad 2^7$	
$e_{16,2}, e_{16,3}$	$2^9 + 2^{38} + 2^{48}, \qquad 2^{21} + 2^{63}$	
$e_{16,4}, e_{16,5}$	$2^{63}, 2 + 2^9 + 2^{30} + 2^{38} + 2^{40} + 2^{48} + 2^{55}$	
$e_{16,6}, e_{16,7}$	$2^{63}, \ 2^9 + 2^{13} + 2^{34} + 2^{42}$	

* both positive and negative are OK

Table 5. Differential Trail of Round 32 and 33 for 33-round Distinguisher

Intermediate values	Differences	Signed Bit-wise Differences
$v_{32,0}, v_{32,1}$	$2^9 + 2^{42},\quad 2^7$	$v_{32,0}[10, 43], v_{32,1}[8]$
$v_{32,2}, v_{32,3}$	$2^9 + 2^{38} + 2^{48},\quad 2^{21}$	$v_{32,2}[10, -39, 40, 49], v_{32,3}[22]$
$v_{32,4}, v_{32,5}$	$0,\ 2 + 2^9 + 2^{30} + 2^{38} + 2^{48} + 2^{55}$	$v_{32,5}[2, 10, 31, -39, -40, 41, 49, 56]$
$v_{32,6}, v_{32,7}$	$0,\ 2^9 + 2^{13} + 2^{34} + 2^{42}$	$v_{32,7}[10, 14, 35, 43]$
$e_{32,0}, e_{32,1}$	$2^9 + 2^{42},\quad 2^7$	$e_{32,1}[8]$
$e_{32,2}, e_{32,3}$	$2^9 + 2^{38} + 2^{48},\quad 2^{21} + 2^{63}$	$e_{32,3}[22, *64]$
$e_{32,4}, e_{32,5}$	$2^{63},\ 2 + 2^9 + 2^{30} + 2^{38} + 2^{48} + 2^{55}$	$e_{32,5}[2, 10, 31, 39, 49, 56]$
$e_{32,6}, e_{32,7}$	$2^{63},\ 2^9 + 2^{13} + 2^{34} + 2^{42}$	$e_{32,7}[10, 14, 35, 43]$
$v_{33,0}$	$2^9 + 2^{21} + 2^{38} + 2^{48} + 2^{63}$	$v_{33,0}[10, 22, 39, 49, *64]$
$v_{33,1}$	$2^7 - 2^9 + 2^{42} + 2^{53}$	$v_{33,1}[8, -10, 43, 54]$
$v_{33,2}$	$2 + 2^9 + 2^{30} + 2^{38} + 2^{48} + 2^{55} + 2^{63}$	$v_{33,2}[2, -10, 11, 31, 39, -49, 50, 56, *64]$
$v_{33,3}$	$8 - 2^9 - 2^{13} - 2^{15} - 2^{34} - 2^{42}$ $-2^{46} - 2^{50} + 2^{63}$	$v_{33,3}[8, -10, -14, -16, -35, -43,$ $-47, -51, *64]$
$v_{33,4}$	$2^9 + 2^{13} + 2^{34} + 2^{42} + 2^{63}$	$v_{33,4}[10, 14, 35, 43, *64]$
$v_{33,5}$	$2 + 2^3 - 2^9 - 2^{20} - 2^{28} - 2^{30} + 2^{38}$ $+2^{48} + 2^{55} - 2^{57} + 2^{63}$	$v_{33,5}[2, 4, -10, -21, -29, -31, 39,$ $49, 56, -58, *64]$
$v_{33,6}$	$2^7 + 2^9 + 2^{42}$	$v_{33,6}[8, 10, 43]$
$v_{33,7}$	$-2^9 + 2^{21} + 2^{35} - 2^{38} - 2^{48} + 2^{57} + 2^{63}$	$v_{33,7}[-10, 22, 36, -39, -49, 58, *64]$
$e_{33,0}$	$2^9 + 2^{21} + 2^{38} + 2^{48} + 2^{63}$	
$e_{33,1}$	$2^7 - 2^9 + 2^{42} + 2^{53}$	
$e_{33,2}$	$2 + 2^9 + 2^{30} + 2^{38} + 2^{48} + 2^{55}$	
$e_{33,3}$	$8 - 2^9 - 2^{13} - 2^{15} - 2^{34} - 2^{42}$ $-2^{46} - 2^{50}$	
$e_{33,4}$	$2^9 + 2^{13} + 2^{34} + 2^{42} + 2^{63}$	
$e_{33,5}$	$2 + 2^3 - 2^9 - 2^{20} - 2^{28} - 2^{30} + 2^{38}$ $+2^{48} + 2^{55} - 2^{57}$	
$e_{33,6}$	$2^7 + 2^9 + 2^{42} + 2^{63}$	
$e_{33,7}$	$-2^9 + 2^{21} + 2^{35} - 2^{38} - 2^{48} + 2^{57} + 2^{63}$	

* both positive and negative are OK

Table 6. One of the Differential Trails of Round 16-34 for 34-round Distinguisher

Intermediate values	Differences	Signed Bit-wise Differences
$e_{16,0}$	$2^3 + 2^{13} + 2^{17} + 2^{19} + 2^{21} + 2^{27} + 2^{37}$ $+2^{39} + 2^{45} + 2^{49} + 2^{55} + 2^{58} + 2^{59} + 2^{63}$	
$e_{16,1}$	$-2^3 - 2^{13} - 2^{17} - 2^{19} - 2^{39} - 2^{45}$ $-2^{55} - 2^{58}$	$e_{16,1}[-4, -14, -18, -20, -40, -46,$ $-56, -59]$
$e_{16,2}$	$2 + 2^4 + 2^9 + 2^{13} + 2^{23} + 2^{29} + 2^{34} + 2^{37}$ $+2^{40} + 2^{49} + 2^{62}$	
$e_{16,3}$	$-2^4 - 2^{13} - 2^{23} - 2^{29} - 2^{37} - 2^{49} - 2^{62}$	$e_{16,3}[-5, -14, -24, -30, -38, -50, -63]$
$e_{16,4}$	$2^4 + 2^7 + 2^{52} + 2^{58}$	
$e_{16,5}$	$-2^4 - 2^{52} - 2^{58}$	$e_{16,5}[-5, -53, -59]$
$e_{16,6}$	$2^{13} + 2^{23} + 2^{34} + 2^{40} + 2^{50}$	
$e_{16,7}$	$-2^{34} - 2^{40} - 2^{50}$	$e_{16,7}[-35, -41, -51]$
$e_{17,0}, e_{17,1}$	$2 + 2^9 + 2^{34} + 2^{40}, \quad -2 - 2^{40}$	$e_{17,0}[2, 10, 35, 41], e_{17,1}[-2, -41]$
$e_{17,2}, e_{17,3}$	$2^7, \quad -2^7$	$e_{17,2}[8], e_{17,3}[-8]$
$e_{17,4}, e_{17,5}$	$2^{13} + 2^{23}, \quad -2^{13} - 2^{23}$	$e_{17,4}[14, 24], e_{17,5}[-14, -24]$
$e_{17,6}$	$2^{21} + 2^{27} + 2^{37} + 2^{49} + 2^{59} + 2^{63}$	$e_{17,6}[22, 28, 38, 50, 60, *64]$
$e_{17,7}$	$-2^{21} - 2^{49} - 2^{59}$	$e_{17,7}[-22, -50, -60]$
$e_{18,4}, e_{18,5}$	$2^{27} + 2^{37} + 2^{63}, \quad -2^{27} - 2^{37}$	$e_{18,4}[28, 38, *64], e_{18,5}[-28, -38]$
$e_{18,6}, e_{18,7}$	$2^9 + 2^{34}, \quad -2^{34}$	$e_{18,6}[10, 35], e_{18,7}[-35]$
$e_{19,2}, e_{19,3}$	$2^{63}, \quad 0$	$e_{19,2}[*64]$
$e_{19,4}, e_{19,5}$	$2^9, \quad -2^9$	$e_{19,4}[10], e_{19,5}[-10]$
$v_{20,0}, v_{20,5}, v_{20,7}$	$2^{63}, \quad 2^{63}, \quad 2^{63}$	$v_{20,0}[*64], v_{20,5}[*64], v_{20,7}[*64]$
$e_{20} \sim v_{28}$	0	
$e_{28,6}, e_{28,7}$	$2^{63}, \quad 2^{63}$	$e_{28,6}[*64], e_{28,7}[*64]$
$e_{29,2}, e_{29,3}$	$0, \quad 2^{23}$	$e_{29,3}[24]$
$e_{30,0}, e_{30,1}$	$2^{23}, \quad 0$	$e_{30,0}[24]$
$e_{30,6}, e_{30,7}$	$0, \quad 2^9 + 2^{23}$	$e_{30,7}[10, 24]$
$e_{31,0}, e_{31,1}$	$0, \quad 2^{23}$	$e_{31,1}[24]$
$e_{31,2}, e_{31,3}$	$0, \quad 2^2 + 2^9 + 2^{23} + 2^{52}$	$e_{31,3}[3, 10, 24, 53]$
$e_{31,4}, e_{31,5}$	$2^9 + 2^{23}, \quad 0$	$e_{31,4}[10, 24]$
$e_{31,6}, e_{31,7}$	$2^{23}, \quad 0$	$e_{31,6}[24]$
$v_{32,0}, v_{32,1}$	$2^2 + 2^9 + 2^{23} + 2^{52}, \quad -2^{23} + 2^{31}$	$v_{32,0}[3, 10, 24, 53], v_{32,1}[-24, 32]$
$v_{32,2}, v_{32,3}$	$2^9 + 2^{23}, \quad -2^{23}$	$v_{32,2}[10, 24], v_{32,3}[-24]$
$v_{32,4}, v_{32,5}$	$2^{23}, \quad 2^9 - 2^{23}$	$v_{32,4}[24], v_{32,5}[10, -24]$
$v_{32,6}, v_{32,7}$	$2^{23}, \quad 2^2 + 2^9 + 2^{37} + 2^{44} + 2^{52} + 2^{58}$	$v_{32,6}[24], v_{32,7}[3, 10, 38, 45, 53, 59]$
$e_{32,0}, e_{32,1}$	$2^2 + 2^9 + 2^{23} + 2^{52}, \quad -2^{23} + 2^{31}$	$e_{32,1}[-24, 32]$
$e_{32,2}, e_{32,3}$	$2^9 + 2^{23}, \quad -2^{23}$	$e_{32,3}[-24]$
$e_{32,4}, e_{32,5}$	$2^{23} + 2^{63}, \quad 2^9 - 2^{23} + 2^{63}$	$e_{32,5}[10, -24, *64]$
$e_{32,6}, e_{32,7}$	$2^{23} + 2^{63}, \quad 2^2 + 2^9 + 2^{37} + 2^{44} + 2^{52} + 2^{58}$	$e_{32,7}[3, 10, 38, 45, 53, 59]$
$e_{33,0}$	2^9	$e_{33,0}[10]$
$e_{33,1}$	$2^2 + 2^5 - 2^9 + 2^{13} + 2^{31} + 2^{52}$	$e_{33,1}[3, 6, -10, 14, 32, 53]$
$e_{33,2}$	2^9	$e_{33,2}[10]$
$e_{33,3}$	$2^2 + 2^9 - 2^{10} + 2^{17} + 2^{23} + 2^{25} + 2^{31} + 2^{37}$ $+2^{39} + 2^{44} + 2^{46} + 2^{52} + 2^{58} + 2^{63}$	$e_{33,3}[3, 10, -11, 18, 24, 26, 32, 38,$ $40, 45, 47, 53, 59, *64]$
$e_{33,4}$	$2^2 + 2^9 + 2^{23} + 2^{37} + 2^{44} + 2^{52} + 2^{58} + 2^{63}$	$e_{33,4}[3, 10, 24, 38, 45, 53, 59, *64]$
$e_{33,5}$	$-2^9 + 2^{18} + 2^{28} + 2^{42}$	$e_{33,5}[-10, 19, 29, 43]$
$e_{33,6}$	$2^2 + 2^9 + 2^{31} + 2^{52}$	$e_{33,6}[3, 10, 32, 53]$
$e_{33,7}$	$-2^9 + 2^{59}$	$e_{33,7}[-10, 60]$

Table 6. *(continued)*

$v_{34,0}$	$2^2 + 2^{17} + 2^{23} + 2^{25} + 2^{31} + 2^{37} + 2^{39}$ $+2^{44} + 2^{46} + 2^{52} + 2^{58} + 2^{63}$	$v_{34,0}[3, 18, 24, 26, 32, 38, 40,$ $45, 47, 53, 59, *64]$
$v_{34,1}$	$1 + 2^2 + 2^5 + 2^{13} + 2^{21} + 2^{31} + 2^{35} + 2^{38}$ $+2^{42} + 2^{46} + 2^{52}$	$v_{34,1}[1, 3, 6, 14, 22, 32, 36, 39,$ $43, 47, 53]$
$v_{34,2}$	$2^2 + 2^{18} + 2^{23} + 2^{28} + 2^{37} + 2^{42} + 2^{44} + 2^{52}$ $+2^{58} + 2^{63}$	$v_{34,2}[3, 19, 24, 29, 38, 43, 45, 53,$ $59, *64]$
$v_{34,3}$	$2^2 + 2^{31} + 2^{37} + 2^{51} + 2^{52} + 2^{59}$	$v_{34,3}[3, 32, 38, 52, 53, 60]$
$v_{34,4}$	$2^2 + 2^{31} + 2^{52} + 2^{59}$	$v_{34,4}[3, 32, 53, 60]$
$v_{34,5}$	$2^2 + 2^{18} + 2^{28} + 2^{32} + 2^{37} + 2^{44} + 2^{52}$ $+2^{56} + 2^{58} + 2^{63}$	$v_{34,5}[3, 19, 29, 33, 38, 45, 53,$ $57, 59, *64]$
$v_{34,6}$	$2^2 + 2^5 + 2^{13} + 2^{31} + 2^{52}$	$v_{34,6}[3, 6, 14, 32, 53]$
$v_{34,7}$	$1 + 2^7 + 2^9 + 2^{15} + 2^{17} + 2^{21} + 2^{23}$ $+2^{25} + 2^{26} + 2^{29} + 2^{31} + 2^{36}$ $+2^{39} + 2^{46} + 2^{50} + 2^{63}$	$v_{34,7}[1, 8, 10, 16, 18, 22, 24,$ $26, 27, 30, 32, 37,$ $40, 47, 51, *64]$
$e_{34,0}$	$2^2 + 2^{17} + 2^{23} + 2^{25} + 2^{31} + 2^{37} + 2^{39}$ $+2^{44} + 2^{46} + 2^{52} + 2^{58} + 2^{63}$	
$e_{34,1}$	$1 + 2^2 + 2^5 + 2^{13} + 2^{21} + 2^{31} + 2^{35} + 2^{38}$ $+2^{42} + 2^{46} + 2^{52}$	
$e_{34,2}$	$2^2 + 2^{18} + 2^{23} + 2^{28} + 2^{37} + 2^{42} + 2^{44} + 2^{52}$ $+2^{58}$	
$e_{34,3}$	$2^2 + 2^{31} + 2^{37} + 2^{51} + 2^{52} + 2^{59} + 2^{63}$	
$e_{34,4}$	$2^2 + 2^{31} + 2^{52} + 2^{59}$	
$e_{34,5}$	$2^2 + 2^{18} + 2^{28} + 2^{32} + 2^{37} + 2^{44} + 2^{52}$ $+2^{56} + 2^{58}$	
$e_{34,6}$	$2^2 + 2^5 + 2^{13} + 2^{31} + 2^{52} + 2^{63}$	
$e_{34,7}$	$1 + 2^7 + 2^9 + 2^{15} + 2^{17} + 2^{21} + 2^{23}$ $+2^{25} + 2^{26} + 2^{29} + 2^{31} + 2^{36}$ $+2^{39} + 2^{46} + 2^{50} + 2^{63}$	

* both positive and negative are OK

Table 7. Sufficient Conditions of the Trail in Table 4

$e_{0,5,33} = 1; e_{0,5,49} = 1; e_{0,3,4} = 1; e_{0,3,10} = 1; e_{0,3,40} = 1; e_{0,3,43} = 1;$ $e_{0,1,0} = 1; e_{0,1,8} = 1; e_{0,1,30} = 1; e_{0,1,36} = 1; e_{0,1,58} = 1;$ $e_{0,7,15} = 1; e_{0,7,31} = 1$
$e_{1,4,4} = 0; e_{1,2,4} = 0; e_{1,2,52} = 0; e_{1,0,46} = 0; e_{1,0,15} = 0; e_{1,6,12} = 0;$ $e_{1,6,18} = 0; e_{1,6,40} = 0; e_{1,6,54} = 0; e_{1,4,52} = 0; e_{1,6,46} = 0; e_{1,0,12} = 0;$ $e_{1,0,40} = 0$
$e_{2,4,15} = 0; e_{2,4,54} = 0; e_{2,6,15} = 0; e_{2,2,18} = 0; e_{2,0,15} = 0$
$e_{3,2,54} = 0; e_{3,4,54} = 0$
$e_{14,5,9} = 0$
$e_{15,5,38} = 0; e_{15,2,46} = 0; e_{14,5,48} = 0; e_{15,2,9} = 0; e_{15,3,42} = 0$
$v_{16,0,9} = 0; v_{16,0,43} = 0; v_{16,2,9} = 0; v_{16,2,38} = 0; v_{16,2,48} = 0;$ $v_{16,1,7} = 0; v_{16,7,34} = 0; v_{16,0,13} = 0; e_{15,3,38} = 0; e_{15,3,7} = 0;$ $e_{15,5,1} = 0; e_{15,5,30} = 0; e_{15,5,40} = 0; v_{16,5,55} = 0; v_{16,2,1} = 0;$ $v_{16,2,30} = 0; v_{16,2,40} = 0; v_{16,3,21} = 0$

Table 8. Sufficient Conditions of the Trail in Table 5

$v_{32,0,9} = 0$; $v_{32,0,43} = 0$; $v_{32,2,9} = 0$; $v_{32,2,38} = 1$; $v_{32,2,39} = 0$; $v_{32,2,48} = 0$; $v_{32,1,7} = 0$; $v_{32,7,34} = 0$; $v_{32,0,13} = 0$; $e_{31,3,38} = 0$; $e_{31,3,7} = 0$; $e_{31,5,17} = 0$; $e_{31,5,46} = 0$; $e_{31,5,47} = 1$; $e_{31,5,56} = 0$; $v_{32,5,55} = 0$; $v_{32,2,1} = 0$; $v_{32,2,30} = 0$; $v_{32,2,40} = 0$; $v_{32,3,21} = 0$
$e_{32,1,7} = 0$; $e_{32,7,9} = 0$; $e_{32,7,13} = 0$; $e_{32,7,34} = 0$; $e_{32,7,42} = 0$; $e_{32,5,1} = 0$; $e_{32,5,9} = 0$; $e_{32,5,30} = 0$; $e_{32,5,38} = 0$; $e_{32,5,48} = 0$; $e_{32,5,55} = 0$; $e_{32,3,21} = 0$
$v_{33,6,7} = 0$; $v_{33,6,9} = 0$; $v_{33,6,42} = 0$; $e_{32,1,25} = 0$; $e_{32,1,27} = 1$; $e_{32,1,60} = 0$; $v_{32,6,53} = 0$; $v_{33,0,9} = 0$; $v_{33,0,21} = 0$; $v_{33,0,38} = 0$; $v_{33,0,48} = 0$; $e_{32,3,37} = 1$; $v_{33,0,57} = 0$; $v_{33,0,35} = 0$; $e_{32,3,2} = 1$; $e_{32,3,12} = 1$; $e_{32,3,49} = 1$; $v_{33,2,1} = 0$; $v_{33,2,9} = 1$; $v_{33,2,10} = 0$; $v_{33,2,30} = 0$; $v_{33,2,38} = 0$; $v_{33,2,48} = 1$; $v_{33,2,49} = 0$; $v_{33,2,55} = 0$; $e_{32,5,49} = 1$; $v_{33,2,3} = 0$; $e_{32,5,54} = 0$; $v_{33,2,20} = 1$; $v_{33,2,28} = 1$; $e_{32,5,11} = 1$; $e_{32,5,19} = 0$; $e_{32,5,29} = 1$; $e_{32,5,36} = 0$; $v_{33,2,57} = 1$; $v_{33,4,9} = 0$; $v_{33,4,13} = 0$; $v_{33,4,34} = 0$; $v_{33,4,42} = 0$; $v_{33,4,7} = 0$; $e_{32,7,36} = 1$; $e_{32,7,40} = 1$; $v_{33,4,15} = 1$; $e_{32,7,61} = 1$; $e_{32,7,5} = 1$; $v_{33,4,46} = 1$; $v_{33,4,50} = 1$

Integral Attacks on Reduced-Round ARIA Block Cipher

Yanjun Li[1,2], Wenling Wu[1], and Lei Zhang[1]

[1] State Key Laboratory of Information Security,
Institute of Software, Chinese Academy of Sciences, Beijing 100190, P.R. China
Graduate University of Chinese Academy of Sciences, Beijing 100049, P.R. China
[2] Beijing Electronic Science and Technology Institute, Beijing 100070, P.R. China
{liyanjun,wwl,zhanglei1015}@is.iscas.ac.cn

Abstract. The security of ARIA against integral attack is analyzed in this paper. First we modify the 3-round integral distinguishers proposed by Li *et al.*, and by analyzing the property of the diffusion layer of ARIA we present new 4-round integral distinguishers. Moreover, based on the 4-round integral distinguishers and the partial sum technique we improve integral attack result on 6-round ARIA and propose integral attack on 7-round ARIA. The results are the best integral attack results on reduced-round ARIA so far.

Keywords: Block cipher, Distinguisher, Integral attack, ARIA, Partial sum technique.

1 Introduction

The block cipher ARIA was designed by a group of Korean experts in 2003 based on SPN structure, which was established as a Korean Standard by the Ministy of Commerce, Industry and Energy [2]. It supports the block length of 128 bits and a variable key length of 128/192/256 bits. The security of ARIA was initially analyzed by the algorithm designers, including differential cryptanalysis, linear cryptanalysis, impossible differential cryptanalysis, truncated differential cryptanalysis and square attack. Later Biryukov *et al.* performed an evaluation of ARIA, but they focused on truncated differential cryptanalysis and dedicated linear cryptanalysis [1]. Wu *et al.* firstly found a non-trivial 4-round impossible differential which leads to a 6-round attack of ARIA with 2^{121} chosen plaintexts and 2^{112} encryptions [12], which was improved by Li *et al.* with $2^{120.5}$ chosen plaintexts and $2^{104.5}$ encryptions [10]. Then Fleischmann *et al.* proposed boomerang attack on 6-round ARIA requiring about 2^{57} chosen plaintexts, however, which required about $2^{171.2}$ encryptions [3].

The integral attack has many interesting features. It can saturate S-Box Layer, and Round Key Addition Layer will not affect this property of saturation. However, Diffusion Layer influences the length of the integral distinguisher. Integral attack was extended from square attack, which is one of the best attacks on AES[5]. Ferguson *et al.* in [8] improved this attack to 8 rounds version of

J. Kwak et al. (Eds.): ISPEC 2010, LNCS 6047, pp. 19–29, 2010.
© Springer-Verlag Berlin Heidelberg 2010

Rijndael-128 with the partial sum technique and the herd technique. Knudsen and Wagner first proposed the definition of integral and analyzed it as a dual to differential attacks particularly applicable to block ciphers with bijective components[6]. Several years later, Muhammad *et al.* presented bit-pattern based integral attack [7]. The integral attack applied to many kinds of block ciphers so far, such as Rijndeal, MISTY, Serpent. In [9] Li *et al.* gave 3-round integral distinguishers of ARIA and attack to 6-round with $2^{124.4}$ data complexity and $2^{169.4}$ time complexity.

For ARIA, the S-Box Layer and the Diffusion Layer are different from those of AES, so the integral attack on ARIA is different from that on AES. In this paper, we modify the 3-round integral distinguishers proposed in [9], and by analyzing the property of the diffusion layer of ARIA we present new 4-round integral distinguishers. Using the partial sum technique proposed by Ferguson[8], we also improve integral attack on 6-round ARIA with the data complexity of $2^{99.2}$ and the time complexity of $2^{71.4}$ based on the 4-round distinguishers. Moreover, we first propose the integral attack on 7-round ARIA with the data complexity of $2^{100.6}$ and the time complexity of $2^{225.8}$.

This paper is organized as follows: Section 2 provides a brief description of ARIA and the notations used throughout this paper. Section 3 describes the new 4-round integral distinguishers. Section 4 describes the attacks on 6-round ARIA and 7-round ARIA. Finally, Section 5 concludes this paper.

2   Preliminaries

2.1   Description of ARIA

ARIA is a SPN style block cipher, and the number of rounds are 12/14/16 corresponding to key length of 128/192/256 bits. In this paper the input and output of round function are treated as 4×4 matrices, which also can be treated as a 16-byte vector over $F_{2^8}^{16}$.

The round function of ARIA includes three basic operations: Round Key Addition, Substitution Layer and Diffusion Layer. For N-round ARIA the round function is iterated $N - 1$ times, and in the last round the Diffusion Layer is replaced by the Round Key Addition. For the detail of key scheduling algorithm, the interested readers can refer to [2].

The three basic operations are defined as follows:

Round Key Addition (RKA): The 128-bit round key is XORed to the state. The round keys are derived from the master key by means of key scheduling.

Substitution Layer (SL): A non-linear byte substitution operation is applied to each byte of the state independently. In ARIA this is implemented by two S-boxes S_1 and S_2 defined by affine transformations of the inverse function over F_{2^8}. ARIA applies two types of S-Box for odd and even rounds.

Diffusion Layer (DL): The diffusion layer is a function P: $F_{2^8}^{16} \rightarrow F_{2^8}^{16}$, which is given by

$$(y_0, y_1, \cdots, y_{15})^T = M(x_0, x_1, \cdots, x_{15})^T,$$

where M is given as follows

$$M = \begin{bmatrix}
0 & 0 & 0 & 1 & 1 & 0 & 1 & 0 & 1 & 1 & 0 & 0 & 0 & 1 & 1 & 0 \\
0 & 0 & 1 & 0 & 0 & 1 & 0 & 1 & 1 & 1 & 0 & 0 & 1 & 0 & 0 & 1 \\
0 & 1 & 0 & 0 & 1 & 0 & 1 & 0 & 0 & 0 & 1 & 1 & 1 & 0 & 0 & 1 \\
1 & 0 & 0 & 0 & 0 & 1 & 0 & 1 & 0 & 0 & 1 & 1 & 0 & 1 & 1 & 0 \\
1 & 0 & 1 & 0 & 0 & 1 & 0 & 0 & 1 & 0 & 0 & 1 & 0 & 0 & 1 & 1 \\
0 & 1 & 0 & 1 & 1 & 0 & 0 & 0 & 0 & 1 & 1 & 0 & 0 & 0 & 1 & 1 \\
1 & 0 & 1 & 0 & 0 & 0 & 0 & 1 & 0 & 1 & 1 & 0 & 1 & 1 & 0 & 0 \\
0 & 1 & 0 & 1 & 0 & 0 & 1 & 0 & 1 & 0 & 0 & 1 & 1 & 1 & 0 & 0 \\
1 & 1 & 0 & 0 & 1 & 0 & 0 & 1 & 0 & 0 & 1 & 0 & 0 & 1 & 0 & 1 \\
1 & 1 & 0 & 0 & 0 & 1 & 1 & 0 & 0 & 0 & 0 & 1 & 1 & 0 & 1 & 0 \\
0 & 0 & 1 & 1 & 0 & 1 & 1 & 0 & 1 & 0 & 0 & 0 & 0 & 1 & 0 & 1 \\
0 & 0 & 1 & 1 & 1 & 0 & 0 & 1 & 0 & 1 & 0 & 0 & 1 & 0 & 1 & 0 \\
0 & 1 & 1 & 0 & 0 & 0 & 1 & 1 & 0 & 1 & 0 & 1 & 1 & 0 & 0 & 0 \\
1 & 0 & 0 & 1 & 0 & 0 & 1 & 1 & 1 & 0 & 1 & 0 & 0 & 1 & 0 & 0 \\
1 & 0 & 0 & 1 & 1 & 1 & 0 & 0 & 0 & 1 & 0 & 1 & 0 & 0 & 1 & 0 \\
0 & 1 & 1 & 0 & 1 & 1 & 0 & 0 & 1 & 0 & 1 & 0 & 0 & 0 & 0 & 1
\end{bmatrix}.$$

2.2 Notations

We introduce some notations used in ARIA. The plaintext is denoted as P and c_i is the i+1-th byte of the ciphertext C. Other notations that will be used in this paper are described as follows:

$b_i^{(r)}$: the i+1-th byte of the output of RKA in r-th round.

$s_i^{(r)}$: the i+1-th byte of the output of SL in r-th round.

$m_i^{(r)}$: the i+1-th byte of the output of DL in r-th round.

$k^{(r)}$: the subkey of the r-th round.

$k'^{(r)}$: This is a simple linear transform of the round key $k^{(r)}$. XORing $k'^{(r)}$ into the state before the diffusion operation is equivalent to XORing $k^{(r)}$ into the state after the diffusion operation (when looking at encryption direction).

3   4-Round Integral Distinguishers

3.1   Integral Attack

Let A be a set of elements. An integral over A is defined as the sum of all elements in A. The aim of integral attack is to predict the values in the sums of the chosen bytes after a certain number of rounds of encryption. The following definitions are essential[9]:

Active Set. A set $\{x_i | x_i \in F_{2^n}, 0 \le i \le 2^n - 1\}$ is active, if for any $0 \le i < j \le 2^n - 1$, $x_i \ne x_j$.

Passive Set. A set $\{x_i | x_i \in F_{2^n}, 0 \leq i \leq 2^n - 1\}$ is passive, if for any $0 < i \leq 2^n - 1$, $x_i = x_0$.

Balanced Set. A set $\{x_i | x_i \in F_{2^n}, 0 \leq i \leq 2^n - 1\}$ is balanced, if the sum of all element of the set is 0, that is $\sum_{i=0}^{2^n-1} x_i = 0$.

3.2 4-Round Integral Distinguishers

Lemma 1 [9]. If $m_0^{(0)}$ takes all values of F_{2^8} and $m_i^{(0)}$ s are constants where $1 \leq i \leq 15$, then $s_6^{(3)}, s_9^{(3)}, s_{15}^{(3)}$ are balanced.

The result shown in Lemma 1 can be simply denoted by [0, (6, 9, 15)]. Table 1 lists all possible values for [a, (b, c, d)] which means that if only the a-th byte of input takes all values of F_{2^8} and other bytes are constants, then $s_b^{(3)}, s_c^{(3)}$ and $s_d^{(3)}$ are balanced.

Table 1. [9]. All possible values for [a, (b, c, d)]

Active byte	Balanced bytes
0	6, 9, 15
1	7, 8, 14
2	4, 11, 13
3	5, 10, 12
4	2, 11, 13
5	3, 10, 12
6	0, 9, 15
7	1, 8, 14
8	1, 7, 14
9	0, 6, 15
10	3, 5, 12
11	2, 4, 13
12	3, 5, 10
13	2, 4, 11
14	1, 7, 8
15	0, 6, 9

Lemma 2. If $m_0^{(0)}, m_5^{(0)}, m_8^{(0)}, m_{13}^{(0)}$ take all values of $F_{2^8}^4$ and other $m_i^{(0)}$s are constants, then $m_2^{(3)}, m_5^{(3)}, m_{11}^{(3)}, m_{12}^{(3)}$ are balanced.

Proof. According to the function P in diffusion layer, we will get the following equations:

$$\begin{cases} m_2^{(3)} = s_1^{(3)} \oplus s_4^{(3)} \oplus s_6^{(3)} \oplus s_{10}^{(3)} \oplus s_{11}^{(3)} \oplus s_{12}^{(3)} \oplus s_{15}^{(3)} \\ m_5^{(3)} = s_1^{(3)} \oplus s_3^{(3)} \oplus s_4^{(3)} \oplus s_9^{(3)} \oplus s_{10}^{(3)} \oplus s_{14}^{(3)} \oplus s_{15}^{(3)} \\ m_{11}^{(3)} = s_2^{(3)} \oplus s_3^{(3)} \oplus s_4^{(3)} \oplus s_7^{(3)} \oplus s_9^{(3)} \oplus s_{12}^{(3)} \oplus s_{14}^{(3)} \\ m_{12}^{(3)} = s_1^{(3)} \oplus s_2^{(3)} \oplus s_6^{(3)} \oplus s_7^{(3)} \oplus s_9^{(3)} \oplus s_{11}^{(3)} \oplus s_{12}^{(3)} \end{cases}$$

From Table 1, we have got $[0, (6, 9, 15)], [5, (3, 10, 12)], [8, (1, 7, 14)], [13, (2, 4, 11)]$, and the bytes of $s_1^{(3)}, s_2^{(3)}, s_3^{(3)}, s_4^{(3)}, s_6^{(3)}, s_7^{(3)}, s_9^{(3)}, s_{10}^{(3)}, s_{11}^{(3)}, s_{12}^{(3)}, s_{14}^{(3)}, s_{15}^{(3)}$ are balanced. So the bytes of $m_2^{(3)}, m_5^{(3)}, m_{11}^{(3)}$ and $m_{12}^{(3)}$ are balanced.   □

Using the result shown in Lemma 2, we can construct some 3-round distinguishers. Furthermore, 4-round distinguishers will be given by adding one round before 3-round distinguishers. The following lemma is useful.

Lemma 3. If the bytes of $x_0, x_1, x_3, x_4, x_6, x_7, x_8, x_9, x_{10}, x_{13}, x_{14}, x_{15}$ take all values of $F_{2^8}^{12}$ and other bytes are constants, then after the transformation of P these values will form 2^{64} sets and in each set the bytes of y_0, y_5, y_8, y_{13} will take all values of $F_{2^8}^4$ while the other 12 bytes are constants.

Proof. From the matrix M we find that the value of variables y_0, y_5, y_8, y_{13} aren't affected by the values of x_2, x_5, x_{11}, x_{12}, so we let x_2, x_5, x_{11}, x_{12} be constants, and the other bytes take all values of $F_{2^8}^{12}$. According to the function P we will get the following 16 equations without considering the constants:

$$
\begin{bmatrix}
0\,0\,1\,1\,1\,0\,1\,1\,0\,1\,1\,0 \\
0\,0\,0\,0\,0\,1\,1\,1\,0\,0\,0\,1 \\
0\,1\,0\,1\,1\,0\,0\,0\,1\,0\,0\,1 \\
1\,0\,0\,0\,0\,1\,0\,0\,1\,1\,1\,0 \\
1\,0\,0\,0\,0\,0\,1\,0\,0\,0\,1\,1 \\
0\,1\,1\,1\,0\,0\,0\,1\,1\,0\,1\,1 \\
1\,0\,0\,0\,0\,1\,0\,1\,1\,1\,0\,0 \\
0\,1\,1\,0\,1\,0\,1\,0\,0\,1\,0\,0 \\
1\,1\,0\,1\,0\,1\,0\,0\,1\,1\,0\,1 \\
1\,1\,0\,0\,1\,0\,0\,0\,0\,0\,1\,0 \\
0\,0\,1\,0\,1\,0\,1\,0\,0\,1\,0\,1 \\
0\,0\,1\,1\,0\,1\,0\,1\,0\,0\,1\,0 \\
0\,1\,0\,0\,1\,1\,0\,1\,0\,0\,0\,0 \\
1\,0\,1\,0\,1\,1\,1\,0\,1\,1\,0\,0 \\
1\,0\,1\,1\,0\,0\,0\,1\,0\,0\,1\,0 \\
0\,1\,0\,1\,0\,0\,1\,0\,1\,0\,0\,1
\end{bmatrix}
\times
\begin{bmatrix}
x_0 \\ x_1 \\ x_3 \\ x_4 \\ x_6 \\ x_7 \\ x_8 \\ x_9 \\ x_{10} \\ x_{13} \\ x_{14} \\ x_{15}
\end{bmatrix}
=
\begin{bmatrix}
y_0 \\ y_1 \\ y_2 \\ y_3 \\ y_4 \\ y_5 \\ y_6 \\ y_7 \\ y_8 \\ y_9 \\ y_{10} \\ y_{11} \\ y_{12} \\ y_{13} \\ y_{14} \\ y_{15}
\end{bmatrix}.
$$

The coefficient matrix of above equations can be denoted as $[A_0, A_1, \cdots, A_{15}]^T$, where A_i denotes the i-th row vector. After linear transformation of this coefficient matrix we find $A_1, A_2, A_3, A_4, A_6, A_7, A_9, A_{10}$ have the following properties:

(1) $A_1, A_2, A_3, A_4, A_6, A_7, A_9, A_{10}$ are independent of A_0, A_5, A_8, A_{13}, and the rank of the matrix composed of these vectors is 12.

(2) $A_1, A_2, A_3, A_4, A_6, A_7, A_9, A_{10}$ and $A_{11}, A_{12}, A_{14}, A_{15}$ are linear dependent, i.e. $A_{11}, A_{12}, A_{14}, A_{15}$ can be represented as follows:

$$A_{11} = A_2 \oplus A_4 \oplus A_6 \oplus A_7$$
$$A_{12} = A_1 \oplus A_4 \oplus A_9$$
$$A_{14} = A_1 \oplus A_2 \oplus A_3 \oplus A_7$$
$$A_{15} = A_2 \oplus A_4 \oplus A_7 \oplus A_9 \oplus A_{10}.$$

The above properties assure that when the bytes of $x_0, x_1, x_3, x_4, x_6, x_7, x_8,$ $x_9, x_{10}, x_{13}, x_{14}, x_{15}$ take all values of $F_{2^8}^{12}$ and x_2, x_5, x_{11}, x_{12} are constants, we will get 2^{96} different values on the right of above equations, which will form 2^{64} sets and in each set the bytes of y_0, y_5, y_8, y_{13} will take all values of $F_{2^8}^4$, and the other bytes are constants. $\qquad\square$

Based on Lemma 2 and Lemma 3, we can construct a new 4-round distinguisher as depicted in Theorem 1.

Theorem 1. If the bytes of $m_2^{(0)}, m_5^{(0)}, m_{11}^{(0)}, m_{12}^{(0)}$ are constants and other bytes take all values of $F_{2^8}^{12}$, then the bytes of $m_2^{(4)}, m_5^{(4)}, m_{11}^{(4)}, m_{12}^{(4)}$ are balanced.

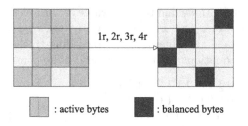

□ : active bytes   ■ : balanced bytes

Fig. 1. A New 4-Round Distinguisher

Considering all possible values in Table 1, there are other 4-round distinguishers. For example, the bytes of $m_0^{(0)}, m_1^{(0)}, m_{10}^{(0)}, m_{11}^{(0)}$ are constants and other bytes take all values of $F_{2^8}^{12}$, then the bytes of $m_0^{(4)}, m_1^{(4)}, m_{10}^{(4)}, m_{11}^{(4)}$ are balanced. We can construct 24 4-round distinguishers in all.

4   Attacks on Reduced-Round ARIA

4.1   Integral Attack on 6-Round ARIA

Applying the above 4-round integral distinguisher at Rounds $1 \rightarrow 4$ (in **Theorem 1**), we can present an integral attack on 6-round ARIA, which is illustrated in Fig.2.

1. Choose a structure of plaintexts. The bytes of $m_0^{(0)}, m_1^{(0)}, m_3^{(0)}, m_4^{(0)}, m_6^{(0)},$ $m_7^{(0)}, m_8^{(0)}, m_9^{(0)}, m_{10}^{(0)}, m_{13}^{(0)}, m_{14}^{(0)}$ and $m_{15}^{(0)}$ take all values of $F_{2^8}^{12}$. Encrypt all these plaintexts and set 2^{56} counters for the seven bytes value of $c_1, c_4, c_6, c_{10},$ c_{11}, c_{12}, c_{15}, and then the corresponding counter is added by one.
2. For the 2^{96} values of ciphertexts, there are 2^{56} values at most in the bytes of $c_1, c_4, c_6, c_{10}, c_{11}, c_{12}$ and c_{15}. We choose those values whose counters are odd ($a \bigoplus a = 0$). Guessing the corresponding key value, then do a partial decrypt to the single byte of $b_2^{(5)}$, sum this value over all the encryptions, and check if it is equal to zero. In this phase we need the partial sum technique in order to reduce the workfactor of the value $b_2^{(5)}$.

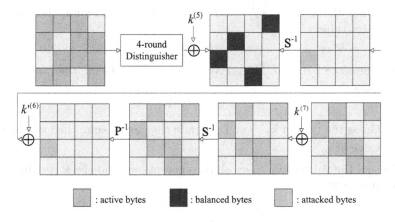

Fig. 2. The Integral Attack on 6-Round ARIA

$$b_2^{(5)} = S_1[S_2(c_1 \oplus k_1^{(7)}) \oplus S_1(c_4 \oplus k_4^{(7)}) \oplus S_1^{-1}(c_6 \oplus k_6^{(7)}) \oplus S_1^{-1}(c_{10} \oplus k_{10}^{(7)})$$

$$\oplus S_2^{-1}(c_{11} \oplus k_{11}^{(7)}) \oplus S_1(c_{12} \oplus k_{12}^{(7)}) \oplus S_2^{-1}(c_{15} \oplus k_{15}^{(7)}) \oplus k_2'^{(6)}].$$

Let $t_0, t_1, t_2, \cdots, t_l$ and $r_0, r_1, r_2, \cdots, r_l$ denote $c_1, c_4, c_6, c_{10}, c_{11}, c_{12}, c_{15}$ and $k_1^{(7)}, k_4^{(7)}, k_6^{(7)}, k_{10}^{(7)}, k_{11}^{(7)}, k_{12}^{(7)}, k_{15}^{(7)}$ respectively. We define

$$x_i := \sum_{j=0}^{i} S[t_j \oplus r_j],$$

where i, j satisfy $l \geq i > j \geq 0$.

For 7 bytes values of ciphertexts which appear odd times, we do the following steps:

(a) Guess the two bytes of $k_1^{(7)}$ and $k_4^{(7)}$, and get the corresponding 6 bytes value, i.e

$$(x_1, c_6, c_{10}, c_{11}, c_{12}, c_{15}).$$

(b) Guess the value of $k_6^{(7)}$, and compute the partial sum, then we get 5 bytes value

$$(x_2, c_{10}, c_{11}, c_{12}, c_{15}).$$

(c) Guess the value of $k_{10}^{(7)}$, and compute the partial sum, then we get 4 bytes value

$$(x_3, c_{11}, c_{12}, c_{15}).$$

(d) Guess the value of $k_{11}^{(7)}$, and compute the partial sum, then we get 3 bytes value

$$(x_4, c_{12}, c_{15}).$$

(e) Guess the value of $k_{12}^{(7)}$, and compute the partial sum, then we get 2 bytes value

$$(x_5, c_{15}).$$

(f) Guess the byte of $k_{15}^{(7)}$, and compute the partial sum, then we get 8 bits value

$$(x_6).$$

(g) Guess the byte of $k_2'^{(6)}$, and compute the partial sum, then we get 8 bits value of $b_2^{(5)}$.

We sum the value of $b_2^{(5)}$ over all the encryptions, and check the sum if it is equal to zero.

$$\oplus b_2^{(5)} = 0 \tag{1}$$

If Equ.(1) holds, the guessed key bytes might be right, otherwise they are wrong guesses.

3. Choose another structure of plaintexts and repeat Step 1 and Step 2 until those key bytes are uniquely determined.

In Step 1, we choose 2^{96} plaintexts and need encrypt 2^{96} times. In Step 2-(a), we guess 16 bits key, and process 2^{56} ciphertexts, which costs 2^{72} S-box applications. Step 2-(b) costs workfactor as $2^{72} = 2^{16} \times 2^8 \times 2^{48}$ at most. This is same to the other phases of Step 2, so the workfactor of Step 2 is $2^{72} \times 7$ S-box applications. For a wrong key, the probability that it satisfies Equ.(1) is 2^{-8}, and thus after analyzing a structure, the number of wrong keys that can pass Equ.(1) is $(2^{64} - 1) \times 2^{-8} \approx 2^{56}$. Hence to uniquely determine 8 bytes key, we need to analyze 9 structures. So the data complexity is $2^{99.2}$ and the time complexity is $2^{72} \times 7 \times 9/(6 \times 16) = 2^{71.4}$ encryptions.

4.2 Integral Attack on 7-Round ARIA

In this subsection, we describe an integral attack on 7-round ARIA. The attack is based on the above 4-round integral distinguisher (in **Theorem 1**) with additional three rounds at the end (Fig.3).

1. Choose a structure of plaintexts. The bytes of $m_0^{(0)}, m_1^{(0)}, m_3^{(0)}, m_4^{(0)}, m_6^{(0)}$, $m_7^{(0)}$, $m_8^{(0)}, m_9^{(0)}, m_{10}^{(0)}, m_{13}^{(0)}, m_{14}^{(0)}$ and $m_{15}^{(0)}$ take all values of $F_{2^8}^{12}$. Encrypt all these plaintexts and we get 2^{96} ciphertexts.

2. For the 2^{96} values of ciphertexts, we will operate the following steps:

(a) Guess the value of $k^{(8)}$ and operate the inverse of RKA($k^{(8)}$), SL(the 7th round) and DL(the 6th round) in sequence. We will get the 7 bytes of

$$(b_1^{(7)}, b_4^{(7)}, b_6^{(7)}, b_{10}^{(7)}, b_{11}^{(7)}, b_{12}^{(7)}, b_{15}^{(7)}).$$

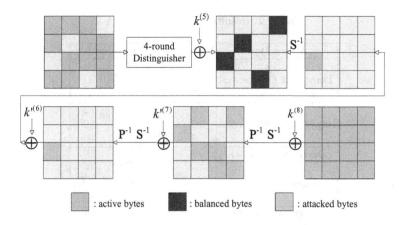

Fig. 3. The Integral Attack on 7-Round ARIA

(b) For the above 7 bytes, we choose those values that the counters are odd, and guess the corresponding 7 bytes of $k'^{(7)}$ and one byte value of $k'^{(6)}$, then operate the inverse of RKA($k'^{(7)}$), SL(the 6th round), DL(the 5th round), RKA($k'^{(6)}$) and SL(the 5th round) just as in step 2 in Sect. 4.1 to get the value of $b_2^{(5)}$.

We sum the value of $b_2^{(5)}$ over all the encryptions, and if the sum is equal to zero, the guessed key bytes might be right, otherwise they are wrong guesses.

3. Choose a new structure of plaintexts and repeat Step 1 and Step 2 until those key bytes are uniquely determined.

In Step 1, we choose 2^{96} plaintexts and need encrypt 2^{96} times. Step 2-(a) costs $2^{128} \times 2^{96}/7 = 2^{224}/7$ encryptions at most, which is the main cost in the attack. Step 2-(b) costs workfactor as $2^{200} \times 7 = 2^{56} \times 2^{16} \times 2^{128} \times 7$ at most. Guessing 24 bytes key, we need to choose 25 structures in total. So the data complexity is $2^{100.6}$ and the time complexity is $2^{224} \times 25/7 = 2^{225.8}$, which only works for the version of the key length 256 bits.

5 Conclusion

The integral attacks on reduced-round of ARIA were described in this paper. We modified the 3-round integral distinguishers for ARIA proposed in [9], based on which we analyzed the property of DL and improved the distinguishers to 4-round. Then we attacked 6-round and 7-round ARIA with the partial sum technique. Table 2 summarizes our integral attacks together with the previously known attacks on ARIA.

According to Table 2, the integral attacks presented in this paper make significant improvements on both data and time complexities. However, the full round ARIA provides a sufficient safety margin against integral attack. The integral attack combined with other cryptanalytic methods might be more effective to ARIA, which will be our future work.

Table 2. Results of attacks on ARIA

Attack type	Rounds	Data	Time	Source
	7	2^{81}	2^{81}	[1]
Truncated Differential	7	2^{100}	2^{100}	[1]
	7	2^{104}	2^{112}	[1]
	6	2^{121}	2^{112}	[12]
Impossible Differential	6	$2^{120.5}$	$2^{104.5}$	[10]
	6	2^{113}	$2^{121.6}$	[10]
Boomerang Attack	6	2^{57}	$2^{171.2}$	[3]
	6	$2^{124.4}$	$2^{169.4}$	[9]
Integral Attack	6	$2^{99.2}$	$2^{71.4}$	Sec.4.1
	7	$2^{100.6}$	$2^{225.8}$	Sec.4.2

Time complexity is measured in encryption units.

Acknowledgments

We would like to thank anonymous referees for their helpful comments and suggestions. The research presented in this paper is supported by the National Natural Science Foundation of China (No. 60873259 and No. 60903212), and Knowledge Innovation Project of The Chinese Academy of Sciences.

References

1. Biryukov, A., De Canniere, C., Lano, J., Ors, S.B., Preneel, B.: Security and Performance Analysis of Aria. Version 1.2. (Janaury 7, 2004)
2. Kwon, D., Kim, J., Park, S., Sung, S.H., et al.: New Block Cipher: ARIA. In: Lim, J.-I., Lee, D.-H. (eds.) ICISC 2003. LNCS, vol. 2971, pp. 432–445. Springer, Heidelberg (2004)
3. Fleischmann, E., Gorski, M., Lucks, S.: Attacking Reduced Rounds of the ARIA Block Cipher. Cryptology ePrint Archive, Report 2009/334 (2009), http://eprint.iacr.org/
4. FIPS 197. Advanced Encryption Standard. Federal Information Processing Standards Publication 197, U.S. Department of Commerce, N.I.S.T (2001)
5. Daemen, J., Knudsen, L., Rijmen, V.: The block cipher Square. In: Biham, E. (ed.) FSE 1997. LNCS, vol. 1267, pp. 149–165. Springer, Heidelberg (1997)
6. Knudsen, L., Wagner, D.: Integral cryptanalysis. In: Daemen, J., Rijmen, V. (eds.) FSE 2002. LNCS, vol. 2365, pp. 112–127. Springer, Heidelberg (2002)
7. Z'aba, M.R., Raddum, H., Henricksen, M., Dawson, E.: Bit-pattern based integral attack. In: Nyberg, K. (ed.) FSE 2008. LNCS, vol. 5086, pp. 363–381. Springer, Heidelberg (2008)
8. Ferguson, N., Kelsey, J., Lucks, S., Schneier, B., Stay, M., Wagner, D., Whiting, D.: Improved cryptanalysis of Rijndael. In: Schneier, B. (ed.) FSE 2000. LNCS, vol. 1978, pp. 213–230. Springer, Heidelberg (2001)
9. Li, P., Sun, B., Li, C.: Integral cryptanalysis of ARIA. In: Information Security and Cryptology-Inscrypt 2009, pp. 1–14 (2009)

10. Li, R., Sun, B., Zhang, P., Li, C.: New Impossible Differentials of ARIA. Cryptology ePrint Archive, Report 2008/227 (2008), http://eprint.iacr.org/
11. Galice, S., Minier, M.: Improving integral attacks against Rijndael-256 upto 9rounds. In: Vaudenay, S. (ed.) AFRICACRYPT 2008. LNCS, vol. 5023, pp. 1–15. Springer, Heidelberg (2008)
12. Wu, W., Zhang, W., Feng, D.: Impossible differential cryptanalysis of Reduced-Round ARIA and Camellia. Journal of Compute Science and Technology 22(3), 449–456 (2007)

A New Class of RC4 Colliding Key Pairs with Greater Hamming Distance

Jiageng Chen* and Atsuko Miyaji**

Japan Advanced Institute of Science and Technology, 1-1 Asahidai, Nomi, Ishikawa
923-1292, Japan
{jg-chen,miyaji}@jaist.ac.jp

Abstract. In this paper, we discovered a new class of colliding key pairs
of RC4, namely, two different secret keys generate the same internal
state after RC4's key scheduling algorithm. This is to our knowledge the
first discovery of RC4 colliding keys with hamming distance greater than
one, that is, the colliding key pairs we found can differ from each other at
three different positions, and the value difference between these positions
needs not be fixed. We analyzed the transition pattern and evaluated the
probability of the existence of this new class of colliding key pairs. Our
result shows that RC4 key collision could be achieved by two keys with
greater hamming distance than the ones found in [1] and [2]. And this
newly discovered class of colliding key pairs reveals the weakness that
RC4's key scheduling algorithm could generate even more colliding keys.
We also proposed an algorithm for searching colliding key pairs within
this new class. Some concrete colliding key pairs are demonstrated in
this paper, among which 55-byte colliding key pair is the shortest one
we found by using our algorithm within one hour time.

1 Introduction

The RC4 stream cipher is one of the most famous ciphers widely used in real
world applications such as Microsoft Office, Secure Socket Layer (SSL), Wired
Equivalent Privacy (WEP), etc. Due to its popularity and simplicity, RC4 has
become a hot cryptanalysis target since its specification was made public on the
Internet in 1994 [3]. Various general weaknesses of RC4 have been discovered in
some previous works including [4,5,6], etc. Another popular cryptanalysis area
for RC4 is in the WEP environment. Such works include [7,8,9,10], etc.

Our paper focuses on RC4 key collisions. It describes the existence of secret
key pairs that generate the same initial states after key scheduling algorithm.
The study of "colliding keys" of RC4 can be dated back to 2000. It was pointed
out by Grosul and Wallach [1] that RC4 has related-key pairs that generate
hundreds of substantially similar output bytes when the key size is close to the
full 256 bytes. In Matsui's paper [2], much stronger key collisions with shorter key

---

* This author is supported by the Graduate Research Program.
** This work is supported by Grant-in-Aid for Scientific Research (B), 20300003.

size were explored. A state transition sequence of the key scheduling algorithm for a related key pair of an arbitrary fixed length which can lead to key collisions was presented.

In both [1] and [2], the colliding keys found only have hamming distance of 1. In this paper, we demonstrate another class of colliding key pairs. Differing from [1] and [2], we showed for the first time that there exist colliding key pairs whose hamming distance is 3, which is greater than 1. That is, two colliding keys we found could differ at three positions and the value differences at these three different positions do not need to be fixed. Our result shows that there exist many more colliding key pairs than previously expected. We estimated the number of colliding key pairs within this newly found class and also we proposed a search algorithm which can be used to easily find such colliding key pairs.

Structure of the paper. In Section 2, we briefly describe the RC4 algorithm followed by some previous works on RC4 key collision in Section 3. In Section 4, we explain our new transition pattern which will lead to the collision. We give probability evaluations in Section 5 and finally we describe an efficient colliding key pair search algorithm. Some techniques needed for the probability analysis, the total number of colliding key pairs we found and some concrete colliding key examples are summarized in the Appendix.

2   Preparation

2.1   Description of RC4

The internal state of RC4 consists of a permutation S of the numbers $0, ..., N-1$ and two indices $i, j \in \{0, ..., N-1\}$. The index i is determined and known to the public, while j and permutation S remain secret. RC4 consists of two algorithms: The Key Scheduling Algorithm (KSA) and the Pseudo Random Generator Algorithm (PRGA). The KSA generates an initial state from a random key K of k bytes as described in Algorithm 1. It starts with an array $\{0, 1, ..., N-1\}$ where $N = 256$ by default. At the end, we obtain the initial state S_{N-1}.

Once the initial state is created, it is used by PRGA to generate a keystream of bytes which will be XORed with plaintext to generate ciphertext. PRGA is described in Algorithm 2. In this paper, we focus only on KSA.

Algorithm 1. KSA	Algorithm 2. PRGA
1: **for** $i = 0$ **to** $N - 1$ **do**	1: $i \leftarrow 0$
2: $S[i] \leftarrow i$	2: $j \leftarrow 0$
3: **end for**	3: **loop**
4: $j \leftarrow 0$	4: $i \leftarrow i + 1$
5: **for** $i = 0$ **to** $N - 1$ **do**	5: $j \leftarrow j + S[i]$
6: $j \leftarrow j + S[i] + K[i \bmod l]$	6: swap$(S[i], S[j])$
7: swap$(S[i], S[j])$	7: keystream byte $z_i = S[S[i] + S[j]]$
8: **end for**	8: **end loop**

2.2 Previous Research on RC4 Key Collisions

Two important studies on RC4 key collisions are [1] and [2]. In [1], the authors pointed out that for secret keys with lengths close to 256 bytes, it's possible for two keys to generate similar internal states after KSA and thus may generate hundreds of similar bytes output during PRGA. Intuition in [1] comes from that for two keys K_1, K_2, assume $K_1[i] = K_2[i]$ except when $i = t$. When t is close to 255, internal state will be substantially similar. However, their discovery cannot be strictly called key collision and their result only works for key length close to 256.

In [2], RC4 key collision for shorter key length was first explained and a 24-byte key collision was found. The key pattern is almost same as in [1], namely, two keys differ at only one byte position ($K_1[i] = K_2[i]$ except when $i = t$) and value difference is $1(K_1[t] = K_2[t] - 1)$. Under the above condition, [2] is able to find a transition pattern that could lead to a total collision after KSA. The intuition behind the transition pattern is that from the first time i touches the different position t, the pattern ensures that there will always be only two differences in the internal state as the key scheduling process goes on. And the difference is absorbed when i touches t for the last time. Please refer to [2] for the detailed description.

Our result shows that RC4 key collision can also be achieved even if the hamming distance between two keys is greater than 1. Also, differing from [2], our transition pattern is a self-absorbing type, which means that once the internal states differences are generated due to the key differences, they will be absorbed very quickly and the internal states returns to the same till i touches the next key difference. We show this interesting pattern in the following section.

3 New Transition Pattern

3.1 Notations and Intuitions

The following are the notations used in this paper.

K_1, K_2: Secret keys which satisfy $K_1[d] = K_2[d] - t$, $K_1[d+1] = K_2[d+1] + t$, $K_1[d+t+1] = K_1[d+t+1] - t$. $K_1[i] = K_2[i]$ for $i \neq d, d+1, d+t+1$.

$S_{1,i}, S_{2,i}$: S-boxes corresponding to $K_1(K_2)$ at time i. When $S_{1,i}[p] = S_{2,i}[p]$ for some p, we use $S_i[p]$ to denote.

$i, j_{1,i}, j_{2,i}$: Internal state. $j_{1,i}(j_{2,i})$ corresponds to $K_1(K_2)$ at time i. When $j_{1,i} = j_{2,i}$, we use j_i to denote.

d: Index of the first position where the values of the two secret keys differ from each other.

t: The value difference between two keys at index $d(t = K_1[d] - K_2[d])$.

k: The length(bytes) of the secret key.

n: The number of times $K_1[d], ..., K_1[d+t+1](K_2[d], ..., K_2[d+t+1])$ appear during the KSA. $n = \lfloor \frac{256+k-1-d}{k} \rfloor$

The colliding key pairs' behavior is influenced by three parameters d, t, n. In order to understand how a key pair with the relation described before can achieve collision after KSA, we explain by illustrating three examples with different d, t, n. In the simple case where $n = 1$ (different positions appear only once during KSA), example 1 and 2 are given to show that collision can be achieved by various d and t. Example 3 shows that in more complex cases where $n > 1$, collisions are still possible. We analyze the key scheduling process for key pairs with the above relation that can lead to collisions. We summarize the transition pattern in the Table 1,2 and 3, which helps in tracking the internal state of RC4 when i touches the different positions of the two keys. The internal state part of each table tracks the information of i, j, K and S-BOX generated by the two keys. Notice that the value of S-BOX denotes the state after the swap. The "Difference" part of each table tells us the difference between two internal states at time i.

3.2   Example 1 ($d = 2, t = 2, n = 1(k = 256)$)

Let's demonstrate the case in which the key length is $k = 256$ byte, $d = 2$ and $t = 2$. Our key pattern requires that $K_1[d] = K_2[d] - t$, $K_1[d+1] = K_2[d+1] + t$, $K_1[d + t + 1] = K_1[d + t + 1] - t$ and all other parts of the key must be the same. Now we describe how the new transition pattern works. First, before i touches index d, in this example we assume $j_1(j_2)$ does not touch d or $d + 2$. When $i = d$, we require $j_{1,2} = d(j_{1,2} = 2)$ and $j_{2,2} = d + 2(j_{2,2} = 4)$. Since $j_{1,2} = j_1 + 2 + K_1[2]$ and $j_{2,2} = j_1 + 4 + K_2[2]$ then according to the key pattern, we know that $K_1[2] = 256 - j_1$ and $K_2[2] = 256 - j_1 + 2$. Therefore, at step $i = d$, $S_1[d]$ will not be swapped and $S_2[d]$ will be swapped to index $d + t$. When i increases to $d + 1$, we need $K_1[d + 1]$ and $K_2[d + 1]$ to absorb the difference between j_1 and j_2. In this example, we let $K_1[3] = X + t$ and $K_2[3] = X$ for some X. When i touches $d + t$, namely, $i = 4$, we need $j_{1,4} = d + t$ and $j_{2,4} = d$, namely, $j_{1,4} = 4$ and $j_{2,4} = 2$ so that the difference between the two S-Boxes is absorbed. Now the internal difference exists only between $j_{1,4}$ and $j_{2,4}$. Finally when $i = d + t + 1$, namely, $i = 5$, then $K_1[d+t+1](Y)$ and $K_2[d+t+1])(Y+2)$ are there to absorb the difference between $j_{1,4}$ and $j_{2,4}$. For the rest of the steps($i > d + t + 1$), the internal state remains the same, until the end of KSA. Table 1 describes the above transition procedure.

Table 1. $d = 2, t = 2, n = 1(k = 256)$

i	$K_1[i]/K_2[i]$	$j_{1,i}/j_{2,i}$	1	2	3	4	5	6	Difference
2	$256 - j_1$	2	*	2	3	4	5	*	$K_1[2] = K_2[2] - 2$
	$256 - j_1 + 2$	4	*	4	3	2	5	*	$j_{1,2} = j_{2,2} - 2, S_1 \neq S_2$
3	$X + 2$	$X + 7$	*	2	$S[X + 7]$	4	5	*	$K_1[3] = K_2[3] + 2$
	X	$X + 7$	*	4	$S[X + 7]$	2	5	*	$j_{1,3} = j_{2,3}, S_1 \neq S_2$
4	$256 - X - 7$	4	*	2	$S[X + 7]$	4	5	*	$K_1[4] = K_2[4]$
	$256 - X - 7$	2	*	2	$S[X + 7]$	4	5	*	$j_{1,4} = j_{2,4} + 2, S_1 = S_2$
5	Y	$Y + 9$	*	2	$S[X + 7]$	4	$S[Y + 9]$	*	$K_1[5] = K_2[5] - 2$
	$Y + 2$	$Y + 9$	*	2	$S[X + 7]$	4	$S[Y + 9]$	*	$j_{1,5} = j_{2,5}, S_1 = S_2$

3.3 Example 2 ($d = 3, t = 3, n = 1(k = 256)$)

In Example 2, we change the values d and t to demonstrate that parameters d, t need not be fixed in order to achieve collisions. The transition pattern is summarized in Table 2. It is easy to understand by following Example 1.

Table 2. $d = 3, t = 3, n = 1(k = 256)$

			Internal State					Difference
i	$K_1[i]/K_2[i]$	$j_{1,i}/j_{2,i}$	2 3 4		5	6	7	
3	$256 - j_1$	3	* 3 4		5	6	7	$K_1[3] = K_2[3] - 3$
	$256 - j_1 + 3$	6	* 6 4		5	3	7	$j_{1,3} = j_{2,3} - 3, S_1 \neq S_2$
4	$X + 3$	$X + 10$	* 3 $S[X + 10]$		5	6	7	$K_1[4] = K_2[4] + 3$
	X	$X + 10$	* 6 $S[X + 10]$		5	3	7	$j_{1,4} = j_{2,4}, S_1 \neq S_2$
5	Y	$X + Y + 15$	* 3 $S[X + 10]$	$S[X + Y + 15]$ 6		7		$K_1[5] = K_2[5]$
	Y	$X + Y + 15$	* 6 $S[X + 10]$	$S[X + Y + 15]$ 3		7		$j_{1,5} = j_{2,5}, S_1 \neq S_2$
6	$256 - (X + Y + 15)$	6	* 3 $S[X + 10]$	$S[X + Y + 15]$ 6		7		$K_1[6] = K_2[6]$
	$256 - (X + Y + 15)$	3	* 3 $S[X + 10]$	$S[X + Y + 15]$ 6		7		$j_{1,6} = j_{2,6} + 3, S_1 = S_2$
7	Z	$Z + 13$	* 3 $S[X + 10]$	$S[X + Y + 15]$ 5 $S[Z + 13]$				$K_1[7] = K_2[7] - 3$
	$Z + 3$	$Z + 13$	* 3 $S[X + 10]$	$S[X + Y + 15]$ 5 $S[Z + 13]$				$j_{1,7} = j_{2,7}, S_1 = S_2$

3.4 Example 3 ($d = 4, t = 2, n = 2(k = 128)$)

Notice that Examples 1 and 2 directly apply to the situations where the three different positions of the key appear only once during the KSA, such as the 256-byte key. However, when the three different positions of the key appear more than once, in other words, when the key becomes short, extra conditions need to be satisfied in order to achieve collision. Table 3 is one example for $k = 128, d = 4, t = 2$; in this case, the different positions of the key will appear twice during KSA. This example will give us all the techniques for even shorter keys. In order to extend the pattern to normal situations, we use abstract values such as a, b instead of specific values. The transition pattern is summarized in table 3.

In this example, index $4, 5, 7$ is the first appearance ($n = 1$) of the different positions of the key, while index $132, 133, 135$ is the second appearance ($n = 2$). After i touches index 135, the two internal states become same for the rest of KSA. Because the key pairs are determined during the first appearance (index $4, 5, 7$), index $132, 133, 135$ have to use the same keys as index $4, 5, 7$. So it is very natural to think that in order for the transition pattern to work for shorter keys, there are some extra conditions that need to be satisfied and the requirement for those extra conditions come from the fact that keys are determined in the first appearance and could not be changed from that point. According to the transition table 3, we can derive $j_{1,134} = j_{1,133} + K_1[6] + S_{1,133}[134] = (X + S[133] + 134) + (254 - X - a - b) + (j_3 - j_{131} + 134 + a - d)$, thus $S[133] = a + b + j_{131} - j_3 - a + d - 132$. We also know from the table that $S[132] = j_3 - j_{131} + 132 + a - d$. This gives us $S[132] + S[133] = a + b$. This is exactly the extra condition that our transition sequence should satisfy in the case of $n = 2$. In summarizing, the following conditions should be satisfied in order to achieve a

Table 3. $d = 4, t = 2, n = 2(k = 128)$

i	$K_1[i]/K_2[i]$	$j_{1,i}/j_{2,i}$	Internal State				Difference
			4	5	6	7	
4	$d - a - j_3$	d	a	b	$a + 2$	$S[7]$	$K_1[4] = K_2[4] - 2$
	$d - a - j_3 + 2$	$d + 2$	$a + 2$	b	a	$S[7]$	$j_{1,4} = j_{2,4} - 2, S_1 \neq S_2$
5	$X + 2$	$X + b + d + 2$	a	$S_1[X + b + d + 2]$	$a + 2$	$S[7]$	$K_1[5] = K_2[5] + 2$
	X	$X + b + d + 2$	$a + 2$	$S_2[X + b + d + 2]$	a	$S[7]$	$j_{1,5} = j_{2,5}, S_1 \neq S_2$
6	$254 - X - a - b$	$d + 2$	a	$S_1[X + b + d + 2]$	$a + 2$	$S[7]$	$K_1[6] = K_2[6]$
	$254 - X - a - b$	d	a	$S_2[X + b + d + 2]$	$a + 2$	$S[7]$	$j_{1,6} = j_{2,6} + 2, S_1 = S_2$
7	Y	$Y + d + 2 + S[7]$	a	$S_1[X + b + d + 2]$	$a + 2$	$S_1[Y + d + 2 + S[7]]$	$K_1[7] = K_2[7] - 2$
	$Y + 2$	$Y + d + 2 + S[7]$	a	$S_2[X + b + d + 2]$	$a + 2$	$S_2[Y + d + 2 + S[7]]$	$j_{1,7} = j_{2,7}, S_1 = S_2$

i	$K_1[i]/K_2[i]$	$j_{1,i}/j_{2,i}$	Internal State				Difference
			132	133	134	135	
132	$d - a - j_3$	132	$j_3 - j_{131} + 132 + a - d$	$S[133]$	$j_3 - j_{131} + 134 + a - d$	$S[135]$	$K_1[132] = K_2[132] - 2$
	$d - a - j_3 + 2$	134	$j_3 - j_{131} + 134 + a - d$	$S[133]$	$j_3 - j_{131} + 132 + a - d$	$S[135]$	$j_{1,132} = j_{2,132} - 2, S_1 \neq S_2$
133	$X + 2$	$X + S[133] + 134$	$j_3 - j_{131} + 132 + a - d$	$S[X + S[133] + 134]$	$j_3 - j_{131} + 134 + a - d$	$S[135]$	$K_1[133] = K_2[133] + 2$
	X	$X + S[133] + 134$	$j_3 - j_{131} + 134 + a - d$	$S[X + S[133] + 134]$	$j_3 - j_{131} + 132 + a - d$	$S[135]$	$j_{1,133} = j_{2,133}, S_1 \neq S_2$
134	$254 - X - a - b$	134	$j_3 - j_{131} + 132 + a - d$	$S[X + S[133] + 134]$	$j_3 - j_{131} + 134 + a - d$	$S[135]$	$K_1[134] = K_2[134]$
	$254 - X - a - b$	132	$j_3 - j_{131} + 132 + a - d$	$S[X + S[133] + 134]$	$j_3 - j_{131} + 134 + a - d$	$S[135]$	$j_{1,134} = j_{2,134} + 2, S_1 = S_2$
135	Y	$Y + 134 + S[135]$	$j_3 - j_{131} + 132 + a - d$	$S[X + S[133] + 134]$	$j_3 - j_{131} + 134 + a - d$	$S[Y + 134 + S[135]]$	$K_1[135] = K_2[135] - 2$
	$Y + 2$	$Y + 134 + S[135]$	$j_3 - j_{131} + 132 + a - d$	$S[X + S[133] + 134]$	$j_3 - j_{131} + 134 + a - d$	$S[Y + 134 + S[135]]$	$j_{1,135} = j_{2,135}, S_1 = S_2$

collision for case $d = 4, t = 2, n = 2(k = 128)$. All the conditions could be derived from the transition table 3 except for the little tricky one $S[132] + S[133] = a + b$, which we have just calculated.

$$
\begin{cases}
S_3[4] + 2 = S_3[6] & (1) \\
j_{1,4} = 4(j_{2,4} = 6) & (2) \\
j_5 \neq 4, 6 & (3) \\
j_{1,6} = 6(j_{2,6} = 4) & (4) \\[6pt]
S_{131}[132] + 2 = S_{131}[134] & (5) \\
j_{1,132} = 132(j_{2,132} = 134) & (6) \\
j_{133} \neq 132, 134 & (7) \\
S_{131}[132] + S_{131}[133] = a + b & (8) \\
j_{1,134} = 134(j_{2,134} = 132) & (9)
\end{cases}
$$

Notice that (5) and (8) will give (9), so actually we only need (1) to (8). From the above analysis, we could easily derive the sufficient and necessary conditions for our transition pattern, namely,

1. $j_{d+pk} = d + pk$ for $p = 0, ..., n - 1$. (corresponding to (2),(6))
2. $j_{d+pk+t} = d + pk + t$ for $p = 0$. (corresponding to (4),(9))
3. $S_{d+pk}[d + pk] + t = S_{d+pk}[d + pk + t]$ for $p = 0, ..., n - 1$. (corresponding to (1),(5))
4. $(S_{d+pk}[d+pk] + \cdots + S_{d+pk}[d+pk+t-1]) \bmod 256 = S_d[d] + \cdots + S_d[d+t-1]$ for $p = 1, ..., n - 1$. (corresponding to (8))
5. $j_{d+pk+1}, ..., j_{d+pk+t-1} \neq d + pk, d + pk + t$ for $p = 0, ..., n - 1$. (corresponding to (3),(7)).

4   Probability Analysis

In this section, we give probability estimation for our transition pattern.

Assume that K_1 and K_2 form a k byte key pair which has the following properties: $K_1[d] = K_2[d] - t$, $K_1[d + 1] = K_2[d + 1] + t$, $K_1[d + t + 1] = K_1[d + t + 1] - t$ for some t, d and n. From the previous section, we know the conditions for our transition pattern. Now we formalize some conditions into events for convenience in the analysis.

Event A: $j_{d+pk} = d + pk$ for $p = 0, 1, 2, ..., n - 1$.
Event B: $S_{d+pk}[d + pk] + t = S_{d+pk}[d + pk + t]$ for $p = 0, 1, ..., n - 1$
Event C: $(S_{d+pk}[d + pk] + \cdots + S_{d+pk}[d + pk + t - 1]) \bmod 256 = S_d[d] + \cdots + S_d[d + t - 1]$ for $p = 1, 2, ..., n - 1$.
Event D: $j_{d+pk+1}, ..., j_{d+pk+t-1} \neq d + pk, d + pk + t$ for $p = 0, ..., n - 1$.

Lemma 1. *The probability of Event A is*

$$
P(A) = P(j_{d+pk} = d + pk) = \frac{1}{256} \text{ for } p = 0, 1, ..., n - 1
$$

Proof. Here we assume that j behaves randomly, thus $P(j_{d+pk} = p + dk) = \frac{1}{256}$.

Lemma 2. *The probability of Event B is*

$$P(B_{d,k,p}) = \frac{255}{256} \times \left(\frac{254}{256}\right)^{d+pk-1} + \frac{1}{256} \ \text{for} \ p = 0, ..., n-1$$

Proof. There are two cases that could lead to $S_{d+pk}[d+pk]+t = S_{d+pk}[d+pk+t]$.

Case 1(Event D): $S_{d+pk}[d+pk]$ and $S_{d+pk}[d+pk+t]$ have not been swapped before. The probability for this case(Event D) is $\left(\frac{254}{256}\right)^{d+pk-1}$.

Case 2(Event E): $S_{d+pk}[d+pk]$ and $S_{d+pk}[d+pk+t]$ have been touched before i touches $d+pk$. The probability of Event E is the complement of Event D, namely, $1 - \left(\frac{254}{256}\right)^{d+pk-1}$.

According to the law of total probability, we have
$$P(B) = P(B|D)P(D) + P(B|E)P(E)$$
$$= 1 \times \left(\frac{254}{256}\right)^{d+pk-1} + \frac{1}{256} \times \left(1 - \left(\frac{254}{256}\right)^{d+pk-1}\right)$$
$$= \frac{255}{256} \times \left(\frac{254}{256}\right)^{d+pk-1} + \frac{1}{256}$$

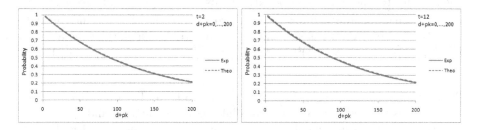

Fig. 1. Event B

Figure 1 shows the experimental and theoretical results with $d+pk$ from 3 to 200. From the figure, we can see that the theoretical result agrees with the experimental result very well. Notice that the probability of Event B is not affected by value t.

Before evaluating Event C, let's first look at the following Lemma 3.

Lemma 3. *The probability of $S_v[v']$ in round v equals to some value $u(u < v$ or $u = v', v' \geq v)$ is as follows:*
(1) When $u = v'$, then

$$P(S_v[v'] = u) = \left(\frac{255}{256}\right)^v$$

(2) When $u < v$, then
$$P(S_v[v'] = u) = \left(\frac{255}{256}\right)^{v-1} \times \frac{1}{256} + \sum_{t_1=u+1}^{v-1}\left(\frac{255}{256}\right)^{v-2} \times \left(\frac{1}{256}\right)^2$$
$$+ \sum_{t_1=u+1}^{v-2}\sum_{t_2=t_1+1}^{v-1}\left(\frac{255}{256}\right)^{v-3} \times \left(\frac{1}{256}\right)^3 + \cdots + \sum_{t_1=u+1}^{v-(n-1)} \cdots \sum_{t_{n-1}=t_{n-2}+1}^{v-1}\left(\frac{255}{256}\right)^{v-n}$$
$$\times \left(\frac{1}{256}\right)^n$$
    where $n = v - u$.

Proof. (1) When $u = v'$, $S_v[v'] = v'$ means after round v, $S[v']$ remains untouched. Thus the probability is $\left(\frac{255}{256}\right)^v$.

(2) When $u < v$, u will be in index v' after v rounds(i touches $v - 1$). In order for this to happen, first, we need u to remain untouched before i touches it, otherwise u will be swapped somewhere before i and the chance for it to be swapped to index v' will be lost. The probability of this is $(\frac{255}{256})^u$. Then when i touches u, we have several choices, either to swap u directly to index v' (we call this one hop), or to swap u to an intermediate index t_1 between index u and v, and then when i touches t_1, u can be swapped to index v' (we call this two hops), etc. As you may guess, there exist maximum $v - u$ hops. We analyze one-hop, two-hop and three-hop cases here.

One hop: When i touches u, u is swapped to index v' with probability $\frac{1}{256}$ and remains untouched for $v - u - 1$ rounds. Thus the probability is $(\frac{255}{256})^u \times \frac{1}{256} \times (\frac{255}{256})^{v-u-1} = (\frac{255}{256})^{v-1} \times \frac{1}{256}$

Two hops: When i touches u, u is first swapped to index t_1 between index u and v with probability $\frac{1}{256}$. For $t_1 - u - 1$ rounds, index t_1 remains untouched. Then when i touches t_1, u is swapped to index v' with probability $\frac{1}{256}$ and then index v' remains untouched for $v - t_1 - 1$ rounds. Notice that the intermediate index t_1 can vary between $u + 1$ and $v - 1$, thus the probability of the above is $\sum_{t_1=u+1}^{v-1}(\frac{255}{256})^u \times \frac{1}{256} \times (\frac{255}{256})^{t_1-u-1} \times \frac{1}{256} \times (\frac{255}{256})^{v-t_1-1} = \sum_{t_1=u+1}^{v-1}(\frac{255}{256})^{v-2} \times (\frac{1}{256})^2$

Three hops: The analysis is the same as for two hops. The only difference for three hops is that we have two intermediate indices t_1 and t_2, and t_1 can vary between index $u + 1$ and $v - 2$ and t_2 can vary between index $t_1 + 1$ and $v - 1$. Thus the probability is $\sum_{t_1=u+1}^{v-2} \sum_{t_2=t_1+1}^{v-1}(\frac{255}{256})^u \times \frac{1}{256} \times (\frac{255}{256})^{t_1-u-1} \times \frac{1}{256} \times (\frac{255}{256})^{t_2-t_1-1} \times \frac{1}{256} \times (\frac{255}{256})^{v-t_2-1} = \sum_{t_1=u+1}^{v-2} \sum_{t_2=t_1+1}^{v-1}(\frac{255}{256})^{v-3} \times (\frac{1}{256})^3$.

For cases of more than 4 hops, the above analysis works in the same way. By summing these results together, we get our final result.

We tested 4 sets of data where (v, v') equal to $(64, 64), (64, 74), (128, 128)$ or $(128, 138)$ respectively. The theoretical result agrees well with the experimental result, except for a few points as shown in Figure 2. This result is sufficient for our probability evaluation.

Now we are ready to calculate Event C by using the above Lemma and partition techniques. Refer to Appendix A for a more specific description of the integer partitioning algorithm.

Lemma 4. *The probability of Event C is*

$$P(C_{d,k,p}) = \sum_{i=0}^{\#(\mathcal{Q}(X)-\mathcal{I}(X))} \prod_{j=0}^{t-1}(P_{d+pk}[d + pk + j] = q_{ij})$$

where $\mathcal{Q}(X)$ denotes the partition function with input X the number to be partitioned, and the output is a set of t-element tuples. Each tuple represents a t distinct element partition of X. Let $PS = S_d[d] + \cdots + S_d[d + t - 1]$ and

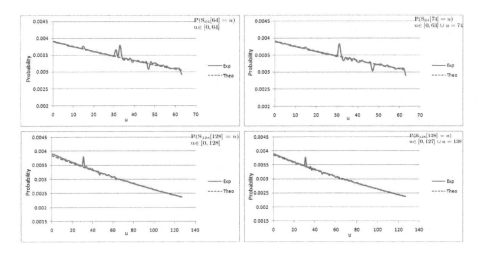

Fig. 2. Theorem 3

$PD = (d + pk) + \cdots + (d + pk + t - 1).$ $X \in \{q = \{0, ..., \lfloor \frac{PD-PS}{256} \rfloor\}|PS + 256 \times q\}.$ $\mathcal{I}(X)$ denotes the subset of $\mathcal{Q}(X)$ which satisfies the following conditions: $S_{d+pk}[d + pk], ..., S_{d+pk}[d + pk + t - 1] > d + pk$ and $S_{d+pk}[d + pk] \neq d + pk, ..., S_{d+pk}[d + pk + t - 1] \neq d + pk + t - 1.$ q_{ij} denotes the jth element in tuple i of set $\mathcal{Q}(X) - \mathcal{I}(X)$.

Proof. According to the definition of Event C, our goal is to partition the sum $S_d[d] + \cdots + S_d[d+t-1]$ and calculate the probability that the t-element partition will be in position $d+pk, ..., d+pk+t-1$. Here, one thing to notice is that when the difference between $(d+pk) + \cdots + (d+pk+t-1)$ and $S_d[d] + \cdots + S_d[d+t-1]$ is larger than $256 * q$ for some $q \geq 0$, than the partition of $S_d[d] + \cdots + S_d[d+t-1] + 256 * q$ is also a possible partition for positions $d + pk, ..., d + pk + t - 1$. Thus the input of partition function $\mathcal{Q}(X)$ can vary depending on the relation between PS and PD. The subset $\mathcal{I}(X)$ indicates partitions that will never occur in the situation of RC4. This is easy to see because before i touches index $d + pk$, $S[d + pk], ..., S[d + pk + t - 1]$ could never become a value greater than index $d + pk$ except for the value of the index itself, which is the case in which these values have never been swapped before. Thus $\mathcal{Q}(X) - \mathcal{I}(X)$ denotes all the legal partitions.

$\prod_{j=0}^{t-1}(P_{d+pk}[d + pk + i] = q_{ij})$ is the probability of each legal partition being in positions $d + pk, ..., d + pk + t - 1$. The probability is calculated by using Lemma 3, and we have t elements for each partition, so we need to multiply them together. Since there are a total $\#(\mathcal{Q}(X) - \mathcal{I}(X))$ partitions, by summing them together, we get the probability of Event C.

Figure 3 represents the experimental and theoretical probability of $S_d[d] + S_d[d + 1] + \cdots + S_d[d + t - 1] \equiv S_{d+k}[d + k] + S_{d+k}[d + k + 1] + \cdots + S_{d+k}[d + k+t - 1] \pmod{256}$ for fixed k, t and various d.

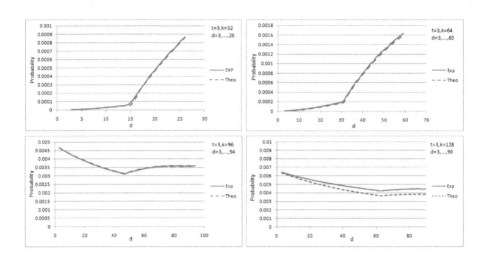

Fig. 3. Event C

Lemma 5. *The probability of Event D is*

$$P(D_t) = \left(\frac{254}{256}\right)^{t-1}$$

Proof. There are $t - 1$ places between index $d + pk$ and $d + pk + t$. When i touches these positions, j should not touch $d + pk$ and $d + pk + t$. This gives us the probability $\left(\frac{254}{256}\right)^{t-1}$.

Theorem 1. *Assume that K_1 and K_2 form a k-byte key pair which has the following properties: $K_1[d] = K_2[d] - t$, $K_1[d + 1] = K_2[d + 1] + t$, $K_1[d + t + 1] = K_1[d + t + 1] - t$ for some fixed t, d and n. Then the probability that K_1 and K_2 are a colliding key pair is*

$$P_{col}(t, d, k) = (P(A))^{n+1}(P(D_t))^n \prod_{p=0}^{n-1} P(B_{d,k,p}) \prod_{p=1}^{n-1} P(C_{d,k,p})$$

Proof. Recall the conditions we summarized in the previous section. What we are doing here is just combining all the conditions. When $p = 0$, there is no restriction on Event C. The probability is $(P(A))^2 P(B)P(D)$. When $p \geq 1$, according to the previous analysis, we have $\prod_{p=1}^{n-1} P(A)P(B)P(C)P(D)$. By multiplying these two cases together, we get our result.

Since parameters d and t are not required to be fixed in our pattern, the total probability should include various d and t. This gives us the following Corollary.

Corollary 1. *Assume that K_1 and K_2 form a k-byte key pair which has the following properties: $K_1[d] = K_2[d] - t$, $K_1[d + 1] = K_2[d + 1] + t$, $K_1[d + t + 1] = K_1[d + t + 1] - t$. Then the probability that K_1 and K_2 are a colliding key pair is*

$$P_{col}(t,d,k) = \sum_{d=0}^{k-4}\sum_{t=2}^{k-d-2}(P(A))^{n+1}(P(D_t))^n\prod_{p=0}^{n-1}P(B_{d,k,p})\prod_{p=1}^{n-1}P(C_{d,k,p})$$

Proof. Let's look at the bounds for d and t. First, for every fixed d, the max value t has to satisfy $d+t = k-2$, and the smallest value of t is 2 in our pattern. Thus $2 \le t \le k-d-2$. Then we look at d. d could start from 0. The max d is such d that $t = 2$, so we have $d+2 = k-2$ which gives us $0 \le d \le k-4$.

Corollary 1 gives us the total collision probability of two keys with length k satisfying conditions $K_1[d] = K_2[d]-t$, $K_1[d+1] = K_2[d+1]+t$ and $K_1[d+t+1] = K_1[d+t+1]-t$. Thus the number of colliding key pairs could be calculated by multiplying 2^{8*k}. Since calculating Event C is time consuming and involves exponential time partition algorithm, to evaluate all d and t is a time-consuming job. We approximate by evaluating some fixed d and t. We choose d,t such that for a given k, they make the different positions of the key pair appear least often in the KSA. For example, for $k = 24$, we choose $d = 17, t = 2$ so that the different positions of the key pair appear 10 times not 11 times during KSA. The probability of the 10 times dominates, so we can ignore the 11 times d,t. Our results can be seen as an approximate lower bound of the total number of this new kind of colliding key pairs, and also we compare our work with the results in [2]. Future work is required for a more precise evaluation. Please refer to Appendix B for the detailed results. The values in parentheses in our result denote the chosen values of d and t.

5   An Efficient Search Technique

Searching for such colliding key pairs randomly will hardly generate any results. Finding the colliding key pairs we found involved some detection tricks. Recall the necessary conditions of the transition pattern we have to satisfy, namely, Event A, Event B, Event C and Event D. For Event B and Event C, we can control them to let them occur with much higher probability. We do this as follows: assume when i touches index $d-1$, $S[d], ..., S[d+t-1]$ have not been swapped, thus we can pre-compute the sum $S_d[d]+\cdots+S_d[d+t-1] = d+\cdots+(d+t-1)$. Then we compute $n-1$ partitions of the sum, namely, $(q_{i,1}, ..., q_{i,t}), i \in [1, n-1], d$ for Event C. Also for Event B we can calculate $p_i = q_{i,1}+t$ according to the partitions we calculated. Now we need to adjust two secret keys during KSA so that the values of p and q will be swapped to the corresponding positions $S[d+pk], ..., S[d+pk+t]$ during the first appearance of the secret key. After the secret key begins to duplicate during KSA, we only hope that those positions $d+pk, ..., d+pk+t$ will not be touched before i touches them and Event A occurs.

The above algorithm gives us a much more efficient way to search for this new class of colliding key pairs. The key point here is that we can control the behavior of the keys to satisfy our conditions in the process of the first key appearance in KSA. However, as the length of the key becomes shorter, in other words, as the number of appearances of the key increases, we'll have less control over the behavior during the KSA process. By using our algorithm, we are able to find a 55-byte colliding key pair within one hour. Refer to Appendix C for some concrete colliding key pairs we found.

6 Conclusion

We discovered a new class of colliding key pairs with properties differing from those discovered in [2]. Our new transition pattern requires relatively loose conditions on the key pairs, namely, our colliding key pairs can differ at more than one position and the value difference can also be more than one. We gave probability evaluations of our colliding key pairs and showed the scale of this new class of colliding key pairs. An efficient search algorithm was proposed which can allow us to find 55-byte colliding key pairs easily. We leave finding even shorter colliding key pairs and more precise probability evaluation as future work.

References

1. Grosul, A.L., Wallach, D.S.: A Related-Key Cryptanalysis of RC4. Technical Report TR-00-358, Department of Computer Science, Rice University (2000), http://cohesion.rice.edu/engineering/computerscience/tr/TRDownload.cfm?SDID=126
2. Matsui, M.: Key collisions of the RC4 stream cipher. In: Dunkelman, O., Preneel, B. (eds.) Fast Software Encryption. LNCS, vol. 5665, pp. 38–50. Springer, Heidelberg (2009)
3. Anonymous: RC4 Source Code. CypherPunks mailing list (September 9 (1994), http://cypherpunks.venona.com/date/1994/09/msg00304.html, http://groups.google.com/group/sci.crypt/msg/10a300c9d21afca0
4. Roos, A.: A Class of Weak Keys in the RC4 Stream Cipher (1995), http://marcel.wanda.ch/Archive/WeakKeys
5. Mantin, I., Shamir, A.: A Practical Attack on Broadcast RC4. In: Matsui, M. (ed.) FSE 2001. LNCS, vol. 2355, pp. 152–164. Springer, Heidelberg (2002)
6. Paul, S., Preneel, B.: A New Weakness in the RC4 Keystream Generator and an Approach to Improve Security of the Cipher. In: Roy, B., Meier, W. (eds.) FSE 2004. LNCS, vol. 3017, pp. 245–259. Springer, Heidelberg (2004)
7. Fluhrer, S., Mantin, I., Shamir, A.: Weaknesses in the Key Scheduling Algorithm of RC4. In: Vaudenay, S., Youssef, A.M. (eds.) SAC 2001. LNCS, vol. 2259, pp. 1–24. Springer, Heidelberg (2001)
8. Klein, A.: Attacks on the RC4 Stream Cipher. Designs, Codes and Cryptography 48(3), 269–286 (2008)
9. Tews, E., Weinmann, R.P., Pyshkin, A.: Breaking 104 Bit WEP in Less than 60 Seconds. In: Kim, S., Yung, M., Lee, H.-W. (eds.) WISA 2007. LNCS, vol. 4867, pp. 188–202. Springer, Heidelberg (2008)
10. Vaudenay, S., Vuagnoux, M.: Passive-Only Key Recovery Attacks on RC4. In: Adams, C., Miri, A., Wiener, M. (eds.) SAC 2007. LNCS, vol. 4876, pp. 344–359. Springer, Heidelberg (2007)

A   Integer Partition Techniques

We refer to "The Art of Computer Programming Vol 4" regarding integer partition techniques. The partitions of an integer are the ways to write it as a sum of positive integers. The following Algorithm 3 calculates all partitions of integer n into a fixed number of parts. This algorithm was featured in C.F. Hindenburg's 18th-century dissertation [Infinitinomii Dignitatum Exponentis Indeterminati]. This algorithm generates all integer t-tuples $a_1...a_t$ such that $a_1 \geq \cdots \geq a_t \geq 1$ and $a_1 + \cdots + a_t = n$.

Algorithm 3. Partition n into t parts (Pa(n,t))

1: **[Initialize.]** Set $a_1 \leftarrow n - t + 1$ and $a_j \leftarrow 1$ for $1 < j \leq t$. Set $a_{t+1} \leftarrow -1$.
2: **[Visit.]** Visit the partition $a_1...a_t$. Then go to 4 if $a_2 \geq a_1 - 1$.
3: **[Tweak a_1 and a_2].** Set $a_1 \leftarrow a_1 - 1, a_2 \leftarrow a_2 + 1$, return to 2.
4: **[Find j.]** Set $j \leftarrow 3$ and $s \leftarrow a_1 + a_2 - 1$. Then, if $a_j \geq a_1 - 1$,
   set $s \leftarrow s + a_j, j \leftarrow j + 1$, repeat until $a_j < a_1 - 1$.
5: **[Increase a_j].** Terminate if $j > m$. Otherwise set $x \leftarrow a_j + 1, a_j \leftarrow x$,
   $j \leftarrow j - 1$.
6: **[Tweak $a_1...a_j$].** While $j > 1$, set $a_j \leftarrow x, s \leftarrow s - x$ and $j \leftarrow j - 1$.
   Finally set $a_1 \leftarrow s$ and return to 2.

For example, Pa(11,4) will generate the following partitions:

$$8111, 7211, 6311, 5411, 6221, 5321, 4421, 4331, 5222, 4322, 3332$$

Use it twice, namely, Pa(n,t) and Pa(n,t-1) to include 0 value cases in the partitions, and perform the permutation on each tuple $(a_1...a_t)$ to cover all the cases. Then this is our $\mathcal{Q}$ function.

B   Number of Colliding Key Pairs

Table 4 shows the number of newly discovered colliding key pairs, compared with [2]'s results. The values in the parentheses denote d and t. "-" means colliding key pairs do not exist theoretically.

Table 4. log_2 (number of colliding key pairs)

k	[2]	Ours(d,t)	k	[2]	Ours(d,t)	k	[2]	Ours(d,t)	k	[2]	Ours(d,t)	k	[2]	Ours(d,t)
15	-	-	25	106.9	9.2(7,2)	35	211.2	147.8(12,2)	45	306.4	267.9(32,2)	55	394.9	367.9(37,2)
16	-	-	26	120.7	13.5(3,2)	36	219.6	153.1(5,2)	46	314.9	275.7(27,2)	56	403.2	375.9(33,2)
17	2.7	-	27	130.5	45.8(14,2)	37	232.3	159.6(3,2)	47	323.3	283.4(22,2)	57	411.5	383.9(29,2)
18	18.5	-	28	139.2	49.6(5,2)	38	242.0	194.0(29,2)	48	331.6	291.1(17,2)	58	419.7	391.8(25,2)
19	34.0	-	29	153.0	83.8(25,2)	39	250.7	201.8(23,2)	49	339.9	298.3(12,2)	59	427.9	399.7(21,2)
20	48.7	-	30	162.5	91.0(17,2)	40	259.2	209.4(17,2)	50	348.1	305.4(7,2)	60	436.1	407.6(17,2)
21	58.8	-	31	171.2	97.2(9,2)	41	267.6	216.5(11,2)	51	356.3	311.7(3,2)	61	444.2	415.4(13,2)
22	73.7	-	32	179.7	108.8(3,2)	42	275.9	223.1(5,2)	52	368.7	343.7(49,2)	62	452.4	423.1(9,2)
23	83.0	-	33	193.7	133.7(26,2)	43	287.7	229.8(3,2)	53	377.8	351.8(45,2)	63	460.5	429.1(4,2)
24	97.7	4.7(17,2)	34	202.6	141.0(19.2)	44	297.6	259.7(37,2)	54	386.4	359.8(41,2)	64	468.6	444.9(3,2)

C   Some Concrete Colliding Key Pairs

We demonstrate 4 colliding key pairs in this section with n from 1 to 4. "-" denotes that K_1 and K_2 have the same value.

C.1 $k = 132, d = 125, t = 5, n = 1$

$K_1[000] \sim K_1[023]$: d6 0d c0 2c ab d2 86 09 15 ec 7c d5 69 cd 3b 75 6e b2 34 b9 8f d1 fd b0
$K_2[000] \sim K_2[023]$: -
$K_1[024] \sim K_1[047]$: 65 42 ab 48 df fd 7b c9 79 0a 25 44 35 86 5c 9b 45 5a a7 e5 6b 2b 43 6c
$K_2[024] \sim K_2[047]$: -
$K_1[048] \sim K_1[071]$: 76 94 e8 41 f6 ec bb c9 e4 2e 62 b5 d8 11 17 e3 05 e7 c9 fd c1 36 3d 80
$K_2[048] \sim K_2[071]$: -
$K_1[072] \sim K_1[095]$: 53 00 38 f5 11 58 65 cd 73 43 2e 64 ea 25 d2 0e 75 26 8b a1 7a 10 a0 06
$K_2[072] \sim K_2[095]$: -
$K_1[096] \sim K_1[119]$: c6 2e 05 28 9e 60 23 9c 04 b1 ae 7e 58 f3 93 22 66 72 a4 f8 50 2f 22 1b
$K_2[096] \sim K_2[119]$: -
$K_1[120] \sim K_1[131]$: 39 09 b4 f6 03 a5 4e 08 c7 f3 b2 84
$K_2[120] \sim K_2[131]$: - - - - - aa 49 - - - - - 89

C.2 $k = 85, d = 5, t = 3, n = 2$

$K_1[00] \sim K_1[23]$: 5a 54 aa ff 51 4e e8 b6 50 bf d7 8e 35 0b 47 2e 17 a1 8c 86 db cf fb 3c
$K_2[00] \sim K_2[23]$: - - - - - 51 e5 - - c2 - - - - - - - - - - - - - -
$K_1[24] \sim K_1[47]$: 13 52 22 1a e0 5d 7d a3 91 d8 4c 45 21 c3 f2 f2 d6 ec c0 d9 ea c4 5f 95
$K_2[24] \sim K_2[47]$: -
$K_1[48] \sim K_1[71]$: 3e b6 6b 30 30 6d 78 9c df 79 7c 81 44 e7 65 10 af d6 95 38 9d dd 97 6f
$K_2[48] \sim K_2[71]$: -
$K_1[72] \sim K_1[84]$: 9f 5c 87 94 ce 80 4d 44 a9 6b b4 fc 3a
$K_2[72] \sim K_2[84]$: - - - - - - - - - - - - -

C.3 $k = 66, d = 58, t = 2, n = 3$

$K_1[00] \sim K_1[23]$: 83 db 06 ee 00 8d 7d cb e5 0c 3a b7 33 ec 8f 93 c5 7d 8d 95 64 c5 d9 19
$K_2[00] \sim K_2[23]$: -
$K_1[24] \sim K_1[47]$: 18 45 54 82 be e1 eb 03 4f 96 75 08 b5 6e c6 81 36 16 0d 15 77 8a a2 6b
$K_2[24] \sim K_2[47]$: -
$K_1[48] \sim K_1[65]$: 6f 49 53 96 67 6b cd 0b 88 09 40 db b0 7b 8d 7f 68 0d
$K_2[48] \sim K_2[65]$: - - - - - - - - - - - 42 d9 - 7d - - - -

C.4 $k = 55, d = 36, t = 2, n = 4$

$K_1[00] \sim K_1[23]$: 89 2d b4 26 2c 12 3b 51 09 87 49 92 88 38 d9 3d e1 7d 4e 35 11 99 fc 76
$K_2[00] \sim K_2[23]$: -
$K_1[24] \sim K_1[47]$: f7 35 46 79 89 b3 00 dd 15 16 a9 14 35 05 b2 5f f6 a0 09 66 d9 08 e4 76
$K_2[24] \sim K_2[47]$: - - - - - - - - - - - - - 37 03 - 61 - - - - - - -
$K_1[48] \sim K_1[54]$: 17 7e 2b 7a 69 5b 69
$K_2[48] \sim K_2[54]$: - - - - - - -

On the Security of NOEKEON against Side Channel Cube Attacks

Shekh Faisal Abdul-Latip[1,2], Mohammad Reza Reyhanitabar[1],
Willy Susilo[1], and Jennifer Seberry[1]

[1] Center for Computer and Information Security Research,
School of Computer Science and Software Engineering,
University of Wollongong, Australia
{sfal620,rezar,wsusilo,jennie}@uow.edu.au
[2] Faculty of Information and Communication Technology,
Universiti Teknikal Malaysia Melaka, Malaysia
shekhfaisal@utem.edu.my

Abstract. In this paper, we investigate the security of the NOEKEON block cipher against side channel cube attacks. NOEKEON was proposed by Daemen et al. for the NESSIE project. The block size and the key size are both 128 bits. The cube attack, introduced by Dinur and Shamir at EUROCRYPT 2009, is a new type of algebraic cryptanalysis. The attack may be applied if the adversary has access to a single bit of information that can be represented by a *low degree* multivariate polynomial over $GF(2)$ of secret and public variables. In the side channel attack model, the attacker is assumed to have access to some leaked information about the internal state of the cipher as well as the plaintext and ciphertext. Adopting the notion of a single bit leakage as formalized by Dinur and Shamir, we assume that the attacker has only one bit of information about the intermediate state after each round. Using this side channel attack model, we show that it is possible to extract 60 *independent* linear equations over 99 (out of 128) key variables. To recover the whole 128-bit key, the attack requires only about 2^{10} chosen plaintext and $O(2^{68})$ time complexity.

Keywords: Algebraic cryptanalysis, block ciphers, cube attacks, NOEKEON, side channel attacks.

1 Introduction

Almost any cryptosystem can be represented by a system of multivariate polynomial equations over a finite field, e.g. $GF(2)$. The cube attack, formalized by Dinur and Shamir at EUROCRYPT 2009 [9], is a generic type of algebraic attacks. The attack aims to derive low-degree equations that can be exploited for constructing distinguishers, e.g. [2], and/or key recovery attacks, e.g. [9, 2]. An interesting feature of the cube attack is that it only requires a black-box access to a target cryptosystem and may be applied even if only a few output bits can be accessed by an adversary.

J. Kwak et al. (Eds.): ISPEC 2010, LNCS 6047, pp. 45–55, 2010.

For a properly designed ("good") cipher, whose algebraic representation over GF(2) is of degree d (i.e. the maximum degree of the output bits represented as boolean functions is d), the cube attack will require about 2^d computations. Therefore, *in general*, the attack's success depends on whether this computational complexity is feasible or not; however we note that this "generic complexity" does not imply that the attack may not be successful for specific cases. The cube attack has been successfully applied (for key recovery) against a reduced-round variant of the Trivium [6] stream cipher in [9] and (as a distinguisher) against a reduced-round variant of the MD6 hash function [14] in [2].

In trying to apply cube attacks to block ciphers, the main problem is that the degree of the polynomial representing a ciphertext bit grows exponentially with the number of rounds in the cipher. Hence, the cube attack usually becomes ineffective after a few rounds if one considers only the standard attack model that is used in the well-known statistical attacks such as the Differential and Linear attacks. Nevertheless, considering the practical implementations of the block cipher, especially in resource limited systems such as smart cards, there is a stronger attack model, namely the side channel attack model, where the adversary is given more power by having access to some "*limited*" information leaked about the internal state of the cipher. This information leakage can be via physical side channels, such as timing, electrical power consumption, electromagnetic radiation, probing, etc.

Dinur and Shamir in [10] proposed a side channel attack model, where the adversary is assumed to have access to "*only one bit of information*" about the internal state of the block cipher after each round. This one bit of information can be, for example, a single bit of the internal state itself or a bit of information about the Hamming weight of the internal state. They showed that the cube attack in this single-bit-leakage side channel model can recover the secret key of the Serpent [1] and AES [7] block ciphers much easier than the previously known side channel attacks. Recently, Yang et al. at CANS 2009 [15] investigated the side channel cube attack on the PRESENT block cipher [5]. It is worth noticing that the single-bit-leakage side channel cube attack against a block cipher is different from a cube attack against a reduced-round variant of the cipher; while in the former the adversary has access to only one bit of information about the internal state, in the latter the adversary has access to the whole internal state after a reduced number of rounds.

In this paper, we investigate the security of the NOEKEON block cipher [8] against the cube attack in the single-bit-leakage side channel attack model. NOEKEON is designed to be efficient and secure on a wide range of platforms including the environment with limited resources such as smart cards. The designers of NOEKEON have shown how the cipher can be adapted to provide an anti-DPA variant of NOEKEON which is secure against differential power analysis (DPA) attacks. However, the implementation cost for the anti-DPA version is almost twice that of a normal NOEKEON implementation. They also noticed that to prevent higher-order DPA attacks one will have to use even less efficient variants. If the cipher were to be implemented in a time-critical system, it is likely that this kind of anti-DPA variants not to be implemented due to the efficiency/security trade-off. Many papers on side channel attacks such as in [12, 13] also concentrate on countermeasures which minimize the leakage from the implementation.

We note that these kind of countermeasures against specific types of side channel attacks (e.g. timing attack or DPA) do not remove the possibility of all side channel attacks such as electromagnetic radiations, probing, etc. In this paper we do not consider these specific issues and countermeasures about the actual physical aspects of the implementation attacks and how information leakage can be measured. Rather, we assume the single-bit-leakage side channel model as an abstract attack model, and concentrate on investigating the security of ciphers against cube attacks in this attack model.

Our Contribution. We investigate the security of the NOEKEON block cipher against cube attacks in the single-bit-leakage side channel attack model. First, we show how to determine the appropriate round to find most of the key bits. Using a single bit of the internal state after the second round, we extract 60 *independent* linear equations over 99 key variables. To recover the whole 128-bit key, the attack requires about 2^{10} chosen plaintext and $O(2^{68})$ time complexity.

Organization of the Paper. In Section 2 and 3, we review the cube attack and the construction of NOEKEON block cipher, respectively. Section 4 contains the main contribution of this paper, where we provide the details of the side channel cube attack on NOEKEON. Section 5 concludes the paper and provides some open problems for future research.

2   A Review on the Cube Attack

In algebraic attacks, one aims at recovering the secret key in cryptosystems by manipulating and solving the underlying algebraic equations. Solving a system of multivariate equations over a finite field $\mathbb{F}$, in general, is known to be an NP-hard problem [11]. However, it has been demonstrated that finding solutions faster than by the exhaustive search may be possible if the algebraic equations have a relatively low algebraic degree when considered as multivariate polynomial equations. An ideal situation is when one can derive enough number of independent linear equations which are easily solvable (e.g. by Gaussian elimination); the cube attack aims at doing this.

The main point of the cube attack is that, the multivariate "master" polynomial $p(v_1, \cdots, v_m, k_1, \cdots, k_n)$, representing an output bit of a cryptosystem over GF(2) of secret variables k_i (key bits) and public variables v_i (i.e. plaintext or initial values), may induce algebraic equations of lower degrees, in particular *linear* equations. The cube attack provides a method to derive such lower degree (especially linear) equations, given the master polynomial only as a black-box which can be evaluated on the secret and public variables.

Let's ignore the distinction between the secret and public variables' notations and denote all of them by $x_i, \cdots, x_\ell$, where $\ell = m + n$. Let $I \subseteq \{1, ..., \ell\}$ be a subset of the variable indexes, and t_I denote a monomial term containing multiplication of all the x_i's with $i \in I$. By factoring the master polynomial p by the monomial t_I, we have:

$$p(x_1, \cdots, x_\ell) = t_I \cdot p_{S(I)} + q(x_1, \cdots, x_\ell) \tag{1}$$

where $p_{S(I)}$, which is called the *superpoly* of t_I in p, does not have any common variable with t_I, and each monomial term t_J in the residue polynomial q misses at least one variable from t_I. A term t_I is called a "*maxterm*" if its superpoly in p is linear polynomial which is not a constant, i.e. $deg(p_{S(I)}) = 1$.

The main observation of the cube attack is that, if we sum p over t_I, i.e. by assigning all the possible combinations of $0/1$ values to the x_i's with $i \in I$ and fixing the value of all the remaining x_i's with $i \notin I$, the resultant polynomial equals to $p_{S(I)} \pmod 2$. More formally, a subset I of size s (where $s \leq \ell$) defines a boolean cube C_I containing 2^s boolean vectors which are formed by assigning all 2^s values to the x_i's with $i \in I$, and leaving all the remaining variables (i.e. x_i's with $i \notin I$) undetermined. For example, if $I = \{1, 2\}$ then $C_I = \{(0, 0, x_3, \cdots, x_\ell), (0, 1, x_3, \cdots, x_\ell), (1, 0, x_3, \cdots, x_\ell), (1, 1, x_3, \cdots, x_\ell)\}$. Any vector $\mathbf{w} \in C_I$ defines a derived polynomial $p_{|\mathbf{w}}$ with $\ell - s$ variables whose degree may be the same or lower than the degree of the master polynomial p. Summing the 2^s derived polynomials over $GF(2)$ defined by the vectors in the cube C_I, we get a new polynomial p_I defined by $p_I \triangleq \sum_{\mathbf{w} \in C_I} p_{|\mathbf{w}}$. The following theorem states the main observation used by the cube attack.

Theorem 1 (The Main Observation [9]). *Given a polynomial p over $GF(2)$ with ℓ variables, and any index subset $I \subseteq \{1, \cdots, \ell\}$, we have $p_I = p_{S(I)}$.*

Given access to a cryptographic function with public and secret variables, this observation enables an attacker to recover the value of the secret variables (k_i's) in two steps, namely preprocessing and online phase, which are described in the sequel.

PREPROCESSING PHASE. During the preprocessing phase, the attacker first finds sufficiently many maxterms, i.e. t_I's, such that each t_I consists of a subset of public variables $v_1, \cdots, v_m$. To find the maxterms, the attacker performs a probabilistic linearity test on $p_{S(I)}$ over the secret variables $k_i \in \{k_1, \cdots, k_n\}$ while the value of the public variables not in t_I are fixed (to 0 or 1). For example, the BLR test of [4] can be used for this purpose. This test requires the attacker to choose a sufficient number of vectors $\mathbf{x}, \mathbf{y} \in \{0, 1\}^n$ independently and uniformly at random representing samples of n-bit key, and then for each pair of vectors $\mathbf{x}$ and $\mathbf{y}$, the attacker sums the polynomial p over t_I to verify whether or not each one of them satisfies the relation:

$$p_{S(I)}[\mathbf{0}] + p_{S(I)}[\mathbf{x}] + p_{S(I)}[\mathbf{y}] = p_{S(I)}[\mathbf{x} + \mathbf{y}] \tag{2}$$

If all the vectors $\mathbf{x}$ and $\mathbf{y}$ satisfy the relation, with high probability $p_{S(I)}$ is linear over the secret variables; that is, t_I is a maxterm. Then the next step is to derive linearly independent equations in the secret variables k_i's from $p_{S(I)}$ that are closely related to the master polynomial p, such that, solving them enables the attacker to determine the values of the secret variables.

ONLINE PHASE. Once sufficiently many linearly independent equations in the secret variables are found, the preprocessing phase is completed. In the online phase, the attacker's aim is to find the value of the right-hand side of each linear equation by summing the black box polynomial p over the same set of maxterms t_I's which are obtained during the preprocessing phase. Now, the attacker can easily solve the resultant system of the linear equations, e.g. by using the Gaussian elimination method, to determine the values of the secret (key) variables.

3 A Brief Description of the NOEKEON Block Cipher

NOEKEON [8] is a block cipher with a block and key length of 128 bits. It produces a ciphertext after iterating a round function 16 times, followed by a final output function. The specification of NOEKEON [8], provides a key schedule which converts the 128-bit "Cipher Key" (i.e. the original key) into a 128-bit "Working Key", which is used in the round function. However, the use of the key schedule is optional. If related-key attack scenarios [3] are not of a concern, then the key schedule is not applied (i.e. the Cipher Key is used directly as the Working Key), and the cipher is called to be used in the "direct-key mode". Otherwise, it operates in the "indirect-key mode", where the Cipher Key is processed by the key schedule algorithm to produce the Working Key.

A graphical representation of the round function of NOEKEON is shown in Fig. 1. It consists of two linear functions, Θ and Π (as illustrated in the figure), and a nonlinear function Γ which is described shortly. We describe the encryption mode of the cipher. The description of the cipher in the decryption (i.e. inverse) mode is also quite straightforward, where the inverse of the component functions are used (we refer to [8] for a complete description of the cipher). The constants C_1 and C_2 are two round constants. C_2 is set to zero during the encryption process and C_1 is set to zero during the decryption process. The constant C_1 that is used during the encryption process can be computed in recursive way as follows:

```
C₁⁰ = 0x80;
if (C₁ʳ & 0x80 != 0) then C₁ʳ⁺¹ = C₁ʳ ≪ 1 ^ 0x1B
else C₁ʳ⁺¹ = C₁ʳ ≪ 1;
```

Let $A_r = A_r^0 A_r^1 A_r^2 A_r^3$ denote the 128-bit internal state after round r; where A_r^i's are 32-bit words, and A_0 contains the input plaintext P to the cipher. Then NOEKEON encryption algorithm can be described as follows:

$$\text{For } r = 0;\ r < 16;\ r{+}{+}$$
$$A_{r+1} = \Pi^{-1}(\Gamma(\Pi(\Theta(A_r, K))));$$
$$A_{17} = \Theta(A_{16}, K)$$

where A_{17} denotes the 128-bit output ciphertext, and $K = K_0K_1K_2K_3$ is the 128-bit working key (K_i's are 32-bit words).

The nonlinear transformation Γ operates on 32 4-tuples of bits (4-bit boxes) using a S-box which is shown in Table 1 (4-bit values are represented by a hexadecimal number). The 4-bit boxes which are input to the S-Boxes, at the round r, are formed by selecting four bits from the words $A_r^0, A_r^1, A_r^2, A_r^3$, that are in the same position. For example, box 1 consists of the first bit from each word, box 2 contains the second bit from each word, and so on.

Table 1. Specification of the S-box in the function Γ

Input:	$x_3x_2x_1x_0$	0	1	2	3	4	5	6	7	8	9	A	B	C	D	E	F
Output:	$y_3y_2y_1y_0$	7	A	2	C	4	8	F	0	5	9	1	E	3	D	B	6

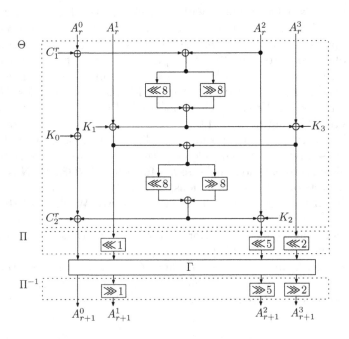

Fig. 1. The round function of NOEKEON

4   The Side Channel Cube Attack on NOEKEON

4.1   Finding the Efficient Round for Side Channel Attacks

In order to apply the single-bit-leakage side channel cube attack on the NOEKEON block cipher, we need to find out the round in which the cipher begins achieving complete diffusion. This enables us to find most of the key variables from low degree master polynomials in early rounds of the encryption process.

To do this, we determine the number of key variables that can be found within the master polynomials representing each bit of the internal state after each round; i.e. the master polynomials representing $A_r^j[i]$ for $1 \leq r \leq 16, 0 \leq j \leq 3$, and $0 \leq i \leq 31$.

The following lemma is a corollary of the main observations supporting the cube attack as described in Sec. 2.

Lemma 1. *Let p be a given (black-box) master polynomial over GF(2) in ℓ variables $x_1, \cdots, x_\ell$; $I \subseteq \{1, \cdots, \ell\}$; $s = |I|$, and t_I denote the multiplication of x_i's with $i \in I$. Let $p_I \triangleq \sum_{\mathbf{w} \in C_I} p_{|\mathbf{w}}$ be the derived polynomial obtained by summing p over the cube C_I (see Sec. 2). t_I appears in p, either as a monomial or as a common subterm of some monomials, if and only if there exist at least a vector $\mathbf{x} \in \{0,1\}^{\ell-s}$ which satisfies $p_I[\mathbf{x}] = \sum_{\mathbf{w} \in C_I} p_{|\mathbf{w}}[\mathbf{x}] = 1$.*

Proof. If t_I is neither a monomial nor a common subterm of some monomials in the master polynomial p, then each monomial term in p must miss at least one variable from t_I (i.e an x_i with $i \in I$). Therefore, in the summation of p over the cube C_I each monomial will be summed an even number of times, and hence will be canceled out as the coefficients are from GF(2); that is, $p_I \equiv 0$ (and hence for all $\mathbf{x} \in \{0,1\}^{\ell-s}$ we have $p_I[\mathbf{x}] = 0$). To complete the proof, simply note that if t_I appears as a monomial or a common subterm of some monomials in p, then p can be factored as $p(x_1, \cdots, x_\ell) = t_I \cdot p_{S(I)} + q(x_1, \cdots, x_\ell)$, where $p_{S(I)}$ is either the constant 1 (when t_I is an independent monomial in p) or a polynomial over at most $\ell - s$ variables (when t_I is a common subterm of some monomials). From Theorem 1 we know that $p_I = p_{S(I)}$, and hence $p_I[\mathbf{x}] = p_{S(I)}[\mathbf{x}] = 1$ for *at least* a vector $\mathbf{x} \in \{0,1\}^{\ell-s}$.   □

This lemma essentially provides the underlying idea for the following probabilistic test, proposed originally in [2], to detect whether a given t_I appears either as a monomial or as a common subterm of some monomials within a master polynomial p:

Step 1: select a value of vector $\mathbf{x} = (x_{s+1}, \cdots, x_\ell) \in \{0,1\}^{\ell-s}$.
Step 2: sum the polynomial $p(x_1, \cdots, x_\ell)$ over the cube C_I (i.e. over all values of $(x_1, \cdots, x_s)$, where $s = |I|$), to get $p_I[\mathbf{x}]$ ($= p_{S(I)}[\mathbf{x}]$).
Step 3: repeat the previous two steps N times and record the values of $p_I[\mathbf{x}]$.

A random master polynomial p is expected to contain at least a monomial $x_1 \cdots x_s \cdots x_j$ ($j \geq s$) in which $t_I = (x_1, \cdots, x_s)$ is either the monomial itself (for $j = s$) or a subterm of the monomial (for $j > s$), with high probability. Hence, after a sufficiently large number of repetitions N, one would find at least one nonzero superpoly $p_{S(I)}$ with high probability. However if t_I is neither a term nor a common subterm in p, the superpoly $p_{S(I)}$ will always evaluate to zero.

We apply this test to *estimate* the the number of key variables within the master polynomials representing each bit of the internal state; i.e. the master polynomials representing $A_r^j[i]$ for $1 \leq r \leq 16, 0 \leq j \leq 3$, and $0 \leq i \leq 31$. To determine whether a key variable k_i, $0 \leq i \leq 127$, exists in a master polynomial p, the following process is repeated for each i ($0 \leq i \leq 127$). Let $t_I = k_i$, randomly choose "sufficiently many" vectors $\mathbf{x} \in \{0,1\}^{128+127}$ (i.e. the space for 128 bits of the plaintext and the secret variables excluding k_i), and sum the polynomial p over t_I for each sample vector $\mathbf{x}$. If at least one sample vector $\mathbf{x}$ results in $p_I = 1$, then from Lemma 1, we can conclude that the key variable k_i exists within the master polynomial p. In our experiment, only after testing about 300 random sample vectors, we have been able to successfully determine that a high portion of the key variables exist in the master polynomials after only two rounds, as shown in Table 2.

Table 2. The number of key variables within the black box polynomials

	$A_r^0[i]$	$A_r^1[i]$	$A_r^2[i]$	$A_r^3[i]$
	$0 \leq i \leq 31$	$0 \leq i \leq 31$	$0 \leq i \leq 31$	$0 \leq i \leq 31$
1st round ($r = 1$)	28	28	28	21
2nd round ($r = 2$)	127	127	127	123
$3^{rd} - 16^{th}$ round ($r \geq 3$)	128	128	128	128

We also need to estimate the degree d of each (black-box) master polynomial in order to verify whether the cube attack can be efficiently implemented. For this purpose, we construct the boolean functions representing output bits of the NOEKEON's S-boxes. Let x_i and y_i be, respectively, the input and output bits of the S-box, for $i = 0, 1, 2, 3$. Each output bit y_i can be represented as a boolean function, as follows.

$$y_0 = x_0 + x_1 + x_2 + x_0 x_1 + x_0 x_2 + x_0 x_3 + x_1 x_3 + x_2 x_3 + x_0 x_2 x_3 + 1$$
$$y_1 = x_2 + x_3 + x_0 x_1 + x_1 x_2 + x_0 x_2 x_3 + x_1 x_2 x_3 + 1$$
$$y_2 = x_0 + x_1 + x_1 x_2 + x_2 x_3 + 1$$
$$y_3 = x_0 + x_1 x_2$$

It is easy to see that the highest degree of the four boolean functions is 3, which correspond to y_0 and y_1. Since the only nonlinear transformations in NOEKEON are the S-boxes (used by the function Γ), we can estimate the degree d of the master polynomial for any round. If we consider a single bit leakage after the third round, the degree of the master polynomials would be approximately between 16 and (the maximum) 256, which is not suitable for our side channel attack model, as it may be unlikely in practice to obtain a leakage that falls within the internal state bits with low degree master polynomials. However if we consider the degree after the second round, it turns out that the degrees of the master polynomials are considerably low, i.e. between 4 and 27. Considering that diffusion process is also almost complete after the second round (refer to Table 2), it turns out that the second round is an appropriate round for the single-bit-leakage side channel attack purpose.

4.2 Finding Maxterm Equations

As an example of the single-bit-leakage attack, in this section we provide the results of the analysis to find maxterm equations from a master polynomial associated with the first bit of the internal state after the second round, i.e. $A_2^0[0]$. (We note that this process can also be straightforwardly applied to any other single bit position in the internal state after the second round, i.e. considering the master polynomial of any $A_2^j[i]$ for $0 \leq j \leq 3$, and $0 \leq i \leq 31$).

Table 3. Cube indexes for maxterms and the linear superpoly for each maxterm

Cube Indexes	Maxterm Equation	Cube Indexes	Maxterm Equation
{11,75,82}	k_{39}	{0,53,60,97}	$k_{113} + k_{89} + k_{57} + k_{49} + k_{33}$
{27,82,91}	k_{55}	{0,4,39,62}	$k_{98} + k_{34} + k_{26} + k_{10} + k_2 + 1$
{1,34,42,127}	k_{100}	{1,4,34,58}	$k_{119} + k_{111} + k_{95} + k_{71} + k_{55} + k_{47}$
{0,4,49,126}	k_{102}	{1,3,25,66}	$k_{118} + k_{110} + k_{94} + k_{70} + k_{54} + k_{46}$
{2,7,36,107}	k_{105}	{0,1,24,99}	$k_{116} + k_{108} + k_{92} + k_{68} + k_{52} + k_{44}$
{1,34,42,79}	k_{108}	{0,20,31,99}	$k_{112} + k_{96} + k_{80} + k_{64} + k_{48} + k_{32}$
{105,118,126}	$k_{107} + 1$	{0,28,39,62}	$k_{114} + k_{106} + k_{50} + k_{42} + k_{26} + k_2$
{2,23,36,123}	k_{121}	{0,5,22,86}	$k_{113} + k_{97} + k_{81} + k_{65} + k_{49} + k_{33}$
{0,12,49,126}	k_{110}	{82,86,123}	$k_{114} + k_{106} + k_{90} + k_{66} + k_{50} + k_{42}$
{118,121,126}	k_{123}	{0,2,75,87}	$k_{115} + k_{107} + k_{91} + k_{67} + k_{51} + k_{43}$
{1,34,58,119}	k_{124}	{3,4,62,76}	$k_{116} + k_{61} + k_{60} + k_{52} + k_{36} + k_{28}$
{5,33,62,85}	$k_{126} + 1$	{70,82,123}	$k_{120} + k_{96} + k_{80} + k_{72} + k_{56} + k_{32}$
{4,13,37,126}	k_{33}	{20,84,119}	$k_{122} + k_{74} + k_{66} + k_{58} + k_{50}$
{104,120,126}	k_{36}	{0,2,15,67}	$k_{122} + k_{106} + k_{58} + k_{42} + k_{26} + k_{10}$
{96,104,126}	k_{44}	{1,3,9,66}	$k_{123} + k_{107} + k_{91} + k_{75} + k_{59} + k_{43}$
{0,7,8,64}	k_{60}	{1,4,34,42}	$k_{126} + k_{118} + k_{78} + k_{70} + k_{62} + k_{54}$
{0,6,50,67}	k_{63}	{2,3,101,125}	$k_{116} + k_{60} + k_{52} + k_{45} + k_{37} + k_{12} + k_4$
{2,31,36,107}	k_{97}	{0,7,9,107}	$k_{120} + k_{104} + k_{96} + k_{56} + k_{40} + k_{32} + k_0 + 1$
{0,3,101,125}	$k_{98} + 1$	{1,4,13,126}	$k_{118} + k_{110} + k_{102} + k_{78} + k_{54} + k_{46} + k_{38} + 1$
{46,121,126}	$k_{99} + 1$	{1,5,92,99}	$k_{125} + k_{109} + k_{101} + k_{69} + k_{61} + k_{45} + k_{37}$
{0,8,47,74}	$k_{103} + k_{38}$	{1,2,44,107}	$k_{127} + k_{119} + k_{111} + k_{63} + k_{56} + k_{55} + k_{47} + k_{23} + 1$
{2,89,96,101}	$k_{118} + k_{53}$	{1,2,60,89}	$k_{119} + k_{111} + k_{55} + k_{47} + k_{40} + k_{32} + k_{31} + k_7 + 1$
{0,7,8,90}	$k_{119} + k_{54}$	{1,36,99,126,127}	$k_{111} + k_{103} + k_{56} + k_{47} + k_{39} + k_{32} + k_{31} + k_{23}$
{0,8,47,66}	$k_{127} + k_{62}$	{3,38,114,124,127}	$k_{57} + k_{41} + k_{33} + k_1$
{30,82,123}	$k_{98} + k_{90} + k_{74} + k_{66} + k_{34}$	{27,54,122,124,127}	$k_{121} + k_{33} + k_{25} + k_9 + k_1 + 1$
{0,10,19,95}	$k_{99} + k_{91} + k_{75} + k_{67} + k_{35}$	{105,108,120,124,126,127}	$k_{92} + k_{61} + k_{28} + 1$
{0,1,64,99}	$k_{100} + k_{92} + k_{76} + k_{68} + k_{36}$	{57,120,121,124,126,127}	$k_{113} + k_{57} + k_{49} + k_{33} + k_{25} + 1$
{4,6,11,34}	$k_{103} + k_{95} + k_{79} + k_{71} + k_{39} + 1$	{102,113,122,124,126,127}	$k_{121} + k_{65} + k_{57} + k_{41} + k_{33} + 1$
{6,62,68,74}	$k_{104} + k_{80} + k_{72} + k_{64} + k_{40}$	{94,121,122,124,126,127}	$k_{108} + k_{60} + k_{44} + k_{37} + k_{36} + k_4$
{0,5,6,70}	$k_{105} + k_{81} + k_{73} + k_{65} + k_{41}$	{78,113,114,124,126,127}	$k_{127} + k_{119} + k_{79} + k_{71} + k_{63} + k_{55}$

By running the preprocessing phase of the attack (on a single PC) for several weeks, we have been able to find collectively thousands of maxterm equations using different cubes sizes, where most of them were found to be redundant and linearly dependent equations. To filter the equations and obtain only linearly independent equations among them, we used the well-known Gaussian elimination. The elimination gives us only 60 linearly independent equations over 99 key variables. Table 3 shows the indexes of variables in the maxterms and the corresponding linearly independent equations that we have obtained. (The indexes for both the plaintext and the key variables start from index 0, namely the MSB, until 127).

As shown in the table, the maxterms start to appear within t_I's of size 3; we have 2 maxterms of size 3, 50 maxterms of size 4, 3 maxterms of size 5, and 5 maxterms of size 6. Hence, the total number of the chosen plaintexts for the online phase of the cube attack is $2 \times 2^3 + 50 \times 2^4 + 3 \times 2^5 + 5 \times 2^6 \approx 2^{10.27}$. Considering that we have 60 linearly independent equations over the key variables, the total time complexity to find the correct 128-bit key reduces to $O(2^{68})$ (compared to the $O(2^{128})$ for an exhaustive key search attack).

5 Conclusions

We investigated the security of the direct-key mode of the NOEKEON block cipher against cube attacks in the (single-bit-leakage) side channel attack model. Our analysis shows that one can recover the 128-bit key of the cipher, by considering a one-bit information leakage from the internal state after the second round, with time complexity of $O(2^{68})$ evaluations of the cipher, and data complexity of about 2^{10} chosen plaintexts. At this step, we have been able to find 60 linearly independent equations over 99 key variables, but from an initial observation, it seems that some nonlinear equations of low degree especially of degree 2 can also be easily found, which may further reduce the complexity of the attack. We leave extending the attack and exploiting such quadratic equations for a future research.

References

[1] Anderson, R., Biham, B., Knudsen, L.: Serpent: A Proposal for the Advanced Encryption Standard. In: First Advanced Encryption Standard (AES) Conference (1998)

[2] Aumasson, J.-P., Dinur, I., Meier, W., Shamir, A.: Cube Testers and Key Recovery Attacks on Reduced-Round MD6 and Trivium. In: Dunkelman, O. (ed.) Fast Software Encryption. LNCS, vol. 5665, pp. 1–22. Springer, Heidelberg (2009)

[3] Biham, E.: New Types of Cryptanalytic Attacks Using Related Keys. In: Helleseth, T. (ed.) EUROCRYPT 1993. LNCS, vol. 765, pp. 229–246. Springer, Heidelberg (1994)

[4] Blum, M., Luby, M., Rubinfield, R.: Self-Testing/Correcting with Application to Numerical Problems. In: STOC, pp. 73–83. ACM, New York (1990)

[5] Bogdanov, A., Knudsen, L.R., Leander, G., Paar, C., Poschmann, A., Robshaw, M.J.B., Seurin, Y., Vikkelsoe, C.: PRESENT: An Ultra-Lightweight Block Cipher. In: Paillier, P., Verbauwhede, I. (eds.) CHES 2007. LNCS, vol. 4727, pp. 450–466. Springer, Heidelberg (2007)

[6] De Cannière, C., Preneel, B.: TRIVIUM. In: Robshaw, M.J.B., Billet, O. (eds.) New Stream Cipher Designs. LNCS, vol. 4986, pp. 244–266. Springer, Heidelberg (2008)

[7] Daemen, J., Rijmen, V.: AES Proposal: Rijndael. Technical Evaluation, CD-1: Documentation (1998)

[8] Daemen, J., Peeters, M., Van Assche, G., Rijmen, V.: Nessie Proposal: NOEKEON. In: First Open NESSIE Workshop (2000), http://gro.noekeon.org

[9] Dinur, I., Shamir, A.: Cube Attacks on Tweakable Black Box Polynomials. In: Joux, A. (ed.) EUROCRYPT 2009. LNCS, vol. 5479, pp. 278–299. Springer, Heidelberg (2009)

[10] Dinur, I., Shamir, A.: Side Channel Cube Attacks on Block Ciphers. Cryptology ePrint Archive, Report 2009/127 (2009), http://eprint.iacr.org/2009/127

[11] Fraenkel, A.S., Yesha, Y.: Complexity of Problems in Games, Graphs, and Alge-
     braic Equations. Discr. Appl. Math. 1, 15–30 (1979)
[12] Mamiya, H., Miyaji, A., Morimoto, H.: Efficient Countermeasures against RPA,
     DPA, and SPA. In: Joye, M., Quisquater, J.-J. (eds.) CHES 2004. LNCS, vol. 3156,
     pp. 243–319. Springer, Heidelberg (2004)
[13] Mangard, S.: Hardware countermeasures against DPA – A statistical analysis
     of their effectiveness. In: Okamoto, T. (ed.) CT-RSA 2004. LNCS, vol. 2964,
     pp. 222–235. Springer, Heidelberg (2004)
[14] Rivest, R., Agre, B., Bailey, D.V., Crutchfield, C., Dodis, Y., Fleming, K.E.,
     Khan, A., Krishnamurthy, J., Lin, Y., Reyzin, L., Shen, E., Sukha, J.,
     Sutherland, D., Tromer, E., Yin, Y.L.: The MD6 Hash Function - A Proposal
     to NIST for SHA-3, http://groups.csail.mit.edu/cis/md6/
[15] Yang, L., Wang, M., Qiao, S.: Side Channel Cube Attack on PRESENT. In:
     Miyaji, A., Echizen, I., Okamoto, T. (eds.) CANS 2009. LNCS, vol. 5888,
     pp. 379–391. Springer, Heidelberg (2009)

On Fast and Approximate Attack Tree Computations

Aivo Jürgenson[1,2] and Jan Willemson[3]

[1] Tallinn University of Technology, Raja 15, Tallinn 12618, Estonia
aivo.jurgenson@eesti.ee
[2] Cybernetica, Akadeemia 21, Tallinn 12618, Estonia
[3] Cybernetica, Aleksandri 8a, Tartu 51004, Estonia
jan.willemson@gmail.com

Abstract. In this paper we address the problem of inefficiency of exact attack tree computations. We propose several implementation-level optimizations and introduce a genetic algorithm for fast approximate computations. Our experiments show that for attack trees having less than 30 leaves, the confidence level of 89% can be achieved within 2 seconds using this algorithm. The approximation scales very well and attack trees of practical size (up to 100 leaves) can be analyzed within a few minutes.

1 Introduction

Structural methods for security assessment have been used for several decades already. Called *fault trees* and applied to analyse general security-critical systems in early 1980-s [1], they were adjusted for information systems and called *threat logic trees* by Weiss in 1991 [2]. In the late 1990-s, the method was popularized by Schneier under the name *attack trees* [3]. Since then, it has evolved in different directions and has been used to analyze the security of several practical applications, including PGP [4], Border Gateway Protocol [5], SCADA systems [6], e-voting systems [7], etc. We refer to [8,9] for good overviews on the development and applications of the methodology.

Even though already Weiss [2] realized that the attack components may have several parameters in practice, early studies mostly focused on attack trees as a mere attack dependence description tool and were limited to considering at most one parameter at a time [3,10,11]. A substantial step forward was taken by Buldas *et al.* [12] who introduced the idea of game-theoretic modeling of the attacker's decision making process based on several interconnected parameters like the cost, risks and penalties associated with different elementary attacks. This approach was later refined by Jürgenson and Willemson by first extending the parameter domain from point values to interval estimates [13] and then by creating the first semantics for multi-parameter attack trees, consistent with the general framework of Mauw and Oostdijk [11,14].

Even though being theoretically sound, the results of Jürgenson and Willemson are rather discouraging from an engineering point of view. Even with all the

J. Kwak et al. (Eds.): ISPEC 2010, LNCS 6047, pp. 56–66, 2010.

optimizations proposed in [14], they are still able to analyze the trees of at most 20 leaves in reasonable time and this may not suffice for many practical applications. Hence, the aim of this paper is to improve their results in two directions. First, we implement several additional optimizations and second, we create and test a genetic algorithm for fast approximations.

The paper is organized as follows. First, in Section 2 we will briefly define attack trees and the required parameters. Then Section 3 will explain our new set of optimizations, which in turn will be tested for performance in Section 4. Section 5 will cover our genetic algorithm and finally Section 6 will draw some conclusions.

2   Attack Trees

Basic idea of the attack tree approach is simple – the analysis begins by identifying one *primary threat* and continues by dividing the threat into subattacks, either all or some of them being necessary to materialize the primary threat. The subattacks can be divided further etc., until we reach the state where it does not make sense to divide the resulting attacks any more; these kinds of non-splittable attacks are called *elementary attacks* and the security analyst will have to evaluate them somehow.

During the splitting process, a tree is formed having the primary threat in its root and elementary attacks in its leaves. Using the structure of the tree and the estimations of the leaves, it is then (hopefully) possible to give some estimations of the root node as well. In practice, it mostly turns out to be sufficient to consider only two kinds of splits in the internal nodes of the tree, giving rise to AND- and OR-nodes. As a result, an AND-OR-tree is obtained, forming the basis of the subsequent analysis. We will later identify the tree as a (monotone) Boolean formula built on the set of elementary attacks as literals.

The crucial contribution of Buldas *et al.* [12] was the introduction of four game-theoretically motivated parameters for each leaf node of the tree. This approach was later optimized in [14], where the authors concluded that only two parameters suffice. Following their approach, we consider the set of elementary attacks $\mathcal{X} = \{X_1, X_2, \ldots, X_n\}$ and give each one of them two parameters:

- p_i – success probability of the attack X_i,
- Expenses$_i$ – expected expenses (i.e. costs plus expected penalties) of the attack X_i.

Besides these parameters, there is a global value Gains expressing the benefit of the attacker if he is able to materialize the primary threat.

3   Efficient Attack Tree Computations

Let us have the attack tree expressed by the monotone Boolean formula $\mathcal{F}$ built on the set of elementary attacks $\mathcal{X} = \{X_1, X_2, \ldots, X_n\}$. In the model of [14], the expected outcome of the attacker is computed by maximizing the expression

$$\text{Outcome}_\sigma = p_\sigma \cdot \text{Gains} - \sum_{X_i \in \sigma} \text{Expenses}_i \qquad (1)$$

over all the assignments $\sigma \subseteq \mathcal{X}$ that make the Boolean formula $\mathcal{F}$ true. Here p_σ denotes the success probability of the primary threat and as shown in [14], this quantity can be computed in time linear in the number n of elementary attacks. The real complexity of maximizing (1) comes from the need to go through potentially all the 2^n subsets $\sigma \subseteq \mathcal{X}$. Of course, there are some useful observations to make.

- The Boolean function $\mathcal{F}$ is monotone and we are only interested in the satisfying assignments σ. Hence, it is not necessary to consider subsets of non-satisfying assignments.
- In [14], Theorem 1, it was proven that if for some AND-node in the attack tree the assignment σ evaluates some of its children as true and others as false, this σ can be disregarded without affecting the correct outcome.

We start the contributions of the current paper by additionally noting that the DPLL algorithm [15], used in [14] to generate all the satisfying assignments, introduces a lot of unnecessary overhead. The formula $\mathcal{F}$ first needs to be transformed to CNF and later maintained as a set of clauses, which, in turn, are sets of literals. Since set is a very inconvenient data structure to handle in the computer, we can hope for some performance increase by dropping it in favor of something more efficient.

In our new implementation, we keep the formula $\mathcal{F}$ as it is – in the form of a tree. The assignments σ are stored as sequences of ternary bits, i.e. strings of three possible values t, f and u (standing for true, false and undefined, respectively). The computation rules of the corresponding ternary logic are natural, see Table 1.

Table 1. Computation rules for ternary logic

&	t	f	u		∨	t	f	u
t	t	f	u		t	t	t	t
f	f	f	f		f	t	f	u
u	u	f	u		u	t	u	u

In its core, our new algorithm still follows the approach of DPLL – we start off with the assignment $[u, u, \ldots, u]$ and proceed by successively trying to evaluate the literals as f and t. Whenever we reach the value t for the formula $\mathcal{F}$, we know that all the remaining u-values may be arbitrary and it is not necessary to take the recursion any deeper. Similarly, when we obtain the value f for the formula $\mathcal{F}$, we know that no assignment of u-values can make $\mathcal{F}$ valid. Thus the only case where we need to continue recursively, is when we have $\mathcal{F} = u$. This way we obtain Algorithm 1, triggered by `process_satisfying_assignments([u, u, ..., u])`.

Even though being conceptually simple, Algorithm 1 contains several hidden options for optimization. The first step to pay attention to lies already in line 2,

---

Algorithm 1. Finding the satisfying assignments

Require: Boolean formula $\mathcal{F}$ corresponding to the given AND-OR-tree
1: **Procedure** process_satisfying_assignments(σ)
2:    Evaluate $\mathcal{F}(\sigma)$
3:    **if** $\mathcal{F}(\sigma) = \mathsf{f}$ **then**
4:        Return;
5:    **end if**
6:    **if** $\mathcal{F}(\sigma) = \mathsf{t}$ **then**
7:        Output all the assignments obtained from σ by setting all its u-values to t and
         f in all the possible ways;
         Return;
8:    **end if**
9:    //reaching here we know that $\mathcal{F}(\sigma) = \mathsf{u}$
10:   Choose X_i such that $\sigma(X_i) = \mathsf{u}$
11:   process_satisfying_assignments($\sigma/[X_i := \mathsf{f}]$);
12:   process_satisfying_assignments($\sigma/[X_i := \mathsf{t}]$);

---

the evaluation of $\mathcal{F}(\sigma)$. The evaluation process naturally follows the tree structure of $\mathcal{F}$, moving from the leaves to the root using the computation rules given by Table 1. However, taking into account Theorem 1 of [14] (see the second observation above), we can conclude that whenever we encounter a node requiring evaluation of t&f or f&t, we can abort this branch of the recursion immediately, since there is a global optimum outcome in some other branch.

In the implementation, this kind of exception to evaluation is modelled as additional data type shortcut-false to the already existing true, false and undefined Boolean types. If the situation is encountered during the recursive evaluation of $\mathcal{F}$, shortcut-false is returned immediately to the highest level and the entire branch of processing is dropped.

Another, somewhat more obvious optimization lies within the line 10 of Algorithm 1. Of course it would be the simplest to pick the next undefined literal randomly (or in some predefined order, which gives the same result for randomly-generated test trees). However, intuitively this approach is one of the worst possible, since the working time of the algorithm depends on the number of the generated satisfying assignments. Hence, the algorithm will be faster if we can systematically disregard larger recursive branches. This is the reason why we first assign undefined literals as f on line 11 and check first, if the whole formula has become non-satisfied.

Still, a clever choice of the order of the undefined literals to specify can speed up this process even further. We implemented and tested several possible strategies.

1. Random – the next undefined literal is picked randomly.
2. Most-AND – for each undefined literal we compute the number of AND-nodes on the path from the corresponding leaf to the root and pick the onest with the highest score first.

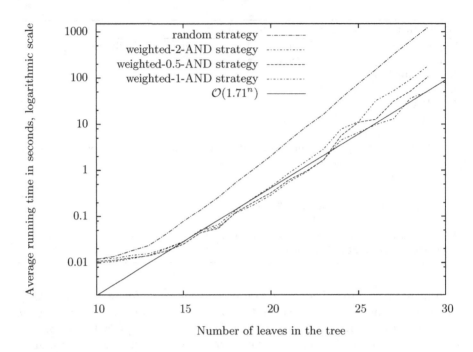

Fig. 1. Performance test results of different strategies for choosing undefined literals

3. Weighted-AND – the ordering routine is similar to Most-AND, but all the AND-nodes on the path do not have an equal weight. The intuition behind this approach is that when we can exclude a larger subtree, we should be able to cut off more hopeless recursion branches as well, hence it makes more sense to prefer paths with AND-nodes closer to the root. Thus we gave each node on the distance i from the root the weight $1/c^i$, where c is a predefined constant. In our experiments we used the values $c = 2$. For comparison, we also ran tests with $c = 0.5$ and $c = 1$. (Not that the Most-AND strategy is equivalent to the Weighted-AND strategy with $c = 1$).

4   Performance Analysis

Somewhat surprisingly it turned out that giving more weight to the AND nodes which are closer to the root node does not necessarily help. The weighting constant $c = 0.5$ gave also very good results and in some cases better than the Weighted-2-AND strategy.

We generated random sample attack trees with 5 leaves up to 29 leaves, at least 100 trees in each group, and measured the solving time with our optimized realization and with different strategies. The results are depicted in Fig. 1.

To estimate the complexity of our algorithms, we used the least-squares method to fit a function $a^{-1} \cdot b^n$ to the running times of our best strategy method. Since there is no reasonable analytical way to establish the time complexity of our algorithm, this approach provided a quick and easy way to estimate it. The found parameters to fit the data points of the best solution (the (1)-AND method) optimally were $a = 109828$ and $b = 1.71018$. Hence we can conclude that the average complexity of our algorithm with our generated sample data is in the range of $\sim \mathcal{O}(1.71^n)$.

The average complexity estimations for all strategies were the following:

- Random strategy – $\mathcal{O}(1.90^n)$
- Weighted-2-AND strategy – $\mathcal{O}(1.78^n)$
- Weighted-1-AND strategy – $\mathcal{O}(1.71^n)$
- Weighted-0.5-AND strategy – $\mathcal{O}(1.75^n)$

However, it should be noted that differences between the Weighted-c-AND strategies were quite small and within the margin of error. Therefore, no conclusive results can be given regarding the different weighting constants. It is clear though that all the tested strategies are better than just choosing the leafs in random.

Currently the world's best #3-SAT problem solving algorithm by Konstantin Kutzkov ([16]) has the worst-case complexity $\mathcal{O}(1.6423^n)$. As #SAT problems can be parsinomically and in polynomial time converted to the #3-SAT problems (see [17], chapter 26), we can roughly compare our algorithm complexity and the #3-SAT problem solver complexity.

Direct comparison is however not possible for several reasons. First, our estimate is heuristic and is based on experimental data. Second, we are not only counting all the possible SAT solutions to the formula $\mathcal{F}$, but we actually have to generate many of them. At the same time, we are using optimizations described in Section 3.

Comparison with the result of Kutzkov still shows that our approach works roughly as well as one would expect based on the similarity of our problem setting to #SAT. It remains an open problem to develop more direct comparison methods and to find out whether some of the techniques of #SAT solvers could be adapted to the attack trees directly.

5 Approximation

Even though reimplementation in C++ and various optimization techniques described in Section 3 helped us to increase the performance of attack tree analysis significantly compared to [14], we are still practically limited to the trees having at most 30 leaves. Given the exponential nature of the problem, it is hard to expect substantial progress in the exact computations.

In order to find out, how well the exact outcome of the attack tree can be approximated, we implemented a genetic algorithm (GA) for the computations. (See [18] for an introduction into GAs.) Let us have an attack tree described by the Boolean formula $\mathcal{F}$ and the set of leaves $\mathcal{X} = \{X_1, X_2, \ldots, X_n\}$ having the parameters as described in 3. We will specify the following concepts for our GA.

Individual: Any subset $\sigma \subseteq \mathcal{X}$. The individuals are internally represented by bitstrings of length n, where 1 in position i means that $X_i \in \sigma$ and 0 in position i means that $X_i \notin \sigma$.

Live individual: $\sigma \subseteq \mathcal{X}$ such that $\mathcal{F}(\sigma := \mathsf{t}) = \mathsf{t}$, i.e. such that the value of $\mathcal{F}$ is t when all the literals of σ are set to t and all the others to f.

Dead individual: $\sigma \subseteq \mathcal{X}$ such that $\mathcal{F}(\sigma := \mathsf{t}) = \mathsf{f}$.

Generation: A set of p live individuals (where p is a system-wide parameter to be determined later).

Fitness function: Outcome$_\sigma$. Note that σ must be alive in order for the fitness function to be well-defined.

Crossover: In order to cross two individuals σ_1 and σ_2, we iterate throughout all the elementary attacks X_i ($i = 1, \ldots, n$) and decide by a fair coin toss, whether we should take the descendant's ith bit from σ_1 or σ_2.

Mutation: When an individual σ needs to be mutated, a biased coin is flipped for every leaf X_i ($i = 1, \ldots, n$) and its status (included/excluded) in σ will be changed if the coin shows heads. Since σ is internally kept as a bit sequence, mutation is accomplished by simple bit flipping.

In order to start the GA, the first generation of p live individuals must be created. We generate them randomly, using the following recursive routine.

1. Consider the root node.
2. If the node we consider is a leaf, then include it to σ and stop.
3. If the node we consider is an AND-node, consider all its descendants recursively going back to Step 2.
4. If the node we consider is an OR-node, flip a fair coin for all of them to decide whether they should be considered or not. If none of the descendants was chosen, flip the coin again for all of them. Repeat until at least one descendant gets chosen. Continue with Step 2.

It is easy to see that the resulting σ is guaranteed to be live and that the routine stops with probability 1.

Having produced our first generation of individuals $\sigma_1, \ldots, \sigma_p$ (not all of them being necessarily distinct), we start the reproduction process.

1. All the individuals σ_i are crossed with everybody else, producing $\binom{p}{2}$ new individuals.
2. Each individual is mutated with probability 0.1 and for each one of them, the bias 0.1 is used.
3. The original individuals $\sigma_1, \ldots, \sigma_p$ are added to the candidate (multi)set. (Note that this guarantees the existence of p live individuals).
4. All the candidates are checked for liveness (by evaluating $\mathcal{F}(\sigma = \mathsf{t})$) and only the live ones are left.
5. Finally, p fittest individuals are selected for the next generation.

The reproduction takes place for g rounds, where g is also a system-wide parameter yet to be determined.

Next we estimate the time complexity of our GA.

- Generating p live individuals takes $\mathcal{O}(np)$ steps.
- Creating a new candidate generation by crossing takes $\mathcal{O}(np^2)$ steps.

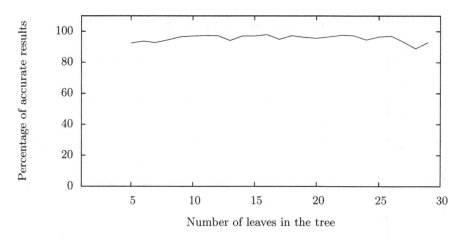

Fig. 2. Accuracy of genetics algorithm with $p = 2n$ and $g = 2n$

- Mutating the candidate generation takes $\mathcal{O}(np^2)$ steps.
- Verifying liveliness takes $\mathcal{O}(np^2)$ steps.
- Computing the outcomes of live individuals takes $\mathcal{O}(np^2)$ steps.
- Sorting out the p best individuals out of the $\binom{p}{2} + p$ individuals takes $\mathcal{O}(p^2 \log p))$ steps.

Since these steps are repeated for g generations, we can find the overall time complexity to be $\mathcal{O}(gp^2(\log p + n))$.

Of course, a GA does not guarantee that the final outcome is the best one globally. To find out, how large populations and how many iterations one has to use to hit the global maximum outcome with some degree of certainty, we performed series of tests.

First we generated a sample random set of about 6000 trees (having $n = 5 \ldots 29$ leaves) and computed the exact outcome for each one of them as described in Sections 3 and 4. Next we ran our GA for population sizes $p = 5, 10, 15, \ldots, 60$ and the number of iterations $1, 2, \ldots, 200$. We recorded the average running times and attacker's estimated outcomes, comparing the latter ones to the exact outcomes computed before.

As a result of our tests we can say that GA allows us to reach high level of confidence (say, with 90% accuracy) very fast. There are many possible reasonable choices for $p = p(n)$ and $g = g(n)$. For example, taking $p = 2n$ and $g = 2n$ allowed us to reach 89% level of confidence for all the tree sizes of up to 29 leaves (see Fig. 2). By accuracy we here mean the ratio of the trees actually computed correctly by our GA when compared to the exact outcome.

The theoretical time complexity of our GA is in this case $\mathcal{O}(n^4)$, which in reality required up to roughly 2 seconds for trees with less than 30 leaves on 2.33 GHz Intel Xeon processor. The same approach also enables us to process moderate size attack trees (70-80 leaves) in reasonable time (1-2 minutes). Attack trees of this size are helpful in analyzing real-life information systems and the

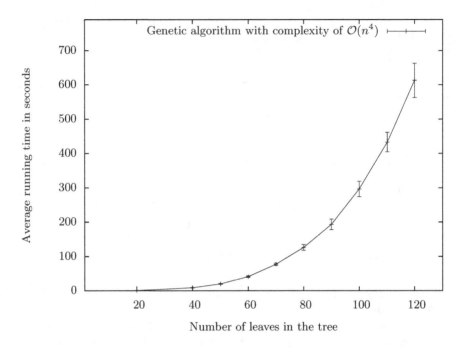

Fig. 3. Performance results of the genetic algorithm

multi-parameter attack trees can be now used in practical security analysis. The performance results for larger trees are given in Fig. 3. For each data point we generated 10 random trees and the average running times were measured for the genetic algorithm with parameters $p = 2n$ and $g = 2n$. The error bars represent the standard deviation of the average running time.

6   Conclusions and Further Work

In this paper we reviewed the method proposed by Jürgenson and Willemson for computing the exact outcome of a multi-parameter attack tree [14]. We proposed and implemented several optimizations and this allowed us to move the horizon of computability from the trees having 20 leaves (as in [14]) to the trees with roughly 30 leaves.

However, computing the exact outcome of an attack tree is an inherently exponential problem, hence mere optimizations on the implementation level are rather limited. Thus we also considered an approximation technique based on genetic programming. This approach turned out to be very successful, allowing us to reach 89% of confidence within 2 seconds of computation for the trees having up to 29 leaves. The genetic algorithm is also very well scalable, making it practical to analyze even the trees having more than 100 leaves.

When running a genetic approximation algorithm, we are essentially computing a lower bound to the attacker's expected outcome. Still, an upper bound (showing that the attacker can not achieve *more* than some amount) would be much more interesting in practice. Hence, the problem of finding efficient upper bounds remains an interesting challenge for future research.

Another interesting direction is extending the model of attack tree computations. For example, Jürgenson and Willemson have also considered the serial model, where the attacker can make his decisions based on previous success or failure of elementary attacks [19]. It turns out that finding the best permutation of the elementary attacks may turn computing the optimal expected outcome into a super-exponential problem, hence the use of good approximation methods becomes inevitable in that setting.

Acknowledgments

This research was supported by the European Regional Development Fund through the Estonian Center of Excellence in Computer Science, EXCS, and Estonian Science Foundation grant no 8124.

References

1. Vesely, W., Goldberg, F., Roberts, N., Haasl, D.: Fault Tree Handbook. US Government Printing Office, Systems and Reliability Research, January, Office of Nuclear Regulatory Research, U.S. Nuclear Regulatory Commission (1981)
2. Weiss, J.D.: A system security engineering process. In: Proceedings of the 14th National Computer Security Conference, pp. 572–581 (1991)
3. Schneier, B.: Attack trees: Modeling security threats. Dr. Dobb's Journal 24(12), 21–29 (1999)
4. Schneier, B.: Secrets & Lies. Digital Security in a Networked World. John Wiley & Sons, Chichester (2000)
5. Convery, S., Cook, D., Franz, M.: An attack tree for the border gateway protocol. IETF Internet draft (February 2004), http://www.ietf.org/proceedings/04aug/I-D/draft-ietf-rpsec-bgpattack-00.txt
6. Byres, E., Franz, M., Miller, D.: The use of attack trees in assessing vulnerabilities in SCADA systems. In: International Infrastructure Survivability Workshop (IISW 2004). IEEE, Lisbon (2004)
7. Buldas, A., Mägi, T.: Practical security analysis of e-voting systems. In: Miyaji, A., Kikuchi, H., Rannenberg, K. (eds.) IWSEC 2007. LNCS, vol. 4752, pp. 320–335. Springer, Heidelberg (2007)
8. Edge, K.S.: A Framework for Analyzing and Mitigating the Vulnerabilities of Complex Systems via Attack and Protection Trees. PhD thesis, Air Force Institute of Technology, Ohio (2007)
9. Espedahlen, J.H.: Attack trees describing security in distributed internet-enabled metrology. Master's thesis, Department of Computer Science and Media Technology, Gjøvik University College (2007)
10. Moore, A.P., Ellison, R.J., Linger, R.C.: Attack modeling for information security and survivability. Technical Report CMU/SEI-2001-TN-001, Software Engineering Institute (2001)

11. Mauw, S., Oostdijk, M.: Foundations of attack trees. In: Won, D.H., Kim, S. (eds.) ICISC 2005. LNCS, vol. 3935, pp. 186–198. Springer, Heidelberg (2006)
12. Buldas, A., Laud, P., Priisalu, J., Saarepera, M., Willemson, J.: Rational Choice of Security Measures via Multi-Parameter Attack Trees. In: López, J. (ed.) CRITIS 2006. LNCS, vol. 4347, pp. 235–248. Springer, Heidelberg (2006)
13. Jürgenson, A., Willemson, J.: Processing multi-parameter attacktrees with estimated parameter values. In: Miyaji, A., Kikuchi, H., Rannenberg, K. (eds.) IWSEC 2007. LNCS, vol. 4752, pp. 308–319. Springer, Heidelberg (2007)
14. Jürgenson, A., Willemson, J.: Computing exact outcomes of multi-parameter attack trees. In: Meersman, R., Tari, Z. (eds.) OTM 2008, Part II. LNCS, vol. 5332, pp. 1036–1051. Springer, Heidelberg (2008)
15. Davis, M., Logemann, G., Loveland, D.: A machine program for theorem proving. Communications of the ACM 5(7), 394–397 (1962)
16. Kutzkov, K.: New upper bound for the #3-sat problem. Inf. Process. Lett. 105(1), 1–5 (2007)
17. Kozen, D.: The design and analysis of algorithms. Springer, Heidelberg (1992)
18. Goldberg, D.E.: Genetic Algorithms in Search, Optimization and Machine Learning. Addison-Wesley Longman Publishing Co., Inc, Boston (1989)
19. Jürgenson, A., Willemson, J.: Serial model for attack tree computations. In: Proceedings of ICISC 2009 (2009)

Width-3 Joint Sparse Form

Katsuyuki Okeya[1], Hidehiro Kato[2], and Yasuyuki Nogami[2]

[1] Hitachi, Ltd., Systems Development Laboratory,
292, Yoshida-cho, Totsuka-ku, Yokohama, 244-0817, Japan
katsuyuki.okeya.ue@hitachi.com

[2] Okayama University, Tsushima–naka, Okayama-shi, 700-8530, Japan
{kato,nogami}@cne.okayama-u.ac.jp

Abstract. The joint sparse form (JSF) is a representation of a pair of integers, which is famous for accelerating a multi-scalar multiplication in elliptic curve cryptosystems. Solinas' original paper showed three unsolved problems on the enhancement of JSF. Whereas two of them have been solved, the other still remains to be done. The remaining unsolved problem is as follows: To design a representation of a pair of integers using a larger digit set such as a set involving ± 3, while the original JSF utilizes the digit set that consists of $0, \pm 1$ for representing a pair of integers. This paper puts an end to the problem; width-3 JSF. The proposed enhancement satisfies properties that are similar to that of the original. For example, the enhanced representation is defined as a representation that satisfies some rules. Some other properties are the existence, the uniqueness of such a representation, and the optimality of the Hamming weight. The non-zero density of the width-3 JSF is $563/1574(= 0.3577)$ and this is ideal. The conversion algorithm to the enhanced representation takes $O(\log n)$ memory and $O(n)$ computational cost, which is very efficient, where n stands for the bit length of the integers.

Keywords: elliptic curve cryptosystem, multi-scalar multiplication, joint sparse form (JSF).

1 Elliptic Curve Cryptosystems and Representations of Integers

Elliptic curve cryptosystems (ECCs) are known for their high security with short bit length [Kob87, Mil86]. One of dominant operations in ECC is a scalar multiplication, which computes the point dP from a point P on an elliptic curve and a scalar d.

1.1 Integer Representations in Scalar Multiplication

There are lots of publications on the way to compute a scalar multiplication efficiently. One of the most natural ways is the binary method in which the scalar d is represented in a binary and an elliptic doubling, or an elliptic doubling and addition are performed depending on each bit of the scalar. Thus, the Hamming weight of the scalar d influences the computational cost.

J. Kwak et al. (Eds.): ISPEC 2010, LNCS 6047, pp. 67–84, 2010.
© Springer-Verlag Berlin Heidelberg 2010

One of the properties of elliptic curves is that for a point P, its inversion $-P$ is easily computed. Therefore, the scalar is often represented with a signed binary representation whose coefficients are 0, 1, -1, where -1 corresponds to an addition of $-P$, and the scalar multiplication is computed using this representation. Furthermore, if the memory is sufficiently available, not only ± 1 but also ± 3 and ± 5 can be used for representing the scalar. In this way, the set of numbers which are used in the representation is called the digit set and denoted by $\mathcal{D}$. A representation using the digit set $\mathcal{D}$ is called a $\mathcal{D}$ representation. In the case of $\mathcal{D} = \{0, 1\}$, the $\mathcal{D}$ representation is the well-known binary representation. If $\mathcal{D} = \{0, \pm 1\}$, it is a signed binary representation. A $\mathcal{D}$ representation for a scalar d is not necessarily unique. For instance, in the case of $\mathcal{D} = \{0, \pm 1\}$, $7 = (111)_2 = (100\bar{1})_2$, where $\bar{1} = -1$.

The use of a representation with the minimal Hamming weight reduces the computational cost. So, for a given $\mathcal{D}$, to find out a $\mathcal{D}$ representation with the minimal Hamming weight is an important problem. On this problem, there are lots of results. If $\mathcal{D} = \{0, 1\}$, since the representation is unique, the problem is trivial. Next, in the case of $\mathcal{D} = \{0, \pm 1\}$, the well-known non-adjacent form (NAF) has the minimal Hamming weight [Rei60, MO90]. NAF has a property that non-zeros are not consecutive. A more general case such as $\mathcal{D} = \{0, \pm 1, \pm 3, \cdots, \pm 2^{w-1} \mp 1\}$ is also well-known; a width-w NAF (wNAF) has the minimal Hamming weight [Sol00]. In wNAF representation, for arbitrary consecutive w bits, there is at most one non-zero. Note that NAF is the special case of wNAF; $w = 2$. Furthermore, for most of $\mathcal{D}$ used in ECC, the above problem was solved.

1.2   Representations of a Pair of Integers in Multi-scalar Multiplication

Another dominant operation is a multi-scalar multiplication. A multi-scalar multiplication is a generalization of a scalar multiplication, and for points P, Q and scalars u, v, the point $uP + vQ$ is computed. A further generalization is an operation with plural points and the same number of scalars. A multi-scalar multiplication is utilized for verifying the elliptic curve signature such as ECDSA. Some other applications are to speed up a scalar multiplication in which the scalar is converted by the comb [LL94] and/or GLV [GLV01] method(s) into a pair of scalars. One of advantages to use a multi-scalar multiplication is the reduction of elliptic doublings, compared with the case that two scalar multiplications are performed independently.

The digit set $\mathcal{D}$ for a multi-scalar multiplication $uP + vQ$ is two-dimensional. That is, $\mathcal{D} \subset \mathcal{D}_u \times \mathcal{D}_v$, where $\mathcal{D}_u$, $\mathcal{D}_v$, and '$\times$' are the digit sets for u, v, and a product of sets, respectively. An example is $\mathcal{D}_u = \mathcal{D}_v = \{0, \pm 1\}$, $\mathcal{D} = \mathcal{D}_u \times \mathcal{D}_v = \{(0,0), (0,\pm 1), (\pm 1, 0), (\pm 1, \pm 1), (\pm 1, \mp 1)\}$. Let $\mathcal{D}^{w=k} = \{(d_0, d_1) | d_0, d_1 \in \{0, \pm 1, \pm 3, \cdots, \pm 2^{k-1} \mp 1\}\}$. The above example is the case $\mathcal{D} = \mathcal{D}^{w=2}$.

For a pair of integers (u, v), let $\begin{bmatrix} u_{n-1}, u_{n-2}, \cdots, u_0 \\ v_{n-1}, v_{n-2}, \cdots, v_0 \end{bmatrix}$ be its $\mathcal{D}$ representation; $u = \sum_{j=0}^{n-1} u_j 2^j$, $v = \sum_{j=0}^{n-1} v_j 2^j$, $u_j \in \mathcal{D}_u$, $v_j \in \mathcal{D}_v$, and $(u_j, v_j) \in \mathcal{D}$. Algorithm 1 computes a multi-scalar multiplication using the $\mathcal{D}$ representation. Note, $\mathcal{O}$, ECDBL and ECADD stand for the point at infinity, an elliptic doubling and an elliptic addition, respectively.

Algorithm 1

Require: Points P, Q, scalars u, v.
Ensure: Multi-scalar multiplication $uP + vQ$
1: $R_{t_1 t_2} \leftarrow t_1 P + t_2 Q, \forall (t_1, t_2) \in \mathcal{D} \setminus \{(0,0)\}$
2: $X \leftarrow \mathcal{O}$
3: **for** $j = n - 1$ down to 0
4:     $X \leftarrow \text{ECDBL}(X)$
5:     **if** $(u_j, v_j) \in \mathcal{D} \setminus \{(0,0)\}$
6:        $X \leftarrow \text{ECADD}(X, R_{u_j v_j})$
7: **return** X.

The joint Hamming weight $JHW_{\mathcal{D}}(R)$ for a $\mathcal{D}$ representation R of (u, v) is defined as the number of non-zero columns in the representation, which corresponds to the number of elliptic additions. The joint Hamming density (or non-zero density) is given by $JHD_{\mathcal{D}} := JHW_{\mathcal{D}}/n$.

1.3 Joint Sparse Form

In the case that the digit set is $\mathcal{D}^{w=2}$, Solinas [Sol01] proposed a joint sparse form (JSF) which is one of the most appropriate among $\mathcal{D}^{w=2}$ representations. For a pair of integers $(u^{(0)}, u^{(1)})$, JSF is defined as a $\mathcal{D}^{w=2}$ representation $\begin{bmatrix} u_{n-1}^{(0)}, u_{n-2}^{(0)}, \cdots, u_0^{(0)} \\ u_{n-1}^{(1)}, u_{n-2}^{(1)}, \cdots, u_0^{(1)} \end{bmatrix}$ that satisfies the following three properties:

(JSF1) For any consecutive three columns, at least one is the zero column.
(JSF2) Adjacent terms do not have opposite signs.
(JSF3) If $u_{j+1}^{(i)} u_j^{(i)} \neq 0$, then $u_{j+1}^{(1-i)} = \pm 1$, $u_j^{(1-i)} = 0$.

Then, JSF has the following three properties:

(Existence) For arbitrary pair of integers, there exists a JSF.
(Uniqueness) For arbitrary pair of integers, at most one JSF exists.
(Optimality) JSF has the minimal joint Hamming weight.

On the other hand, Solinas' paper stated unsolved problems on some of prospective enhancements of JSF.

1. *Left-to-right generation.* The usual JSF is generated from right-to-left. Since Algorithm 1 computes from left-to-right, a left-to-right generation of the representation unleashes the buffers for the converted representation.

2. *JSF for 3 or more scalars.* Since the comb method divides a scalar into several integers, such an enhancement is useful.
3. *JSF for a larger digit set.* If memory is sufficiently available, one can compute more points and store them. Thus, such an enhancement provides us with further speeding up.

  − Regarding 1. left-to-right generation, Heuberger et al. [HKP$^+$04] showed an enhancement, namely, this was solved.
  − Regarding 2. JSF for 3 or more scalars, Proos [Pro03] showed an enhancement, namely, this was also solved.
  − Regarding 3. JSF for a larger digit set, there are several proposals [Ava02, KZZ04, DOT05], however, none of them proves the optimality. Therefore, this problem remains *unsolved*.

Since these representations are used for computing a multi-scalar multiplication, there are some strict conditions for a conversion algorithm that outputs the most appropriate representations from inputted integers. In other words, although an algorithm outputs the minimal JHW, it is useless if it has a large cost.

One is the requirement for the memory issue. In a multi-scalar multiplication, the points corresponding to $\mathcal{D}$ are computed and stored on the memory. The required memory is $\#\mathcal{D} \cdot n$, namely the order is $O(n)$, where n is the bit length. Hence, the requirement for the memory issue of the conversion algorithm is the order is smaller than $O(n)$, or the memory is smaller than $\#\mathcal{D} \cdot n$. Otherwise, a larger digit set can be used for speeding up (ignoring the computational cost for preparing the precomputation table, which is independent from n).

The other is the requirement for the computational cost. In a multi-scalar multiplication, an elliptic doubling is computed per bit of the scalar. An elliptic doubling requires a constant number of n-bit finite field multiplications. Thus, the multi-scalar multiplication has $O(n^3)$ computational complexity. Hence, the requirement for the computational cost is that the order is negligibly smaller than $O(n^3)$.

2   Width-3 Joint Sparse Form

This section proposes a JSF for the digit set $\mathcal{D}^{w=3}$; width-3 JSF.

Notations

$$u^{(i)}_{[j_1,j_2]} = \sum_{j=j_2}^{j_1} u^{(i)}_j 2^{j-j_2}, \ u^{(i)}_{(j_1,j_2)} = (u^{(i)}_{j_1}, u^{(i)}_{j_1-1}, \cdots, u^{(i)}_{j_2}).$$

$$U_j = \begin{bmatrix} u^{(0)}_j \\ u^{(1)}_j \end{bmatrix}, \ O = \begin{bmatrix} 0 \\ 0 \end{bmatrix}, \ U_{(j_1,j_2)} = \begin{bmatrix} u^{(0)}_{j_1}, u^{(0)}_{j_1-1}, \cdots, u^{(0)}_{j_2} \\ u^{(1)}_{j_1}, u^{(1)}_{j_1-1}, \cdots, u^{(1)}_{j_2} \end{bmatrix}.$$

Definition 1. *A JSF of a pair of integers $(u^{(0)}, u^{(1)})$ for the digit set $\mathcal{D}^{w=3}$ (3JSF) is defined as the $\mathcal{D}^{w=3}$ representation U in which for any non-zero $u^{(i)}_j$, exactly one of the following seven properties (3JSF1)-(3JSF7) holds:*

(3JSF1) $u_j^{(1-i)} = 0$, $U_{j+1} = U_{j+2} = O$.

(3JSF2) $u_j^{(1-i)} = 0$, $U_{j+1} = O$, $u_{j+2}^{(0)} u_{j+2}^{(1)} \neq 0$.

(3JSF3) $u_j^{(1-i)} = 0$, $u_{j+1}^{(0)} u_{j+1}^{(1)} \neq 0$.

If $u_{[j+3,j]}^{(i)} = \pm 7, \pm 9$, then $U_{j+3} = O$, $u_{j+4}^{(0)} = u_{j+4}^{(1)}$ (mod 2).

(3JSF4) $u_j^{(1-i)} \neq 0$, $U_{j+1} = U_{j+2} = O$, and $JHW(U_{(j+4,j+3)}) \leq 1$.

(3JSF5) $u_j^{(1-i)} \neq 0$, $U_{j+1} = O$, $u_{j+2}^{(0)} u_{j+2}^{(1)} \neq 0$, and $u_{j+2}^{(i)}$ satisfies *(3JSF4)*.

$u_j^{(i)}$ is not transferable to *(3JSF4)*. That is to say, for any $V_{(n-1,j)}$ with
$V_{(n-1,j)} \neq U_{(n-1,j)}$ and $v_{[n-1,j]}^{(i')} = u_{[n-1,j]}^{(i')}$ $(i' = 0,1)$, $v_j^{(i)} \neq 0$ does not
satisfy *(3JSF4)*.

(3JSF6) $u_j^{(1-i)} \neq 0$, $U_{j+1} = U_{j+2} = O$. $u_{[j+6,j+3]}^{(i')} = \pm 7, \pm 9$ $(i' = 0$ or $1)$.
$u_j^{(i)}$ is not transferable to *(3JSF5)*.

(3JSF7) $u_j^{(1-i)} \neq 0$, $U_{j+1} = O$, $u_{j+2}^{(0)} u_{j+2}^{(1)} \neq 0$. $u_{j+2}^{(i)}$ satisfies one of *(3JSF5)*,
(3JSF6), *(3JSF7)*. $u_j^{(i)}$ is not transferable to any of *(3JSF4)*, *(3JSF5)*, *(3JSF6)*.

The above definition is well-defined; (1) Every two properties are not satisfied simultaneously. (2) (3JSF7) is recursive but terminative since the bit length n is finite and there exists j such that $u_j^{(i)}$ satisfies (3JSF5) or (3JSF6). In addition, it is easy to see that $u_j^{(i)}$ with (3JSF6) is not transferable to (3JSF4).

Furthermore, 3JSF satisfies the following properties which are similar to the definition of JSF for the digit set $\mathcal{D}^{w=2}$.

Corollary 1. *3JSF further satisfies the following properties.*

(Distribution of zero columns) For any consecutive three columns, at least one is the zero column. Furthermore, $m \geq 2$, for any consecutive $2m$ columns, at least m column are zeros.
(Duality of non-zeros (1)) If $u_{j+1}^{(i')} u_j^{(i)} \neq 0$, then $u_{j+1}^{(1-i')} \neq 0$, $u_j^{(1-i)} = 0$.
(Duality of non-zeros (2)) If $u_{j+2}^{(i')} u_j^{(i)} \neq 0$, then $u_{j+2}^{(1-i')} \neq 0$.

Remark 1. While (JSF2) is irreducibility, it may be switched to duality of non-zeros; if $u_{j+1}^{(1-i)} u_j^{(i)} \neq 0$, then $u_{j+1}^{(i)} = \pm 1$, $u_j^{(1-i)} = 0$. This change doesn't affect the JHW. Combined with (JSF3), it makes duality of non-zeros (1).

3JSF is supposed to satisfy the three properties of JSF for the digit set $\mathcal{D}^{w=2}$. In fact, the following theorem holds.

Theorem 1. *3JSF satisfies the following three properties.*

(Existence) For any pair of integers, there exists 3JSF.
(Uniqueness) For any pair of integers, at most one 3JSF exists.
(Optimality) 3JSF has the minimal JHW in the $\mathcal{D}^{w=3}$ representations of the pair of integers.

3   Existence

In order to prove the existence, we construct an algorithm that outputs a 3JSF for arbitrary pair of integers. The proposed algorithm has the five states (A-E), and the initial state is A. Each state reads several left columns from the current bit position (indicated by j), converts them and outputs some of them. Then it moves to the next state. The conversions in the every state are combinations of the following three basic conversions (SW, ZF, DI):

- (Sliding Window) $SW(U_{(j_1,j_2)}) = \begin{bmatrix} SW(u^{(0)}_{(j_1,j_2)}) \\ SW(u^{(1)}_{(j_1,j_2)}) \end{bmatrix}$, where $SW(u^{(i)}_{(j_1,j_2)}) =$

$(\underbrace{0,0,\cdots,0}_{j_1-j'}, u^{(i)}_{[j_1,j']}, \underbrace{0,\cdots,0}_{j'-j_2})$ for the smallest j' $(j_1 \geq j' \geq j_2)$ such that

$u^{(i)}_{j'} \neq 0$.

- (Zero-Free) $ZF(U_{(j_1,j_2)}) = \begin{bmatrix} ZF(u^{(0)}_{(j_1,j_2)}) \\ ZF(u^{(1)}_{(j_1,j_2)}) \end{bmatrix}$, where $ZF(u^{(i)}_{(j_1,j_2)}) = (\underbrace{s, \bar{s}, \bar{s}, \cdots, \bar{s}}_{j_1-j'},$

$u^{(i)}_{j'} - 2s, u^{(i)}_{j'-1}, u^{(i)}_{j'-2}, \cdots, u^{(i)}_{j_2})$, $s = sgn(u^{(i)}_{j'})$ for the largest j' $(j_1 \geq j' \geq j_2)$ such that $u^{(i)}_{j'} \neq 0$, and $\bar{s}$ denotes $-s$. [1]

- (Dual Inversion) $DI((u^{(i)}_{j+4}, 0, 0, \pm3, \pm1)) = (u^{(i)}_{j+4} \pm 1, 0, 0, \mp3, \mp3)$. (double signs correspond)

These basic conversions are conversions of representations. That is, the converted representation $V_{(j_1,j_2)}$ satisfies $v^{(i)}_{[j_1,j_2]} = u^{(i)}_{[j_1,j_2]}$ $(i = 0, 1)$.

First of all, a binary representation is converted to Booth recoding [Boo51]. Booth recoding is a signed binary representation, and ignoring 0s, the signs of the consecutive non-zeros are opposite (i.e. 1 and -1 are alternately appeared) and the most and the least significant non-zeros are different. Booth recoding is derived from the computation of the bitwise $2d - d$ for the binary representation of d.

Next, for the converted Booth recoding, the following conversions are applied at each state. At the initial state initializes j as $j = 0$. At the time when $j \geq n$ is satisfied, the flow is terminated. Since j is increased whenever the flow returns to the same state, the proposed algorithm always terminates.

The input is given by $U_{(n-1,0)}$ and the converted representation is stored on the same $U_{(n-1,0)}$. In case the input needs to be preserved, the input is copied to the output area only as needed, then convert it.

Note that, since the conversion to Booth recoding and the copy to the output area can be performed from right to left, the conversion and the copy only as needed at each state provide us with the right-to-left algorithm.

For simplicity, $JHW(SW(U_{(j+b,j+a)}))$ and $\begin{bmatrix} U_{(j+a,j)} \leftarrow ZF(U_{(j+a,j)}) \\ U_{(j+a-1,j)} \leftarrow SW(U_{(j+a-1,j)}) \end{bmatrix}$ [2]

are abbreviated to $\omega(b, a)$ and $U_{(j+a,j)} \leftarrow \overline{SW}(U_{(j+a,j)})$, respectively.

---

[1] $sgn(\cdot)$ is the signum function; $sgn(x) = x/|x|$ if $x \neq 0$, 0 otherwise.
[2] After ZF conversion, SW conversion is applied.

– State A: (Initial state)
  • The case (A-1): $U_j = O$
    1. $j \leftarrow j + 1$.
    2. Move to State A.
  • The case (A-2): $u_j^{(i)} \neq 0$, $u_{[j+2,j]}^{(1-i)} = 0$
    1. $U_{(j+2,j)} \leftarrow SW(U_{(j+2,j)})$.
    2. $j \leftarrow j + 3$.
    3. Move to State A.
  • The case (A-3): $u_j^{(i)} \neq 0$, $u_{j+2}^{(1-i)} \neq 0$, $u_{[j+1,j]}^{(1-i)} = 0$
    1. $U_{(j+2,j)} \leftarrow \overline{SW}(U_{(j+2,j)})$.
    2. $j \leftarrow j + 2$.
    3. Move to State B.
  • The case (A-4): $u_j^{(i)} \neq 0$, $u_{j+1}^{(1-i)} \neq 0$, $u_j^{(1-i)} = 0$, $u_{[j+3,j]}^{(i)} = \pm 7$
    1. Move to State D.
  • The case (A-5): $u_j^{(i)} \neq 0$, $u_{j+1}^{(1-i)} \neq 0$, $u_j^{(1-i)} = 0$, $u_{[j+3,j]}^{(i)} \neq \pm 7$
    1. $U_{(j+1,j)} \leftarrow ZF(U_{(j+1,j)})$.
    2. $j \leftarrow j + 1$.
    3. Move to State B.
  • The case (A-6): $u_j^{(i)} \neq 0$, $u_j^{(1-i)} \neq 0$
    1. Move to State B.

– State B: ($u_j^{(0)} u_j^{(1)} \neq 0$)
  • The case (B-1): $\omega(4, 3) \leq 1$
    1. $U_{(j+2,j)} \leftarrow SW(U_{(j+2,j)})$.
    2. $j \leftarrow j + 3$.
    3. Move to State E.
  • The case (B-2): $\omega(4, 3) = 2$
    1. Move to State C.

– State C: ($u_j^{(0)} u_j^{(1)} \neq 0$, $\omega(4, 3) = 2$)
  • The case (C-1): $\omega(6, 5) \leq 1$
    1. $U_{(j+2,j)} \leftarrow \overline{SW}(U_{(j+2,j)})$.
    2. $U_{(j+4,j+2)} \leftarrow SW(U_{(j+4,j+2)})$.
    3. $j \leftarrow j + 5$.
    4. Move to State E.
  • The case (C-2): $\omega(6, 5) = 2$, $u_{[j+6,j+3]}^{(i)} = \pm 7$
    1. $U_{(j+2,j)} \leftarrow SW(U_{(j+2,j)})$.
    2. $j \leftarrow j + 3$.
    3. Move to State D.
  • The case (C-3): $\omega(6, 5) = 2$, $u_{[j+6,j+3]}^{(i)} \neq \pm 7$
    1. $U_{(j+2,j)} \leftarrow \overline{SW}(U_{(j+2,j)})$.
    2. $j \leftarrow j + 2$.
    3. Move to State C.

– State D: ($u_{[j+3,j]}^{(i)} = \pm 7$)
  • The case (D-1): $u_{j+4}^{(1-i)} = 0$

    1. $U_{(j+1,j)} \leftarrow ZF(U_{(j+1,j)})$.

    2. $U_{(j+3,j+1)} \leftarrow SW(U_{(j+3,j+1)})$.

    3. $u^{(i)}_{(j+4,j)} \leftarrow DI(u^{(i)}_{(j+4,j)})$ if $u^{(i)}_{j+4} \neq 0$.

    4. $j \leftarrow j + 5$.

    5. Move to State A.

- The case (D-2): $u^{(1-i)}_{j+4} \neq 0$

    1. $U_{(j+1,j)} \leftarrow Z\bar{F}(U_{(j+1,j)})$.

    2. $U_{(j+3,j+1)} \leftarrow SW(U_{(j+3,j+1)})$.

    3. $u^{(i)}_{(j+4,j)} \leftarrow DI(u^{(i)}_{(j+4,j)})$ if $u^{(i)}_{j+4} = 0$.

    4. $j \leftarrow j + 4$.

    5. Move to State B.

– State E: $(\omega(1,0) \leq 1)$

- The case (E-1): $U_j = O$

    1. $j \leftarrow j + 1$.

    2. Move to State A.

- The case (E-2): $u^{(i)}_j \neq 0$, $u^{(1-i)}_{[j+2,j]} = 0$

    1. $U_{(j+2,j)} \leftarrow SW(U_{(j+2,j)})$.

    2. $j \leftarrow j + 3$.

    3. Move to State A.

- The case (E-3): $u^{(i)}_j \neq 0$, $u^{(1-i)}_{j+2} \neq 0$, $u^{(1-i)}_{[j+1,j]} = 0$

    1. $U_{(j+2,j)} \leftarrow \overline{SW}(U_{(j+2,j)})$.

    2. $j \leftarrow j + 2$.

    3. Move to State B.

- The case (E-4): $u^{(i)}_j \neq 0$, $u^{(1-i)}_j \neq 0$

    1. Move to State B.

First, we will confirm the output is a $\mathcal{D}^{w=3}$ representation. All the conversions at every states are combinations of the basic conversions from Booth recoding. In particular, one of the following conversions is applied: (1) 3-bit SW conversion from a 3-bit Booth recoding. (2) ZF conversion. (3) 2-bit SW conversion after ZF conversion. (4) DI conversion after ZF and 3-bit SW conversions. Thus, every cases output values belong to $\mathcal{D}^{w=3}$.[3]

Next, we will confirm the output satisfies (3JSF1)-(3JSF7). The outputs at every transitions are categorized by the values of U_j as follows:

1. Blank. A-4,6, B-2, E-4
2. O. A-1, E-1
3. One is non-zero and the other is zero. A-2,3,5, D-1,2, E-2,3
4. Both are non-zeros. B-1, C-1,2,3

---

[3] In the case of (4), after ZF and SW conversions, the sign of $u^{(i)}_{j+4}$ is different from that of $u^{(i)}_{j+1}$ if $u^{(i)}_{j+4} \neq 0$. Thus the remaining part keeps Booth recoding after DI conversion. If $u^{(i)}_{j+4} = 0$, a similar argument is applied to $u^{(i)}_{j'} \neq 0$ with the smallest $j'(> j + 4)$.

The cases 1. and 2. obviously satisfy the rules. In the case of 3., one non-zero is outputted by A-2,3,5, E-2,3, and three non-zeros are done by D-1,2. Focus on the non-zero in the former. A-2 and E-2 satisfy (3JSF1). A-3 and E-3 satisfy (3JSF2). A-5 satisfies (3JSF3), but doesn't the latter condition of (3JSF3). Next, focus on the right non-zero in the latter. Since $u^{(i)}_{[j+3,j]} = \pm 7, \pm 9$, D-1,2 satisfy (3JSF3). The left non-zeros $u^{(i)}_{j+1}$, $u^{(1-i)}_{j+1}$ satisfy $U_{j+2} = U_{j+3} = O$. In addition, $JHW(U_{(j+5,j+4)}) \leq 1$ since $u^{(i)}_{j+4} = u^{(1-i)}_{j+4}$ (mod 2). Thus (3JSF4) is satisfied.

Next, we will confirm the case 4. B-1 satisfies (3JSF4). In the case of C-1, $U_{j+1} = O$, $u^{(0)}_{j+2} u^{(1)}_{j+2} \neq 0$, $U_{j+3} = U_{j+4} = O$. Focusing on $u^{(i)}_{j+2}$ and $u^{(1-i)}_{j+2}$, they satisfy (3JSF4) since $JHW(U_{(j+6,j+5)}) \leq 1$. Thus, $u^{(i)}_j$ and $u^{(1-i)}_j$ do (3JSF5). In the case of C-2, $U_{j+1} = U_{j+2} = O$. Since the succeeding D outputs $U_{(j+6,j+3)}$ with $u^{(i)}_{[j+6,j+3]} = \pm 7, \pm 9$ or $u^{(1-i)}_{[j+6,j+3]} = \pm 7, \pm 9$, (3JSF6) is satisfied. In the case of C-3, $U_{j+1} = O$, $u^{(0)}_{j+2} u^{(1)}_{j+2} \neq 0$. The succeeding C converts $u^{(i)}_{j+2}$ and $u^{(1-i)}_{j+2}$ based on the next transition (C-1,2,3). If it is C-1 or C-2, they satisfy (3JSF5) or (3JSF6), so $u^{(i)}_j$ and $u^{(1-i)}_j$ do (3JSF7). The flow doesn't terminate just after C-3 since $JH\dot{W}(U_{(j+6,j+5)}) = 2$. Thus, there exists a C-3 transition whose succeeding transition is C-1 or C-2. Tracking back to the first C-3, $u^{(i)}_j$ and $u^{(1-i)}_j$ satisfy (3JSF7).

Therefore, the output satisfies (3JSF1)-(3JSF7).

4 Efficiency

This section discusses JHD, the memory usage, and the computational cost.

First, we will consider JHD of the output. Fig. 1 shows the transition graph of the algorithm, which is a finite Markov chain. Each arrow shows a transition. A fractional number near by an arrow is a transition probability, and (x, y) is information on the outputted columns, where x and y stand for JHW and the number of columns, respectively. Although the input is in Booth recoding, the digits are independent; 0 and non-zero are with probability 1/2. Note, the sign of non-zero is determined based on the adjacent non-zero.

JHD is computed using the properties of a finite Markov chain. Since the finite Markov chain of Fig. 1 is irreducible and aperiodic, there exists the stationary distribution

$$(A, B, C, D, E) = \frac{1}{423}(112, 133, 38, 47/4, 513/4),$$

which is the solution of

$$\begin{bmatrix} A \\ B \\ C \\ D \\ E \end{bmatrix} = \begin{bmatrix} \frac{1}{4} + \frac{1}{8} & \frac{1}{8} + \frac{3}{16} + \frac{1}{4} & 0 & \frac{1}{16} & 0 \\ 0 & 0 & \frac{1}{4} & 0 & \frac{3}{4} \\ 0 & 0 & \frac{1}{8} & \frac{1}{8} & \frac{3}{4} \\ \frac{1}{2} & \frac{1}{2} & 0 & 0 & 0 \\ \frac{1}{3} + \frac{1}{6} & \frac{1}{6} + \frac{1}{3} & 0 & 0 & 0 \end{bmatrix} \begin{bmatrix} A \\ B \\ C \\ D \\ E \end{bmatrix}.$$

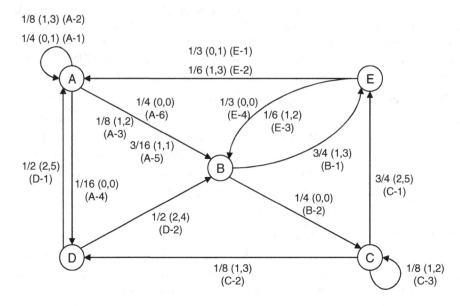

Fig. 1. The transition graph of the proposed algorithm

Average JHW and length per transition are as follow:

$$(\text{Average JHW/transition}) = 563/846$$
$$(\text{Average length/transition}) = 1574/846$$

Thus, $JHD_{\mathcal{D}^{w=3}} = 563/1574 \ (= 0.3577)$.

For confirming the correctness of the theoretical estimate, we experimented on 1.28 billion bits. Table 1 shows the result.

The total number of transitions and JHW are 687965610 and 457841714, respectively. So the average {JHW, length} per transition and JHD are 0.66550, 1.86056 and 0.35769, which are very close to 563/846, 1574/846 and 563/1574, respectively. The stationary distribution and transition probabilities are also very close to the theoretical values.

Memory Usage: Under the assumption that input and output areas are assigned beforehand, we estimate the internal buffers. For doing that, we count up internal variables and the maximum bit length to be read at each transition.

On variables, there is one; j for the current bit position. Its bit length is $\log n$, where n stands for the bit length of the representation. On the maximum bit length to be read, C-x transitions requires 7-bit Booth recoding, namely, 8-bit binary representation, which is maximum. Thus, it is constant independent from n. Therefore, the memory usage is $O(\log n)$, which is smaller than $O(n)$.

Computational Cost: For doing that, we estimate the computational cost for each transition and the number of transitions until the end.

Table 1. The experimental results on the distribution

state	transitions	prob.
A	182164428	0.2648
A-1	45548792	0.2500
A-2	22774395	0.1250
A-3	22770833	0.1250
A-4	11384830	0.0625
A-5	34152309	0.1875
A-6	45533269	0.2500

state	transitions	prob.
B	216304453	0.3144
B-1	162222553	0.7500
B-2	54081900	0.2500
C	61807446	0.0898
C-1	46355840	0.7500
C-2	7726060	0.1250
C-3	7725546	0.1250

state	transitions	prob.
D	19110890	0.0278
D-1	9558368	0.5002
D-2	9552522	0.4998
E	208578393	0.3032
E-1	69516208	0.3333
E-2	34766665	0.1667
E-3	34769893	0.1667
E-4	69525627	0.3333

Each transition requires the following amount of computational cost.

1. Selection of transitions
2. Total amount of the basic conversions
3. Bit position renewal
4. Selection of the next state
5. Test for termination

For 1. and 4., the computational costs are constant, since numbers of states and transitions are constant. For 2., the maximum bit length to be read is 4, the number of kinds of converted values (i.e. coefficient) is 5, and the maximum number of basic conversions is 4. Thus, the computational cost is constant. For 3. and 5., since the variable j is updated/read, the computational cost for the worst case is $O(\log n)$. However, the probability of the worst case is $1/n$, and the average computational cost is constant. Thus, the computational cost for each transition is $O(1)$.

The number of transitions until the end is $O(n)$, since the average length per transition is a positive constant (1574/846). Therefore, the computational cost is $O(n)$, which is smaller than $O(n^3)$.

For confirming the efficiency of the proposed algorithm, we implemented it on a computer using the NTL library [NTL]. The CPU was Intel® Core 2 2.66GHz. The program was composed of two modules; the conversion into 3JSF and computation of $uP + vQ$ using the 3JSF representation. 256-bit elliptic curves were used, and u, v, P, Q were randomly chosen and given just before the computation. The precomputation table stored the points correspond to $\mathcal{D}^{w=3}$ in affine coordinates. The elliptic addition and doubling were computed in Jacobian coordinates with mixed coordinates technique. In this setting, the conversion into 3JSF took $27.2\mu sec$ and the total timing was $2674.7\mu sec$. The timings were averaged over 100000 executions. So, the overhead of the conversion is not big. Note, the program of the conversion was straightforwardly implemented since it had been aimed for confirming the correctness of the algorithm, and was not optimized.

5   Optimality

In order to prove the optimality, for a 3JSF U, we consider any V with a smaller JHW than U, and derive contradiction. For the complete proofs for optimality and uniqueness, see the appendix.

In the proof, contradiction is derived in each case that a non-zero $u_0^{(1)}$ satisfies the condition (3JSFx). The proof will be done by induction regarding the bit length n of U. That is to say, for any n' smaller than n, with assuming that a 3JSF U' with the bit length n' has the minimal JHW, we will show U has the minimal JHW. The following lemma ensures the choice $U' = U_{(n-1,n-n')}$.

Lemma 1 (Sustainability). *The proposed algorithm is sustainable. That is, the output that the flow is temporarily halted at any state and continued from the initial state, is the same to that without the temporary halt. Furthermore, for any n', the output for $(u_{[n-1,n-n']}^{(0)}, u_{[n-1,n-n']}^{(1)})$ coincides with $U_{(n-1,n-n')}$.*

In the proof, we will show that the prospective carries on V do not contribute the reduction of JHW using the following lemma.

Lemma 2 (Subadditivity). *The minimal JHW (MJHW for short) for a pair of integers satisfies subadditivity. That is, for any pairs of integers $U = (u^{(0)}, u^{(1)})$ and $V = (v^{(0)}, v^{(1)})$, $MJHW(U + V) \leq MJHW(U) + MJHW(V)$, where $U + V$ stands for $(u^{(0)} + v^{(0)}, u^{(1)} + v^{(1)})$. Furthermore, if $u^{(0)} = u^{(1)}$ (mod 2), then $MJHW((u^{(0)} + d, u^{(1)}))), MJHW((u^{(0)}, u^{(1)} + d)) \geq MJHW(U)$ for any $d \in \{\pm 1, \pm 3\}$.*

6   Conclusion

This paper enhanced a JSF to the digit set $\mathcal{D}^{w=3}$. 3JSF is defined as a representation that satisfies seven properties (3JSF1)-(3JSF7). We ensured 3JSF is a natural enhancement of the usual JSF. In addition, 3JSF satisfies the existence, the uniqueness, and the optimality properties as JSF does. 3JSF has the minimal joint Hamming density $0.3577 (= 563/1574)$ among all the $\mathcal{D}^{w=3}$ representations. The algorithm to compute a 3JSF requires $O(\log n)$ memory and $O(n)$ computational complexity, where n is the bit length.

A further direction of this topic will be to construct a JSF for the digit set $\mathcal{D}^{w=k}$ with general k. Some other directions will be left-to-right generation and three or more scalars in addition to width-3. An unsigned version is also a good research topic.

Acknowledgement

We would like to thank Camille Vuillaume, Erik Dahmen, and anonymous reviewers for their helpful comments.

References

[Ava02]   Avanzi, R.: On multi-exponentiation in cryptography, Cryptology ePrint Archive: Report 2002/154 (2002)

[Boo51]   Booth, A.: A signed binary multiplication technique. Quarterly Journal of Mechanics and Applied Mathematics 4(2), 236–240 (1951)

[DOT05]   Dahmen, E., Okeya, K., Takagi, T.: An Advanced Method for Joint Scalar Multiplications on Memory Constraint Devices. In: Molva, R., Tsudik, G., Westhoff, D. (eds.) ESAS 2005. LNCS, vol. 3813, pp. 189–204. Springer, Heidelberg (2005)

[GLV01]   Gallant, R.P., Lambert, J.L., Vanstone, S.A.: Faster Point Multiplication on Elliptic Curves with Efficient Endomorphism. In: Kilian, J. (ed.) CRYPTO 2001. LNCS, vol. 2139, pp. 190–200. Springer, Heidelberg (2001)

[HKP+04]   Heuberger, C., Katti, R., Prodinger, H., Ruan, X.: The Alternating Greedy Expansion and Applications to Left-To-Right Algorithms in Cryptography. Theoret. Comput. Sci. 341, 55–72 (2005)

[Kob87]   Koblitz, N.: Elliptic Curve Cryptosystems. Math. Comp. 48, 203–209 (1987)

[KZZ04]   Kuang, B., Zhu, Y., Zhang, Y.: An Improved Algorithm for uP+vQ using JSF_3. In: Jakobsson, M., Yung, M., Zhou, J. (eds.) ACNS 2004. LNCS, vol. 3089, pp. 467–478. Springer, Heidelberg (2004)

[LL94]   Lim, C., Lee, P.: More flexible exponentiation with precomputation. In: Desmedt, Y.G. (ed.) CRYPTO 1994. LNCS, vol. 839, pp. 95–107. Springer, Heidelberg (1994)

[Mil86]   Miller, V.S.: Use of elliptic curves in cryptography. In: Williams, H.C. (ed.) CRYPTO 1985. LNCS, vol. 218, pp. 417–426. Springer, Heidelberg (1986)

[MO90]   Morain, F., Olivos, J.: Speeding up the computations on an elliptic curve using addition-subtraction chains. Inform. Theor. Appl. 24, 531–543 (1990)

[NTL]   Shoup, V.: NTL: A Library for doing Number Theory (version 5.5.2), http://www.shoup.net/ntl/

[Pro03]   Proos, J.: Joint Sparse Forms and Generating Zero Columns when Combing, Technical Report of the Centre for Applied Cryptographic Research, University of Waterloo - CACR, CORR 2003-23 (2003), http://www.cacr.math.uwaterloo.ca

[Rei60]   Reitwiesner, G.W.: Binary arithmetic. Advances in Computers 1, 231–308 (1960)

[Sol00]   Solinas, J.A.: Efficient Arithmetic on Koblitz Curves. Designs, Codes and Cryptography 19, 195–249 (2000)

[Sol01]   Solinas, J.A.: Low-weight binary representations for pairs of integers, Technical Report of the Centre for Applied Cryptographic Research, University of Waterloo - CACR, CORR 2001-41 (2001), http://www.cacr.math.uwaterloo.ca

A   Uniqueness

In order to prove the uniqueness, for arbitrary two 3JSFs, we derive contradiction from the coincidence of the remainders by powers of 2 at the bit position which differs the values.

Let U and V be two different 3JSFs. Then $u^{(i)}_{[n-1,0]} = v^{(i)}_{[n-1,0]}$ for $i = 0, 1$ holds. Since two 3JSFs are different, there exists j with $u^{(i)}_j \neq v^{(i)}_j$. Let j be anew the smallest one among such indexes j. Ignoring digits smaller than j, without loss of generality, we may assume $j = 0$. In addition, we may further assume $i = 1$, if necessary, $u^{(0)}$ and $u^{(1)}$, $v^{(0)}$ and $v^{(1)}$ are exchanged respectively. To put it plainly, $u^{(1)}_0 \neq v^{(1)}_0$.

Since $u^{(1)}_{[n-1,0]} = v^{(1)}_{[n-1,0]}$, $u^{(1)}_0 = v^{(1)}_0$ (mod 2). If $u^{(1)}_0$ is even, $u^{(1)}_0 = v^{(1)}_0$, which contradicts the assumption. Thus, it is odd. If necessary, exchange of u and v, and sign inversion of u and v, every cases are reduced to the following four cases: $(u^{(1)}_0, v^{(1)}_0) = (\bar{3}, \bar{1}), (\bar{3}, 3), (\bar{1}, 1), (\bar{1}, 3)$.

- The case $(\bar{3}, \bar{1})$: Since $u^{(1)} = v^{(1)}$ (mod 4), $(u^{(1)}_1, v^{(1)}_1) = (0, x)$ or $(x, 0)$, where x stands for non-zero. In the case for $(0, x)$ (the case for $(x, 0)$ is similar), since non-zeros $v^{(1)}_1$, $v^{(1)}_0$ are consecutive, $v^{(1)}_{[1,0]} = \pm 7$ or ± 9 (3JSF3). In addition, $v^{(0)}_1 \neq 0$, $v^{(0)}_0 = 0$. Because of $u^{(1)}_1 = 0$, $u^{(1)}_0$ satisfies (3JSFx) except for (3JSF3), so $u^{(0)}_1 = 0$. On the other hand, $2 = v^{(0)}_{[n-1,0]} = u^{(0)}_{[n-1,0]} = u^{(0)}_0$ (mod 4), which is contradiction. In the case for $(u^{(1)}_0, v^{(1)}_0) = (\bar{3}, 3)$, $(\bar{1}, 1)$ is similar.
- The case $(\bar{1}, 3)$: There are two cases; $(u^{(1)}_1, v^{(1)}_1) = (x, x)$ or $(0, 0)$
  - The case (x, x): Since $u^{(1)}_0$ and $v^{(1)}_0$ satisfy (3JSF3), $u^{(0)}_0 = v^{(0)}_0 = 0$, $u^{(1)}_1 = \bar{3}$, $u^{(0)}_1 \neq 0$, $v^{(1)}_1 = 3$, $v^{(0)}_1 \neq 0$, $U_2 = U_3 = V_2 = V_3 = O$, $u^{(0)}_4 = u^{(1)}_4$ (mod 2), $v^{(0)}_4 = v^{(1)}_4$ (mod 2). Since $16u^{(1)}_4 - 7 = u^{(1)}_{[n-1,0]} = v^{(1)}_{[n-1,0]} = 16v^{(1)}_4 + 9$ (mod 32), $u^{(1)}_4 \neq v^{(1)}_4$ (mod 2). On the other hand, since $2u^{(0)}_1 = u^{(0)}_{[n-1,0]} = v^{(0)}_{[n-1,0]} = 2v^{(0)}_1$ (mod 16), $u^{(0)}_1 = v^{(0)}_1$. Thus, $16u^{(0)}_4 + 2u^{(0)}_1 = u^{(0)}_{[n-1,0]} = v^{(0)}_{[n-1,0]} = 16v^{(0)}_4 + 2v^{(0)}_1$ (mod 32), so $u^{(0)}_4 = v^{(0)}_4$ (mod 2). Hence, $u^{(1)}_4 = v^{(1)}_4$ (mod 2), which is contradiction.
  - The case $(0, 0)$: Since $4u^{(1)}_2 - 1 = u^{(1)}_{[n-1,0]} = v^{(1)}_{[n-1,0]} = 4v^{(1)}_2 + 3$ (mod 8), $u^{(1)}_2 \neq v^{(1)}_2$ (mod 2). In the case for $(u^{(1)}_2, v^{(1)}_2) = (0, x)$ (the case for $(x, 0)$ is similar), since $u^{(1)}_0$ satisfies one of (3JSF1) (3JSF4) (3JSF6), $u^{(0)}_1 = u^{(0)}_2 = 0$. On the other hand, since $v^{(1)}_0$ satisfies one of (3JSF2) (3JSF5) (3JSF7), $v^{(0)}_1 = 0$, $v^{(0)}_2 \neq 0$. $u^{(0)}_0 = u^{(0)}_{[n-1,0]} = v^{(0)}_{[n-1,0]} = 4 + v^{(0)}_0$ (mod 8), so $u^{(0)}_0 v^{(0)}_0 \neq 0$. Hence, whereas $u^{(1)}_0$ satisfies one of (3JSF4) (3JSF6), $v^{(1)}_0$ satisfies one of (3JSF5) (3JSF7), which is contradiction.

In any case, contradiction is derived, therefore, non-existence of two different 3JSFs, namely, the uniqueness has been proved.

B   Optimality

First, we will prove two lemmas.

Proof (of Lemma 1). The former is clear. On the latter, the cases of transitions with JHW ≤ 1 are obvious. For the left non-zero column of transitions with JHW $= 2$, the succeeding transitions are as follows: The case of C-1: A $\rightarrow$ A-6 $\rightarrow$ B-1 $\rightarrow$ E. The case of D-1: A $\rightarrow$ A-6 $\rightarrow$ B-1 $\rightarrow$ E-1 $\rightarrow$ A. The case of D-2: A $\rightarrow$ A-6 $\rightarrow$ B-1 $\rightarrow$ E-4 $\rightarrow$ B. These outputs coincide with their originals. □

Proof (of Lemma 2). Without loss of generality, we can assume $JHW(V) = 1$. The general case is deduced by the induction regarding JHW. Let (x, y) be a non-zero column of V and the corresponding column of U be (x', y'), where $x \neq 0$. In the case of $y = 0$, it's trivial if $x' = 0$. If $x' \neq 0$, then $x + x'$ can be written by the form $d \cdot 2^k$, $d \in \{\pm 1, \pm 3\}$. Replaced by d, the same argument is applied. Since the bit length is finite, this iteration terminates. Except for the leftmost carry, non-zeros do not increase. In the case of $y \neq 0$, the same discussion is applied. Remind the column at the original position becomes zero, which decrease JHW by one.

On the latter, suppose $MJHW((u^{(0)} + d, u^{(1)})) = MJHW(U) - 1$, and let $U'_{(n-1,0)}$ be a representation of $(u^{(0)} + d, u^{(1)})$. Then, $u_0'^{(0)} \neq u_0'^{(1)}$ (mod 2). $JHW(U'_{(n-1,1)})$ should be $MJHW(U) - 2$. If $u_0'^{(0)} \neq 0$, adding $-d$ makes a zero column at the position of $j = 0$, which contradicts $MJHW(U)$. If $u_0'^{(0)} = 0$, adding $-d$ doesn't increase JHW, which contradicts $MJHW(U)$. □

In order to prove the optimality, for a 3JSF U, we consider any V with a smaller JHW than U, and derive contradiction. From the assumption, $u_{[n-1,0]}^{(i)} = v_{[n-1,0]}^{(i)}$ for $i = 0, 1$ holds.

Since two representations are different, there exists j such that $u_j^{(i)} \neq v_j^{(i)}$. Let j be anew the smallest one among such indexes j. Ignoring digits smaller than j, without loss of generality, we may assume $j = 0$. In addition, we may further assume $i = 1$, if necessary, $u^{(0)}$ and $u^{(1)}$, $v^{(0)}$ and $v^{(1)}$ are exchanged respectively. To put it plainly, $u_0^{(1)} \neq v_0^{(1)}$.

Since $u_{[n-1,0]}^{(1)} = v_{[n-1,0]}^{(1)}$, $u_0^{(1)} = v_0^{(1)}$ (mod 2). If $u_0^{(1)}$ is even, $u_0^{(1)} = v_0^{(1)}$, which contradicts the assumption. Therefore, it is odd, namely, non-zero.

In what follows, contradiction is derived in each case that a non-zero $u_0^{(1)}$ satisfies the condition (3JSFx). The proof will be done by the induction regarding the bit length n of U. That is to say, for any n' smaller than n, with assuming that a 3JSF U' with the bit length n' has the minimal JHW, we will show U has the minimal JHW.

- The case (3JSF1): $v_0^{(1)} \neq 0$, $v_{[2,0]}^{(0)} = 0$ (mod 8). Since $v_{[2,0]}^{(1)} = u_{[2,0]}^{(1)} = u_0^{(1)}$ mods 8 and $v_0^{(1)} \neq u_0^{(1)}$, $JHW(V_{(2,1)}) \geq 1$, where mods stands for the modular reduction with the smallest residue in absolute value. Especially, $JHW(V_{(2,0)}) \geq JHW(U_{(2,0)}) + 1$. Because of Lemma 1 and the induction hypothesis, $JHW(U_{(n-1,3)})$ has the MJHW. Since $-21 \leq v_{[2,0]}^{(1)} \leq 21 (= 3 \cdot 2^2 + 3 \cdot 2 + 3)$, $-3 \leq v_{[n-1,3]}^{(1)} - u_{[n-1,3]}^{(1)} \leq 3 (= \lceil 21/8 \rceil)$. Thus, Lemma 2 implies $JHW(V_{(n-1,3)}) \geq JHW(U_{(n-1,3)}) - 1$. Therefore, $JHW(V_{(n-1,0)}) \geq JHW(U_{(n-1,0)})$, which is contradiction.

- The case (3JSF2): $v_0^{(1)} \neq 0$, $v_{[2,0]}^{(0)} = 4$ (mod 8). $U_{(n-1,2)}$ has the MJHW.

  - The case $v_1^{(1)} \neq 0$: Since $-3 \leq v_{[n-1,2]}^{(1)} - u_{[n-1,2]}^{(1)} \leq 3$, $JHW(V_{(n-1,2)}) \geq JHW(U_{(n-1,2)}) - 1$. Therefore, $JHW(V_{(n-1,0)}) \geq JHW(U_{(n-1,0)})$, which is contradiction.
  - The case $v_1^{(1)} = 0$: $-1 \leq v_{[n-1,2]}^{(1)} - u_{[n-1,2]}^{(1)} \leq 1$. Since $u_2^{(0)} = u_2^{(1)}$ (mod 2), $JHW(V_{(n,0)}) \geq JHW(U_{(n,0)})$, which is contradiction.

- The case (3JSF3): $v_0^{(1)} \neq 0$, $v_{[1,0]}^{(0)} = 2$ (mod 4).

  - The case $u_{[1,0]}^{(1)} \neq \pm 7, \pm 9$: $U_{(n-1,1)}$ has the MJHW. Since $u_0^{(1)} = \pm 1$, $-2 \leq v_{[n-1,1]}^{(1)} - u_{[n-1,1]}^{(1)} \leq 2$. For $-1 \leq v_{[n-1,1]}^{(1)} - u_{[n-1,1]}^{(1)} \leq 1$, $JHW(V_{(n-1,0)}) \geq JHW(U_{(n-1,1)}) + 1 = JHW(U_{(n-1,0)})$, which is contradiction. For $v_{[n-1,1]}^{(1)} - u_{[n-1,1]}^{(1)} = \pm 2$, $U_{(n-1,3)}$ has the MJHW. If $JHW(V_{(2,0)}) = 3$, then $-3 \leq v_{[n-1,3]}^{(1)} - u_{[n-1,3]}^{(1)} \leq 3$. $JHW(V_{(n-1,0)}) \geq JHW(U_{(n-1,3)}) - 1 + 3 = JHW(U_{(n-1,0)})$, which is contradiction. If $JHW(V_{(2,0)}) = 2$, then $-1 \leq v_{[n-1,3]}^{(1)} - u_{[n-1,3]}^{(1)} \leq 1$. Since $u_3^{(0)} = u_3^{(1)}$ (mod 2), $JHW(V_{(n-1,0)}) \geq JHW(U_{(n-1,3)}) + 2 = JHW(U_{(n-1,0)})$, which is contradiction.
  - The case $u_{[1,0]}^{(1)} = \pm 7, \pm 9$: $U_{(n-1,4)}$ has the MJHW.
    * The case $JHW(V_{(3,0)}) = 4$: $-3 \leq v_{[n-1,4]}^{(i)} - u_{[n-1,4]}^{(i)} \leq 3$ $(i = 0, 1)$. $JHW(V_{(n-1,0)}) \geq JHW(U_{(n-1,4)}) - 2 + 4 = JHW(U_{(n-1,0)})$, which is contradiction.
    * The case $JHW(V_{(3,0)}) = 3$: $-2 \leq v_{[n-1,4]}^{(i)} - u_{[n-1,4]}^{(i)} \leq 2$ $(i = 0, 1)$. Since $u_4^{(0)} = u_4^{(1)}$ (mod 2), $JHW(V_{(n-1,0)}) \geq JHW(U_{(n-1,4)}) - 1 + 3 = JHW(U_{(n-1,0)})$, which is contradiction.
    * The case $JHW(V_{(3,0)}) = 2$: $v_{[n-1,4]}^{(0)} = u_{[n-1,4]}^{(0)}$, $-1 \leq v_{[n-1,4]}^{(1)} - u_{[n-1,4]}^{(1)} \leq 1$. Since $u_4^{(0)} = u_4^{(1)}$ (mod 2), $JHW(V_{(n-1,0)}) \geq JHW(U_{(n-1,4)}) + 2 = JHW(U_{(n-1,0)})$, which is contradiction.

- The case (3JSF4): $U_{(n-1,3)}$ has the MJHW.

  - The case $JHW(V_{(2,0)}) = 3$: $-3 \leq v_{[n-1,3]}^{(i)} - u_{[n-1,3]}^{(i)} \leq 3$ $(i = 0, 1)$. Thus, $JHW(V_{(n-1,0)}) \geq JHW(U_{(n-1,3)}) - 2 + 3 = JHW(U_{(n-1,0)})$, which is contradiction.
  - The case $JHW(V_{(2,0)}) = 2$: $-2 \leq v_{[n-1,3]}^{(i)} - u_{[n-1,3]}^{(i)} \leq 2$ $(i = 0, 1)$. If $u_3^{(0)} = u_3^{(1)}$ (mod 2), $JHW(V_{(n-1,0)}) \geq JHW(U_{(n-1,3)}) - 1 + 2 = JHW(U_{(n-1,0)})$, which is contradiction. Otherwise, $u_3^{(0)} \neq u_3^{(1)}$ (mod 2). $U_{(n-1,5)}$ has the MJHW. If $JHW(V_{(4,3)}) = 2$, $-3 \leq v_{[n-1,5]}^{(i)} - u_{[n-1,5]}^{(i)} \leq 3$ $(i = 0, 1)$. $JHW(V_{(n-1,0)}) \geq JHW(U_{(n-1,5)}) - 2 + 4 = JHW(U_{(n-1,0)})$,

which is contradiction. The case $JHW(V_{(4,3)}) = 1$: Since $-2 \le v^{(i)}_{[n-1,5]} - u^{(i)}_{[n-1,5]} \le 2$ $(i = 0, 1)$ and $u_5^{(0)} = u_5^{(1)}$ (mod 2), $JHW(V_{(n-1,0)}) \ge JHW(U_{(n-1,5)}) - 1 + 3 = JHW(U_{(n-1,0)})$, which is contradiction.

- The case $JHW(V_{(2,0)}) = 1$: $v_0^{(1)} = v_{[2,0]}^{(1)} = u_{[2,0]}^{(1)} = u_0^{(1)}$ mods 8, which is contradiction.

- The case (3JSF5): $U_{(n-1,5)}$ has the MJHW.
  - The case (5-4) $JHW(V_{(4,0)}) \ge 4$: Since $-3 \le v^{(i)}_{[n-1,5]} - u^{(i)}_{[n-1,5]} \le 3$ $(i = 0, 1)$, $JHW(V_{(n-1,0)}) \ge JHW(U_{(n-1,5)}) - 2 + 4 = JHW(U_{(n-1,0)})$, which is contradiction.
  - The case (5-3) $JHW(V_{(4,0)}) = 3$: Since $-2 \le v^{(i)}_{[n-1,5]} - u^{(i)}_{[n-1,5]} \le 2$ $(i = 0, 1)$ and $u_5^{(0)} = u_5^{(1)}$ (mod 2), $JHW(V_{(n-1,0)}) \ge JHW(U_{(n-1,5)}) - 1 + 3 = JHW(U_{(n-1,0)})$, which is contradiction.
  - The case (5-2) $JHW(V_{(4,0)}) = 2$: Remind non-transferability to (3JSF4). Since $JHW(V_{(4,3)}) = 0$, $v^{(i)}_{[n-1,5]} = u^{(i)}_{[n-1,5]}$ $(i = 0, 1)$. $JHW(V_{(n-1,0)}) \ge JHW(U_{(n-1,5)}) + 2 = JHW(U_{(n-1,0)})$, which is contradiction.
  - The case (5-1) $JHW(V_{(4,0)}) = 1$: Contradict the non-transferability to (3JSF4).

- The case (3JSF6): $U_{(n-1,7)}$ has the MJHW.
  - The case (6-5) $JHW(V_{(6,0)}) \ge 5$: Since $-3 \le v^{(i)}_{[n-1,7]} - u^{(i)}_{[n-1,7]} \le 3$ $(i = 0, 1)$, $JHW(V_{(n-1,0)}) \ge JHW(U_{(n-1,7)}) - 2 + 5 = JHW(U_{(n-1,0)})$, which is contradiction.
  - The case (6-4) $JHW(V_{(6,0)}) = 4$: Remind non-transferability to (3JSF4). Since $-2 \le v^{(i)}_{[n-1,7]} - u^{(i)}_{[n-1,7]} \le 2$ $(i = 0, 1)$ and $u_7^{(0)} = u_7^{(1)}$ (mod 2), $JHW(V_{(n-1,0)}) \ge JHW(U_{(n-1,7)}) - 1 + 4 = JHW(U_{(n-1,0)})$, which is contradiction.
  - The case (6-3) $JHW(V_{(6,0)}) = 3$: Since it's not transferable to (3JSF4)(3JSF5), $v^{(i)}_{[n-1,7]} = u^{(i)}_{[n-1,7]}$ $(i = 0, 1)$. $JHW(V_{(n-1,0)}) \ge JHW(U_{(n-1,7)}) + 3 = JHW(U_{(n-1,0)})$, which is contradiction.
  - The case (6-2) $JHW(V_{(6,0)}) \le 2$: Contradict the non-transferability to (3JSF4).

- The case (3JSF7): Since the bit length is finite, there exists $u_j^{(1)}$ that satisfies (3JSF5) or (3JSF6). Let m be the number of iterations of (3JSF7) to get to the non-zero; $j = 2m$.
  - The case $u_{2m}^{(1)}$ satisfies (3JSF5): $U_{(n-1,2m+5)}$ has the MJHW.
    * The case $JHW(V_{(2m+4,0)}) \ge m + 4$: (5-4) is applied.
    * The case $JHW(V_{(2m+4,0)}) = m + 3$: (5-3) is applied.
    * The case $JHW(V_{(2m+4,0)}) = m + 2$: Remind the non-transferability to (3JSF6), and (5-2) is applied.
    * The case $JHW(V_{(2m+4,0)}) \le m+1$: Contradict the non-transferability to (3JSF4).

- The case $u_{2m}^{(1)}$ satisfies (3JSF6): $U_{(n-1,2m+7)}$ has the MJHW.
  * The case $JHW(V_{(2m+6,0)}) \geq m+5$: (6-5) is applied.
  * The case $JHW(V_{(2m+6,0)}) = m+4$: (6-4) is applied.
  * The case $JHW(V_{(2m+6,0)}) = m+3$: (6-3) is applied.
  * The case $JHW(V_{(2m+6,0)}) \leq m+2$: Contradict the non-transferability to (3JSF4).

Therefore, the optimality of U has been proved.

Accelerating Inverse of $GF(2^n)$ with Precomputation[*]

Xu Lei[1,2] and Lin Dongdai[1]

[1] State Key Laboratory of Information Security, Institute of Software,
Chinese Academy of Sciences, Beijing, China
[2] Graduate University of Chinese Academy of Sciences, Beijing, China
xuleimath@gmail.com, ddlin@is.iscas.ac.cn

Abstract. In this paper we propose a method to accelerate the inverse of $GF(2^n)$ with some precomputation. Our method works for both almost inverse and Montgomery inverse of $GF(2^n)$, and is faster than previous methods. Furthermore, the precomputation is done only one time for a fixed finite field and can be done efficiently.

Keywords: $GF(2^n)$, almost inverse, Montgomery inverse.

1 Introduction

Finite field arithmetic is becoming increasingly important in today's computer systems, particularly for implementing cryptographic operations, such as the Diffie-Hellman key exchange algorithm ([1]) and the elliptic curve cryptography ([11],[13]). Among all the finite fields, prime fields with large characteristic ($GF(p)$) and binary fields with large extension degree ($GF(2^n)$) are important in cryptography.

For cryptographic applications, the most frequently used arithmetic of finite fields operations are addition, multiplication, and inverse. Compared with addition and multiplication, inverse of finite fields is much more expensive ([17], [18],[15],[6]). Many techniques are developed to avoid inverse operations, such as using projective coordinates to represent rational points on elliptic curves. But sometimes inverse is unavoidable. For example, in order to use parallelized ρ method ([14]) to calculate the elliptic curve discrete logarithm, we have to choose affine coordinates to represent rational points. In this situation inverse is essential for points additions. So accelerating the inverse is meaningful for cryptographic applications. In this paper we only consider the inverse of $GF(2^n)$.

Many algorithms have been proposed to calculate the inverse of $GF(2^n)$. The most well known method is extend Euclidean algorithm ([10]), which is derived

---

[*] This work was supported by the Grand Project of Institute of Software(NO. YOCX285056), the National Natural Science Foundation of China(NO. 60970152), and the National High Technology Research and Development Program of China(NO. 2007AA01Z447).

J. Kwak et al. (Eds.): ISPEC 2010, LNCS 6047, pp. 85–95, 2010.

from Euclidean algorithm that first appears in Euclid's *Elements* about two thousand years ago. Binary Euclidean algorithm ([10]), also known as Stein's algorithm, is another well known method used to calculate inverse of $GF(2^n)$. It gains a measure of efficiency over the ancient Euclidean algorithm by replacing divisions and multiplications with shifts, which are cheaper for software implementation. In 1988 Toshiya Itoh and Shigeo Tsujii gave a method(ITI) to calculate the inverse of $GF(q^m)$ using normal basis ([7]). Although it does not perform a complete inverse, it reduces inverse of $GF(q^m)$ to inverse of $GF(q)$, and it is assumed that subfield inverse can be done relatively easily. The ITI algorithm is applicable to finite fields $GF(2^m)$ given in a normal basis representation, where m is composite number. In 2002 Jorge Guajardo and Christof Paar extend this method to polynomial basis ([3]). The disadvantage of this method is that it cannot work when the extension degree is prime, which is the usual case for elliptic curve cryptography. In 1991 Alain Guyot introduced the idea of almost inverse ([5]) to calculate inverse of prime fields $GF(p)$. This idea was extended to $GF(2^n)$ by Richard Schroeppel et al in [15] in 1995. Almost inverse is an improvement of binary Euclidean algorithm. Specifically, the algorithm works in two phases. In order to find the inverse of $a \in GF(2^n)$, firstly a polynomial g and a positive integer k are computed satisfying $ag \equiv x^k \ mod \ f$. Then a reduction is applied to obtain $a^{-1} = x^{-k}g \ mod \ f$. In [15] the authors only considered a very special irreducible polynomial $x^{155} + x^{62} + 1$ and gained a very fast reduction algorithm. But their algorithm cannot apply to ordinary irreducible polynomials. In [9], Burton S. Kaliski introduced the Montgomery inverse by combing the idea of Montgomery representation and almost inverse. Montgomery inverse is similar to almost inverse in essence. The only difference is that Montgomery inverse need to calculate $a^{-1}x^n$ instead of a^{-1} in the reduction phase. Kaliski's algorithm for reduction is general but is bit-level and not so efficient. E. Savaş and K. Koç in [2] gave a general improvement of reduction method by eliminating bit-level operations and making use of Montgomery product.

In this paper, we propose another improvement for reduction with some precomputation. Our algorithm works for both almost inverse and Montgomery inverse, and is applicable to all irreducible polynomials. Our algorithm eliminates the bit-level operations of reduction in a different way and is faster than previous methods. In addition, for irreducible polynomials with special structure, such as some pentanomials proposed by NIST ([16]), our method can achieve more on time and space efficiency.

The rest of this paper is organized as follows. Section 2 gives a brief introduction of polynomial basis representation of $GF(2^n)$. Section 3 sketches previous methods for the reduction methods for almost/Montgomery inverse. Section 4 gives detailed information about our improved algorithm. In Section 5 we compared our algorithm with previous algorithms through both theoretic analysis and experiment research. Finally we draw a conclusion and give some comments in Section 6.

2   Polynomial Basis

The elements of the field $GF(2^n)$ can be represented in several different ways ([12]). Polynomial basis is suitable for software implementation. Using polynomial basis, an element a of $GF(2^n)$ is a polynomial of length n, i.e., of degree less than or equal to $n-1$, written as

$$a(x) = \sum_{i=0}^{n-1} a_i x^i = a_{n-1}x^{n-1} + a_{n-2}x^{n-2} + \cdots + a_1 x + a_0,$$

where the coefficients $a_i \in GF(2)$. These coefficients are also referred as the bits of a, and the element a is represented as $a = (a_{n-1}a_{n-2}\cdots a_1 a_0)$. For software implementation, the bits of a are partitioned into blocks of equal length. Let w be the word size of the computer, and s a positive integer such that $(s-1)w < n \leq sw$. Then we can write a in s words, where each word is of length w. Thus, we have $a = (A_{s-1}A_{s-2}\cdots A_1 A_0)$, where each A_i is of length w such that

$$A_i = a_{iw+w-1}a_{iw+w-2}\cdots a_{iw+1}a_{iw}.$$

Notice that the $sw - n$ highest bits of A_{s-1} remain unused.

The addition of two elements a and b in $GF(2^n)$ is performed by adding the polynomials $a(x)$ and $b(x)$, where the coefficients are added in the field $GF(2)$. This is equivalent to bit-wise XOR operation on the vectors a and b. Let $f(x)$ be the irreducible polynomial of degree n over the field $GF(2)$, the product $c = a \cdot b$ in $GF(2^n)$ is obtained by computing

$$c(x) = a(x)b(x) \ mod \ f(x),$$

where $c(x)$ is a polynomial of length n, representing the element $c \in GF(2^n)$. The inverse $c = a^{-1}$ in $GF(2^n)$ is obtained by computing

$$c(x)a^{-1}(x) \equiv 1 \ mod \ f(x),$$

where $c(x)$ is a polynomial of length n, representing the element $c \in GF(2^n)$.

3   Previous Reduction Methods for Almost/Montgomery Inverse

In this section, we describe previous methods for reduction, i.e., given field element $a^{-1}x^k$ and positive integer k, compute a^{-1} or $a^{-1}x^n$, where $n \leq k \leq 2n$ ([9]).

Kaliski's Reduction Algorithm. Kaliski's reduction algorithm is simple and straightforward. It is applicable to both almost inverse and Montgomery inverse. The algorithm reduce $a^{-1}x^k$ bit by bit. In concrete, it always tries to divide $a^{-1}x^k$ by x. If $a^{-1}x^k$ is indivisible by x, then add $f(x)$ to $a^{-1}x^k$ and do the division. The algorithm terminates when appropriate number of xs is reduced.

The bit-level characteristic of Kaliski's reduction algorithm can be seen more clear from pseudo code. We give the almost inverse edition in Algorithm 1. From the algorithm description, we can see that one division by x is done per iteration(line 4 or line 7). If g is indivisible by x, a polynomial addition is needed (line 7).

Algorithm 1. Kaliski's Reduction Algorithm for Almost Inverse

---

  Input: $a^{-1}x^k \ mod \ f$ and integer $k(n \leq k \leq 2n)$
  Output: $a^{-1} \ mod \ f$

1 $g \leftarrow a^{-1}x^k \ mod \ f$;
2 **for** $i \leftarrow 0$ *to* k **do**
3   **if** $x|g$ **then**
4 | $g \leftarrow g/x$;
5   **end**
6   **else**
7 | $g \leftarrow (g+f)/x$;
8   **end**
9 **end**

E. Savaş and K. Koç's Reduction Algorithm. E. Savaş and K. Koç in [2] proposed to use Montgomery multiplication(s) to replace the slow bit-level reduction procedure of Kaliski. The efficiency of their algorithms for reduction only depend on the efficiency of Montgomery multiplication. So we give a brief summary of Montgomery representation of $GF(2^n)$ and corresponding operations at first.

Montgomery Representation of $GF(2^n)$. $\forall a \in GF(2^n)$, the Montgomery representation of a is $a(x)r(x) \ mod \ f(x)$, where $f(x)$ is the irreducible polynomial generates $GF(2^n)$, $r(x)$ is a polynomial over $GF(2)$ and is prime to $f(x)$.

Montgomery Multiplication. $\forall a, b \in GF(2^n)$, the Montgomery multiplication is defined as $a \cdot b \cdot r^{-1}$. The selection of $r(x) = x^n$ and $r(x) = x^{iw}((i-1)w < n \leq iw)$ turns out to be very useful in obtaining fast software implementations.

Although the original algorithms of E. Savaş and K. Koç in [2] were for inverse of prime fields, they were easy to be adopted to $GF(2^n)$ ([4]). Let $n \leq m = iw$, and $(i - 1)w < m$, w the word size of the computer, they gave three algorithms using this idea:

1. Given a, f, n and m, where $degree(a(x)) \in [1, m-1]$, calculate $a^{-1}x^m \ mod \ f$. In this case, one or two Montgomery multiplications are needed for reduction.
2. Given a, f, n and m, where $degree(a(x)) \in [1, m-1]$, calculate $a^{-1} \ mod \ f$. In this case, one or two Montgomery multiplications are needed for reduction.
3. Given ax^m and f, calculate $a^{-1}x^m \ mod \ f$. In this case, two or three Montgomery multiplications are needed for reduction.

Note that the definition of Montgomery inverse in [2] is a little different from that of [9]. Specifically, $a^{-1}x^m$ was defined as Montgomery inverse instead of $a^{-1}x^n$. But they are essentially the same. For detailed information about these algorithms, we refer the readers to [2].

4   Our Refinement of Reduction Algorithm

Notice the sole purpose of the reduction phase of almost/Montgomery inverse calculation of $GF(2^n)$ is reducing some or all the x's from $a^{-1}x^k \bmod f$, and word-level reduction is more efficient than bit-level reduction. In this section we propose our algorithm for reduction, which is a word-level and quite different from previous method. And our method is faster than previous methods.

The key point of our refinement is constructing a table from $f(x)$ and using this table to replace the bit-level operations with word-level operations. Our method works for both almost inverse and Montgomery inverse of $GF(2^n)$.

4.1   Construction of the Precomputed Table

Denote the word size of the computer by w. We have mentioned in Section 2 that a binary polynomial can be represented by an array of words. For example, let $w = 8$, then binary polynomial $x^8 + x + 1$ can be represented by an array of two words, i.e. [00000001][00000011]. The bits of the array correspond to coefficients of the polynomial. Notice that the right most bit of the right most word corresponding to the const term of the binary polynomial.

The precomputed table TBL contains binary polynomials calculated from $f(x)$, and TBL is addressed using the right most words of these polynomials. We first give the properties of TBL, and then give method to construct TBL.

TBL should satisfy the following conditions:

1. The number of binary polynomials in TBL is 2^w, w is the word size.
2. $\forall g_i \in \text{TBL}(0 \le i \le 2^w - 1)$, we have $f|g_i$.
3. The right most word of the binary polynomials saved in TBL runs over $\{0,1\}^w$.

We give an efficient algorithm to construct TBL from $f(x)$. For efficient software implementation on general purpose processor, TBL is organized as an array of binary polynomials and each polynomial is an array of words. In other words, TBL can be seen as a two dimension array, and the right most word of each polynomial(regards as integer) is its subscripts in the array. When the context is clear, we use TBL[i] to represent the polynomial saved in TBL[i]. Notice that we save an zero polynomial in TBL[0].

TBL is constructed in three steps:

1. Multiply $f(x)$ by $x^i(0 \le i \le w - 1)$, the result is stored in TBL[2^i].
2. Process the result of step 1 to make sure that for the right most word of TBL[2^i], every bit is zero except the ith bit. This can be achieved in the

following way. Note that for the right most word of TBL$[2^i]$, all bits that are on the right of the ith bit are already zero. We process from TBL$[2^0]$ to TBL$[2^{w-1}]$. When we arrive at TBL$[2^i]$, check the ith bit of polynomial TBL$[2^j](0 \leq j < i)$. If it is 1, then add TBL$[2^i]$ to TBL$[2^j]$.

3. As in step 2, we process from TBL$[2^0]$ to TBL$[2^{w-1}]$. When we arrive at TBL$[2^i](0 \leq i < w)$, for each $j \in [0, 2^i)$, add TBL$[j]$ to TBL$[2^i]$ and save the result to TBL$[2^i + j]$.

Theorem 1. *TBL constructed using the above method satisfies all the three requirements mentioned at the beginning of this section.*

Proof

1. It is obvious that TBL contains 2^w polynomials(including the zero polynomial saved in TBL$[0]$).
2. In fact, all the polynomials in TBL are in the form of $\sum_{i=0}^{2^w-1} c_i f(x)x^i$, $c_i \in \{0,1\}$, so they are divisible by $f(x)$.
3. Regarding a word as integer, in order to prove that he right most word of the binary polynomials saved in TBL runs over $\{0,1\}^w$, we have only to prove that the right most word of the polynomial TBL$[i]$ corresponds to integer i. This is because there are 2^w polynomials in TBL, the right most words of these polynomials must run over $\{0,1\}^w$. In step 1) of the construction of TBL, w polynomials are obtained. They are saved in TBL$[2^i], 0 \leq i < w$. Notice that the constant term of $f(x)$ is 1 and TBL$[2^i] = f(x)x^i$, so the right most i bits of TBL$[2^i]$ are all zeros and the ith bit is 1. In step 2), the undesired 1 at ith bit is eliminated by adding TBL$[2^i]$. This operation may introduce some additional 1s on the left of the ith bit, however, these 1s will be eliminated in the following operations by adding some TBL$[2^j]$ where $i < j < w$.

   By now we have w polynomials TBL$[2^i](0 \leq i < w)$ and the right most word of TBL$[2^i]$ has only the ith bit set to 1, which corresponds to integer 2^i.

   Then we use mathematical induction to derive our conclusion. Obviously, TBL$[0]$, TBL$[1]$, and TBL$[2]$ satisfy the requirement. Suppose we have constructed polynomials TBL$[0]$, TBL$[1]$, ..., TBL$[t](t < 2^w - 1)$, and we want to calculate TBL$[t + 1]$. If $t + 1$ is a power of 2, then it has already been saved in TBL. Otherwise according to our construction method

$$\text{TBL}[t + 1] = \text{TBL}[2^{\lfloor log_2(t+1) \rfloor}] + \text{TBL}[t + 1 - 2^{\lfloor log_2(t+1) \rfloor}].$$

For example,

$$\text{TBL}[3] = \text{TBL}[2] + \text{TBL}[1]$$
$$\text{TBL}[5] = \text{TBL}[4] + \text{TBL}[1]$$
$$\text{TBL}[6] = \text{TBL}[4] + \text{TBL}[2]$$
$$\text{TBL}[7] = \text{TBL}[4] + \text{TBL}[3]$$

Note that $2^{\lfloor log_2(t+1) \rfloor}$ is less than $t + 1$ because $t + 1$ is not a power of 2, and $t + 1 - 2^{\lfloor log_2(t+1) \rfloor}$ is also less than $t + 1$ because $2^{\lfloor log_2(t+1) \rfloor} > 0$, so the right most word of TBL$[t + 1]$ is $2^{\lfloor log_2(t+1) \rfloor} + t + 1 - 2^{\lfloor log_2(t+1) \rfloor} = t + 1$. This finish our proof.

In fact, the right most word of the polynomials saved in TBL can be ignored, because this information can be derived from its subscript in TBL.

4.2   Accelerating the Inverse of $GF(2^n)$ with Precomputed Table

The way to use TBL to accelerate process of reduction is straightforward. Suppose we need to reduce $a^{-1}x^k \bmod f$ to $a^{-1}x^t \bmod f$, where $t < k$, and the right most word of $a^{-1}x^k \bmod f$ is W. Then we can reduce $x^w \bmod f$ from $a^{-1}x^k \bmod f$ at a time when $t + w < k$ by adding TBL[W] to $a^{-1}x^k \bmod f$ and discarding the right most word of $a^{-1}x^k \bmod f$.

Algorithm 2 gives detailed description of this process.

Algorithm 2. Our Refined Algorithm for Reduction

Input: $a^{-1}x^k \bmod f$, integer $k(n \le k \le 2n)$, pre-computed table TBL, integer
        $t(0 \le t < k)$
Output: $a^{-1}x^t \bmod f$

1 $g \leftarrow a^{-1}x^k \bmod f$;
2 **while** $k > t$ **do**
3 | $W \leftarrow$ the right most word of g;
4 | **if** $t + w < k$ **then**
5 | | $g \leftarrow g + $ TBL[W];
6 | | Discard the right most word of g;
7 | | $k \leftarrow k - w$;
8 | **end**
9 | **else**
10 | | $W' \leftarrow$ right $k - t$ bits of W;
11 | | $g \leftarrow g + $ TBL[W'];
12 | | $g \leftarrow g/x^{k-t}$;
13 | **end**
14 **end**
15 **return** g

Note that Algorithm 2 has an integer t as input, so can be used for both almost inverse and Montgomery inverse by tuning the value of t.

4.3   Further Improvements for Special Irreducible Polynomials

The above method of constructing the precomputed table and calculating the inverse are for general irreducible polynomial $f(x)$. If the irreducible polynomial has some special structure, such as polynomials proposed by NIST ([16]), we can achieve further improvements due to their features.

Take $f(x) = x^{163} + x^7 + x^6 + x^3 + 1$ for example. If we set $w = 8$, then only the right most word and left most word are nonzero. So we don't need to save entire polynomials in TBL. In fact, 3 words are enough for each polynomial in TBL: one words for the precomputation result of $x^7 + x^6 + x^3 + 1$ and two words for that of x^{163}. correspondingly, we only need to add corresponding words to $a^{-1}x^k \bmod f$ instead of the whole polynomials.

For irreducible polynomials that all their nonzero terms reside in different words, such as trinomials $x^{233} + x^{74} + 1$ and $x^{409} + x^{87} + 1$ proposed in [16], our method is not appropriate. In this case, the method of [15] is faster and without the burden of precomputation.

5   Analysis and Comparisons

Note that we focus on reduction phase of calculation of almost/Montgomery inverse of $GF(2^n)$. In other words, given $a^{-1}x^k \bmod f$, we consider the cost of calculating $a^{-1}x^t \bmod f$, where $t < k$. As in the previous sections, let the word size be w.

We first give theoretic analysis of the cost of these algorithms for reduction.

1. Bit-level Algorithm for Reduction (Algorithm 1). Though the output of this algorithm is $a^{-1} \bmod f$, it can be modified easily to output $a^{-1}x^t \bmod f$. Suppose there is a 50% probability that we need to calculate $g \leftarrow (g + f)/x$(line 7 of Algorithm 1). Then the total cost includes $(k-t)/2$ polynomial additions, and $(k - t)$ divisions by x. For one polynomial addition, we need $\lceil n/w \rceil$ XORs. For one division by x, we need $\lceil n/w \rceil$ Right Shifts and $\lceil n/w \rceil$ XORs. In conclusion, $(k - t)\lceil n/w \rceil$ Right Shifts and $\frac{3(k-t)}{2}\lceil n/w \rceil$ XORs are needed. However, some tricks can be used to improve the calculation. When there are two or more consecutive 0's at the right end of the middle result, two or more divisions by x can be done with the same cost of one division.
2. E. Savaş and K. Koç's Method for Reduction. In order to analysis the method of E. Savaş and K. Koç ([2]), we just need to consider the cost of Montgomery multiplication. In [8], Çetin K. Koç and Tolga Acar gave a rigorous analysis of word-level Montgomery multiplication of two binary polynomials of degree n. Let MULGF2 denote multiplying two 1-word(w-bit) polynomials to get a 2-word polynomial, the authors suggested to use 2 tables for this operation. The cost of MULGF2 is two table reads. Let $s = \lceil n/w \rceil$, the word-level Montgomery multiplication cost is $(2s^2 + s)$ MULGF2 operations and $4s^2$ XOR operations ([8]).
3. Our Algorithm for Reduction (Algorithm 2). If $w|(k - t)$, $\lceil (k - t)/w \rceil$ polynomial additions are needed(line 5 of Algorithm 2). When $w \nmid (k - t)$, another polynomial addition(line 11 of Algorithm 2) and an extra division with x^i(line 12 of Algorithm 2, i is an integer and $0 < i < w$) are needed. So in the worst case, $\lceil (k-t)/w \rceil + 1$ polynomial additions and 1 division by x^i are needed. As mentioned in the analysis of Algorithm 1, one polynomial addition comprises $\lceil n/w \rceil$ XORs, and one division by x^i comprises $\lceil n/w \rceil$ Right Shifts and $\lceil n/w \rceil$ XORs. So the total cost includes $(\lceil (k-t)/w \rceil + 2)\lceil n/w \rceil$ XORs and $\lceil n/w \rceil$ Right Shifts.

The results are summarized in Table 1.

Table 1. Cost of Calculating $a^{-1}x^t \bmod f$ from $a^{-1}x^k \bmod f$

Algorithms to be Compared	Number of Operations		
	XOR	Right Shift	MULGF2
Bit-Level Algorithm for Reduction Algorithm 1	$\frac{3(k-t)}{2}\lceil n/w \rceil$	$(k-t)\lceil n/w \rceil$	none
Montgomery Multiplication	$4\lceil n/w \rceil^2$	none	$2\lceil n/w \rceil^2 + \lceil n/w \rceil$
Our Algorithm for Reduction Algorithm 2	$(\lceil (k-t)/w \rceil + 2)\lceil n/w \rceil$	$\lceil n/w \rceil$	none

Notice that $n \le k \le 2n$, $0 \le t < k$

From Table 1, it easy to see that our method is faster than the bit level method. But there is a spot of trouble comparing the cost of Montgomery multiplication and our method from theoretic view because they have different basic operations. We implement our Algorithm 2 and word-level Montgomery multiplication in C. Note that the implementation of word-level Montgomery multiplication comes from [8]. The experiment is done on a Lenovo X200 laptop with Intel P8600 processor. The operating system is Windows XP, and the programming environment is Visual Studio 2008.

In the implementation, we set $w = 8$. Besides using table lookup for MULGF2, the authors also suggested using big word size in [8]. However, when the word size is 16, the table size is about 2^{33} bits and is not bearable. So the choice of $w = 8$ is appropriate. In this situation, the size of our precomputed TBL is about $255 \cdot n$ bits, which is acceptable for modern computers.

Table 2. Experimental Result

Field Size n	Our Method(Algorithm 2)		Word-Level Montgomery Multiplication	
	Debug version	Release version	Debug version	Release version
320 bits	0.0838095 μs	0.0164825 μs	12.2041 μs	0.686679 μs
640 bits	0.22654 μs	0.055873 μs	53.9169 μs	3.11799 μs

We summarize the experimental result in Table 2. The first column is the size of the finite field, the second and third column are time cost of running Algorithm 2 100 times and running Word-Level Montgomery Multiplication 100 times respectively. For each algorithm, we include the result of using different compile options. Note that we only record the running time of one Montgomery multiplication, but some times more than one Montgomery multiplication may be needed for one inverse of $GF(2^n)$. So E. Savaş and K. Koç's algorithm for reduction may take two or three times of that listed in Table 2. We also notice that although our method is faster in all cases, when turning on the compiler optimization option, the speed up of Montgomery multiplication is much larger than our method. The possible reason for this phenomenon is that our method is straight forward and has little room for compiler optimization.

6   Conclusion

In this paper we proposed a method to accelerate inverse of $GF(2^n)$ with some precomputations. The analysis and experiment show that our method is faster than previous methods, and the precomputation has only to be executed one time for a fixed $GF(2^n)$. Though the precomputed table has to be stored in memory, the space cost is acceptable. Furthermore, our method can achieve more on time and space efficiency for some special irreducible polynomials.

References

1. Diffe, W., Hellman, M.E.: New Directions in Cryptography. IEEE Transactions on Information Theory 22(6), 644–654 (1976)
2. Savaş, E., Koç, K.: The Montgomery Modular Inverse-Revisited. IEEE Transactions on Computer 49(7), 763–766 (2000)
3. Guajardo, J., Paar, C.: Itoh-Tsujii Inversion in Standard Basis and its Application in Cryptography and Codes. Designs, Codes and Cryptography 25(2), 207–216 (2002)
4. Gutub, A.A.A., Tenca, A.F., Savaş, E., Koç, Ç.K.: Scalable and Unifed Hardware to Compute Montgomery Inverse in $GF(p)$ and $GF(2^n)$. In: Kaliski Jr., B.S., Koç, Ç.K., Paar, C. (eds.) CHES 2002. LNCS, vol. 2523, pp. 484–499. Springer, Heidelberg (2003)
5. Guyot, A.: OCAPI: Architecture of a VLSI Coprocessor for the GCD and the Extended GCD of Large Numbers. In: Proc. 10th IEEE Symposium on Computer Arithmetic, pp. 226–231. IEEE, Los Alamitos (1991)
6. Hankerson, K.F.D., López, J., Menezes, A.: Field Inversion and Point Halving Revisited. IEEE Transactions on Computers 53(8), 1047–1059 (2004)
7. Itoh, T., Tsujii, S.: A Fast Algorithm for Computing Multiplicative Inverses in $GF(2^m)$ Using Normal Bases. Information and Computation 78, 171–177 (1988)
8. Koç, Ç.K., Acar, T.: Montgomery Multiplication in $GF(2^k)$. Designs, Codes and Cryptography 14(1), 57–69 (1998)
9. Kaliski, B.S.: The Montgomery Inverse and its Applications. IEEE Transactions on Computers 44(8), 1064–1065 (1995)
10. Knuth, D.E.: The Art of Computer Programming, Seminumerical Algorithms, 2nd edn., vol. 2. Addison-Wesley, Reading (1981)
11. Koblitz, N.: Elliptic Curve Cryptosystems. Mathematics of Computation 48 (1987)
12. Lidl, R., Niederreiter, H.: Finite Fields. Cambridge University Press, Cambridge (1997)
13. Miller, V.S.: Use of elliptic curves in cryptography. In: Williams, H.C. (ed.) CRYPTO 1985. LNCS, vol. 218, pp. 417–426. Springer, Heidelberg (1986)
14. van Oorschot, P.C., Wiener, M.J.: Parallel Collision Search with Application to Hash Functions and Discrete Logarithms. In: 2nd ACM Conference on Computer and Communications Security, pp. 210–218. ACM, New York (1994)
15. Schroeppel, R., Orman, H., O'Malley, S., Spatscheck, O.: Fast Key Exchange with Elliptic Curve Systems. In: Coppersmith, D. (ed.) CRYPTO 1995. LNCS, vol. 963, pp. 43–56. Springer, Heidelberg (1995)
16. FIPS 186-2 Digital Signature Standard (DSS)

17. Win, E.D., Bosselaers, A., Vandenberghe, S., Gersem, P.D., Vandewalle, J.: A Fast Software Implementation for Arithmetic Operations in $GF(2^n)$. In: Kim, K.-c., Matsumoto, T. (eds.) ASIACRYPT 1996. LNCS, vol. 1163, pp. 75–76. Springer, Heidelberg (1996)
18. Win, E.D., Mister, S., Preneel, B., Wiener, M.: On the Performance of Signature Schemes Based on Elliptic Curves. In: Buhler, J.P. (ed.) ANTS 1998. LNCS, vol. 1423, pp. 252–266. Springer, Heidelberg (1998)

Concurrent Error Detection Architectures for Field Multiplication Using Gaussian Normal Basis⋆

Zhen Wang, Xiaozhe Wang, and Shuqin Fan

Department of Applied Mathematics,
Zhengzhou Information Science and Technology Institute,
No. 742, P.O. Box 1001, Zhengzhou, 450002, P.R. China
{longdizhen,xiaozhe.wng,shuqinfan78}@gmail.com

Abstract. In this investigation, we present a semisystolic type-t(t is even) Gaussian normal basis(GNB) multiplier. Compared with the only existing bit parallel semisystolic even type GNB multiplier, our multiplier saves 10% space complexity and has 50% increase on throughput under the same time complexity. Based on the proposed multiplier, two multipliers with concurrent error detection(CED) capability are developed using two different schemes. The second multiplier with CED capability outperforms previous related works and can be further simply modified to correct certain multiple errors for GNB with type $t \geq 6$. Moreover, both the multipliers with CED capability have a high fault coverage. Our results show that any single-cell fault can be detected.

Keywords: finite field multiplication, Gaussian normal basis, concurrent error detection(CED), systolic multiplier.

1 Introduction

Finite field arithmetic has gained much of attention in cryptography, especially public key cryptography based on complex arithmetic such as Elliptic Curve Cryptosystems[1]. The main arithmetic operation in finite field is multiplication since addition is done easily and other arithmetic operations, inversion and exponentiation, can be done with consecutive multiplications. Therefore, efficient implementation of multiplication is crucial for cryptographic applications. Binary fields $GF(2^m)$ are more attractive compared with prime field in practical applications, since they are suitable for hardware implementation. On the other hand, it is possible that the computation goes wrong due to either natural causes or adversarial attacks by injecting fault(s) into the circuits. Also, fault-based

---

⋆ The research is supported by the National High Technology Research and Development Program of China (2009AA01Z417), the National Basic Research Program of China(2007CB807902), Program for New Century Excellent Talents in University(NCET-07-0384) and Foundation for the Author of National Excellent Doctoral Dissertation of China (FANEDD-2007B74).

J. Kwak et al. (Eds.): ISPEC 2010, LNCS 6047, pp. 96–109, 2010.

cryptanalysis has been proven to be a threat against cryptosystems security [4]-[7]. Therefore, besides efficiency, hardware architecture for multiplication with an acceptable security should be considered.

To achieve the efficiency of finite field multiplication, the basis to represent the field element has an important role. The most commonly used bases include polynomial basis (PB) or stand basis, dual basis (DB) and normal basis (NB). As compared to other two bases, the major advantage of NB is simple squaring arithmetic by shift operation. Thus, the NB multipliers are very effectively applied on inverse and exponentiation. The first NB multiplier was invented by Massey and Omura[8]. Following that, various architectures for normal basis multiplication over $GF(2^m)$ have been proposed, such as bit-level style[9][10],digit-level style [11][12] and parallel style[13][14]. As a special class of normal basis, Gaussian normal basis(GNB) has received considerable attention for its low complexity, which has been included by many standards, such as NIST[2] and IEEE[3]. Kwon[15] proposed the first novel systolic type-2 GNB multiplier using the self duality of the normal basis. Unlike Kwon, without using self duality, Bayat-Sarmadi[16] also announced a semisystolic type-2 GNB multiplier. However, type-2 GNBs over $GF(2^m)$ take up a small proportion as shown in [3], about 16% for $2 \leq m \leq 1000$. Also, the four, i.e., $m \in \{163, 283, 409, 571\}$, of five $GF(2^m)$ fields recommended by NIST for elliptic curve digital signature(ECDSA)[2] have GNBs of even type $t \geq 4$. For these reasons, it is important to study the multiplication using GNB of general type. However, the only existing bit parallel systolic multiplier using GNB of general type is that of Chiou[17]. In this investigation, we present a semisystolic even type GNB multiplier, which has an outstanding performance when compared with related previous works. Compared with Chiou's work[17], our multiplier saves 10% space complexity and has 50% increase on throughput. But both the multipliers have the same time complexity.

To achieve an acceptable security of multiplication architecture, error detection is adopted so that the failures can be fully or partially detected. The acknowledged error detection techniques include space redundancy scheme such as parity checking and time redundancy approaches such as recomputing with shifted operands (RESO). Both the error detection methods have been widely used in number of architectures such as non-systolic style [18]-[22] and systolic style [16][17][23][24]. Fenn[18] proposed the first bit-serial NB multiplier with error detection using parity checking method. Specially, for Gaussian normal basis, the same error detection method is employed by Lee[22] to design several kinds of, bit-parallel, sequential and digit-serial, concurrent error detection (CED) architectures. However, the bit-parallel architecture is designed for specific fields and hard to extend its size. Compared with parity checking method, RESO is more efficient for systolic architectures with high throughput. By applying this technique, two semisystoic GNB multipliers with CED capability have been presented in [16] and [17]. In our investigation, based on the proposed multiplier, two multipliers with CED capability are developed using two different methods. The first multiplier with CED, based on RESO method, requires only one more round when compared with the multiplier without CED, while in [17] two extra rounds are needed. The second multiplier with CED is designed for GNB of type $t \geq 4$ and outperforms previous works, which not only takes only one round to complete both multiplication and error detection but also has no space redundancy except necessary equality checkers. Furthermore, the second multiplier with CED can be simply modified to correct certain multiple errors for GNB of type $t \geq 6$. It's worth mentioning that although the second multiplier with CED is only applicable for GNB of type $t \geq 4$, it still has important applications as aforementioned. Both the proposed multipliers with CED have a low space-time overhead and can detect any single-cell fault.

The organization of this paper is as follows: In section 2, some preliminaries about Gaussian normal basis and RESO method are reviewed. Then a semisystolic type-t(t is even) GNB multipliers is proposed in section 3. In section 4, we present two different methods to make the proposed semisystolic GNB multiplier to have concurrent error detection capability, where the second method is applicable for GNB of type $t \geq 4$. Conclusions are finally drawn in section 5.

2   Preliminaries

In this section, a review about Gaussian normal basis representation and RESO method is given.

2.1   Gaussian Normal Basis Representation

Normal basis representation has the computational advantage that squaring can be done by simple shift operations. Multiplication, on the other hand, can be cumbersome in general. For this reason, it is common to specialize to a class of normal basis, called Gaussian normal basis, for which multiplication is both simple and efficient. Moreover, It is pointed that GNBs exist for $GF(2^m)$ whenever m is not divisible by eight[28].

Definition 1. *([27]) Let $p = mt + 1$ be a prime number. A Gauss period of type (m, t) over F_2 is defined as $\beta = \gamma + \gamma^\alpha + \cdots + \gamma^{\alpha^{t-1}}$, where γ and α are primitive $mt + 1$-th, t-th roots in $GF(2^{p-1})$ and F_p respectively.*

Theorem 1. *([27])Let k denotes the multiplicative order of 2 module p. If $\gcd(mt/k, m) = 1$, then the set $I_1 = \{\beta, \beta^2, \cdots, \beta^{2^{m-1}}\}$ generated by type (m, t) Gaussian period β is a normal basis for finite field $GF(2^m)$, called type-t Gaussian normal basis.*

The type value t of a Gaussian normal basis can be used to measure the complexity of the multiplication. The smaller the type value, the more efficient the multiplication. In [3], for each $m(2 \leq m \leq 1000)$ not divisible by eight, the smallest type value t among Gaussian normal basis for $GF(2^m)$ is given. It is shown that even type-t GNBs take up a big proportion, about 75%. Thus, finite fields $GF(2^m)$ with even type-t Gaussian normal basis are studied in this paper.

2.2 Gaussian Normal Basis with Even Type

Consider GNB with even type t for $GF(2^m)$, from definition 1,

$$I_1 = \{\beta, \beta^2, \cdots, \beta^{2^{m-1}}\} = \{\sum_{i=0}^{t-1} \gamma^{\alpha^i}, \sum_{i=0}^{t-1} \gamma^{2\alpha^i}, \cdots, \sum_{i=0}^{t-1} \gamma^{2^{m-1}\alpha^i}\}.$$

Since α is a primitive t-th root and t is an even integer, then we have $\alpha^{t/2} = -1$ and $\sum_{i=0}^{t-1} \gamma^{2^j \alpha^i} = \sum_{i=0}^{t/2-1}(\gamma^{2^j \alpha^i} + \gamma^{-2^j \alpha^i})$. Thus, normal basis I_1 can be extended to an intermediate 'basis', denoted by I_2:

$$I_2 = \{\gamma + \gamma^{-1}, \gamma^\alpha + \gamma^{-\alpha}, \cdots, \gamma^{\alpha^{t/2-1}} + \gamma^{-\alpha^{t/2-1}}, \cdots, \gamma^{2^{m-1}} + \gamma^{-2^{m-1}},$$
$$\gamma^{2^{m-1}\alpha} + \gamma^{-2^{m-1}\alpha}, \cdots, \gamma^{2^{m-1}\alpha^{t/2-1}} + \gamma^{-2^{m-1}\alpha^{t/2-1}}\}.$$

Since $\{\pm 2^j \alpha^i : 0 \le j \le m-1, 0 \le i \le t/2-1\}$ and $\{\pm i : 1 \le i \le mt/2\}$ are the same set but with a different order in $F_p[28]$ and $\gamma^p = 1$, then the *basis* I_2 can be converted to the following *basis* I_3:

$$I_3 = \{\gamma + \gamma^{-1}, \gamma^2 + \gamma^{-2}, \cdots, \gamma^{mt/2} + \gamma^{-mt/2}\}.$$

In fact, conversions between I_1 and I_3 representation, referred to as palindromic representation[17][29], is simple. For $1 \le i \le mt$, denote

$$<i> = \begin{cases} i, & 1 \le i \le mt/2; \\ mt + 1 - i, & mt/2 < i \le mt. \end{cases}$$

If one element $A \in GF(2^m)$ represented by both I_1 and I_3, $A = \sum_{i=0}^{m-1} A_i \beta^{2^i} = \sum_{j=1}^{mt/2} a_j(\gamma^j + \gamma^{-j})$, then the relationship between the coefficients is as follows:

$$a_j = A_i(1 \le j \le mt/2, 0 \le i \le m-1) \Leftrightarrow \exists k(0 \le k \le t-1), \text{s.t.}, <2^i \alpha^k> = j \tag{1}$$

Remark 1. Let $A = \sum_{j=1}^{mt/2} a_j(\gamma^j + \gamma^{-j}) = (a_1, a_2, \cdots, a_{mt/2})$ is an element of $GF(2^m)$ in I_3 representation, then squaring and square root of A can be obtained by simple permutation as follows, where $i = \lfloor \frac{mt}{4} \rfloor$,

$$A^2 = \begin{cases} (a_{mt/2}, a_1, a_{mt/2-1}, a_2, \cdots, a_{mt/2-j+1}, a_j, \cdots, a_{mt/4+1}, a_{mt/4}), & 4|mt; \\ (a_{mt/2}, a_1, a_{mt/2-1}, a_2, \cdots, a_{mt/2-i+1}, a_i, a_{i+1}), & 4 \nmid mt, \end{cases}$$

$$A^{1/2} = (a_2, a_4, \cdots, a_{2i}, a_{<2i+1>}, \cdots, a_3, a_1).$$

2.3 RESO Method

RESO is a time redundancy-based error detection method[25][26]. Suppose x be the input to a computation unit f and $f(x)$ be the desired output. Also let D and E respectively, be decoding and encoding function such that $D(f(E(x))) = f(x)$. Now two computation steps are needed. The result of the first computation step by $f(x)$ is stored in a register and then compared with the result of the second computation step by $D(f(E(x)))$. A mismatch between results of these two computation steps indicates an error. Since decoding function D and encoding function E are usually simple shift operations in this error detection method, thus it is very cost-effective. Furthermore, the RESO method can detect both permanent as well as intermittent failures. The fault model assumed in RESO method is the functional fault model. The functional fault model assumes that any faults are confined to a small area of the circuit and that the precise nature of these faults is not known. This model is very appropriate for VLSI circuits.

3   Proposed Semisystolic Even Type GNB Multiplier

In this section, a semisystolic even type-t GNB multiplier is proposed. Following that, a comparison for various bit parallel systolic GNB multipliers is presented.

3.1   Semisystoic GNB Multiplier

Let A, B be two Gaussian normal elements of the field $GF(2^m)$ given by I_3 representation, i.e., $A = \sum_{i=1}^{mt/2} a_i(\gamma^i + \gamma^{-i})$ and $B = \sum_{j=1}^{mt/2} b_j(\gamma^j + \gamma^{-j})$. It is easy to check that

$$(\gamma^i + \gamma^{-i})(\gamma^j + \gamma^{-j}) = (\gamma^{i+j} + \gamma^{-(i+j)}) + (\gamma^{i-j} + \gamma^{-(i-j)}) \tag{2}$$

and

$$\sum_{i=1}^{mt/2} a_i(\gamma^i + \gamma^{-i}) = \sum_{i=1}^{mt} a_{<i>}\gamma^i. \tag{3}$$

Since $\gamma^{(mt+1)} = 1$, the power of γ in Eq.(2), i.e., $\pm(i+j)$, $\pm(i-j)$ can be confined from $-mt/2$ to $mt/2$.

Let C be the product of A and B, then the product can be computed as follows:

$$C = AB = \sum_{j=1}^{mt/2} b_j A(\gamma^j + \gamma^{-j}) = \sum_{j=1}^{mt/2} b_j A^{(j)}, A^{(j)} = A(\gamma^j + \gamma^{-j}).$$

Following Eq.(2), we know that the constant term of $A^{(j)}$ is 0. Moreover, for $1 \leq i \leq mt/2$, γ^i and γ^{-i} always have the same coefficient c_i, so we can only focuse on the former.

$A^{(j)} = A\gamma^j + A\gamma^{-j}$

$= \gamma^j \sum_{i=1}^{mt/2} a_i(\gamma^i + \gamma^{-i}) + \gamma^{-j} \sum_{i=1}^{mt} a_{<i>}\gamma^i$

$= (a_{j-1}+a_{<j+1>})\gamma + \cdots + (a_1+a_{<2j-1>})\gamma^{j-1} + (a_0+a_{<2j>})\gamma^j + (a_1+a_{<2j+1>})\gamma^{j+1}$

$+ \cdots + (a_{n-j} + a_{<n+j>})\gamma^n + \cdots + (a_{mt/2-j}+a_{<mt/2+j>})\gamma^{mt/2} + Part[\gamma^{-i}]$

$= \sum_{l=1}^{mt/2} (a_{|l-j|} + a_{<j+l>})(\gamma^l + \gamma^{-l})$

where $|\cdot|$ denotes the absolute value of $\cdot$, $a_0 = 0$ and $Part[\gamma^{-i}]$ indicates the γ^{-i} part of $A^{(j)}$ with the same coefficients as γ^i. Thus we have

$$C = AB = \sum_{j=1}^{mt/2} b_j A^{(j)} = \sum_{l=1}^{mt/2} \sum_{j=1}^{mt/2} b_j(a_{|l-j|} + a_{<j+l>})(\gamma^l + \gamma^{-l}).$$

Therefore each coefficient of C can be given by

$$c_l = \sum_{j=1}^{mt/2} b_j(a_{|l-j|} + a_{<j+l>}), 1 \le l \le mt/2.$$

Let $c_l^{(i)} = \sum_{j=1}^{i} b_j(a_{|l-j|} + a_{<j+l>})$, then

$$c_l^{(i)} = c_l^{(i-1)} + b_i(a_{|l-i|} + a_{<i+l>}). \tag{4}$$

Observing expression (4), an even type-t GNB multiplication algorithm is addressed as follows.

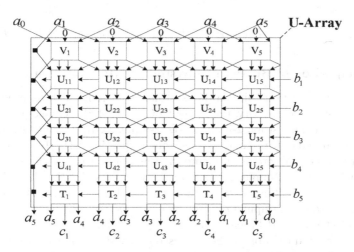

Fig. 1. The proposed semisystolic GNB multiplier for $GF(2^5)$

Algorithm 1.(even type-t GNB multiplication)
Input: $A = \sum_{i=1}^{mt/2} a_i(\gamma^i + \gamma^{-i})$, $B = \sum_{j=1}^{mt/2} b_j(\gamma^j + \gamma^{-j})$, $a_0 = 0$
Output: $C = AB = \sum_{j=1}^{mt/2} c_j(\gamma^j + \gamma^{-j})$.
  1. Initialization: $c_j^{(0)} = 0, j = 1, 2, \cdots, mt/2$;
  2. for $j = 1$ to $mt/2$
       $D_j^{(0)} = a_{|j-1|} + a_{<j+1>}$;
  3. for $k = 1$ to $mt/2 - 1$
       for $j = 1$ to $mt/2$ compute parallel

$$\{c_j^{(k)} = c_j^{(k-1)} + b_k D_j^{(k-1)}, D_j^{(k)} = a_{|j-k-1|} + a_{<j+k+1>}\}$$

4. for $j = 1$ to $mt/2$,

$$c_j^{(mt/2)} = c_j^{(mt/2-1)} + b_{mt/2} D_j^{(mt/2-1)}.$$

Then final value $c_j^{(mt/2)} = c_j$, for $1 \le j \le mt/2$.

Following Algorithm 1, a semisystolic GNB multiplier is proposed and shown in Fig. 1, where ■ denotes one bit latch (flip-flop). For convenience, the structure for $GF(2^5)$, where a type-2 GNB exists, as an example is presented. The details of $V_j, U_{i,j}, T_j (1 \le i \le 4, 1 \le j \le 5)$ are shown in Fig. 2, where $\oplus$ and $\otimes$ denote XOR and AND gate respectively.

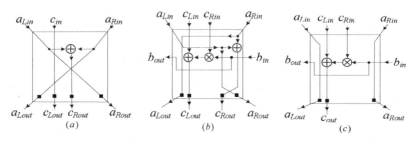

Fig. 2. Three cells of the proposed multiplier (a). V cell (b). U cell (c). T cell

3.2   Comparison of Bit Parallel Systolic GNB Multipliers

A comparison for various bit parallel systolic GNB multipliers is presented in Table 1. For space complexity, the following CMOS VLSI technology is adopted to take count of transistors: 2-input AND, 2-input XOR, 2-input OR and 1-bit latch are composed of $6, 6, 6$ and 8 transistors, respectively[31]. To estimate time complexity, some real circuits are employed as done in [17] such as M74HC08 (STMicroelectronics, 2-input AND gate, $t_{PD} = 7ns$ (TYP.))[32], M74HC86 (STMicroelectronics, 2-input XOR gate, $t_{PD} = 12ns$ (TYP.))[33], M74HC32 (STMicroelectronics, 2-input OR gate, $t_{PD} = 8ns$(TYP.))[34] and M74HC279 (STMicroelectronics, SR Latch, $t_{PD} = 13ns$ (TYP.))[35].

As demonstrated in Table 1, the proposed semisystolic multiplier saves 15.6% space complexity and 27% time complexity when compared with Kwon's systolic multiplier[15] for the case of type 2. Compared with the semisystolic type-2 GNB multiplier[16], the proposed multiplier in Fig. 1 has a lower cell delay, which brings about 27% time complexity saved. Both the multipliers in [17] and ours are designed for GNBs with even type and have the same time complexity, but our multiplier saves 10% space complexity and has 50% increase on throughput.

4   Proposed Semisystolic GNB Multiplier with CED

In the previous section, we have presented a semisystolic even type-t GNB multiplier. In the following, we will introduce how to make the proposed multiplier to have concurrent error detection(CED) capability.

Table 1. Comparison of various systolic GNB multipliers

multipliers	Kwon[15]	Bayat-Sarmadi[16]	Chiou[17]	proposed multiplier(Fig.1)
t(type-t GNB)	2	2	$even$	$even$
array type	systolic	semisystolic	semisystolic	semisystolic
number of cells	m^2	m^2	$(mt)^2/2 + mt/2$	$(mt)^2/4 + mt/2$
Space complexity				
2-input AND	$2m^2 + m$	m^2	$(mt)^2/2 + mt/2$	$(mt)^2/4$
3-input XOR	$2m^2 + 2m$	0	0	0
2-input XOR	0	$2m^2$	$(mt)^2/2 + 5mt/2 + 1$	$(mt)^2/2$
latch	$5m^2 + 2m - 2$	$9m^2/2 - 3m/2$	$9(mt)^2/8 + 7mt/4 + 1$	$9(mt)^2/8 + 9mt/4$
total transistor counts	$64m^2 + 34m - 16$	$54m^2 - 12m$	$15(mt)^2 + 32mt + 14$	$13.5(mt)^2 + 18mt + 8$
Time complexity				
cell delay	$T_A + T_{3X} + T_L$	$T_A + 2T_X + T_L$	$T_A + T_X + T_L$	$T_A + T_X + T_L$
latency	$m + 1$	m	$mt/2 + 1$	$mt/2 + 1$
total delay(unit:ns)	$44m + 44$	$44m$	$16mt + 32$	$16mt + 32$
throughput(unit:1/$cycle$)	1	1	1/2	1

Note: The latches for synchronizing inputs are also counted in.

4.1 Type-t GNB Multiplier with CED for All Even t

The technology of Recomputing with Shifted Operands (RESO) is employed to design the semisystolic GNB multipliers with CED capability. As shown in Fig. 3, to achieve CED capability, two rounds are necessary. $C = A \cdot B$ and $C^2 = E(A)E(B) = A^2 \cdot B^2$ are computed at the first and second round, respectively. From Remark 1, encoding function E is cost-free permutation and the result C can also be obtained by taking square root of C^2 by simple permutation (i.e., Square Root Permutation in Fig. 3). Thus, an error will be detected if both results derived by computing $C = A \cdot B$ and $C = (A^2 \cdot B^2)^{1/2}$ are inconsistent.

An XOR-OR architecture is employed for the equality checker and assumed to be error-free or designed self-checking[30]. Also, the equality checker can be designed in a pipelined manner to alleviate the long checker delay as suggested in [16]. Since that is not the point here, traditional equality checker with one level of OR unit is used for illustration as shown in Fig. 5. One equality checker with size $mt/2 + 1$ and two equality checkers with size $mt/2$ are used for checking A and B, C respectively. As aforementioned, the functional fault model is assumed. The fault will be felt at the cell level in terms of changed logical output value, which means that a faulty cell has error output(s). Then for simplicity, the sing-cell fault is considered throughout this paper.

Theorem 2. *The proposed semisystolic GNB multiplier with CED capability (Fig. 3) can detect any single-cell fault.*

Proof. If a single-cell fault occurs, then the faulty behavior can be classified into the following three cases:

1. *Error on b_{out}.*
   In this case, the single faulty cell can be either U or T cell. Suppose the faulty cell be $U_{i,j}(1 \leq i \leq mt/2 - 1, 1 \leq j \leq mt/2)$. Since the output b_{out} of cell $U_{i,j}$ is a go-through line from input b_{in}, thus the error on b_{out} of cell $U_{i,j}$

can be detected by comparing b_{in} of cell $U_{i,mt/2}$ and b_{out} of $U_{i,1}$. Similarly, T cell's error of this kind can be detected.

2. Error(s) on a_{Lout} or/and a_{Rout}.
   It is obviously that $a_i(1 \leq i \leq mt/2)$ are loaded into the U-Array in two different lines and can be got at the neighboring outputs of U-Array(see Fig. 1). Thus the error(s) on a_{Lout} or/and a_{Rout} can be detected by comparing the neighboring outputs of U-Array. As for a_0, if there is an error at $a_0's$ line, then a_0 is equal to one so that the error can be detected by equality checker.

3. Error(s) on c_{Lout} or/and c_{Rout}, Error on c_{out}.
   Since these erroneous output(s) only propagate in the same column of cells, that is to say the error(s) will affect a single output bit of result C. Suppose in the first round, the error(s) will affect the output bit c_j. Then in the second round, the error(s) will affect the output c_k, where $<2k> = j$. Thus, the error can not be detected only when $k = j$, which implies $<2j> = j$, i.e., $2j = j$ or $mt + 1 - 2j = j$. Since $1 \leq j \leq mt/2$ and $mt + 1$ is a prime, so $<2j> = j$ is impossible. Therefore, the error can be detected by comparing c_k or c_j of the first computation and second computation. To illustrate this, an example for $GF(2^5)$ is given in Table 2, where a type-2 GNB exists.

Table 2. Error detection procedure for $GF(2^5)$

first computation(C)		c_1	c_2^*	c_3	c_4	c_5
second computation(C^2)		c_5	c_1^*	c_4	c_2	c_3
square root permutation		c_1^*	c_2	c_3	c_4	c_5
equality checker	XOR	1	1	0	0	0
	OR			1		

Notes: (1) The result is assumed to be $C = \sum_{i=1}^{5} c_i(\gamma^i + \gamma^{-i})$. (2)Suppose $U_{i,2}$ be the faulty cell and the * parts denote the erroneous outputs.

4.2 Better Error Detection Strategy for GNB Multiplier with Type $t \geq 4$

Among even type-t GNB multipliers, type-2 GNB multipliers are both time-efficient and space-saved. But fields $GF(2^m)$ existing type-2 GNB is limited, about 16% for $2 \leq m \leq 1000$. For practical applications, we always have to resort to GNB with type $t > 2$. For instance, among the five NIST-suggested fields for ECDSA[2], the four of them have GNB of even type $t \geq 4$, i.e., type-4 GNB for $GF(2^{163})$, type-6 GNB for $GF(2^{283})$, type-4 GNB for $GF(2^{409})$ and type-10 GNB for $GF(2^{571})$. Therefore in this part, based on the proposed multiplier in Fig. 1, we will introduce a better error detection strategy for GNB of type $t \geq 4$. Using a precomputed permutation module, the multiplier takes only one round to complete both multiplication and error detection while the multiplier in [17] requires four rounds. Furthermore, this multiplier with CED capability can be simply modified to correct certain multiple errors for GNB with type $t \geq 6$.

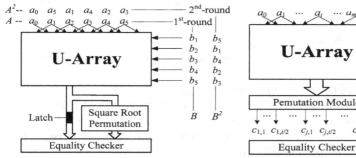

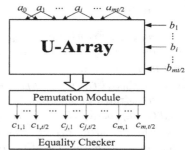

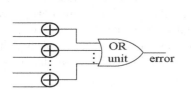

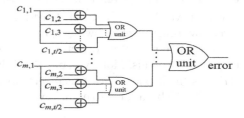

Fig. 3. Semisystolic GNB multiplier with CED($GF(2^5)$ as an example)

Fig. 4. Semisystolic GNB multiplier with CED for type $t \geq 4$

Fig. 5. Equality checker with one level of OR unit in Fig. 3

Fig. 6. Equality checker with two levels of OR units in Fig. 4

As illustrated above, the product C of A and B in the multiplier(Fig. 1) is given by palindromic representation I_3. Clearly, C can be further converted back to normal basis representation I_1 using expression (1):

$$C = \sum_{i=1}^{mt/2} c_i(\gamma^i + \gamma^{-i}) = \sum_{j=0}^{m-1} C_j \left(\sum_{i=0}^{t/2-1} (\gamma^{2^j \alpha^i} + \gamma^{-2^j \alpha^i}) \right).$$

Thus for GNB multiplier with type $t \geq 4$, any output coefficient c_i must agree with the other $t/2-1$ output coefficients if the result is correctly computed, which means these $t/2$ coefficients always have the same value C_j for some $j \in [0, m-1]$. Following that, an alternative error detection method for multiplier(Fig. 1) can be given and shown in Fig. 4. The Permutation Module in Fig. 4 , carrying out permutation operations precomputed for specific m and t, is used to gather the $t/2$ coefficients with the same value. In addition, similar with the multiplier with CED in section 4.1, one equality checker with size $mt/2 + 1$ and one with size $mt/2$ are used to check A and B respectively. The difference is that the equality checker for C is composed of two levels of OR uints as shown in Fig. 6.

Theorem 3. *The proposed semisystolic GNB multiplier with CED capability (Fig. 4) can detect any single-cell fault.*

Proof. If a single-cell fault occurs, then the faulty behavior can be classified into the following two cases:

1. *Error on b_{out}, Error(s) on a_{Lout} or/and a_{Rout}.*
   Since this kind of error(s) is on global lines, then it(they) can be detected as done in Theorem 2.
2. *Error on c_{out}, Error(s) on c_{Lout} or/and c_{Rout}.*
   As demonstrated in Theorem 2, the error(s) will affect a single output bit of result C, supposed to be c_i. Since there are other $t/2-1$ output bits having the same value as error-free c_i, then the error(s) can be detected by comparing c_i and any one output bit of the other $t/2-1$ bits.

In fact, the error detection scheme used above can be regarded as 'space redundancy' by duplicating $t/2$ modules to compute each coefficient $C_j (0 \le j \le m-1)$ concurrently. Therefore, if the error(s) on global lines is/are neglected[23], the scheme have the capability of detecting $t/2 - 1$ errors and correcting $\lfloor \frac{t/2-1}{2} \rfloor$ errors by using a well-known majority voter. Take $t = 6$ for example, this strategy takes one round to correct one single-cell fault, while the multiplier in [17] employs six rounds. Moreover, our multiplier has a lower space complexity than [17]. The multipliers with concurrent error correction(CEC) capability can be used effectively in fault tolerant cryptosystems.

Table 3. Comparison of various systolic GNB multipliers with CED capability

multipliers	Bayat-Sarmadi[16]	Chiou[17]	Fig.3	Fig.4
t(type-t GNB)	2	even	even	even($t \ge 4$)
array type	semisystolic	semisystolic	semisystolic	semisystolic
number of cells	m^2	$(mt)^2/2 + mt/2$	$(mt)^2/4 + mt/2$	$(mt)^2/4 + mt/2$
fault model	single-bit fault	single-cell fault	single-cell fault	single-cell fault
CED scheme	RESO	RESO	RESO	--
Space complexity				
2-input AND	m^2	$(mt)^2/2 + mt/2$	$(mt)^2/4$	$(mt)^2/4$
2-input XOR	$2m^2 + m$	$(mt)^2/2 + 5mt + 3$	$(mt)^2/2 + 3mt/2$	$(mt)^2/2 + 3mt/2 - m$
latch	$9m^2/2 - m/2$	$9(mt)^2/8 + 11mt/4 + 2$	$9(mt)^2/8 + 11mt/4 + 1$	$9(mt)^2/8 + 9mt/4 + 1$
2-input OR	$m - 1$	$5mt/2 - 1$	$3mt/2 - 2$	$3mt/2 - m - 1$
total transistor counts	$54m^2 + 8m - 6$	$15(mt)^2 + 70mt + 28$	$13.5(mt)^2 + 40mt - 4$	$13.5(mt)^2 + 36mt - 12m + 2$
space overhead(%)	0.1	0.1	0.1	0.07
Time complexity				
cell delay	$T_A + 2T_X + T_L$	$T_A + T_X + T_L$	$T_A + T_X + T_L$	$T_A + T_X + T_L$
latency	$m + 1$	$mt/2 + 3$	$mt/2 + 2$	$mt/2 + 1$
equality checker delay	$T_X + \lceil log_2 m \rceil T_O$	$T_X + \lceil log_2(mt + 1) \rceil T_O$	$T_X + \lceil log_2(mt/2 + 1) \rceil T_O$	$T_X + \lceil log_2(mt/2 - m) \rceil T_O$
total delay(unit:ns)	$44m + 8\lceil log_2 m \rceil + 56$	$16mt + 8\lceil log_2(mt + 1) \rceil + 108$	$16mt + 8\lceil log_2(mt/2 + 1) \rceil + 76$	$16mt + 8\lceil log_2(mt/2 - m) \rceil + 44$
time overhead(%)	1.0	0.6	0.5	0.3
throughput(unit:1/$cycle$)	$1/2$	$1/4$	$1/2$	1
fault coverage	100%	100%	100%	100%

Note: The space and time overhead are computed for the case of $m = 283$ and $t = 6$.

4.3   Comparison of Various Systolic GNB Multipliers with CED

In the previous section, the proposed semisystolic GNB multiplier (Fig. 1), by RESO method, is equipped with CED capability for general type t(Fig. 3). Specially for GNB with type $t \ge 4$, an alternative simpler but better error detection strategy is presented in Fig. 4 using one extra precomputed Permutation Module. To better evaluate their performance, a comparison with existing bit parallel systolic GNB multipliers with CED is given and shown in Table 3. As done in section 3.2, the same CMOS VLSI technology and real circuits are referred to estimate space and time complexity. As demonstrated, similar to the other two multipliers with CED in [16] and [17], very low space-time overhead is needed for the proposed multiplier to achieve CED capability. For instance, for $m = 283$ and $t = 6$, only about 0.1% space complexity and 0.5% time complexity are added for the multiplier in Fig. 3, while 0.07% and 0.3% for the multiplier in Fig. 4. Compared with the multiplier with CED in [17], both the proposed multipliers with CED in Fig. 3 and Fig. 4 saves 10% space complexity and have a higher throughput. The multiplier with CED capability in Fig. 4 is considered to be the best among the listed architectures. Also, as aforementioned, this class of multipliers with CED designed for GNB of type $t \geq 4$ have important applications.

5   Conclusion

This paper proposed a semisystolic type-$t(t$ is even) GNB multiplier over $GF(2^m)$, which is suitable for VLSI implementation and has an outstanding performance. Compared with the only existing bit parallel semisystolic even type-t GNB multiplier[17], the proposed multiplier saves 10% space complexity and has 50% increase on throughput under the same time complexity. Following that, the multiplier is equipped with concurrent error detection capability based on RESO method. Specially for GNB with type $t \geq 4$, another better method is employed to make the proposed multiplier fault-detected, which takes only one round to complete both multiplication and error detection while other listed architectures in Table 3 require at least two rounds. Also, the multiplier with CED based on the second method can be further simply modified to correct certain multiple errors for GNB with type $t \geq 6$. It is shown that no much than 0.1% space overhead and 0.5% time overhead are needed for the proposed multiplier to achieve CED capability for the case of $m = 283$ and $t = 6$. Futhermore, the fault coverage for single-cell fault of the proposed multipliers with CED capability is 100%.

References

1. Hankerson, D., Menezes, A., Vanstone, S.: Guide to Elliptic Curve Cryptography. Springer, Heidelberg (2004)
2. Nat'l Inst. of Standards and Technology, Digital Signature Standard(DSS), FIPS Publication 186-3 (2009)
3. IEEE Standard 1363-2000, IEEE Standard Specifications for Public-Key Cryptography (2000)
4. Boneh, D., DeMillo, R., Lipton, R.: On the Importance of Checking Cryptographic Protocols for Faults. In: Fumy, W. (ed.) EUROCRYPT 1997. LNCS, vol. 1233, pp. 37–51. Springer, Heidelberg (1997)
5. Kelsey, J., Schneier, B., Wagner, D., Hall, C.: Side-channel Cryptanalysis of Product Ciphers. In: Quisquater, J.-J., Deswarte, Y., Meadows, C., Gollmann, D. (eds.) ESORICS 1998. LNCS, vol. 1485, pp. 97–110. Springer, Heidelberg (1998)

6. Biehl, I., Meyer, B., Müller, V.: Differential Fault Attacks on Elliptic Curve Cryptosystems. In: Bellare, M. (ed.) CRYPTO 2000. LNCS, vol. 1880, pp. 131–146. Springer, Heidelberg (2000)
7. Blömer, J., Otto, M., Seifert, J.P.: Sign Change Fault Attacks on Elliptic Curve Cryptosystems. In: Breveglieri, L., Koren, I., Naccache, D., Seifert, J.-P. (eds.) FDTC 2006. LNCS, vol. 4236, pp. 36–52. Springer, Heidelberg (2006)
8. Massey, J.L., Omura, J.K.: Computational Method and Apparatus for Finite Field Arithmetic, US patent 4,587,627 (1986)
9. Agnew, G.B., Mullin, R.C., Onyszchuk, I.M., Vanstone, S.A.: An Implementation for a Fast Public-Key Cryptosystem. J. Cryptology 3, 63–79 (1991)
10. Feng, G.-L.: A VLSI Architecture for Fast Inversion in $GF(2^m)$. IEEE Trans. Computers 38, 1383–1386 (1989)
11. Gao, L., Sobelman, G.E.: Improved VLSI Designs for Multiplication and Inversion in $GF(2^m)$ over Normal Bases. In: 13th IEEE International ASIC/SOC Conference, pp. 97–101. IEEE Press, New York (2000)
12. Reyhani-Masoleh, A., Hasan, M.A.: Low Complexity Word-Level Sequential Normal Basis Multipliers. IEEE Trans. Computers 54, 98–110 (2005)
13. Koç, Ç.K., Sunar, B.: Low-Complexity Bit-Parallel Canonical and Normal Basis Multipliers for a Class of Finite Fields. IEEE Trans. Computers 47, 353–356 (1998)
14. Reyhani-Masoleh, A., Hasan, M.A.: A New Construction of Massey-Omura Parallel Multiplier over $GF(2^m)$. IEEE Trans. Computers 51, 511–520 (2002)
15. Kwon, S.: A Low Complexity and a Low Latency Bit Parallel Systolic Multiplier over $GF(2^m)$ Using an Optimal Normal Basis of Type II. In: 16th IEEE Symposium on Computer Arithmetic, pp. 196–202. IEEE Press, New York (2003)
16. Bayat-Sarmadi, S., Hasan, M.A.: Concurrent Error Detection in Finite-Filed Arithmetic Operations Using Pipelined and Systolic Architectures. IEEE Trans. Computers 58, 1553–1567 (2009)
17. Chiou, C.W., Chang, C.C., Lee, C.Y., Hou, T.W., Lin, J.M.: Concurrent Error Detection and Correction in Gaussian Normal Basis Multiplier over $GF(2^m)$. IEEE Trans. Computers 58, 851–857 (2009)
18. Fenn, S., Gossel, M., Benaissa, M., Taylor, D.: On-Line Error Detection for Bit-Serial Multipliers in $GF(2^m)$. J. Electronic Testing: Theory and Applications 13, 29–40 (1998)
19. Reyhani-Masoleh, A., Hasan, M.A.: Fault Detection Architectures for Field Multiplication Using Polynomial Bases. IEEE Trans. Computers 55, 1089–1103 (2006)
20. Lee, C.Y., Meher, P.K., Patra, J.C.: Concurrent Error Detection in Bit-Serial Normal Basis Multiplication over $GF(2^m)$ Using Multiple Parity Prediction Schemes. IEEE Trans. VLSI (2009) (in Press)
21. Lee, C.Y.: Concurrent Error Detection in Digital-Serial Normal Basis Multiplication over $GF(2^m)$. In: 22nd IEEE International Conference on Advanced Information Networking and Applications, pp. 1499–1504. IEEE Press, New York (2008)
22. Lee, C.Y.: Concurrent Error Detection Architectures for Gaussian Normal Basis Multiplication over $GF(2^m)$. J. VLSI: Integration 43, 113–123 (2010)
23. Lee, C.Y., Chiou, C.W., Lin, J.M.: Concurrent Error Detection in a Polynomial Basis Multiplier over $GF(2^m)$. J. Electronic Testing 22, 143–150 (2006)
24. Lee, C.Y., Chiou, C.W., Lin, J.M.: Concurrent Error Detection in a Bit-Parallel Systolic Multiplier for Dual Basis of $GF(2^m)$. J. Electronic Testing 21, 539–549 (2005)
25. Patel, J.H., Fung, L.Y.: Concurrent Error Detection in ALU's by Recomputing with Shifted Operands. IEEE Trans. Computers 31, 589–595 (1982)

26. Patel, J.H., Fung, L.Y.: Concurrent Error Detection in Multiply and Divide Arrays. IEEE Trans. Computers 32, 417–422 (1983)
27. Feisel, S., von zur Gathen, J., Shokrollahi, M.A.: Normal Bases via General Gauss Periods. Math. Comput. 68, 271–290 (1999)
28. Ash, D.W., Blake, I.F., Vanstone, S.A.: Low Complexity Normal Bases. Discrete Appl. Math. 25, 191–210 (1989)
29. Blake, I.F., Roth, R.M., Seroussi, G.: Efficient Arithmetic in $GF(2^m)$ through Palindromic Representation. Technical Report, HPL-98-134 (1998)
30. McCluskey, E.J.: Design Techniques for Testable Embedded Error Checkers. IEEE Computer 23, 84–88 (1990)
31. Weste, N., Eshraghian, K.: Principles of CMOS VLSI Design: A system Perspective. Addison-Wesley, Reading (1985)
32. M74HC08, Quad 2-Input AND Gate, STMicroelectronics (2001), http://www.st.com/stonline/products/literature/ds/1885/m74hc08.pdf
33. M74HC86,Quad Exclusive OR Gate, STMicroelectronics (2001), http://www.st.com/stonline/products/literature/ds/2006/m74hc86.pdf
34. M74HC32, Quad 2-Input OR gate, STMicroelectronics (2001), http://www.st.com/stonline/products/literature/ds/1944/m74hc32.pdf
35. M74HC279, Quad $\bar{S}$-$\bar{R}$ Latch, STMicroelectronics (2001), http://www.st.com/stonline/products/literature/od/1937/m74hc279.pdf

The Elliptic Curve Discrete Logarithm Problems over the p-adic Field and Formal Groups

Masaya Yasuda

Fujitsu Laboratories Ltd.
4-1-1, Kamikodanaka, Nakahara-ku,
Kawasaki, 211-8588, Japan
myasuda@labs.fujitsu.com

Abstract. The hardness of the elliptic curve discrete logarithm problem (ECDLP) on a finite field is essential for the security of all elliptic curve cryptographic schemes. The ECDLP on a field K is as follows: given an elliptic curve E over K, a point $S \in E(K)$, and a point $T \in E(K)$ with $T \in \langle S \rangle$, find the integer d such that $T = dS$. A number of ways of approaching the solution to the ECDLP on a finite field is known, for example, the MOV attack [5], and the anomalous attack [7,10]. In this paper, we propose an algorithm to solve the ECDLP on the p-adic field $\mathbb{Q}_p$. Our method is to use the theory of formal groups associated to elliptic curves, which is used for the anomalous attack proposed by Smart [10], and Satoh and Araki [7].

Keywords: ECDLP, formal groups, the anomalous attack.

1 Introduction

In 1985, Neal Koblitz and Victor Miller independently proposed using elliptic curves to design public-key cryptographic systems (see [3,4,6]). The hardness of the elliptic curve discrete logarithm problem (ECDLP) on a finite field is essential for the security of all elliptic curve cryptographic schemes, for example, elliptic curve-based signature, public-key encryption, and key establishment schemes. The ECDLP on a field K is as follows: given an elliptic curve E defined over K, a point $S \in E(K)$, and a point $T \in E(K)$ with $T \in \langle S \rangle$, find the integer d such that $T = dS$. A number of ways of approaching the solution to the ECDLP on a finite field is known. However, no efficient algorithm is known for the ECDLP on a finite field except several special cased including the supersingular cases and the anomalous cases (see [1,5,7,8,10]). In this paper, we consider the ECDLP on the p-adic number field $\mathbb{Q}_p$.

In his paper [2], Gaudry proposed a method for solving the ECDLP on $\mathbb{Q}_p$ using the p-adic elliptic logarithm. For an elliptic curve E over $\mathbb{Q}_p$, the p-adic elliptic logarithm of E is given by

$$\log_E(z) = \int \omega(z)dz \in \mathbb{Q}_p[[z]],$$

J. Kwak et al. (Eds.): ISPEC 2010, LNCS 6047, pp. 110–122, 2010.

where $\omega(z)$ is the Laurent series for an invariant differential $\omega \in H^0(E, \Omega_E)$ (see [9]). Let $E_1(\mathbb{Q}_p)$ be the subgroup of $E(\mathbb{Q}_p)$ defined by $\ker \pi$, where π is the reduction map. The map

$$E_1(\mathbb{Q}_p) \to \mathbb{Q}_p^+, \quad (x, y) \mapsto \log_E(z)$$

is a group homomorphism, where $\mathbb{Q}_p^+$ denotes the additive group of $\mathbb{Q}_p$ and $z = -\frac{x}{y}$. Consider a composition of the following maps

$$E(\mathbb{Q}_p) \xrightarrow{N_p} E_1(\mathbb{Q}_p) \xrightarrow{\log_E(z)} \mathbb{Q}_p^+,$$

where N_p denotes the multiplication by $N_p = \widetilde{E}(\mathbb{F}_p)$ (let $\widetilde{E}$ be the reduced curve of E). His method is to reduce the ECDLP on $\mathbb{Q}_p$ to the discrete logarithm problem (DLP) on $\mathbb{Q}_p^+$ by using the above map.

In using his method, we need to compute the coefficients of $\log_E(z)$. However, it seems to be unfamiliar to compute the coefficients of $\log_E(z)$. In this paper, we propose a method for solving the ECDLP on $\mathbb{Q}_p$ only using operations familiar for elliptic curve cryptography (for example, the scalar multiplication for elliptic curves). Our method is to consider the filtration $\{E_n(\mathbb{Q}_p)\}_{n \geq 1}$ of $E_1(\mathbb{Q}_p)$ defined as follows: For $n \geq 1$, we define a subgroup $E_n(\mathbb{Q}_p)$ of $E(\mathbb{Q}_p)$ by

$$E_n(\mathbb{Q}_p) = \{P \in E(\mathbb{Q}_p) \mid v_p(x(P)) \leq -2n\} \cup \{O\},$$

where v_p is the normalized p-adic valuation and $x(P)$ is the x-coordinate of P (note that $E_n(\mathbb{Q}_p)$ for $n = 1$ is the same as what we previously defined). Then we have

$$E_1(\mathbb{Q}_p) \supset E_2(\mathbb{Q}_p) \supset E_3(\mathbb{Q}_p) \supset \cdots,$$
$$\mathbb{F}_p^+ \qquad\quad \mathbb{F}_p^+ \qquad\quad \mathbb{F}_p^+$$

where $E_n(\mathbb{Q}_p)/E_{n+1}(\mathbb{Q}_p) \simeq \mathbb{F}_p^+$ for $n \geq 1$. We consider the following diagram:

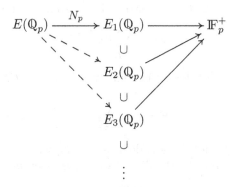

We note that the maps on the right hand side are induced by isomorphisms $E_n(\mathbb{Q}_p)/E_{n+1}(\mathbb{Q}_p) \simeq \mathbb{F}_p^+$. Using the above diagram, we give an algorithm for solving the ECDLP on $\mathbb{Q}_p$, which is an extension of the anomalous attack proposed by Smart [10], and Satoh and Araki [7].

2   Mathematical Foundations

An elliptic curve over a field K is a pair (E, O), where E is a curve defined over K of genus 1 and O is a point of E defined over K. Let $E(K)$ denote the set of K-rational points of E. The set $E(K)$ forms an abelian group where O is the identity element, and the group law is given by elements of the function field $K(E)$. Let $K[E]_O$ be the local ring of E at O. Taking the completion of $K[E]_O$ at its maximal ideal leads to a power series ring in one variable, $K[[z]]$, for some uniformizier z at O. By expressing the group law on E in z, we obtain a power series $F(X, Y) \in K[[X, Y]]$ which is called the *formal group law* associated to E. A formal group law might be described as "a group law without any group elements". Such objects are called *formal groups*. In this section, we review on the theory of formal groups associated to elliptic curves (see [9, Chapter IV] for details).

2.1   Introduction to Elliptic Curves

The *elliptic curves* is the curves of genus 1 with a specified basepoint. As is well known, every such curve E can be written as the locus in $\mathbb{P}^2$ of an equation of the form

$$Y^2 Z + a_1 XYZ + a_3 Y Z^2 = X^3 + a_2 X^2 Z + a_4 X Z^2 + a_6 Z^3$$

with the specified basepoint $O = [0 : 1 : 0]$. Using non-homogeneous coordinates $x = \frac{X}{Z}$ and $y = \frac{Y}{Z}$, we usually write the Weierstrass equation

$$y^2 + a_1 xy + a_3 y = x^3 + a_2 x^2 + a_4 + a_6. \tag{1}$$

for E. We say that E is *defined over* a field K if $a_1, a_2, \cdots, a_6 \in K$.

Let E be an elliptic curve defined over K. The *divisor group* of E, denoted $\mathrm{Div}(E)$, is the free abelian group generated by the points of E. Thus every element $D \in \mathrm{Div}(E)$, called a *divisor*, can be written as a formal sum

$$D = \sum_{P \in E} n_P (P)$$

with $n_P \in \mathbb{Z}$ and $n_P = 0$ for all but finitely many $P \in E$. The *degree* of D is defined by

$$\deg D = \sum_{P \in E} n_P.$$

Let $\overline{K}(E)$ be the function field of E defined over $\overline{K}$, where $\overline{K}$ is a fixed algebraic closure of K. For $f \in \overline{K}(E)^*$, the divisor $\mathrm{div}(f)$ is given by

$$\mathrm{div}(f) = \sum_{P \in E} \mathrm{ord}_p(f)(P),$$

where $\mathrm{ord}_P(f)$ is the order of the zero or pole of f at P. We call a divisor D is *principal* if it has the form $D = \mathrm{div}(f)$ for some $f \in \overline{K}(E)^*$. We note that the set of principal divisors is the subgroup of $\mathrm{Div}^0(E)$. Let $\mathrm{Div}^0(E)$ be the subgroup of $\mathrm{Div}(E)$ of degree zero and let $\mathrm{Pic}^0(E)$ be the quotient of $\mathrm{Div}^0(E)$ by the subgroup of principal divisors.

Consider the map

$$\kappa : E \to \mathrm{Pic}^0(E), \quad P \mapsto [(P) - (O)],$$

where $[D]$ denotes the class of $D \in \mathrm{Div}^0(E)$. It is well known that κ is an isomorphism as sets (see [9, Proposition 3.4] for the proof). We can define a group law $+$ on E such that the diagram

$$
\begin{array}{ccc}
E \times E & \xrightarrow{\ \kappa \times \kappa\ } & \mathrm{Pic}^0(E) \times \mathrm{Pic}^0(E) \\
{\scriptstyle +}\downarrow & & \downarrow{\scriptstyle +} \\
E & \xrightarrow[\ \kappa\ ]{} & \mathrm{Pic}^0(E)
\end{array}
$$

is commutative. Therefore κ is an isomorphism as groups. Let $P_1 = (x_1, y_1)$ and $P_2 = (x_2, y_2)$ be points of E. We take the line L through P_1 and P_2. The line L has an equation of the form

$$L : y = \lambda x + \nu, \quad \exists \lambda, \nu \in \overline{K}.$$

Let $f = y - (\lambda x + v) \in \overline{K}(E)$. Then we have

$$\mathrm{div}(f) = (P_1) + (P_2) + (P_3) - 3(O),$$

where $P_3 = (x_3, y_3)$ is the third point of $L \cap E$. Since

$$\kappa(P_1 + P_2 + P_3) = \kappa(P_1) + \kappa(P_2) + \kappa(P_3) = [\mathrm{div}(f)] = 0 \text{ in } \mathrm{Pic}^0(E),$$

we have

$$P_1 + P_2 + P_3 = 0. \tag{2}$$

This gives a formula for the addition law on E (see [9, Chapter III] for explicit formulas).

The map

$$\mathrm{sum} : \mathrm{Div}^0(E) \to E, \quad D = \sum_i n_i(P_i) \mapsto \sum_i n_i P_i$$

induces the map $\mathrm{Pic}^0(E) \to E$, which is the inverse to the isomorphism κ. Thus we have an exact sequence

$$1 \longrightarrow \overline{K}^* \longrightarrow \overline{K}(E)^* \xrightarrow{\ \mathrm{div}\ } \mathrm{Div}^0(E) \xrightarrow{\ \mathrm{sum}\ } E \longrightarrow 0. \tag{3}$$

In the case $K = \mathbb{C}$, there exists a lattice $\Lambda \subset \mathbb{C}$ and a complex analytic isomorphism (see [9, Chapter VI] for details)

$$\phi : \mathbb{C}/\Lambda \to E.$$

There exists an exact sequence on $\mathbb{C}/\Lambda$ as well as (3) and the diagram

$$
\begin{array}{ccccccccc}
1 & \longrightarrow & \mathbb{C}^* & \longrightarrow & \mathbb{C}^*(\Lambda) & \xrightarrow{\text{div}} & \text{Div}^0(\mathbb{C}/\Lambda) & \xrightarrow{\text{sum}} & \mathbb{C}/\Lambda & \longrightarrow & 0 \\
& & \| & & \downarrow & & \downarrow & & \downarrow{\scriptstyle\phi} & & \\
1 & \longrightarrow & \mathbb{C}^* & \longrightarrow & \mathbb{C}^*(E) & \xrightarrow{\text{div}} & \text{Div}^0(E) & \xrightarrow{\text{sum}} & E & \longrightarrow & 0
\end{array}
$$

is commutative (see [9, Chapter VI] for details). We note that the composition map $\phi^{-1} \circ \text{sum} : \text{Div}^0(E) \to \mathbb{C}/\Lambda$ is given by

$$
D = \sum_i (P_i - Q_i) \mapsto \sum_i \int_{Q_i}^{P_i} \omega \bmod \Lambda,
$$

where ω is an invariant differential defined by $dx/(2y + a_1 x + a_3)$.

2.2   The Definition of the Formal Group Law Associated to an Elliptic Curve

Let E be an elliptic curve given by a Weierstrass equation (1). By making a change of variables

$$
z = -\frac{x}{y} \text{ and } w = -\frac{1}{y} \left(\Leftrightarrow x = \frac{z}{w} \text{ and } y = -\frac{1}{w} \right),
$$

we see that the Weierstrass equation (1) becomes

$$
w = z^3 + a_1 zw + a_2 z^2 w + a_3 w^2 + a_4 zw^2 + a_6 w^3. \tag{4}
$$

We note that the specified basepoint O on E is now the point $(z, w) = (0, 0)$ and z is a uniformizier at O. By substituting the equation (4) into itself recursively, we can express w as a power series in z as follows:

$$
\begin{aligned}
w &= z^3 + (a_1 z + a_2 z^2) w + (a_3 + a_4 z) w^2 + a_6 w^3 \\
&= z^3 + (a_1 z + a_2 z^2)[z^3 + (a_1 z + a_2 z^2)w + (a_3 + a_4 z)w^2 + a_6 w^3] \\
&\quad + (a_3 + a_4 z)[z^3 + (a_1 z + a_2 z^2)w + (a_3 + a_4 z)w^2 + a_6 w^3]^2 \\
&\quad + a_6 [z^3 + (a_1 z + a_2 z^2)w + (a_3 + a_4 z)w^2 + a_6 w^3]^3 \\
&= z^3 + a_1 z^4 + (a_1^2 + a_2) z^5 + (a_1^3 + 2a_1 a_2 + a_3) z^6 + \cdots \\
&= z^3 (1 + A_1 z + A_2 z^2 + \cdots),
\end{aligned} \tag{5}
$$

where $A_n \in \mathbb{Z}[a_1, \ldots, a_6]$ is a polynomial in the coefficients of E. Using the power series w in z as above, we find *Laurent series* for x and y as follows:

$$
\begin{aligned}
x(z) &= \frac{z}{w} = \frac{1}{z^2} - \frac{a_1}{z} - a_2 - a_3 z - (a_4 + a_1 a_3) z^2 + \cdots \\
y(z) &= -\frac{1}{w} = -\frac{1}{z^3} + \frac{a_1}{z^2} + \frac{a_2}{z} + a_3 + (a_4 + a_1 a_3) z + \cdots.
\end{aligned}
$$

The pair $(x(z), y(z))$ provides a "formal solution" to the Weierstrass equation (1). Similarly, the invariant differential ω has an expansion

$$\omega(z) = \frac{dx}{2y + a_1 x + a_3} = (1 + a_1 z + (a_1^2 + a_2)z^2 + (a_1^3 + 2a_1 a_2 + 2a_3)z^3$$
$$+ (a_1^4 + 3a_1^2 a_2 + 6a_1 a_3 + a_2^2 + 2a_4)z^4 + \cdots)dz. \quad (6)$$

We note that the series $x(z), y(z)$ and $\omega(z)$ have coefficients in $\mathbb{Z}[a_1, \ldots, a_6]$ (see [9, Chater IV]).

We consider the addition law on E in the (z, w)-plane. Let $P_1 = (z_1, w_1)$ and $P_2 = (z_2, w_2)$ be points of E in the (z, w)-plane. Take the line L through P_1 and P_2 and let $P_3 = (z_3, w_3)$ be the third point of $L \cap E$. The line L has slope

$$\lambda = \frac{w_2 - w_1}{z_2 - z_1} = \sum_{n=3}^{\infty} A_{n-3} \frac{z_2^n - z_1^n}{z_2 - z_1} \in \mathbb{Z}[a_1, \ldots, a_6][[z_1, z_2]]$$

(Note that w_i has an expression (5) as a power series in z_i). Let $v = w_1 - \lambda z_1 \in \mathbb{Z}[a_1, \ldots, a_6][[z_1, z_2]]$. Then the equation of L is given by $w = \lambda z + v$. Substituting this into the equation (4) gives a cubic in z, two of whose roots are z_1 and z_2. Therefore we see that the third root z_3 can be expressed as a power series in z_1 and z_2 as follows:

$$z_3 = -z_1 - z_2 + \frac{a_1 \lambda + a_3 \lambda^2 - a_2 v - 2a_4 \lambda v - 3a_6 \lambda^2 v}{1 + a_2 \lambda + a_4 \lambda^2 + a_6 \lambda^3} \in \mathbb{Z}[a_1, \ldots, a_6][[z_1, z_2]].$$

By the formula (2) for the additive group law on E, we have $-P_3 = P_1 + P_2$. In the (x, y)-plane, the inverse of (x, y) is $(x, -y - a_1 x - a_3)$ (see [9, Chapter III]). Hence the inverse of (z, w) will have z-coordinate (remember $z = -x/y$)

$$\iota(z) = \frac{x(z)}{y(z) + a_1 x(z) + a_3} = \frac{z^{-2} - a_1 z^{-1} - \cdots}{-z^{-3} + 2a_1 z^{-2} + \cdots} \in \mathbb{Z}[a_1, \ldots, a_6][[z]].$$

This gives the formal addition law

$$\widehat{E}(z_1, z_2) = \iota(z_3)$$
$$= z_1 + z_2 - a_1 z_1 z_2 - a_2(z_1^2 z_2 + z_1 z_2^2)$$
$$- (2a_3 z_1^3 z_2 - (a_1 a_2 - 3a_3)z_1^2 z_2^2 + 2a_3 z_1 z_2^3) + \cdots \quad (7)$$

on E. Set $X = z_1, Y = z_2$. Then we have $\widehat{E}(X, Y) \in \mathbb{Z}[a_1, \ldots, a_6][[X, Y]]$, which is the formal group law associated to E.

2.3   The Formal Group Associated to an Elliptic Curve

Let E be an elliptic curve given by a Weierstrass equation (1) with coefficients in a ring R. Then we see that $\widehat{E}(X, Y) \in R[[X, Y]]$ and $\widehat{E}(X, Y)$ satisfies the following conditions:

1. $\widehat{E}(X, Y) = X + Y + (\text{terms of degree} \geq 2)$.
2. $\widehat{E}(X, \widehat{E}(Y, Z)) = \widehat{E}(\widehat{E}(X, Y), Z)$.
3. $\widehat{E}(X, Y) = \widehat{E}(Y, X)$.

Let $\mathcal{E}$ be the formal group associated to E (Here the term *formal group* means the same as formal group law). Let R be a complete local ring and let K be the quotient field of R. Let M be the maximal ideal of R and let k be the residue field R/M (In the case $R = \mathbb{Z}_p$, we have $K = \mathbb{Q}_p, M = p\mathbb{Z}_p$ and $k = \mathbb{F}_p$). We let $\mathcal{E}(M)$ denote the set M with the group operations

$$x \oplus y = \widehat{E}(x, y) \text{ and } \ominus x = \iota(x) \quad \forall x, y \in M.$$

(Since $\widehat{E}(X, Y)$ satisfies the above conditions, we can define the group operations on $\mathcal{E}(M)$ well.) Similary, for $n \geq 1$, $\mathcal{E}(M^n)$ is the subgroup of $\mathcal{E}(M)$ consisting of the set M^n. The power series $x(z)$ and $y(z)$ give a group homomorphism

$$\mathcal{E}(M) = M \to E(K), \quad z \mapsto (x(z), y(z)), \tag{8}$$

which gives a subgroup $E_1(K)$ of $E(K)$. The subgroup $E_1(K)$ is a key tool in the next section.

3   The ECDLP on $\mathbb{Q}_p$

The elliptic curve discrete logarithm problem (ECDLP) on a field K is: given an elliptic curve E defined over K, a point $S \in E(K)$, and a point $T \in \langle S \rangle$, find the integer d with $T = dS$. In this section, we consider the ECDLP on $\mathbb{Q}_p$ and propose an algorithm for solving the ECDLP on $\mathbb{Q}_p$.

3.1   The p-adic Elliptic Logarithm

Let p be a prime number and let E be an elliptic curve defined over $\mathbb{Q}_p$ given by a Weierstrass equation (1) with coefficients in $\mathbb{Z}_p$. The *p-adic elliptic logarithm* of E is given by

$$\log_E(z) = \int \omega(z)dz$$

$$= z + \frac{a_1}{2}z^2 + \frac{a_1^2 + a_2}{3}z^3 + \cdots \in \mathbb{Q}_p[[z]].$$

The p-adic elliptic logarithm induces a group homomorphism

$$\log_E : \mathcal{E}(p\mathbb{Z}_p) \to \mathbb{Q}_p^+, \quad z \mapsto \log_E(z),$$

where $\mathbb{Q}_p^+$ denotes the additive group of $\mathbb{Q}_p$ (see [9, Proposition 6.4 of Chapter IV]).

We consider a method for solving the ECDLP on $\mathbb{Q}_p$ using the p-adic elliptic logarithm (see [2]). Reducing the coefficients of E modulo p, we can obtain a curve $\widetilde{E}$ over $\mathbb{F}_p$. For simplicity, we assume that $\widetilde{E}$ is an elliptic curve. Let $\pi : E(\mathbb{Q}_p) \to \widetilde{E}(\mathbb{F}_p)$ be the reduction map (see [9, Chapter VII] for its definition). Then we have an exact sequence of abelian groups (see [9, Proposition 2.1 of Chapter VII])

$$0 \to E_1(\mathbb{Q}_p) \to E(\mathbb{Q}_p) \xrightarrow{\pi} \widetilde{E}(\mathbb{F}_p) \to 0, \tag{9}$$

where $E_1(\mathbb{Q}_p) = \ker \pi$. The map

$$E_1(\mathbb{Q}_p) \to \mathcal{E}(p\mathbb{Z}_p), \quad (x,y) \mapsto -\frac{x}{y} \tag{10}$$

is an isomorphism, which is the inverse of the map (8). Let N_p be the order of the group $\widetilde{E}(\mathbb{F}_p)$. We consider a composition of the following maps

$$E(\mathbb{Q}_p) \xrightarrow{N_p} E_1(\mathbb{Q}_p) \simeq \mathcal{E}(p\mathbb{Z}_p) \xrightarrow{\log_E} \mathbb{Q}_p^+,$$

where N_p denotes the multiplication by N_p. Then we can reduces the ECDLP on $\mathbb{Q}_p$ to the DLP on $\mathbb{Q}_p^+$ by using the above map.

3.2   Our Method

The problem in the above method is that we need to compute the coefficients of the p-adic elliptic logarithm $\log_E(z)$. To compute the coefficients of $\log_E(z)$, it is necessary to obtain the followings:

1. the coefficients of Laurent series $x(z), y(z)$ for x and y.
2. the coefficients of $\omega(z)$ (remember $\omega(z) = dx(z)/(2y(z) + a_1 x(z) + a_3)$).

For many people (for examples, cryptographers), it seems to be unfamiliar to compute the above objects. Here we propose the other method for solving the ECDLP on $\mathbb{Q}_p$.

Let p be a prime number and let E be an elliptic curve defined over $\mathbb{Q}_p$. We say that a Weierstrass equation (1) for E is *minimal* if $v_p(\Delta)$ is minimal subject to the condition $a_1, \ldots, a_6 \in \mathbb{Z}_p$, where v_p is the normalized p-adic valuation and Δ is the discriminant of E. Note that every elliptic curve defined over $\mathbb{Q}_p$ has a minimal Weierstrass equation (see [9, Proposition 1.3 of Chapter VII]). For simplicity, we assume that the Weierstrass equation for E is minimal and the reduced curve $\widetilde{E}$ is an elliptic curve defined over $\mathbb{F}_p$. For $n \geq 1$, we define a subgroup of $E(\mathbb{Q}_p)$ by

$$E_n(\mathbb{Q}_p) = \{P \in E(\mathbb{Q}_p) \mid v_p(x(P)) \leq -2n\} \cup \{O\},$$

where $x(P)$ is the x-coordinate of P (note that $E_n(\mathbb{Q}_p)$ for $n = 1$ is the same as what we previously defined). For $n \geq 1$, the subgroup $E_n(\mathbb{Q}_p)$ of $E_1(\mathbb{Q}_p)$ corresponds to the subgroup $\mathcal{E}(p^n \mathbb{Z}_p)$ of $\mathcal{E}(p\mathbb{Z}_p)$ under the isomorphism (10).

Therefore we have the diagram

$$
\begin{array}{ccc}
E_1(\mathbb{Q}_p) & \simeq & \mathcal{E}(p\mathbb{Z}_p) \\
\cup & & \cup \\
E_2(\mathbb{Q}_p) & \simeq & \mathcal{E}(p^2\mathbb{Z}_p) \\
\cup & & \cup \\
E_3(\mathbb{Q}_p) & \simeq & \mathcal{E}(p^3\mathbb{Z}_p) \\
\cup & & \cup \\
\vdots & & \vdots
\end{array}
$$

which is an extension of the isomorphism (10). Since the formal group law $\widehat{E}(X,Y)$ satisfies $\widehat{E}(X,Y) = X + Y + (\text{terms of degree} \geq 2)$, we have

$$
\begin{aligned}
x \oplus y &= \widehat{E}(x,y) \\
&\equiv x + y \bmod p^{2n}\mathbb{Z}_p, \quad \forall x,y \in p^n\mathbb{Z}_p
\end{aligned}
$$

for $n \geq 1$. Then the map

$$
\mathcal{E}(p^n\mathbb{Z}_p)/\mathcal{E}(p^{n+1}\mathbb{Z}_p) \overset{\mathrm{id}}{\to} p^n\mathbb{Z}_p/p^{n+1}\mathbb{Z}_p \simeq \mathbb{F}_p^+ \tag{11}
$$

is an isomorphism of groups for $n \geq 1$, where "id" denotes the identity map on sets. Therefore the group $\mathcal{E}(p\mathbb{Z}_p)$ has a filtration

$$
\underset{\mathbb{F}_p^+}{\mathcal{E}(p\mathbb{Z}_p)} \supset \underset{\mathbb{F}_p^+}{\mathcal{E}(p^2\mathbb{Z}_p)} \supset \underset{\mathbb{F}_p^+}{\mathcal{E}(p^3\mathbb{Z}_p)} \supset \cdots
$$

with isomorphisms (11).

We now consider the ECDLP on $\mathbb{Q}_p$. Fix $S \in E(\mathbb{Q}_p)$ and $T \in \langle S \rangle$. For simplicity, we assume that the order of S is infinite. Our idea to solve the ECDLP on $\mathbb{Q}_p$ is as follows: We first consider the following diagram:

We note that the maps on the right hand side are induced by isomorphisms (11).

1. We consider a composition of the following maps:

$$h_p : E(\mathbb{Q}_p) \overset{N_p}{\to} E_1(\mathbb{Q}_p) \simeq \mathcal{E}(p\mathbb{Z}_p).$$

Let h_1 be a composition of the following maps:

$$h_1 : E(\mathbb{Q}_p) \overset{h_p}{\to} \mathcal{E}(p\mathbb{Z}_p) \to \mathbb{F}_p^+.$$

Set $s_1 = h_1(S), t_1 = h_1(T) \in \mathbb{F}_p$. Compute $d_0 \in \mathbb{Z}$ with $0 \le d_0 \le p-1$ and $d_0 \equiv t_1 \cdot s_1^{-1} \bmod p$.

2. Set $S_1 = pS$ and $T_1 = T - d_0 S$. Then we have $h_p(S_1), h_p(T_1) \in \mathcal{E}(p^2 \mathbb{Z}_p)$. We can transfer $h_p(S_1), h_p(T_1)$ to $s_2, t_2 \in \mathbb{F}_p$ like in Step 1. Compute $d_1 \in \mathbb{Z}$ with $0 \le d_1 \le p-1$ and $d_1 \equiv t_2 \cdot s_2^{-1} \bmod p$.

3. Set $S_2 = pS_1$ and $T_2 = T_1 - d_1 S_1$. Then we have $h_p(S_2), h_p(T_2) \in \mathcal{E}(p^3 \mathbb{Z}_p)$. We compute $d_2 \in \mathbb{Z}$ like in Step 2.

4. We compute S_n, T_n and d_n until $T_n = 0$. Since

$$
\begin{aligned}
T_n &= T_{n-1} - d_{n-1} S_{n-1} \\
&= (T_{n-2} - d_{n-2} S_{n-2}) - d_{n-1} p S_{n-2} = T_{n-2} - (d_{n-2} + d_{n-1} p) S_{n-2} \\
&\cdots \\
&= T - \sum_{i=0}^{n-1} d_i p^i S,
\end{aligned}
$$

we have $T = dS$ with $d = \sum_{i=0}^{n-1} d_i p^i$.

Remark 1. We shall review here on the anomalous attack (see [7] for details). Let $\widetilde{E}$ be an elliptic curve defined over $\mathbb{F}_p$. Fix an elliptic curve E which is a lifting of $\widetilde{E}$ to $\mathbb{Q}_p$. For any lifting $u : \widetilde{E}(\mathbb{F}_p) \to E(\mathbb{Q}_p)$, let $\lambda_E(u)$ be a composition of the following maps

$$\lambda_E(u) : \widetilde{E}(\mathbb{F}_p) \overset{u}{\to} E(\mathbb{Q}_p) \overset{N_p}{\to} E_1(\mathbb{Q}_p) \overset{\log_E}{\to} p\mathbb{Z}_p \overset{\bmod p^2}{\to} \mathbb{F}_p^+,$$

where $N_p = \widetilde{E}(\mathbb{F}_p)$. Satoh and Araki showed that $\lambda_E(u)$ is a group homomorphism independent of the choice of u if $\widetilde{E}$ is anomalous (i.e. $N_p = p$) [7, Theorem 3.2]. Then we can reduce the ECDLP on $\mathbb{F}_p$ to the DLP on $\mathbb{F}_p^+$ if $\widetilde{E}$ is anomalous. Since $\log_E(z) \equiv z \bmod z^2$, we see that a composition of the maps

$$E(\mathbb{Q}_p) \overset{N_p}{\to} E_1(\mathbb{Q}_p) \overset{\log_E(z)}{\to} p\mathbb{Z}_p \overset{\bmod p^2}{\to} \mathbb{F}_p^+$$

is the same as h_1 which is defined as above. Therefore we see that our method for solving the ECDLP on $\mathbb{Q}_p$ is an extension of the anomalous attack.

Algorithm 1. Solving the ECDLP on $\mathbb{Q}_p$

Input: (E, S, T), where E is an elliptic curve defined over $\mathbb{Q}_p$ with good reduction, $S \in E(\mathbb{Q}_p)$ of infinite order and $T \in \langle S \rangle$. For simplicity, we assume that $h_p(S) \notin E_2(\mathbb{Q}_p)$ and $T \in \langle S \rangle_+ = \{dS \mid d \in \mathbb{Z}_{\geq 0}\}$.

Output: The integer d with $T = dS$.

1: $N_p \leftarrow \sharp\widetilde{E}(\mathbb{F}_p)$, where $\widetilde{E}$ is the reduced elliptic curve of E.
2: Compute $N_p S = (x, y)$ and set $a = -\frac{x}{py} \bmod p$. By the assumption $h_p(S) \notin E_2(\mathbb{Q}_p)$, we have $a \not\equiv 0 \bmod p$.
3: Set $n = 0, \ell = 1, S' = S, T' = T$.
4: **while** $T' \neq 0$ **do**
5:     Compute $N_p T' = (x, y)$ and set $w = -\frac{x}{y}$.
6:     Set $b = \frac{w}{p^\ell}$.
7:     Compute $d_n = b \cdot a^{-1} \bmod p$ and let d_n with $0 \leq d_n \leq p - 1$ and $d_n \equiv \bar{d}_n \bmod p$.
8:     $T' \leftarrow T' - d_n S', S' \leftarrow pS'$.
9:     $n \leftarrow n + 1, \ell \leftarrow \ell + 1$.
10: **end while**
11: Compute $d = \sum_{i=0}^{n-1} d_i p^i$.
12: Return d.

3.3 Our Algorithm

We note that

$$h_p(Q) = -\frac{x}{y} \in \mathcal{E}(\mathbb{Q}_p), \quad N_p Q = (x, y)$$

for any $Q \in E(\mathbb{Q}_p)$. We give an algorithm for solving the ECDLP on $\mathbb{Q}_p$ in Algorithm 1. We mainly need the following operations to compute Algorithm 1:

- counting the order of the reduced elliptic curve $\widetilde{E}$ over $\mathbb{F}_p$ (Step 1).
- group operations on E over $\mathbb{Q}_p$ (Step 5 and Step 8).

We have that the integer sequence $\{d_i\}_{0 \leq i \leq n-1}$ satisfies $d = \sum_{i=0}^{n-1} d_k p^k$ with $0 \leq d_i \leq p-1$. Therefore the expected number of iterations in Step 4 is estimated at $\log_p d$. Hence it takes approximately

(counting $\widetilde{E}(\mathbb{F}_p)$) $+ 2\log_p d \cdot \log p$-(group operations on E over $\mathbb{Q}_p$)

to compute Algorithm 1. Moreover, if we assume that $d < A$ for some A, it takes approximately

(counting $\widetilde{E}(\mathbb{F}_p)$) $+ 2\log_p A \cdot \log p$-(group operations on E over $\mathbb{Q}_p$)

to compute Algorithm 1.

In general, it takes very long time to compute a group operation on E over $\mathbb{Q}_p$. But in the following example, we can compute the integer d with $T = dS$ using group operations on E mod p^5.

Example 1. Suppose $p = 547$, $E : y^2 = x^3 + 3x$, $S = (x_1, y_1)$ and $T = (x_2, y_2)$ with

$$\begin{cases} x_1 = 137 + 410p + 136p^2 + 410p^3 + 136p^4 + O(p^5), \\ y_1 = 341 + 478p + 341p^2 + 478p^3 + 341p^4 + O(p^5), \\ x_2 = 97 + 358p + 346p^2 + 320p^3 + 323p^4 + O(p^5), \\ y_2 = 47 + 512p + 514p^2 + 409p^3 + 431p^4 + O(p^5). \end{cases}$$

In the notation of Algorithm 1, we have $d_0 = 508$, $d_1 = 46$, $d_2 = 1$. Therefore we obtain $d = d_0 + d_1 p + d_2 p^2 = 324879$.

4   Conclusion and Future Work

In his paper [2], Gaudry proposed a method for the ECDLP on $\mathbb{Q}_p$ using the p-adic elliptic logarithm. In his method, we need to compute the coefficients of the p-adic elliptic logarithm. On the other hand, we propose an algorithm for solving the ECDLP on $\mathbb{Q}_p$ using the filtration of elliptic curves over $\mathbb{Q}_p$, which is an extension of the anomalous attack. To compute our algorithm, we mainly need the following operations (we do not need to compute the p-adic elliptic logarithm):

- counting the order of the reduced elliptic curve $\widetilde{E}$ over $\mathbb{F}_p$.
- group operations on E over $\mathbb{Q}_p$.

Considering the ECDLP on $\mathbb{F}_p$, we can reduce the ECDLP on $\mathbb{F}_p$ to the ECDLP on $\mathbb{Q}_p$ if we could construct a good lifting map $u : \widetilde{E}(\mathbb{F}_p) \to E(\mathbb{Q}_p)$. However, in general, it is very difficult to construct a good lifting map (see §4.1 below). It is our subject of future investigation to construct a good lifting map by using the filtration of elliptic curves over $\mathbb{Q}_p$, which is used for solving the ECDLP on $\mathbb{Q}_p$ in Algorithm1.

4.1   The ECDLP on $\mathbb{F}_p$ and the ECDLP on $\mathbb{Q}_p$

Let p be a prime number and let $\widetilde{E}$ be an elliptic curve defined over $\mathbb{F}_p$. Let $\widetilde{S}$ be a rational point of $\widetilde{E}$ of prime order r and let $\widetilde{T} \in \langle \widetilde{S} \rangle$. The ECDLP on $\mathbb{F}_p$ is to compute the integer d with $\widetilde{T} = d\widetilde{S}$. The hardness of the ECDLP on $\mathbb{F}_p$ is essential for the security of all elliptic curve cryptography schemes. We here consider the method for reducing the ECDLP on $\mathbb{F}_p$ to the ECDLP on $\mathbb{Q}_p$.

The case $r = p$

In this case, we note that $\widetilde{E}$ is anomalous. We can solve the ECDLP on $\mathbb{F}_p$ efficiently using the map $\lambda_E(u)$ in Remark 1 (see [7, Corollary 3.8]).

The case $r \neq p$

In this case, we need to construct a lifting $u : \widetilde{E}(\mathbb{F}_p) \to E(\mathbb{Q}_p)$ with $T = \langle S \rangle$ where E is an elliptic curve which is a lifting of $\widetilde{E}$ to $\mathbb{Q}_p$, $S = u(\widetilde{S})$ and $T = u(\widetilde{T})$.

- We first consider the case where u is a canonical lifting (for example, the elliptic Teichmüller lifting which is a group homomorphism). In this case, we have $T \in \langle S \rangle$. However, since $h_P(S), h_p(T) = 0$ in the group $\mathcal{E}(p\mathbb{Z}_p)$, we cannot solve the ECDLP on $\mathbb{Q}_p$ using the p-adic elliptic logarithm or our method.
- We next consider the case where u is not a canonical lifting (for example, Hensel's lifting which is not a group homomorphism). In this case, we cannot construct u with $T \in \langle S \rangle$ efficiently. Therefore we cannot reduce the ECDLP on $\mathbb{F}_p$ to the ECDLP on $\mathbb{Q}_p$ efficiently.

Therefore we cannot reduce the ECDLP on $\mathbb{F}_p$ to the ECDLP on $\mathbb{Q}_p$ efficiently in this case.

Acknowledgements

We would like to thank the anonymous referees for their useful comments.

References

1. Blake, I., Seroussi, G., Smart, N.: Elliptic Curves in Cryptography. Cambridge University Press, Cambridge (1999)
2. Gaudry, P.: Some remarks on the elliptic curve discrete logarithm (2003), http://www.loria.fr/~gaudry/publis/liftDL.ps.gz
3. Hankerson, D., Menezes, A., Vanstone, S.: Guide to Elliptic Curve Cryptography, Springer Professional Computing (2004)
4. Koblitz, N.: Elliptic curve cryptosystems. Math. Comp. 48, 203–209 (1987)
5. Menezes, A., Okamoto, T., Vanstone, S.: Reducing elliptic curve logarithms to logarithms in a finite field. IEEE Transactions on Information Theory 39, 1639–1646 (1993)
6. Miller, V.S.: Use of elliptic curves in cryptography. In: Williams, H.C. (ed.) CRYPTO 1985. LNCS, vol. 218, pp. 417–426. Springer, Heidelberg (1986)
7. Satoh, T., Araki, K.: Fermat quotients and the polynomial time discrete log algorithm for anomalous elliptic curves. Comm. Math. Univ. Sancti Pauli 47, 81–92 (1998)
8. Semaev, I.: Evaluation of discrete logarithms in a group of p-torsion points of an elliptic curve in characteristic p. Math. Comp. 67, 353–356 (1998)
9. Silverman, J.H.: The Arithmetic of Elliptic Curves. In: Graduate Texts in Math. Springer, Heidelberg (1986)
10. Smart, N.P.: The discrete logarithm problem on elliptic curves of trace one. J. Crypto. 12, 110–125 (1999)

A New Efficient Algorithm for Computing All Low Degree Annihilators of Sparse Polynomials with a High Number of Variables*

Lin Xu[1,2], Dongdai Lin[1], and Xin Li[1,2,3]

[1] The State Key Laboratory of Information Security, Institute of Software,
Chinese Academy of Sciences, Beijing, P.R. China, 100080
[2] Graduate University of Chinese Academy of Sciences,
Beijing, P.R. China, 100039
[3] School of Computer Science, China Mining University of Technology,
Xuzhou, P.R. China, 221008
{xulin,ddlin,lixin}@is.iscas.ac.cn

Abstract. Algebraic attacks have proved to be an effective threat to block and stream cipher systems. In the realm of algebraic attacks, there is one major concern that, for a given Boolean polynomial f, if f or $f + 1$ has low degree annihilators. Existing methods for computing all annihilators within degree d of f in n variables, such as Gauss elimination and interpolation, have a complexity based on the parameter $k_{n,d} = \sum_{i=0}^{d} \binom{n}{i}$, which increases dramatically with n. As a result, these methods are impractical when dealing with sparse polynomials with a large n, which widely appear in modern cipher systems.

In this paper, we present a new tool for computing annihilators, the characters $w.r.t.$ a Boolean polynomial. We prove that the existence of annihilators of f and $f + 1$ $resp.$ relies on the zero characters and the critical characters $w.r.t.$ f. Then we present a new algorithm for computing annihilators whose complexity relies on $k'_{f,d}$, the number of zero or critical characters within degree d $w.r.t. f$. Since $k'_{f,d} \ll k_{n,d}$ when f is sparse, this algorithm is very efficient for sparse polynomials with a large n. In our experiments, all low degree annihilators of a random balanced sparse polynomial in 256 variables can be found in a few minutes.

Keywords: algebraic attack, annihilator, algebraic immunity, boolean polynomial, computational algebra.

1   Introduction

The key idea of algebraic attacks is to set up an overdefined system of multivariate algebraic equations verified by the key bits and try to solve it[1][2][3][4][5]. In recent years, algebraic attacks have proved to be quite effective in some cases.

---

* This work is partly supported by the National Natural Science Foundation of China under Grant No. 60970152, the Grand Project of Institute of Software: YOCX285056, and National 863 Project of China(No. 2007AA01Z447).

Algebraic attacks raise a new fundamental issue of determining whether or not a given Boolean polynomial has low degree annihilators. For instance, it is well known that algebraic attacks are powerful on LFSR-based stream ciphers[3], which consist of a linear feedback function(denoted by L) and a nonlinear combining function(denoted by f, and in degree D). Let $(s_0, \ldots, s_{n-1})$ be the initial state, then the output of the cipher is given by:

$$
\begin{cases}
b_0 & = f(s_0, s_1, \ldots, s_{n-1}) \\
b_1 & = f(L(s_0, s_1, \ldots, s_{n-1})) \\
\ldots & \\
b_{m-1} & = f(L^{m-1}(s_0, s_1, \ldots, s_{n-1}))
\end{cases}
$$

Given $(b_0, \ldots, b_{m-1})$, the complexity of solving $(s_0, \ldots, s_{n-1})$ is exponential in D. However, if there exists a polynomial $g \neq 0$ in degree $d < D$ such that $f \cdot g = 0$ (or $(f + 1) \cdot g = 0$), we can solve the left equation below(or the right one, correspondingly) instead, whose complexity is only exponential in d[3]. Here g is called an *annihilator* of f(or $f + 1$)[5].

$$
\begin{cases}
0 & = g(L^{i_1}(s_0, s_1, \ldots, s_{n-1})) \; (b_{i_1} = 1) \\
0 & = g(L^{i_2}(s_0, s_1, \ldots, s_{n-1})) \; (b_{i_2} = 1) \\
\ldots & = \ldots \\
0 & = g(L^{i_k}(s_0, s_1, \ldots, s_{n-1})) \; (b_{i_k} = 1)
\end{cases}
\qquad
\begin{cases}
0 & = g(L^{j_1}(s_0, s_1, \ldots, s_{n-1})) \; (b_{j_1} = 0) \\
0 & = g(L^{j_2}(s_0, s_1, \ldots, s_{n-1})) \; (b_{j_2} = 0) \\
\ldots & = \ldots \\
0 & = g(L^{j'_k}(s_0, s_1, \ldots, s_{n-1})) \; (b_{j'_k} = 0)
\end{cases}
$$

Therefore, for algebraic attacks to work, it is crucial that there exists one or more low degree annihilators of f or $f + 1$. The smallest degree for which this happens is called the *algebraic immunity* of f, which quantifies the immunity of f against algebraic attacks[5].

Currently, for computing low degree annihilators, Gauss elimination is mostly used[6]. Its time and space complexity are *resp.* $O(k_{n,d}^{log_2 7})$(with Strassen algorithm) and $O(k_{n,d}^2)$, in which

$$
k_{n,d} = \sum_{i=0}^{d} \binom{n}{i}.
$$

In addition, interpolation is also proposed for checking the existence of low degree annihilators[7]. With a careful implementation, and for polynomials with a high algebraic immunity, it has a better time complexity, $O(k_{n,d}^2)$.

These methods perform well when n is small. But when $n \geq 64$, $k_{n,d}$ grows very large so that they become impractical. An interesting example is the combing function(denoted by f_{toyo}) in the stream cipher Toyocrypt:

$$
f_{toyo}(s_0, \ldots, s_{127}) = s_{127} + \sum_{i=0}^{62} s_i s_{\alpha_i} + s_{10} s_{23} s_{32} s_{42} +
$$

$$
s_1 s_2 s_9 s_{12} s_{18} s_{20} s_{23} s_{25} s_{26} s_{28} s_{33} s_{38} s_{41} s_{42} s_{51} s_{53} s_{59} + \prod_{i=0}^{62} s_i,
$$

$\{\alpha_0, \ldots, \alpha_{62}\}$ is some permutation of $\{63, \ldots, 125\}$. Simply by noticing the largest three terms in f_{toyo} have common variables s_{23} and s_{42}, N.T.Courtois easily found two annihilators with degree 3 of f_{toyo}[3]. However, when above methods are used, since $n = 128$ and $d = 3$, the time cost for computing all annihilators is about 2^{50}, while as much as 8GB memory is required!

In fact, sparse Boolean polynomials in rather large n, like f_{toyo}, are definitely interesting in cryptography. They appear in various cipher designs as a source of nonlinearity. And unfortunately, existing methods are not capable of efficiently checking whether or not they have low degree annihilators.

It is believed that, the complexity of computing all annihilators within degree d of f in n variables is at least $O(k_{n,d})$[8], because roughly there are $k_{n,d}$ different possibilities. However, in this paper, we will show that this is not always true. These $k_{n,d}$ possibilities are not separated, but tensely related with each other when f is sparse. As a result, only a small *critical* part of them(for example, 0.3% in the case of f_{toyo}) need to be checked.

The key idea of this paper originates from F_5 algorithm by J.C.Faugére[9]([10] is a more detailed version). It is widely believed that Gröbner bases algorithm can be used for computing annihilators[11], however it is still unknown whether or not they perform better than above methods. And this paper indirectly gives a positive answer to this question.

This paper is organized as follows. Section 2 introduces the basic definitions and notations regarding Boolean polynomials and their annihilators. Section 3 and Section 4 present the theory of characters *w.r.t.* a Boolean polynomial, and then reveal the relation between different categories of characters *w.r.t.* f and the annihilators of f or $f+1$. Section 5 gives the full description of our algorithm for computing annihilators, and its performance is shown in Section 6.

2 Preliminary

In this paper, we denote by $\mathbb{N}^+$ the set of positive natural numbers $\{1, 2, \ldots\}$, and by $\mathbb{F}_2$ the binary finite field $\{0, 1\}$. A mapping $f(x_1, \ldots, x_n)$ from $\mathbb{F}_2^n$ into $\mathbb{F}_2$ with $n \in \mathbb{N}^+$ is called a *Boolean polynomial* in n variables, which is actually a polynomial in the quotient ring

$$\mathcal{R}[x_1, \ldots, x_n] = \mathbb{F}_2[x_1, \ldots, x_n]/\langle x_1^2 - x_1, \ldots, x_n^2 - x_n \rangle.$$

We denote $\mathcal{R}[x_1, \ldots, x_n]$ simply by $\mathcal{R}$. It is well known that each Boolean polynomial $f \in \mathcal{R}$ has an unique expression, called the *algebraic normal form*(ANF) of f,

$$f = a_1 \cdot x_1^{\nu_{1,1}} \cdot \ldots \cdot x_n^{\nu_{1,n}} + \ldots + a_m \cdot x_1^{\nu_{m,1}} \cdot \ldots \cdot x_n^{\nu_{m,n}} (a_i, \nu_{i,j} \in \mathbb{F}_2).$$

Each $x_k^{\nu_{k,1}} \cdot \ldots \cdot x_n^{\nu_{k,n}} (1 \leq k \leq m)$ with $a_k = 1$ is called a *term* in f. We say f is *sparse*, *iff.* the number of terms in $f \ll 2^n$. In this paper, the set of terms is denoted by $\mathcal{T}$. For $t_1, t_2 \in \mathcal{T}$, we say t_1 and t_2 are *coprime*, *iff.* they have no common variable. We denote by $\mathcal{R}^*$ the set of non-zero Boolean polynomials. The *total degree* of a term $t \in \mathcal{T}$ and a non-zero Boolean polynomial $f \in \mathcal{R}^*$, are *resp.* denoted by $deg(t)$ and $deg(f)$. Finally, for $f \in \mathcal{R}^*$, $\langle f \rangle$ denotes the ideal of $\mathcal{R}$ generated by f.

Definition 1. (Annihilator)
    For $f \in \mathcal{R}$, $c \in \mathcal{R}$ is an annihilator of f iff. $c \cdot f = 0$.   □

In this paper, the set of annihilators of f, and the set of annihilators within degree $D(D \in \mathbb{N}^+)$ of f, are *resp.* denoted by $An(f)$ and $An_D(f)$.

Theorem 1. $An(f) = \langle f + 1 \rangle$.   □

Theorem 1[5] reveals that we can obtain all annihilators of f by computing $\langle f + 1 \rangle$. However, for f in n variables, the complexity of computing $\langle f + 1 \rangle$ is exponential in n. Thus Theorem 1 has few practical value and we will present some enhanced versions of it in later sections.

Definition 2. (Algebraic Immunity)
    For $f \in \mathcal{R}^*$, the algebraic immunity of f, denoted by $AI(f)$, is defined as

$$\min\{deg(c) : c \in An(f) \cup An(f + 1), c \neq 0\}.$$ □

As mentioned in Introduction, we are actually interested in the annihilators of f or $f + 1$ with the lowest degree, $AI(f)$. For convenience, $An_{AI(f)}(f)$ and $An_{AI(f)}(f + 1)$ are simply denoted by $An^\star(f)$ and $An^\star(f + 1)$ in following sections. It is just the main aim of this paper to efficiently compute them.

3   Characters *w.r.t.* a Boolean Polynomial

In following two sections, we present the theoretical foundation of our new method for computing annihilators. Briefly, given a nonzero Boolean polynomial f, an unique term $\sigma \in \mathcal{T}$ is assigned to each element t in $LT\langle f \rangle$. σ is called the *character* of t *w.r.t.* f. We will show that the existence of annihilators of f and $f + 1$ completely relies on the behavior of the characters *w.r.t.* f.

We start by the definition of the term order, which is a basic concept in commutative algebra[12]. We have slightly modified it for the Boolean case.

Definition 3. (Term Order) *A term order is a total order $\leq$ on $\mathcal{T}$ such that $1 \leq \mathcal{T}$ for all $t \in \mathcal{T}$, and for $t_1, t_2, u \in \mathcal{T}$, u and t_2 are coprime, $t_1 \leq t_2 \Rightarrow u \cdot t_1 \leq u \cdot t_2$.*   □

For $t \in \mathcal{T}$, we denote by $prev(t)$ the predecessor of t in $\mathcal{T}$ *w.r.t.* $\leq$. For $f \in \mathcal{R}^*$, the maximum term *w.r.t.* $\leq$ in f, called the *leading term* of f, is denoted by $lt(f)$. For $F \subseteq \mathcal{R}$, we denote by $LT(F)$ the set of leading terms of nonzero polynomials in F. Then obviously following lemma holds for any term order.

Lemma 1. $f \in \mathcal{R}^*$ and $t \in \mathcal{T}$, $lt(t \cdot f) = t \cdot lt(f)$ if t and $lt(f)$ are coprime.   □

We choose the graded lexicographical order(DL) as our term order used throughout this paper[1]. For details about DL, we refer to [12].

Next, as a preparation, we define the bounded closures of a Boolean polynomial f, which are a series of subsets of $\langle f \rangle$.

Definition 4. (Bounded Closure) *Let $f \in \mathcal{R}^*$, $\sigma \in \mathcal{T}$. The σ-closure of f, denoted by $\langle f \rangle_{\leq \sigma}$, is defined as*

$$\{c \cdot f \mid c \in \mathcal{R}, c = 0 \text{ or } lt(c) \leq \sigma\}. \qquad \square$$

For convenience, we also use following notations for bounded closures:

$$\langle f \rangle_{<\sigma} = \langle f \rangle_{\leq prev(\sigma)} = \{c \cdot f \mid c \in \mathcal{R}, c = 0 \text{ or } lt(c) < \sigma\},$$

$$\langle f \rangle_{\leq d} = \{c \cdot f \mid c \in \mathcal{R}, c = 0 \text{ or } deg(c) \leq d\}, d \in \mathbb{N}^+.$$

Proposition 1. *Let $f \in \mathcal{R}^*$, $\sigma, \sigma' \in \mathcal{T}$, then the followings hold:*

a. $0 \in \langle f \rangle_{\leq \sigma}$
b. $\langle f \rangle_{<\sigma} \subseteq \langle f \rangle_{\leq \sigma} \subseteq \langle f \rangle$
c. $\sigma \leq \sigma' \Longrightarrow \langle f \rangle_{\leq \sigma} \subseteq \langle f \rangle_{\leq \sigma'}$
d. $f, g \in \langle f \rangle_{\leq \sigma} \Longrightarrow f + g \in \langle f \rangle_{\leq \sigma}$
e. $LT\langle f \rangle_{\leq \sigma} = LT\langle f \rangle_{\leq \sigma'} \Longleftrightarrow \langle f \rangle_{\leq \sigma} = \langle f \rangle_{\leq \sigma'}$
f. *there exists at most one term in $LT\langle f \rangle_{\leq \sigma}$ but not in $LT\langle f \rangle_{<\sigma}$.*

Proof. (a) (b) (c) and (d) are trivial by Definition 4.

(e). $\Leftarrow$ is trivial. $\Rightarrow$: assuming there exist $\sigma < \sigma'$ such that $LT\langle f \rangle_{\leq \sigma} = LT\langle f \rangle_{\leq \sigma'}$ and $\langle f \rangle_{\leq \sigma} \neq \langle f \rangle_{\leq \sigma'}$. We have $\langle f \rangle_{\leq \sigma} \subseteq \langle f \rangle_{\leq \sigma'}$ by (c), and thus there exists a $p_1 \in \mathcal{R}$ such that $p_1 \in \langle f \rangle_{\leq \sigma'}$ and $p_1 \notin \langle f \rangle_{\leq \sigma}$, and then $p_1 \neq 0$ by (a). On the other hand, since $lt(p_1) \in LT\langle f \rangle_{\leq \sigma} = LT\langle f \rangle_{\leq \sigma'}$, there exists a $q_1 \in \langle f \rangle_{\leq \sigma'}$ such that $lt(q_1) = lt(p_1)$. Let $p_2 = p_1 + q_1$, we have $p_2 \notin LT\langle f \rangle_{\leq \sigma}$ by (d), $p_2 \neq 0$ by (a) and $lt(p_2) < lt(p_1)$. Similarly, there exists a $q_2 \in \langle f \rangle_{\leq \sigma'}$ such that $lt(q_2) = lt(p_2)$ and we have $p_3 = p_2 + q_2$ such that $p_3 \neq 0$ and $lt(p_3) < lt(p_2)$.... In this way, an infinite strictly descending list of terms in $\mathcal{T}$ can be generated: $lt(p_1) > lt(p_2) > lt(p_3) > \ldots$. However, $\mathcal{T}$ is a finite set and thus there is a contradiction. Therefore we have $\langle f \rangle_{\leq \sigma} = \langle f \rangle_{\leq \sigma'}$.

(f). For any $t_1, t_2 \in LT\langle f \rangle_{\leq \sigma} - LT\langle f \rangle_{<\sigma}$, there exist $c_1, c_2 \in \mathcal{R}^*$ such that $lt(c_1 \cdot f) = t_1, lt(c_2 \cdot f) = t_2$ and $lt(c_1) = lt(c_2) = \sigma$. Since $lt(c_1 + c_2) < \sigma$, we have $(c_1 + c_2) \cdot f \in \langle f \rangle_{<\sigma}$ and thus $lt(c_1 \cdot f + c_2 \cdot f) \in LT\langle f \rangle_{<\sigma}$. Since $t_1, t_2 \notin LT\langle f \rangle_{<\sigma}$, we have $lt(c_1 \cdot f + c_2 \cdot f) \neq t_1$ or t_2, which means $lt(c_1 \cdot f) = lt(c_2 \cdot f)$, and finally $t_1 = t_2$. $\qquad \square$

Definition 5. (Zero Character) *Let $f \in \mathcal{R}^*$, $\sigma \in \mathcal{T}$. σ is a zero character w.r.t. f, iff.*

$$\langle f \rangle_{\leq \sigma} = \langle f \rangle_{<\sigma}. \qquad \square$$

---

[1] In fact, any other term order in *total degree*, such as the graded reverse lexicographical order(DRL), is also a valid choice here, and nothing else in this paper needs to do any change.

We denote by $\mathcal{S}_f^0$ the set of zero characters $w.r.t.$ f, and by $\mathcal{S}_f^+$ the set $\mathcal{T} - \mathcal{S}_f^0$. Following theorem reveals that, the existence of annihilators of f equals to the existence of zero characters $w.r.t.$ f.

Theorem 2. $\sigma \in \mathcal{S}_f^0$, iff. there exists an annihilator c of f such that $lt(c) = \sigma$.

Proof. $\Rightarrow$: since $\sigma \in \mathcal{S}_f^0$, we have $\sigma \cdot f \in \langle f \rangle_{\leq \sigma} = \langle f \rangle_{<\sigma}$, which means there exists a $c' \in \mathcal{R}^*$ such that $lt(c') < \sigma$ and $c' \cdot f = \sigma \cdot f$. Let $c = \sigma + c'$, we have $c \cdot f = c' \cdot f + \sigma \cdot f = 0$. Therefore c is an annihilator of f and $lt(c) = \sigma$.

$\Leftarrow$: let c an annihilator of f and $lt(c) = \sigma$. For any polynomial $c' \cdot f \in \langle f \rangle_{\leq \sigma}$, if $lt(c') < \sigma$, obviously we have $c' \cdot f \in \langle f \rangle_{<\sigma}$. And if $lt(c') = \sigma$, we also have $c' \cdot f = c' \cdot f + c \cdot f = (c' + c) \cdot f \in \langle f \rangle_{<\sigma}$ since $lt(c' + c) < \sigma$. Therefore $\langle f \rangle_{\leq \sigma} = \langle f \rangle_{<\sigma}$ and finally $\sigma \in \mathcal{S}_f^0$. □

Corollary 1. $\sigma \in \mathcal{S}_f^0, \sigma \mid \sigma' \Rightarrow \sigma' \in \mathcal{S}_f^0$.

Proof. Since $\sigma \in \mathcal{S}_f^0$, there exists an annihilator c of f such that $lt(c) = \sigma$ by Theorem 2. Let $c' = (\sigma'/\sigma) \cdot c$, obviously c' is also an annihilator of f. And since σ'/σ and σ are coprime, we have $lt(c') = (\sigma'/\sigma) \cdot lt(c) = \sigma'$ by Lemma 1. Finally we have $\sigma' \in \mathcal{S}_f^0$ by Theorem 2. □

Corollary 2. $LT(An^\star(f)) = \{\sigma \in \mathcal{S}_f^0 : deg(\sigma) = AI(f)\}$. □

Corollary 2 will be used for computing $An^\star(f)$ in Section 5.

Now we are ready to define the characters $w.r.t.$ a Boolean polynomial.

Definition 6. (Character) Let $f \in \mathcal{R}^*$, $t \in LT\langle f \rangle$. The character of t $w.r.t.$ f, denoted by $ch_f(t)$, is defined as

$$\min\{lt(c) \mid c \in \mathcal{R}^*, lt(c \cdot f) = t\}.$$ □

Proposition 2. Let $f \in \mathcal{R}^*$, $t, t' \in LT\langle f \rangle$, then the followings hold:
  a. $ch_f(t) = \sigma \Longleftrightarrow t \in LT\langle f \rangle_{\leq \sigma}, t \notin LT\langle f \rangle_{<\sigma}$
  b. $ch_f(t) \in \mathcal{S}_f^+$
  c. $\sigma \in \mathcal{S}_f^+ \Longrightarrow \exists t \in LT\langle f \rangle, ch_f(t) = \sigma$
  d. $ch_f(t_1) = ch_f(t_2) \Longrightarrow t_1 = t_2$
  e. ch_f is a bijective mapping from $LT\langle f \rangle$ to $\mathcal{S}_f^+$.

Proof. (a) is trivial by Definition 6.

(b). We have $LT\langle f \rangle_{\leq ch_f(t)} \neq LT\langle f \rangle_{<ch_f(t)}$ by (a). Therefore $\langle f \rangle_{\leq ch_f(t)} \neq \langle f \rangle_{<ch_f(t)}$ and thus $ch_f(t) \notin \mathcal{S}_f^0$.

(c). For $\sigma \in \mathcal{S}_f^+$, we have $\langle f \rangle_{\leq \sigma} \neq \langle f \rangle_{<\sigma}$ and thus $LT\langle f \rangle_{\leq \sigma} \neq LT\langle f \rangle_{<\sigma}$ by Proposition 1.e. Therefore there exists a $t \in LT\langle f \rangle_{\leq \sigma}$ such that $t \notin LT\langle f \rangle_{<\sigma}$, and finally $ch_f(t) = \sigma$ by (a).

(d) directly follows (a) and Proposition 1.f.

(e). ch_f is a mapping from $LT\langle f \rangle$ to $\mathcal{S}_f^+$ by (b) ; ch_f is surjective by (c); ch_f is injective by (d). Thus ch_f is a bijective mapping from $LT\langle f \rangle$ to $\mathcal{S}_f^+$. □

We denote the reverse mapping of ch_f by gen_f. Then every term $\sigma \in \mathcal{T}$ is either a zero character w.r.t. f, or the character of $gen_f(\sigma)$ w.r.t. f by Proposition 2. When we say *characters w.r.t. f* in this paper, we mean both types.

Theorem 3. $\sigma \in \mathcal{S}_f^+ \Rightarrow gen_f(\sigma) \geq \sigma$.

Proof. Let $t = gen_f(\sigma)$, by Definition 6, there exists a $c \in \mathcal{R}^*$ such that $lt(c) = \sigma$ and $lt(c \cdot f) = t$. Let $g = c \cdot f$ and multiple both sides of $g = c \cdot f$ with f, since $f \cdot f = f$ we have $(c + g) \cdot f = 0$, and thus $c + g$ is an annihilator of f. Assuming $lt(c) > lt(g)$, we have $lt(c + g) = lt(c) \in \mathcal{S}_f^0$ by Theorem 2. However, we also have $\sigma = lt(c) \in \mathcal{S}_f^+$ and there is a contradiction. Therefore $\sigma = lt(c) \leq lt(g) = t = gen_f(\sigma)$. $\square$

With Theorem 3, we get Theorem 1 improved.

Corollary 3. $An_D(f + 1) = \{g \in \langle f \rangle_{\leq D} : deg(g) \leq D\}$.

Proof. By Theorem 1, we have

$$An_D(f + 1) = \{g \in \langle f \rangle : deg(g) \leq D\}.$$

Let $g \in \langle f \rangle$ and $deg(g) \leq D$, since $ch_f(lt(g)) \leq lt(g)$ by Theorem 3, we have $deg(ch_f(lt(g))) \leq deg(lt(g)) = deg(g) = D$ by the definition of DL. Therefore $g \in \langle f \rangle_{\leq D}$ and finally

$$An_D(f + 1) = \{g \in \langle f \rangle_{\leq D} : deg(g) \leq D\}. \qquad \square$$

Now, for computing $An_D(f + 1)$, not $\langle f \rangle$, but only $\langle f \rangle_{\leq D}$ is required. We can just incrementally compute $\langle f \rangle_{\leq 1}$, $\langle f \rangle_{\leq 2}$, ..., and check whether or not there exist polynomials with degree 1, 2, ... respectively in them until one or more polynomials in degree d are found in $\langle f \rangle_{\leq d}$. Then all annihilators of $f + 1$ with the lowest degree are obtained.

4   Critical Characters and Bounded Bases

As shown in Section 3, if all $\langle f \rangle_{\leq \sigma}$ with $deg(\sigma) \leq d$ are given, it is straightforward in theory to detect whether or not f or $f + 1$ has annihilators within degree d. By Theorem 2, we can obtain annihilators of f by checking for each σ whether or not $\langle f \rangle_{\leq \sigma} \neq \langle f \rangle_{<\sigma}$. And by Corollary 3, we can obtain annihilators of $f + 1$ simply by retrieving polynomials within degree d from $\langle f \rangle_{\leq d}$.

There are $k_{n,d}$ different σ-s within degree d, and thus this method seems still having a complexity based on $k_{n,d}$. However, in this section, we will show only a small *critical* part of these $k_{n,d}$ characters are really essential when computing annihilators, while the others can be directly excluded.

Definition 7. (Critical Character)
Let $f \in \mathcal{R}^*$, we recursively define a series of set $(\mathcal{S}_{f,\sigma}^\star)_{\sigma \in \mathcal{T}}$,
  a. $\mathcal{S}_{f,1}^\star = \{1\}$;
  b. if $\sigma \neq 1$, $\mathcal{S}_{f,\sigma}^\star$ is defined with $\mathcal{S}_{f,prev(\sigma)}^\star$ as below. Let

$$\sigma_b = \max\{\sigma' \in \mathcal{S}^{\star}_{f,prev(\sigma)} : \sigma' \mid \sigma\},$$

then we define

$$\mathcal{S}^{\star}_{f,\sigma} = \begin{cases} \mathcal{S}^{\star}_{f,prev(\sigma)} \cup \{\sigma\} & \text{iff. } \sigma \in \mathcal{S}^{+}_{f} \text{ and } (\sigma/\sigma_b) \cdot gen_f(\sigma_b) \neq gen_f(\sigma). \\ \mathcal{S}^{\star}_{f,prev(\sigma)} & \text{otherwise.} \end{cases}$$

We say $\sigma \in \mathcal{T}$ is a critical character w.r.t. f, iff. $\sigma \in \mathcal{S}^{\star}_{f,\sigma}$. □

We denote by $\mathcal{S}^{\star}_{f}$ the set of critical characters *w.r.t.* f. And for $\sigma \in \mathcal{T}$, we denote the *maximum* divisor of σ in $\mathcal{S}^{\star}_{f}$ by $base_f(\sigma)$.

Proposition 3. *Let $f \in \mathcal{R}^{*}$, $\sigma \in \mathcal{S}^{+}_{f}$, $\sigma_B = base_f(\sigma)$, then the followings hold:*

    a. $gen_f(\sigma) = (\sigma/\sigma_B) \cdot gen_f(\sigma_B)$.
    b. σ/σ_B and $gen_f(\sigma_B)$ are coprime.

Proof. (a). If $\sigma \in \mathcal{S}^{\star}_{f}$, we have $\sigma_B = \sigma$ and (a) obviously holds. And if $\sigma \notin \mathcal{S}^{\star}_{f}$, (a) is trivial by Definition 7.

(b). Assuming σ/σ_B and $gen_f(\sigma_B)$ are not coprime so that they have a common variable x_i. Let $\sigma' = \sigma_B \cdot x_i$, we have $\sigma_B \mid \sigma' \mid \sigma$, and then since $\sigma \in \mathcal{S}^{+}_{f}$ we have $\sigma' \in \mathcal{S}^{+}_{f}$ by Corollary 1. We also have $\sigma' \notin \mathcal{S}^{\star}_{f}$ because $\sigma' \mid \sigma$ and the maximum divisor of σ in $\mathcal{S}^{\star}_{f}$ is $\sigma_B < \sigma'$. Meanwhile, since $\sigma' \mid \sigma$, all divisors of σ' are also divisors of σ, therefore we have $base_f(\sigma') = base_f(\sigma) = \sigma_B$, and thus $gen_f(\sigma') = gen_f(\sigma_B) \cdot x_i = gen_f(\sigma_B)$ by (a). Now there is a contradiction because gen_f is injective. Therefore σ/σ_B and $gen_f(\sigma_B)$ have no common variable. □

With Proposition 3, we get Theorem 1 further improved.

Corollary 4. *$LT(An^{\star}(f+1)) \subseteq \{gen_f(\sigma) : \sigma \in \mathcal{S}^{\star}_{f}, deg(\sigma) \leq AI(f)\}$.*

Proof. Firstly we have $LT(An^{\star}(f+1)) \subseteq \{gen_f(\sigma) : \sigma \in \mathcal{T}, deg(\sigma) \leq AI(f)\}$ by Corollary 3. And for any $t \in LT(An^{\star}(f+1))$, t has the lowest degree in $LT\langle f \rangle$ by the definition of $AI(f)$. Therefore there cannot exist a divisor of t in $LT\langle f \rangle$ other than t, and thus $ch_f(t)$ must be a critical character by Proposition 3.a. □

Corollary 2 and Corollary 4 together compose the foundation of our algorithm in Section 5: $An^{\star}(f)$ and $An^{\star}(f+1)$ *resp.* rely on the zero characters with the lowest degree and the critical characters within degree $AI(f)$. When f is sparse, critical characters *w.r.t.* f within a small degree d are also very sparse in all $k_{n,d}$ characters, which guarantees the efficiency of our method(see Section 6 for details). Following proposition shows the criterions for detecting them.

Proposition 4. *Let $f \in \mathcal{R}^{*}$, $\sigma \in \mathcal{T}$, let $\sigma_b = \max\{\sigma' \in \mathcal{S}^{\star}_{f} : \sigma' \mid \sigma, \sigma' < \sigma\}$, then $\sigma \in \mathcal{S}^{\star}_{f}$ or σ is a zero character w.r.t. f with the lowest degree, only if either of the following conditions holds,*
    a. σ/σ_b and $gen_f(\sigma_b)$ are coprime, and $(\sigma/\sigma_b) \cdot gen_f(\sigma_b) \in LT\langle f \rangle_{<\sigma}$.
    b. $\sigma/\sigma_b = x_i$ and $x_i \in gen_f(\sigma_b)$.

Proof. Supposing σ/σ_b and $gen_f(\sigma_b)$ are coprime, we have $(\sigma/\sigma_b) \cdot gen_f(\sigma_b) \in LT\langle f \rangle_{\leq \sigma}$. Then assuming $(\sigma/\sigma_b) \cdot gen_f(\sigma_b) \notin LT\langle f \rangle_{<\sigma}$, we have $gen_f(\sigma) = (\sigma/\sigma_b) \cdot gen_f(\sigma_b)$ by Proposition 3.a and thus $\sigma \notin \mathcal{S}_f^\star$ and $\sigma \notin \mathcal{S}_f^0$. Therefore there is a contradiction and finally we have $(\sigma/\sigma_b) \cdot gen_f(\sigma_b) \in LT\langle f \rangle_{<\sigma}$.

Now supposing σ/σ_b and $gen_f(\sigma_b)$ are not coprime, which means they have common variable x_i. Assuming $\sigma \neq \sigma_b \cdot x_i$ and let $\sigma' = \sigma_b \cdot x_i$, we have $\sigma_b \mid \sigma' \mid \sigma$. (1) Supposing $\sigma' \in \mathcal{S}_f^+$, we have $\sigma' \notin \mathcal{S}_f^\star$ because $\sigma' \mid \sigma$ and the maximum divisor of σ in $\mathcal{S}_f^\star$ is $\sigma_b < \sigma'$. Meanwhile, since $\sigma' \mid \sigma$, all divisors of σ' are also divisors of σ, therefore we have $base_f(\sigma') = base_f(\sigma) = \sigma_b$, and thus $gen_f(\sigma') = gen_f(\sigma_b) \cdot x_i = gen_f(\sigma_b)$. Now there is a contradiction because gen_f is injective. Finally we have $\sigma = \sigma_b \cdot x_i$. (2) Supposing $\sigma' \in \mathcal{S}_f^0$, we have $\sigma \in \mathcal{S}_f^0$ by Corollary 1. Since σ has the lowest degree we have $\sigma' = \sigma$ and thus $\sigma = \sigma_b \cdot x_i$ also holds.

Therefore, either (a) or (b) holds when $\sigma \in \mathcal{S}_f^\star$ or σ is a zero character *w.r.t.* f with the lowest degree. □

Finally, in Section 5, bounded closures will be represented as their bounded bases, which are defined as below.

Definition 8. (Bounded Bases)
    Let $f \in \mathcal{R}^*$, $\sigma \in \mathcal{T}$. *Bounded bases of* $\langle f \rangle_{\leq \sigma}$ *are a subset of* $\mathcal{T} \times \mathcal{R}^* \times \mathcal{R}^*$, *and for each* $\sigma' \in \mathcal{S}_f^\star$ *and* $\sigma' \leq \sigma$, *there exists one* $(\sigma', c, p) \in G$ *such that* $p = c \cdot f$, $lt(c) = \sigma'$ *and* $lt(p) = gen_f(\sigma')$. □

Proposition 4 can be translated into following proposition under bounded bases.

Proposition 5. *Let* $f \in \mathcal{R}^*$, $\sigma \in \mathcal{T}$, G *is bounded bases of* $\langle f \rangle_{<\sigma}$. *Then* $\sigma \in \mathcal{S}_f^\star$ *or* σ *is a zero character w.r.t.* f *with the lowest degree, only if either of the followings holds,*
    a. *there exist* $g_1 = (\sigma_1, c_1, p_1), g_2 = (\sigma_2, c_2, p_2) \in G$, *such that,*
    a.1. μ_1 *and* σ_1 *are coprime,* μ_2 *and* σ_2 *are coprime.*
    a.2. $\mu_1 \cdot \sigma_1 \neq \mu_2 \cdot \sigma_2$.
    a.3. $\sigma = \max(\mu_1 \cdot \sigma_1, \mu_2 \cdot \sigma_2)$.
    in which $\mu_i = \frac{lt(p_1) \cdot lt(p_2)}{lt(p_i)}$, $i = 1, 2$.
    b. *there exist* $g = (\sigma', c, p) \in G$ *and a variable* $x_i \in lt(p)$ *such that* $\sigma = \sigma' \cdot x_i$.

Proof. Let $\sigma_b = \max\{\sigma' \in \mathcal{S}_f^\star : \sigma' \mid \sigma, \sigma' < \sigma\}$, and supposing σ/σ_b and $gen_f(\sigma_b)$ are coprime. Let $t = (\sigma/\sigma_b) \cdot gen_f(\sigma_b)$, we have $t \in LT\langle f \rangle_{<\sigma}$ by Proposition 4. It is easy to check the elements in G with characters σ_b and $base_f(ch_f(t))$ are g_1 and g_2 for (a).

And if σ/σ_b and $gen_f(\sigma_b)$ are not coprime, we have $\sigma/\sigma_b = x_i$ and $x_i \in gen_f(\sigma_b)$ by Proposition 4. Then the element in G with the character σ_b is g for (b). □

5   Description of the Algorithm

Now, we are ready to show our algorithm for computing annihilators. Briefly, for a given Boolean polynomial f, bounded bases of $\langle f \rangle_{\leq \sigma}$ for each critical character

σ are incrementally computed by Algorithm 3. Potential zero characters and critical characters $w.r.t.$ f are predicted with Proposition 5 by Algorithm 4, and are checked one by one in the DL order by Algorithm 2.

Firstly, given bounded bases of $\langle f \rangle_{<\sigma}$ and any term $t \in \mathcal{T}$, Algorithm 1 checks whether or not $t \in LT\langle f \rangle_{<\sigma}$.

Algorithm 1. BoundedBasis

Input: $t \in \mathcal{T}$, $f \in \mathcal{R}^*$, $\sigma \in \mathcal{T}$, BoundedBases: bounded bases of $\langle f \rangle_{<\sigma}$.
Output:
$$\begin{cases} (\sigma_0, c_0, p_0) \in \text{BoundedBases}; & t \in LT\langle f \rangle_{<\sigma} \\ \quad lt((\sigma/\sigma_0) \cdot p_0) = t, lt((\sigma/\sigma_0) \cdot c_0) < \sigma. & \\ \Phi. & otherwise \end{cases}$$

1 **foreach** $(\sigma', c', p') \in$ BoundedBases **do**
2   **if** $lt(p') \mid t$ **and** $\mathbf{coprime}(t/lt(p'), \sigma')$ **and** $(t/lt(p')) \cdot \sigma' < \sigma$ **then**
3      $\llcorner$ **return** (σ', c', p')

4 **return** Φ

The correctness of Algorithm 1 relies on the followings:

(a). For any $(\sigma', c', p') \in BoundedBases$, if the three conditions in *Line 2* hold, let $p = (t/lt(p')) \cdot p'$, we have $p \in \langle f \rangle_{<\sigma}$ and $lt(p) = t$, therefore $t \in LT\langle f \rangle_{<\sigma}$ and (σ', c', p') is what we need.

(b). Reversely, if $t \in LT\langle f \rangle_{<\sigma}$, at least the element with character $base_f(ch_f(t))$ in *BoundedBases* satisfies the three conditions in *Line 2*.

Next, given bounded bases of $\langle f \rangle_{<\sigma}$, Algorithm 2 checks whether or not σ is a zero character with the lowest degree, or a critical character $w.r.t.$ f. $gen_f(\sigma)$ will be computed in the later case.

In Algorithm 2, *Line 4-7* check whether or not $gen_f(\sigma) = (\sigma/\sigma_0) \cdot gen_f(\sigma)$. If so we have $\sigma \in \mathcal{S}_f^+$ and $\sigma \notin \mathcal{S}_f^*$, which means that σ will not bring an annihilator and *BoundedBases* are also bounded bases of $\langle f \rangle_{\leq \sigma}$. Algorithm 2 immediately returns Φ in this case. Otherwise, we have $\sigma \in \mathcal{S}_f^*$ or $\sigma \in \mathcal{S}_f^0$, and then Algorithm 2 tries to compute $gen_f(\sigma)$. Note that in *Line 9-10* and *Line 14-15*, $c \cdot f = p$ and $p \in \langle f \rangle_{\leq \sigma}$ are maintained, while $lt(p)$ strictly descends until $p = 0$ which means $\sigma \in \mathcal{S}_f^0$, or $lt(p) \notin LT\langle f \rangle_{<\sigma}$ which means $gen_f(\sigma) = lt(p)$.

Algorithm 3 is the main loop of the computation. The lowest degree of known annihilators of f or $f + 1$ is saved in *AlgebraicImmunity* (initiated with $deg(f)$ because $f + 1$ is always an annihilator of f). *ToDo* records all potential critical or zero characters in future predicted by Algorithm 4. And the bounded bases are recorded in *BoundedBases*, which is maintained by Algorithm 3 and provided to other algorithms.

In *Line 7-8*, the minimal element σ_{todo} in *ToDo* is retrieved, and then Algorithm 2 is called to try computing $gen_f(\sigma_{todo})$(*Line 11*). If σ_{todo} is confirmed by Algorithm 2 to be a zero character, an annihilator of f is discovered by Corollary

Algorithm 2. Gen

Input: $\sigma \in \mathcal{T}$, $f \in \mathcal{R}^*$, BoundedBases: bounded bases of $\langle f \rangle_{<\sigma}$.
Output:

$$\begin{cases} (\sigma, c, 0) \in (\mathcal{T}, \mathcal{R}, \mathcal{R}) : lt(c) = \sigma, \; c \cdot f = 0; & \sigma \in \mathcal{S}_f^0 \\ (\sigma, c, c \cdot f) \in (\mathcal{T}, \mathcal{R}, \mathcal{R}) : lt(c) = \sigma, lt(c \cdot f) = gen_f(\sigma); & \sigma \in \mathcal{S}_f^\star \\ \Phi. & otherwise \end{cases}$$

1 $(\sigma_0, c_0, p_0) := \max_{\sigma'}\{(\sigma', c', p') \in \text{BoundedBases} : \sigma' \mid \sigma\}$
2 $c := (\sigma/\sigma_0) \cdot c_0$
3 $p := (\sigma/\sigma_0) \cdot p_0$
4 **if** $\mathbf{coprime}(\sigma/\sigma_0, lt(p_0))$ **then**
5 $\quad$ Basis := **BoundedBasis**$(lt(p), f, \sigma, \text{BoundedBases})$
6 $\quad$ **if** Basis $= \Phi$ **then**
7 $\quad\quad$ $\lfloor$ **return** Φ
8 $\quad$ $(\sigma', c', p') := \text{Basis}$
9 $\quad$ $c := c + (\sigma/\sigma') \cdot c'$
10 $\quad$ $p := p + (\sigma/\sigma') \cdot p'$
11 Basis := **BoundedBasis**$(lt(p), f, \sigma, \text{BoundedBases})$
12 **while** Basis $\neq \Phi$ **do**
13 $\quad$ $(\sigma', c', p') := \text{Basis}$
14 $\quad$ $c := c + (\sigma/\sigma') \cdot c'$
15 $\quad$ $p := p + (\sigma/\sigma') \cdot p'$
16 $\quad$ Basis := **BoundedBasis**$(lt(p), f, \sigma, \text{BoundedBases})$
17 **return** (σ, c, p)

2($Line\ 16\text{-}18$). Or if σ is confirmed to be a critical character, a potential anni-hilator of $f + 1$ is obtained by Corollary 4 and it will be checked($Line\ 20\text{-}21$). In the later case, $BoundedBases$ will also be renewed($Line\ 23$) and new poten-tial characters will be added to $ToDo$ via a call to Algorithm 4($Line\ 22$). The main loop goes until an annihilator in degree d of f or $f + 1$ is found. Then we have $AI(f) = d$, and the computation ends after all other (linearly independent) annihilators in degree d are found($Line\ 9\text{-}10$).

Proposition 6. *After dealing with σ_{todo}, the value of BoundedBases is bounded bases of $\langle f \rangle_{\leq \sigma_{todo}}$.*

Proof. Before dealing with σ_{todo}, the value of $BoundedBases$ is supposed to be bounded bases of $\langle f \rangle_{<\sigma_{todo}}$. If $\sigma_{todo} \notin \mathcal{S}_f^\star$, $BoundedBases$ is also bounded bases of $\langle f \rangle_{\leq \sigma_{todo}}$. Or if $\sigma_{todo} \in \mathcal{S}_f^\star$, the correctness of Algorithm 2 guarantees a cor-responding (σ_{todo}, c, p) will be added to $BoundedBases$. □

Corollary 5. *That makes the proof of the correctness of Algorithm 3.* □

Finally, algorithm 4 predicts potential characters or zero characters in future with Proposition 5.

Algorithm 3. Main

Input: $f \in \mathcal{R}^*$.
Output: $AI(f)$, (the maximum linearly independent subset of) $An^*(f)$ and $An^*(f+1)$.

1   AlgebraicImmunity $:= deg(f)$
2   Annihilators$_1$ $:= \Phi$
3   BoundedBases $:= \Phi$
4   ToDo $:=$ **PotentialCriticalCharacters**$((1, 1, f),$ BoundedBases$)$
5   **append** $(1, 1, f)$ **to** BoundedBases
6   **while** ToDo $\neq \Phi$ **do**
7      $\sigma_{todo} := \min(\text{ToDo})$
8   ToDo $:=$ ToDo $\setminus \{\sigma_{todo}\}$
9   **if** $deg(\sigma_{todo}) >$ AlgebraicImmunity **then**
10   **break**
11   NewBasis $:=$ **Gen**$(\sigma_{todo}, f,$ BoundedBases$)$
12   **if** NewBasis $= \Phi$ **then**
13   **continue**
14      $(\sigma, c, p) :=$ NewBasis
15   **if** $p = 0$ **then**
16   **if** AlgebraicImmunity $> deg(\sigma_{todo})$ **then**
17   AlgebraicImmunity $:= deg(\sigma_{todo})$
18   **append** c **to** Annihilators$_1$
19   **else**
20   **if** AlgebraicImmunity $> deg(p)$ **then**
21   AlgebraicImmunity $:= deg(p)$
22   ToDo $:=$ ToDo $\cup$ **PotentialCriticalCharacters**$((\sigma, c, p),$ BoundedBases$)$
23   **append** (σ, c, p) **to** BoundedBases
24   Annihilators$_2$ $:= \{ p : (\sigma, c, p) \in$ BoundedBases, $deg(p) :=$ AlgebraicImmunity $\}$
25   **return** AlgebraicImmunity, Annihilators$_1$, Annihilators$_2$

Algorithm 4. PotentialCriticalCharacters

Input: $(\sigma_1, c_1, g_1) \in (\mathcal{T}, \mathcal{R}, \mathcal{R})$, BoundedBases: bouned bases of $\langle f \rangle_{<\sigma}$.
Output: potential critical or zero characters (σ_1, c_1, g_1) brings.

1   ToDo $:= \Phi$
2   **foreach** $(\sigma_2, c_2, g_2) \in$ BoundedBases **do**
3      $\mu_i := \dfrac{lcm(lt(g_1), lt(g_2))}{lt(g_i)}$ for $i=1,2$
4   **if** **coprime**(μ_1, σ_1) and **coprime**(μ_2, σ_2) and $\mu_1 \cdot \sigma_1 \neq \mu_2 \cdot \sigma_2$ **then**
5   ToDo $:=$ ToDo $\cup \{ \max(\mu_1 \cdot \sigma_1, \mu_2 \cdot \sigma_2) \}$
6   **foreach** variable $x \in lt(g_1)$ and $x \notin \sigma_1$ **do**
7   ToDo $:=$ ToDo $\cup \{x \cdot \sigma_1\}$
8   **return** ToDo

Proposition 7. *Characters returned by Algorithm 4 are always larger than σ_1.*

Proof. Firstly, since $x \notin \sigma_1$, $x \cdot \sigma_1$ added to *ToDo* in *Line 7* is obviously larger than σ_1. And then since $\mu_1 \cdot \sigma_1 \geq \sigma_1$, the characters added to *ToDo* in *Line 5* at least can not be smaller than σ_1. Assuming $\mu_1 \cdot \sigma_1 = \sigma_1$ and $\mu_1 \cdot \sigma_1 > \mu_2 \cdot \sigma_2$, since μ_1 and σ_1 are coprime, we have $\mu_1 = 1$. And since $lt(\mu_2 \cdot g_2) = \mu_2 \cdot lt(g_2) = \mu_1 \cdot lt(g_1) = lt(g_1)$, we have $ch_f(lt(g_1)) \leq \mu_2 \cdot \sigma_2 < \mu_1 \cdot \sigma_1 = \sigma_1$. there is a contradiction with $ch_f(lt(g_1)) = \sigma_1$ by the correctness of Algorithm 2. Therefore we have either $\mu_1 \cdot \sigma_1 > \sigma_1$ or $\mu_2 \cdot \sigma_2 > \mu_1 \cdot \sigma_1 \geq \sigma_1$ and finally $\max(\mu_1 \cdot \sigma_1, \mu_2 \cdot \sigma_2) > \sigma_1$. □

Corollary 6. *That makes the proof of the termination of Algorithm 3.* □

6   Complexity Issues and Benchmarks

As mentioned before, there are $k_{n,d}$ different characters within degree d *w.r.t.* f. By the algorithm in Section 5, all these characters can be classified into three categories: firstly, if a character σ is not predicted by Algorithm 4 in the entire process(type I), obviously it brings no time cost; secondly, if σ is predicted, but later confirmed to be neither a critical character nor a zero character(type II), it is immediately discarded in Algorithm 2 and the time cost is trivial; finally, if $\sigma \in \mathcal{S}_f^+$ or $\sigma \in \mathcal{S}_f^\star$(type III), Algorithm 2 needs to try computing $gen_f(\sigma)$ in a costly loop, which is the main time cost of our algorithm.

We define the new parameter $k'_{f,d}$ as follows,

$$k'_{f,d} = |\{\sigma \ : \ \sigma \in \mathcal{S}_f^\star \cup \mathcal{S}_f^0, deg(\sigma) \leq d\}|, \ d \leq AI(f).$$

Then the time complexity of our algorithm relies on $k'_{f,d}$ instead of $k_{n,d}$. Meanwhile, the space requirement of our algorithm mainly comes from *BoundedBases*, and the number of polynomials in it equals to the number of critical characters within degree d, which is roughly (slightly smaller than) $k'_{f,d}$. Therefore, the time and space complexity of our algorithm are both based on $k'_{f,d}$, and the superiority of our algorithm is determined by the difference in value of $k'_{f,d}$ and $k_{n,d}$. We have implemented our algorithm in C++. And the values of $k'_{f,d}$ for various polynomials are collected in a series of experiments. Firstly, as an example, Table 1 shows the result for $f_{toyo}(\alpha_i = 125 - i)$.

As shown here, for $d = 3$, we need to check only 1,067 instead of all 349,633 possibilities. Running on a Pentium Core 2 Duo at 2.4G, the computation ends in less than 2 seconds after all the four annihilators in degree 3 are discovered.

Table 1. $k'_{f,d}$ v.s. $k_{n,d}(f_{toyo})$

d	$k_{n,d}$	type I	type II	type III($k'_{f,d}$)	$k'_{f,d}/k_{n,d}$
1	129	65	0	64	49.6%
2	8,257	7,379	437	441	5.3%
3	349,633	347,904	662	1,067	0.3%

Table 2. $k'_{f,d}$(in average) vs. $k_{n,d}$ (random sparse polynomials)

n	$d = 3$		$d = 4$		$d = 5$	
	$k_{n,d}$	$k'_{f,d}(\approx)$	$k_{n,d}$	$k'_{f,d}(\approx)$	$k_{n,d}$	$k'_{f,d}(\approx)$
20	1,351	**470**	6,196	**1,400**	21,700	**3,300**
32	5,489	**620**	41,449	**2,100**	242,825	**4,000**
64	43,745	**840**	679,121	**2,600**	$\sim 10^7$	**4,300**
128	349,633	**870**	$\sim 10^7$	**2,700**	$\sim 10^8$	**4,500**
256	$\sim 10^6$	**920**	$\sim 10^8$	**3,100**	$\sim 10^9$	**5,700**

Table 3. Performance on random sparse polynomials

n	$d = 3$	$d = 4$	$d = 5$
20	**1s**, 2MB	**5s**, 10MB	**18s**, 35MB
32	**2s**, 4MB	**6s**, 13MB	**28s**, 46MB
64	**2s**, 5MB	**8s**, 28MB	**33s**, 84MB
128	**2s**, 10MB	**15s**, 59MB	**40s**, 144MB
256	**3s**, 19MB	**23s**, 140MB	**84s**, 430MB

And we test our implementation on random (balanced) sparse polynomials. Finally we have $k'_{f,d} \ll k_{n,d}$ in general cases as shown in Table 2, while the performance is given in Table 3.

7 Conclusion

In this paper, we propose a new algorithm for computing low degree annihilators. It is very efficient for sparse Boolean polynomials with a large number of variables. Our experiments show that, in this specified case, the new algorithm performs significantly better than existing methods. And even for polynomials with as many as 256 variables, all low degree annihilators can be found in only a few minutes.

Acknowledgement

We thank anonymous reviewers for their encouragement and valuable comments.

References

1. Courtois, N.T., Pieprzyk, J.: Cryptanalysis of block ciphers with overdefined systems of equations. In: Zheng, Y. (ed.) ASIACRYPT 2002. LNCS, vol. 2501, pp. 267–287. Springer, Heidelberg (2002)
2. Courtois, N.: Fast algebraic attacks on stream ciphers with linear feedback. In: Boneh, D. (ed.) CRYPTO 2003. LNCS, vol. 2729, pp. 176–194. Springer, Heidelberg (2003)
3. Courtois, N., Meier, W.: Algebraic attacks on stream ciphers with linear feedback. In: Biham, E. (ed.) EUROCRYPT 2003. LNCS, vol. 2656, pp. 346–359. Springer, Heidelberg (2003)

4. Faugère, J.C., Joux, A.: Algebraic cryptanalysis of hidden field equation (HFE) cryptosystems using Gröbner bases. In: Boneh, D. (ed.) CRYPTO 2003. LNCS, vol. 2729, pp. 44–60. Springer, Heidelberg (2003)
5. Meier, W., Pasalic, E., Carlet, C.: Algebraic attacks and decomposition of boolean functions. In: Cachin, C., Camenisch, J.L. (eds.) EUROCRYPT 2004. LNCS, vol. 3027, pp. 474–491. Springer, Heidelberg (2004)
6. Armknecht, F., Cayrel, P.L., Gaborit, P., Ruatta, O.: Improved algorithm to find equations for algebraic attacks for combiners with memory. In: Third International Workshop on Boolean Functions: Cryptography and Applications, Proceedings of BFCA, pp. 81–98 (2007)
7. Armknecht, F., Carlet, C., Gaborit, P., Kunzli, S., Meier, W., Ruatta, O.: Efficient computation of algebraic immunity for algebraic and fast algebraic attacks. In: Vaudenay, S. (ed.) EUROCRYPT 2006. LNCS, vol. 4004, pp. 147–164. Springer, Heidelberg (2006)
8. Didier, F., Tillich, J.P.: Computing the algebraic immunity efficiently. In: Robshaw, M.J.B. (ed.) FSE 2006. LNCS, vol. 4047, pp. 359–374. Springer, Heidelberg (2006)
9. Faugère, J.C.: A new efficient algorithm for computing Gröbner bases without reduction to zero(F5). In: Proceedings of the 2002 international symposium on Symbolic and algebraic computation, pp. 75–83 (2002)
10. Stegers, T., Buchmann, J.: Faugere's F5 algorithm revisited. Thesis for Diplom-Mathematiker (2005)
11. Faugère, J.C., Ars, G.: An algebraic cryptanalysis of nonlinear filter generators using Gröbner bases. Rapport de Recherche INRIA, 4739 (2003)
12. Becker, T., Weispfenning, V., Kredel, H.: Gröbner Bases: a computational approach to commutative algebra. Springer, Heidelberg (1991)

Host-Based Security Sensor Integrity in Multiprocessing Environments

Thomas Richard McEvoy[1] and Stephen D. Wolthusen[1,2]

[1] Information Security Group, Department of Mathematics, Royal Holloway,
University of London, Egham Hill, Egham TW20 0EX, UK
[2] Norwegian Information Security Laboratory, Gjøvik University College,
P.O. Box 191, N-2802 Gjøvik, Norway

Abstract. Attack and intrusion detection on host systems is both a last
line of defence and provides substantially more detail than other sensor
types. However, any host-based sensor is likely to be a primary target
for adversaries to ensure concealment and evasion of defensive measures.
In this paper we therefore propose a *novel defence mechanism for host-
based sensors* utilising *true concurrent observation of state* at key locations of operating systems and security controls, *including a self-defence
mechanism*. This is facilitated by the ready availability of multi-core and
multi-processor systems in symmetric and non-uniform architectures for
general-purpose computers.

This obviates the need for specialised hardware components or overhead imposed by virtualisation approaches and has the added advantage
of becoming increasingly difficult to foil as the number of concurrent observation threads increases whilst being highly scalable itself. We describe
a formal model of this *observation* and *self-observation mechanism*. The
analysis of the observations is supported by a causal model, which we describe briefly. Using causal models enables us to detect complex attacks
using dynamic obfuscation as it relies on higher-order semantics and also
allows the system to deal with non-linearity in memory writes which is
characteristic of multiprocessing systems. We conclude with a brief description of experimental validation, demonstrating both high, adaptable
performance and the ability to detect attacks on the mechanism itself.

1 Introduction

Skilled and knowledgeable attackers implement deception techniques post in-
cursion with great rapidity, targeting state reporting and intrusion detection
mechanisms, leading to a strong requirement to assure their functionality.

Techniques for achieving concealment have evolved primarily in response
to improved detection techniques. Initially, subversion and concealment was
achieved in user space by subverting key executables. Now, in general, attacks
are implemented by inserting malicious code or by violating data structure integrity [1,2] in kernel space. In addition, recent "proof of concept" attacks have
included the use of off-CPU processing and virtualisation techniques [3,4,5].

J. Kwak et al. (Eds.): ISPEC 2010, LNCS 6047, pp. 138–152, 2010.

These also implicate operating system structures, albeit at low-level. Therefore, at least initially, detection attempts should concentrate on determining the integrity of operating system structures and relevant third party security applications as its loss constitutes clear evidence of intrusion [6]. The increase in the sophistication of attacker methods creates a requirement for considerable knowledge of kernel states to uncover any attempts. At the same time, the threat of attack on auditing mechanisms has led to attempts to conceal the presence of those mechanisms by isolating them the system and hence from direct attack [7,8]. This approach of "security by obscurity" often leads to a loss of granularity w.r.t system states. It also creates considerable computational overheads to re-create such states. Furthermore, such methods do not take into account the requirement to assure the integrity of the detection mechanism itself.

Here, we propose to address these problems by taking advantage of multiprocessing (including multi-core) capabilities, which we instantiate for the case of operating systems. Using *lossless, asynchronous communication channels in shared memory*, each sensor (or observer thread) – belonging to a designated group – may measure and exchange data regarding key features with other sensors. Any inconsistencies between observations will be registered initially as transitions in state. As can be seen easily, any subversion attempt will be *non-atomic* in nature, so that the **forced linearisation of observations and attacker actions** on being written to shared memory means that illegitimate states will be readily detected by such an approach owing to **probabilistic interleaving of operations**. The observation strategy represents an important extension of a technique of Wang *et al.* [9] by adding the ability to take snapshots of different levels of abstraction and different subsystems concurrently to uncover operating system and application inconsistencies.

This has the following advantages over the state of the art: First, it may be implemented natively to its environment and does not require hardware modifications to host systems to implement or reside as an external VMM. Second, it consists of multiple, concurrent observation threads (taking advantage of the inexpensive processing power of multi-core and multi-processor platforms) making it difficult to achieve a total subversion of its function in less than detection time even for a small number of concurrent observers. Third, it is capable of self-observation, ensuring its own resilience using the same approach. Finally, as both individual processing steps and the serialisation of memory access is very difficult to determine, this element of stochastic behaviour results in additional difficulty for adversaries. We note that the usefulness of this approach may be limited on small-scale multiprocessing platforms due to natural performance constraints, but on larger-scale platforms (e.g. with more than 8 concurrent processing units) offers a computationally inexpensive means of detecting operating state inconsistencies.

The remainder of this paper is structured as follows: In section 2, we discuss related work on subversion detection in operating systems while in section 3, we describe the problems posed by subversion and concealment, particularly on modern operating systems. In section 4, we outline our approach to detection followed by a more formal description and model in section 5. Experiments and results are then described in section 6 followed by a concluding discussion and outline of future work in section 7.

2   Related Work

The initial evolution of subversion and concealment methods can be followed in [1,6]. More subtle and complex approaches have developed recently [2,3,4,5]. Concealment renders the symptoms of attack transient in nature making them difficult to detect by sampling methods such as those demonstrated by Petroni [10]. Attacks of this type show the limitations of static approaches, e.g. w.r.t attempts at removing obfuscation [11]. We argue that such attacks follow a predictable pattern post-intrusion targeting known security mechanisms [6] and key data structures and processes [12]. Even attacks which have novel features will likely incorporate previous tactics [13]. Therefore, we may anticipate, at least partially, the action of *even novel* attacks. This analysis represents a primary area of interest owing to the potential for damage [14].

Approaches to defending security mechanisms have in general concentrated on creating distinct security domains within host systems by, for example, use of co-processors [8,15,16,17] or VMMs [7,18,19,20,21,10,22]. The advantages of such approaches are that they render the detection mechanism, in general, immune to tampering and may obfuscate their presence. Their disadvantages are that they may be unable to interpose themselves between the malicious process [15]. They place reliance on "security through obscurity" rather than integrity mechanisms and because they operate asynchronously, they suffer limitations in their ability to reconstruct kernel states, particularly in the face of non-linearity [23]. Moreover, they still do *not* direct efforts at assuring their own integrity.

Our detection strategy represents an important extension of techniques described by Wang *et al.* [9] and Loscocco *et al.* [24] where kernel states were checked for consistency at different APIs. We add additional checks between distinct kernel subsystems and use concurrency to catch even momentary inconsistencies in state transitions. Our technique is related to the use of multi-threaded techniques for integrity checking as exampled by Opplinger *et al.*, [25] and Nightingale *et al.* [26]. Such approaches lose the advantage of complete isolation from malicious software, but gain finer granularity of accessible operating system states. They are also able to interpose themselves between malicious software and its target.

The analysis of observations is based on extending previous work on the analysis of distributed processing based on best effort asynchronous communication channels [27]. A key part of this extension is the recognition that multiprocessor systems share some common features with distributed systems [28], in particular, that the forced linearization of processing states in shared memory results in a set of partial orders which to be understood must be analysed with regard to causality.

3   Problem

Attacks are inevitably accompanied by concealment and obfuscation strategies. Auditing, state reporting, intrusion detection and other security applications are a primary target of such attempts, both to avoid detection and as part of an anti-forensics strategy. Security and audit mechanisms do not, in general, direct efforts at ensuring their own integrity. Instead, *current architectures are based on the assumption of their own integrity* and concentrate on protecting the integrity of their mechanisms by wholly or partially isolating these from the environment and in some cases by relying on "security through obscurity". However, we must assume that a capable attacker will be knowledgeable of any detective mechanisms. Because the symptoms of attack may be distributed throughout the host system [2, 12], considerable domain knowledge is required to be able to analyse and uncover such attacks. A highly granular view of host operations is needed to achieve this. Difficulties are increased because memory management techniques in multiprocessing systems lead to non-linearity in state transitions.

Concealment is achieved using strategies (and consequently coding techniques) common to all attackers. Such techniques may be dynamic such as the use *polymorphism* and *metamorphism*, to bypass signature-based detection [29], [30]. Active attacks on audit systems may also create contradictory views of the global state of the operating system which exist concurrently. The attacker has a true view of the system state while defenders are presented with a benign face. This can affect both processing [1] and data structures [2]. Detecting these contradictions, after concealment techniques have been applied, represents a severe problem in commonly used computational models (see e.g. [31, 32]) as any illegitimate states are subsequently indistinguishable from legitimate ones. The level of difficulty is increased because multiprocessing operating systems are characterised by non-linearity – that is, computation on such systems must be regarded as a set of partial orders where memory management may force one of a set of potential linearisations on the outcome [23]. Various linearisations are possible. This renders naive attempts at heuristic analysis and sampling techniques ineffective, while dynamic obfuscation undermines the validity of signature based techniques. A semantic analysis based on cause and effect is hence required to uncover inconsistent linearisations.

We therefore propose an approach which is capable of detecting inconsistent states in such systems by *concurrently observing and comparing* results at different layers of abstraction and between distinct system mechanisms and data structures. This detection mechanism must then also be resilient to attacks and capable of assigning semantic meaning to operational states both with respect to obfuscation and concealment and the non-linearity of multiprocessor systems; this is achieved making deliberate use of shared memory access linearisations in the underlying hardware. Finally, to prevent the recursion of the initial problem, i.e. defending the integrity of security mechanisms, the mechanism must observe and validate its own states.

4   Approach

We assume that we are able to identify key operating system structures in relation to security and state reporting mechanisms which are probable targets of attacks; while this is non-trivial, the set of relevant states will typically be small and well-known. We further assume that we can express the behavior, including any causal interdependencies, of such structures using a set of suitable transition graphs [27]. This will enable the expression of a set of legitimate behaviors as a partial order with respect to causality using the "happened before" relation to establish logical time [28]. By subtraction, any other behaviors constitute a subset of anomalous partial orders which may represent novel attacks. We also assume that any subversion attempt will contain non-atomic sequences of operations, particularly altering state by way of more than a single memory access; these represent a transition period during which a set of illegitimate states will occur. Under concurrent observation, forced linearisations of such states with observations by a set of sensor processes will probabilistically enable (see Section 5) the detection of inconsistent transitions.

To achieve concurrent observation, we create a set of observer ensembles. Each ensemble represents a partition of observer processes which measure state for a given kernel feature and communicate their observations with other members of the ensemble. Any inconsistencies in measurement are logged. Such inconsistencies are assumed to be state transitions. These are analysed in real time against pertinent transition graphs, but can also be employed in other mechanisms. In this paper, we concentrate on describing the *observer mechanism* rather than the subsequent application of analytical techniques. Our approach anticipates the potential growth in scale of multiprocessing systems [33] and represents a computationally inexpensive approach to detection as observers may be distributed across multiple processing units. It also has defensive advantages compared to other approaches, as will be described in section 5.5.

5   Model

In the following, we provide a formal description of the mechanism's operation, its architecture and communication strategy. We also briefly outline the analysis technique and provide a probability model for its observational success and conclude with an outline of its defensive capability. We note that the model anticipates the use of this approach in large-scale systems and with complex process interactions. The experimental results we present seek to establish its feasibility as an approach, using some basic examples of concealment techniques (cf. 6) and demonstrate the positive scalability effects.

5.1   Observer Definition

We define a set of observers Ω. Each observer $O \in \Omega$ is an instance $O_{u,v,w}(m)$ where u is the observed (e.g. kernel) feature, v is the observation role, w is the instance of this function and $m \in M$ is a vector representing the measurement function and other role/task parameters e.g. processing unit assignments, number of instances to assign to this task, cpu assignation and so forth. Each observer $O \in \Omega$ uses algorithm 1 in its basic operation.

Intuitively, the observer takes a measurement and communicates its findings to all other **concurrent observers** assigned to the same observation role as itself, noting that such observers are to be distributed to as many independent processing units as are available. It receives observations for every corresponding observer and, after comparison, logs any inconsistencies in observation. Finally, it waits a random period up to a specified time limit before recurring.

Algorithm 1. OBSERVE($measure()$, $NTasks$, $Period$, $OwnId$)

```
 1: u = 0
 2: while continue() do
 3:     u = measure()
 4:     ...
 5:     send(i, OwnId)
 6:     for i = 0, i ≤ NTasks, i + + do
 7:         receive(w, JobId)
 8:         if u ≠ w then
 9:             ...
10:             log(u, w, OwnId, JobId)
11:         end if
12:     end for
13:     wait(Period − (Period modulus RandomNumber))
14: end while
```

It should be noted that **each observer is stateless**. This enables the system to scale well compared to potential future demands [33].

5.2   Messaging, Synchronisation and Time Keeping

For large scale multiprocessing systems, the utilisation of synchronisation primitives in shared memory for interprocess communication is unfeasible. Instead, we substitute a communication model analogous to a best effort asynchronous system which we simulate in shared memory.

Let $\mathcal{M}$ be the observer mechanism. $\mathcal{M}$ consists of a set of N processes $\{P_1, P_2, \ldots, P_N\}$ which are our observer threads and a set of unidirectional channels C. Each channel $c \in C$ connects two processes. We can view the topology of the resulting system as a directed graph in which the vertices represent the processes and the edges represent the channels. A bi-directional channel may be represented as two unidirectional edges [28].

We divide $\mathcal{M}$ into partitions of observers (ensembles) which are linked by bi-directional channels. Let $\overrightarrow{G} = V(E)$ be a graph. Let V be an ensemble of observers. Let E be the set of channels of V. Let $\overrightarrow{G}$ be a complete graph $\overrightarrow{K}$ connected by bi-directional channels.

The implementation of this messaging architecture enables the use of well-known algorithms for "weakly" synchronizing process action, keeping logical time and taking global snapshots in state [28, 27]. These may be realised by additional coding to the basic algorithm 1 as required.

5.3 Dataset Analysis

During observation, any inconsistency in measured states results in a log being created. Let O_i and O_j be two communicating observers whose states differ during a single round of observation, then $V_{o_i,o_j} = \{(o_i, o_j), (o_j, o_i)\}$ is a vector which results from their comparison of states. In fact, V_{o_i,o_j} consists of two ordered pairs of observations from each observer O_i and O_j of their observed and received values.

Let V_O and W_O be the set of all such vectors which results from two distinct rounds of observation. If we know the initial state, say S, of the operating system characteristic under observation, then V_O and U_O should provide us with sufficient knowledge to determine a set of partial orders $(S', \rightsquigarrow)$ resulting from S which are the set of reported transitions in state, eliminating any repeated 2-tuples. We can compare this set of transitions with the expected behavior of the system in state S [27] to determine the existence of any anomalous states. Analysis is cumulative. We may miss some observations – see 5.4 – but can provide a probability distribution over a current set of linearisations.

We note that this form of analysis also enables us to deal with the non-linear presentation of computational states in the face of dynamic obfuscation techniques such as polymorphism and metamorphism as it addresses process semantics rather than specific signatures or anomalies.

5.4 Observational Probabilities

For the lossless asynchronous messaging architecture we describe, the probability of observing a single transition is given. Let L be the length of an observation round. Assume a transition event occurs at some point during L. Observer threads may take a measurement at any time during L **where the linearisation of transition and observation is non-deterministic** owing to both randomness in processing units and memory access sequencing. Let p be the probability of observing before the transition event T. Let q be the probability of observing after the transition event T. Then the probability of detecting $P(T)$ is the same as the probability of at least one observation event occurring before T and at least one observation event occuring after T. Let n be the number of observer threads. It follows that $P(T) = 1 - (p^n + q^n)$ – that is, T is not observed if all state measurements take place either before or after T.

Given a transition between a legitimate and an illegitimate state, which will subsequently be reversed to give the appearance of legitimacy, what is the probability of detecting the malicious state? In fact, by letting q be the probability of an observer taking a measurement during an illegitimate transition in state and p be the probability of observing any legitimate state, we see that the same binomial distribution applies. It follows that the probability of observing any transition in state will in general increase as the number of concurrent observers. For large scale multiprocessing systems, this probability may be rendered arbitrarily high.

However, *such arbitrary increases in the probability of success are unlikely to be achievable on small scale systems* as constraints are naturally introduced for such systems where process scheduling overheads rapidly come to dominate. This observation technique is, therefore, primarily designed for observations of state in a host system with larger numbers of independent processing units (hyperthreading, dies, cores). On smaller platforms, optimum detection rates will be a trade-off between the frequency of observation rounds and the efficiency of the observational functions, suggesting that observations for a given frequency will rise to a maximum and then either stabilise or fall away.

Finally, *observational probabilities should not be confused with detection probabilities*. The results of observation are cumulative over several rounds, leading up to a detection event. Detection probabilities are therefore much higher and, as a result of deductive and inductive reasoning over observations, detection can take place even in the presence of missing observations, although confidence levels in the results will be lowered.

5.5 Resilience to Attack

We show that the multiplicity of observers and the multiplicity of communication channels results in raising the barrier to subversion of the mechanism. This primary advantage is underpinned by the ability to self-observe.

Let n be the minimum number of observers per ensemble and N be the number of processors. Let $n > N$. It follows, assuming that the subversion of each observer is non-trivial, that an adversary has insufficient computational capability to simultaneously undermine the observers belonging to any ensemble in the mechanism i.e. assuming the adversary commandeers N processors, the condition that N is strictly less than n prevents their concurrent subversion.

Let O be an observer ensemble. Let $o_1, o_2, \ldots, o_n \in O$ be observers. Each observer o_i communicates its findings with every other observer o_j. Let $|O| = n$. There exist $n(n - 1)$ ordered pairs of data readings. Any alteration of an already observed value during a round will instantly reveal subversive activity. The attacker must successfully subvert $n(n - 1)$ individual channels to control the outcome for a single ensemble. Clearly, we present the attacker with a combinatorial barrier to subversion. The ability of the mechanism to self observe arises because it is possible to assign a set of independent observers to functions in relation to this task. This underpins the advantages bestowed by self validation by providing further integrity checks.

6   Experimental Results

We implemented a basic version of the proposed mechanism as a loadable kernel module in Linux on a VMware platform on a 2-core Intel system. We used basic concealment techniques to evaluate functionality [1, 34]. In particular, we were interested in demonstrating: First, that it could implement concurrent observations of different APIs within the operating system. Second, that it could observe distinct, but related, kernel features concurrently. Third, that it was capable of self observation. We also wished to establish that we could arbitrarily raise the probability of observation by increasing the number of observers up to natural performance constraints (due to the limited nature of the platform). The cumulative nature of observations subsequently raises the probability of detection. In particular, the concurrent observation of distinct, but related, kernel features enables this potential.

6.1   Cross-Sectional Observation

In a cross-sectional view of operating states, we examine observations of semantically related values at different APIs and compare results.

We selected the virtual file system as an example of a kernel subsystem which consists of several layers of abstraction. A classic attack is to "hook" the system call table functions which invoke kernel functionality in this area to selectively hide static file structures. A more sophisticated attack at a lower level of abstraction – demonstrated by e.g. the *adore_ng* rootkit – is to subvert the function pointers for the *readdir()* function, leaving the system table unaltered.

We created 3 observer ensembles, which used "clean" copies of kernel code to measure root directory size at 3 different APIs, including the system call table, *getdents64()* and *readdir()* functions. We could increase the numbers of observers in each ensemble and also vary the period of time between observation rounds.

In an initial trial, we subverted the system call table. This resulted in immediate and ongoing reporting of inconsistencies, showing that where a lower level API which retained integrity was compared with a subverted higher one, the anomaly is invariably detectable.

Subsequently, we selected to subvert the `readdir()` function to hide a randomly named file in the root directory[1]. The simulated attack created and then hid the file such that any subversion would cause a momentary transition in root directory size, but would not be detectable thereafter. 100 transitions were observed per trial. For measuring a single characteristic, we took as our hypothesis that observation rates greater than 65% would be acceptable *given likely constraints on performance* – see 5.4. Figure 1 shows the results.

These results show that it is possible to achieve a satisfactory observational probability for observing transitions in values between lower and higher level APIs and detecting any inconsistencies.

---

[1] This feature is common to several attacks.

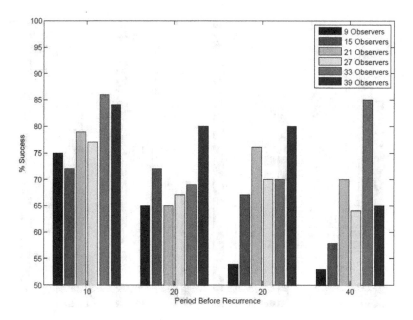

Fig. 1. Observations of Root Directory Size at Distinct APIs

6.2   Cross-System Observation

The second experiment represented an extension of the first in which we considered other related kernel features which might be implicated in a concealment attack but not necessarily belong to the same kernel subsystem. This experiment is, in miniature, a trial in raising detection probabilities through cumulative observations.

We added additional observer ensembles to measure the integrity of the system call table used hashed values for comparison and also checked the read/write permission flag for the table (which has to be altered to change the table).

For this experiment, we simulated a more complete attack where more than one kernel substructure (i.e. the system call table, its read/write flag and the `readdir()` functionality) might be altered and subsequently the alteration reversed. Each trail consisted of 100 transitions of the LKM simulating attacker actions by first altering and then reversing the alteration to these structures. We recorded a successful *detection* if 2 out of 3 of the characteristics were observed in transition. It should be noted that additional opportunities were provided to observe the attack because the reversal of the system call table and read/write flags was obvious to the mechanism. This is a characteristic of some concealment techniques that we can happily take advantage of. We set the target for success higher at 90% as we were taking advantage of cumulative observational probabilities. The results are shown in Figure 2.

These results demonstrate how cumulative observations from distinct observer groups result in acceptably high levels of detection. Here it is much clearer that

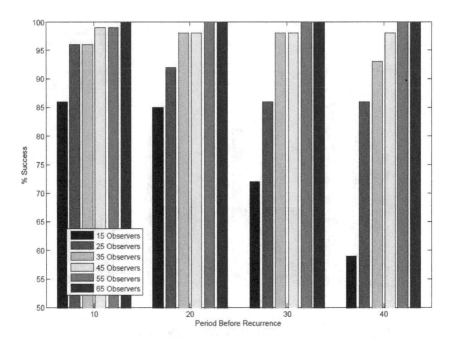

Fig. 2. Comparing the Consistency of Related Kernel Features

increasing the number of observers is the dominant strategy for increasing the probability of detection. These results show that we can concurrently measure semantically related kernel structures and underscore the high cumulative probability of detecting anomalous transitions.

6.3   Self-observation

In the final experiment, we evaluated the ability of the mechanism to self-observe. A LKM was created to delete observer threads in groups and replace them with inert threads. 100 observer threads were instantiated as "sacrifical victims" in addition to an ensemble of threads for self-observation. Observer threads measured a hash of the mechanism's process PIDS. Acceptable rates of observation were set as before at 65% for the measurement of a single characteristic, given potential performance constraints. Several trials were undertaken. The results are shown in Figure 3.

These results clearly demonstrate the effectiveness of self-observation. However, we also see scheduling constraints causing observational values to peak and then fall off for increasing numbers of observer threads with a clear relation to the period allowed for observation – see section 5.4 for an explanation. This is a predictable result, which would not be encountered on larger-scale platforms (e.g. with 8 or more cores).

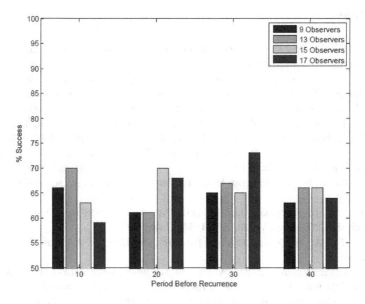

Fig. 3. Self Observation - Measuring Process PID Consistency

7   Conclusions and Future Work

In this paper, we have presented a novel mechanism for observing transitions the key characteristics of state reporting mechanisms and third-party security applications in order to assure their integrity. We use multiple observers to compare and log any inconsistencies in observed characteristics. We demonstrated the feasibility of the approach, using basic examples of concealment techniques, and provided a model for detection probabilities. We also outlined, *for more complex interactions*, how the data set may subsequently be analysed (including interactions with other key features), using techniques originally developed for distributed processing systems [27].

The mechanism is intended to be utilised on larger scale multiprocessor hosts [2] such as are anticipated in future [33] to assure the integrity of on state reporting, audit and security mechanisms and add confidence to detection efforts and also to post incident forensics analysis.

Future work divides into three areas: First, to implement the tool on larger scale platforms to determine performance characteristics; Second, to develop functionality in relation to specific state reporting mechanisms and security applications. Third, we see a potential in developing the approach in relation to other features common to modern hosts such as 'off CPU' processing centers, where an interaction between observers in off CPU processing centres and in operating system structures could have the potential to defeat modern approaches to concealing subversion attempts such as in [3, 4, 5].

---

[2] Results on small scale platforms are inevitably limited.

References

1. Hoglund, G., Butler, J.: Rootkits: Subverting the Windows Kernel. Addison-Wesley Professional, Reading (2005)
2. Petroni, N.L., Fraser, T., Walters, A., Arbaugh, W.A.: An Architecture for Specification-Based Detection of Semantic Integrity Violations in Kernel Dynamic Data. In: Proceedings of the 15th USENIX Security Symposium (2006)
3. King, S.T., Chen, P.M., Wang, Y.-M., Verbowski, C., Wang, H.J., Lorch, J.R.: SubVirt: Implementing malware with virtual machines. In: 2006 IEEE Symposium on Security and Privacy (S&P 2006), vol. 0, pp. 314–327. IEEE Computer Society, Los Alamitos (2006)
4. Rutkowska, J.: Beyond the cpu: Defeating hardware based ram acquisition. Defcon (2007)
5. Heasman, J.: Implementing and Detecting an ACPI BIOS Root Kit. In: Briefing at Black Hat 2005, Las Vegas, NV, USA (July 2005)
6. Szor, P.: The Art of Computer Virus Research and Defense. Addison-Wesley, Reading (2005)
7. Garfinkel, T., Rosenblum, M.: A Virtual Machine Introspection Based Architecture for Intrusion Detection. In: Proceedings of the 10th Annual Network And Distributed System Security Symposium (NDSS 2003), Internet Society, San Diego (2003)
8. Yee, B., Tygar, J.D.: Secure Coprocessors in Electronic Commerce Applications. In: Geer, D.E. (ed.) Proceedings of the First USENIX Workshop on Electronic Commerce, p. 14. USENIX Press, New York (1995)
9. Wang, Y.-M., Beck, D., Vo, B., Roussev, R., Verbowski, C.: Detecting Stealth Software with Strider GhostBuster. In: 2005 International Conference on Dependable Systems and Networks (DSN 2005), pp. 368–377. IEEE Computer Society, Los Alamitos (2005)
10. Petroni Jr., N.L., Hicks, M.: Automated Detection of Persistent Kernel Control-Flow Attacks. In: di Vimercati, S.D.C., Syverson, P. (eds.) Proceedings of the 14th ACM Conference on Computer and Communications Security (CCS 2007), pp. 103–115. ACM Press, New York (2007)
11. Christodorescu, M., Jha, S., Seshia, S.A., Song, D., Bryant, R.E.: Semantics-Aware Malware Detection. In: Proceedings of the 2005 IEEE Symposium on Security and Privacy (S&P 2005), pp. 32–46. IEEE Press, Piscataway (2005)
12. Baliga, A., Kamat, P., Iftode, L.: Lurking in the Shadows: Identifying Systemic Threats to Kernel Data. In: Proceedings of the 2007 IEEE Symposium on Security and Privacy (S&P 2007), pp. 246–251. IEEE Press, Piscataway (2007)
13. Chuvakin, A.: An overview of unix rootkits. White Paper, iDefense Laboratories, iDefence Inc., 14151 Newbrook Suite, Chantilly, VA 20151 (2003)
14. Wilhelm, J., cker Chiueh, T.: A Forced Sampled Execution Approach to Kernel Rootkit Identification. In: Kruegel, C., Lippmann, R., Clark, A. (eds.) RAID 2007. LNCS, vol. 4637, pp. 219–235. Springer, Heidelberg (2007)
15. Zhang, X., van Doorn, L., Jaeger, T., Perez, R., Sailer, R.: Secure Coprocessor-Based Intrusion Detection. In: Muller, G., Jul, E. (eds.) Proceedings of the 10th ACM SIGOPS European Workshop, pp. 239–242. ACM Press, New York (2002)
16. Molina, J., Arbaugh, W.: Using Independent Auditors as Intrusion Detection Systems. In: Deng, R.H., Qing, S., Bao, F., Zhou, J. (eds.) ICICS 2002. LNCS, vol. 2513, pp. 291–302. Springer, Heidelberg (2002)

17. Williams, P.D., Spafford, E.H.: CuPIDS: An Exploration of Highly Focused, Co-Processor-based Information System Protection. Computer Networks 51(5), 1284–1298 (2007)

18. Riley, R., Jiang, X., Xu, D.: Guest-Transparent Prevention of Kernel Rootkits with VMM-Based Memory Shadowing. In: Lippmann, R., Kirda, E., Trachtenberg, A. (eds.) RAID 2008. LNCS, vol. 5230, pp. 1–20. Springer, Heidelberg (2008)

19. Dinaburg, A., Royal, P., Sharif, M., Lee, W.: Ether: Malware Analysis via Hardware Virtualization Extensions. In: Ning, P., Syverson, P., Jha, S. (eds.) Proceedings of the 15th ACM Conference on Computer and Communications Security (CCS 2008), pp. 51–62. ACM Press, New York (2008)

20. Huang, Y., Stavrou, A., Ghosh, A.K., Jajodia, S.: Efficiently Tracking Application Interactions using Lightweight Virtualization. In: Nieh, J., Stavrou, A. (eds.) Proceedings of the 1st ACM Workshop on Virtual Machine Security (VMSec 2008), pp. 19–28. ACM Press, New York (2008)

21. Jiang, X., Wang, X., Xu, D.: Stealthy Malware Detection through VMM-based "out-of-the-box" Semantic View Reconstruction. In: De Capitani di Vimercati, S., Syverson, P. (eds.) Proceedings of the 14th ACM Conference on Computer and Communications Security (CCS 2007), pp. 128–138. ACM Press, New York (2007)

22. Riley, R., Jiang, X., Xu, D.: Multi-Aspect Profiling of Kernel Rootkit Behavior. In: Proceedings of the 4th ACM European Conference on Computer Systems, pp. 47–69. ACM Press, Nuremberg (2008)

23. Thober, M., Pendergrass, J.A., McDonell, C.D.: Improving Coherency of Runtime Integrity Measurement. In: Proceedings of the 3rd ACM Workshop on Scalable Trusted Computing, pp. 51–60. ACM Press, Alexandria (2008)

24. Loscocco, P., Wilson, P.W., Pendergrass, J.A., McDonell, C.D.: Linux Kernel Integrity Measurement using Contextual Inspection. In: Proceedings of the 2007 ACM Workshop on Scalable Trusted Computing, pp. 21–29. ACM Press, Alexandria (2007)

25. Oplinger, J., Lam, M.S.: Enhancing Software Reliability with Speculative Threads. In: Gharachorloo, K. (ed.) Proceedings of the 10th International Conference on Architectural Support for Programming Languages and Operating Systems (ASPLOS XIII), pp. 184–196. ACM Press, New York (2002)

26. Nightingale, E.B., Peek, D., Chen, P.M., Flinn, J.: Parallelizing Security Checks on Commodity Hardware. In: Eggers, S., Larus, J. (eds.) Proceedings of the 13th International Conference on Architectural Support for Programming Languages and Operating Systems (ASPLOS XIII), pp. 308–318. ACM Press, New York (2008)

27. for review), A (Anonymised for review). In (Anonymised for review) (September 2008)

28. Garg, V.K.: 1. In: Elements of Distributed Computing. John Wiley and Sons Inc., Chichester (2002)

29. Moser, A., Kruegel, C., Kirda, E.: Exploring multiple execution paths for malware analysis. In: IEEE Symposium on Security and Privacy, vol. 0, pp. 231–245 (2007)

30. Ring, S., Cole, E.: Taking a Lesson from Stealthy Rootkits. IEEE Security and Privacy 02(4), 38–45 (2004)

31. Moser, A., Kruegel, C., Kirda, E.: Limits of Static Analysis for Malware Detection. In: Proceedings of the 23rd Annual Computer Security Applications Conference (ACSAC 2007), pp. 421–430. IEEE Press, Miami Beach (2007)

32. Cavallaro, L., Saxena, P., Sekar, R.: On the Limits of Information Flow Techniques for Malware Analysis and Containment. In: Zamboni, D. (ed.) DIMVA 2008. LNCS, vol. 5137, pp. 143–163. Springer, Heidelberg (2008)
33. Asanovic, K., Bodik, R., Catanzaro, B.C., Gebis, J.J., Husbands, P., Keutzer, K., Patterson, D.A., Plishker, W.L., Shalf, J., Williams, S.W., Yelick, K.A.: The landscape of parallel computing research: A view from berkeley. Technical Report UCB/EECS-2006-183, EECS Department, University of California, Berkeley (December 2006)
34. Ivan Sklyarov: 21. In: Programming Linux Hacker Tools Uncovered. A-LIST, LLC (2007)

Using Purpose Capturing Signatures to Defeat Computer Virus Mutating

Xiaoqi Jia[1,*], Xi Xiong[2], Jiwu Jing[1], and Peng Liu[2]

[1] The State Key Laboratory of Information Security,
Graduate University of Chinese Academy of Sciences, China
[2] The Pennsylvania State University, University Park, USA
{xjia,xxx111,pliu}@ist.psu.edu, jing@is.ac.cn

Abstract. Nowadays computer viruses become more and more difficult to be identified. Modern computer viruses use various mutation techniques such as polymorphism and metamorphism to evade detection. Previous researches in mutated computer virus detection have limitations in that: 1) most of them cannot handle advanced mutation techniques; 2) the methods based on source code analysis are less practical. 3) some methods are unable to detect computer viruses immediately. In this paper, we present a new dynamic approach to detect and analyze computer viruses based on Virtual Machine technology. We show that 1) how to generate *Purpose Capturing Signatures* based on the information of runtime values (*execution value sequence*, EVS) and control flows (*execution control sequence*, ECS); 2) how to detect and analyze computer viruses using the purpose-capturing signatures. To our best knowledge, it is the first method to perform computer virus detection and analysis using the EVS and ECS. Our experimental evaluation demonstrates that this approach is able to use one signature to detect all mutations of the corresponding virus efficiently.

Keywords: Computer Virus, Mutated Virus Detection.

1   Introduction

Nowadays computer viruses are more and more difficult to be identified. Most contemporary computer virus detectors are based on syntactic fingerprints to identify and prevent the execution of known computer viruses. However, modern virus writers use various mutation techniques such as polymorphism and metamorphism to evade detection. Virus writers can transform computer viruses in several ways [1,2,3,4,5,6,7,8]: 1) furnish the code to different forms, but keep the same semantic function; 2) pack the malicious payload using compression

* The work of Xiaoqi Jia and Peng Liu was supported by United States AFOSR FA9550-07-1-0527 (MURI), ARO MURI: Computer-aided Human Centric Cyber Situation Awareness, NSF CNS-0905131, and AFRL FA8750-08-C-0137. This work was also supported by National Natural Science Foundation of China under Grant No. 70890084/G021102.

J. Kwak et al. (Eds.): ISPEC 2010, LNCS 6047, pp. 153–171, 2010.

or encryption, leaving only the instructions to decrypt the payload in the code segment; 3) change the order of instructions which are included in the body of the virus; 4) "dillute" computer virus signatures by inserting nonessential instructions; 5) make the virus dynamically change itself upon each infection; 6) make the virus code dynamically disassemble, mutate and then reassemble itself while running.

Identifying virus mutations is a difficult task. To our best knowledge, no existing technology can automatically deal with mutated computer viruses well. Commercial anti-virus products usually suffer from the woe of "one fingerprint per virus mutation", which makes computers less secure due to inability to detect unknown mutations and the often seen delay in adopting anti-virus database updates. Mutation-insensitive signatures are highly desired but they often draw many false positives. Therefore, to defeat computer virus mutating, computer virus detectors and analyzers should satisfy three basic requirements as follows. R1) Resiliency to virus mutation techniques. As mentioned in [9,10,11,12,13,14], many if not most existing detectors and analyzers cannot handle mutations without new signatures. R2) No requirement for the source code of suspects. R3) Be able to detect computer viruses immediately. Some detectors or analyzers detect a computer virus after the damage has been caused.

In this paper, we present a new dynamic approach for mutation-resistant virus detection and analysis which satisfies all the above requirements. When observing various runtime behaviors of computer viruses based on the Virtual Machine technology, we find that some runtime values and control flow information of a computer virus cannot be mutated without changing the specific purpose of the virus. Based on this observation, we generate *Purpose Capturing Signatures* which consiste of uniquely defined *execution value sequence* (EVS) and *execution control sequence* (ECS). Our approach preserves the precision of signature-based detection while avoiding the woe of "one fingerprint per virus mutation". What sets our approach apart is the way it lets one to use one signature to accurately detect all mutations of the corresponding virus. By nature a signature-based approach, the rational of our approach is distinct from that of anomaly detection approaches. As a result, our approach does not suffer from the "high false positive rate" problem of anomaly detection techniques. Moreover, our approach is orthogonal to the approaches that use vulnerability signatures [15]. With a focus on the purpose of each virus, no vulnerability knowledge is used in our signature generation process.

Accordingly, our new anti-virus method consists of two key components: (1) a *generator* that automatically generates purpose-capturing signatures, and (2) a *matcher* that automatically matches a virus mutation against a purpose-capturing signature. Given a known virus in its original form or any known mutated form as input, the generator generates the corresponding purpose-capturing signature of this virus. This signature captures a set of unique runtime characteristics of the virus. Once the virus-like code of a suspect gets executed, The generator will "record" the corresponding execution sequence blocks of the suspect. The matcher uses a specific similarity measuring algorithm to compare

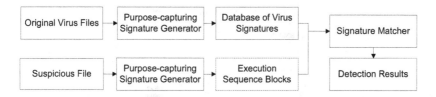

Fig. 1. Architecture of generating and usage of purpose-capturing signatures

the recorded execution sequence blocks with the purpose-capturing signatures of the known viruses. The comparison should result in alarms for virus mutations. According to our experiment results, even though a piece of malicious code is mutated, its purpose-capturing ECS and EVS still have high similarity with those generated from the original virus code in the same environment.

Our Contributions: We present a new computer virus detection and analysis technique based on VM analysis: C1) It detects the virus based on EVS and ECS. It is believed that this is the first investigation that takes advantage of both runtime values and control flows of a virus for in-time detection. C2) It can detect mutated computer viruses and is resilient to various advanced mutation techniques. C3) It doesn't rely on the vulnerability knowledge. C4) This technique is practical which works on the binary directly and doesn't rely on the source code. C5) It can monitor the execution of mutated computer viruses and analyze them.

The rest of the paper is organized as follows. Our algorithm are made clear in Section 2. The design and implementation of our tool are described in Section 3. In Section 4, evaluation results are presented. In Section 5, we discuss our approach and future directions. In Section 6, we describe the related work. We conclude the paper in Section 7.

2   Purpose Capturing Signatures

A virus should contain a set of key instructions in order to achieve its malicious purpose. For example, a linux virus named *caline* intents to propagate itself by inserting its code after the code segment of ELF files. In order to achieve this purpose, it contains key instructions such as *open, mmap, write* system calls which can be captured as INT 0x80 or SYSENTER instruction during execution, and certain machine instructions which calculate the code segment position or patch the PHDR and SHDR of the ELF file. If an executable file or a legitimate application with input file contains similar instructions which result in the similar behaviors (e.g., calculating the code segment position, inserting the same code, and patching the PHDR and SHDR) when being executed in the same environment, it has been infected by the same category of virus as caline.

Intuition behind Purpose-Capturing Signatures: A computer virus is either part of an executable file or part of a data file used as input to a legitimate

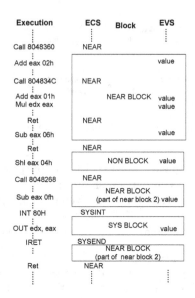

Fig. 2. Generation of Purpose Capturing Signature

application. We call both the executable file and the legitimate application a *run-time reservoir* of the virus. By observing the runtime behavior of a virus based on the Virtual Machine technology, we find that some *runtime values* which are output values written in output operands of the machine instructions (e.g. caline virus which patches the PHDR position contains several ADD and port operation instructions) and control sequence (e.g. caline has several INT 80H instructions which represent system calls) keep the same among all the mutations in order to serve the same malicious purpose. Code packing and encryption techniques do not modify the original instruction sequences which are generated and executed during execution. Substitution and emulation techniques only change the form of the virus program which means that it cannot change those runtime values and control sequences. Irrelevant code insertion, code splitting and merging can produce additional values and control instructions during runtime which may add elements to runtime values and control sequences, but do not delete key elements from them. Instruction reordering and control flow obfuscation techniques can only change the order between the runtime values and control sequences that do not have any dependences with each other.

According to the observation above, we generate purpose-capturing signatures of computer viruses based on information of runtime values and control flows. We define the runtime output operands of key instructions (an exception is port operation instructions, see details in Section 2.1) which are necessary operations (highly related to achieving its purpose) for a virus to transform the system's state (before the virus runs its code) to the desired infected state as an *execution value sequence* (EVS). Similarly, we define the sequence of instructions which change the execution flow of a virus as an *execution control sequence* (ECS).

In x86 architecture, control instructions include INT, SYSENTER, SYSEXIT, varieties of Call, Return and Jump instructions.

Basic Assumptions on Purpose-Capturing Signature Database: As shown in Figure 1, we need to generate a purpose-capturing signature database of known viruses which is used to identify mutated versions of the known viruses. We assume that a known virus, after being analyzed, will be manually confirmed by a human analyst in terms of its exact location inside the body of its runtime reservoir. Therefore, our generator can be precisely activated when the first instruction of the virus is executed.

2.1 Execution Value Sequence

The EVS is a sequence of values which are output operands of instructions. In x86 architecture, not all the instructions are highly related to the purpose of a virus. Therefore, we are only interested in the values whose updating represents the necessary procedure of the virus' purpose, such as mathematical (*ADD, MUL, SUB, DIV, INC, etc*), logical (*AND, XOR, OR, etc*), address calculation (*LEA*), bitshift (*SAR, SHR, SHL, etc*), rotate (*ROL, RCR, etc*) and port operations (*OUT, OUTS, IN, etc*) in our x86 architecture implementation. The EVS includes values, the operation and the port numbers for the port operations while only values for the other operations. For example, we log the value in EAX, port number in DX and operation for the instruction of {OUT dx,eax}, and only value of EAX for {ADD eax, edx}. We also exclude some meaningless values following the methods described in Section 2.3.

2.2 Execution Control Sequence

Since attackers can use mutation techniques such as instruction insertion, instruction reordering and code packing, we cannot rely on the order of values in an EVS to make detection decisions. However, if we ignore the order of values in the EVS, the similarity of two EVS will increase. In order to decrease false alarm probability, the ECS is introduced.

The ECS is a sequence of control instructions and their related information. Our ECS emphasizes on providing abstracted information to do detection and analysis with combination of the EVS. In this section, we introduce the form of ECS and the method to extract the ECS from code execution. In x86 architecture, we find that the control sequence which consists of a set of control flow instructions can be divided into three groups. One is defined as SYS group including system enter (*SYSENTER*), system exit (*SYSEXIT*), interrupt (*INT*) and interrupt return (*IRET*) instructions. The second group is defined as FAR group including far call, far return and unconditional far jump instructions. The third is defined as NEAR group including near call, near return and unconditional near jump instructions.

The rules for generating ECS are as follows. As shown in Figure 2, a control instruction is recorded in the format (symbol of an instruction, parameter 1, parameter 2, parameter 3). *SYSENTER* represents system enter and *SYSCALL* represents interrupt instruction whose interrupt number is *80H*. Both of them have three parameters: parameter 1 is the system call number, parameter 2 is the address of the instruction following the executing instruction, and parameter 3 is the address of the instruction which is to be executed according to the current instruction. *SYSINT* represents interrupt instructions excluding *INT 80H*. It also has three parameters and the only different parameter comparing with SYSCALL is parameter 1 which is the interrupt number here. *SYSEXIT* and *SYSEND* stand for system exit and interrupt return instructions respectively with two parameters each which have the same meaning with parameter 2, 3 of SYSENTER. *FAR* or *NEAR* stands for each FAR or NEAR instruction belonging to the corresponding group as described above. Their two parameters are the same as SYSEND.

2.3   Generating Purpose-Capturing Signatures for Viruses and Execution Sequence Blocks for Suspects

The EVS and ECS are recorded by the purpose-capturing signature generator concurrently. After getting the EVS and ECS, the EVS is divided into several blocks by the ECS. Ideally, we can find pairs of symbols in ECS such as interrupt and interrupt return, call and return, indicating the boundaries of the blocks which are either interrupt handlers, or function calls in the code and libraries. We call consecutive EVS inside a corresponding instruction pair as a block. As shown in Figure 2, the EVS is divided into the multi-level blocks between the symbols of ECS. Those blocks which represent the purpose of a computer virus are called a purpose-capturing signature. We call those blocks execution sequence blocks for a suspicious file.

As shown in Figure 1, the generator generates not only signatures for viruses, but also execution sequence blocks for suspicious files. We show the details that how to divide the EVS into multi-level blocks according to the information of ECS. We analyze the ECS to eliminate effects of those mutation techniques. Firstly, we mark corresponding SYSINT/SYSCALL and SYSEND as a pair if parameter 2 of SYSINT/SYSCALL is the same as parameter 2 of SYSEND. The SYSENTER and SYSEXIT pair is marked similarly. These SYS pairs will divide the EVS into several blocks. We define the blocks inside the corresponding SYS pairs as *SYS BLOCK* while others as *NON SYS BLOCK*. Secondly, for the instructions inside the corresponding ECS block of NON SYS BLOCK, we mark corresponding FAR as a pair if parameter 1 of one FAR is the same as another's parameter 2 based on the same logic. We define the consecutive sequence values of EVS inside those corresponding pairs as *FAR BLOCK* while others inside NON SYS BLOCK as *NON FAR BLOCK*. Similarly, in NON FAR BLOCK, we mark corresponding NEAR as a pair. We define the consecutive sequence values inside those corresponding pairs as *NEAR BLOCK* while others inside NON FAR BLOCK as *NON NEAR BLOCK*.

Remark: The attackers can insert some meaningless instructions after the call instruction and let the corresponding return instruction return to the address of meaningless instructions (e.g. NOP) or the first meaningful instruction after the call instruction. To solve this problem, we need to add a static analysis component to find the address of the first meaningful instruction after each control instruction by statically analyzing the code in the memory of the VM. Then we also need to record this address as a new parameter of each instruction. We will finish this work in the future.

2.4   Refining Techniques in Purpose-Capturing Signature Generation

As shown in Figure 1, we need to generate execution sequence blocks for a suspicious file. In order to remove noise to reduce false positive probability, we introduce the following techniques into the VM based purpose-capturing signature generator.

1) We do dynamic fine-grained instruction level taint analysis to get the refined EVS and ECS based on our previous work [16] to locate all the effects of the suspicious file and reduce the noise introduced by other unrelated instructions. If the suspicious file is an executable file, we let it run directly inside the "sandbox" and mark the related memory loaded by the executing suspicious file as the taint seed. If the suspicious file is a data file, we let the corresponding application run with the file as input inside the VM and mark the memory in which the data file is stored as the taint seed. Besides, considering the packing techniques, we also mark the newly generated code as different taint seeds. Starting with tainting the seeds, our analyzer in the VM propagats the taint to every byte (e.g., in registers, memory cells, and files) deriving from the seeds. We will detail our Dynamic Taint Analyzer in Section 3.

2) Packing techniques are commonly used for computer viruses to hide malicious code. We need to remove the noise introduced before and during unpacking execution. With help of the taint analysis method, we remove the sequences of instructions which are related to the unpacking purpose and label each element in the EVS and the ECS with the packed-level. When identifying the blocks described as above, we should consider the effects of packing techniques, which means that we cannot treat two control instructions as a pair if they are at different packed-levels. We will detail our Code Unpack Analyzer in Section 3.

We also use other techniques to refine the runtime sequences. The sequences generated through dynamic taint analysis may still contain some non-important values to the semantic of the suspicious file. In order to eliminate those values, following strategies are made. Firstly, if a group of consecutive instructions always modify the same registers or the same memory cells, only the last value of those consecutive instructions needs to be recorded in the EVS. For example, we only need to record the last value in the group of consecutive instructions { *add eax, 01h; sub eax 0f3dbh; push eax; inc eax; pop eax; add eax, 12h* }. Secondly, some operations which are generated by mutation tools are meaningless and need to be neglected. For example, the values of instructions such as multiplying or dividing a pointer by another pointer should not be recorded. Thirdly, some operation values are meaningless such as calculating new *ESP* after a function call and need to be neglected.

2.5 Matching Purpose-Capturing Signatures against Virus Suspects

We assume that the user (or other intrusion detection tools) will tell the virus detector which (executable or data) files are suspicious. Our sandbox virus detector only analyzes the suspicious files instead of monitoring the execution of every program.

Our matching technique is totally different from the traditional virus fingerprint matching which is a direct byte-by-byte matching (e.g., seeing whether the exact bytes contained in a fingerprint appear in the body of a suspect). The matching we do is an *indirect* matching between the purpose of a known virus and that of a suspect. We never match against the bytes contained in the body of a suspect.

We do similarity calculation in which we compare the execution sequence blocks of the suspicious file with the purpose-capturing signatures of known computer viruses. In order to get the comparison results, we define V as the set of values in one block, so that V_{1n} means the set of values in the nth block of the purpose-capturing signature of a known computer virus while V_{2m} means the set of values in the mth block of the suspicious file's execution sequence blocks, and $|V|$ means the number of values in this set. Then we can get the similarity score P of the two blocks.

$$P_{nm}[V_{1n}, V_{2m}] = \frac{|V_{1n} \cap V_{2m}|}{|V_{1n}|}$$

As mentioned above, execution sequence blocks of a suspicious file which contain several SYS BLOCKs, FAR BLOCKs, NEAR BLOCKs and NON NEAR BLOCKs have been generated. To compare execution sequence blocks with purpose-capturing signatures of known computer viruses, firstly, we find the related SYS BLOCKs in them by comparing the interrupt number or system call number. If several SYS BLOCKs have the same interrupt number or system call number, the maximum similarity of those blocks needs to be calculated. We define the number of the SYS BLOCKs which have the same interrupt number or system call number as Ni_1 and Ni_2. Then the similarity of those blocks is

$$P_{SYSi} = max\{\frac{\sum_{m,n} P_{nm}}{min[Ni_1, Ni_2]}\}$$

For example, if one signature has two SYS BLOCKs with system call number 4 which represents the write system call while the execution sequence blocks have three, we need to calculate P_{SYS4} which is the maximum of $[(P_{11} + P_{22})/2,$ $(P_{11} + P_{23})/2, (P_{12} + P_{21})/2, (P_{12} + P_{23})/2, (P_{13} + P_{21})/2, (P_{13} + P_{22})/2]$ so that we can get the corresponding SYS BLOCK relation which makes the similarity maximum.

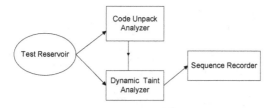

Fig. 3. Purpose-Capturing Signature Generator

Secondly, we calculate the corresponding block relations and similarities of FAR BLOCKs and NEAR BLOCKs by the same method. Finally, we merge remaining blocks into one block and calculate the similarity. Therefore, the similarity between the execution sequence blocks of the suspicious file and the purpose-capturing signature of a virus is the average similarity of all the corresponding blocks. For the detection purpose, if the similarity is greater than the threshold, we treat the suspicious file as containing the virus.

Remark: All the call and return instructions of functions written inside the code can be removed by duplicating the code body of functions to every place where the call happens. However, this method will significantly increase the size of the virus. So it is usually not adopted by the virus writers. Furthermore, to solve this problem, we just do not rely on this kind of calls when we generate the signatures for the viruses. We only use system calls, interrupts and calls to dynamic libraries to generate signatures.

3   Design and Implementation

Our tool which contains purpose-capturing signature generator and signature matcher is implemented based on x86 CPU architecture.

3.1   Purpose-Capturing Signature Generator

The purpose-capturing signature generator is implemented atop QEMU which is a machine emulator running in the Full System Emulation mode. QEMU works as a dynamic translator, which enables us to monitor each executing instruction. In our tool, the environment to generate purpose-capturing signature database and to generate execution sequence blocks of a suspicious file should be the same. To achieve this purpose, we use the same image file of QEMU to make generation processes consistent.

When analyzing a suspicious file, the execution of the file is monitored by our generator from the VM level. The generator can monitor the memory and disk of the VM. In order to generate the purpose-capturing signatures, the related suspicious memory cells and disk sectors should be located first to remove the noise. There are two ways to solved this problem. One is to locate disk sectors which store suspicious files. Then the generator can get corresponding memory

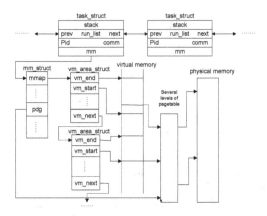

Fig. 4. Reconstruction Method

addresses by monitoring disk operations from the VM level. The other one is to reconstruct the high-level information directly from the memory.

Reconstruction: QEMU defines a structure *env* to emulate the target CPU of the VM. All the registers of the CPU running the guest Operating System can be found in this structure. We implement reconstruction of linux OS. As shown in Figure 4, the kernel stack of the current running process can be located through the register *tr*. The *thread_info* structure which includes a pointer pointing to the *task descriptor* (defined as *task_struct* in Linux) resides at the bottom of the kernel stack. Through the task descriptor, all the information related to a process can be obtained. Furthermore, all the processes can be located from the pointer *tasks* in the task descriptor. At last, all the management information of the guest OS such as memory management information can be obtained. With help of reconstruction, the purpose-capturing signature generator can locate the processes loaded by the executable file or the memory space which contains a data file used as input of a legitimate application.

After locating this information, the purpose-capturing signature generator starts to generate the signatures during the execution. As shown in Figure 3, we implement three components of the purpose-capturing signature generator which are the Dynamic Taint Analyzer, the Code Unpack Analyzer and the Sequence Recorder respectively and make them as parts of QEMU. The Dynamic Taint Analyzer provides a method to identify the sequences related to the runtime reservoir and removes noise. The Code Unpack Analyzer identifies packed executable code. The Sequence Recorder automatically records EVS and ECS to generate signatures.

Dynamic Taint Analyzer. To precisely locate the effects of the malicious code and reduce the noise introduced by mutation techniques and the environment, the dynamic taint analyzer uses fine grained instruction level dynamic taint analysis which maintains a flag for each memory and disk cell. The flag has

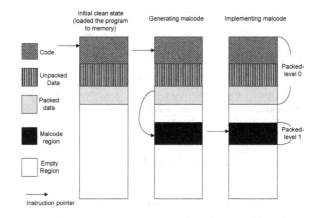

Fig. 5. Generate the Packed-level During Execution

two states: dirty and clean. To minimize the memory consumption, the dynamic taint analyzer maintains a pagetable-like structure to store the flags.

The dynamic taint analyzer analyzes the source and destination of each instruction and shows two kinds of taint propagation flows in a VM: the data taint flow and the control taint flow. From the view of the data flow, for an instruction involving a source operand and a destination operand, the dynamic taint analyzer will taint the destination if the data stored in the source is dirty, the value used to find the source/destination is dirty or the memory cells of this instruction are dirty. For an instruction only involving a destination operand, the dynamic taint analyzer will taint the destination if the memory cells of this instruction are dirty. For the control flow, if the condition of the currently executing instruction is dirty, or the destination address of the redirection is dirty, the dynamic taint analyzer will taint the corresponding event of the control flow redirection. The dynamic taint analyzer can gradually construct an instruction level dependency graph by analyzing each executed instruction.

Code Unpack Analyzer. Packing techniques are commonly used for computer viruses to hide malicious code. As shown in Figure 5, this kind of computer viruses needs to generate malicious code when executing. Therefore, the sequences which are not generated by the malicious code are treated as noise. In order to reduce this kind of noise, the code unpack analyzer needs to determine the newly generated code when executing.

The code unpack analyzer collects all the memory writing and monitors the execution flow while the aimed code is being executed. During execution, it precisely identifies the newly generated code and the instruction causing the control-flow transfer by monitoring the instruction execution through VM level. Then it provides the packed-level information to the dynamic taint analyzer. For example, as shown in Figure 5, once code or data is executed from a memory area that is newly written by the taint code or data, the code unpack analyzer

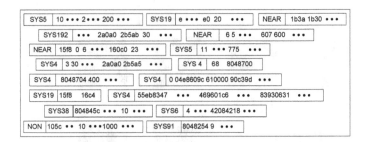

Fig. 6. Signature Example

calculates the packed-level and sets it as another seed, then transfers the information to the dynamic taint analyzer. An exception is that if a process loads a dynamic link library, we do not set the library as the newly generated code.

Sequence Recorder. The sequence recorder records the EVS and ECS to generate purpose-capturing signatures of known viruses or execution sequence blocks of suspicious files which may contain packed-level information if the file uses packing techniques. The sequence recorder utilizes the information from the dynamic taint analyzer to remove unrelated sequences. It only records the sequences which are tainted and not related to new code generation. In our implementation, it records these sequences after running each guest instruction. After that, it follows the method described in Section 2 to generate the purpose-capturing signature of the virus and execution sequence blocks of the suspicious file. A signature example is shown in Figure 6.

3.2   Signature Matcher

The signature matcher detects viruses according to the method described in Section 2.5. It is an independent program outside QEMU.

Regarding detection, all our tool does is to let a given virus suspect or its reservoir run inside a VM so that we can extract its EVS and ECS and match them against the signature database. In terms of how the virus suspects are identified, the user can simply follow his or her common sense: an executable file or a data file from an unknown or not-fully-trusted source (e.g., a web site, an email attachment) should be firstly fishbowled by our tool.

4   Evaluation

In this section, we present details on the evaluation of our computer virus detection and analysis system. Our signature generator is implemented based on VM QEMU (linux version 0.9.0) which runs in Full System Emulation mode by adding 13000 lines of C code. QEMU uses dynamic binary translation to emulate kinds of CPU in the Full System Emulation mode. We only focus on the

Table 1. Virus Size and Signature File Size

Virus Name	Size of Virus	Size of Signature	Virus Name	Size of Virus	Size of Signature
Arches	4.2KByte	1.3KByte	Alaeda	20.4KByte	2.3KByte
Arian	3.2KByte	1.1KByte	Caline	18.1KByte	2.8KByte
Califax	22KByte	3.4KByte	Dateseg	20.5KByte	2.6KByte
Derfunf.a	18.7KByte	1.9KByte	Gripa	4.4KByte	1.4KByte
laurung	12.6KByte	2.0KByte	Lacrimae	9.2KByte	1.9KByte
Nel	18.1KByte	3.0KByte	Osf	41KByte	4.0KByte
Radix	57.7KByte	3.6KByte	Rapeme	13.7KByte	1.1KByte

x86 CPU architecture. For our prototype, current implementation of signature generator does not use the *translation block cache* technique, which makes the performance 30 times slower than the original QEMU. Our signature generator is 2.3 times slower than the QEMU without translation block cache.

4.1 Virus Mutation Detection Results

For the virus data file used as input to a legitimate application, it should use the exploitable buffer overflow, the race condition or other exploitable bugs in the legitimate application to trigger the execution of code hidden within it. However, with protection features such as execute disable bit and/or address space layout randomization, it is very difficult for the virus to exploit this type of bugs. Moreover, our tool can easily detect this kind of viruses by finding that code inside the data file is executed. Therefore, we only analyzed the executable files in our recent experiments. After downloading a file into our tool, we manually set the file name as the seed parameter to the signature generator, then ran the file to do analysis. In order to make generation processes consistent, we just used the same image file of QEMU which was the disk of the guest for each execution.

In our experiments, the purpose-capturing signature database of computer viruses was generated by ourselves. The signatures were generated from the original form of computer viruses.

Linux Virus: We generated purpose-capturing signatures of 42 different original linux viruses. Examples are shown in Table 1. As mentioned in section 3.1, with help of the reconstruction component, the memory cells of suspicious processes were marked as taint seeds. We also used *Linux Mutation Engine [LiME]* with code encrytion, instruction insertion and replacement methods, and *Binobfuscator* with all the mutation methods mentioned in Section 2 to generate mutated viruses. All the 42 similarity results between the one-level mutated virus and the original virus are almost 1. Results are shown in Figure 7(a). We also tested our method with multi-level mutation. We mutated each virus by both two mutation tools three times each following the order (Binobf, LiME, Binobf, LiME, Binobf, LiME). As shown in Figure 7(a), all the similarity results between the multi-level mutated virus and the original one are still almost 1. Therefore, our tool is able to correctly identify all the mutated virus samples.

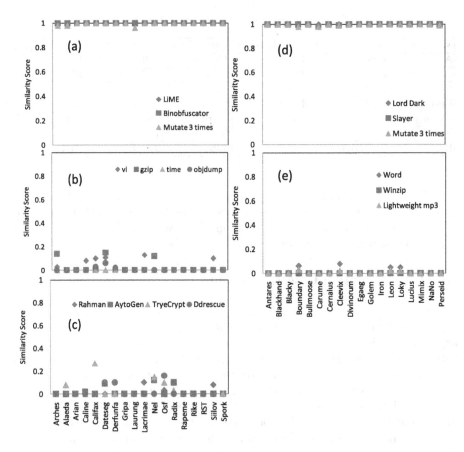

Fig. 7. Experiment Results: (a) Linux Virus Examples, (b) Similarity Score Examples between Linux System Utilities and Viruses, (c) Similarity Score Examples between Other Benign Linux Executable Files and Viruses, (d) Windows Virus Examples, (e) Similarity Score Examples between Windows Utilities and Viruses

False Positive: We firstly tested four linux system utilities *vi*, *gzip*, *date* and *objdump* as counter examples. For vi, we randomly wrote and pasted 2000 characters and saved to a file. For gzip, we used it to compress a txt file. For objdump, we used it to dissemble an executable file *ls*. For all the system utilities, our generator marked the memory cells of processes loaded by the executable file as taint seeds. The results are shown in Figure 7(b). Every similarity result is lower than 0.25. Then we downloaded four benign, free executable files from internet and tested them by the same method. As shown in Figure 7(b) and Figure 7(c), our tool is able to clearly distinguish the benign linux files from viruses.

Windows Virus: We also tested 120 Windows Viruses to show the capability of our tool. In Windows environment, our tool disables the windows virtual memory to prevent memory swapping. As mentioned in section 3.1, the memory cells loaded from the disk sectors which store suspicious files are marked as taint seeds. We also used *Lord Dark Mutation Engine* and *Slayer Confusion Engine* to generate mutated viruses. All the similarity results between the one-level mutated virus and the original virus are almost 1. We also mutated each virus by both two mutation tools three times each following the order (Lord Dark, Slayer, Lord Dark, Slayer, Lord Dark, Slayer). All the similarity results between the multi-level mutated virus and the original one are still almost 1. The result examples are shown in Figure 7(d).

False Positive: We tested windows system utilities and free windows executable file samples such as *office utilities, winzip* and *mp3 player* to measure the false positive probability. As shown in Figure 7(e), every similarity result is lower than 0.25.

Comparison with anti-virus tools: We used a Linux anti-virus tool Sophos trial version [17] and a Windows anti-virus tool Kaspersky 6.0 to scan all the original virus files and got true positive alerts. However, those anti-virus tools did not raise any alarm for all the mutated virus files.

Performance: Although the overhead of our generator is significantly increased without translation block cache of QEMU, the performance of our tool is still acceptable. In our experiments, the time for getting the detection result of each suspicious file is between 20 seconds to 6 minutes on the 2.13 GHz computer with 2 GB memory.

5   Discussion

In this section, we discuss the limitations and the techniques that we will develop in future.

1) Our tool focuses on detecting mutated versions of known viruses. It heavily relies on the purpose-capturing signature database to detect viruses. Therefore, the database should be as complete as possible for the practical application. This problem can be solved with help from anti-virus companies.

2) Our purpose-capturing signature generator is based on VM techniques. VM techniques isolate the virus running inside the VM from the VM monitor and the host operating system. We assume that the virus can compromise everything inside the VM, but cannot break out of the VM and compromise the VM monitor and the host operating system. However, in reality the virus may break out of the VM by exploiting bugs of it. This problem can be solved by fixing these bugs or providing limited interface to the untrusted VM.

3) Viruses may evade detection by hiding their malicious purposes. Attackers can set conditions in viruses which deactivate the malicious code if the conditions are satisfied. For example, our generator is based on VM techniques, and viruses are able to know whether they are running inside a VM [18]. Therefore, attackers can set a condition that when the virus confirms that it is running in a VM, it turns to another execution path to evade detection. This problem can be solved by adding a path analyzer component which can set the condition at the path

branch to explore all the execution paths. Moser [19] also provides a solution to solve this problem.

4) The limitation of runtime overhead can be addressed by turning on the QEMU translation block cache to speed up the VM. Moreover, most PC users do not have tons of untrusted email attachments (or executable files) on a daily base, and they typically do not require the tool to be extremely fast or scalable.

6   Related Work

We group the malware detection and analysis techniques into three categories: traditional signature based, behavior based and cross view based detection. Signature based malware detection is commonly used in the real world. There are numerous researchers focusing on this technique. Christodorescu [12] used annotation of program instructions to provide an abstraction from the code and detect the patterns of mutation. Their second paper [13] replaced the annotation by a more complicated set of techniques to provide different levels of resilience to mutated variants. Bonfante [20] and Kaczmarek [21] proposed an malware detector based on control flow graphs which provided some abstraction on the signature to help detection. Polygraph [22] targeted polymorphic worms and automatically determined appropriate signatures. Their signatures included multiple disjoint content substrings such as protocol framing and some obfuscated code. Compared to those signature based techniques, our approach takes advantage of both runtime values and control flows to extract the purpose of the virus and detect it. Moreover, by using Virtual Machine technique, our approach is implemented completely outside of the victim system. We can detect the virus which uses rootkit hidden techniques based on Virtual Machine-level knowledge, while above detection techniques cannot.

Behavior based malware detection techniques identify the malware by observing its behaviors and system states. There are a variety of behavior based detection techniques. Some of them rely on the examination of detection points. System virginity verifier [23] focused on hooks usually used by rootkits and other malwares. GateKeeper [24] checked auto-start extensibility points in the registry to find unauthorized restart-surviving behaviors. However, this kind of detection techniques can be easily evaded by misleading information which can cheat the detector. Some malware analysis efforts such as BitBlaze [25], Panorama [26] and Polyglot [27] made heavy use of virtualized and emulated environments, and analyzed the behavior of the software. Cluster [28] extracted behavioral profiles by abstracting system calls, their dependences, and the network activities to a generalized representation consisting of OS objects and OS operations. However, the defect of this kind of techniques is obvious, which is that it cannot detect the malware until the damage has been caused. In contrast, our approach overcomes these weaknesses. 1) Our tool is based on two execution sequences, which does not provide a target detection point for the virus to avoid. 2) Our tool can detect the virus immediately which does not rely on the damage-caused behaviors.

The cross-view based rootkit detection techniques such as Rootkit Revealer [29] and Strider Ghostbuster [30], detect hidden files and processes by comparing two level views of the system. The upper-level view is obtained from calling common operating system APIs, while the lower-level view is obtained from system states in the kernel, virtual machine level or hardware. This kind of techniques can only detect the hidden entities, while our approach can detect all the viruses no matter they are hidden or not.

7 Conclusions

Modern virus writers use various mutation techniques to evade detection. In this paper, we present an approach to detect and analyze computer viruses based on VM technology. Our approach of detection is based on both the EVS and the ECS. To our best knowledge, it is the first method to effectively detect virus mutations based on these two sets of information. Our approach is resilient to various advanced mutation techniques. Moreover, it works on the binary directly and doesn't rely on the source code, operating system or other anti-virus software. We believe that our approach will offer indispensable assistance to virus detectors and analysts, and enable them to quickly comprehend the purposes of mutated viruses.

References

1. Cohen, F.B.: Operating system protection through program evolution. Computers & Security 12(6) (1993)
2. Collberg, C., Thomborson, C., Low, D.: Manufacturing cheap, resilient, and stealthy opaque constructs. In: Principles of Programming Languages (POPL 1998), San Diego, CA, USA (1998)
3. Linn, C., Debray, S.: Obfuscation of executable code to improve resistance to static disassembly. In: Proceedings of the 10th. ACM Conference on Computer and Communications Security (CCS 2003), Washingtion DC, USA (2003)
4. Majumdar, A., Thomborson, C., Drape, S.: A survey of control-flow obfuscations. In: Bagchi, A., Atluri, V. (eds.) ICISS 2006. LNCS, vol. 4332, pp. 353–356. Springer, Heidelberg (2006)
5. Popov, I., Debray, S., Andrews, G.: Binary obfuscation using signals. In: Proceedings of 16th USENIX Security Symposium on USENIX Security Symposium (Security 2007), Berkeley, CA, USA, pp. 1–6 (2007)
6. Szor, P., Ferrie, P.: Hunting for metamorphic. In: Proceedings of Virus Bulletin Conference, pp. 123–144 (2001)
7. Sharif, M., Lanzi, A., Giffin, J., Lee, W.: Impeding malware analysis using conditional code obfuscation. In: Proceedings of the Network and Distributed System Security Symposium (NDSS 2008), San Diego, CA, USA (2008)
8. Sharif, M., Lanzi, A., Giffin, J., Lee, W.: Automatic Reverse Engineering of Malware Emulators. In: Proceedings of The 2009 IEEE Symposium on Security and Privacy (Oakland 2009), Oakland, CA, USA (2009)
9. Detristan, T., Ulenspiegel, T., Malcom, Y., von Underduk, M.S.: Polymorphic shellcode engine using spectrum analysis. Phrack 11(61) (2003),
   http://www.phrack.org

10. Mohanty, D.: Anti-virus evasion techniques and countermeasures (2005),
    http://www.hackingspirits.com/eth-hac/papers/whitepapers.asp
11. Christodorescu, M., Jha, S.: Testing malware detectors. In: Proceedings of the ACM
    SIGSOFT International Symposium on Software Testing and Analysis, ISSTA 2004
    (2004)
12. Christodorescu, M., Jha, S.: Static analysis of executables to detect malicious pat-
    terns. In: Proceedings of USENIX Security Symposium(Security 2003), Washing-
    tion DC, USA (2003)
13. Christodorescu, M., Jha, S., Seshia, S.A., Song, D., Bryant, R.E.: Semantics-aware
    malware detection. In: Proceedings of the 2005 IEEE Symposium on Security and
    Privacy (Oakland 2005), Oakland, CA, USA (2005)
14. Wroblewski, G.: General method of program code obfuscation. PhD thesis, In-
    stitute of Engineering Cybernetics, Wroclaw University of Technology, Wroclaw,
    Poland (2002)
15. Brumley, D., Wang, H., Jha, S., Song, D.: Creating Vulnerability Signatures Us-
    ing Weakest Pre-conditions. In: Proceedings of Computer Security Foundations
    Symposium, Italy (2007)
16. Jia, X., Zhang, S., Jing, J., Liu, P.: Using Virtual Machines to Do Cross-Layer
    Damage Assessment. In: Proceedings of the ACM Workshop on Virtual Machine
    Security (VMSEC 2008), in association with ACM CCS, Washingtion DC, USA
    (2008)
17. Sophos (2009),
    http://www.sophos.com/products/enterprise/endpoint/
    security-and-control/8.0/linux/
18. Klein, T.: VMware Fingerprint Suite (2008),
    http://www.trapkit.de/research/vmm/scoopydoo/index.html
19. Moser, A., Kruegel, C., Kirda, E.: Exploring multiple execution paths for mal-
    ware analysis. In: IEEE Symposium on Security and Privacy (Oakland 2007),
    pp. 231–245 (2007)
20. Bonfante, G., Kaczmarek, M., Marion, J.: Architecture of a Morphological Malware
    Detector. Journal in Computer Virology 5(3), 263–270 (2008)
21. Bonfante, G., Kaczmarek, M., Marion, J.: Control Flow to Detect Malware. In:
    Inter-Regional Workshop on Rigorous System Development and Analysis (2007)
22. Newsome, J., Karp, B., Song, D.: Polygraph: Automatically generating signatures
    for polymorphic worms. In: IEEE Symposium on Security and Privacy, pp. 226–241
    (2005)
23. Rutkowska, J.: System virginity verifier: Defining the roadmap for malware detec-
    tion on windows systems. In: Hack in the Box Security Conference (2005)
24. Wang, Y.M., Roussev, R., Verbowski, C., Johnson, A., Wu, M.W., Huang, Y.,
    Kuo, S.Y.: Gatekeeper: Monitoring Auto-Start Extensibility Points (ASEPs) for
    spyware management. In: Proceedings of the Large Installation System Adminis-
    tration Conference, LISA 2004 (2004)
25. Song, D., Brumley, D., Yin, H., Caballero, J., Jager, I., Kang, M.G., Liang, Z.,
    Newsome, J., Poosankam, P., Saxena, P.: BitBlaze: A new approach to computer
    security via binary analysis. In: Sekar, R., Pujari, A.K. (eds.) ICISS 2008. LNCS,
    vol. 5352, pp. 1–25. Springer, Heidelberg (2008)
26. Yin, H., Song, D., Egele, M., Kruegel, C., Kirda, E.: Panorama: Capturing System-
    wide Information Flow for Malware Detection and Analysis. In: Proceedings of
    ACM Conference on Computer and Communications Security (CCS 2007), Alexan-
    dria, Virginia, USA (2007)

27. Caballero, J., Yin, H., Liang, Z., Song, D.: Polyglot: Automatic Extraction of Protocal Message Format Using Dynamic Vinary Analysis. In: Proceedings of ACM Conference on Computer and Communications Security (CCS 2007), Alexandria, Virginia, USA (2007)
28. Bayer, U., Comparetti, P.M., Hlauschek, C., Kruegel, C., Kirda, E.: Scalable, Behavior-Based Malware Clustering. In: Proceedings of the Network and Distributed System Security Symposium (NDSS 2009), California, USA (2009)
29. Revealer (2008), http://www.sysinternals.com/Files/RootkitRevealer.zip
30. Wang, Y., Beck, D., Vo, B., Roussev, R., Verbowski, C.: Detecting stealth software with strider ghostbuster. In: Proceedings of the 2005 International Conference on Dependable Systems and Networks (DSN 2005), pp. 368–377 (2005)

Rate-Based Watermark Traceback: A New Approach*

Zongbin Liu[1], Jiwu Jing[1], and Peng Liu[2]

[1] The State Key Laboratory of Information Security, Graduate University of
Chinese Academy of Sciences, China
{zbliu,jing}@lois.cn
[2] The Pennsylvania State University, University Park, USA
pliu@ist.psu.edu

Abstract. Network based intrusions have become a serious threat to
Internet users. Despite many sophisticated defense techniques, attacks
continue to increase. At present, in order to hide the source of the attack, many attackers prefer a stepping stone to launch their attack due
to the anonymous nature of the Internet. The size, header and content of
an IP packet will be changed because of the stepping stone and all these
changes make it more difficult to trace the source of attacks. Currently,
researchers study the time interval between IP packets and embed the
watermark into the packet stream by adjusting the time interval between
IP packets to trace the source of attacks. In this paper we study the previous watermarking schemes based on inter packet delay and propose a
novel watermark scheme based on the rate of packets. For the first time
we used weak signal detection model and cluster technology to resume
the watermark, so as to avoid the present schemes which are based on
precision time synchronization or packet number. Simulation tests show
that the novel watermark is robust and can countermine the time perturbation, packet losing perturbation and packet padding perturbation
caused by an attacker on purpose.

Keywords: Stepping stone, IPD, watermark.

1   Introduction

Although nowadays there are many techniques and laws to defend network attacks, network based intrusions still increase every day. Network based intrusions
have become a serious threat to the users of the Internet, especially those attackers who use intermediate host [1](stepping stone) to avoid tracing. This gives the
attacker more courage to launch their attack, and also makes the tracing more
difficult. The attacker usually uses many stepping stones to increase the difficulty of tracing to them. The stepping stone is located in different areas, and

* The work is supported by the National Natural Science Foundation of China under
Grant No. 70890084/G021102; and the National High-Tech Research and Development Plan of China under Grant No. 2006AA01Z454.

undergoes many changes, especially the packet through the stepping stone which changes things such as the packet header, size and content. This is also the main difference from the IP trace back problem [2,3]. In IP trace back technology, the source IP address will be changed by the attacker on purpose, but the other information of the packet stream remains unchanged. However, almost all the characteristics of the packet stream will be changed through the stepping stone. At present, in order to defend against such an attack, there are two main ideas proposed in the literature [4]:

Host-based trust model: In this model, the stepping stone participates in the tracing. In other words, stepping stone can be trusted, by tracing every log of the stepping stones to find the source of the attack; however, there are some shortcomings in this model. First of all, it cannot be traced in a timely way, so tracing efficiency is low. Secondly, this scheme must monitor the entire stepping stone chain, so if one of the stepping stones is out of monitoring, the whole tracing process will be broken. Thirdly, if the stepping stone was controlled by the attacker, the log of the intermediate host is not reliable. Based on these shortcomings, the Host Based tracing back technique is quite limited.

Network-based trust model [5,6,7,8,4,9,10]. The previous works analyze the invariable characteristics (e.g., inter packet delay(IPD) of the packet flow through the stepping stone [4], and embed watermark into the packet flows so that each flow will carry a unique watermark even if it flows through malicious stepping stones. From the evaluation results reported in the previous works, those schemes have good tracing effectiveness in some cases, however, in other cases those schemes did not perform very well. They did not perform very well because most tracing schemes are based on the precision time synchronization or precision packet number to embed or detect watermark.

This paper proposed a novel packet stream watermark method based on the packet rate. The new watermark method is very effective defending against the time perturbation, packet losing and packet padding which were introduced by the attacker on purpose. Simulation shows that the novel watermark is more successful when defending against bigger time perturbation, bigger packet losing and packet padding.

The remainder of the paper is organized as follows. Section 2 presents the related work of the stepping stone tracing technology. Section 3 presents the watermark based on the packet rate and the watermark detection model. Section 4 presents the simulation result by MATLAB. Section 5 presents the analysis of the watermark model. Section 6 concludes the paper.

2   Related Work

The problem of the stepping stone detection was first proposed by Staniford-Chen and Heberlein [11]. Their main idea was to look into the packet content to find the same flow through the stepping stone. However, as advanced technology involved, such as SSH, the traffic was encrypted, the tracing method must accommodate the new technology. Zhang and Paxson [12] proposed an algorithm based on the distinctive characteristics (packet size, timing) of the interactive traffic, not on connection contents, so it can be used to find stepping stone even when traffic is encrypted. He et al. [13] also gave two algorithms to detect stepping stone encrypted connection with bounded memory and bounded time delay perturbation.

Some other paper gave some scenario based on Inter-packet delays (IPDs). Wang et al. [4] proposed a correlation scheme to show that IPDs of both encrypted and unencrypted, interactive connections are preserved across many router hops and stepping stones. Wang and Reeves [8] designed a watermark scheme to be robust against timing perturbations which were introduced by adjusting the timing of selected packets of the flow, but only when the delay perturbation is not very big, the watermark could remain in the stepping stone connection.

Pyun [6] proposed a watermark scheme for purpose of tracing the traffic in the presence of repacketizaion. In other words, the repacketize flow can be taken as the flow which loses packets, however, when adding chaff packets into a flow, the watermark will be inefficient.

Wang et al. [5] proposed a watermark scheme to attack on low-latency anonymous communication system [14] by injecting unique watermark into the inter packet timing domain of a packet flow. The watermark is robust against packet dropping, repacketizaion and flow splitting.

Yu et al. [15] developed a flow marking technique for invisible trace back based on Direct Sequence Spread Spectrum. By interfering with a sender's traffic and marginally varying its rate, an investigator can embed a secret spread signal into the sender's traffic, however, this scheme need a very precision time synchronization.

Peng et al. [16]developed attack techniques to infer some important watermark parameters in [5,15] proposed methods, and to recover and duplicate embedded watermarks. Consequently the watermark was destroyed. This proposed method can use to destroy the watermark based on the time interval. The resulting techniques enabled an attacker to defeat the tracing system in certain cases by removing watermarks from the stepping stone connections.

However, not all of these previous approaches can effectively detect stepping stones. When big time perturbation, packet losing and packet padding occur, most of the previous work based on precision packet number or precision time synchronization could be defeated.

3   Rate-Based Watermark

The proposed scheme is based on the packet rate of the packet stream. Compared to the previous works, the proposed approach is in general much more effective in coping with (or tolerating) large time perturbation, packet losing and packet padding. This technique uses weak signal detection model and fuzzy cluster technique to extract the watermark embedded into the packet stream. In this watermark scheme, we denote the low rate of packet stream as the low frequency of the carrier wave, and the high rate of the packet stream as the high frequency of the carrier wave. By controlling the rate of the packet stream we embed the watermark into the packet stream. In the paper, we assume that all perturbations in the packet stream are the noise of the channel, because both of packet perturbation and time perturbation introduced by attacker will change the interval of the packets. The network delay will also change the interval of the packets, when packet stream passes through many stepping stones, the perturbation will grow larger. When detecting watermark, we first use weak signal detection model to get the threshold of the high rate and low rate. Then we use the cluster technique to get the watermark embedded in the packet stream.

3.1 Data Source Mode

We use the notation F to denote the packet stream that was embedded watermark; Let V_H be the high rate of the packet stream, and V_L be the low rate of the packet stream. Let T be the continuance of the high rate packets or low rate packets continuance. We denote that the high rate packets during time interval T as watermark bit 1 embedded into the packet stream; and the low packets rate during time interval T as bit 0. Let z_{iL} be the time interval between the $(i + 1)^{th}$ and i^{th} packet when the transfer speed is low, and let z_{iH} be the time interval between the $(i + 1)^{th}$ packet and i^{th} packet when the transfer speed is high. The embedded watermark flow can be defined as:

$$\{\overbrace{Z_{0L}, Z_{1L}, \ldots \ldots}^{0} \overbrace{Z_{iH}, Z_{i+1H}, \ldots}^{1}\} \tag{1}$$

3.2 Channel Model

During transmission the packet stream could face some perturbations, mainly as follows:

- Due to the network delay, the interval between packets could be changed.
- Due to the the quality of network, some packets may be lost during transformation, so the time interval between packets would change by this way.
- The attacker may introduce random time perturbation when packet stream pass through the stepping stone.
- The attacker may repacketize the packets through the stepping stone, drop some packets or add some extra useless packets into the stream when stream passes through the stepping stone; these ways could change the time interval between packets in the packet flow.

Dropping packets or repacketization will make the time interval between the packets larger. On the other hand, the packets padding will cause the time interval to be larger or shorter. The packet stream that pass through every stepping stone may be interfered by these perturbations. Based on these, we assume that the sum of all of these time perturbations follow the normal probability distribution:

$$f(x) = \frac{1}{\sqrt{2\pi}\sigma} e^{-\frac{(x-\mu)^2}{2\sigma^2}} \tag{2}$$

3.3   Watermark Detection Model

Hypothesis testing model. In hypothesis testing [17], a decision is made based on the observation of a random variable as to which of several hypotheses to accept. In binary hypothesis testing the choice is made between two hypotheses:

H_0: denotes low rate;

H_1: denotes high rate;

One observation y of a random variable Y whose probability density function (pdf) under each hypothesis is known. In this binary case there are two alternative hypotheses. Thus we wish to determine $f(H_0|y)$ and $f(H_1|y)$ the probability of each of the hypothesis, given the observation y. If $f(H_0|y) > f(H_1|y)$, we decide low rate was present, and then conversely we decide high rate if $f(H_1|y) > f(H_0|y)$. We denote these pdf's as: $f(y|H_0)$ and $f(y|H_1)$.

Using Bayes' theorem, we can write:

$$f(H_0|y) = \frac{f(y|H_0)f(H_0)}{f(y)} \tag{3}$$

Where $f(H_i)$ is the probability of hypothesis H_i and $f(y)$ is the pdf of them; by the theorem of total probability, $f(y)$ can be written as:

$$f(y) = f(y|H_0)P(H_0) + f(y|H_1)P(H_1) \tag{4}$$

A similar equation is:

$$f(H_1|y) = \frac{f(y|H_1)f(H_1)}{f(y)} \tag{5}$$

Let $f(H_0) = \pi_0$ and $f(H_1) = \pi_1$, then we can determine from above

$$f(y|H_0)\pi_0 > f(y|H_1)\pi_1 \tag{6}$$

If the inequality is reversed, then we decide a decision rule D, i.e. a function H_1 is correct. We will let D_0 be the event associated with the "decision" of choosing H_0 and D_1 be the corresponding event associated with H_1. Because the π_0 and π_1 is a fixed value after embedding the watermark. So if we can get the value of $f(y|H_0)$ and $f(y|H_1)$, we can make a decision the rate is High speed or low speed.

However, if we assume that the distribution of time perturbation is

$$f(w) = \frac{1}{\sqrt{2\pi}\sigma} e^{-\frac{(w-\mu)^2}{2\sigma^2}} \tag{7}$$

We denote the data stream carrying an embedded watermark as X, based on the above, the signal to detect is $Y = x + W$ where

$$x = \begin{cases} H \text{ under } H_1 \\ L \text{ under } H_0 \end{cases} \tag{8}$$

pdf of Y under H_0 and H_1:

$$f(y|H_0) = f(w)|_{w=y+L} = \frac{1}{\sqrt{2\pi}\sigma} e^{-\frac{(y+L-\mu)^2}{2\sigma^2}} \tag{9}$$

$$f(y|H_1) = f(w)|_{w=y+H} = \frac{1}{\sqrt{2\pi}\sigma} e^{-\frac{(y+H-\mu)^2}{2\sigma^2}} \tag{10}$$

And the likelihood ratio is:

$$L(y) = exp(\frac{(y+L-\mu)^2}{2\sigma^2} - \frac{(y+H-\mu)^2}{2\sigma^2}) \tag{11}$$

If we know μ and σ, from (11) we can get the decision threshold. By the decision threshold, we can classify the inter packet delay of the packet stream.

Next we will focus on how to estimate the μ of the noise distribution. Let the time interval of adjacent packets be random variable X; let random variable Y denotes the noise signal; let random variable Z denotes the time interval to be classified. In order to get μ of the noise distribution function, we must first get the mean of Z. The following theory can help us get the mean of Z.

Corollary of the law of large numbers 1. *Let $X_1, X_2, \ldots, X_n, \ldots$ be a sequence of independent and identically distributed random variables, if $E(X_i) = \mu, D(X_i) = \sigma^2 (i = 1, 2, 3, \ldots)$*

$$\overline{X} = \frac{1}{n} \sum_1^n X_i, \overline{X} \to^p \mu. \tag{12}$$

Because the inter packet delay is independent and follows identical distribution. If the packet stream packets number are large enough, through the corollary of the law of large numbers we can estimate $E(Z)$. So when getting $E(Z)$, we can also assess $E(Y)$ and the variance of the distribution of the noise signal. Consequently the decision threshold can use the likelihood ration(11) to obtain.

Detect watermark. When getting the decision threshold θ, we can classify the inter packet delay of the packet stream. If the time interval is greater than θ, the time interval should be identified as low-speed time interval, if the time interval not greater than θ the time interval should be identified as high-speed time interval. Next the method will deal with the result from above step with the following algorithm, let T_H be the high-speed data packet interval; let T_L be the low speed data packet interval.

1. If detecting inter packet delay lower than T_H, the inter packet delay should remain unchanged.

2. If detecting inter packet delay lower than the threshold θ but greater than T_H, the inter packet delay should adjust to T_H;
3. If detecting inter packet delay greater than T_L, the inter packet delay should adjust to T_L;
4. If detecting inter packet delay greater than threshold θ, but lower than T_L, the inter packet delay should remain unchanged.

Considering the four cases above, the elapsed time of packet stream carrying embedded watermark is enlarged by the time perturbation. By the above processing, we can squeeze the elapsed time of the receive packet stream. Let L be the squeezed elapsed time of received packet stream. Then let L be equally sliced into N fixed length intervals, with N lower than T, here T is the duration of high rate packets(or duration of low rate packets.) In the experiment they are the same. Next, the rate of packet in fixed length interval can be calculated. The fixed length is L/N. When getting the rates on every time interval L/N, we can use the cluster technique to cluster these rates in fixed time interval. Once obtaining the centers of the clusters, the center can be classified into two parts, and then the watermark information can be extracted. From Fig.1 we can easily find the embedded bit information is $LHLHL$(01010).

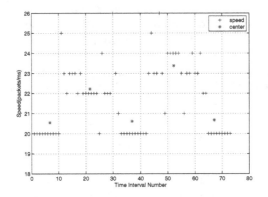

Fig. 1. Cluster result of FCM

The experiment shows that we can effectively reduce the time perturbation by the above processing. The next step is extracting the watermark from the processed inter packet delays. According to the ON-OFF [12]characteristics of the stepping stone, we assume that the detecting client can get the whole packet flow in which the watermark is embedded.

This paper chooses the fuzzy cluster algorithm to extract the watermark. The verge of the different interval rates is not very clear because the time perturbation, so we choose the fuzzy cluster algorithm to cluster the last small interval rates to obtain the embedded watermark. Next, we will give a brief description of fuzzy cluster. The Fuzzy C-Means [18] cluster algorithm is one of the most widely used fuzzy clustering algorithms. Fuzzy C-Mean Cluster(FCM) algorithm process is as follows. The FCM algorithm attempts to partition a finite collection of elements $X = x_1, x_2, \ldots, x_n$ into a collection of c fuzzy cluster with respect to some given criterion. Given a finite set of data, the algorithm return a list of c cluster centers V, such that $V = v_i, i = 1, 2, \ldots, c$ and a partition matrix U such that $U = u_{ij}, i = 1, 2, \ldots, c, j = 1, 2, \ldots, n$ Where u_{ij} is a numerical value in $[0, 1]$ that tells the degree to which the element x_j belongs to the ith cluster.

The algorithm steps are below:

Step 1. select the number of clusters $c(2 \leq c \leq n)$, exponential weight $\mu(1 < \mu < \infty)$, initial partition matrix U^0, and the termination criteria ε. Also, set the iteration index 1 to 0.

Step 2. calculate the fuzzy cluster centers $v_i^l | i = 1, 2, , c$ by using U^l.

Step 3. calculate the new partition matrix U^{l+1} by using $v_i^l | i = 1, 2, \ldots, c$.

Step 4. calculate the new partition matrix $\Delta = U^{l+1} - U^l = max_{ij} |u_{ij}^{l+1} - U_{ij}^l|$. If $\Delta > \varepsilon$, then set l=1+l and to step 2. if $\Delta \leq \varepsilon$, then stop.

4   Evaluation by Simulation

The above section has given a detailed description of the *Rate-based* flow watermark technique which is for tracing back stepping stone. In this section, this novel technique is simulated by the MATLAB.

4.1   Signal Source Model

Let V_H be the high speed of the packet stream, and V_L be the low speed of the packet stream. The duration of high speed packet stream and low rate packet stream both are T. When packet transfer speed is high, the transferred packets number during T are $T * V_H$; on the other hand, when transferred speed is low, the total transferred packets number are $T * V_L$. The inter packet delay of high speed packets is $\frac{1}{V_H}$, and the inter packet delay of low speed packets is $\frac{1}{V_L}$. We use the following vector to simulate the inter packet delay of the packet stream:

$$\theta = (1 : \frac{1}{V_H} : T, T : \frac{1}{V_L} : 2T, T : \frac{1}{V_H} : 3T, \ldots, (m - 1)T : \frac{1}{V_L} : mT) \quad (13)$$

Where $1 : \frac{1}{V_H} : T$ denotes from 1 increase to T by step length $\frac{1}{V_H}$. Let $1 : \frac{1}{V_H} : T$ denotes 1, $T : \frac{1}{V_L} : 2T$ denotes 0 *etc.* From this way the watermark information can be embedded into the θ. From the the above method, we can generate the data to simulate the data stream that embedded watermark.

4.2   Channel Model

There are two main perturbations in the transferring channel:

First, the time delay was introduced by both the attacker on purpose and network delay. In order to simulate this perturbation, we generated a series of random numbers to simulate the time perturbation, then added these random numbers which denote the time perturbation into the θ (13);

Second, by randomly adding or omitting some variables in θ, we want to simulate the perturbation which was introduced by the attacker, such as the adding packet or dropping packet.

4.3   Simulation Result

1. Detecting rate $v.s. \frac{1}{V_L} - \frac{1}{V_H} = \gamma$

Let T be the elapsed time of one bit watermark information as defined in 1, in the experiment, $\frac{1}{V_H} = 30ms$; T is respectively 10s, 15s, 20s, 25s and 30s ; $\frac{1}{V_L} - \frac{1}{V_H} = \gamma$; γ is respectively 5ms, 10ms, 15ms, 20ms, 25ms and 30ms. The mean of time perturbation is near 200ms. In the experiment we embedded 5 bits of watermark information; Table.1 shows that if the γ is bigger, the right detecting

Table 1. Detection Rate $v.s.$ $1/V_L - 1/V_H = \gamma$

D.R	$T = 10s$	$T = 15s$	$T = 20s$	$T = 25s$	$T = 30s$
$\gamma = 5ms$	84%	94%	100%	100%	100%
$\gamma = 10ms$	100%	100%	100%	100%	100%
$\gamma = 15ms$	100%	100%	100%	100%	100%
$\gamma = 20ms$	100%	100%	100%	100%	100%
$\gamma = 30ms$	100%	100%	100%	100%	100%

rate is higher. In order to upgrade the detecting rate, we can choose a bigger γ when embedding watermark into packet stream. However, if we choose a bigger γ, the watermark is difficult to embed into the stream. At the same time, if the γ is too big, the watermark is visible if the attacker collects enough packets. Table.1 shows that if the γ is less than $5ms$, the detecting rate becomes decreased. From signal detection aspect, the signal was too small, it was submerged by the noise signal(the mean of the noise signal is 200ms in the experiment). The useful signal was too weak to extract.

2. Detecting rate $v.s$ **Time perturbation**

In the experiment, $\frac{1}{V_L} - \frac{1}{V_H} = \gamma$; γ is respectively 5ms, 10ms, 15ms, 20ms, 25ms and 30ms. Let elapsed time of one bit watermark information $T = 15s$. The time distribution which obeys the normal distribution, the mean of the time distribution is respectively 40ms, 80ms, 120ms, 200ms, 270ms, 310ms, 380ms, 470ms, 550ms and 640ms. In the Fig.2, the mean of time perturbation is the x axis. The y axis represents the detecting rate of the watermark detection.

In the experiment, the mean amplitude of the noise signal is larger than the useful signal itself. From the result of the simulation, as Fig.2 shows the algorithm we proposed tolerated time perturbation. When the packet stream pass through many stepping stones, the time perturbation is growing larger and larger; this algorithm can extract watermark from packet stream despite the time perturbation being so large, because we use weak signal detecting model to detect the watermark, so the proposed algorithm tolerate the bigger time

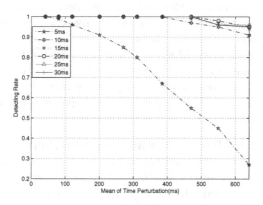

Fig. 2. Detecting rate *v.s.* Time perturbation

perturbation. However Fig.2 also shows that if γ is too small, the detecting rate will decrease. This reason is similar as in Table 1, if the useful signal too weak, but the noise signal too larger, it is hard to get useful signal from the channel.

3. Detecting rate *v.s.* Packet Losing perturbation

In the previous context, we have discussed two kinds of packet perturbation: packet losing and packet padding. In this experiment we will simulate the watermark detecting rate under packet losing perturbation. Like prior experiments, we still choose $T = 15ms$, $\frac{1}{V_L} - \frac{1}{V_H} = \gamma$, γ is respectively 10ms, 15ms, 20ms and 30ms. The packet losing rate is respectively 5%, 10%, 20%, 30%, 40%, 50% and 60%.

Table 2. Detecting Rate *v.s.* Packet Losing perturbation

D.R	$\gamma = 10ms$	$\gamma = 15ms$	$\gamma = 20ms$	$\gamma = 30ms$
$L.R = 5\%$	100%	100%	100%	100%
$L.R = 10\%$	100%	100%	100%	100%
$L.R = 20\%$	100%	100%	100%	100%
$L.R = 30\%$	100%	100%	100%	100%
$L.R = 40\%$	100%	100%	100%	100%
$L.R = 50\%$	99%	99%	99%	99%
$L.R = 60\%$	99%	97%	97%	98%

In Table 2, R.D denotes the detecting rate, and L.R denotes packet losing rate. From the result of the simulation, the algorithm tolerated the packet losing. So either this algorithm tolerated SSH tools which will repacketize the packets or the attacker drops the packets on purpose when packet stream pass through the stepping stone. The previous work[5] proposed method tolerated less than 11% packet repacketizaion. However, our watermark technique tolerated more than 50% packet losing.

This algorithm can tolerate the packet losing perturbation, because of two main reasons. Firstly, the packet losing will change the inter packet delay, the way same as the time perturbation, because this algorithm can tolerate the time perturbation, so the algorithm can also tolerate packet losing perturbation. Secondly, the watermark detection model use fuzzy cluster to extract embedded information, which does't live on precision packet number compared to previous work. In the above discussion, the algorithm this paper proposed can tolerate packet losing perturbation.

4. Detecting rate *v.s.* Packet Padding perturbation

In the above section, we discussed the influenza of packet losing perturbation to the packet stream watermark. In this section we give another kind of packet perturbation: packet padding. In the experiment, we choose $\frac{1}{V_L} - \frac{1}{V_H} = \gamma$; γ is respectively 10ms, 15ms, 20ms and 30ms; the packet padding rate is respectively 5%, 10%, 15%, 20%, 25%, and 30%. The main different between the packet losing perturbation and packet padding perturbation is that packet padding perturbation will introduced time delay to the whole packet stream, so this attack is more difficult to defend than packets losing perturbation. We assume that adding a packet will induce a random time delay. In the test we randomly chose each time delay which is less than 500ms for the inter packet delay has a upper boundary. In Table 3, P.R denotes packet padding rate, D.R denotes the

Table 3. Detecting Rate *v.s.* Packet Padding perturbation

D.R	$\gamma = 10ms$	$\gamma = 15ms$	$\gamma = 20ms$	$\gamma = 30ms$
$P.R = 5\%$	100%	100%	100%	100%
$P.R = 10\%$	100%	100%	100%	100%
$P.R = 15\%$	100%	100%	100%	100%
$P.R = 20\%$	95%	99%	99%	99%
$P.R = 25\%$	97%	98%	98%	96%
$P.R = 30\%$	96%	95%	96%	95%

detecting rate. From Table 3, we can find that the detecting rate is not good as the result of Table 2. The main reason is that packet padding not only influenced the adjacent packets, but also influence the the whole inter packet delay of the packets flow. So the detecting rate is not well as Table 2. However, from the experiment result, we can see that the algorithm still can tolerate 15% packet padding.

5. Detecting Rate *v.s.* Packet Losing and Time Perturbation

This experiment introduced both time perturbation and packet losing perturbation; we choose $T = 15ms$, $\frac{1}{V_L} - \frac{1}{V_H} = \gamma$; γ is respectively 10ms and 15m. The packet losing rate is respectively 5%, 10%, 15%, 20%, 25%, 30% and 40%. The mean of time perturbation is respectively 80ms, 120ms, 200ms, 270ms, 310ms and 470ms. The experiment result as show in Table 4 and Table 5.

Table 4. Detecting Rate *v.s.* Packet Losing and Time Perturbation

when $\frac{1}{V_L} - \frac{1}{V_H} = 10ms$

D.R	M.T = 80ms	M.T = 120ms	M.T = 200ms	M.T = 270ms	M.T = 310ms	M.T = 470ms
L.R = 5%	100%	100%	100%	100%	100%	99%
L.R = 10%	100%	100%	100%	100%	99%	95%
L.R = 15%	100%	100%	100%	99%	96%	94%
L.R = 20%	100%	100%	100%	99%	96%	94%
L.R = 25%	100%	100%	99%	99%	97%	98%
L.R = 30%	100%	100%	100%	97%	97%	89%

Table 5. Detecting Rate *v.s.* Packet Losing and Time Perturbation

when $\frac{1}{V_L} - \frac{1}{V_H} = 15ms$

D.R	M.T = 80ms	M.T = 120ms	M.T = 200ms	M.T = 270ms	M.T = 310ms	M.T = 470ms
L.R = 5%	100%	100%	100%	100%	100%	100%
L.R = 10%	100%	100%	100%	100%	100%	100%
L.R = 15%	100%	100%	100%	100%	100%	100%
L.R = 20%	100%	100%	100%	100%	98%	99%
L.R = 25%	100%	100%	100%	99%	96%	98%
L.R = 30%	100%	100%	100%	99%	96%	98%

In Table 4 and Table 5, M.T denotes the mean of the time perturbation. Table 4 and Table 5 show that algorithm is effective when there is a concurrence of time perturbation and packet losing perturbation. As we have discussed before, the packet losing is time perturbation essentially; So the concurrence of time and packet losing perturbation will increase the time perturbation, because the algorithm can tolerate time perturbation as discussed in above section. So in this experiment, the result of the experiment is still good.

6. Detecting Rate *v.s.* Packet Padding and Time Perturbation

The experiment introduce both time perturbation and packet padding perturbation; we choose $T = 15ms$, $\frac{1}{V_L} - \frac{1}{V_H} = \gamma$; γ is respectively 10ms and 15m. The packet padding rate is respectively 5%, 10%, 15%, 20%, 25% and 30%. The mean of time perturbation is respectively 80ms, 120ms, 200ms, 270ms, 310ms and 470ms.

Table 6 and Table 7 show that the algorithm is effective under the concurrence of time perturbation and packet padding perturbation, when packet padding rate and time perturbation are not too large. Compared to other experiment results above, this result is not good, because the packet padding not only influenced the adjacent packets, but also influenced all the time interval of packets in the packet stream. Thus it will influence the cluster result, so the detecting rate is not as good. When time perturbation is introduced concurrently, the detecting rate will decreased more. But from Table 6 and Table 7, the technique still can defend 10% packet padding rate and time perturbation that is less than 200ms.

Table 6. Detecting Rate *v.s.* Packet Padding and Time Perturbation

when $\frac{1}{V_L} - \frac{1}{V_H} = 10ms$

D.R	$M.T = 80ms$	$M.T = 120ms$	$M.T = 200ms$	$M.T = 270ms$	$M.T = 310ms$	$M.T = 470ms$
$P.R = 5\%$	100%	100%	100%	96%	94%	90%
$P.R = 10\%$	100%	100%	98%	96%	94%	86%
$P.R = 15\%$	99%	96%	94%	93%	90%	85%
$P.R = 20\%$	99%	96%	94%	91%	88%	83%
$P.R = 25\%$	98%	97%	90%	85%	82%	78%
$P.R = 30\%$	95%	84%	81%	80%	77%	65%

Table 7. Detecting Rate *v.s.* Packet Padding and Time Perturbation

when $\frac{1}{V_L} - \frac{1}{V_H} = 15ms$

D.R	$M.T = 80ms$	$M.T = 120ms$	$M.T = 200ms$	$M.T = 270ms$	$M.T = 310ms$	$M.T = 470ms$
$P.R = 5\%$	100%	100%	100%	100%	98%	96%
$P.R = 10\%$	100%	100%	100%	100%	97%	91%
$P.R = 15\%$	100%	100%	99%	97%	94%	85%
$P.R = 20\%$	100%	100%	98%	96%	93%	88%
$P.R = 25\%$	100%	99%	97%	96%	94%	93%
$P.R = 30\%$	99%	97%	95%	93%	90%	84%

5   Analysis

5.1   Resilience against Time Perturbation and Packet Perturbation

In the process of data transmission, the network itself will bring time delay. What's more packet stream suffered from time perturbation by the attacker on purpose when packet stream pass through the stepping stone; the stepping stone may repacketize the packets or add some useless packets. All of these perturbation will cause the time interval between packets be changed. Especially, the packets pass through many stepping stones, the time perturbation will become larger. When we take this problem into account, we used the weak signal detection model and cluster method to extract the watermark, because the cluster method is used to get embedded watermark information, so the watermark detecting technique doesn't need the precision packet number. From the simulation, we found the watermark can tolerate bigger time perturbation and packet perturbation.

5.2   Defense against the "Visible" Attack

The method proposed in this paper proposed is based on packet rate. If the attacker can collect enough packets, the watermark is visible. Some proposed methods [5] used this weakness to attack the watermark method which based on IPD. Fortunately, our novel watermark is based on weak signal detection model, so in order to make the watermark invisible, we added some time perturbations on purpose. If the attacker doesn't know the watermark bits number and $\frac{1}{V_L} - \frac{1}{V_H}$, then the attacker couldn't use the cluster method to extract the watermark information.

6   Conclusion

Tracing intrusion connection through the stepping stones has been a challenge work until now, especially because the time perturbation and packet perturbation introduced both by the the network itself and the attacker on purpose make this problem more difficult to solve. However, the flow watermark based on the time interval between packets is a good way to deal with this problem, as we know many previous schemes based on time interval between packet can solve some perturbations under some hypotheses. The contribution of this paper is that we analyze previous watermark techniques, and propose a novel flow watermark detection model to deal with the problem which we have referred in the above context. From the simulation result, the novel watermark technique can tolerate the perturbation discussed above.

This paper's main innovation is that we used the hypothesis testing model to get the decision threshold. In the paper we also use the cluster method to extract watermark from the packet stream. From this way we can extract watermark without precision packet number and precision time synchronization comparing to the previous works. Also, this paper proposed algorithm can extract watermark in less than 2 minutes packet stream. Wang [5] proposed method needs 10 minutes packet stream to recover the watermark. The article proposed scheme assumed that the beginning and the end of the packet stream can be detected by the detecting client, according to ON-OFF characteristics of the stepping stone connection. In the future work we will omit these hypotheses, and develop more robust watermark technique.

References

1. Sekar, V., Xie, Y., Maltz, D., Reiter, M., Zhang, H.: Toward a framework for internet forensic analysis. In: Proc. of ACM HotNets-III (2004)
2. Yaar, A., Perrig, A., Song, D.: FIT: fast internet traceback. In: Proceedings IEEE INFOCOM 2005. 24th Annual Joint Conference of the IEEE Computer and Communications Societies, vol. 2 (2005)
3. Strayer, W., Jones, C., Schwartz, B., Mikkelson, J., Livadas, C., Technol, B., Cambridge, M.: Architecture for multi-stage network attack traceback. In: The IEEE Conference on Local Computer Networks, 2005. 30th Anniversary, p. 8 (2005)
4. Wang, X., Reeves, D., Wu, S.: Inter-packet delay based correlation for tracing encrypted connections through stepping stones. In: Gollmann, D., Karjoth, G., Waidner, M. (eds.) ESORICS 2002. LNCS, vol. 2502, pp. 244–263. Springer, Heidelberg (2002)
5. Wang, X., Chen, S., Sybase, I., Dr, O., Jajodia, S.: Network flow watermarking attack on low-latency anonymous communication systems
6. Pyun, Y., Park, Y., Wang, X., Reeves, D., Ning, P.: Tracing traffic through intermediate hosts that repacketize flows. In: IEEE INFOCOM 2007. 26th IEEE International Conference on Computer Communications, pp. 634–642 (2007)
7. Zhang, L., Persaud, A., Johnson, A., Guan, Y.: Detection of stepping stone attack under delay and chaff perturbations. In: 25th IEEE International Performance, Computing, and Communications Conference, IPCCC 2006, p. 10 (2006)

8. Wang, X., Reeves, D.: Robust correlation of encrypted attack traffic through step-ping stones by manipulation of interpacket delays. In: Proceedings of the 10th ACM conference on Computer and communications security, pp. 20–29. ACM, New York (2003)

9. Donoho, D., Flesia, A., Shankar, U., Paxson, V., Coit, J., Staniford, S.: Multiscale stepping-stone detection: Detecting pairs of jittered interactive streams by exploit-ing maximum tolerable delay. In: Wespi, A., Vigna, G., Deri, L. (eds.) RAID 2002. LNCS, vol. 2516, pp. 17–35. Springer, Heidelberg (2002)

10. Wang, X.: Tracing intruders behind stepping stones. PhD thesis (2004)

11. Staniford-Chen, S., Heberlein, L.: Holding intruders accountable on the internet. In: 1995 IEEE Symposium on Security and Privacy, Proceedings, pp. 39–49 (1995)

12. Zhang, Y., Paxson, V.: Detecting stepping stones. In: Proceedings of the 9th USENIX Security Symposium, pp. 171–184 (2000)

13. He, T., Tong, L.: Detecting encrypted stepping-stone connections. IEEE Transac-tions on Signal Processing, Part 1 55(5), 1612–1623 (2007)

14. Dingledine, R., Mathewson, N., Syverson, P.: Tor: The second-generation onion router. In: Proceedings of the 13th conference on USENIX Security Symposium, vol. 13, p. 21. USENIX Association, Berkeley (2004)

15. Yu, W., Fu, X., Graham, S., Xuan, D., Zhao, W.: Dsss-based flow marking tech-nique for invisible traceback. In: IEEE Symposium on Security and Privacy, SP 2007, pp. 18–32 (2007)

16. Peng, P., Ning, P., Reeves, D.: On the secrecy of timing-based active watermarking trace-back techniques

17. Helstrom, C.: Statistical theory of signal detection. Pergamon Press, Oxford (1968)

18. Dembele, D., Kastner, P.: Fuzzy C-means method for clustering microarray data (2003)

Locally Multipath Adaptive Routing Protocol Resilient to Selfishness and Wormholes

Farshid Farhat, Mohammad-Reza Pakravan,
Mahmoud Salmasizadeh, and Mohammad-Reza Aref

Department of Electrical Engineering, Sharif University of Technology, Tehran, Iran
{farhat,pakravan,salmasi,aref}@ee.sharif.edu

Abstract. Locally multipath adaptive routing (LMAR) protocol, classified as a new reactive distance vector routing protocol for MANETs is proposed in this paper. LMAR can find an ad-hoc path without selfish nodes and wormholes using a random search algorithm in polynomial-time. Also when the primary path fails, it discovers an alternative safe path if network graph remains connected after eliminating selfish/malicious nodes. The main feature of LMAR to seek safe route free of selfish and malicious nodes in polynomial time is its searching algorithm and flooding stage that its generated traffic is equiloaded compared to single-path routing protocols but its ability to bypass the attacks is much better than the other multi-path routing protocols. LMAR concept is introduced to provide the security feature known as availability and a simulator has been developed to analyze its behavior. Efficiency of the route discovery stage is analyzed and compared with the previous algorithms.

Keywords: Ad-hoc Wireless Networks Security, Efficient Local-Multipath Adaptive Routing Protocol, Resilience to Selfishness and Wormholes, On-demand Distance Vector Routing.

1 Introduction

Mobile Ad-hoc Networks (MANETs) are characterized by mobile hosts connected by wireless links communicating with each other without any infrastructure such as access point or base station. MANETs have many applications in a wide area of situations. MANET applications include military and emergency instances to establish an integrated network in an infrastructure-less location. Also MANETs are used for sensor networks, civilian applications, and ubiquitous computing. We could imagine most of the applications of infrastructure-based networks for MANETs with mobility feature. Each ad-hoc node can only communicate with its neighbor nodes within its radio range. Each node to send a message to the node out of its radio range has to ask its neighbor nodes' help. So a multi-hop path between source and destination must be discovered. As the hosts of MANET move randomly, the topology of the MANET changes. MANET is usually established for impromptu decisions to achieve the specific goal. As mentioned we could conclude the main characteristics of MANET such as: wireless autonomous nodes, ad-hoc-based network, multi-hop routing protocols, mobility, and infrastructure-less.

J. Kwak et al. (Eds.): ISPEC 2010, LNCS 6047, pp. 187–200, 2010.

Many routing protocols have been suggested to find multi-hop routes between some nodes. But selfish and malicious nodes can disrupt found paths easily. Routing protocol designers try to secure their schemes by using cryptography methods like confidentiality, integrity, authentication and non-repudiation. But these methods are not enough to establish connection. One of the main security services mentioned in network security is availability that is needed to assure establishing connection. Providing availability service is a challenging issue like DoS attack resiliency and cannot be achieved by using cryptography methods lonely.

We propose locally multipath adaptive routing (LMAR) protocol which finds safe ad-hoc routes free of selfish nodes and wormholes. Utilizing a reactive approach, proposed routing protocol uses an adaptive rerouting method to bypass selfish/malicious nodes, and also guarantees establishing a safe connection in polynomial-time if network graph remains connected after eliminating wormholes and selfish nodes.

In following sections, first we briefly review in section 2 some of key concepts such as on-demand routing, multipath routing, node selfishness and wormholes in MANETs. In section 3, we present the key concepts of our proposed approach; LMAR. We explain the network model, problem definition, attack scenario and solution strategy. We describe the structure of LMAR in section 4. Simulation results are given in section 5.

2 Fundamental Concepts

In this section we explain some fundamental concepts like on-demand distance vector routing, multipath routing, selfishness in ad-hoc networks and wormhole attacks on MANETs.

2.1 On-Demand Distance Vector Routing

Routing protocols in wireless networks are usually based on either distance vector or source routing and not link state routing algorithms. Routing algorithms in conventional networks require periodic broadcast of routing information by each router like Destination Sequenced Distance Vector (DSDV) [1] as a proactive (periodic) routing protocol. In distance vector routing, each router broadcasts to all of its neighboring routers the prospected distance to all other non-neighboring nodes. The neighboring routers then compute the shortest path to each node, like Ad-hoc On-demand Distance Vector Routing (AODV) [2] as a reactive (on-demand) routing protocol.

Another famous concept of routing is source routing, a technique where the source of the packet determines the complete sequence of the nodes of the established route. Each intermediate node attaches its address to the header of the packet like what happened to Dynamic Source Routing (DSR) [3]. In link-state routing, each router broadcasts to all of its neighboring routers its view of the status of each of its adjacent links; the neighboring nodes then compute the shortest distance to each node based upon the complete topology of the network like Optimized Link State Routing (OLSR) [4]. Some protocols like DSDV, called as proactive, are suitable for network environments where there are no node power consumption constraints. In MANETs where nodes have power constraints and the network has a much more dynamic nature, reactive or on-demand routing protocols are usually used. Routing table update procedure of on-demand routing protocol are different from the previous proactive approaches. Reactive or on-demand routing protocols establish and sustain paths from one source to its destination on an as needed basis. Compared to the proactive counterparts of the on-demand protocols, the routing discovery overhead is typically lower. On-demand route discovery reduced the cost of route maintenance towards periodic route discovery, because unused routes are not updated. On-demand route discovery is useful when the network traffic is sparse and related to a known subset of nodes. But data traffic suffers from the delay of route discovery and route maintenance procedure. Also these routing algorithms, in contrast with source routing, use a smaller header, because their packets doesn't convey the address list of passing routers except the address of source and destination.

Flooding process helps reactive protocols to discover routes. The traffic source floods an inquiry packet called Route Request Packet (RREQ) into the network to find a route to the desire destination. When an old route breaks because of a link breakage, flooding is also applied to maintain a new route instead of previous route. To have effective performance of reactive protocols flooding procedure should be controlled, because it consumes the most amounts of network resources like bandwidth and nodes' power.

All of above protocols are single path protocols, because they find only one shortest path in the specific topology of the network. If there are selfish nodes that do not cooperate for proper execution of data forwarding, or malicious nodes that collude to make wormholes, active data forwarding paths may be broken. So route discovery process must be performed again. Thus it necessitates flooding RREQs in the network again. In ad-hoc networks with dynamic topology, frequent route maintenance requests cause the high latency of new route discovery stage and affect the performance efficiency adversely.

2.2 Multipath Routing

Multipath on-demand routing protocols try to alleviate single path reactive routing protocols flaws by discovering multiple routes in a single route discovery procedure. Source nodes and intermediate nodes could find multi-paths sent by destination nodes. Route maintenance stage is needed only when all previous paths fail. So route maintenance latency and routing overheads decrease. By storing more available path to destination, higher performance efficiency could be achieved. Multipath routing in wired networks has been suggested to decrease data re-forwarding, control congestion, and deal with QoS issues. Other coercing advantages of applying multipath routing in MANETs are lower latency, higher fault tolerance, lower energy consumption, and higher robustness. Some on-demand multipath routing protocols have been suggested for ad hoc networks, including Shortest Multipath Routing Using Labeled Distances [5], Ad hoc On-demand Multipath Distance Vector (AOMDV) [6], Multipath Dynamic Source Routing (Multipath DSR) [7], Cooperative Packet Caching and Shortest Multipath (CHAMP) [8], Temporally Ordered Routing Algorithm (TORA) [9], Split Multipath Routing (SMR) [10], and Routing

On-demand Acyclic Multipath (ROAM) [11]. SMR and MDSR are on the basis of dynamic source routing whereas AOMDV, ROAM, CHAMP and TORA are destination-sequenced distance vector routing based. Mentioned protocols establish multiple paths upon request, the data traffic could be distributed into multiple routes. But usually a single route is mainly employed and the other routes are applied only when the main route fails.

2.3 Selfishness and Wormholes

Noting the distributed and mostly uncontrolled nature of MANETs, there are possibilities of node misbehavior that can have serious impact on network operation. Active attacks and passive attacks essentially threaten mobile ad-hoc networks (MANETs). In an active attack, the malicious routers have to consume some power to execute the assault, but passive attacks are principally due to lack of cooperation with the purpose of saving energy selfishly. Nodes that perform active attacks with the aim of damaging other nodes by causing network recess are considered to be malicious while nodes that execute passive attacks with the aim of saving battery life for their own communications are considered to be selfish. A selfish node that wants to save battery life for its own communication, may not take part in any communications known as Selfish Type-I or only takes part in the route discovery process to update its routing table, and selfishly doesn't participate in the data forwarding process known as Selfish Type-II [22]. Selfish nodes can endanger the correct network operation by simply not cooperating in the packet forwarding process (this attack is also known as the black hole attack). Single path ad hoc routing protocols can not cope with the selfishness problem when a selfish node exists in the active shortest path. The selfish node doesn't forward the data traffic, so another route discovery process must be implemented to get a new route with possibly cooperative nodes. Accordingly the network performance severely degrades.

The effect of node selfishness on the network throughput and end-to-end delay has been simulated by Michiardi et al [12] when the dynamic source routing protocol is employed. Traditional network security services consist of authentication and access control cannot handle selfishness as well as wormhole attack. Secure cooperation enforcement schemes such as Nuglets as a virtual currency [13], CONFIDANT [14], CORE [15], or Token-based cooperation enforcement [16] seem to offer reasonable solution. In a collaboration enforcement security scheme, router misbehaviour could be caught by the collaboration between numerous nodes supposing that most of routers do network tasks normally. We show that our multipath routing protocol is flexible towards selfishness, because it could bypass selfish nodes and choose cooperative clients.

A further shrewd type of active attack is the establishment of a virtual private connection or tunnel (called as wormhole [17]) between two colluding malicious routers in MANET topology (see Figure 1). This feature allows the wormhole nodes to short-circuit two points of network, so the normal flow of routing messages creates a virtual vertex cut in the network that is controlled by the two colluding attackers. Our protocol could adaptively change paths containing working links instead of wormholes. Malicious nodes can disrupt the correct functioning of a routing protocol or degrade the performance of data forwarding process by discarding attracted traffic. This new type of attack goes under the name of wormhole attack.

To defend against the destructive wormhole attack various works have been done [18,19]. To restrict the travelling space of any message, time-based solution has been proposed in [18]. Time-based mechanisms rely on strict synchronization between the network routers, thus they need to apply some extra equipments like GPS. A collaborative routing protocol through routers share directional messages assuming that routers are supplied with directional antennas is suggested in [19] to protect ad-hoc network against wormhole attacks.

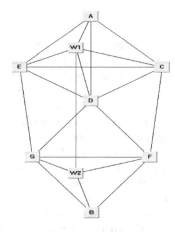

Fig. 1. Wormhole Link between W1 and W2

Khabbazian et al. [23] have been suggested a single-path protocol against wormhole attack. They have been applied per packet*connection process run on all nodes to detect wormholes. In their attack scenario, only 4 consecutive nodes (F-M1-M2-E) have been provided that M1,M2 nodes are malicious and M1-M2 link is wormhole. If the nodes S-F-M1-M2-E-D construct the route from source (S) to destination (D), malicious behavior of M1-M2 affects on nodes F-E to choose as malicious, because they cannot provide the node S with a signed destination ACK or a signed RERR/FR packet too. Our proposed protocol adaptively process per packet and changes the paths between the nodes to avoid wormholes, and it doesn't need to use any extra supplies. Detecting the wormhole attack has been suggested in [20] by a graph theoretic approach and [21] by a statistical approach.

3 Overview of the Approach

In this section we explain our assumptions about the network model and its security attributes. We then clarify the problem that endangers any mobile ad-hoc network. Thereafter we explain our solution strategy.

3.1 Network Model

Our proposed algorithm is implemented in the network layer. It is assumed that neighbor discovery phase has been carried out by an appropriate layer-2 or layer-3 processes. We also assume that an acknowledgement (ACK) reception process will execute in the transport layer or network layer that would indicate correct reception of source packets. When the source does not receive any ACK, it tries another route until it can establish a safe path. Our assumed network topology is a random graph model network, that ad-hoc nodes is randomly placed in their positions. Also it is assumed the nodes characteristics are the same.

3.2 Attack Scenario Model

Passive and active attacks on availability of safe connections are considered in this paper. Other threats against security services like confidentiality, integrity or non-repudiation by eavesdropping or forging packets have not been included, because some of them could be provided by using cryptographic methods. Two kinds of selfish nodes including Type-I and Type-II could be available among the nodes. Behavior of a selfish/malicious node is independent from its neighbor nodes' behavior. In our attack scenario selfishness or wormholeness could happen occasionally by all the nodes so at the time T all nodes divided into ad-hoc and selfish/malicious nodes. Trying to establish selfish/malicious-free connections, ad-hoc nodes by using LMAR change their directions from time-variant selfish nodes at the time T+Δ. Cooperation enforcement schemes need supervising by trusted third party. Third party is like a central bank that gives reputation to its branches. Without any third party, malicious nodes could cheat in reputations. They could generate fake currencies or shows the value of other nodes' reputation lower or higher. So we are not interested in cooperative schemes.

3.3 Problem Definition

As mentioned in Section 2.3, selfishness and wormholes threaten wireless ad-hoc networks. Selfish and malicious nodes participate in route discovery stage properly to update their routing table, but as soon as data forwarding stage begins, they discard data packets ungenerously! We want to suggest a routing scheme to solve these problems by ignoring routes crossing selfish nodes or wormholes. Mobility and its effect on the algorithm have not been widely discussed.

As shown in Figure 1, it is assumed that we want to establish a connection between source (A) and destination (B). Routes such AW1W2B (optimal), AEW1W2B, ACW1W2B, ADW1W2B, AW1W2GB, or AW1W2FB could be best choices for optimal and sub-optimal paths, but non of them would work when the wormhole thread runs, because all the high ranked paths include wormhole link between W1 and W2 (they discard all traffic containing data packets).

3.4 Solution Strategy

Our goal is to establish a connection between the source and the destination. To counter the effects of wormhole attacks and selfishness, LMAR algorithm creates at least one alternative working path that is established by active cooperators from source to destination. LMAR has been designed such that it could explore all available paths from source to destination in the graph of network topology to get a working route. Theoretically if the induced sub-graph of the network topology is connected by removing selfish and malicious nodes, LMAR can discover a locally efficient path from source to destination. Referring to Figure 1, we have to get some reliable links to set up a desired route from A to B. Paths like ADGB, ADFB, AEGB, or ACFB are possible candidates. A flexible routing protocol must determine such paths as alternative routes to bypass the threats of wormholes or the selfishness of other nodes.

4 LMAR Protocol Structure

The design of LMAR is based on on-demand distance vector and multipath routing mentioned in sections 2.1 and 2.2. The protocol phases are divided into 3 parts: Route Discovery and Maintenance, and Data Forwarding.

4.1 Route Discovery and Maintenance

Every router has a clock measuring the number of ticks past first tick (when the router is on). As a source wants to transmit data to a destination and it doesn't know any active path to destination. Source node generates a proper RREQ packet to destination. Then it initiates a timer in transport layer to measure the period (here the number of ticks) between sending a RREQ and receiving its route reply (RREP). Subsequently it broadcasts the RREQ for destination.

The RREQ packets are a tuple with {Request ID (ReqID), Source Address (SrcAdd), Destination Address (DestAdd), Sequence Number (SeqNum), and Expiration Ticks (ExpTicks)}. *ReqID*, *SrcAdd*, and *DestAdd* are random unique identifiers (like IP Addresses or Nonce numbers) for RREQ, source, and destination respectively. As used in AODV, Sequence numbers play a key role in ensuring loop freedom. An incremental sequence number is maintained by every node. Also the highest perceived sequence numbers for each destination node is kept in the routing table. The higher SeqNum shows a new route, so it is one of the parameter used to update routing table. *Tick* is the unit of delay cost in our implementation. Delay cost is defined for links as transmission delay and for routers as processing delay. While RREQ passes a hop, *ExpTicks* showing the lifetime of the RREQ is monotonically decreased. This technique is applied for flooding limitation.

Every intermediate node receiving RREQ checks the destination address. If the destination address is different from its address, it will update its routing table with respect to source address. Note that each RREQ (RREP) arriving at a node during route discovery potentially defines an alternate path back to the source (destination). All routes to the specific node in routing table are always less than the number of neighbors. Each node can receive copies of RREQ from its neighbors, and update its routing table with respect to that destination. As we mentioned neighbor discovery phase has been carried out by an appropriate data-link or network layer processes attaching neighbor's identity as the uploader of the packet in the header of the frame.

Here delay cost instead of hop-count is applied for shortest path gauge. The sequence of paths is sorted with respect to the sequence number then the reception tick (*RecTick*), i.e. first the freshness of sequence number is checked and the path with the fresh SeqNum would be set as the first path. If the SeqNum is not changed, the *RecTick* is considered, and the path with lower *RecTick* would be set as the first path (The repeated neighbor is overwritten in the path list). The abstracted format of routing table simply is depicted below in Table 1. Seeing Table 1, you could find that *Destination Address* is the RREQ or RREP creator address. The address of the RREQ or RREP owner is received by the owner of this routing table. In each table the *Entry Index* specifies the current active entry used for sending data towards the destination, and the default value of *Entry Index* is 1 that points to the first entry.

Table 1. Abstracted Routing Table in LMAR

Destination Address	
Entry Index (Default=1)	
Index	The List of Paths (Entries)
1	{Neighbor1, SeqNum1, RecTick1}
2	{Neighbor2, SeqNum2, RecTick2}
	And so on

After updating the routing table with respect to the source, intermediate node searches for any route to the intended destination of RREQ packet. If the number of paths to destination is equal with the number of neighbors, it will forward the RREQ to the best route with minimum delay cost; otherwise it will broadcast the RREQ to all neighbors. Each router broadcasts the RREQ only once like AODV protocol, but it may receive and process the copies of that to update routing table several times (at most the number of its neighbors). When the first RREQ reaches the destination, it will be processed and the destination will generate RREP packet in response to RREQ packet. RREP packet structure is same as RREQ packet structure. RREP will be broadcast to source again. RREP flooding is necessary to set or update distance vector to the destination in intermediate nodes' routing tables. Also the destination doesn't involve in timeout process, because it couldn't measure the period between sending RREP and getting data packets, due to the fact that data packets never flood in network, so limited number of selfish or malicious nodes could discard them. Intermediate nodes apply the same process with RREP packets like what they do with RREQ packets. They update their routing table with respect to the destination address. If all possible routes to source are available, they will choose the best one to source, otherwise they will broadcast RREP packet again.

When the source gets the RREP packet generated by the destination, it updates its routing table, checks the RREP must not be repeated. Then it measures the period between request and reply, so it could set the ACK timeout period (the number of ticks needed to resend data packets in alternative route). Afterwards the best neighbor (first entry of routing table) as first hop of the shortest path is selected to send the desired traffic towards the destination. When two nodes exit from the coverage range of each other, the available link between them is broken. So each node deletes its previous neighbor address from its routing table. Also when a node reaches the coverage range of another node, they have to set or update their reachable destinations by exchanging their Entry[Index] of their routing tables. Observe that these operations are performed in data link layer. No update packet is broadcast or multicast to other stable neighbors, only moving and separated nodes updates their tables.

4.2 Data Forwarding

As mentioned before, when the source gets a reply from the destination, it initiates data forwarding via the neighbor specified by the Entry[Index] of its routing tables. Also each intermediate node sets the reverse path index back to the source in its routing table. Intermediate node gets the next hop of the best path to the destination, and forwards the data packet to its neighbor. If the data packet eventually arrives at the destination properly, the destination unicasts the ACK packet periodically after receiving multiple fragments of data packets. Sending an ACK from destination to source is a key process by which the presence of wormhole or selfish nodes in the path can be detected. This can be a part of network layer process or transport layer (e.g. using TCP ACK).

When ACK process reports an unestablished connection between source and destination which can be a sign of the presence of a wormhole or a selfish node in the path, a new route should be used. Therefore, the source chooses the next index of its routing table entries to establish a new route to destination. If all of entries are selected at least once, it means that the source has searched its table at least once (one round search reaches so the entry index sets to 1). Since then the source sets the *Change Path* flag in the header of next resent data packets to warn intermediate nodes for choosing alternative route to the destination. The interveners, which do not search all of its entries, reset the flag for subsequent nodes not to change their index, but if any intermediate node searched all of its routing table entries, it would keep the flag set adaptively for the next hops to change their index, and would forward the data packet to next neighbor. Observe that with this algorithm all of available paths between the source and the destination will be checked one by one in order to get a possibly safe route for data forwarding.

5 Simulation Results

We developed a simulator on a PC under Windows XP operating system with Visual C++ programming to implement LMAR protocol. The simulation speed is higher than similar simulators like NS-2 or Glomosim, because we only simulate main parameters of our model and some unused codes is not executed periodically. Also our simulator has visual effects to show the topology changes visually. Furthermore simulator developing is cumbersome but the simulator code can be easily debugged in Visual C++ environment.

5.1 Selfishness Resilience

To show the resilience of LMAR to selfishness we set up a uniform-randomly generated network topology containing 50 similar nodes randomly placed over a 100*100 m² area (see Figure 2), so the network topology is a random graph. Source (node 0) and destination node (node 49) are marked by circles in the network. The radio range of all nodes is set to 30 pixels, so they can cover the nodes available in a circle with 30-pixel radius. Nodes mutually covering their radio ranges have been interconnected to each other by a black line. When the packets pass the links, the color of the links is changed. RREQs color the links darker than RREPs do. All nodes' transmission range is 10m.

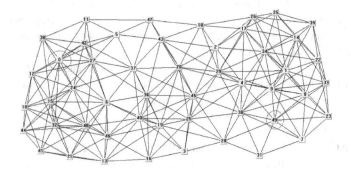

Fig. 2. A sample network topology

When the simulation is performed, RREQs are broadcasted in network (the links go darker), also RREPs are broadcasted (the links go brighter). As shown in Figure 3, in the middle of the simulation we have some dark and bright links together.

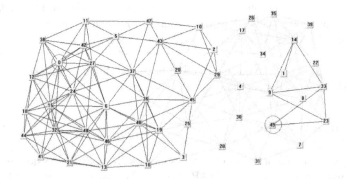

Fig. 3. The broadcasting of RREQs and RREPs

Afterwards node 0 sends the traffic towards node 49 by choosing the shortest path in its routing table. The intermediate nodes send the traffic towards their first index entry, the best path. The purple line (note that the forwarding route is darker than the

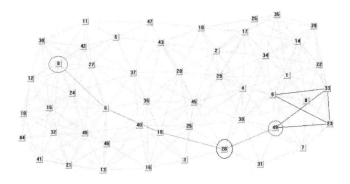

Fig. 4. Established connection with the shortest path

reverse path of ACK packet) in Figure 4 shows the forwarding path from the source to the destination (this line is overwritten by the return path of ACK packet). The ACK packet traverses the reverse path (the green line) back to the source, as the intermediate nodes set the reverse hop back to the source in their routing tables. So the green line of reverse path overcolor the purple line of forwarding path (we only showed the final reverse path in Figure 4).

As node 28 the neighbor of node 49 illustrated in Figure 4 with a black circle around, we change the characteristic of node 28 from *ad-hoc* to *selfish*, and run the simulation again. The details of RREQs and RREPs broadcasting are eliminated and the final result that is the alternative path to forward data is shown in Figure 5.

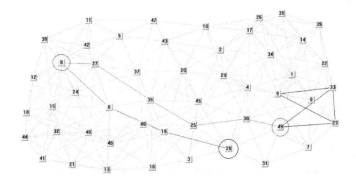

Fig. 5. LMAR resilience to one node selfishness

Now we change the characteristics of nodes 30 another neighbor of node 49 as a selfish node. Our simulator showed that the locally efficient path would be the route containing the nodes of 0-42-37-20-4-49. So we put the node 4 as a selfish node too. As depicted in Figure 6, the number of timeouts or attempts to establish connection increases (purple line shows the tried paths, but only the green path sends the ACK back to the source).

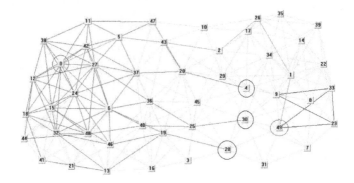

Fig. 6. LMAR resilient to neighbors' selfishness

In spite of the fact that the number of tries to set up connection increases when the number of selfish nodes grow up, every try could change the index entry of intermediate nodes away from selfish nodes (even malicious nodes) spontaneously as mentioned in section 4.2.

5.2 Wormhole Attack Resilience

As illustrated in Figure 7, to show the resilience of LMAR to wormholes we use previous random topology, and add a wormhole link (the red line) between node 24 (the neighbor of node 0) and node 30 (the neighbor of node 49). Obviously the shortest path between node 0 and node 49 would be the path containing the nodes of 0-24-30-49.

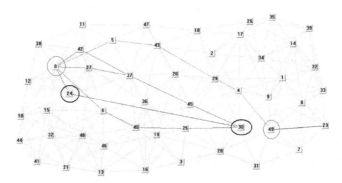

Fig. 7. LMAR resilience to wormhole attack

As seen in Figure 7, node 0 as the source could find a locally efficient route to node 49 as the destination after 5 tries. Also it shows that the wormholes are more dangerous than selfishness, because they attract most of traffics towards themselves. Longer wormholes have a much more severe impact on the network performance and LMAR requires many more steps to converge. When the number of tries increases, the direction of intermediate nodes' index entry switches away from wormhole contributors similar to what happened when the number of selfish nodes increased in the example given before. Our goal is connection establishment or providing availability services. The cost of our aim is the flooding of route discovery stage. So we developed our simulator to show the number of RREQ/RREP transmission. Also one of similar protocol called AOMDV is simulated and the results of our solution are compared to AOMDV below. There are 15 random connections in this scenario and the number of selfish nodes out of prospective connected nodes is incremented one by one.

7 Conclusion

In this paper, we introduced an efficient local-multipath adaptive routing (LMAR) protocol, a routing algorithm to provide availability security service properly. The objective of LMAR design is to provide a mechanism by which network nodes can find alternative paths using a distributed mechanism. This is done using an exhaustive search algorithm. Therefore LMAR can bypass the selfishness of independent nodes that disrupt the data path. In addition LMAR could defeat the wormhole attack by finding alternate routes that bypass the wormholes.

Acknowledgment

This work is partially supported by Iran Telecommunication Research Center (ITRC) in Information Systems and Security Lab (ISSL). Also we thank the Iranian NSF for support and establishing the cryptography chair.

References

1. Perkins, C.E., Bhagwat, P.: Highly Dynamic Destination-Sequenced Distance-Vector Routing (DSDV) for Mobile Computers. In: Proc. of the ACM SIGCOMM (1994)
2. Perkins, C.E., Royer, E.M., Das, S.R.: Ad-hoc On-demand Distance Vector (AODV) routing. In: IETF MANET Group (Janaury 2002)
3. Johnson, D.B., Maltz, D.A., Hu, Y.C., Jetcheva, J.G.: The Dynamic Source Routing Protocol for Mobile Ad-hoc Networks. In: IETF MANET Group (February 2002)
4. Clausen, T., Jacquet, P.: RFC 3626: Optimized link state routing protocol OLSR (October 2003)
5. Balasubramanian, C., Garcia-Luna-Aceves, J.J.: Shortest Multipath Routing Using Labeled Distances. In: Proc. of 1st IEEE MASS (October 2004)
6. Marina, M.K., Das, S.R.: On-Demand multipath distance vector routing in ad hoc networks. In: Proc. IEEE ICNP (2001)
7. Nasipuri, A., Castaneda, R., Das, S.R.: Performance of Multipath Routing for On-Demand Protocols in Mobile Ad Hoc Networks. In: ACM/Kluwer Mobile Networks and Applications MONET (2001)
8. Valera, A., Seah, W., Rao, S.V.: Cooperative packet caching and shortest multipath routing in mobile ad hoc networks. In: Proc. IEEE INFOCOM (2003)
9. Park, V.D., Corson, M.S.: A highly adaptive distributed routing algorithm for mobile wireless networks. In: Proc. IEEE INFOCOM (1997)

10. Lee, S., Gerla, M.: Split Multipath routing with maximally disjoint paths in ad hoc networks. In: Proc. IEEE ICC (2001)
11. Raju, J., Garcia-Luna-Aceves, J.J.: A new approach to on-demand loop-free multipath routing. In: Proc. IC3N (1999)
12. Michiardi, P., Molva, R.: Simulation-based Analysis of Security Exposures in Mobile Ad Hoc Networks. In: Proc. European Wireless Conference (2002)
13. Buttyan, L., Hubaux, J.-P.: Nuglets: a virtual currency to stimulate cooperation in self-organized ad hoc networks, Technical Report DSC/2001/001 (2001)
14. Buchegger, S., Le Boudec, J.-Y.: Nodes Bearing Grudges: Towards Routing Security, Fairness, and Robustness in Mobile Ad Hoc Networks. In: 10th Euro-micro Workshop on Parallel, Distributed and Network-based Processing
15. Michiardi, P., Molva, R.: CORE: A Collaborative Reputation mechanism to enforce node cooperation in Mobile Ad Hoc Networks. In: IFIP - Communication and Multimedia Security Conference (2002)
16. Yang, H., Meng, X., Lu, S.: Self-Organized Network-Layer Security in MANETs
17. Perrig, A., Hu, Y.-C., Johnson, D.B.: Wormhole Protection in Wireless Ad Hoc Networks. Technical Report TR01-384, Dep. of Computer Science, Rice University
18. Hu, Y.-C., Perrig, A., Johnson, D.B.: Packet Leashes: A Defense against Wormhole Attacks in Wireless Ad Hoc Networks. In: Proc. of INFOCOM 2003 (April 2003)
19. Hu, L., Evans, D.: Using Directional Antennas to Prevent Wormhole Attacks. In: Network and Distributed System Security Symposium (NDSS), San Diego (February 2004)
20. Lazos, L., Poovendran, R., Meadows, C., Syverson, P., Chang, L.W.: Preventing Wormhole Attacks on Wireless Ad-hoc Networks: A Graph Theoretic Approach. In: IEEE Wireless Communications and Networking Conference (2005)
21. Song, N., Qian, L., Li, X.: Wormhole Attacks Detection in Wireless Ad-hoc Networks: A Statistical Analysis Approach. In: IPDPS. IEEE, Los Alamitos (2005)
22. Wang, B., Soltani, S., Shapiro, J., Tan, P.: Local detection of selfish routing behavior in ad hoc networks. In: ISPAN. IEEE, Los Alamitos (2005)
23. Khabbazian, M., Mercier, H., Bhargava, V.K.: Wormhole Attack in Wireless Ad Hoc Networks: Analysis and Countermeasure. In: Global Telecommunications Conference. IEEE, Los Alamitos (2006)

Security Analysis and Validation for Access Control in Multi-domain Environment Based on Risk[*]

Zhuo Tang, Shaohua Zhang, Kenli Li, and Benming Feng

School of Computer and Communications, Hunan University, Changsha 410082
hust_tz@126.com

Abstract. Access control system is often described as a state transition system. Given a set of access control policies, a general safety requirement in such a system is to determine whether a desirable property is satisfied in all the reachable states. In this paper, we propose to use security analysis techniques to maintain desirable security properties in the Multi-domain Environment based on risk model (MDR^{2}BAC). We give a precise definition of security analysis problems in MDR^{2}BAC, which is more general than safety analysis that is studied in single-domain. We show the process of dynamic permission adjustment in multi-domain environment, and illustrate two classes of problems in the process which can be reduced to similar analysis in the RT[←,∩] role-based trust-management language, thereby establishing an interesting relationship between MDR^{2}BAC and the RT framework. The reduction gives efficient algorithms for answering most kinds of queries in the two stages of dynamic adjustment permissions.

1 Introduction

Role-based Access Control Model (RBAC) [1] is a widely used access control mechanism, which associates permissions and roles. The risk-based access control model MDR^{2}BAC [2] is based on RBAC, which is one of the direction of the current study. In this model, the risk of strategy determines whether access can be granted to the specified subjects ultimately. The model can calculate the risk rank of an access policy which belongs to the specified subjects by the history of the inter-operations among domains; the security degrees of the operations and the safety factors of the access events. The privilege of the subjects can be adjusted dynamically according to the risk levels of the access events so that the system security properties are maintained [3]. The risk rank in multi-domain environment depends on the confidence in each domain, the security degrees of the objects and the safety factor of the access events.

---

[*] This work is supported by the National Natural Science Foundation of China (Grant Nos. 90715029 and 60603053), the Culti-vation Fund of the Key. Scientific and Technical Innovation Project, Ministry of Education of China (Grant No. 708066), the Program for New Century Excellent Talents in University, NCET.

J. Kwak et al. (Eds.): ISPEC 2010, LNCS 6047, pp. 201–216, 2010.

For the actual demand, the behaviors of the system are not determined by the risk only. For example, a period of the frequent network access may bring the high risk so that some subjects may lose some privileges. The deprivation of these privileges may be unfair, and may not help to the effective run of the system. A security authentication model is needed to monitor the changes in the system and ensure the safety of the system property, and ensure that the behavior of the system is reasonable and effective. The security analysis model uses security analysis techniques to maintain desirable security properties. In this paper, the MDR^2BAC model is equivalent to the state transition system in which the state changes dynamically as the system changes. Security analysis aims to analyze whether the state of system maintains the security properties or the desired state of the system as the dynamic adjustment to reach.

In this paper, we propose to use security analysis in literature [4] to maintain desirable security properties for performing the cross-domain operation in multi-domain environment. In security analysis, an access-control system is always described as a state transition system. In the MDR^2BAC system, state changes occur via administrative operation in every single-domain or inter-domain operations among domains. Security analysis techniques answer questions such as whether an undesirable state is reachable and whether every reachable state satisfies some safety or availability. Examples of undesirable states are a state in which an inter-domain existence such that an un-trusted user gets access and a user who is entitled to access permission but does not get it.

Our contributions in this paper are as follows:

1) We give a precise definition of a family of security analysis problems in MDR^2BAC. In this family, we consider queries that occur in multi-domain environment rather than that occur in single-domain.
2) We introduce risk mechanism to multi-domain environments while the inter-operation occurs among domains. We can count the risk rank between two domains after both are initialized, and adjust the permissions which exceed the risk threshold dynamically.
3) We show that two classes of the security analysis problems in MDR^2BAC can be reduced to similar ones in $RT[\leftarrow,\cap]$, a role-based trust-management language for which security analysis has been studied. The reduction gives efficient algorithms for answering most kinds of queries in the two classes.

The rest of this paper is organized as follows: Related work is discussed in Section 2. In section 3, we give a formal definition of MDR^2BAC model and security analysis. Detailed definitions of every element in security analysis are shown in section 4. Section 5 gives an overview of the process and results for security analysis in MDR^2BAC. We present the $RT[\leftarrow,\cap]$ and the reduction from security analysis in MDR^2BAC to that in $RT[\leftarrow,\cap]$ in section 6. The paper is concluded in section 7.

2   Related Works

In the recent 20 years, people have acquired the plentiful achievement for the research of the access control. Many access control models have been proposed. The most popular models include discretionary access control (DAC), mandatory access controls (MAC) and role based access control (RBAC). In the RBAC family which was proposed by Sandhu in 1996[6], the users' privilege is related with their roles, and the users acquire their privilege through roles. A role is a permission set for a special work station. When the users' privilege needs to be changed, we can do it by revoking the roles or re-distributing the user's roles.

Michael J. Covington et al [7] have proposed the Generalized Role Based Access Control (GRBAC) model. In this model, they extend the traditional RBAC by applying the roles to all the entities in a system. (In RBAC, the role concept is only used for subjects). By defining three types of roles, i.e., Subject roles, Environment roles, and Object roles, GRBAC uses context information as a factor to make access decisions. Guangsen Zhang et al. [8] also uses context parameters in their dynamic role-based access control model under the two key ideas: (1) A user's access privileges should be changed when the user's context changes. (2) A resource must adjust its access policy when the environment context information (e.g., network bandwidth, CPU usage, memory usage) changes. They did not consider the aspect of security in making-decision process and the impact of security problems on the system. These above two papers make the access control be dynamic and flexible but the decision-making process is not as powerful and precise as that in our model MDR^2BAC [2]. In this model, we propose a method to calculate the risk rank of an inter-domain operation in multi-domain environment.

The Nathan Dimmock's paper [9] uses the concept of outcome to calculate cost for each outcome and risk value but they do not consider the context for risk assessment. So it loses the flexibility characteristic in evaluating risk. They did not consider risk as an important factor in their access control mechanism and they did not use risk directly in making decision.

There is little attention to the trust and risk in the access control research [10]. The term trust management system was introduced by Blaze et al. in [11], but the solution it proposes involves an unduly static notion of trust application programmers to choose where to insert code to evaluate their notion of trust, for example at the starting point of a given execution session. Most of the past research combining access control with trust concepts focuses on a trust-management approach in which trust values flow in a manually defined way through access control policy. For example, in literature [12] and [13], the mutual trust relationship is founded by the continuously negotiation. Literature [14] illuminates the relationship between the trust management and distributed access control, and it extends the access control system of OASIS and the access control language. So, the access policy can be decided base on the trust and risk. But the trust mentioned in this paper is defined by the special operation, and the relationship between risk and trust is faint in this paper.

Li et al[4] proposed the notion of security analysis and studied security analysis in the context of $RT[\leftarrow, \cap]$, a role-based trust-management language. They showed that a security analysis instance in $RT[\leftarrow, \cap]$ involving only semi-static queries can be solved efficiently. The work by Koch [15] considers safety in RBAC with the RBAC state and state-change rules posed as graph formalism. They show that safety (defined as whether a given graph can become a subgraph of another graph) is decidable provided that a state-change rule does not both remove and add components to the graph that represents the protection state.

Li and Tripunitara [5] were the first to analyze RBAC. They performed security analysis on two restricted versions of administrative RBAC. These are known as AATU (Assignment And Trusted Users) and AAR (Assignment And Revocation). They proposed two reduction algorithms and studied complexity results for various analysis problems such as safety, availability and containment. But they didn't consider risk and inter-domain operation in Multi-domain environments.

3   Formal Definition of Model Security in MDR^{2}BAC

Formal definition of access control strategy in MDR^{2}BAC is based on state transition system. An access-control strategy is modeled as a state-transition system $<S_{set}, Q_{set}, Ent_{set}, Tr_{set}>$, in which S_{set} is a set of states, Q_{set} is a set of queries, Ent_{set} is a set of entailment relations, on behalf of all queries that meet the conditions of system security certification, and also is a set of state-transition relations that are allowed, Tr_{set} is a set of state-transition rules.

Formal definitions of state-transition system $<S_{set}, Q_{set}, Ent_{set}, Tr_{set}>$ in MDR^{2}BAC are as follows:

1) States (S_{set}). S_{set} is the set of all MDR^{2}BAC, contains all the necessary information in access-control, denoted by: $s \in S_{set}$ if and only if $S_S \in S$, $O_s \in O$, $A_s \in A, D_{S_s} \in D, D_{O_s} \in D, R_s \in R$ and $F_s(S_s, O_s, D_{S_s}, D_{O_s}, R_s) \rightarrow 2^{A_s}$, here S, O, A, D, R denote subjects, objects, access-permissions, domains, and a set of risk rank respectively, mapping $F_s(s,o,d_1,d_2,r_i)=a$ denotes that subject s in domain d_1 has the access-permission a to object o in domain d_2 under the risk rank r_i in the current status.

2) Queries (Q_{set}). Query is a major form to check the security of a system. Query not only provides a access interface on the current state so that we can obtain detailed permission-assignment information about system, but also provides a secure checking interface, that is, predict the behavior of the system in the future, and gives the results of secure checking.

3) Entailment (Ent_{set}). It is defined as follows: $q \propto s$, if, and only if, $s \in S_{set}$, $q \in Q_{set}$ and q are true. Entailment indicates that whether a query is in the desired state. It provides a form as the secure checking result of the system. It responds to the questions such as if the current operation is safety or not and if the current permission-assignment is in existence or not.

4) State-change rules (Tr_{set}). State-change rules are given by a set of commands. It has nothing to do with the specific state, but whether the execution can be successful or the result after the successful execution will depend on the actual distribution of the state. The state-change rules in multi-domain based on risk mainly related to permissions-assignment and dynamic adjustment of permissions.

Formal definitions of security analysis in MDR^{2}BAC are as follows:

Given an access-control strategy $<S_{set}, Q_{set}, Ent_{set}, Tr_{set}>$, the definition of security analysis is $<s, q, tr_{sub}, \prod>$, in which $s \in S_{set}$ is the initial analysis state of security analysis, $q \in Q_{set}$ is the query expression of security analysis, $tr_{sub} \subseteq Tr_{set}$ is a set of state-transition rule that related with the security analysis. It is the subset of Tr_{set}, divided into two categories: 1) related with initial permissions assignment; 2) related with dynamic adjustment of permissions, $\prod \in \{ \exists, \forall \}$ is a quantifier.

1) The existence query. The definition of existence query in the process of security analysis is as follows: $<s, q, tr_{sub}, \exists >$. An instance $<s, q, tr_{sub}, \exists >$ ask whether state s_1 exists in access-control strategy $<S_{set}, Q_{set}, Ent_{set}, Tr_{set}>$ to make $s \rightarrow (r_1 \in tr_{sub}) \ldots \rightarrow (r_n \in tr_{sub}) s_1$ or $s \rightarrow (\mathcal{E}) s_1$ and $q \propto s_1$; the $\rightarrow (r_1 \in tr_{sub})$ denotes a step state-change rule, $\rightarrow (\mathcal{E})$ denotes a direct state-change rule. If the result is true, it shows that the permissions-assignment in query q is reachable under state s and specified rule set tr_{sub}, and the query is verified by the security verification.

2) The arbitrary query. The definition of arbitrary query in the process of security analysis is as follows: $<s, q, tr_{sub}, \forall >$. An instance $<s, q, tr_{sub}, \forall >$ ask whether each state s_1 under access-control strategy $<S_{set}, Q_{set}, Ent_{set}, Tr_{set}>$ make $s \rightarrow (r_1 \in tr_{sub}) \ldots \rightarrow (r_n \in tr_{sub}) s_1$ or $s \rightarrow (\mathcal{E}) s_1$ and $q \propto s_1$. The $\rightarrow (r_1 \in tr_{sub})$ denotes a step state-change rule; $\rightarrow (\mathcal{E})$ denotes direct state-change rule. If the result is true, it shows that the permissions-assignment in query q is necessary under access-control strategy $<S_{set}, Q_{set}, Ent_{set}, Tr_{set}>$, we say the permissions-assignment must be contained in each state.

4   Security Analysis in the Context of Access-Control Strategy in MDR^{2}BAC

In the previous section, we show the access-control strategy in MDR^{2}BAC and definition of security analysis, and describe state machine model of access-control strategy in MDR^{2}BAC and application of security analysis which is based on access-control strategy. On this basis, we can further abstract formal definition of security analysis elements in the context of MDR^{2}BAC, as the basis for analysis and reduction.

4.1   The Definition of State for Security Analysis

The definition of state in the context of MDR^{2}BAC is as follows:

The definition of state in the context of MDR^{2}BAC is a 5-tuple $<URD, RPD, RRD, RD, CC>$. Here, user assignment relation $URD \subseteq U \times R \times D$ associates users with roles in single domain; the permission assignment relation $RPD \subseteq R \times P \times D$ associates permissions with roles in single domain; the role hierarchy relation $RRD \subseteq R \times R \times D$ is a partial order among roles in single domain; $RD \subseteq R \times D_S \times R \times D_O$ is a relation mapping of roles among multi-domains; $CC \subseteq D_S \times D_O \times Z$ denotes the confidence between two domains, in which, U is a set of users, R is a set of roles, P is a set of permissions, D_S is a set of subjects, D_O is a set of objects, $Z \in [0,1]$.

We denote the partial order of roles by $\geq$. $r_1 \geq r_2$ means that a user who is a member of r_1 is also a member of r_2 and r_1 has all the permissions as r_2 has.

The confidence among domains is given by Z in the definition of state. The security degree of the objects and the safety factor of the access events can be considered as a security property constant of each domain, which will be dealt with as a known quantity in security analysis. Below are the definitions of some Known quantity:

1) Security level of role in a single-domain. Role $r \in d:Rank_i$, if and only if, r lies in the i-th layer of role hierarchy, $d \in D$ denotes the domain, $Rank_i$ is a set of roles which lie in the same layer of role hierarchy, they have the same security level, $i = 1, 2, \ldots n$.

2) The safety factor of the access events among domains. The set AF contain all access events.

3) Risk threshold. The risk threshold is denoted by RV. The inter-operations permissions which exceed the threshold will be recycled.

Example 1. We describe the multi-domain environment showed in Fig.1 by the definition of state-transition system.

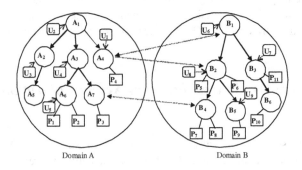

Domain A   Domain B

Fig. 1. It is an example of multi-domain environment, which contains two domains and five inter-domain role mapping

By definition, respectively, given the state of URD, RPD, and RRD members:

$URD = \{(U_2,A_1,A), (U_3,A_2,A), (U_4,A_3,A), (U_1,A_4,A), (U_5,A_6,A), (U_6,B_1,B), (U_8,B_2,B),$
$\qquad (U_7,B_3,B), (U_9,B_5,B)\}$

$RPD = \{(A_4,P_4,A), (A_6,P_1,A), (A_6,P_2,A), (A_7,P_3,A), (B_2,P_5,B), (B_2,P_6,B), (B_3,P_{11},B),$
$\qquad (B_4,P_7,B), (B_4,P_8,B) (B_5,P_9,B), (B_6,P_{10},B)\}$

$RRD = \{(A_1,A_2,A), (A_2,A_5,A), (A_1,A_3,A), (A_1,A_4,A), (A_3,A_6,A), (A_3,A_7,A), (B_1,B_2,B),$
$\qquad (B_1,B_3,B), (B_2,B_4,B), (B_2,B_5,B), (B_3,B_6,B)\}$

$RD = \{(A_4,A,B_2,B), (A_7,A,B_4,B), (B_2,B, A_4,A), (A_4,A,B_1,B), (B_1,B, A_4,A)\}$

We suppose that the confidence in domain A and domain B is 0.43, so $CC =$ $\{(A,B,0.43)\}$. In addition, also the known quantities involved in the multi-domain are needed:

Security level of role in each domain:

$$A:Rank_1 = \{A_1\} = 1; A:Rank_2 = \{A_2,A_3,A_4\} = 2/3; A:Rank_3 = \{A_5,A_6,A_7\} = 1/3;$$
$$B:Rank_1 = \{B_1\} = 1; B:Rank_2 = \{B_2,B_3\} = 2/3; B:Rank_3 = \{B_4,B_5,B_6\} = 1/3;$$

The safety factor of the access events: $AF = \{read = 0.8, copy = 0.6, write = 0.4, execute = 0.2\}$;

Risk threshold: $RV = 0.2$;

We can see that the states can be described clearly throughout the definition of state in the context of MDR^2BAC. This can make the security checking become more convenient.

The most important issue in security checking is finding an object which exists in the system and can be compared with other object. We can use the method that maps the permission and role to user to complete the security checking. So we need to give the following function definitions of inter-domain user set mapping which can map permission and role that is cross-domain to user set of subject.

Definition 1. ($USERS_S$) Given the state $s=<URD,RPD,RRD,RD,CC>$, for every inter-domain mapping in RD, we define a function $USERS_S$: $R_{D_S} \cap P_{D_O} \to 2^{U_{D_S}}$, in which R_{D_S} is the set of role in subject D_S, U_{D_S} is the set of user in subject D_S, P_{D_O} is the set of permission in object D_O.

1) For any $r \in R_{D_S}$ and $u \in U_{D_S}$, $u \in USERS_S[r]$, if, and only if, $(u,r,d_S) \in URD$ or there exists r_1 such that $r_1 \geqq r$ and $(u,r_1,d_S) \in URD$.

2) For any $p \in P_{D_O}$ and $u \in U_{D_S}$, $u \in USERS_S[p]$, if, and only if, $r_1 \in R_{D_O}$ such that $(r_1,p,d_O) \in RPD$ and there exists $r \in R_{D_S}$ such that $(u,r,d_S) \in URD$ and $(r,d_S,r_1,d_O) \in RD$ or there exists $r_2 \geqq r$, $(u,r_2,d_S) \in URD$ and $(r_2,d_S,r_1,d_O) \in RD$, satisfied $F(c,d_O:Rank_i,af) \leq RV$, where $(d_S,d_O,c) \in CC$, $r_1 \in d_O:Rank_i$, $af \in AF$, $i \in \{1,2,\ldots,n\}$, R_{D_O} is the set of roles in object domain, F is the risk rank function. Here, we need not consider the role hierarchy relation in object domain D_O, because $u \in USERS_S[p]$ is subset of users in subject domain.

4.2 The Definition of Query and Entailment

In multi-domain environment, query ask under the current state whether inter-domain role mapping exists, and whether subject has specific permission on object with the risk rank less than the risk threshold.

The query is defined as $uset_1 \lhd uset_2$, $uset_1 \in S$, $uset_2 \in S$, $S \in 2^{U_{D_S}}$ denotes the set of all user in the domain which subjects belong to. According the definition of user set in literature [5], S is defined to be the least set satisfying the following conditions: 1) $funR(r)$ denotes the user set of role R in subject domain D_S, $funP(p)$ denotes the user in subject domain which has inter-domain operation permission p and the permission p is in object domain D_O, $funR(r) \cup funP(p) \in S$ means every role in subject domain and every permission in object domain is a user set of subject domain; 2) $\{u_1, u_2, \ldots, u_k\} \in S$, where $k \geq 0$, and $u_i \in U_{D_S}$ for $1 \leq i \leq k$, i.e., means that a finite set of users in subject domain is a user set of subject domain; 3) $uset_1 \cup uset_2$, $uset_1 \cap uset_2$, means that the set of all user sets is closed with respect to union and intersection. We extend the function $USERS_S$ in a straightforward way to give a valuation for all user sets. The extended function $USERS_S$: $S \rightarrow 2^{U_{D_S}}$ is defined as follows: $USERS_S[\{u_1, u_2, \ldots, u_k\}] = \{u_1, u_2, \ldots, u_k\}$, $USERS_S[uset_1 \cup uset_2] = USERS_S[uset_1] \cup USERS_S[uset_2]$, and $USERS_S[uset_1 \cap uset_2] = USERS_S[uset_1] \cap USERS_S[uset_2]$. We say a query $uset_1 \lhd uset_2$ is semi-static, if one of $uset_1$, $uset_2$ can be evaluated independent of the state, i.e., no role or permission appears in it. The reason we distinguish semi-static queries is that a security analysis instance involving only such queries can be solved efficiently.

Given the state $s \in S_{set}$, and query expression $uset_1 \lhd uset_2$, the entailment is defined by $uset_1 \lhd uset_2 \propto s$ if, and only if, $USERS_S[uset_1] \supseteq USERS_S[uset_2]$. The query result is the left side of the user set contains a set of the right side of the user, so the current state entails the query.

5   Types of Security Analysis and Main Results in MDR²BAC

Given the security analysis instance$<s, q, tr_{sub}, \prod>$, there are two kinds of subsets of state-change rules tr_{sub} in MDR²BAC. These two types of state-change rules correspond to the two stages of implementation process in MDR²BAC access-control strategy. The first type is related to the permission-assignment; the second kind is associated with dynamic adjustment of permissions. Next we will give the definitions and solutions about the two kinds of state-change rules.

5.1   Initial Permissions Assignment (*IPA*)

Initial permissions assignment(*IPA*) involves the role-assignment, the permission-assignment, the initial of security level of object, the initial of confidence among domains and the safety factor of the access events.

We suppose that the constants are given, for the initial state $s \in S_{set}$, the form of state-transition rules tr_{sub} in *IPA* is defined as $can\_assign \subseteq R \times C \times M$, where R is the set of management roles among domains, C is the set of conditions, which are expressions formed by using inter-domain mapping $(r_S, d_S, r_O, d_O) \subseteq RD$, the operators $\cup$ and $\cap$, only the role in subject domain meets the conditions can establish a new inter-domain mapping. M is form of (r_S,d_S,r_O,d_O), meaning we can establish the inter-domain from role r_S in subject domain d_S to role r_O in object domain d_O.

For example, $<r_m,(r_1,A,r_2,B)\cap(r_1,A,r_3,B),(r_1,A,r_4,B)> \in can\_assign$ means that a user that is a member of management role r_m is allowed to establish an inter-domain mapping from role r_1 in domain A to role r_4 in domain B when the condition expression $(r_1,A,r_2,B)\cap(r_1,A,r_3,B)$ is true. The condition expression $(r_1,A,r_2,B)\cap(r_1,A,r_3,B)$ means that the role r_1 in subject domain A must have a mapping to role r_2 in domain B and a mapping to role r_3 in domain B. We can unconditionally establish inter-domain mapping from role r_1 in domain A to role r_4 in domain B when the c is "true".

Definition 2. (Initial Permissions Assignment-*IPA*) Each state-change rule in *IPA* has the form can_assign such that $s = <URD,RPD,RRD,RD,CC>$ is allowed to $s_1 = <URD_1,RPD_1,RRD_1,RD_1,CC_1>$ by $tr_{sub} = can\_assign$, if $URD = URD_1$, $RRD = RRD_1$, $CC = CC_1$, then 1) $RD_1 = RD \cup (r_S,d_S,r_O,d_O)$, and $(r_S,d_S,r_O,d_O) \notin RD$, and there exists $<r_m,c,(r_S,d_S,r_O,d_O)> \in can\_assign$ such that r_m is not empty, r_S satisfies c (i.e., there exists at least one user who is a member of management role r_m, so that a user can establish the inter-domain mapping from role r_S in subject domain d_S to role r_O in object domain d_O where the condition c is satisfied); 2) $RPD_1=RPD \cup R_1P_1D$, for (r_S,d_S,r_O,d_O) in M, and permission p_O is associated with role r_O in object domain d_O, so satisfied $R_1P_1D = (r_S,p_O,d_S)$.

Example 2. Suppose the multi-domain environment of Fig.1 is in the initial of permission stage and state-change rule as follows: $can\_assign = <A_1,(A_4,A,B_2,B)\cap(A_4,A,B_1,B),(A_4,A,B_5,B)>$. Let q be the query $P_9 \lhd \{U_1\}$, then, $P_9 \lhd \{U_1\} \propto s$ is true. Security analysis $<s,q,tr_{sub}, \exists >$ asks whether there exists a reachable state s_1 such that the user U_1 has the permission P_9. The instance is true. This is because the user U_1 has not the permission P_9 under the state s, but the role A_4 satisfied the conditions $(A_4,A,B_2,B)\cap(A_4,A,B_1,B)$ in state-change rule can_assign such that we can establish the inter-domain mapping from role A_4 in subject domain A to role B_5 in object domain B. Then, there exists a reachable state s_1 such that $(A_4,A,B_5,B) \subseteq RD$, $(U_1,A_4,A) \subseteq URD$ and $(B_5,P_9,B) \subseteq RPD$. So the user U_1 has the permission P_9 and the analysis instance is true.

5.2 Risk Rank Counting (*RRC*)

The risk rank is counted by the confidence among domains, history of the inter-operations among domains, the security degree of the objects and the safety factor of the access events under the known inter-domain mapping. The algorithm of *RRC* is as follows:

1. Traverse inter-domain mapping tuple RD, obtain the role r_S in subject domain D_S and role r_O in object domain D_O;
2. Obtain the security degree O_s for role in object domain D_O, so $O_s = D_O :Rank_i = \{r_O\}$;
3. Obtain the permission set p_O for role r_O in object domain D_O. Traverse permission set p_O and the set of safety factor of access events AF, obtain the safety factor of access events A_s for every permission;

4. Establish the revoke set of inter-domain operations $must\_revoke = \emptyset$. It is defined by $must\_revoke \subseteq a \times R_S \times D_S \times R_O \times D_O$, where R_S is role in subject domain D_S, R_O is the role in object domain D_O, a is a operation permission in permission set p_O which is associated with role R_O in object domain D_O. The instance $<a,r_S,d_S,r_O,d_O> \in must\_revoke$ meaning that the operation permission a from role r_S in subject domain d_S to role r_O in object domain d_O beyond the risk threshold RV.

5. For every operation permission $a \in p_O$, according to the definition of risk function $F(C(i,j),O_s, A_s) = O_s \times (1- C(i,j)) \times (1- A_s)$, we count the risk rank R_i of operation permission a between subject s in subject domain D_S and object o in object domain D_O, denoted as $R_i = risk\_count(s,o,a,d_S,d_O)$, where $C(i,j)$ is the confidence among domains, initial $C(i,j) = CC_{D_S \times D_O}$ and can be counted by the method in literature [2]. If $R_i \geq RV$, meaning that the risk rank of inter-domain operation exceeds the risk threshold, so we add the member $<a,r_S,d_S,r_O,d_O>$ to set $must\_revoke$.

5.3 Dynamic Permissions Regulating (DPR)

Dynamic permissions regulating (DPR) revokes the inter-domain operation permission which exceeds the risk threshold by the permission revoke function after the RRC stage.

The form of state-transition rules tr_{sub} in DPR is denoted by $must\_remove \subseteq R_M \times A \times R_S \times D_S \times R_O \times D_O$, where R_M is the set of role management, A is the set of a which is the operation permission that must be revoked in $must\_revoke$. The instance $<r_m,a,r_S,d_S,r_O,d_O> \in must\_remove$ meaning that a user in role management set r_m has right to revoke the inter-domain operation permission a between role r_S in subject domain d_S and role r_O in object domain d_O, where r_S, d_S, r_O, d_O, a associated with the member $<a,r_S,d_S,r_O,d_O>$ in the set of $must\_revoke$.

Definition 3. (Dynamic Permissions Regulating-DPR) The state-change rule has the form $must\_remove$ in DPR stage, such that a state-change from $s = <URD,RPD,RRD,RD,CC>$ to $s_1 = <URD_1, RPD_1,RRD_1,RD_1,CC_1>$ is allowed by state-change rule $tr_{sub} = must\_remove$. If $URD = URD_1$, $RRD = RRD_1$, $CC = CC_1$, $RD = RD_1$, then, $RPD = RPD_1 \cup \{(r_S,a,d_S)\}$, where $a \in A$, r_S is role in subject domain d_S, and satisfied $(r_S,a,d_S) \notin RPD_1$, and exists $<r_m,a,r_S,d_S,r_O,d_O> \in must\_remove$ such that $USERS_S[r_m]$ is not empty and satisfied $<a,r_S,d_S,r_O,d_O> \in must\_revoke$ (i.e., there exists at least one user in role r_m that can revoke the operation permission a which belongs to role r_S in subject domain).

Example 3. Let the query q be $P_9:write \lhd \{U_1\}$. We have established an inter-domain mapping from role A_4 in subject domain A to role B_5 in object domain B in Example 2. Then, the role A_4 has the permissions P_9 that keep by role B_5. We suppose that permission P_9 is comprised of operation set $\{read,copy,write\}$. For operation permission $a = write$, if $R_i = risk\_count(s,o,write,A,B) \geq RV$, so $<write,A_4,A,B_5,B> \in must\_revoke$, and $<r_m,write,A_4,A,B_5,B> \in must\_remove$, meaning that a user in management role r_m must remove the operation permission $write$ from the role A_4 in domain A. So satisfied $(A_4,P_9:write,A) \notin RPD$, and the security analysis instance is false.

6 Reductions Algorithm for Security Analysis in MDR²BAC

In this section, we solve *IPA* and *DPR*. We can use the method which based on $RT[\leftarrow,\cap]$ to perform the security checking and security analysis and give the reduction algorithm in multi-domain environment.

6.1 Syntax of $RT[\leftarrow,\cap]$

A role in $RT[\leftarrow,\cap]$ is denoted by a principal (corresponding to a user in MDR²BAC) followed by a role name, separated by a dot. For example, when U is a principal and r is a role name, $U.r$ is a role.

Roles are defined by statements. For the $RT[\leftarrow,\cap]$ in multi-domain environment, we have five kinds of statement as follows:

1) Simple Member: $U.r \leftarrow U_1$, meaning that U_1 is a member of U's r role;
2) Simple Inclusion: $U.r \leftarrow U_1.r_1$, meaning that U's r role includes U_1's r_1 role;
3) Linking Inclusion: $U.r \leftarrow U.r_1.r_2$, meaning that $U.r$ includes $U_1.r_2$, for every U_1 that is a member of $U.r_1$;
4) Intersection Inclusion: $U.r \leftarrow U_1.r_1 \cap U_2.r_2$, meaning that $U.r$ includes every principal who is a member of both $U_1.r_1$ and $U_2.r_2$;
5) Inter-domain Operation: $U.r_O \leftarrow U.r_S$, meaning that every user of role $U.r_S$ in subject domain is a member of role $U.r_O$ in object domain where the inter-domain mapping is existence.

For the states of access-control and query in $RT[\leftarrow,\cap]$, we use the definition in literature [5]. So we can obtain the security analysis results which are proofed in literature [5].

6.2 Reduction Algorithm in MDR²BAC

In this section, we perform security analysis through reducing the *IPA* and *DPR* to the $RT[\leftarrow,\cap]$. Each reduction is an efficient computable mapping from an instance of *IPA/DPR* to a security instance in $RT[\leftarrow,\cap]$.

6.2.1 Reduction for *IPA*

The reduction algorithm *IPA_Reduce* is given in Algorithm 1, it uses the subroutines defined in Algorithm 2. Given an instance $<s = <URD,RPD,RRD,RD,CC>$, $q = uset_1 \lhd uset_2$, $tr_{sub} = can\_assign$, $\prod \in \{ \exists, \forall \}>$, *IPA_Reduce* takes $<s,q,tr_{sub}>$ and outputs $<s^T,q^T,tr_{sub}{}^T>$, such that the $RT[\leftarrow,\cap]$ analysis instance $<s^T,q^T,tr_{sub}{}^T,\prod>$ has the same answer as the original *IPA* instance.

In the reduction, we use one principal for every user that appears in s, and the special *Sys* to represent the MDR²BAC system. The $RT[\leftarrow,\cap]$ role names used in the reduction include the MDR²BAC roles in every domain and permissions in state s and some additional temporary role names. The $RT[\leftarrow,\cap]$ role $Sys.r$ represents the MDR²BAC role r, and the $RT[\leftarrow,\cap]$ role $Sys.p$ represents the MDR^2BAC permission p. Each $(u,r,d) \in URD$ is translated into the $RT[\leftarrow,\cap]$ statement $Sys.r \leftarrow u$. Each $r_1 \geqq r_2$ is translated into the $RT[\leftarrow,\cap]$ statement $Sys.r_2 \leftarrow Sys.r_1$. Each $(r,p,d) \in RPD$ is translated into the $RT[\leftarrow,\cap]$ statement $Sys.p \leftarrow Sys.r$. Each (r_S,d_S,r_O,d_O) is translated into the $RT[\leftarrow,\cap]$ statement $Sys.p_O \leftarrow Sys.r_S$ (as role r_S in subject domain d_S has the permissions that possessed by role r_O in object domain d_O).

Each $<r_m,c,(r_S,d_S,r_O,d_O)> \in can\_assign$ is translated into $Sys.r_O \leftarrow Sys.r_m.r_O \cap Sys.r_S$ $\cap Sys.c$. The intuition is that a user u_m, who is a member of management role r_m assigning the user u_S who is a member of role r_S in subject domain d_S to be a member of role r_O in object domain d_O, is represented as adding the $RT[\leftarrow,\cap]$ statement $u_m.r_O \leftarrow u_S$. As u_m is a member of the $Sys.r_m$ role, the user u_S is added as a member to the $Sys.r_O$ role, if, and only if, the condition c is satisfied.

Example 4. Consider the state-change rule we discussed in Example 2, in which tr_{sub} is: $can\_assign = <A_1,(A_4,A,B_2,B) \cap (A_4,A,B_1,B),(A_4,A,B_5,B)>$. Let s be the MDR^2BAC state (shown in Fig.1) and let q be the query $P_9 \lhd \{U_1\}$. We then represent the output of IPA_Reduce ($<s,q,tr_{sub}>$) as $<s^T,q^T,tr_{sub}{}^T>$. q^T is $Sys.P_9 \lhd \{U_1\}$. The following RT statements in s^T result from URD:

$Sys.A_1 \leftarrow U_2$ $Sys.A_2 \leftarrow U_3$ $Sys.A_3 \leftarrow U_4$ $Sys.A_4 \leftarrow U_1$ $Sys.A_6 \leftarrow U_5$ $Sys.B_1 \leftarrow U_6$
$Sys.B_2 \leftarrow U_8$ $Sys.B_5 \leftarrow U_9$ $Sys.B_3 \leftarrow U_7$

The following RT statements in s^T result from RPD:

$Sys.P_4 \leftarrow Sys.A_4$ $Sys.P_1 \leftarrow Sys.A_6$ $Sys.P_2 \leftarrow Sys.A_6$ $Sys.P_3 \leftarrow Sys.A_7$ $Sys.P_5 \leftarrow Sys.B_2$
$Sys.P_6 \leftarrow Sys.B_2$ $Sys.P_{11} \leftarrow Sys.B_3$ $Sys.P_7 \leftarrow Sys.B_4$ $Sys.P_8 \leftarrow Sys.B_4$ $Sys.P_9 \leftarrow Sys.B_5$
$Sys.P_{10} \leftarrow Sys.B_6$

The following RT statements in s^T result from RRD:

$Sys.A_2 \leftarrow Sys.A_1$ $Sys.A_3 \leftarrow Sys.A_1$ $Sys.A_4 \leftarrow Sys.A_1$ $Sys.A_5 \leftarrow Sys.A_2$ $Sys.A_6 \leftarrow Sys.A_3$
$Sys.A_7 \leftarrow Sys.A_3$ $Sys.B_2 \leftarrow Sys.B_1$ $Sys.B_3 \leftarrow Sys.B_1$ $Sys.B_4 \leftarrow Sys.B_2$ $Sys.B_5 \leftarrow Sys.B_2$
$Sys.B_6 \leftarrow Sys.B_3$

The following RT statements in s^T result from RD:

$Sys.P_5 \leftarrow Sys.A_4$ $Sys.P_7 \leftarrow Sys.A_7$ $Sys.P_8 \leftarrow Sys.A_7$ $Sys.P_3 \leftarrow Sys.B_4$ $Sys.P_4 \leftarrow Sys.B_1$

The following RT statements in s^T result from can_assign:

$Sys.NewRole_1 \leftarrow Sys.B_1 \cap Sys.B_2 \cap Sys.A_4$ $Sys.NewRole_2 \leftarrow Sys.A_1.B_5$
$Sys.B_5 \leftarrow Sys.NewRole_1 \cap Sys.NewRole_2$

It is clear that the security instance $<s^T,q^T,tr_{sub}{}^T, \exists >$ is true. The user U_1 has not possessed the permission P_9 in state s^T, but state $s_1{}^T$ is reachable such that the inter-domain role mapping (A_4,A,B_5,B) comes into existence, and satisfies $Sys.P_9 \leftarrow U_1$, meaning the user U_1 possesses permission P_9.

```
1   IPA_Reduce(<s  =  <URD,   RPD,   RRD,   RD,   CC  >,q  =
uset₁ ◁ uset₂, tr_sub = can_assign>)
2 { /* Initial of  sᵀ */
3    sᵀ = ∅; qᵀ = Trans(uset₁,sᵀ) ◁ Trans(uset₂,sᵀ);
4    foreach (uᵢ,rⱼ,dₖ) ∈ URD       { sᵀ += Sys.rⱼ←uᵢ};
5    foreach (rᵢ,pⱼ,dₖ) ∈ RPD     { sᵀ += Sys.pⱼ←Sys.rᵢ }
6    foreach (rᵢ,rⱼ,dₖ) ∈ RRD     { sᵀ += Sys.rⱼ←Sys.rᵢ }
7    foreach (rₛ,dₛ,rₒ,dₒ) ∈ RD { sᵀ += Sys.rₒ←Sys.rₛ }
8    foreach <rₘ,c,(rₛ,dₛ,rₒ,dₒ)> ∈ can_assign
9       {    if c is satisfied or c==true
10          { sᵀ += Sys.rₒ←Sys.rₛ }}
11   return <sᵀ,qᵀ,tr_subᵀ>;
12 } /*end IPA_Reduce*/
```

Algorithm 1. Algorithm for *IPA_Reduce*

```
13 Trans(s,sᵀ)
14 { /*return an RT role corresponding to the user set s*/
15   if s is an MDR²BAC role then return Sys.s;
16   else if s is an MDR²BAC permission then return Sys.s;
17   else if s is a set of users then {
18            name = newName();
19            foreach u ∈ s;
20            sᵀ += Sys.name←u;
21            return Sys.name;  }
22   else if (s = s₁ ∪ s₂) then {
23            name = newName();
24            sᵀ += Sys.name←Trans(s₁,sᵀ);
25            sᵀ += Sys.name←Trans(s₂,sᵀ);
26            return Sys.name;  }
27   else if (s = s₁ ∩ s₂) then {
28            name = newName();
29            sᵀ += Sys.name←Trans(s₁,sᵀ)∩Trans(s₂,sᵀ);
30            return Sys.name; }
31 }/* end Trans*/
```

Algorithm 2. Algorithm for Trans

6.2.2 Reduction for *DPR*

The reduction algorithm *DPR_Reduce* is given in Algorithm 3. Given an *DPR* instance $<s=<URD, RPD,RRD,RD,CC>,q = uset_1 \lhd uset_2, tr_{sub} = must\_remove, \prod \in \{ \exists, \forall \}>$, *DPR_Reduce* takes$<s,q,tr_{sub}>$ and outputs $<s^T,q^T,tr_{sub}^T>$, such that the $RT[\leftarrow,\cap]$ analysis instance $<s^T,q^T,tr_{sub}^T,\prod>$ has the same answer as the original *DPR* instance.

Example 5. Consider the state-change rule and example in Example 4. The state s^T in *RT* is shown in Example 4 after the operation *can_assign*. Let P_9 be made up of operation set {*read,copy, write*}, and let *q* be the query P_9: $write \lhd A_4$. We then represent the output of *DPR_Reduce*$(<s,q,tr_{sub}>)$ as$<s^T,q^T,tr_{sub}^T>$. q^T is $Sys.P_9:write \leftarrow Sys.A_4$. For the operation permission *a=write*, we suppose its risk rank value exceed the risk threshold after *RRC* stage, denoted by $R_i=risk\_count(s,o,write,A,B)\geq RV$. Then$< write,A_4,A,B_5,B >\in must\_revoke$, and $<r_m,write,A_4,A,B_5,B >\in must\_remove$.

It is clear that the security instance $<s^T,q^T,tr_{sub}^T, \forall >$ is false. Though the expression $Sys.P_9:write \leftarrow Sys.A_4$ come into existence in stage s^T, but the permission P_9: *write* which belongs to role A_4 exceed the risk threshold *RV* in *RRC* stage. So the regular expression $<r_m,write,A_4,A,B_5,B >\in must\_remove$ comes into existence in the reachable state s_1^T such that management role revokes the operation P_9: *write* of A_4. Then, the statement $Sys.P_9:write \leftarrow Sys.A_4$ is not satisfied.

```
32  DPR_Reduce(<s   =   <URD,   RPD,   RRD,   RD,   CC >,q   =
uset₁◁uset₂,tr_sub = must_remove>)
33 { /* Initial of  sᵀ */
34      sᵀ = ∅;  qᵀ = Trans(uset₁,sᵀ) ◁ Trans(uset₂,sᵀ);
must_remove= ∅;
35      foreach (uᵢ,rⱼ,dₖ)∈URD       { sᵀ += Sys.rⱼ←uᵢ};
36      foreach (rᵢ,pⱼ,dₖ)∈RPD       { sᵀ += Sys.pⱼ←Sys.rᵢ }
37      foreach (rᵢ,rⱼ,dₖ)∈RRD       { sᵀ += Sys.rⱼ←Sys.rᵢ }
38      foreach (rₛ,dₛ,rₒ,dₒ)∈RD     { sᵀ += Sys.rₒ←Sys.rₛ }
39      foreach <a,rₛ,dₛ,rₒ,dₒ>∈must_revoke {
40          must_remove +=  <rₘ,a,rₛ,dₛ,rₒ,dₒ>;}
41      foreach<rₘ,a,rₛ,dₛ,rₒ,dₒ>∈must_remove{
42          sᵀ -=Sys.a←Sys.rₛ;  }
43      return <sᵀ,qᵀ,tr_sub^T>;
44 } /*end DPR_Reduce*/
```

Algorithm 3. Algorithm for *DPR_Reduce*

7 Conclusion

This paper proposed a safety analysis model for access-control in multi-domain environment based on risk. The analysis model takes the access-control strategy and its behaviors in system as a state transition system to model. Then, we can give a precise definition and evaluate the safety of system operation, and thus establish rules to provide safeguard for specific safe operation and especially for the inter-domain operations. More specifically, we have defined two classes of security analysis problems in MDR^{2}BAC, namely *IPA* and *DPR*, base on the model for MDR^{2}BAC. We have also shown that *IPA* and *DPR* can be reduced to similar analysis problems in the $RT[\leftarrow,\cap]$ trust-management language. The reduction gives efficient algorithms for answering most kinds of queries in these two classes. We can show that the general *IPA* and *DPR* problem is coNP-complete problem in almost and can be solved efficiently if the q is semi-static.

Much work remains to be done for understanding security analysis in MDR^{2}BAC. The family of MDR^{2}BAC security analysis defined in this paper can be parameterized with more sophisticated models, e.g., those that allow negative preconditions, those that allow changes to the role hierarchy or role-permission assignments, and those that allow the specification of constraints, such as mutually exclusive roles.

References

1. Joshi, J.B.D., Bertino, E.: Hybrid Role Hierarchy for Generalized Temporal Role Based Access Control Model. In: Proceedings of the 26th Annual International Computer Software and Applications Conference (COMPSAC 2002), Oxford, England, August 26-29 (2002)
2. Tang, Z., Li, R., Lu, Z., Wen, Z.: Dynamic Access Control Research for Inter-operation in Multi-domain Environment Based on Risk. In: Kim, S., Yung, M., Lee, H.-W. (eds.) WISA 2007. LNCS, vol. 4867, pp. 277–290. Springer, Heidelberg (2008)
3. Li, R., Tang, Z., Lu, Z.: A Request-driven Policy Framework for Secure Interoperation in Multi-domain Environment. International Journal of Computer Systems Science & Engineering 23(3), 193–206 (2008)
4. Li, N., Mitchell, J.C., Winsborough, W.H.: Beyond proof-of-compliance: Security analysis in trust management. Journal of the ACM 52(3), 474–514 (2005)
5. Li, N., Tripunitara, M.V.: Security Analysis in Role-Based Access Control. ACM Transactions on Information and System Security 9(4), 391–420 (2006)
6. Sandhu, R., Coyne, E.J., Feinstein, H.L., Youman, C.E.: Role Based Access Control Models. Computer 29(2) (February 1996)
7. Moyer, M.J., Covington, M.J., Ahamad, M.: Generalized role-based access control for securing future applications. In: 23rd National Information Systems Security Conference (NISSC 2000), Baltimore, Md, USA (October 2000)
8. Zhang, G., Parashar, M.: Context-Aware Dynamic Access Control for Pervasive Applications. In: Proceedings of the Communication Networks and Distributed Systems Modeling and Simulation Conference (CNDS 2004), Western MultiConference (WMC), San Diego, CA, USA (January 2004)
9. Dimmock, N., Belokosztolszki, A., Eyers, D., Bacon, J., Moody, K.: Using Trust and Risk in Role-Based Access Control Policies. In: Proceedings of Symposium on Access Control Models and Technologies (2004)

10. Grandison, T., Sloman, M.: A Survey of Trust in Internet Applications. IEEE Communications Surveys 3(4), 2–16 (Fourth Quarter 2000)
11. Blaze, M., Feigenbaum, J., Lacy, J.: Decentralized trust management. In: Proceeding of IEEE Conference on Security and Privacy. AT&T (May 1996)
12. Li, N., Mitchell, J.C., Winsborough, W.H.: Design of a role-based trust management framework. In: 2002 IEEE Symposium on Security and Privacy, pp. 114–131. IEEE, Los Alamitos (2002)
13. Yao, W.T.-M.: Fidelis: A policy-driven trust management framework. In: Nixon, P., Terzis, S. (eds.) iTrust 2003. LNCS, vol. 2692, pp. 301–317. Springer, Heidelberg (2003)
14. Dimmock, N., Belokosztolszki, A., Eyers, D., et al.: Using Trust and Risk in Role-Based Access Control Policies. In: SACMAT 2004, New York, USA, June 2-4 (2004)
15. Koch, M., Mancini, L.V., Parisi-Presicce, F.: Decidability of safety in graph-based models for access control. In: Gollmann, D., Karjoth, G., Waidner, M. (eds.) ESORICS 2002. LNCS, vol. 2502, pp. 229–243. Springer, Heidelberg (2002)

A Proposal of Appropriate Evaluation Scheme for Exchangeable CAS (XCAS)[*,**]

Yu-na Hwang, Hanjae Jeong, Sungkyu Cho, Songyi Kim,
Dongho Won, and Seungjoo Kim[***]

Information Security Group,
School of Information and Communication Engineering, Sungkyunkwan University,
300 Cheoncheon-dong, Jangan-gu, Suwon, Gyeonggi-do, 440-746, Korea
{ynhwang,hjjeong,skcho,s2kim,dhwon,skim}@security.re.kr

Abstract. A conditional access system (CAS) only allows appropriate users to get access to contents. The advent of exchangeable CAS (XCAS) that updated version of CAS is developed. But the standards or evaluation schemes for XCAS are absent, so many interoperability problems among XCAS of each company may have to be occurred. Therefore, a specific scheme that can evaluate the security and suitability of exchangeable conditional access systems has been requested. In this paper, we propose an appropriate evaluation scheme for XCAS. The evaluation scheme includes an evaluation purpose and four components to evaluate the evaluation target, the evaluation process, the evaluation subject, and the evaluation cost involved.

Keywords: XCAS, exchangeable CAS, Conditional Access System, CC, Common Criteria, CMVP, EMV, PCIDSS, DCAS, downloadable CAS.

1 Introduction

The profitability of a multiple service operator (MSO) strongly depends on the techniques that it uses to filter out illegal access to its pay channels broadcast by satellite or cable. A conditional access system (CAS) only allows appropriate users to access content. When implementing its CAS, an MSO makes a password and scrambles the content, then transmits the scrambled content based on the password. Only those users who know the password can use it to descramble the password and receive normal content. Set-top boxes use passwords they receive from built-in chips or smart cards to automatically descramble content. However, users who own these boxes cannot change MSOs without also changing the set-top boxes. The advance of

---

[*] "This research was supported by the MKE(Ministry of Knowledge Economy), Korea, under the ITRC(Information Technology Research Center) support program supervised by the NIPA(National IT Industry Promotion Agency)" (NIPA-2009-(C1090-0902-0016)).

[**] This work was supported by Defense Acquisition Program Administration and Agency for Defense Development under the contract UD070054AD.

[***] Corresponding author.

J. Kwak et al. (Eds.): ISPEC 2010, LNCS 6047, pp. 217–228, 2010.

smart cards made it easier for users to change MSOs, but the heat produced from the card while set-top box was operating has created errors [1-4].

To solve this problem, researchers designed a new type of conditional access system in which hardware such as smart cards handles the descrambling process in a CAS, and software handles the descrambling process in an exchangeable conditional access system (XCAS). One of the strengths of this method that users do not have to change their set-top box, but simply download new filtering process software from a new MSO whenever they want to change MSOs.

But because XCAS protocols or standards currently don't exist, each company develops its own type of software, which will cause many interoperability problems in the future. Therefore we request and propose an appropriate evaluation scheme for XCAS to evaluate security, suitability and other factors.

In the first part of the paper, we analyze existing evaluation schemes. In the second part of the paper we propose an appropriate evaluation scheme for XCAS. We describe XCAS Chapter 2, and analyze existing evaluation schemes in Chapter 3. In Chapter 4 we propose an evaluation scheme for XCAS and follow up with a conclusion in Chapter 5.

2   Related Works

This chapter includes an overview of CAS first, and a description of XCAS second.

2.1   CAS

CAS solves the problem of content security by only allowing paid subscribers to watch specific channels of scrambled content. In CAS, a server generates scrambled content and recipients can descramble this content. A Control Word Generator in the server makes a Control Word (CW) and then the server scrambles data with the given CW and sends it to the recipients. The server then converts the CW into an Entitlement Control Message (ECM) and sends it. The server also converts the service key to an Entitlement Management Message (EMM) using a secret key built into the smart card owned by the recipient, and transmits it as well. A Subscriber Management System (SMS) manages and distributes the secret keys. On the recipient side, recipients recover content using an inverse process. The set-top box decrypts the service key with the secret key, decrypts the CW with the service key, and finally descrambles the transmitted data with the CW [1-4].

2.2   XCAS

Fig. 1 is a general overview of an XCAS.

Existing systems use methods based on hardware like set-top boxes or smart cards for certification, but with XCAS the set-top box only needs to download and install the appropriate software. This makes communication between the MSO and the user quite necessary. So XCAS needs much stronger security to guarantee the security and safety of the communications between the MSO and the user [1-4].

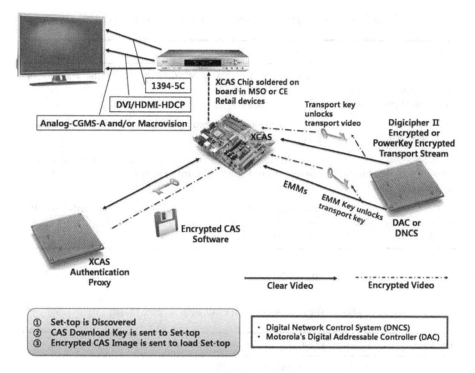

Fig. 1. A general overview of an XCAS [2]

Downloadable CAS (DCAS), what the National Cable & Telecommunications Association (NCNA) developed as one of their Next Generation Network Architectures (NGNAs), appears similar to XCAS. The three largest American MSOs - Comcast Corporation, Cox Communications Inc., and Time Warner Cable - are the main players in NGNA. Now they are aiming to create an Integrated Multimedia Architecture that leads the innovation of goods and reduction of costs with no investment in hybrid fiber-coaxial (HFC) network infrastructure which makes up the present cable TV network. The NGNA Security Model also downloads software which differs greatly from existing systems. Systems based on hardware are remotely adjustable, and under a software-based system, access control systems can be updated by downloading new software [1-4].

XCAS is gradually becoming the replacement for existing CAS. But there aren't any standards or evaluation schemes for XCAS. So many difficulties have arisen when trying to get several different kinds of XCAS to work together [1-4].

3 Analysis of Existing Evaluation Schemes

In this chapter, we analyze four kinds of evaluation schemes. The four evaluation schemes are shown below.

Table 1. Analysis target of the existent evaluation scheme [9-12][15]

Division	Description
CMVP (Cryptographic module verification program)	Enforced in America, a standard to verify the stability of cryptographic modules
CC (Common criteria)	An international standard (ISO/IEC 15408) for computer security certification
PCIDSS (Payment card industry data security standard)	A worldwide information security standard assembled by the Payment Card Industry Security Standards Council (PCI SSC)
EMV (Europay, MasterCard, VISA)	A standard for interoperation of IC cards ("Chip cards") and IC capable POS terminals and ATMs, for authenticating credit and debit card payments

Table 2 is shows the results of the analysis of each evaluation scheme.

Table 2. The analysis of each evaluation scheme [5-16]

Division	Evaluation Target	
CC	IT product with security functionality	
CMVP	cryptographic module	
PCIDSS	transaction information for credit cards	
EMV	IC cards	
Division	Feature	
CC	an international standard	
	many evaluation criteria that is used each country is combined to CC	
CMVP	CMVP is developed to evaluation for cryptographic module	
PCIDSS	global security criteria for credit card	
EMV	IC card standard based on ISO 7816	
Division	Evaluation Level	Evaluation process
CC	O	3 steps
CMVP	O	3 steps
PCIDSS	X	3 steps
EMV	X	3 steps
Division	Evaluation subject	
	Applicant	Evaluation Authority Certification Authority

Table 2. (*continued*)

CC	The company that develops IT products with security functionality	Corporate that satisfies the Requirements of CA and CCRA	Body that sets the standards and monitors the quality of evaluations conducted by bodies within a specific community and implements the CC for that community by means of an evaluation scheme
CMVP	The company that develops cryptographic module	CMT Laboratory	NIST (USA), CSE (Canada)
PCIDSS	Shop, Internet shopping mall that can use credit card	Authority that is able to perform the PCIDSS security audit	VISA etc. Global Card brands
EMV	IFM provider	Accredited Laboratories that are accredited by EMVCo. , LLC.	EMVCo. , LLC.

Division	Advantage
CC	CCRA participant shares evaluation result of other participants
CMVP	CMVP evaluates cryptographic algorithms to physical security of cryptographic module
PCIDSS	Evaluation criteria for the payment system of credit cards
EMV	EMV resolves interoperability problem between products of each country/company
	EMV supports various multi- applications

Division	Weakness
CC	CC does not have evaluation methods for cryptographic modules
	CC demands too many evaluation deliverables
CMVP	CMVP does not have evaluation method for total system
PCIDSS	The mean of requirements still does not specify
EMV	This standard is too complex

4 Proposed Evaluation Scheme for XCAS

In this chapter, we describe an appropriate evaluation scheme for XCAS. The evaluation scheme includes an evaluation purpose and four components to evaluate the evaluation target, the evaluation process, the evaluation subject, and the evaluation cost involved.

DCI (Digital Cinema Initiatives), a venture company established by a collaboration of film firms all over the world including Hollywood, as the center, is a leading company recognized as a standard of digital cinema. DCI does not have an evaluation scheme for XCAS, but they do have CMVP Level 3 requirements for cryptographic equipment. CMVP also shows each levels of operating environments for cryptographic modules. To qualify for CMVP Level 3, a cryptographic module has to operate in an environment above CC Evaluation Assurance Level 3 (EAL 3) with the addition of a Trusted Path (FTP_TRP.1) and an informal Target of Evaluation (TOE) Security Policy Model (ADV_SPM.1). So in this paper an evaluation scheme is proposed that can meet CMVP Level 3 and CC EAL3 [5-8] [17-19].

The proposed evaluation scheme did not exist in the past and requires relatively strict evaluation deliverables. So a manufacturer of XCAS could have severe initial difficulties to get certified. Therefore, we think the ideal way would be to have a two-step evaluation scheme. The first step would have easier requirements for some of the evaluation deliverables. The second step at the international level would be a strict interpretation of the requirements. A XCAS manufacturer could qualify for the first step of basic evaluation deliverables, and when ready for international business, could be evaluated with additional evaluation deliverables.

4.1 Evaluation Purpose and Target

Object of evaluation scheme proposed in this paper is certificating suitability of solution developed by various companies. Yet, there is not any international standard as well as Korea's standard; various MSOs are developing their own XCAS. Despite these actual circumstances, there is no standard and evaluation scheme which can verify suitability such as security and safety. So in this chapter, an appropriate evaluation scheme for XCAS is proposed, to make right users use XCAS safely.

The proposed evaluation scheme is targeted to XCAS developed by companies, and the later follows the performance of the verification according to the process described.

4.2 Evaluation Process

Fig. 2 is the process of evaluation in the proposed scheme.

① Company that developed XCAS prepares the evaluation deliverables for certification from Certification Authority (CA).
② When the evaluation deliverables are prepared, applicant fills out the form required by Evaluation Authority (EA) and transmits it to them.
③ If applicant requests evaluation to EA, EA reports it to CA.
④ EA and CA have to know all the details about the contract of evaluation such as period, scope, cost and etc. So the three parties must create a contract together. For harmony, the applicant should provide an explanation about evaluation deliverables to the EA.
⑤ Evaluation of the deliverables provided should be performed first, before the XCAS test.

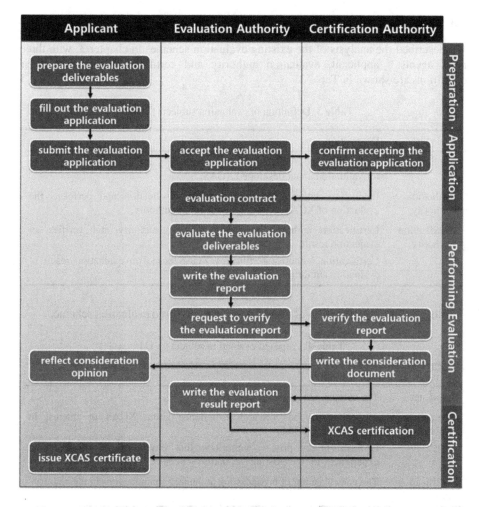

Fig. 2. Proposed evaluation process

⑥ Evaluation report written out by EA ought to pass the investigation of CA to guarantee fairness of the evaluation and review.

⑦ CA should check the report and results about evaluations performed by EA. After checking, CA should comment on their opinions by drawing up a consideration document.

⑧ Next step depends on a consideration document written by CA. If there is a modification opinion, applicant has to make corrections and should be evaluated again. No modification opinion means the evaluation for XCAS is well performed well and has no errors, so EA writes out an Evaluation Report.

⑨ The certificate will be issued normally to applicants by CA when CA completes investigation about the evaluation performed by EA.

4.3 Evaluation Subject

We described the analysis of the existing evaluation schemes in chapter 3, with three main agents - applicant, evaluation authority and certification authority. Their definitions are shown in Table 3.

Table 3. Definition of evaluation subjects [5-7]

Division	Description
Applicant	Applicant prepares the evaluation deliverables and applies the evaluation for validation about developed XCAS.
Evaluation Authority	Evaluation authority accepts to do the evaluation and performs the evaluation of XCAS replacing certification authority.
Certification Authority	Certification authority assigns evaluation authority and verifies an evaluation result.
	Certification authority certificates XCAS based on evaluation result of evaluation authority.

Table 4 shows the selection of each agent of the proposed evaluation scheme.

Table 4. Proposed evaluation subject [4-11]

Division	Description
Applicant	The company that develops XCAS
Evaluation Authority	Authority that has research experience about XCAS or interest in evaluation for XCAS.
	Government or private authorities that have certification/evaluation experiences for the existing evaluation scheme.
Certification Authority	The control center of broadcasting and telecommunications in the country

Obviously, the company that developed an XCAS becomes the applicant, since they want to get validation of the developed XCAS. In the selection of EA, an evaluation in Step 1 is relatively simple compared to the one in Step 2 because it is an introduction stage. So in Step 1, it is possible that CA designates a private or public institution as EA which has studied or shown interest in XCAS. In Step 2, evaluation performing ability is emphasized because it is required to submit the evaluation deliverables at an international level. Therefore, the institution chosen as EA has to have experienced XCAS evaluation during the time of Step 1 and have the experts and environment to perform an accurate evaluation. But those institutions with no experience in Step 1 can perform as EA with the permission of CA under the condition of providing expert knowledge and human resources to evaluate XCAS. CA has to be selected as the control center of broadcasting and telecommunications in the country. The CA selected ought to be responsible for the chapter of the EA and the management of the evaluation.

4.4   Evaluation Deliverable

Table 5 shows the evaluation deliverables of evaluation schemes analyzed above, according to CMVP Level 3 and CC EAL 3 [5-8].

Table 5. The evaluation deliverables of existing evaluation schemes for Level 3 [5-8]

CC(EAL 3)	CMVP(Level 3)
The security target	N/A
The configuration management documentation	The configuration management
The functional specification	N/A
The delivery documentation	N/A
The TOE design	Basic and details design
The security architecture description	Product and source program or hardware design
The preparative user guidance	N/A
The development security documentation	N/A
The operational user guidance	Product using guidance
The life-cycle definition documentation	N/A
The test documentation	Test procedure and result

Table 6. The evaluation deliverables for each evaluation step

CC(EAL 3)	Step 1	Step 2
The security target	O	O
The functional specification	O	O
The TOE design	O	O
The security architecture description	O	O
The test documentation	O	O
The delivery documentation	N/A	O
The preparative user guidance	N/A	O
The development security documentation	N/A	O
The operational user guidance	N/A	O
The life-cycle definition documentation	N/A	O
The configuration management documentation	N/A	O

Step 1 requires only the basic evaluation deliverables to evaluate XCAS. But Step 2 has to require additional evaluation deliverables to perform a much more strict evaluation compared to Step 1.

Regarding this, we propose the evaluation deliverables for each step as outlines in Table 6.

4.5 Evaluation Cost

Evaluation cost is proposed according to the policies or laws of the country that evaluates XCAS using the proposed evaluation scheme.

The following is an example of a computation method for the evaluation cost. The computation method of evaluation cost is proposed based on the policies and laws of Korea. It is appropriate to apply computation method for evaluation cost of CC with a computational method. No matter what is evaluated, the cost of acquiring evaluation equipment is the same because the target of the proposed evaluation scheme is only XCAS.

The terms of evaluation vary related to what each step is. The proposed evaluation scheme for XCAS does not require many papers, and in this point is similar to the CC evaluation in Korea. Because Step 2 in the proposed scheme is similar to EAL 3 of CC, the period of the proposed evaluation scheme in Step 2 is estimated to be 82 days. We arrived at this figure by calculating the computation method of the evaluation for Korea [10]. We can also get an estimate of Step 1 by comparing it to the estimated result of Step 2. Step 1 has 5 kinds of evaluation deliverables and Step 2 has 11, so we can estimate 37 days as appropriate Step 1 evaluation.

Considering these facts, we can propose a basis of the computation method for evaluation cost and consideration parameters.

Table 7. Proposed consideration parameter of evaluation cost for Korea [10]

Division	Foundation
Pay per Day per Worker	EA Policy
Number of Workers	1 Person
Evaluation Term	Step 1 : 37 days, Step 2 : 82 days
Complexity	According to Evaluation Target
Cost of Acquiring Evaluation Equipment	Real Cost
Miscellaneous Costs	Real Cost

Worker pay is adjustable depending on the EA policy.

Using the above parameters of evaluation cost and EA confirms the payment per day, personnel expenses, indirect cost for administration, technique cost and direct cost out of the cost for the evaluation equipment. The results of these calculations are listed in Table 8 [10].

Table 8. Proposed computation method of evaluation cost for Korea [10]

Division	Computation method
Personnel Expenses	Σ{evaluation term×pay per worker-day}
Cost for Evaluation Equipment	cost for acquiring evaluation equipment×(evaluation term/the life of an equipment)
Indirect Cost for Administration	personnel expenses×110%
Technique Cost	(personnel expenses + indirect cost for administration)×20%
Total Constant Cost	personnel expenses + direct cost (the cost for evaluation equipment) + Indirect cost for administration + technique cost
Total Cost	(total constant cost×complexity) + the others cost

This calculation is relatively easier for applicants to understand compared to the computation method of the evaluation for Korean CC cost, so it's rationally appropriate for the evaluation cost of XCAS. The computation method of the evaluation for Korean CC cost can be used anytime whether it is the first or second evaluation. The size of the enterprise or the classification of complexity of the evaluation target doesn't matter either.

5 Conclusion

We proposed an evaluation scheme for XCAS that followed an analysis of existing evaluation schemes. The proposed evaluation scheme allowed strengths of the existing systems and appropriated for XCAS. The system also has two enforcement steps. Because of this, XCAS companies will first be able to qualify for the Step 1 scheme with just five evaluation deliverables. The system intends to verify the security, safety and suitability of the developed XCAS and raise the intensity of the certification by requiring evaluation deliverables meeting an international level in Step 2 of evaluation. This two-stage system is deal according to a consideration of the conditions.

Using the proposed evaluation scheme for XCAS, we evaluate many XCAS. Due to this proposed evaluation, many kinds of XCAS are expected to be evaluated with a common rule and will be a great help to revitalized and spread XCAS.

References

1. OpenCableTM Technical Reports, DCAS System Overview Technical Report, OC-TR-DCAS-D02-060912 (2006)
2. NCTA DCAS Report to FCC (November 2005)
3. http://www.opencable.com/dcas
4. http://www.klabs.re.kr
5. ISO/IEC 15408-1, Information technology — Security techniques — Evaluation criteria for IT security — Part 1: Introduction and general model

6. ISO/IEC 15408-2, Information technology — Security techniques — Evaluation criteria for IT security — Part 2: Security functional requirements
7. ISO/IEC 15408-3, Information technology — Security techniques — Evaluation criteria for IT security — Part 3: Security assurance requirements
8. NIST, FIPS 140-2: Security Requirements For Cryptographic Modules (May 2001)
9. http://www.nist.gov
10. http://www.kisa.or.kr
11. http://www.niap-ccevs.org
12. http://www.emvco.com
13. EMVCo, LLC. EMVCo Type Approval – Contact Terminal Level 1 – Administrative Process Version 5.0 (January 2009)
14. EMVCo, LLC. EMVCo Type Approval – Contact Terminal Level 2 – Administrative Process Version 2.0 (January 2009)
15. https://www.pcisecuritystandards.org
16. PCI Security Standard Council, Payment Card Industry (PCI) Data Security Standard: Requirements and Security Assessment Procedures Version 1.2.1 (July 2009)
17. http://www.dcimovies.com
18. Digital Cinema Initiatives, LLC, Digital Cinema System Specification Compliance Test Plan Version 1.1 (May 2009)
19. Digital Cinema Initiatives, LLC, Digital Cinema System Specification Version 1.2 (March 2008)

A Trustworthy ID Management Mechanism in Open Market

Inkyung Jeun and Dongho Won*

Sungkyunkwan University,
300 Cheoncheon-dong, Jangan-gu, Suwon, Gyeonggi-do, 440-746 Korea
{ikjeun,dhwon}@security.re.kr

Abstract. The Peer-to-Peer(P2P) network has been growing dramatically in popularity over the last decade. In this paper we present the trustworthy Identity(ID) management method to provide reliable P2P open market service. In particular, we focus on the duplicated joining, privacy issues and non-repudiation problems in service. For safe usage of the P2P based e-commerce, the security issues about the identity management in P2P network which given the inherently untrustworthy nature, should be highlighted most of all, and this paper proposed the method for resolving the vulnerability in ID management of the P2P open market.

1 Introduction

As e-Commerce on the Internet becomes more and more popular, C2C(Customer-to-customer(C2C)) based open market have become quite popular during the recent years. The success of eBay[1] could be a good example of how eagerly Internet users were waiting for appearance of C2C-based e-commerce[2]. A growing number of online commercial transactions occur in peer-to-peer(P2P) environments, which is the structure of coordinated by peer's free participation. P2P network have been proposed for a wide variety of application, including file-sharing, web cashing, distributed computation, etc. In these days, C2C based e-commerce using P2P network is widely used because the peers can join or leave the P2P network at any time. Free subscription and withdrawal guarantees the anonymity of each peer but can also pose a threat to e-Commerce where monetary transaction is performed, because free-riders[3] can get a new ID without proper verification, and the same peer can get several IDs in duplicate to take part in the P2P network. So, P2P network does not efficiently provide all the services required by e-commerce transaction such as reliability and identification[6].

Recently, Auction which is representative P2P e-commerce provider of Korea had an accident of personal information exposure[5]. About ten million people's personal information was stolen, so the customers started a lawsuit against Auction. As we can see this accident, trust, security and privacy issues should be researched extensively for open market. There are many researches deal with the

---

* Corresponding author.

J. Kwak et al. (Eds.): ISPEC 2010, LNCS 6047, pp. 229–240, 2010.

230 I. Jeun and D. Won

trust issues in P2P network. Most existing researches propose that the trust of peers in P2P network is depend on a reputation of peer. Of course, the reputation is the most important factor for deciding the trust of peer. But the identity itself is also very important, especially in the e-commerce service as we mentions above. Also, most existing trust model of P2P network are developed for general-purpose P2P applications like as file-sharing. In fact, little work has been done in establishing trust in e-commerce applications.

Some service providers verify the identity of the peer that participates in the P2P network using their RN(Registration Number), SSN(Social Security Number), and financial information like as a credit card number, in order to resolve the problem of duplicated ID issuance. However, the personal information like the RN is very sensitive, and should be submitted to the trusted service provider only. Therefore, it is difficult to use this information on the P2P open market without discretion, which tries to provide the flexible service usage environment. If this personal information is disclosed, it can be stolen or misused on the Internet. Consequently, it cannot be the information that identifies each individual uniquely. In addition, identification by the PKI(Public Key Infrastructure)[7] can prevent indiscrete issuance and duplicated issuance of the ID. However, it requires relatively heavy PKI infrastructure such as issuance, renewal, and disposal of a certification, and users without a certificate cannot access to the requested service. This paper intend to provide of the identity of an entity, that participates in the P2P network, without disclosing personal information, using the identity information from CTA (Central Trusted Authority), and to propose a method of ID issuance that ensures one-to-one mapping with each entity.

The rest of this paper is organized as follows. We shall describe the ID threats and security requirement in P2P open market service in Section 2. In Section 3, we shall describe our ID management model and suggest some assumption . In Section 4, we shall explain P2P e-commerce service scenario and protocol, and we shall analysis our model in Section 5. And this paper will make a conclusion in Section 6.

2 Related Works

2.1 Reviews of P2P System

Existing P2P systems employ centralized or decentralized service architectures[4]. For the centralized system, a central server is present to provide the directory service. Napster[8] and eDonkey are example of centralized systems. Peers can connect other peers after they receive the location information of peers from the central server. This paper will focus on the centralized systems.

The decentralized systems is classified the pure centralized model and the supernode model. Pure decentralized model has no centralized directory and nodes can join the service by randomly connecting to the existing participants. Each node acts as a server to handle requests of other nodes, and at the same time acts as a client to receive services provided by other nodes. Gnutella is a typical example of pure decentralized systems. Supernode model have no fixed central directory server but the supernode provides file indexing services for their connected peers known as leaf nodes, with less computer resources. When the leaf nodes perform searching, they will first search for the files in the file index kept by the supernode. An example using this model is FastTrack.

2.2   ID-Related Threats in P2P Open Market

In this section, we first state the threats in a P2P network, followed by the requirements for providing a secure P2P e-Commerce service. Recently, the potential of the P2P network, which is based on such characteristics as "open, dynamic, and anonymous," has been recognized, receiving attention as a new internet service infrastructure in various areas. However, it's not easy to implement the reliable and effective entity authentication method due to the nature of the P2P network[9]. Without a reliable ID generation and management and a proper authentication procedure, the P2P open market can be exposed to the following ID-related vulnerabilities.

Whitewashing: Whitewashing, the most conspicuous vulnerability, is causing serious problems on the Internet these days. The P2P network is established with free participation of the peer, thus providing the benefit of securing anonymity[16]. Conversely, it is possible that peers can receive a new ID at a low cost and take part in the P2P network.

ID spoofing: ID spoofing is a technique that the malicious peer deceives its ID to attack another target system. The attacker can use the obtained ID as one to access the target peer, and can pretend to be a responder peer while communicating between two peers, in order to maintain the unauthorized communication. This attack cannot be traced easily, since the current p2p service allows ID issuance without any effective limitation. Thus, if ID issuance is allowed without any rules, ID theft cannot be prevented actively. Consequently, the ID verification system should be reinforced in P2P network.

Repudiation: Even when an attacker uses an ID maliciously using the vulnerable authentication method, the identity of the attacker cannot be verified if the attacker denies using that ID. Therefore, the owner of the ID can repudiate any action that he committed in a cyber space.

Privacy: In the P2P network, there is no outright definition as to who shares whose information due to the nature of the distributed environment, nor there is any definition of the management subject of the user's personal information. In this environment, the personal information should not be provided to or managed by the network or service provider more than is necessary[10][11]. Especially, the RN or bank account number is deal with very carefully, because they are very sensitive information.

2.3   Targeted Requirements

In order to enable P2P e-commerce like e-Bay, it is essential to provide security functionalities such as confidentiality, integrity including the following requirements.

– *Uniqueness:* ID of the peer who participates in P2P service should be issued uniquely. Even though duplicated subscription is allowed, it should be possible to identify the user as for each subscription.
– *Privacy:* The personal information of the peer should not be disclosed[12]. And, activities of the peer who uses the P2P network should not be traced by the service providers.
– *Scalability:* Because the P2P service allows the participation and withdrawal of the various subjects due to the characteristics of the network, the service should be applicable to several subjects conveniently. Also, the performance should not decrease as the load increases.
– *Authentication:* All peers who can be a buyer and seller, should have an identity to verify them in the e-commerce. And the system should be capable to verify of the identity exactly.
– *Non-repudiation:* Buyers and sellers should not be allowed to repudiate their goods purchase and sales behavior.

3   ID Management Model in the P2P Open Market

As the number of the SPs(Service Provider) providing the escrow service has been increasing according with the rising demand for the P2P-based open market, various problems have arisen due to the limitations of P2P network. For example, certain users can falsely increase the price of an item they are selling by receiving several IDs from the SP and pretending to be a different user, for the purpose of selling his/her item at a higher price. Even worse, the seller can provide an item that is different from the one initially proposed, or the buyer may want to cancel the transaction because the product is damaged. In the latter case, the buyer may not be able to cancel the transaction because he/she cannot trace the ID of the seller of the item. This can occur because an ID can be issued indiscreetly due to the characteristics of the P2P electronic transaction, which has a limited capability of identifying the counterpart, even though user's identification is indispensable for the safe e-commerce.

This chapter proposes mechanism that checks for duplicated subscription of the user in the P2P e-Commerce environment, using the PII(Personal Identify Information) that enables the identification of the individual without disclosing the individual's personal information, while identifying the user uniquely like the RN and using the robust identification method. The CTA issues and manages the PII for the P2P entity through association with the open market SPs, and provides the personal information of the entity that is required to provide a service to the SP under the user's authorization. The SP provides a broker function so that the transaction between entities on the P2P network can be made. If the entity registers the item to be traded with the SP or wants to buy that item, the SP enables the transaction to go ahead after authenticating each entity.

3.1   Service Model

The P2P e-Commerce service model proposed by this paper is composed of CTA, SP, and $peer$ as follows.

CTA(Central Trusted Authority): The CTA is the trusted third party that stores and manages the personal information and the identification information of each peer in the P2P e-Commerce environment. The CTA issues the personal identification information(PII) for the peer that participates in service, verifies the validity of the user's PII, and generates and sends the duplicated joining verification information to the open market service provider. CTA is a central authority, so the safety of CTA should be guaranteed in our service model.

SP(Service Provider): The SP is a broker that provides P2P-based open market service through linkage with the CTA and share the secret key. The SP arranges the agreement with the CTA in advance for issuing of user's PII and requests the personal information. All SPs have a SP identity number which is assigned by it's CTA. SPs are same as e-Bay and Auction service provider in real environment.

Peer: The peer is a user who wants to use P2P open market service. The peer is the P2P entity that registers the item to be sold with the SP, which is a broker, or selects and buys the item registered in SP. The peer can use a personal computer or mobile device to connect our P2P open market service. The peer is not a device, but just a person who has a identity like as RN or real name.

3.2   Notaion

For easy of explanation, we use the following notations to describe our P2P open market service model in this paper.

PII_i	Personal Identity Information of i
PI_i	Personal Information of i, like as real name, e-mail address, etc.
VI	user Verification Information
DI	Duplicated joining Information
SPI	SP Identification number
$\|\|$	Concatenation
$H()$	Hash function
$HMAC()$	Hash MAC function
SK_{CTA}	Secret Key of CTA
SS	Secret Key between CTA and SP
$X \rightarrow Y : m$	message m is sent from X to Y
$E_K()$	a encryption function under secret key K
$PU_X()$	an asymmetric-key of X
f	verification result flag of PII_i, the value can be true or false

3.3   Assumption

P2P e-commerce is more and more popular in these days.But as we investigated in Section 2, the current P2P network has some ID management problems.In this paper, we propose an efficient and reliable ID management method using in P2P network. To achieve this, we assume some facts as follows.

1. The peer that wants to buy or sell the items by joining in P2P open market should be register the personal information to the CTA in advance and receive the PII from CTA using the out-of-band method. Section 4.1 describes the detailed procedure of receiving the PII.
2. The CTA is the trusted agency that stores and manages identification and personal information of the peer that participates in the service. There can be several $CTAs$ to prevent the problem of centralization of the personal information that can occur when one agency possesses the personal information of all users. The CTA identifier is allocated in advance and used to identify several $CTAs$. But in this paper, we assume there is only one CTA for a convenient.
3. Also, CTA and SP should contract in advance and share a secret symmetric key(SS) used to transfer the data between the SP and CTA. And the CTA issues an identifier SI to the SP. SP has a public key and a private key pair, which is used to transfer message between SP and $peer$. The public key is used to encrypt the message by peer, and the private key of SP is used to decrypt it.
4. The personal information required to provide P2P open market is minimized. The real name and his/her address, phone number are used to provide e-commerce.

4   Service Scenario

The proposed service model is divided into 3 processes : First one is a personal information registration process, and a selling and purchase process, and a duplication joining verification process. The duplication joining verification process is performed in the selling and purchase process to verify of seller and buyer's identity.

4.1   Personal Information Registration Process

Every peer who wishes to joining in P2P e-commerce needs to register himself to CTA and issues his/her PII.

Next is the detailed step of the registration process.

Step1. The peer should visit CTA and requests PII_{peer} issuance. Then, the CTA will request the peer to provide the identity proof(using resident registration number(RN), driver's license number, bank account number, or credit card number) issued by the third trusted agency in order to identify the peer. The type of the identity proof information can be variety.

Step2. Once the CTA has identified the peer, the peer registers the personal information needed for PII_{peer} issuance to the CTA database, such as peer's real name, RN, and phone number, address, etc. Then, the peer sets and stores the password(PW_{peer}) corresponding the PII_{peer} in the CTA, which is needed to identify the peer.

Step3. The CTA verifies validity of the personal information of the peer, and generates the PII_{peer}. At this time, the PII_{peer} is configured as below, using the $CTAidentifier$ and the R(random number). The $CTAidentifier$ is the used to identify the CTA, if there are several $CTAs$. The digit can be determined by the number of $CTAs$ in service domain. The $CTAidentifier$ is a unique value. The R is the random number generated by the CTA arbitrarily.

$$PII_{peer} = CTAidentifier \| R$$

As we can see here, the PII_{peer} contains any personal information. As the $CTAidentifier$ can be assumed to be the unique value for each CTA, the PII_{peer} is made to include the random number R, so the value cannot be inferred easily. The CTA saves the peer's personal information in the database, using the PII_{peer} as a primary key.

Step4. The CTA sends the PII_{peer} to the peer.This can be done by on-line or off-line.

4.2 Item Selling and Purchase Process

The Fig.1 describes the item selling and purchase scenario of the P2P open market using the PII.

First, the detailed step for item selling is as follows

1. $Peer1$ requests the sale of an item SP.At this time, $Peer1$ encrypts PII_{peer1} received from the CTA, item selling request message (M_{sell}), PW_{p1} registered in the CTA, ID to be registered in the SP, and the item list to be sold $item_{p1}$ using SP's public key, and sends them to SP.
   [**S-1**] $p1 \rightarrow SP : E_{PU_{sp}}(M_{sell}, PW_{p1}, ietm_{p1}, ID_{p1}, PII_{peer1})$
2. The SP that receives [S-1] decrypts the message with its private key to check it. Afterwards, the SP requests the CTA to provide the verification of PII_{peer1} and duplicated joining verification information(DI_{peer1}) in order to identify $Peer1$, and the personal information like as the real name or home address needed to offer the requested service. At this time, the request message uses the secret key SS, which is shared between SP and CTA in advance.
   [**S-2**] $SP \rightarrow CTA : E_{SS}(PII_{peer1})$
3. The CTA verifies PII_{peer1} in [S-2] to determine whether it is valid or not. If PII_{peer1} is valid, it generates DI_{peer1} If it's invalid, the result flag(f) sets false and sent it to SP. The DI_{peer1} is created as below.
   $DI_{peer1} = HMAC_{SK}(H(RN\|SI))$
   The RN is a user's unique ID such as his/her resident registration number, driver's license number, or student ID number. This is the value saved in

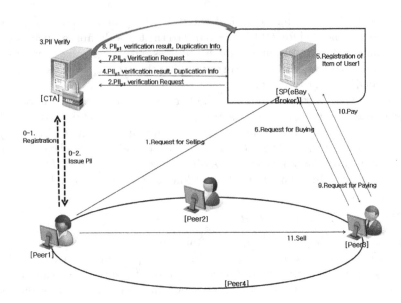

Fig. 1. P2P Open Market Service using PII

the CTA's database while issuing the PII_{peer1} after user submits the RN to the CTA. The CTA shares the SI and SK with the SP in advance. Even though DI_{peer1} is generated using the RN that is the unique identification information of $Peer1$, it is generated by $HMAC[9]$ using the SK, which is the CTA's secrete key and the value that hashed the RN and the SI is used as the $HMAC$ input value. Therefore, it is difficult to infer the RN from the DI_{peer1}. In addition, if the SP changes, DI_{peer1} is generated using the different SI value. So it is impossible to know where the $Peer1$ registered using the DI_{peer1} value.

4. The CTA sends PII_{peer1} verification result(f) and DI_{peer1}, PW_{p1} and the personal information such as which real name to the SP.

   [S-3] $CTA \rightarrow SP : E_{SS}(f, DI_{peer1}, PW_{p1}, PII_{peer1})$

5. The SP authenticates $Peer1$ by comparing PW_{p1}, which is the user password in [S-3], with the one sent by the user from [S-1]. In addition, the SP checks the DI_{peer1} received from the CTA to see whether the user is correct one who is not registered yet. Then, it allows ID issuance to $Peer1$, and registers ID of $Peer1$, PI_{peer1}, and item to sell. Section 4.3 describes how to check the duplicated subscription of $Peer1$ using the DI_{peer1} value.

Next is the detailed process for buying the item

6. $Peer3$ checks the item registered by $Peer1$ through consultation with the SP. To purchase that item, $Peer3$ sends the message of buying(M_{buy1}) and PII_{peer3}, PW_{p3}, and the ID to register to the SP. Also this message is encrypted using public key of SP.

[B-1] $p3 \rightarrow SP : E_{PU_{sp}}(M_{buyl}, PW_{p3}, ID_{p3}, ietm_{p3}, PII_{peer3})$

7. Upon receiving **[B-1]**, the SP checks the message by decrypting it with its private key. Afterwards, the SP requests the CTA to provide the verification information regarding PII_{peer3} and it's duplicated joining verification information (DI_{peer3}) to identify $Peer3$, and the user's personal information needed to provide service. The request message also uses the secret key SS in this case, which is shared between SP and CTA in advance.

   [B-2] $SP \rightarrow CTA : E_{SS}(PII_{peer3})$

8. The CTA verifies PII_{peer3} and then sends the verification result of PII_{peer3}, the duplicated joining verification information(DI_{peer3}), user password PW_{p3}, and personal information needed for service to the SP. The same DI generation method in (3) is used.

   [B-3] $CTA \rightarrow SP : E_{SS}(f, DI_{peer3}, PW_{p3}, PI_{peer3})$

9. When the SP receives **[B-3]**, the SP checks duplicated joining of $Peer3$ using the information obtained from the CTA like the procedure in (5). If the user is not registered in duplicate, the SP registers the ID of $peer3$ and the PI_{peer3} and then sends the payment request to $Peer3$.

10. $Peer3$ makes a payment to the SP.

11. The transaction is complete when $Peer1$ sends the goods to $Peer3$.

4.3   Duplicated Joining Verification Process Using DI

The next section explains the procedure that SP checks whether the peer is subscribed or not, using the DI received from the CTA. DI is used to guarantee one-to-one mapping of peer and it's ID to prevent duplicated ID issuance in one P2P open market service , and to confirm that one peer has been issued with several IDs.

1. The SP searches its database to look for the peer that corresponds to the real name of the peer received from the CTA. Database can enhance its efficiency by searching for the peer who uses the same real name, instead of using the DI_{peer} value first. If the real name of the peer is not used, peer's duplicated subscription can be verified via the DI_{peer} verification procedure without a real name search.

2. If no peer is found with the same real name after database search, the PI_{peer1} and DI_{peer1} are saved, and the ID is issued to Peer i.

3. If the $peer_s$(s: number of subscribers with the same real name) with the same real name is found, $DI(Dli, 1 \leq i \leq s)$ of the subscriber concerned is compared with the received DI_{peer1}.
   $DIi ? = DII_{peer1}$ $(1 \leq i \leq s)$

4. If the same DI is found, the peer is a already subscribed user. Therefore, the enrollment process of the peer is terminated.

5. If the same DI is not found, PII_{peer1} and DI_{peer1} are saved, and the ID is issued to $Peer1$.

5 Analysis

This chapter analyzes our proposed model satisfies the requirements proposed at chapter 2. For the P2P e-Commerce service that provides reliable ID management function, identification and unique ID issuance should be supported without disclosing the personal information of the peer participating in service, also peer's activities should be traceable,if needed.

5.1 System Implementation and Evaluation

Here, we will discuss the system implementation result for the evaluation of our proposed model. Our test bed for the evaluation consists of two service platforms. One is for the open market service provider, the other is for the *CTA*. Next table shows the system construction and configuration.

Module	SP Server	CTA Server
OS	Windows 2003	Linux 2.6.18-53.1.21.el5xen
RAM	2G	2G
DBMS	MySQL5.1	Oracle10 XE
Application Server	tomcat 6.0.18	tomcat 6.0.18
CPU	Intel CPU E4500 @2.20GHz	Intel E4500 @2.20GHz

We use here two groups of peer, one group use only his ID/PW and the other group use *PII* to identify himself. To evaluate of performance in the real P2P network, we assume 10, 100, 500, 1000 peers simultaneously. That is 10, 100, 500, and 1000 peers request to SP at the same time. To generate the requests simultaneously, we use jakarta-jmeter program.

Next figure show the response time of each request. When we use *PII*,the response time is five times longer than using ID/PW. But our proposed model provide the uniqueness and identity of peers and the response time is enough short to provide service, it merits careful consideration.

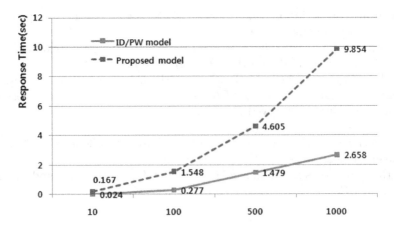

5.2 Satisfaction of Requirements

- **Uniqueness:** The *SP* checks whether the peer is already subscribed or not, by receiving the *DI* from the *CTA* before issuing the ID for each peer. As the *DI* is generated using the RN which is peer's unique identification information, and the *SI* value that is uniquely assigned to each *SP*. So the same *DI* value is generated to the same peer, because its RN value is same. If the peer is already registered in the *SP*, the *SP* already has the *DI* value of the peer concerned, it can prevent duplicated subscription because it can check whether there is any peer having the same *DI* value with the one received from the *CTA*. Even the peer with the same *DI* value, the *SP* can check the same identity. Therefore, threats against the electronic transaction can be prevented in advance which can be caused by indiscreet ID issuance.
- **Privacy:** The *PII* does not contain any personal information of the peer, but it can verify the identity of peer. Consequently,the threat of personal information leak can be prevented, which may occur by submitting the resident's registration number or a PKI certification for user identification.
- **Scalability:** The model proposed by this paper allows free participation of the *CTAs* and the *SPs*. As the *CTA* identifier and the *SP* identifier are used when *PII* and *DI* are generated considering participation of several *CTAs* and *SPs*, the *CTA* and the *SP* that wants to participate in service can receive the identifier, which doesn't match other agencies.
- **Non-reputation:** The *SP* receives the password of the peer that is registered in advance, when issuing the *PII* for the peer who wants ID issuance. This password is saved in the *CTA*, and sent to the *SP* when the *CTA* sends the *DI* and the necessary personal information after verifying the peer's *PII*. That is, because the user requesting ID issuance can be assumed to know both *PII* and password, unless the peer's *PII* and password are completely disclosed, non-repudiation of peer can be prevented.
- **Flexibility:** As the *PII* is generated using the random number created by the *CTA*, the user can request to re-issue or dispose the *PII* if it is leaked, stolen, or lost. The peer's request is saved in the *CTA*'s peer information so when the *PII* verification request is received after the *PII* disposal request, the request will be deemed invalid, which enables to prevent the *PII* disclosure problem.

6 Conclusion

This paper proposed the ID management technique that can resolve the problem of whitewashing and repudiation, which may occur due to a difficulty in identifying the user uniquely in the P2P network, and indiscreet issuance of the ID because of the above-mentioned problem. Recently, P2P service is not limited to file sharing service but expanded to various areas, such as VoIP, game, and virtual office. For safe usage of the P2P network, the P2P network security issue should be highlighted most of all, and this paper proposed the method of resolving the vulnerabilities in ID management of the P2P network.

References

1. eBay Inc. ebay (2003), `http://www.ebay.com`
2. Datta, A., et al.: Beyond web of trust: Enabling P2P E-commerce. In: Proceedings of the IEEE International Conference on E-Commerce (CEC 2003), IEEE, Los Alamitos (2003)
3. Feldman, M., et al.: Free-Riding and White-washing in Peer-to-Peer Systems. In: The 3rd Annual Workshop on Economics and information Security, SEIS 2004 (2004)
4. Sur, S., Jung, J.W., et al.: A fair and reliable P2P E-commerce model based on collaboration with distributed peers. In: Pal, A., Kshemkalyani, A.D., Kumar, R., Gupta, A. (eds.) IWDC 2005. LNCS, vol. 3741, pp. 380–391. Springer, Heidelberg (2005)
5. Auction Inc. emph (2009), `http://www.auction.co.kr`
6. Kwok, S.H., et al.: A Server-mediated Peer-to-peer System. In: ACM SIGccom Exchanges (April 2005)
7. Housley, R., et al.: Internet X.509 Public Key Infrastructure Certificate and Certificate Revocation List (CRL) Profile. In: RFC3280, IETF (April 2002)
8. The Napster homepage (2009), `http://www.hapster.com/`
9. Milojicic, D.S., Kalogeraki, V., et al.: Peer-to-Peer Computing, HPL-2002-57 (2002)
10. Mondal, A., Kitsuregawa, M.: Privacy, Security and Trust in P2P environment: A Perspective. In: Database and Expert Systems Applications, DEXA 2006 (2006)
11. Belenkiy, M., et al.: Making p2p accountable without losing privacy. In: Workshop on Privacy in the Electonic Society. ACM, New York (2007)
12. Choi, D., et al.: A Personal Information Leakage Prevention Method on the Internet. In: ISCE 2006 (2006)

BioID: Biometric-Based Identity Management

Byoung-Jin Han[1], Dong-Whi Shin[1], Hyoung-Jin Lim[2],
In-Kyung Jeun[1], and Hyun-Chul Jung[1]

[1] Korea Internet & Security Agency (KISA), Seoul, Korea
{bjhan,shindh,ikjeun,hcjung}@kisa.or.kr
[2] Financial Security Agency (FSA), Seoul, Korea
hjlim@fsa.or.kr

Abstract. Multiple identities for an individual make a problem. There
are too many identities to control by human. Identity management helps
to solve the problem. OpenID and Cardspace are well known identity
management technologies. As the summary, OpenID reduce the number
of identities of the individual and Cardspace help to manage identities
easily. Biometrics help to overcome the threats for lost and forget on
the methods of what you know and what you have. In this paper, we
propose the identity management using a biometric technique. BioID,
uses an advantage both the biometric technique and ID management, is
the new identity management mechanism. BioID is also inter-operable
with OpenID. BioID gives users convenience that they only input their
biometric feature like as touch finger, check iris, and so on. Then, BioID
is passed to the service provider and users enjoy the services.

1 Introduction

As the growth of the Internet, the activity on the Internet gains importance
as the activity of real-life. For the activity on the Internet, the methods to
distinguish the individual are needed. In the real-life, individuals have one name
to activity. However, in the Internet, individuals have several identities. Thus
the individuals can use different identity for the different service. Like as this,
those of multiple identities for an individual make a problem. There are too
many identities to control by human.

To solve the problem, the identity management technology is emerged. The
main issues of the identity management are consists of managing multiple identity, secure authentication, managing privacy data, provide anonymity, etc.

OpenID and Cardspace are well known identity management technologies.
As the summary, OpenID reduce the number of identities of the individual and
Cardspace help to manage identities easily.

By the way, biometrics gain interest and is used in immigration control system the day after 9.11. Biometrics uses the characteristics of human body such
as permanence, uniqueness, and universality and automated authenticate the
individuals. Biometrics help to overcome the threats for lost and forget on the
methods of what you know and what you have.

J. Kwak et al. (Eds.): ISPEC 2010, LNCS 6047, pp. 241–250, 2010.

The identity management technologies have an advantage on the use of identity easily. However, they mostly based on password security and inherited the threats of password nature.

In this paper, we propose the identity management using a biometric technique. BioID, uses an advantage both the biometric technique and ID management, is the new identity management. The BioID employs OpenID concept to inter-operability and manages the stored biometric information safely using the re-issuable biometric technique.

The rest of this paper is organized as follows: In Section 2, we briefly review the background knowledge such as identity management and biometrics; In Section 3, we present BioID overview, strategy, scenario, and discussion; Finally in Section 4, we conclude this paper.

2   Backgrounds

2.1   OpenID

In the introduction, we mentioned that the OpenID's main concept is to minimize a number of identities the user manages. The OpenID chooses a URL to uniquely identify a web user. This means that the user was aware of the resources. Also, this means the end users involved in the authentication mechanism[1]. The components for OpenID service are user, service provider (SP), and OpenID provider (OP). The existing service provider performed both the role of SP and the role of OP. And all authentication information is passed through the user [2,3]. The following is OpenID protocol.

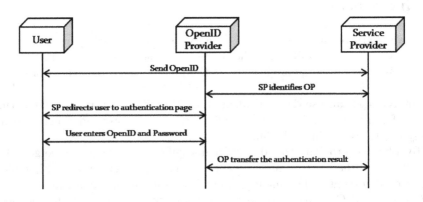

Fig. 1. The OpenID Protocol

1) User sends OpenID to SP or OP domain, which the user issued from.
2) SP identifies OP from OpenID or OP domain and SP associates with OP.
3) SP redirects user to OP authentication page.

4) The user enters OpenID password or OpenID and password pair. OP authenticates OpenID user.
5) OP transfers the user authentication information to SP. SP provides service for OpenID user.

2.2 OpenID Security Issue

Linkability and Traceability. The linkability and traceability are the probability that can be analyzed or got the user orientation information or the other information through user identity relation analysis by any attacker. The linkability and traceability issues in OpenID will not be OpenID own problems. Because the concept of OpenID is that the user manages a single OpenID to all the OpenID support SP, the linkability and traceability problem is presented. Eventually the concept of single identity management brings both advantage and disadvantage.

Anonymous OpenID. The some OP provides the anonymous OpenID for the above linkability and traceability issue. Thus, by using the anonymous OpenID it is hard to get the user information using OpenID linkability and traceability property. However, the anonymous OpenID generated by OP is changed to the random string form, the user cannot remember, for the linkability and traceability issue solution. In addition to some anonymous OpenID is not true anonymous OpenID. Because the anonymous OpenID does not be changed, though the anonymous is the complicated string. In addition, the user can not choose the level of anonymous because the OP provides the anonymous property of an anonymous OpenID.

Phishing. The OpenID protocol redirect user to OP that you submit in the user-SP. Because the user believes the SP, the OP, SP redirects, is trusted by the user. However, the user almost will not be able to distinguish between real OP site and phishing OP site. Therefore if the user not be able to distinguish between real OP site and phishing OP site, the OpenID authentication information of

Fig. 2. Anonymous OpenID

the user is exposed through the phishing OP site. Because a high probability of ID and password equality on other site, are exposed at the phishing OP site, the information can be exploited at security incidents.

2.3   Biometric System

Biometric systems recognize individuals based on their biological and behavioral characteristics. The favorite biological characteristics are fingerprints, face, iris, hand geometry, veins in the hands, retina, DNA, and palm prints. These characteristics are considered to satisfy the following desirable properties [4].

  - **Universality:** Every individual should have the characteristic;
  - **Uniqueness:** Each individual should have a different characteristic;
  - **Permanence:** The characteristics should not show any variation that may be caused by the ageing process.

For convenience' sake, the following terms and definitions apply.

  - **Biometric Template:** A set of stored biometric features that are directly comparable to the biometric features of a recognition biometric sample;
  - **Biometric Sample:** Analog or digital representation of biometric characteristics prior to the feature extraction process, obtained from a biometric capturing device and a biometric capturing subsystem;
  - **Biometric Reference:** One or more stored biometric samples, biometric templates or biometric models attributed to a subject and used for comparison.

Biometric verification and identification are powerful techniques against reputation and have been widely used in various security systems. For the authentication and/or identification of an individual, a biometric system processes a probe sample and one or multiple stored biometric reference(s). The biometric reference could be a biometric sample or a set of biometric features. However, such biological biometric characteristics are intrinsically immutable, so when they are stolen or leaked, a permanent compromise may result.

2.4   Cancellable Biometrics

A strong security and privacy concern for biometric systems relates to cancellable biometrics. Cancellable means the renewability and revocability of biometric references. Because individuals have a limited number of irises and fingers, identity theft makes the corresponding biometric references unsuitable for future use. Due to its quality of permanence, a biometric reference that has been compromised once remains compromised forever [5,6].

The risk of biometric references being compromised can be mitigated by developing methods that allow cancellable biometric references. If various different biometric references can be extracted from the same biometric sample, then the biometric reference can be cancelled and renewed in the vent that it becomes compromised.

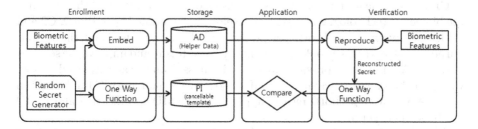

Fig. 3. High level description of cancellable biometrics

In the cancellable biometric system we employed, the biometric reference consists of two data elements: a pseudo identity (PI) and the corresponding auxiliary data (AD). Both data elements are generated during enrolment and should be stored, because both are required for verification.

3   Biometric-Based Identity Management Mechanism

In this paper, we propose a novel identity management mechanism based on biometrics technology which called BioID. As we already mentioned earlier, existing ID management mechanisms provide convenience for managing variety identities, but its security level depends on the secrecy of the password. However, biometrics provides authentication using universality, uniqueness, and permanence of parts of human body. We merge two technologies on their good points, and propose basic concept of BioID like as below.

C1. Biometrics technologies are used for authenticating users.
C2. Users can create several IDs for each modality they use.
C3. Users can create several IDs on the same modality they use.
C4. Use Cancellable Biometrics for enhancing security.
C5. Anonymous BioID can be provided.
C6. Keep synchronization with OpenID specification.

C1 does not means that the biometrics only be used on authentication, but also it can apply the various research results on the biometrics area to build BioID architecture. C2 and C3 let the individual can have multiple BioID for its purpose. C4 cover the weak point of biometrics, because it helps to protect from the threat of the biometric information leakage by using renewability. It also helps to make the biometric template fresh like as a periodic password renewal. The anonymous BioID in C5 can be realized by using one-time biometric template, biometric encryption, and cancellable biometric. Finally, BioID keep synchronization with OpenID specification. BioID can be inter-operable with OpenID or can be act as a kind of OpenID provider.

Those six basic concepts are foundation of the BioID. BioID can enhance the security on identity management mechanism and expand base of the biometrics.

C1 does not mean the biometric is only used for authentication, rather it means the biometric technologies are used to develop the functionality of BioID. C2 and C3 let us have multiple BioID per person and choose and use it for the various purposes. C4 solves the problem of biometric data storing and improve the security of BioID. Anonymity is provided by C5. It is an issue on privacy area and related with Linkability and Tracability. OpenID also provide anonymity. C6 and C7 mean interoperability that BioID mostly apply with OpenID specification and BioID can be a OpenID provider.

As far, we describe the overview of BioID. BioID improves the security level of identity management system and expands the basis of biometrics. Now we introduce two strategies to realize BioID.

3.1 Strategies for BioID

Independent. According to 'Independent' strategy, BioID is developed by its own way. It concentrates on distinguish the unique features of BioID with basis of OpenID concept. Thus, the BioID provider means the provider of specific modality of biometrics. In other words, the vendors of biometric authentication such as fingerprint recognition, face recognition will be a BioID provider and provide their service to the customer. The providers compete and the customers choose a provider. This strategy has several merits. Most of all, it can help the biometric venders that the unique and convenience biometric technique make the vendor a popular BioID provider. This stimulates the vender's initiativeness. However BioID cannot be co-operated with OpenID well on this strategy. It is a problem of interoperability and it may effect on the number of BioID users.

Convergence. According to 'Convergence' strategy, BioID is developed as a kind of OpenID provider. BioID apply with the OpenID specification. For the authentication, users choose the BioID as an OpenID provider. Then, check the modality and perform authentication. At here authentication methods may be limited by standardized or voted techniques. Because this strategy follows OpenID, the number of users may be easily guaranteed. Users will use the BioID because of its convenience, security, curiosity, and so on. However the biometric vendors will take a negative attitude to develop a brand new technology because it uses standardized or voted techniques to authentication. It is also hard to standardize or vote the technique itself.

We provide those two strategies. Each of those strategies has merits and demerits. For the purpose of stimulating the various attempts and emphasizing the features of biometrics, the first strategy 'Independent' has an advantage. However for the purpose of guaranteeing the number of users and maintaining the interoperability, the second strategy 'Convergence' has an advantage. Of course, there may be other strategies and it is hard to select only one strategy. In this paper, we provide the 6-step scenario based on the 'Independent' strategy for the variety and emphasizing the biometric features.

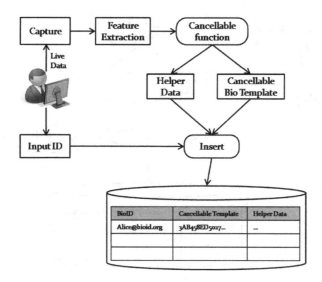

Fig. 4. BioID Creation (Enrollment) Process

3.2   Scenarios

BioID Creation. The first step is a join. For using a BioID, the user selects and signs in the BioID provider.

1) First of all, the user selects a modality and an authentication mechanism. And then user prepares a biometric sensor.
2) The biometric sensor acquires biometric features and template.
3) The acquired biometric features and auxiliary data are used to generate the cancellable biometric template. The cancellable biometric template will be authentication information.
4) After input the BioID, both the BioID and the template are stored. The form of BioID will be an OpenID form.

Login and Service Join. Though the most login process is similar to OpenID login process, a login process is changed for the use of biometric on login process.

1) The user enters the provider name on the service provider web site.
2) The service provider redirects to the ID provider.
3) The user authenticates in ID provider using a biometric sensor.
4) Enter an auxiliary data as occasion demands.
   A. If the biometric template is not changed for a long time, ID provider performs the reissue procedure and updates the biometric template.
5) If the authentication is success, select the BioID.
6) The ID provider transmits the selected BioID to the service provider.

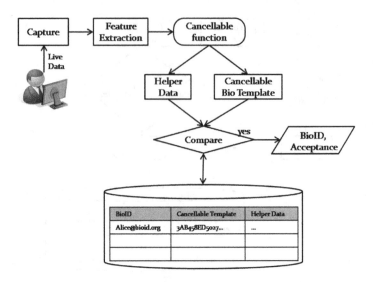

Fig. 5. BioID Login (Verification) Process

Identity Addition (on the same ID provider). When the user wants to add another ID on the same ID provider, the process is similar in the login/join process.

1) The user enters the ID provider name, the user already had, on the service provider.
2) The service provider redirects to the ID provider.
3) The user authenticates in ID provider using a biometric sensor.
4) Enter an auxiliary data as occasion demands.
   A. If the biometric template is not changed for a long time, ID provider performs the reissue procedure and updates the biometric template.
5) If the authentication is success, add the BioID.
6) If the user selects the additional BioID, the ID provider transmits it to the service provider.

Identity Addition (on the other provider). When the user wants to add another ID on the other ID provider, the process is similar in the login/join process. The other provider is able to use the same modality or the different modality.

1) First of all, the user selects a user favor modality and authentication process. And then user prepares a biometric sensor.
2) The biometric sensor acquires biometric template and features.
3) The acquired biometric features and auxiliary data are used to generate the cancellable biometric template. The cancellable biometric template will be authentication information.
4) After input the BioID, both the BioID and the template are stored. The form of BioID will be an OpenID form.

Anonymous Login. On the anonymous login process, the login process is some different from an OpenID login process.

1) The user enters the provider name on the service provider web site.
2) The service provider redirects to the ID provider.
3) The user selects an anonymous login button.
4) The user authenticates in the ID provider using a biometric sensor.
   A. The authentication process is composed of two parts. First, enter the auxiliary data like a normal login process.
   B. If the authentication is success, generate an onetime template using reissue biometric OTT, biometric encryption, and reissue mechanism.
5) After the onetime template is created, an arbitrary value will be an anonymous BioID.
6) The user selects the created anonymous BioID and the ID provider transmits the information to the service provider.

Withdraw. The withdraw process is two cases. One is the service withdraw and the other is the provider withdraw.

1) After the login process, the service withdraw follows the withdraw process for each service page.
2) After the authentication using the biometric information, the provider withdraw start with the withdraw button/link click.

Until now, we examine six procedures. In this paper, don't provide the implementation and detail algorithm because of the limit of paper space and research progress situation. The security and semantics of proposed BioID mechanism is mentioned in discussion.

3.3 Discussion

BioID mechanism is an alternative of identity management and also is alternative of biometric authentication. It means that BioID make the identity management easier and the biometric information centralized. As mentioned earlier, use of biometric information gives us convenience with threats of suffering heavy loss. BioID centralize the biometric information on the provider and protect the information safely by using protection technique such as cancellable biometrics.

BioID mechanism can overcome the authentication level between the biometric modalities. Because the authority of biometric authentication is depend on the provider (same as vender for 'independent' strategy), the value of FAR, FRR may be a competitive power and it is an area of the market economy. BioID only shows the result of authentication. It is the reason why BioID overcome the authentication level between the biometric modalities.

In this paper, we describe the scenario based on the strategy 'Independent'. As mentioned in strategy section, strategy 'Independent' has an advantage on the variety of authentication methods.

1) Each vender can create the BioID provider which uses their own hardware and software.

2) Biometric authentication is not preferred on open network authentication. It is because of the variety of hardware and software which depends on the vender. BioID can overcome the problem and make the biometric authentication easier on open network. It is because the venders can be a BioID provider if they follow the BioID specification. Since the service providers only receive the BioID and acceptances, the variety of authentication method is a competition power of venders.

4 Conclusion

In this paper, we proposed the identity management using a biometric technique. BioID, uses an advantage both the biometric technique and ID management, is the new identity management. We were able to check the BioID mechanism by six basic concept, two strategies, and six scenarios of the proposed BioID. The BioID gathers the distributed biometric information from service providers. And the biometric information is stored safely using the re-issuable biometric technique. Also, the BioID mechanism overcomes the difference of authentication level by modality. In the strategy 'Independent', it supports a base for using the biometric information on the open network and brings characteristic of biometric vendor into relief. Finally, the most important thing is that the user is able to use the physical characteristic using the biometric information instead of remembering a password and using a secondary tool. For the future work, we will research BioID algorithm and an anonymous ID creation mechanism using a onetime template.

Acknowledgement

This research was supported by the TTA(Telecommunications Technology Association) (2010-P1-30).

References

1. OpenID, http://openid.co.kr (accessed December 2009)
2. OpenID Authenitcation 2.0,
   http://openid.net/specs/openid-authenication-2_0.html (accessed December 2009)
3. OpenID - next big thing lots of problems,
   http://bendrath.blogspot.com/2007/04/openid-next-big-thing-with-lots-of.html (accessed December 2009)
4. Pavesic, N., Savic, T., Ribaric, S.: Multimodal Biometric Authentication System Based on Hand Features. In: From Data and Information Analysis to Knowledge Engineering, pp. 630–637. Springer, Heidelberg (2006)
5. Ratha, N.K., Connell, J.H., Bolle, R.M.: Enhancing security and privacy in biometric-based authentication systems. IBM Systems Journal 40(3), 614–634 (2001)
6. Li, Q., Sutcu, Y., Memon, N.: Secure sketch for biometric templates. In: Lai, X., Chen, K. (eds.) ASIACRYPT 2006. LNCS, vol. 4284, pp. 99–113. Springer, Heidelberg (2006)

Privacy Preserving of Trust Management Credentials Based on Trusted Computing[*]

Bin Wu[1,3], Dengguo Feng[1,2], and Meijiao Duan[1,3]

[1] State Key Laboratory of Information Security,
Graduate University of Chinese Academy of Sciences, 100039 Beijing, China
[2] State Key Laboratory of Information Security,
Institute of Software, Chinese Academy of Science, 100190 Beijing, China
[3] National Engineering and Research Centre of Information Security,
100190 Beijing, China
{wubin,feng,duanmeijiao}@is.iscas.ac.cn

Abstract. Privacy disclosure of forward direction credentials and backward direction credentials is an important security defect in existing trust management systems. In this paper, a novel distributed privacy preserving scheme for trust management credentials is proposed to solve this problem. Based on the trusted computing technology, the scheme provides the sealed protection for the credentials with privacy sensitive information and guarantees all the Deduced Composite Credential Constructing Units running in participant platforms untampered. In the process of collecting credentials, the deduced composite of multiple credentials replaces the single credential as the irreducible constituent to prevent the uncontrolled disclosure of privacy attributes. By modifying the traditional privacy preserving pattern, our scheme avoids the inadvertent disclosure of credential privacy attributes and provides a reliable solution for many privacy sensitive fields such as medical, business, and so on.

Keywords: privacy preserving, trust management, trusted computing, attribute credential.

1 Introduction

In Internet authorization scenarios, there are a large number of participant entities which belong to different domains and do not know each other. Thus, the style of authorization has become significantly different from that in centralized systems or distributed systems which are closed or relatively small. To satisfy the cross-domain authorization decisions' requirement in large scale and heterogeneous scenarios, several trust-management (TM) systems have been proposed in recent years, such as SPKI/SDSI [1,2], Delegation Logic [3,4] and RT [5,6]. These

---

[*] Supported by the National Natural Science Foundation of China under Grant No. 60803129; The Next Generation Internet Business and Equipment Industrialization Program under Grant No. CNGI-09-03-03.

J. Kwak et al. (Eds.): ISPEC 2010, LNCS 6047, pp. 251–263, 2010.
© Springer-Verlag Berlin Heidelberg 2010

TM systems support attribute-based access control (ABAC) by credentials that specify attributes of entities and rules for deriving entities' attributes. Because these credentials are digitally signed, they can serve to introduce strangers to one another without contacting with any trusted third part on-line. In this approach, TM systems make an authorization decision by finding a chain of credentials that grants the authority from the source to the requester in a logical way. However, attributes in practical application may be sensitive (such as medical or financial data), then this approach will lead to two kinds of privacy disclosure of credential, we call them the *privacy disclosure of forward direction credentials* and the *privacy disclosure of backward direction credentials*.

The privacy disclosure of forward direction credentials happens when a credential without privacy contents is required by an access control policy and its forward direction (we use the direction to be consistent with the underlying logic programming, which is similar with literature [5]) credentials contain some privacy attributes. In traditional privacy preserving scheme, it is assumed that one entity can reveal his credential as long as it contains no privacy attribute. However, this assumption ignores the fact that the entity's privacy may be contained in other credentials of the same credential chain (e.g. forward direction credentials) and be revealed by other entities casually. For example, a fictitious industrial group GroupA cooperates with an organization OrgB. OrgB regulates the cooperation archives with an access control policy "the employee in GroupA's majority-owned subsidiary company which operates international business outsourcing can access the archives". When an employee Alice tries to prove that she is entitled to the archives, she can show the credential "Alice is the employee of company T" to OrgB. Meanwhile, the following three forward direction credentials need to be collected to form the credential chain: "company T is GroupA's subsidiary company", "company T is GroupA's majority-owned subsidiary" and "company T operates international business outsourcing in GroupA". It is observed that the credential "Alice is the employee of company T" contains no privacy attribute, but its forward direction credentials reveal the privacy of GroupA's subsidiary company (e.g. company's shareholder information, business direction and so on).

Similarly, if a credential without privacy is required by a policy, its backward direction credentials can also reveal the privacy contents; we call this the *privacy disclosure of backward direction credentials*. For the example above, OrgB can define a new access control policy for a data table: "the senior customer of machinery manufacturing industrial group can access the data table". Here, GroupA is a machinery manufacturing industrial group, and the definition of GroupA's senior customer depends on the other credentials issued by GroupA's subsidiary company T: "the customer's transaction with company T amounts to 15 million dollar at least", "the customer has a registered capital of 5 billion dollar" and "the number of collaborative projects with company T is more than 4". When a senior customer of GroupA wants to access the data table and OrgB tries to make access control decisions, the credential "GroupA is a machinery manufacturing industrial group" and its three backward direction credentials which contains the sensitive transaction privacy and capital status are collected all together. Thus, OrgB not only obtains the credential chain for authorization decision but also learns company T's commercial privacy by exploiting the privacy disclosure of backward direction credentials.

In this paper, we address these problems associated with privacy preserving of credential chain in TM systems. A novel privacy preserving scheme for trust management credentials is proposed, in which the deduced composite of multiple credentials replaces the single credential as the irreducible constituent of credential discovery to prevent the uncontrolled disclosure of privacy attributes in the acquisition of credentials. The trusted computing technology [7] allows one participant platform to attest its configuration and state to another, in our scheme this feature has been used to ensure that the Deduced Composite Credential Constructing Unit (DCCCU) can trust and import the results of deduced composite credentials returned by other platforms' DCCCUs. Based on the secure storage protected by TPM (Trusted Platform Module), our scheme prevents the sensitive credentials being obtained by other participants, and consequently provides a comprehensive protection of privacy information in distributed TM system.

The rest of this paper is organized as follows. In Section 2, we discuss related work. In Section 3, we introduce the basic elements in the privacy preserving scheme. In Section 4, we describe the architecture of participant platform based on the trusted computing. In Section 5, we present the scheme's details in implementation, including the goal, the credential workflow and the algorithms. We conclude the paper in Section 6.

2   Related Work

In the literature, a number of solutions for privacy preserving have been proposed. Bonatti et al. [8] introduced a uniform framework to regulate service access and information release over the Internet. Their framework contains a language with formal semantics and a policy filtering mechanism to let the participants exchange their requirements in a privacy preserving way. A service accessibility rule in their model is composed of two parts: a prerequisite rule and a requisite rule. To protect both the participants' privacy, the model enforces a specific ordering between prerequisite and requisite rules. The participant will not disclose a requisite rule until the requester satisfies a corresponding prerequisite rule. Yu et al. [9] presented a similar privacy protection approach based on the incremental exchange of credentials and requests for credentials in order to safeguard the contents of credentials and policies. Seamons et al. [10] identified privacy disclosure of two kinds of sensitive credentials, possession-sensitive credentials and attribute-sensitive credentials. Several modifications was proposed in this paper to help prevent the inadvertent privacy disclosure for those credentials or credential attributes that have been designated as sensitive. Yu [11] proposed policy filtering and policy migration as two techniques to alleviate the privacy disclosure of possession-sensitive credential and attribute-sensitive credential in his Ph.D. thesis. Winsborough et al. [12,13] introduced a framework based on Ack policies to protect sensitive credentials. In their approach, for each sensitive credential, no matter whether Alice possesses it or not, she has an Ack policy. Alice only acknowledges whether she has a credential or not after the corresponding Ack policy is satisfied. Ack policy can prevent inference attacks through simple observation of behavior, but the management overhead is high. For each sensitive credential Alice possesses, she now needs an access control policy for its disclosure and also an Ack policy to determine with whom she can discuss this credential. Moreover, it is a hard task to design and maintain good policies, especially for individual users.

The previous work focuses on protecting the possession-sensitive credential or attribute-sensitive credential itself. They does not address the problem of protecting privacy attributes contained in the backward direction credentials and forward direction credentials, which is a great vulnerability of TM systems.

3   Basic Elements

In the ABAC-enabled TM systems, there are many basic elements to support distributed authorization decisions. We now formally give these definitions.

3.1   Entity

An *entity* is also called principals in some literatures, which denotes a participant in the TM system. An entity can issue credentials and make requests to other entities. Moreover, any entity in the TM system can determine which entity issued a particular credential or request. Clearly, public/private key pairs in public-key cryptosystem make this possible. In this paper, we use *ENTITYS* to denote the set of all entities in system.

3.2   Attribute

An *attribute* is the characteristic of the entity that can be universally recognized by all entities. In ABAC systems, an entity can allow another entity to access the resources by asserting that another entity has a certain attribute. An attribute takes the form of an entity followed by an attribute name, separated by a dot, like *A.attr*. Each entity *A* has the authority to define who has the attribute of the form *A.attr*. We use *ATTRS* to denote the set of all attributes.

3.3   Credential

A *credential* specifies attributes of entities or rules for deriving entities' attributes. Through a credential, entity *A* can assert his judgment *J* about the attribute of another entity *B*. We call *A* the issuer, *B* the subject, and *J* the statement. In TM system, the statement is a fact or a rule. The fact specifies which attributes the subject has in the form of predicate, while the rule expresses the deriving relationships between entities and attributes. We can depict the syntax of credential in Backus-Naur Form as follows, in which $< pred\_symb >$, $< entity >$, $< constant >$, $< var >$ and $< attribute >$ represent a predicate symbol, an entity, a constant, a variable, and an attribute respectively:

```
<credential>::= <issuer> "says" <statement>
<issuer>::= <entity>
<statement>::= <fact >| <rule>
<fact>::= <predicate>
<rule>::= <predicate> ":-" <body_formula>
<list of X>::= <X>|<X> "," <list of X>
<predicate>::= <pred_symb> "(" <list of term> ")"
<body_formula>::= < list of predicate >
<term>::= <entity>|<attribute>|<constant>|<var>
```

3.4   Deduced Composite Credential

For two adjoining credentials and more, our scheme can combine them into one deduced composite credential (DCC) by imposing the resolution on their statements. The process of resolution aims at deducing new statement from those existing credentials' facts and rules. After the resolution, the newly deduced statement can also be translated into a digitally signed credential, which asserts the issuer's judgments about the attributes. If the new deduced composite credential can be combined together with its adjoining forward direction credentials or backward direction credentials, our scheme continues the construction of the deduced composite credentials as well. With such a recursive fashion, our scheme can combine multiple credentials' agreements and judgments in a logical way. By collecting the related DCC, the authorization decision can be made eventually without privacy disclosure. We now give a fictitious example to illustrate the effect of DCC in our scheme, and present the definition later.

Example 1. A fictitious service, EService, offers a discount to the depositors of preferred banks of its parent organization, EOrg. EOrg considers banks whose transaction with EOrg amounts to at least 15 million dollar to be preferred banks. EOrg issues a credential to BankA stating that the BankA's transaction with EOrg amounts to 25 million dollar. BankA issues a credential to Alice stating that Alice is a depositor in BankA. These are represented by four credentials:

$$EService \, says \, isMember(EService, discount, X): -isMember(EOrg, \atop preferred\_bank, Y), isMember(Y, depositor, X). \tag{1}$$

$$EOrg \, says \, isMember(EOrg, preferred\_bank, Y): -isGreaterThan \atop (EOrg, transaction\_value, Y, \$15 \, million). \tag{2}$$

$$EOrg \, says \, isEqual(EOrg, transaction\_value, BankA, \$25 \, million). \tag{3}$$

$$BankA \, says \, isMember(BankA, depositor, Alice). \tag{4}$$

The credential (1) contain no privacy attributes, but its backward direction credentials (2) and (3) have the financial privacy information of EOrg and BankA, which should not be obtained by other participants. When Alice wants to get Eservice's discount, the acquisition of credential (2) and (3) will not be allowed in consideration of preserving privacy; therefore, nobody can certify that Alice is a depositor of EOrg's preferred banks even if she can be certified a depositor in BankA by the credential (4). Thus, due to the absence of credential (2) and (3), Alice is wrongly deprived of the eligibility for Eservice's discount.

In order to make the proper authorization decisions without revealing the privacy in credential (2) and (3), our scheme introduces the DCC. From the logic viewpoint, the meaning of credential (2) is "if a bank has at least 15 million dollar transaction with EOrg, then it is a preferred bank of EOrg", while credential (3) can certify that BankA has 25 million dollar transaction with EOrg. Thus, regarding the credential (2) and (3) as the precondition, EOrg can deduce a statement "BankA is a preferred bank of EOrg" which contains no privacy attribute. In this way, EOrg signs the new statement with its private key and releases it in the form of DCC to certify that BankA is a preferred bank of EOrg. We can formulate the DCC's definition as following:

Definition 1 (Deduced Composite Credential). *Given credential set $\mathcal{C}$, statement set $\mathcal{S} = \{s_i | s_i = Cred_i.statement, Cred_i \in \mathcal{C}\}$, if $(\mathcal{T} \subseteq \mathcal{S}) \wedge (\mathcal{T} \Rightarrow \mathcal{G}) \wedge (\mathcal{T} \cap \mathcal{G} = \Phi)$, then elements in $\mathcal{G}$ are called deduced statements, where $\Rightarrow$ is a deductive reasoning notation. The credentials in set $\mathcal{C}^{\mathcal{D}} = \{Cred_i | Cred_i = Sign(g_i), g_i \in \mathcal{G}\}$ are called deduced composite credentials.*

According to Definition 1, with the credential (2) and credential (3) as input credential set $\mathcal{C}$, the following DCC can be produced:

$$EOrg \; says \; isMember(EOrg, preferred\_bank, BankA). \tag{5}$$

As Eservice obtains the DCC (5) from EOrg, together with the credential (4) held with Alice herself, it can be concluded that Alice is entitled to the Eservice's discount according to her depositor status of EOrg's preferred banks.

4   Architecture of Participant Platform

Figure 1 shows the architecture of participant platform based on the trusted computing. The Trusted Computing Base (TCB) in our platform is made up of trusted hardware layer, virtual machine hypervisor layer and trusted service layer. The application instances run in the isolated compartments above the TCB.

TPM in trusted hardware layer is able to check the authenticity and state of the components, allowing other platform to verify the trustworthiness of local platform. PCR (platform configure register)[7] inside TPM is used to store the check value of those components. The system can update the value of PCR with operation of $TPM\_Extend()$.

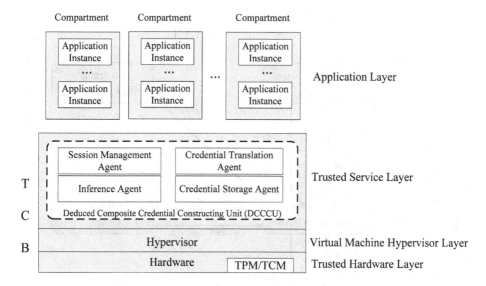

Fig. 1. Architecture of Participant Platform

The virtual machine hypervisor layer manages multiple virtual machines, providing the isolation of compartments based on the same hardware platform and the trust establishment from TPM to virtual machines. Virtualization technology especially Xen[14] allows the resources of a single physical platform to be efficiently divided into multiple virtual parts in a safe fashion, but without sacrificing either performance or functionality. We design the virtual machine hypervisor layer to measure the virtual machine kernel, kernel modules, application instances in compartments, and establish the trust chain based on the TPM.

The DCCCU runs as a kernel service in the trusted service layer, handling the credential chain discovery request from application instances in compartments. It is comprised of four components as follows:

1. Session Management Agent (SMA). The SMA agent receives and parses the credential search request (CSR) from other platforms' SMA, takes out the input credentials from the CSR, and sends them to the credential translation agent. When the credential translation agent returns the DCCs, the SMA agent will assemble the credential search response with these DCCs to reply the requester. The SMA agent provides the interfaces SMA_CREATE_CSReq and SMA_CREATE_CSResp to create a credential search request session and a credential search response session respectively.
2. Credential Translation Agent (CTA). The CTA agent manages all kinds of credentials, including credentials stored in the local platform, credentials received from other entities, and DCCs constructed by inference agent. The CTA agent supplies three interfaces $CTA\_TRANS\_TO\_RULE$, CTA_VERIFY_CRED and CTA_SIGN_CRED to implement the function of

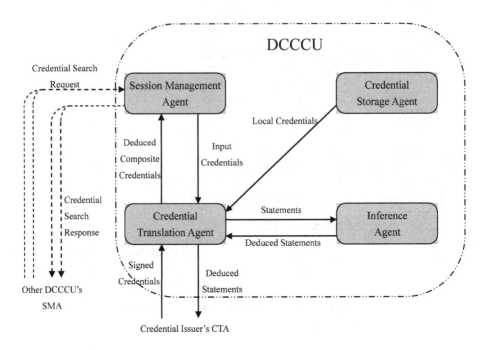

Fig. 2. The credential processing flow in the DCCCU

mutual translation between the credentials' statements and the logical rules, the verification of credentials and the signature of DCCs respectively.

3. Inference Agent (IA). The inference agent receives the translated rules from the CTA agent as the logic premises, and provides the function of deducing consequences from these premises. Eventually, the inference agent returns the conclusions which contain a group of deduced statements. The inference agent supplies the interface IA_DEDUCE with the set of logical rules as the input parameter and the set of conclusions as the output parameter to implement the core function of deducing conclusions from the rule premises.

4. Credential Storage Agent (CSA). The CSA agent is the infrastructure providing the sealed storage and query services of local credentials. Differing from the existing schemes, the credentials with privacy are not allowed to be obtained by other entity freely. Therefore, all the credentials are saved in the secure storage protected by TPM. The CSA agent provides the interface $CSA\_LOAD\_CREDENTIAL$, $CSA\_ADD\_CREDENTIAL$, $CSA\_DEL\_CREDENTIAL$ and so on to access and manage the credentials saved in the depository.

The credential processing flow within the four components in DCCCU is shown in Figure 2.

5   Implementation

In this section, we first define the goal of credential search in our scheme, which form the theoretic basis of our algorithms. Then, we briefly present the credential search process. Finally, we give the details of the algorithm executed by DCCCU during the credential search phase.

5.1   Goal

When a requester R submits a request to access a particular resource stored in entity A, and it is the access policy associated with the resource to authorize the requester who has the attribute of $A.attr$ to access the resource, then the DCCCU in entity A's platform needs to search credentials from other platforms to determine whether R has the attribute of $A.attr$. We call this the *goal of credential search*.

Definition 2 (Goal of Credential Search). *Given requester R and desired attribute $A.attr$, search for a set $\mathcal{C}$ of credentials such that $R \in \mathcal{M}_\mathcal{C}(A.attr)$, where $\mathcal{M}_\mathcal{C}(A.attr) = \mathsf{expr}[\mathcal{S}_\mathcal{C}](A.attr) = \mathcal{S}_\mathcal{C}(A.attr)$ as defined in [5].*

In order to protect the privacy in the forward direction credentials and backward direction credentials, the set $\mathcal{C}^\mathcal{D}$ of deduced composite credentials replaces the set $\mathcal{C}$ of credentials as the irreducible constituent in credential search. The following theorem guarantees the equivalence of the set $\mathcal{C}$ and the set $\mathcal{C}^\mathcal{D}$ in the credential search.

Theorem 1 (Equivalence of Set $\mathcal{C}$ and $\mathcal{C}^\mathcal{D}$). *Given resource provider A, requester R, attribute $A.attr$ and a set $\mathcal{C}$ of credentials, $R \in \mathcal{M}_\mathcal{C}(A.attr)$ if and only if there exists a set $\mathcal{C}^\mathcal{D}$ of DCCs such that $R \in \mathcal{M}_{\mathcal{C}^\mathcal{D}}(A.attr) = \mathcal{S}_{\mathcal{C}^\mathcal{D}}(A.attr)$.*

Proof. Necessity: Given any finite credential set $\mathcal{C}$ having $R \in \mathcal{M}_\mathcal{C}(A.attr)$, let $\langle C_1, C_2, C_3 \ldots C_n \rangle, C_i \in \mathcal{C}, t = 1, 2, \ldots n$ be the forward sequence of $\mathcal{C}$. Let $C_{i_1}, C_{i_2}, C_{i_3}, \ldots C_{i_j}, 1 \leq i_1 < i_2 < \ldots < i_j \leq n$ be the non-zero subset of $\mathcal{C}$ with each element having a deductive relationship with its backward element, as presented by $\langle C_{i_k}, C_{i_k+1} \rangle \mapsto C_{i_k}^\mathcal{D}, k = 1, 2, \ldots j$, where $C_{i_k}^\mathcal{D}, k = 1, 2, \ldots j$ denotes the DCCs of credentials C_{i_k} and C_{i_k+1}. We have $\langle C_1, C_2, \ldots, C_{i_1}, C_{i_1+1}, \ldots, C_{i_2}, C_{i_2+1}, \ldots, C_{i_j}, C_{i_j+1}, \ldots C_n \rangle \mapsto \langle C_1, C_2, \ldots, C_{i_1}^\mathcal{D}, \ldots, C_{i_2}^\mathcal{D}, \ldots, C_{i_j}^\mathcal{D}, \ldots C_n \rangle$. Consequently, the set of DCCs $\mathcal{C}^\mathcal{D} = \{\langle C_1, C_2, \ldots, C_{i_1}^\mathcal{D}, \ldots, C_{i_2}^\mathcal{D}, \ldots, C_{i_j}^\mathcal{D}, \ldots C_n \rangle\}$ has $R \in \mathcal{M}_{\mathcal{C}^\mathcal{D}}(A.attr) = \mathcal{S}_{\mathcal{C}^\mathcal{D}}(A.attr)$ satisfied.

Sufficiency: Let $\langle C_1, C_2, \ldots, C_{i_1}^\mathcal{D}, \ldots, C_{i_2}^\mathcal{D}, \ldots, C_{i_j}^\mathcal{D}, \ldots C_n \rangle$ denote the forward sequence of set $\mathcal{C}^\mathcal{D}$ which satisfies $R \in \mathcal{S}_{\mathcal{C}^\mathcal{D}}(A.attr)$. We prove the sufficiency by contradiction. If the credential set $\mathcal{C}$ doesn't make $R \in \mathcal{M}_\mathcal{C}(A.attr)$ hold, there must be at least one DCC $C_{i_k}^\mathcal{D}(1 \leq k \leq j)$such that $(\langle C_{i_k}, C_{i_k+1} \rangle \mapsto C_{i_k}^\mathcal{D}) \bigwedge (C_{i_k} \notin \mathcal{C}) \bigvee ((\langle C_{i_k}, C_{i_k+1} \rangle \mapsto C_{i_k}^\mathcal{D}) \bigwedge (C_{i_k+1} \notin \mathcal{C})$. But this is contrary to $(C_{i_k} \in \mathcal{C}) \bigwedge (C_{i_k+1} \in \mathcal{C})$ which is set as condition. As a result, the credential set $\mathcal{C}$ must have $R \in \mathcal{M}_\mathcal{C}(A.attr)$ satisfied.

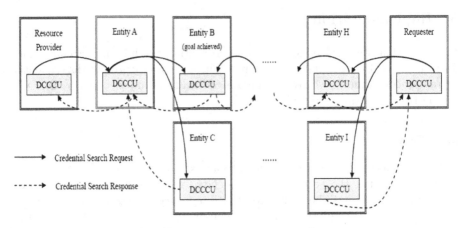

Fig. 3. Credential search process based on DCC

Theorem 1 guarantees that the DCC set $\mathcal{C}^{\mathcal{D}}$ can replace credential set $\mathcal{C}$ in credential search and the results of two methods are consistent. So we can rewrite the goal of credential search as follows:

Definition 3 (Goal of Credential Search Based on DCC). *Given requester R and desired attribute $A.attr$, search for a set $\mathcal{C}^{\mathcal{D}}$ of DCCs such that $R \in \mathcal{M}_{\mathcal{C}^{\mathcal{D}}}(A.attr)$.*

5.2   Credential Search Based on DCC

In the credential search based on DCC, there is no special mediator responsible for searching credentials, discovering the credential chain and making access control decisions. The mediator is substituted by a group of individual collaborative DCCCUs running in the participant platforms. The DCCCU is the minimal unit to implement the distributed collaborative credential search and credential chain discovery. All the participant platforms' DCCCUs swap the data of credentials and DCCs in the forms of credential search request and credential search response. By the four steps of "receive-process-deduce-send", the DCCCUs can share all the credentials related to the access request and all the DCCs newly deduced by other DCCCUs.

In Figure 3, we present a representative example of credential search process based on DCC. The flows of credential search request and response illustrate the whole evolvement sequence in credential search process. When a requester R wishes to access a resource in the resource provider A, the DCCCUs running in both sides of the requester and the resource provider start the credential search process at the same time and then transmit the data of credentials and DCCs along the bidirectional credential chain inwards. In the beginning of credential search, only entity A and entity R belong to the participant set. The DCCCUs running in A and R determine whether the goal $R \in \mathcal{M}_{\mathcal{C}^{\mathcal{D}}}(A.attr)$ is achieved. In fact, the goal may not be achieved only through credentials stored in entity

Algorithm 1 (Credential Search Algorithm) $DCCCU\_CRED\_SEARCH()$

Input: A credential search request structure CSR, including: a resource
   requester RR; a resource provider RP; a desired attribute $ATTR$; a
   resource request's ID R_ID and an input credentials set ICS.
Output: A credential search response structure $CSRP$, including: a credential
   search status code SC; a resource request's ID R_ID and a deduced
   composite credentials set $DCCS$.
Procedure:
$CRED := \{\}$;
$CRED := CSA\_LOAD\_CREDENTIAL()$;
 /* **Integrate the data of credentials in the CSR with the local**
credentials. */
$CRED := CRED \cup CSR.ICS$;
/* **Verify the signature of each credential in the set CRED, and**
translate the validated credentials' statements into the logical rules.
*/
$RULE\_SET := CTA\_TRANS\_TO\_RULE(CTA\_VERIFY\_CRED(CRED))$;
if $RULE\_SET \neq \Phi$ then
   $DS\_SET := IA\_DEDUCE(RULE\_SET)$;
   if $RR \in \mathcal{M}_{\mathcal{CD}(RP.ATTR)}$ in DS_SET then
      /* **The goal is achieved. Algorithm returns the new produced**
      DCCs and terminates successfully. */
      $CSRP.SC := success$;
      $CSRP.R\_ID := CSR.R\_ID$;
      $CSRP.DCCS := CTA\_SIGN\_CRED(DS\_SET)$;
      return $CSRP$;
   end
   else
      $SUCCESSOR\_SET := GET\_SUCCESSOR(DS\_SET)$;
      for each successor in $SUCCESSOR\_SET$ **do**
         /* **Form the new CSR request and send it to each**
         successor. */
         $newCSR.RR := CSR.RR$;
         $newCSR.RP := CSR.RP$;
         $newCSR.ATTR := CSR.ATTR$;
         $newCSR.R\_ID := CSR.R\_ID$;
         $newCSR.ICS := CTA\_SIGN\_CRED(DS\_SET)$;
         $out := SMA\_CREATE\_CSReq(newCSReq,successor)$;
         if $out.SC = success$ then
            /* **Receive the new DCCs produced by the successor,**
            and integrate them with the local DCCs. */
            $CSRP.SC := success$;
            $CSRP.R\_ID := out.R\_ID$;
            $CSRP.DCCS := out.DCCS \cup newCSR.ICS$;
            return $CSRP$;
         end
      end
      /* **The goal is not achieved. Algorithm returns the produced**
      DCCs as the intermediate results. */
      $CSRP.SC := stop$;
      $CSRP.R\_ID := CSR.R\_ID$;
      $CSRP.DCCS := CTA\_SIGN\_CRED(DS\_SET)$;
      return $CSRP$;
   end
end
else
   /* **The goal is not achieved while algorithm cannot produce**
   new DCCs any more. Credential search fails. */
   $CSRP.SC := failure$;
   $CSRP.R\_ID := CSR.R\_ID$;
   $SRP.DCCS := \Phi$;
end
end
return $CSRP$;

Algorithm 1. Credential Search Algorithm

A and entity R, so more credentials or DCCs linked with these two entities are needed to produce new deduced statements. In order to query and collect these credentials, the DCCCUs running in A and R start to send the CSR request to the other DCCCUs. Meanwhile these platforms become new members of the participant set. When a new participant's DCCCU receives the CSR request, the DCCCU integrates the new credentials and DCCs encapsulated in the CSR request with its local credentials, and starts the process of logical deducing to achieve the goal defined in Definition 3. If new deduced statements still can not prove $R \in \mathcal{M}_{C^{\mathcal{D}}}(A.attr)$, namely that the goal is still not achieved, the DCCCU will assemble the old CSR request it received and the newly DCCs into a new CSR request, and send the new request to DCCCUs linked with the newly DCCs. With this recursive fashion, the CSR request spreads all over the relevant entities' DCCCUs and contains all relevant DCCs that may affect the achievement of goal. If a DCCCU deduces the result which can prove $R \in \mathcal{M}_{C^{\mathcal{D}}}(A.attr)$, a notification will be sent to the requester R and the resource's owner A indicating that the credential search is successful and R can access the resource in entity A. The detailed description of credential search algorithm is given in Section 5.3.

5.3   Algorithm

We now present the credential search algorithm that can collect distributed credentials and DCCs to construct the credential chains without revealing any privacy information. DCCCU can begin the process with an incomplete set of credentials, then suspend evaluation, issue a credential search request by SMA for credentials and DCCs that could extend the credential chains, then resume the process when additional credentials and DCCs are obtained, and iterate these steps as needed.

6   Conclusion

Aiming at the privacy disclosure of forward direction credentials and backward direction credentials, we present a scheme for preserving credentials' privacy attributes in discovering credential chains. Based on the trusted computing technology, our scheme provides the sealed protection for the credentials with privacy and guarantees the output of DCCCU running in platform is the expected result of its execution which is not manipulated or tampered with. By modifying the traditional credential search pattern, our scheme adopts the deduced composite credential as the irreducible constituent of credential discovery to avoid the inadvertent disclosure of credential privacy attributes.

References

1. Clarke, D., Elien, J., Ellison, C., Fredette, M., Morcos, A., Rivest, R.: Certificate Chain Discovery in SPKI/SDSI. Journal of Computer Security 9(4), 285–322 (2001)
2. Ellison, C., Frantz, B., Lampson, B., Rivest, R., Thomas, B., Ylonen, T.: SPKI certificate theory. IETF RFC 2693 (1999)

3. Li, N.H.: Delegation Logic: A Logic-based Approach to Distributed Authorization. Ph.D. thesis, New York University (2000)
4. Li, N.H., Grosof, B.N., Feigenbaum, J.: A Practically Implementable and Tractable Delegation Logic. In: Proceedings of the 2000 IEEE Symposium on Security and Privacy, pp. 27–42. IEEE Computer Society Press, New York (2000)
5. Li, N.H., Winsborough, W.H., Mitchell, J.C.: Distributed Credential Chain Discovery in Trust Management. Journal of Computer Security 11(1), 35–86 (2003)
6. Li, N.H., Mitchell, J.C., Winsborough, W.H.: Design of a Role-based Trust-management Framework. In: Proceedings of the 2002 IEEE Symposium on Security and Privacy, pp. 114–130. IEEE Computer Society Press, New York (2002)
7. Trusted Computing Group: TPM Main Specification. Version 1.2, Revision 103 (2007), http://www.trustedcomputinggroup.org
8. Bonatti, P., Samarati, P.: Regulating Service Access and Information Release on the Web. In: Proceedings of the 7th ACM Conference on Computer and Communications Security, pp. 134–143. ACM Press, New York (2000)
9. Yu, T., Winslett, M., Seamons, K.E.: Interoperable Strategies in Automated Trust Negotiation. In: Proceedings of the 8th ACM Conference on Computer and Communications Security, pp. 146–155. ACM Press, New York (2001)
10. Seamons, K.E., Winslett, M., Yu, T., Yu, L., Jarvis, R.: Protecting Privacy during On-line Trust Negotiation. In: Dingledine, R., Syverson, P.F. (eds.) PET 2002. LNCS, vol. 2482, pp. 129–143. Springer, Heidelberg (2003)
11. Yu, T.: Automated Trust Establishment in Open Systems. Ph.D. thesis, University of Illinois at Urbana-Champaign (2003)
12. Winsborough, W.H., Li, N.H.: Towards Practical Automated Trust Negotiation. In: Proceedings of the Third International Workshop on Policies for Distributed Systems and Networks, pp. 92–103. IEEE Computer Society Press, New York (2002)
13. Winsborough, W.H., Li, N.H.: Protecting Sensitive Attributes in Automated Trust Negotiation. In: Proceedings of ACM Workshop on Privacy in the Electronic Society, pp. 41–51. ACM Press, New York (2002)
14. Barham, P., Dragovic, B., Fraser, K., Hand, S., Harris, T., Ho, A., Neugebauer, R., Pratt, I., Warfield, A.: Xen and the Art of Virtualization. In: Proceedings of the 19th ACM Symposium on Operating Systems Principles, pp. 164–177. ACM Press, New York (2003)

Mitigating the Malicious Trust Expansion in Social Network Service*

Daren Zha, Jiwu Jing, and Le Kang

SKLOIS, Graduate University of CAS, Yuquan Road,19A, Beijing 100049, China
zdr@is.ac.cn, jing@is.ac.cn,
kangle@is.ac.cn

Abstract. With the growth of Social Network Service(SNS), the trust that plays
the role of connecting people brings both good user experience and threat. Trust
expansion is not only the means by which the SNS users construct their social
network , but also exploited by the attackers to collect victims. Hence, it is desirable to find the differences between malicious and normal behaviors. In this paper
we analyze the malicious trust expansion behavior and notice that the behavior
feature of the malicious users is their weakness. We present the detailed analysis
and propose a creative trust control strategy to restrict the malicious users, which
fully exploit the characteristic of SNS. The conclusions are positively supported
by simulation and experiment in a real SNS scenario.

Keywords: Social Network Service, Trust, Trust Expansion.

1   Introduction

Social Network Service(SNS) is a new rising form of web application in recent years
[10,7]. A typical SNS provides users a trust-based platform to maintain their social
relationships. On this platform each user manages a list that contains all the users he
trusts. He generates and enlarges this list with the method we call trust expansion. The
users and trust relationships consists of a huge complex network, on which people can
conveniently communicate with others.

With the development of SNS, the security problems are also exposed. Because the
SNS gathers a huge amount of real individual information, it attracts various attacks.
However, the effect of all these attacks is determined by the size of the attacker's trust
expansion, because the SNS users only share their information with the users they trust.
This paper focuses on the trust expansion behavior with malicious purposes in the SNS.
Malicious trust expansion is the prelude of any attack that is easy to play but still over-
looked. Fortunately, we noticed that the attackers should adopt some measures to avoid
being exposed. These measures will make a difference in their behavior features.

The primary contributions of our work are:

- We propose a malicious trust expansion model to describe this behavior.

---

* This work is supported by NSF No.70890084/G021102, and 863 Foundation
No.2006AA01Z454.

J. Kwak et al. (Eds.): ISPEC 2010, LNCS 6047, pp. 264–275, 2010.

– We prove our point of view through simulation and real experiment respectively to prove our point of view.
– We are the first to design the evaluation scheme that can effectively identify the abnormal users as suspects.

In our work we propose a malicious trust expansion model to describe this behavior.We also summarize the feature differences between malicious and normal users. Then we make simulation and real experiment respectively to prove our point of view. According to the differences we design a evaluation scheme that can effectively identify the abnormal users as suspects, and then apply a dynamic strategy to restrain them. Each step of our work is supported by simulation or experiment in the real SNS environment.

The remainder of the paper is organized as follows: in section 2 we introduce the related works about the attacks in SNS. In section 3 we discuss the malicious trust expansion and the difference between normal and malicious behavior. In section 4 we raise a trust evaluation scheme, and a delicate strategy to restrict the malicious users. At last In section 5 we make a conclusion.

2 Related Works

H.Jones [7] took Facebook [3] as an example to summarize the main threats to SNS users, such as privacy bleaching [10,2,8] and unauthorized commercial data mining. Millions of people place their real information in SNS, the attacker can easily steal the information, or organize the attacker with high feedback rate. However, the effect of these attacks is completely based on the size of trust list that the attacker can obtain. If the attacker has successfully expanded his trust list to a large size, any countermeasures against his subsequent attack are late and passive. P. Heymann [6] discussed the prevention from spamming in SNS with traditional ways. [13] gave a method to catch malicious users with a honeypot account. These approaches can neither solve the problem of latency nor prevent large scale attacks.

The attack in SNS has something in common with the Sybil attack [14] and Eclipse attack [9,1] in some respects. However, the defence in these approaches are not effective in our issue. For example, [14] presumes that in a Sybil attack the attacker vertices are linked with each other and attack through few edges, but in SNS the situation is opposite, the malicious vertices are likely to be separated to avoid being exposed together, and need many outer edges for attack.

A recommendable method is to rate the reputation of users, and apply the different restraints to them according to their reputation. Some researchers [5,11,16] have proposed several trust inference algorithm to evaluate the reputation of SNS users. But a fatal defect of them is, they assume that each user has made quantized assessments to all his neighbors' reputation as trust rate, and based on the existed reputation between every two adjacent users they can infer the trust value between any two users. But in practice, to pre-rate the trust has no maneuverability. In section 4 we contribute to rate the user reputation objectively.

3   Malicious Trust Expansion

The SNS complex network is based on trust. It can be considered as a graph, the users are the vertices, two vertices are linked by an edge when and only when the two users establish a **trust relationship**(**trust** for short) between them. In SNS the trust means the authority of individual information access between two users. User i trusts user j (labeled $i \rightarrow j$) denotes that j has the authority to visit the individual information of i, and is permitted to send massages in specified format to i. The concept of trust in this paper is different from the definition in [5,11,16] that denotes the user reputation or credit. It only means the legal communication path between users.

If user i and j trusts each other (labeled $i \longleftrightarrow j$), the trust relationship is bidirectional. In most SNSs the trust is forced to be bidirectional, such as Facebook. The establishment of bidirectional trust is a request-response protocol. One side sends a request to the other for building trust, the trust is successfully established when and only when the recipient grants the request. The release of a trust relationship is unidirectional, and either side can unilaterally release a formed trust. Some SNSs, such as Twitter, also adopt uni-directional trust scheme. A user can not apply for trust to other users but only authorize others to have his trust. In this paper we generally discuss the SNSs that adopt bidirectional trust.

SNS users construct their online social network by establishing trusts with others. We call the group of vertices that are connected to vertex i as the **trust list** of i. The sub-network constituted by the vertices in the trust list of i is called the **trust network** of i. The size of trust list equals the degree k_i of i. The process that i expands his trust list size from 0 to k_i is called **trust expansion**. The trust expansion with malicious purposes is called **malicious trust expansion**(for short MTE in the remainder). The vertices that execute malicious trust expansion in SNS network is called **malicious vertices**.

A typical malicious trust expansion is like the process of search engine crawler. The attacker can take advantage of the trust list sharing, starting from several vertices and traversing the whole network. We propose a dynamic model to describe the MTE behavior.

Definition (MTE Model). In the graph of SNS network G, i is a malicious vertex.
Step 1. Connect random $j \in G$ with i.
Step 2. With probability θ

- With probability p, connect random j to i. $j \in G$, the shortest path length between j and i is 2.
- With probability $q = 1 - p$, connect random j to i. $j \in G$, $p >> q$

Step 3. With probability β, remove an edge of i
Step 4. Repeat Step 2.   □

The parameter θ denotes the success rate of trust establishment, β is the rate of trust removal. Malicious users expand trusts through their neighbors most of the time. It is a beneficial strategy, because people tend to trust the ones who are nearer from them in the network graph, the request from friends' friend is more possible to be accepted. Another reason is the attacker can not get many accounts information outside SNS. So the malicious vertices will have a higher parameter p. In this section we discuss the features of MTE, make a experiment in a real SNS, and then simulate the MTE process in a real data set to prove our analysis.

3.1 Features of MTE

The difference between malicious and normal vertices is their trust expansion strategy. Except for that the MTE has a high parameter p, the malicious users always expand trusts selectively. Otherwise, they will encounter unexpected danger. Because the attacker is not really trusted by the victims in real world, if he behaves abnormally, he may be exposed to any one of his neighbors. This risk from a single user is possible to be magnified. Because of the individual information sharing scheme, each SNS user will react to his neighbors' behavior, and the chain reaction may be quite different in different network topological structure. Suppose that user i suspects user j at time t, removes j from trust list, and then informs other neighbors, then at time $t+1$, each user who trusts both i and j will remove j with probability τ. Suppose at time n, the degree of j is $k[n]$, consider following two situations as Figure 1 shows.

Fig. 1. Three kinds of trust network structure

In the 3 situations, the malicious vertex have equal degree but different local clustering coefficients. Local clustering coefficients is an important concept in graph theory, it rates the how close a vertex's neighbors are to being a clique(complete graph). Consider undirected simple graphs on $i = 1, ..., N$ vertices. Let k_i be the degree of a vertex and t_i the number of edges among its neighbors. The standard definition of local clustering coefficient is:

$$c_i = \frac{t_i}{k_i(k_i - 1)}$$

In this paper all the refereed clustering coefficient is local clustering coefficient. We discuss the differences between the 3 situations as follows:

1. $k[0] = m, c(k[0]) = 1$

In this case, the trust network of j is a complete graph. If at time $t = n - 1$ there are c vertices that remove j from their trust lists, then at time $t = n$ the number of vertices which execute the same action is in proportion with $c\tau$. The differential equation is

$$k[n] - k[n - 1] = \tau k[n](k[n - 1] - k[n - 2])$$

when $\tau k[n](k[n - 1] - k[n - 2])$ reaches 1, the degree of j will reduce to 0.

2. $k[0] = m, c(k[0]) = \frac{2}{n}$

Another situation is, the trust network of j is a chain. Most vertex connects to only two vertices and j). In this case, at time $t = n$, the expected reduction of $k[n]$ is $2\tau^n$. The differential equation is

$$k[n] - k[n-1] = -2\tau^n$$

Figure 1 shows the network structure in the above two extreme situations, the vertex labeled 9 is the malicious vertex j. High clustering coefficient will increase the risk that the attacker suffers from, and then the degree k will quickly reduce. In the latter case, the risk declines with time goes. The degree that the attacker loses k_{lost} is at maxium

$$k_{lost} = 2 \sum_{t=0} \tau^t - 1 = \frac{1 - \tau}{i + \tau}$$

3. $k[0] = m, c(k[0]) = 0$

The ideal extreme situation is, if the attacker controls several accounts, each exploits the candidate trust list of others, it is possible to reduce the clustering coefficient to 0. It is quite difficult to achieve, because the users in the trust list will also connect with each other. Moreover, in the case the attackers can not exploit the trust chain, it may reduce the success rate of trust establishment.

Figure 2 shows the degree k changes with time in the first and second situations. The second topological structure will remarkably reduce the lost. Obviously the attackers do not expect the first situation, so they will do their best to make their trust networks resemble the second or third picture of Figure 1 by minimize the clustering coefficient. Although the third one can avoid the risk completely, it differs not much from the second one. So the second topological structure is the most beneficial one for the attackers. In practice this goal is easy to achieve by implement the following strategy.

Lowest Clustering Strategy. For any user u in the candidate trust list, and for any two users in the trust list, if $u \longleftrightarrow v$ and $u \longleftrightarrow w$, do not attempt to establish trust relationship with u.

3.2   Real Experimentation

We experimented the malicious trust expansion in a real SNS site that has 30 million users. The experiment was executed by an automated robot program. The program is coded in C# and uses a MySQL database as data storage. It works according to a predefined work flow, extracts the information on the web page and post data to the server.

The experiment is organized as follows:

1. Register an account on the target SNS as malicious user.
2. Inquire the keyword of the target SNS on Google, and find 5 account information. The 5 users consist of the initial candidate trust list.
3. Send requests to the users in the candidate trust list.
4. Remove the users that accepted our requests from the candidate trust list, and add them to the trust list. Collect their trust lists as new candidate trust.
5. Repeat step 3 per 24 hours.

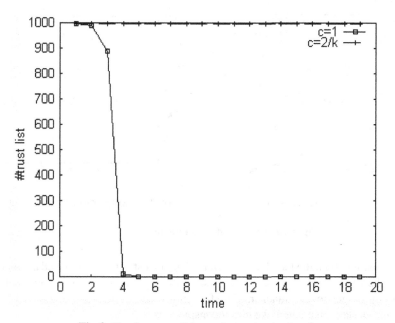

Fig. 2. The decrease of degree in two trust networks

The robot works in an intelligent way. We use a normal account to monitor all the users in the trust list. The size of trust expansion of all these users everyday are recorded and then the average number and deviation in a week are calculated. The frequency of our malicious trust expansion doubles the average number. It can reduce risk from the victims, because the malicious users' behavior is also visible to the normal users, and obvious abnormal behavior will bring about unexpected disaster, the account may be canceled by administrator. Moreover, a cheating tactic is also adopted. When the robot sends request to Bob who was collected from the trust list of Alice, it sends a cheating message like "I'm a friend of Alice". It can achieve a high pass rate.

Figure 3 shows the result of trust expansion. The robot started with 5 trusts. In 30 days it sent 956 requests, and ended with 704 trusts. The overall pass rate is 44.8%. About half users are willing to make friends with strangers and ignore the risk. Moreover, the number of users that sent requests to our account is 274, and the daily requests that our account received seems to be rising. The increment of candidate trust list is large. We collected 119,031 users in 30 days. Compared with this number, the sent requests are trivial. During the whole process the robot did not encounter any prevention by the server. It proves that in a SNS environment where the users are lack of awareness of security, it is easy for the attacker to get a large trust list at short notice.

In addition, we used two accounts to experiment different trust expansion strategies. The first account adopted the lowest clustering strategy, in 30 days it got 732 trust relationships, and lost 7. The second account adopted a strategy that makes the clustering coefficient as much as possible. As a result, in 30 days it obtained 577 trust relationships, but lost 122. Moreover, 19 users sent message to the second account to express

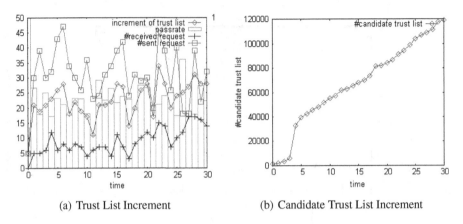

(a) Trust List Increment   (b) Candidate Trust List Increment

Fig. 3. Malicious trust expansion in a real SNS site

their complaint about the fact that we traversed their trust lists, or published a notice that warned their friends not to pass our request. It proves that a large clustering coefficient will bring danger to the attacker. This fact motivates the attacker to use the lowest clustering strategy that can make him inconspicuous.

3.3 Simulation

We make a simulation of malicious trust expansion by applying MTE model to the complex network of a real SNS data. The data set is contributed by [12]. It contains 63,731 vertices and 817,090 edges. The average clustering coefficient is 0.224, and the degree distribution obeys power-law distribution.

We repeat the simulation for several times. Figure 4 gives 5 instances. The X-axis is the degree, in Figure 4(a) the Y-axis is the size of candidate trust list. When the size of trust list reaches 1,000, the size of candidate trust list is more than 20,000. Figure 4(b) shows how the clustering coefficient changes with the degree. With the degree increasing, the clustering coefficient of malicious vertices decrease quickly. The average clustering coefficient distribution of Facebook data set is also given. It illustrates that the malicious vertices possess lower clustering coefficient than the normals that have equal degree when the degree is larger than 8.

4   Delimma Strategy to Restrict MTE

The difficulty in restricting the malicious users is how to distinct them from the normals. It is not proper to classify some users into the malicious until they expose some real baleful purposes. Thus, resilient rules are better countermeasures than strict filters. A common prevention method in practice is simply to restrict the increment of trust per unit time. It can prevent the immoderate attackers that employ robots to send thousand of requests per minute. However, a simple tactic, such as the one that our experiment shows, to determine the behavior frequency by imitating normal users, can help the robot to bypass this barrier. In addition, an over-rigid rule may hurt the user experience.

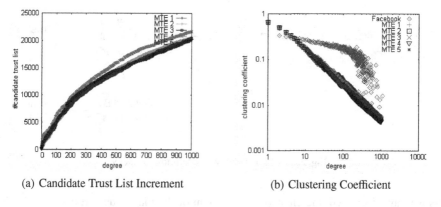

(a) Candidate Trust List Increment   (b) Clustering Coefficient

Fig. 4. Malicious trust expansion in a real SNS site

In this section we propose a delicate scheme called **Delimma Strategy**. As Figure 5 illustrates, the principle of Delimma Strategy is: to objectively rate the trust on the view of the server side. Each user gets an evaluation result. The ones that get worse trust rate are labeled as suspects, then we use an attribute-based access control scheme to restrains the suspect from visiting some part of his candidate trust list. This banned part contains the users that will decrease the suspects' clustering coefficient if they are connected to the suspect. Thus, if the suspect is actually an attacker, he has two choices: he can either choose to establish trust with the users that will increase his clustering coefficient, which will increase the risk as we discussed, or continuously build trust with the users that is farer than 2 links from him (These victims may be collected by other accounts), resulting a severe drop in the clustering coefficient. In this case, we can consider the suspect as malicious users and apply a strict restriction to his behavior. In following section we will introduce the trust evaluation scheme, and discuss the Delimma Strategy in detail.

4.1 Trust Evaluation

In section 3.3 we have discussed the difference between the malicious and normal users. The clustering coefficient actually represents that how much the users in the trust list trust each other. Since the malicious users possess larger clustering coefficient decrement than the normals, the features can be utilized as an evaluation criterion. We make evaluation for all vertices in the network, label the ones that perform worse as suspicious vertices and make a restriction. The filter is constructed as follows:

1. For $n = 5$ to MAX, MAX is the maximum value of permitted degree, sample N vertices that have n edges, and calculate the average clustering coefficient $C_{avg}(n)$ and deviation $C_{dev}(n)$.
2. Calculate the threshold $Threshold\_C(n) = C_{avg}(n) - C_{dev}(n)$
3. For any newly comer j, when j has n edges, if its clustering coefficient $C_j(n)$ is smaller than $Threshold\_C(n)$, label it as a suspect. The value $\frac{Threshold\_C(n)}{C_j(n)}$ is the **suspicions rate**.

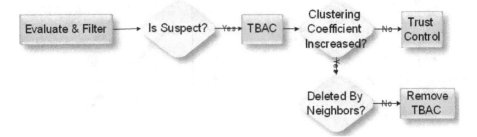

Fig. 5. The Process Flow of Delimma Strategy

As we have discussed, the clustering coefficient of the malicious vertices tends to decrease faster than the normals, so it can filter the malicious users quickly after they joined into the network. Its problem is, since the normal vertices may also have low trust rate long time after they have joined into the network, it may raise some false alarms. If the filter fails to detect the malicious users in early time, it is difficult to be effective later. The time complexity of trust-rate-based filter is $O(n^2)$.

This evaluation scheme has a limitation. Its effect is influenced by the business logic of SNS. In a regulatory SNS environment where the users are not willing to trust the strangers, with average clustering coefficient high, and the average degree low, the detection task is easy to implement.

But if the SNS adopt some business logic such as games to encourage people to collect friends as the resource in the games, the situation will become a mess, and the filter is not that effective.

4.2   Clustering-Coefficient-Based Access Control

An attribute-based access control scheme [15,4] is a significant component of the Delimma strategy. It determines whether the suspects can access the candidate trust resource according to the suspects' clustering coefficient. Suppose the clustering coefficient of i is C, the degree of i is k, the trust list of i is TL_i, the candidate trust list is CTL_i. Then we can get the clustering-coefficient-based access control (CCBAC) Strategy.

Clustering-coefficient-based access control (CCBAC) Strategy
If $C < Threshold\_C$, for $\forall j \in CTL_i$, the set $U_j = \{u | u \longleftrightarrow j, u \in TL_i\}$, if $|U| < Ck$, then forbid i from sending request to j.

Solve the inequality $C > \frac{C(k(k-1))+m}{k(k+1)}$, we conduct that $m < Ck$. So for each $j \in CTL_i$, if there are less than $[m]$ vertices in TL_i that are linked to j, to connect i and j will decrease the clustering coefficient of i. The CCBAC strategy is to stop suspect i from visiting these part of users in CTL_i.

This access control strategy stops the suspect from establishing trust with the users that can help to decrease his clustering coefficient through his neighbors. In other words, it forces the suspect to increase his clustering coefficient. If the suspect is an attacker, he is trapped in a delimma. If he increases his clustering coefficient by building trust with the permitted users, as we discussed in section 3.2, the risk he suffers from will also increase. With this method we deliver the discretion to the normal users, and expect them to discover the attackers. Moreover, if the suspect is not an attacker actually, he will be safe, and the user experience will not be hurt. Another choice for the suspect is to continuously decrease his clustering coefficient by building trust with the users that are far from him in the network. If the attacker maintains several accounts, it is easy to achieve. In this case, the suspect is considered to be malicious because he deliberately gives up trusting the users that many of his neighbors trust. Then a restriction strategy carried out by the server is put into practice.

The clustering-coefficient-based access control strategy has two extra advantages: it stops the suspects from going on exploiting the trust chain. The attacker should give up expanding trust through his neighbors. Second, it can largely reduce the candidate trust scope that the suspect can visit. Figure 6(a) gives the simulation result. The CCBAC strategy can observably reduce the candidate trust list of the suspects.

The removal of clustering-coefficient-based access control can be determined by the following judgement: if the suspects choose to increase his clustering coefficient but are not removed by many of his neighbors, the restriction should be removed, and the banned candidate trust can be visited again.

4.3   Trust Restriction and Reduction

If the clustering-coefficient-based access control strategy fails to encourage the suspects to increase their clustering coefficient, we conclude they are deliberately avoiding doing this, and then apply a rigid restriction to them. Because the suspects are not definitely malicious but only suspicious with some probability, a fixed rule is not proper. We designed a resilient trust expansion control strategy. It contains two parts: restriction and reduction. The former dynamically controls the success rate of trust establishment θ according to the features of vertices. Generally, the greater the difference of the features between the thresholds and individual value, the lower the success rate. In practice the restriction method is flexible, such as to discard the requests for trust establishment with some probability, or to send warnings with varying degrees to the requested side.

Ideally the restriction strategy should reduce the suspicious users' success rate of trust establishment θ to $\gamma\theta$. $\gamma = \frac{C}{threshold\_C}$. γ reflects the departure from the threshold.

The restriction strategy can only put off the attack, so it requires a method that can decrease the degree of suspicious vertices by increasing the parameter β. In practice the reduction strategy is more difficult to execute than restriction, because the system can not forcibly remove the users' trust but only provide users some prompt to motivate the normal users to discover and remove the malicious neighbors. The inter-trust rate conveys such prompt, and it measures the real reputation between two vertices. Suppose the system can transfer this feature to prompt messages, the parameter β of malicious users will increase. An ideal trust reduction should make $\beta = \eta\beta_0, \eta = \frac{threshold\_C}{C}$. If β is larger than 1, it represents the expectation rather than probability.

We implemented the simulation result. Suppose that the suspect does not choose to increase their clustering coefficient, he has to build trusts with the users that are far from him. So in the model the parameter p is set as 0. The trust control strategies are applied to the vertex 5 time step after it was labeled as suspect. Figure 6(b) shows the an example of the two strategies are applied or not. The malicious trust expansion is

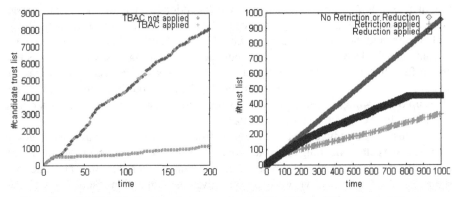

(a) The Effect of CCBAC in limiting the scope of   (b) The Effect of Trust Control Strategy
the candidate trust list

Fig. 6. Simulation to Delimma Strategy

obviously restrained. The circles in the figures specify when the restriction and reduction strategies come into effect. In our experiment we simply do not consider the removal of the restraint.

5   Conclusion

This paper analyzed the weakness malicious trust expansion in SNS, proposed a trust evaluation scheme and a method to restrain the malicious users based on the evaluation. The analysis is supported by experiment. We have several important conclusions: First of all, in real SNS it is easy to organize a malicious trust expansion. Second, The attacker has to make some effects to avoid the danger from other users, and it will make a difference in his feature. Third, the business logic of SNS site is a decisive element of SNS security, and SNS should not encourage the users to expand trust immoderately. In an SNS where the users do not care to add the ones they do not really know in the real world as friends, the security is difficult to be guaranteed. At last, a well-designed access control scheme to restrict the visible candidate trust list is very useful. However, if the attackers realize this shortcoming, they may moderately increase his clustering coefficient by using multi-accounts to construct a fake trust network and forging the clustering coefficient. In future work we will focus on prevention from this deceit that looks like a botnet in SNS.

References

1. Eclipse Attacks on Overlay Networks: Threats and Defenses (2006)
2. Brown, G., Howe, T., Ihbe, M., Prakash, A., Borders, K.: Social networks and context-aware spam. In: CSCW 2008: Proceedings of the ACM 2008 conference on Computer supported cooperative work, pp. 403–412. ACM, New York (2008)
3. Facebook, http://www.facebook.com/

 4. Frikken, K., Atallah, M., Li, J.: Attribute-based access control with hidden policies and hidden credentials. IEEE Transactions on Computers 55, 1259–1270 (2006)
 5. Golbeck, J., Hendler, J.: Inferring trust relationships in web-based social networks. To appear in ACM Transactions on Internet Technology
 6. Heymann, P., Koutrika, G., Molina, H.G.: Fighting spam on social web sites: A survey of approaches and future challenges. IEEE Internet Computing 11(6), 36–45 (2007)
 7. Jones, H., Soltren, J.H.: Facebook: Threats to privacy (December 2005)
 8. Rosenblum, D.: What anyone can know: The privacy risks of social networking sites. IEEE Security and Privacy 5(3), 40–49 (2007)
 9. Singh, A., Castro, M., Druschel, P., Rowstron, A.: Defending against eclipse attacks on overlay networks. In: EW11: Proceedings of the 11th workshop on ACM SIGOPS European workshop, p. 21. ACM, New York (2004)
10. Squicciarini, A.C., Shehab, M., Paci, F.: Collective privacy management in social networks. In: WWW 2009: Proceedings of the 18th international conference on World wide web, pp. 521–530. ACM, New York (2009)
11. Taherian, M., Amini, M., Jalili, R.: Trust inference in web-based social networks using resistive networks. In: ICIW 2008: Proceedings of the 2008 Third International Conference on Internet and Web Applications and Services, pp. 233–238. IEEE Computer Society, Washington (2008)
12. Viswanath, B., Mislove, A., Cha, M., Gummadi, K.P.: On the evolution of user interaction in facebook. In: Proceedings of the 2nd ACM SIGCOMM Workshop on Social Networks WOSN 2009 (August 2009)
13. Webb, S., Caverlee, J., Pu, C.: Social honeypots: Making friends with a spammer near you. In: CEAS (2008)
14. Yu, H., Kaminsky, M., Gibbons, P.B., Flaxman, A.: Sybilguard: defending against sybil attacks via social networks. In: SIGCOMM 2006: Proceedings of the 2006 conference on Applications, technologies, architectures, and protocols for computer communications, pp. 267–278. ACM Press, New York (2006)
15. Zhang, X., Li, Y., Nalla, D.: An attribute-based access matrix model. In: SAC 2005: Proceedings of the 2005 ACM symposium on Applied computing, pp. 359–363. ACM, New York (2005)
16. Ziegler, C.-N., Lausen, G.: Propagation models for trust and distrust in social networks. Information Systems Frontiers 7(4-5), 337–358 (2005)

An Efficient Convertible Undeniable Signature Scheme with Delegatable Verification

Jacob C.N. Schuldt and Kanta Matsuura

Institute of Industrial Science, University of Tokyo,
4-6-1 Komaba, Meguro-ku, Tokyo 153-8505, Japan
{schuldt,kanta}@iis.u-tokyo.ac.jp

Abstract. Undeniable signatures, introduced by Chaum and van Antwerpen, require a verifier to interact with the signer to verify a signature, and hence allow the signer to control the verifiability of his signatures. Convertible undeniable signatures, introduced by Boyar, Chaum, Damgård, and Pedersen, furthermore allow the signer to convert signatures to publicly verifiable ones by publicizing a verification token, either for individual signatures or for all signatures universally. In addition, the signer is able to delegate the ability to prove validity and convert signatures to a semi-trusted third party by providing a verification key. While the latter functionality is implemented by the early convertible undeniable signature schemes, most recent schemes do not consider this despite its practical appeal.

In this paper we present an updated definition and security model for schemes allowing delegation, and highlight a new essential security property, token soundness, which is not formally treated in the previous security models for convertible undeniable signatures. We then propose a new convertible undeniable signature scheme. The scheme allows delegation of verification and is provably secure in the standard model assuming the computational co-Diffie-Hellman problem, a closely related problem, and the decisional linear problem are hard. Our scheme is, to the best of our knowledge, the currently most efficient convertible undeniable signature scheme which provably fulfills all security requirements in the standard model.

Keywords: undeniable signatures, universal/selective convertibility, provable security.

1 Introduction

Undeniable signatures, first introduced by Chaum and van Antwerpen [10], are like ordinary signatures, except that verification of a signature requires interaction with the signer. Unlike ordinary signatures, this enables a signer to control who can verify his signatures and when verification is allowed. This feature makes undeniable signatures attractive when sensitive data or confidential business agreements are being signed, since the signer is guaranteed that only the relevant parties can verify his signature and no outsider will be able to link

J. Kwak et al. (Eds.): ISPEC 2010, LNCS 6047, pp. 276–293, 2010.

him to the signed data. To preserve non-repudiation, an undeniable signature scheme furthermore requires that a signer is able to disavow an invalid signature. Hence, a signer will either be able to confirm or disavow the validity of any signature, and any dispute can be resolved by letting the signer convince a judge about the validity or invalidity of the signature in question. Since their introduction, a number of undeniable signature schemes have been proposed e.g. [9,16,30,25,23,31,22].

In [6], Boyar, Chaum, Damgård and Pedersen introduced convertible undeniable signatures which allow the signer to convert his undeniable signatures into publicly verifiable signatures. Two types of conversions were introduced: *selective conversion* which enables the signer to individually convert signatures, and *universal conversion* which enables the signer to convert all (existing and future) signatures. A signer selectively converts a signature σ on a message m by releasing a token tk_σ which will convince any verifier that σ is indeed a valid signature on m. Likewise, a signer universally converts all signatures by releasing a universal token tk_* which can be used as a token for any signature. This feature is desirable when public verifiability is required after a period of time, which, for example, is the case for the problem of keeping digital records of confidential political decision (e.g. see [14]). Another aspect of the definition in [6] is that the private key material of the signer is divided into two parts: a signing key sk and a verification key vk. The former is only used to sign messages, whereas the latter is used to convert and confirm or disavow signatures. This property is useful in scenarios where the signer is met with more verification requests than he has capacity to handle, or when the signer might become off-line or otherwise unavailable and therefor cannot handle verification requests. In such scenarios, the signer will be able to delegate the verification by releasing vk to a semi-trusted entity who will then have the capacity to verify signatures on behalf of the signer. It is required that the scheme remains unforgeable, even for the semi-trusted entity with the knowledge of vk.

Overview of prior work. The original convertible undeniable signature scheme by Boyar *et al.* [6] was shown to be insecure by Michels, Petersen and Horster [27] when an universal token is released. Michels *et al.* furthermore proposed an updated scheme, but only heuristic arguments for the security of this scheme were presented. Recently, Aimani and Vergnaud [4] provided an analysis of the updated scheme in the generic group model. Furthermore, Damgård and Pedersen [14] proposed two convertible undeniable signature schemes based on El Gamal signatures, but did not give full proofs of invisibility, and Michels and Stadler [28] proposed a scheme based on Schnorr signatures.

The first RSA based scheme was proposed by Gennaro, Rabin and Krawczyk [16] which Miyazaki later improved [29] (see also [17]). Kurosawa and Takagi [24] proposed a (selective convertible only) scheme which they claimed to be the first RSA based scheme secure in the standard model, but it was shown by Phong, Kurosawa and Ogata [33] that the scheme does not provide full invisibility. Phong *et al.* furthermore proposed a new selective and universally convertible RSA based scheme secure in the standard model.

Laguillaumie and Vergnaud [26] defined and proposed a pairing-based time-selective convertible undeniable signatures which allow conversion of signatures constructed in a given time period, and Monnerat and Vaudenay [30] pointed out that their MOVA undeniable signature scheme supports selective conversion although a formal analysis is not given. Recently, Huang, Mu, Susilo and Wu [21] proposed the currently most efficient scheme in the random oracle model which supports both selective and universal conversion. Yuen, Au, Liu and Susilo [37] proposed a selective and universal convertible standard model scheme, but it was shown by Phong, Kurosawa and Ogata [32] that the scheme is not invisible for the standard definition of invisibility (Yuen et al. recently updated their scheme [38] to address this). Phong et al. furthermore proposed two efficient schemes which are claimed to be the first practical discrete logarithm based schemes both providing selective and universal conversion and being provably secure in the standard model. However, as we discuss in Section 4, these schemes do not provide token soundness, and will not be secure against malicious signers. Lastly, Huang and Wong [19] proposed a scheme with even shorter signatures than the schemes by Phong et al., but only prove the scheme to be invisible according to a weaker definition of invisibility which does not guarantee signer anonymity. In fact, it is fairly easy to see that the scheme does not provide anonymity, which will be highlighted in Section 4.

An intuitive approach to the construction of a convertible undeniable signature scheme is to use an encryption scheme to encrypt (parts of) an ordinary signature, and this is indeed the approach used in [14,32]. Aimani [2,3] proposed a generic construction based on a certain class of encryption and signature schemes. However, this approach does not provide selective conversion as described above; while a signer is able to extract a valid public verifiable signature from an undeniable signature, a verifier will not receive any proof that the received publicly verifiable signature corresponds to the undeniable signature i.e. the verifier does not receive a token which allows him to independently verify the undeniable signature, but only a publicly verifiable signature derived from the undeniable signature. It should be noted that a designated confirmer signature, in which the signer holds both signer and confirmer key pairs, will not automatically yield a selective and universal convertible signature scheme for a similar reason; the ability of the confirmer to extract a publicly verifiable signature from an undeniable signature does not necessarily imply the ability to provide a token which will convince a verifier of the validity of the original signature.

All of the early proposed schemes [6,27,14,16] implement the above described separation of the signer's key material into a signer key and verification key, which allows delegation of the verification. However, despite the practical advantages of this property, it is not considered in the formalization, security model or the concrete schemes presented in most recent papers [26,24,21,37,2,33,32] (we note that [19] discuss delegation of verification as an extension). In these schemes, only the ability of the signer to confirm, disavow and convert signatures is considered and no explicit mechanism is provided for delegating this ability.

Note that although the possession of an universal token allows verification of any signature, this does not necessarily provide the ability to efficiently prove validity to a third party in a non-transferable way.

Our Contribution. We present an updated definition and security model for schemes allowing delegation, and highlight a new security property, token soundness, which is not formally treated in previous security models[1]. Token soundness guarantee that a malicious signer (or delegated verifier) cannot produce a token such that an invalid signature/message pair appears valid. This is different from the ordinary completeness requirement which only considers honestly generated tokens, and will furthermore, in combination with unforgeability of undeniable signatures, guarantee unforgeability of message/signature/token tuples (see Section 4). We also note that the recently proposed schemes by Phong, Kurosawa and Ogata [32] do not provide token soundness, and hence allows a malicious signer to fool potential verifiers.

We then propose a convertible undeniable signature scheme which allows verification delegation and is provably secure in the standard model assuming the computational co-Diffie-Hellman problem, a closely related problem (see Section 2), and the decisional linear problem are hard. Our scheme is the most efficient scheme, in terms of signature size, that provably fulfills all security properties of a convertible undeniable signature scheme in the standard model (see Section 6 for a comparison).

2   Preliminaries

Negligible function. A function $\epsilon : \mathbb{N} \to [0,1]$ is said to be *negligible* if for all $c > 0$ there exists an n_c such that for all $n > n_c$ $\epsilon(n) < 1/n^c$.

Bilinear maps. Our scheme makes use of groups equipped with a *bilinear map* (we refer the reader to [5] for a detailed description of these maps). To instantiate our schemes, we consider a generator $\mathcal{G}$ that on input 1^k outputs a description of groups $\mathbb{G}_1$, $\mathbb{G}_2$ and $\mathbb{G}_T$ of prime order p where $2^k < p < 2^{k+1}$, a bilinear map $e : \mathbb{G}_1 \times \mathbb{G}_2 \to \mathbb{G}_T$ and an isomorphism $\psi : \mathbb{G}_2 \to \mathbb{G}_1$. We will use the notation $\mathbb{P} = (e, \mathbb{G}_1, \mathbb{G}_2, \mathbb{G}_T, p, \psi)$ as a shorthand for the output of $\mathcal{G}$.

The discrete logarithm problem. Given a group $\mathbb{G}$ of order p, where $2^k < p < 2^{k+1}$, and random elements $g, h \in \mathbb{G}$, the discrete logarithm problem in $\mathbb{G}$ is defined as computing $x \in \mathbb{Z}_p$ such that $g_2^x = h$. We say that the discrete logarithm problem is *hard* in $\mathbb{G}_2$ if all polynomial time algorithms have negligible probability (in the parameter k) of solving the problem.

The computational co-Diffie-Hellman problem. Given $\mathbb{P} = (e, \mathbb{G}_1, \mathbb{G}_2, \mathbb{G}_T, p, \psi)$, elements $g_2, g_2^a \in \mathbb{G}_2$ and $h \in \mathbb{G}_1$ where a is a random element in $\mathbb{Z}_p$, the

---

[1] We note that [19] independently proposed a similar security property which they refer to as non-claimability, but that our results were made public [35] well ahead of those from [19].

computational co-Diffie-Hellman problem in the bilinear groups $(\mathbb{G}_1, \mathbb{G}_2)$ is to compute $h^a \in \mathbb{G}_1$. We say the computational co-Diffie-Hellman problem is *hard* in $(\mathbb{G}_1, \mathbb{G}_2)$ if all polynomial time algorithms have negligible probability (in the parameter k) of solving the problem.

Besides the above defined problem, we will also consider the following variant: Given $\mathbb{P} = (e, \mathbb{G}_1, \mathbb{G}_2, \mathbb{G}_T, p, \psi)$, elements $g_2, g_2^a, h \in \mathbb{G}_2$ where a is a random element in $\mathbb{Z}_p$, compute $\psi(h^a) \in \mathbb{G}_1$. We will refer to this problem as the computational ψ-Diffie-Hellman problem to distinguish it from the above, and say that the problem is *hard* in $(\mathbb{G}_1, \mathbb{G}_2)$ if all polynomial time algorithms have negligible probability (in the parameter k) of solving the problem.

The decisional linear problem. Given a group $\mathbb{G}$ of order p, where $2^k < p < 2^{k+1}$, and elements $u, v, u^x, v^y, h, h^z \in \mathbb{G}$ where x, y are random elements in $\mathbb{Z}_p$, the decisional linear problem in $\mathbb{G}$ is to decide whether $z = x + y$ or z is a random element in $\mathbb{Z}_p$. We say the decisional linear problem is *hard* in $\mathbb{G}$ if all polynomial time algorithms have negligible probability (in the parameter k) of solving the the problem.

3   Convertible Undeniable Signatures

A convertible undeniable signature (CUS) scheme consists of the following algorithms and protocols:

- Setup: Given input 1^k, this algorithm outputs a set of public parameters *par*.
- KeyGen: Given *par*, this algorithm outputs a public key *pk*, a private verification key *vk* and a private signing key *sk*. The verification key *vk* will be used as private prover input in the confirm/disavow protocols, and to selectively convert signatures, whereas the signing key will only be used to sign messages.
- Sign: Given *par*, *sk* and a message m, this algorithm outputs an undeniable signature σ.
- Convert: Given *par*, *vk* and (m, σ), this algorithm returns a verification token tk_σ for σ if (m, σ) is a valid message/signature pair. Otherwise, the algorithm returns $\perp$.
- Verify: Given *par*, *pk*, (m, σ) and tk_σ, this algorithm returns either accept or reject.
- (Confirm, V_{con}): A pair of interactive algorithms for confirming validity of a signature. Both algorithms take as common input *par*, *pk* and (m, σ). The algorithm Confirm takes as an additional private input the verification key *vk*. While Confirm has no local output, the algorithm V_{con} will output either accept or reject after having interacted with Confirm.
- (Disavow, V_{dis}): A pair of interactive algorithms for disavowing validity of a signature. Similar to the above, both algorithms take as common input *par*, *pk* and (m, σ), and the algorithm Disavow takes the verification key *vk* as an additional private input. Disavow has no local output, but V_{dis} will output either accept or reject after having interacted with Disavow.

Note that the above definition does not explicitly mention how a universal token is generated or how signatures are verified using this token since this functionality follows directly from the separation of the private key material into a signing key sk and a verification key vk. More precisely, a universal token corresponds to vk, and using this, any signature can be verified using the Convert algorithm. We assume that given (pk, vk) it can be verified that vk is a verification key for the public key pk.

We use the notation $\{\texttt{Confirm}(vk) \leftrightarrow \mathsf{V}_{con}\}(par, pk, m, \sigma)$ to denote the interaction between Confirm and V_{con} with the common input (par, pk, m, σ) and the private input vk to the Confirm algorithm (a similar notation is used for Disavow and V_{dis}). We furthermore use $z \leftarrow_2 \{\texttt{Confirm}(vk) \leftrightarrow \mathsf{V}_{con}\}(par, pk, m, \sigma)$ to denote the output of V_{con} upon completion of the protocol i.e. z will be either accept or reject.

Correctness. For a scheme to be correct, it is required that for all parameters $par \leftarrow \texttt{Setup}(1^k)$, all keys $(pk, vk, sk) \leftarrow \texttt{KeyGen}(par)$, all messages $m \in \{0, 1\}^*$, and all signatures $\sigma \leftarrow \texttt{Sign}(par, sk, m)$, that the interaction $z \leftarrow_2 \{\texttt{Confirm}(vk) \leftrightarrow \mathsf{V}_{con}\}(par, pk, m, \sigma)$ yields $z = \texttt{accept}$. Furthermore, it is required that for all $tk_\sigma \leftarrow \texttt{Convert}(par, vk, m, \sigma)$ that $\texttt{Verify}(par, pk, m, \sigma, tk_\sigma) = \texttt{accept}$. Lastly, it is required that for any $(m', \sigma') \notin \{(m, \sigma) : \sigma \leftarrow \texttt{Sign}(par, sk, m)\}$, the interaction $z' \leftarrow_2 \{\texttt{Disavow}(vk) \leftrightarrow \mathsf{V}_{dis}\}(par, pk, m', \sigma')\}$ yields $z' = \texttt{accept}$.

4 Security Model

A CUS scheme is required to provide *token soundness, unforgeability, invisibility* and *non-impersonation*, which will be defined below. Besides this, both the confirm and disavow protocols are required to be *zero-knowledge proofs* [18] to guarantee soundness of the protocols and transcript simulatability. The latter property will in combination with invisibility of the scheme provide what is commonly referred to as non-transferability (see below).

4.1 Token Soundness

The soundness of the confirm and disavow protocols intuitively captures the requirement that a signer cannot "cheat" when interacting with a verifier in

$\texttt{Exp}_{S,\mathcal{A}}^{\text{tk-sound}}(1^k)$
  $par \leftarrow \texttt{Setup}(1^k)$
  $(pk^*, m^*, \sigma^*, tk_\sigma^*, st) \leftarrow \mathcal{A}(par)$
  $z_1 \leftarrow_2 \{\mathcal{A}(st) \leftrightarrow \mathsf{V}_{dis}\}(par, pk^*, m^*, \sigma^*)$
  $z_2 \leftarrow \texttt{Verify}(par, pk^*, m^*, \sigma^*, tk_\sigma^*)$
  if $z_1 = z_2 = \texttt{accept}$
    output 1
  else output 0

$\texttt{Exp}_{S,\mathcal{A}}^{\text{suf-cma}}(1^k)$
  $par \leftarrow \texttt{Setup}(1^k)$
  $(pk, vk, sk) \leftarrow \texttt{KeyGen}(par)$
  $(m^*, \sigma^*) \leftarrow \mathcal{A}^{\mathcal{O}}(par, pk, vk)$
  if $(m^*, \sigma^*) \in \{(m, \sigma); \sigma \leftarrow \texttt{Sign}(par, sk, m)\}$
    output 1
  else output 0

Fig. 1. Token soundness and unforgeability experiments

the confirm or disavow protocol i.e. he cannot convince a verifier that a signature is both valid and invalid. However, it does not guarantee that a cheating signer cannot produce a token tk_σ and a message/signature pair (m, σ) such that $\mathtt{Verify}(par, pk, m, \sigma, tk_\sigma) = \mathtt{accept}$, but (m, σ) can be disavowed. This requirement, which we will refer to as token soundness, is somewhat surprisingly not formally treated in the used security models for convertible undeniable signatures. Token soundness of a CUS scheme S is defined via the experiment $\mathtt{Exp}_{S,\mathcal{A}}^{tk\text{-}sound}(1^k)$ shown in Figure 1. We define the advantage of the algorithm $\mathcal{A}$ as

$$\mathtt{Adv}_{S,\mathcal{A}}^{tk\text{-}sound} = \Pr[\mathtt{Exp}_{S,\mathcal{A}}^{tk\text{-}sound}(1^k) = 1]$$

Definition 1. *A CUS scheme is said to have* token soundness *if for all polynomial time algorithms $\mathcal{A}$, the advantage $\mathtt{Adv}_{S,\mathcal{A}}^{tk\text{-}sound}$ is negligible in the security parameter k.*

We note that the recently proposed schemes by Phong, Kurosawa and Ogata [32] does not provide token soundness as defined above. More specifically, the schemes in [32] make use of NIZK proofs as tokens, and a signer will construct a token for a selective conversion of a signature by generating a NIZK proof of the validity of the signature. However, since the common reference string (CRS) used by the NIZK proofs is stored as part of the public signer key (i.e. the CRS will be generated by the signer), a malicious signer will, by the properties of the NIZK proofs, be able to generate a CRS which is indistinguishable from an honestly generated one, and which allows the signer to simulate the NIZK proofs. Hence, the malicious signer can break the token soundness of the schemes by simulating a NIZK proof for an invalid signature. This scenario can be avoid by letting the verifier generate the CRS, but this will tie a conversion to a single verifier and will not provide public verifiability. Alternatively, the CRS could be generate by a trusted third party. However, both of these options limit the practical applicability of the scheme.

4.2 Unforgeability

Strong unforgeability against a chosen message attack for a CUS scheme S is defined via the experiment $\mathtt{Exp}_{S,\mathcal{A}}^{suf\text{-}cma}(1^k)$ shown in Figure 1. In the experiment, $\mathcal{A}$ has access to the oracle $\mathcal{O} = \{\mathcal{O}_{Sign}\}$ which is defined as follows

- $\mathcal{O}_{Sign}$: Given a message m, the oracle returns $\sigma \leftarrow \mathtt{Sign}(par, sk, m)$.

It is required that $\mathcal{A}$ did not obtain σ^* by submitting m^* to $\mathcal{O}_{Sign}$. Note that since $\mathcal{A}$ is given the verification key vk, $\mathcal{A}$ can convert signatures and run the confirm and disavow protocols by himself, and there is no need to provide $\mathcal{A}$ with oracles for these tasks. The advantage of $\mathcal{A}$ is defined as

$$\mathtt{Adv}_{S,\mathcal{A}}^{suf\text{-}cma} = \Pr[\mathtt{Exp}_{S,\mathcal{A}}^{suf\text{-}cma}(1^k) = 1]$$

$\mathbf{Exp}_{S,\mathcal{A}}^{\text{inv-cma}}(1^k)$
   $par \leftarrow \mathbf{Setup}(1^k)$
   $(pk, vk, sk) \leftarrow \mathbf{KeyGen}(par)$
   $(m^*, st) \leftarrow \mathcal{A}^{\mathcal{O}}(par, pk)$
   $b \leftarrow \{0,1\}$
   if $b = 0$ set $\sigma^* \leftarrow S$
   else set $\sigma^* \leftarrow \mathbf{Sign}(par, sk, m)$
   $b' \leftarrow \mathcal{A}^{\mathcal{O}}(st, \sigma^*)$
   if $b = b'$ output 1
   else output 0

$\mathbf{Exp}_{S,\mathcal{A}}^{\text{imp-cma}}(1^k)$
   $par \leftarrow \mathbf{Setup}(1^k)$
   $(pk, vk, sk) \leftarrow \mathbf{KeyGen}(par)$
   $(m^*, \sigma^*, st) \leftarrow \mathcal{A}^{\mathcal{O}}(par, pk)$
   if $(m^*, \sigma^*) \in \{(m, \sigma); \sigma \leftarrow \mathbf{Sign}(par, sk, m)\}$
     $z \leftarrow_2 \{A(st) \leftrightarrow V_{con}\}(par, pk, m^*, \sigma^*)$
   else
     $z \leftarrow_2 \{A(st) \leftrightarrow V_{dis}\}(par, pk, m^*, \sigma^*)$
   if $z = \mathbf{accept}$
     output 1
   else output 0

Fig. 2. Invisibility and non-impersonation experiments

Definition 2. *A CUS scheme is said to be* strongly unforgeable *if for all polynomial time algorithms $\mathcal{A}$, the advantage* $\mathbf{Adv}_{S,\mathcal{A}}^{suf-cma}$ *is negligible in the security parameter k.*

While the above definition does not involve tokens, it will, in combination with token soundness, guarantee that an adversary without the knowledge of sk cannot produce (m, σ, tk_σ) such that $\mathbf{Verify}(par, pk, m, \sigma, tk_\sigma) = \mathbf{accept}$ without having obtained (m, σ) from the signer. This follows easily from the following observation. If the adversary does produce (m, σ, tk_σ), then if (m, σ) is a valid message/signature pair, the adversary has broken the above defined unforgeability property, whereas if (m, σ) is not a valid message/signature pair, the token soundness of the scheme has been broken, which should not be possible even for an adversary knowing sk.

We furthermore stress the importance of giving $\mathcal{A}$ access to vk in the above definition. This guarantees that if a signer delegates the verification operation by releasing vk to a semi-trusted entity, this entity will not be able to forge new signatures, but only verify existing ones.

4.3 Invisibility

Invisibility against a chosen message attack for a CUS scheme S is defined via the experiment $\mathbf{Exp}_{S,\mathcal{A}}^{\text{inv-cma}}(1^k)$ shown in Figure 2. In the experiment, S denotes the signature space and is defined as $S = \{\sigma : (pk, vk, sk) \leftarrow \mathbf{KeyGen}(par); m \leftarrow \mathcal{M}; \sigma \leftarrow \mathbf{Sign}(par, sk, m)\}$ where $\mathcal{M}$ is the message space given in par. Furthermore, $\mathcal{A}$ has access to the oracles $\mathcal{O} = \{\mathcal{O}_{Sign}, \mathcal{O}_{Conv}, \mathcal{O}_{Conf/Dis}\}$ which are defined as follows:

- $\mathcal{O}_{Sign}$: Defined as in the unforgeability experiment.
- $\mathcal{O}_{Conv}$: Given a message/signature pair (m, σ), this oracle returns $tk_\sigma \leftarrow \mathbf{Convert}(par, vk, m, \sigma)$ if $(m, \sigma) \in \{(m', \sigma') : \sigma' \leftarrow \mathbf{Sign}(par, sk, m')\}$. Otherwise the oracle returns $\perp$.
- $\mathcal{O}_{Conf/Dis}$: Given a message signature pair (m, σ), this oracle interacts with $\mathcal{A}$ by running $\mathbf{Confirm}(par, vk, m, \sigma)$ if $(m, \sigma) \in \{(m', \sigma') : \sigma' \leftarrow$

$\text{Sign}(par, sk, m')\}$. Otherwise, the oracle interacts with $\mathcal{A}$ by running $\text{Disavow}(par, vk, m, \sigma)$.

It is required that $\mathcal{A}$ does not query (m^*, σ^*) to the convert or confirm/disavow oracles. We define the advantage of $\mathcal{A}$ in the experiment as

$$\text{Adv}_{S,\mathcal{A}}^{inv\text{-}cma} = |\Pr[\text{Exp}_{S,\mathcal{A}}^{inv\text{-}cma}(1^k) = 1] - 1/2|$$

Definition 3. *A CUS scheme is said to be* invisible *if for all polynomial time algorithms $\mathcal{A}$ the advantage $\text{Adv}_{S,\mathcal{A}}^{inv\text{-}cma}$ is negligible in the security parameter k.*

Note that the only requirement in the above definition is that $\mathcal{A}$ did not submit (m^*, σ^*) to the convert or confirm/disavow oracles. Hence, a deterministic scheme cannot satisfy the above definition since access to the signing oracle is not restricted (i.e. for a deterministic scheme, an adversary can simply submit m^* to $\mathcal{O}_{Sign}$ and compare the received signature with σ^*). Furthermore, $\mathcal{A}$ is allowed to submit (m^*, σ) where $\sigma \neq \sigma^*$, and (m, σ^*) where $m \neq m^*$ to the convert and confirm/disavow oracles. While a deterministic scheme should be able to satisfy a security definition where these type of queries are allowed, some security models (e.g. [37]) do not allow the former type of query, and thereby further weaken the obtain security. These issues might be a concern in a scenario where the entropy of the signed messages is small i.e. the security of a signature on a message which the signer has previously signed might not be guaranteed. However, with the above security notion, these concerns are eliminated.

Another aspect of the above security notion which we would like to highlight is the definition of $\mathcal{S}$. We note that anyone can sample $\mathcal{S}$ and that when using this definition of $\mathcal{S}$, invisibility implies anonymity i.e. the inability for an adversary to distinguish between signatures constructed by different users (see [15,21] for a formal proof of this). Some schemes (e.g. [14,22,20,19]) use a more restricted definition limiting $\mathcal{S}$ to signatures from the signer i.e. $\mathcal{S} = \{\sigma : m \leftarrow \mathcal{M}; \sigma \leftarrow \text{Sign}(par, sk, m)\}$. This not only removes the guarantee of anonymity, but might also make it difficult for users other than the signer to sample $\mathcal{S}$. The latter can potentially have an impact on the non-transferability of the scheme, which we will discuss below. Regarding anonymity, we note that in the recent scheme by Huang and Wong [19], it is in fact easy to link valid signatures to a signer. This can be seen as follows: A public key in [19] is given by $pk = (g, X = g^x, Y = g^{1/y}, u, k)$, where g is a generator of a group $\mathbb{G}$ of order p and $u \in \mathbb{G}$ is a random element, and a signature is given by $\sigma = (\sigma_1, \sigma_2, \sigma_3) = (H_k(m)^{1/(x+s)}, Y^s, u^s)$ for a random value $s \in \mathbb{Z}_p$. Hence, if σ is a valid signature, it can be checked whether pk is the public key of the signer by checking whether $e(Y, \sigma_3) = e(\sigma_2, u)$ holds.

A note on non-transferability. The security notion non-transferability captures the property that a verifier who learns whether a given signature is valid or not by interacting with the signer in the confirm or disavow protocols, should not be able to prove this knowledge to a third party. More specifically, the verify should be able to "fake" any evidence of the validity of a signature obtain by interacting

$$\text{Exp}_{S,\mathcal{A}}^{\text{tk-imp-cma}}(1^k)$$
$$par \leftarrow \text{Setup}(1^k)$$
$$(pk, vk, sk) \leftarrow \text{KeyGen}(par)$$
$$(m^*, \sigma^*, tk_\sigma^*) \leftarrow \mathcal{A}^\mathcal{O}(par, pk)$$
$$\text{if Verify}(par, pk, m^*, \sigma^*, tk_\sigma^*) = \text{accept}$$
$$\quad \text{output } 1$$
$$\text{else output } 0$$

Fig. 3. Token non-impersonation experiment

with the signer. When introducing convertible undeniable signatures, Boyar, Chaum, Damgård and Pedersen [6] referred to this property as *undeniability* and defined the property as a verifier's ability to produce fake signature/transcript pairs indistinguishable from real ones.

The above definition of invisibility guarantees that a valid signature from a signer cannot be distinguished from any other element in $\mathcal{S}$, and allows any user to sample $\mathcal{S}$. Furthermore, since the confirm and disavow protocols are required to be zero-knowledge proofs, transcript simulatability of these protocols is guaranteed. Hence, it is easy to see that a verifier can produce fake signature/transcript pairs indistinguishable from real ones, implying that non-transferability is already achieved with the above security requirements.

4.4 Non-impersonation

While soundness informally guarantees that a prover cannot "cheat", it does not prevent a third party from impersonating the prover. This was pointed out by Kurosawa and Heng [23], and Huang *et al.* [21] furthermore noticed that, for convertible schemes, this might be an issue for token generation as well.

Non-impersonation against a chosen message attack for a CUS scheme S is defined via the experiment $\text{Exp}_{S,\mathcal{A}}^{\text{imp-cma}}(1^k)$ shown in Figure 2. In the experiment, $\mathcal{A}$ has access to the oracles $\mathcal{O} = \{\mathcal{O}_{Sign}, \mathcal{O}_{Conv}, \mathcal{O}_{Conf/Dis}\}$ defined as in the invisibility definition. It is required that $\mathcal{A}$ does not submit (m^*, σ^*) to the confirm/disavow oracle. We define the advantage of $\mathcal{A}$ in the experiment as

$$\text{Adv}_{S,\mathcal{A}}^{\text{imp-cma}} = \Pr[\text{Exp}_{S,\mathcal{A}}^{\text{imp-cma}}(1^k) = 1]$$

Definition 4. *A CUS scheme is said to be resistant to* impersonation attacks *if for all polynomial time algorithms $\mathcal{A}$, the advantage $\text{Adv}_{S,\mathcal{A}}^{imp-cma}$ is negligible in the security parameter k.*

Token non-impersonation against a chosen message attack for a CUS scheme S is defined via the experiment $\text{Exp}_{S,\mathcal{A}}^{\text{tk-imp-cma}}(1^k)$ shown in Figure 3. $\mathcal{A}$ has access to the oracles $\mathcal{O} = \{\mathcal{O}_{Sign}, \mathcal{O}_{Conv}, \mathcal{O}_{Conf/Dis}\}$ defined as in the above. It is required that $\mathcal{A}$ does not submit (m^*, σ^*) to the conversion oracle. The advantage of $\mathcal{A}$ in the experiment is defined as

$$\text{Adv}_{S,\mathcal{A}}^{\text{tk-imp-cma}} = \Pr[\text{Exp}_{S,\mathcal{A}}^{\text{tk-imp-cma}}(1^k) = 1]$$

Definition 5. *A CUS scheme is said to be resistant to* token impersonation attacks *if for all polynomial time algorithms* $\mathcal{A}$*, the advantage* $\mathbf{Adv}_{S,\mathcal{A}}^{tk-imp-cma}$ *is negligible in the security parameter* k*.*

5   A Concrete Convertible Undeniable Signature Scheme

In this section we present a CUS scheme provable secure in the standard model. Our scheme is based on a similar approach to the basic designated confirmer signature scheme by Schuldt *et al.* [34], but we employ different proof systems and provide a token generation method. Furthermore, our scheme does not require verifiers to hold public/private key pairs and avoids the key registration requirement of [34]. In the description of the scheme we use the notation $ZKPK\{w : R(w)\}$ to mean a zero-knowledge proof of knowledge of w such that the relation $R(w)$ holds. We discuss the implementation details of these proofs below.

- **Setup:** Compute $\mathbb{P} = (e, \mathbb{G}_1, \mathbb{G}_2, \mathbb{G}_T, p, \psi) \leftarrow \mathcal{G}(1^k)$, pick $g_2 \in \mathbb{G}_2$ and set $g_1 \leftarrow \psi(g_2)$. Furthermore, choose a collision resistant hash function family $\mathcal{H} = \{H_{\mathbf{k}} : \{0,1\}^* \to \mathbb{Z}_p\}$ indexed by a key $\mathbf{k} \in \mathcal{K}$. Return $par = (\mathbb{P}, g_1, g_2, \mathcal{H})$.

- **KeyGen :** Given par, pick $\alpha, x, y \leftarrow \mathbb{Z}_p$, $h \leftarrow \mathbb{G}_1$ and $w_2 \leftarrow \mathbb{G}_2$, and set $w_1 \leftarrow g_1^{\alpha}$, $v_1 \leftarrow g_2^{x^{-1}}$ and $v_2 \leftarrow g_2^{y^{-1}}$. Furthermore, pick $u_0, \dots, u_n \leftarrow \mathbb{G}_2{}^2$, and define $F(m) = u_0 \prod_{i=1}^{n} u_i^{m_i}$ where m_i is the ith bit of m. Finally pick a hash key $\mathbf{k} \in \mathcal{K}$ and set $pk = (\mathbf{k}, w_1, w_2, v_1, v_2, h, u_0, \dots, u_n)$, $vk = (x, y)$ and $sk = w_2^{\alpha}$. Return (pk, vk, sk).

- **Sign :** Given input (par, sk, m), where $sk = w_2^{\alpha}$, pick random $a, b, s \leftarrow \mathbb{Z}_p$, compute $t \leftarrow H_{\mathbf{k}}(\psi(v_1)^a || \psi(v_2)^b || m)$ and $M = g_1^s h^t$, and return

$$\sigma = (\psi(v_1)^a, \psi(v_2)^b, \psi(w_2^{\alpha} F(M)^{a+b}), s).$$

- **Convert :** Given (par, vk, m, σ) where $\sigma = (\sigma_1, \sigma_2, \sigma_3, s)$ and $vk = (x, y)$, check that $e(\sigma_3, g_2) = e(w_1, w_2)e(\sigma_1^x \sigma_2^y, F(M))$ where $M = g_1^s h^t$ and $t = H_{\mathbf{k}}(\sigma_1 || \sigma_2 || m)$, and return $\perp$ if this is not the case. Otherwise, return the token $tk_{\sigma} = (\sigma_1^x, \sigma_2^y)$.

- **Verify :** Given $(par, pk, m, \sigma, tk_{\sigma})$ where $pk = (\mathbf{k}, w_1, w_2, v_1, v_2, h, u_0, \dots, u_n)$, $\sigma' = (\sigma_1, \sigma_2, \sigma_3, s)$ and $tk_{\sigma} = (tk_1, tk_2)$, return **accept** if $e(tk_1, v_1) = e(\sigma_1, g_2)$, $e(tk_2, v_2) = e(\sigma_2, g_2)$, and $e(\sigma_3, g_2) = e(w_1, w_2)e(tk_1 tk_2, F(M))$ where $M = g_1^s h^t$ and $t = H_{\mathbf{k}}(\sigma_1 || \sigma_2 || m)$.

- **(Confirm, V_{con}):** Given the common input (par, pk, m, σ), where $\sigma = (\sigma_1, \sigma_2, \sigma_3, s)$ and $pk = (\mathbf{k}, w_1, w_2, v_1, v_2, h, u_0, \dots, u_n)$, and the additional private input $vk = (x, y)$ to the **Confirm** algorithm, (**Confirm**, V_{con}) is executed as

$$ZKPK\{(x, y) : v_1^x = g_2 \wedge v_2^y = g_2 \wedge$$
$$e(\sigma_1, F(M))^x e(\sigma_2, F(M))^y = e(\sigma_3, g_2)/e(w_1, w_2)\}$$

---

[2] We assume that the description of group elements in $\mathbb{G}_1$ is less than n bits.

where $M = g_1^s h^t$ and $t = H_{\mathbf{k}}(\sigma_1||\sigma_2||m)$.

- $(\mathtt{Disavow}, \mathsf{V}_{dis})$: Given same common input as in $(\mathtt{Confirm}, \mathsf{V}_{con})$ and private input $vk = (x, y)$ to the $\mathtt{Disavow}$ algorithm, $(\mathtt{Disavow}, \mathsf{V}_{dis})$ is executed as

$$ZKPK\{(x, y) : v_1^x = g_2 \wedge v_2^y = g_2 \wedge$$
$$e(\sigma_1, F(M))^x e(\sigma_2, F(M))^y \neq e(\sigma_3, g_2)/e(w_1, w_2)\}$$

where $M = g_1^s h^t$ and $t = H_{\mathbf{k}}(\sigma_1||\sigma_2||m)$.

Implementation of ZKPK. We note that it is possible to construct sigma protocols for the confirm and disavow protocols by using a combination of well known sigma protocols for proving knowledge of a discrete logarithm, equality of discrete logarithms, and inequality of discrete logarithms (see [8,7]). The zero-knowledge proofs of knowledge in the above scheme can then be obtained by using the transformation proposed by Cramer *et al.* [12] which converts a sigma protocol into a perfect zero-knowledge proof of knowledge. The resulting zero-knowledge proofs are efficient 4-move protocols, and no additional hardness assumptions are required in the transformation. In the full version [35], we give a more detailed description of how the protocols are implemented.

5.1 Security

The soundness and the zero-knowledge property of the confirm and disavow protocols are guaranteed by the transformation by Cramer *et al.* [12], and we refer the reader to [12] for proofs of these properties.

The token soundness of the scheme is implied by the properties of the bilinear map in combination with the proof of knowledge property of the disavow protocol (which is achieved without requiring any intractability assumptions [12]):

Theorem 6. *If the disavow protocol is a zero-knowledge proof of knowledge, then the above CUS scheme has token soundness.*

The unforgeability of the above CUS scheme is based on the unforgeability of the signature scheme by Waters [36] which we recall in Appendix A.

Theorem 7. *Assume that the hash function family $\mathcal{H}$ is collision resistant, the discrete logarithm problem is hard in $\mathbb{G}_2$, and that Waters signature scheme is (weakly) unforgeable. Then the above CUS scheme is strongly unforgeable.*

We note that Waters' signature scheme is (weakly) unforgeable assuming the computational co-Diffie-Hellman problem is hard [36]. Furthermore, collision resistant hash functions can be constructed based on the discrete logarithm assumption [13], which imply that the unforgeability of the above scheme can be reduced to the computational co-Diffie-Hellman problem alone.

Due to space limitations, the proofs of Theorem 6 and 7 are not given here, but can be found in the full version [35].

Theorem 8. *Assume the above CUS scheme is strongly unforgeable and that the decision linear problem is hard in $\mathbb{G}_2$. Then the above CUS scheme is invisible.*

The proof of the above theorem is given in Appendix B.

Lastly, the following theorems show that the above CUS scheme is resistant to impersonation and token impersonation attacks.

Theorem 9. *Assume the above CUS scheme is strongly unforgeable and that the the discrete logarithm problem is hard in $\mathbb{G}_2$. Then the above CUS scheme is resistant to impersonation attacks.*

Theorem 10. *Assume the above CUS scheme is strongly unforgeable and that the computational ψ-Diffie-Hellman problem is hard in $(\mathbb{G}_1, \mathbb{G}_2)$. Then the above CUS scheme is resistant to token impersonation attacks.*

The strategy of the proof of the first theorem is to make use of the proof of knowledge property of the used proof systems to extract the verification key which, in the simulation, will contain an unknown discrete logarithm. Otherwise, the simulation is very similar to that of Theorem 8, and can easily be derived from this. The strategy of the proof of the second theorem is to return a signature in one of the adversary's signature queries such that a conversion will reveal the solution to a computational ψ-Diffie-Hellman problem[3]. The strong unforgeability of the scheme will ensure that the signature converted by the adversary in a token impersonation attack was constructed by the simulator, and the remaining part of the simulation is similar to that of Theorem 8. We omit the details of the proofs here.

6   Comparison

In Table 1 we compare the recently proposed standard model CUS schemes [38,33,32,19] and our proposed scheme described above. All schemes support selective and universal conversion and are instantiated to provide approximately 80-bits of security. Note that the scheme YALS requires both a verification key and a signature of a one-time signature scheme to be included as part of a undeniable signature, which leads to a slightly larger signature size.

While the schemes PKO-4 and HW have slightly smaller signatures than our scheme, they do not provide both token soundness and anonymity. Hence, our scheme provides the smallest signature size of the CUS schemes which provably satisfies all desired security requirements. Furthermore, we note that the security of our scheme rests on weaker and more natural security assumptions compared to those of PKO-4 and HW.

---

[3] More specifically, a simulator given $\mathbb{P}$ and a ψ-Diffie-Hellman instance $g, g^a, h' \in \mathbb{G}_2$ will set $g_2 \leftarrow g^a$, $v_1 \leftarrow g$, $u_i \leftarrow g^{d_i}$ with random $d_i \leftarrow \mathbb{Z}_p$ for $0 \leq i \leq n$, and generate the remaining elements of *par* and *pk* as in an ordinary scheme. Then, for a message m, the signature $\sigma = (\sigma_1, \sigma_2, \sigma_3, s)$ constructed by picking $r, b, s \leftarrow \mathbb{Z}_p$, setting $\sigma_1 \leftarrow \psi(h')^r$, $\sigma_2 \leftarrow \psi(v_2)^b$, $t \leftarrow H_k(\sigma_1 || \sigma_2 || m)$, $M \leftarrow g_1^s h^t$ (where h is from *pk*) and $\sigma_3 \leftarrow \psi(w_2^a(h')^{r(d_0 + \sum_{i=1}^n d_i M_i)} F(M)^b)$, will have a conversion token of the form $tk_\sigma = (\psi(h')^{ra}, g_1^b)$ for a known value r. This yields the solution $\psi(h')^a$ to the ψ-Diffie-Hellman problem.

Table 1. Comparison of CUS schemes. All pairing-based schemes are assumed to be instantiated with an elliptic curve group equipped with an asymmetric pairing using group elements of size 170 bits, and the RSA-based schemes are assumed to use an RSA group with a 1024 bit modulus. Furthermore, the discrete logarithm-based one-time signature scheme described in [1] and implemented in an elliptic curve group with group elements of size 160 bits, is used to instantiate the YALS [38] scheme. In the assumptions column, the abbreviations sRSA, DNR, DIV, q-SDH, DLIN, CDH, q-HSDH, q-DHSDH and ψ-CDH stands for strong RSA, decisional N-th residuosity, division intractability, q strong Diffie-Hellman, decisional linear, computational Diffie-Hellman, q hidden strong Diffie-Hellman, q decisional hidden strong Diffie-Hellman and computational ψ-Diffie-Hellman (see the respective papers for a description of these assumptions).

Scheme	Signature Size	Token-Soundness	Anonymity	Assumptions
PKO-1 [33]	2128	yes	yes	sRSA + DNR
PKO-2 [33]	2048	yes	yes	sRSA + DIV + DNR
YALS [38]	1180	yes	yes	CDH + DLIN
PKO-3 [32]	680	no	yes	q-SDH + DLIN
PKO-4 [32]	580	no	yes	q-SDH + DLIN
HW [19]	510	yes	no	q-HSDH + q-DHSDH
ours	680	yes	yes	ψ-CDH + DLIN

Lastly we note that while delegation of verification is discussed as an extension to the scheme HW, the confirm and disavow protocols defined for the schemes YALS, PKO-3 and PKO-4 make use of the same private key material as signature generation, preventing delegation of verification. Delegation of verification for PKO-1 and PKO-2 is not discussed in [33], but it seems that these schemes can be extended to provide this.

7   Conclusion

We have given an updated definition and security model for convertible undeniable signature schemes which supports delegation of verification, and highlighted a new security property, token soundness, which is not formally captured by existing security models. We then proposed a new convertible undeniable signature scheme. Our scheme is the most efficient scheme in terms of signature size which provably fulfills all security requirements in the standard model, and is furthermore based on weak and natural security assumptions.

References

1. Abe, M., Cui, Y., Imai, H., Kiltz, E.: Efficient hybrid encryption from id-based encryption. Cryptology ePrint Archive, Report 2007/023 (2007),
   http://eprint.iacr.org/
2. Aimani, L.E.: Toward a generic construction of universally convertible undeniable signatures from pairing-based signatures. In: Chowdhury, D.R., Rijmen, V., Das, A. (eds.) INDOCRYPT 2008. LNCS, vol. 5365, pp. 145–157. Springer, Heidelberg (2008)

3. Aimani, L.E.: Toward a generic construction of convertible undeniable signatures from pairing-based signatures. Cryptology ePrint Archive, Report 2009/362 (2009), http://eprint.iacr.org/
4. Aimani, L.E., Vergnaud, D.: Gradually convertible undeniable signatures. In: Katz, J., Yung, M. (eds.) ACNS 2007. LNCS, vol. 4521, pp. 478–496. Springer, Heidelberg (2007)
5. Boneh, D., Franklin, M.K.: Identity-based encryption from the Weil pairing. In: Kilian, J. (ed.) CRYPTO 2001. LNCS, vol. 2139, pp. 213–229. Springer, Heidelberg (2001)
6. Boyar, J., Chaum, D., Damgård, I., Pedersen, T.P.: Convertible undeniable signatures. In: Menezes, A., Vanstone, S.A. (eds.) CRYPTO 1990. LNCS, vol. 537, pp. 189–205. Springer, Heidelberg (1991)
7. Camenisch, J., Shoup, V.: Practical verifiable encryption and decryption of discrete logarithms. In: Boneh, D. (ed.) CRYPTO 2003. LNCS, vol. 2729, pp. 126–144. Springer, Heidelberg (2003)
8. Camenisch, J., Stadler, M.: Proof systems for general statements about discrete logarithms. Technical Report 260, Institute for Theoretical Computer Science, ETH Zurich (March 1997)
9. Chaum, D.: Zero-knowledge undeniable signatures. In: Damgård, I.B. (ed.) EUROCRYPT 1990. LNCS, vol. 473, pp. 458–464. Springer, Heidelberg (1991)
10. Chaum, D., van Antwerpen, H.: Undeniable signatures. In: Brassard, G. (ed.) CRYPTO 1989. LNCS, vol. 435, pp. 212–216. Springer, Heidelberg (1990)
11. Cramer, R. (ed.): EUROCRYPT 2005. LNCS, vol. 3494. Springer, Heidelberg (2005)
12. Cramer, R., Damgård, I., MacKenzie, P.: Efficient zero-knowledge proofs of knowledge without intractability assumptions. In: Imai, H., Zheng, Y. (eds.) PKC 2000. LNCS, vol. 1751, pp. 354–373. Springer, Heidelberg (2000)
13. Damgård, I.B.: Collision free hash functions and public key signature schemes. In: Price, W.L., Chaum, D. (eds.) EUROCRYPT 1987. LNCS, vol. 304, pp. 203–216. Springer, Heidelberg (1988)
14. Damgård, I., Pedersen, T.P.: New convertible undeniable signature schemes. In: Maurer, U.M. (ed.) EUROCRYPT 1996. LNCS, vol. 1070, pp. 372–386. Springer, Heidelberg (1996)
15. Galbraith, S.D., Mao, W.: Invisibility and anonymity of undeniable and confirmer signatures. In: Joye, M. (ed.) CT-RSA 2003. LNCS, vol. 2612, pp. 80–97. Springer, Heidelberg (2003)
16. Gennaro, R., Krawczyk, H., Rabin, T.: RSA-based undeniable signatures. In: Kaliski Jr., B.S. (ed.) CRYPTO 1997. LNCS, vol. 1294, pp. 132–149. Springer, Heidelberg (1997)
17. Gennaro, R., Rabin, T., Krawczyk, H.: Rsa-based undeniable signatures. J. Cryptology 20(3), 394 (2007)
18. Goldreich, O.: Foundations of Cryptography. Cambridge University Press, Cambridge (2001)
19. Huang, Q., Wong, D.S.: New constructions of convertible undeniable signature schemes without random oracles. Cryptology ePrint Archive, Report 2009/517 (2009), http://eprint.iacr.org/
20. Huang, X., Mu, Y., Susilo, W., Wu, W.: A generic construction for universally-convertible undeniable signatures. In: Bao, F., Ling, S., Okamoto, T., Wang, H., Xing, C. (eds.) CANS 2007. LNCS, vol. 4856, pp. 15–33. Springer, Heidelberg (2007)

21. Huang, X., Mu, Y., Susilo, W., Wu, W.: Provably secure pairing-based convertible undeniable signature with short signature length. In: Takagi, T., Okamoto, T., Okamoto, E., Okamoto, T. (eds.) Pairing 2007. LNCS, vol. 4575, pp. 367–391. Springer, Heidelberg (2007)
22. Kurosawa, K., Furukawa, J.: Universally composable undeniable signature. In: Aceto, L., Damgård, I., Goldberg, L.A., Halldórsson, M.M., Ingólfsdóttir, A., Walukiewicz, I. (eds.) ICALP 2008, Part II. LNCS, vol. 5126, pp. 524–535. Springer, Heidelberg (2008)
23. Kurosawa, K., Heng, S.-H.: 3-move undeniable signature scheme. In: Cramer [11], pp. 181–197
24. Kurosawa, K., Takagi, T.: New approach for selectively convertible undeniable signature schemes. In: Lai, X., Chen, K. (eds.) ASIACRYPT 2006. LNCS, vol. 4284, pp. 428–443. Springer, Heidelberg (2006)
25. Laguillaumie, F., Vergnaud, D.: Short undeniable signatures without random oracles: The missing link. In: Maitra, S., Veni Madhavan, C.E., Venkatesan, R. (eds.) INDOCRYPT 2005. LNCS, vol. 3797, pp. 283–296. Springer, Heidelberg (2005)
26. Laguillaumie, F., Vergnaud, D.: Time-selective convertible undeniable signatures. In: Menezes, A. (ed.) CT-RSA 2005. LNCS, vol. 3376, pp. 154–171. Springer, Heidelberg (2005)
27. Michels, M., Petersen, H., Horster, P.: Breaking and repairing a convertible undeniable signature scheme. In: ACM Conference on Computer and Communications Security, pp. 148–152 (1996)
28. Michels, M., Stadler, M.: Efficient convertible undeniable signature schemes (extended abstract). In: SAC 1997, pp. 231–244. Springer, Heidelberg (1997)
29. Miyazaki, T.: An improved scheme of the gennaro-krawczyk-rabin undeniable signature system based on RSA. In: Won, D. (ed.) ICISC 2000. LNCS, vol. 2015, pp. 135–149. Springer, Heidelberg (2001)
30. Monnerat, J., Vaudenay, S.: Generic homomorphic undeniable signatures. In: Lee, P.J. (ed.) ASIACRYPT 2004. LNCS, vol. 3329, pp. 354–371. Springer, Heidelberg (2004)
31. Monnerat, J., Vaudenay, S.: Short 2-move undeniable signatures. In: Nguyên, P.Q. (ed.) VIETCRYPT 2006. LNCS, vol. 4341, pp. 19–36. Springer, Heidelberg (2006)
32. Phong, L.T., Kurosawa, K., Ogata, W.: New dlog-based convertible undeniable signature schemes in the standard model. Cryptology ePrint Archive, Report 2009/394 (2009), http://eprint.iacr.org/
33. Phong, L.T., Kurosawa, K., Ogata, W.: New RSA-based (Selectively) convertible undeniable signature schemes. In: Preneel, B. (ed.) Progress in Cryptology – AFRICACRYPT 2009. LNCS, vol. 5580, pp. 116–134. Springer, Heidelberg (2009)
34. Schuldt, J.C.N., Matsuura, K.: On-line non-transferable signatures revisited. Cryptology ePrint Archive, Report 2009/406 (2009), http://eprint.iacr.org/
35. Schuldt, J.C.N., Matsuura, K.: An Efficient Convertible Undeniable Signature Scheme with Delegatable Verication. Cryptology ePrint Archive, Report 2009/454 (2009), http://eprint.iacr.org/
36. Waters, B.: Efficient identity-based encryption without random oracles. In: Cramer [11], pp. 114–127
37. Yuen, T.H., Au, M.H., Liu, J.K., Susilo, W.: (Convertible) undeniable signatures without random oracles. In: Qing, S., Imai, H., Wang, G. (eds.) ICICS 2007. LNCS, vol. 4861, pp. 83–97. Springer, Heidelberg (2007)
38. Yuen, T.H., Au, M.H., Liu, J.K., Susilo, W.: (convertible) undeniable signatures without random oracles. Cryptology ePrint Archive, Report 2007/386 (2007), http://eprint.iacr.org/

A   Waters' Signature Scheme

Below we recall the signature scheme by Waters [36]. Note that we make use of an asymmetric bilinear map $e : \mathbb{G}_1 \times \mathbb{G}_2 \to \mathbb{G}_T$ whereas the original scheme in [36] was defined using a symmetric bilinear map $e : \mathbb{G}_1 \times \mathbb{G}_1 \to \mathbb{G}_T$.

- **Setup:** Compute $\mathbb{P} = (e, \mathbb{G}_1, \mathbb{G}_2, \mathbb{G}_T, p, \psi) \leftarrow \mathcal{G}(1^k)$, pick $g_2 \in \mathbb{G}_2$ and set $g_1 \leftarrow \psi(g_2)$. Return $par = (\mathbb{P}, g_1, g_2)$.
- **KeyGen :** Given par, pick $\alpha \leftarrow \mathbb{Z}_p$ and $w_2 \leftarrow \mathbb{G}_2$, and set $w_1 \leftarrow g_1^\alpha$. Furthermore, pick $u_0, \ldots, u_n \leftarrow \mathbb{G}_2$, and define $F(m) = u_0 \prod_{i=1}^n u_i^{m_i}$ where m_i is the ith bit of m. Finally set the public key to $pk = (w_1, w_2, u_0, \ldots, u_n)$ and the private key to $sk = w_2^\alpha$. Return (pk, sk).
- **Sign :** Given input (par, sk, m), where $sk = w_2^\alpha$ pick $r \leftarrow \mathbb{Z}_p$, compute $\sigma_1 \leftarrow g_1^r$ and $\sigma_2 \leftarrow \psi(w_2^\alpha F(m)^r)$, and return the signature $\sigma = (\sigma_1, \sigma_2)$.
- **Verify :** Given par, a public key $pk = (w_1, w_2, u_0, \ldots, u_n)$, a message m and a signature $\sigma = (\sigma_1, \sigma_2)$, return **accept** if $e(\sigma_2, g_2) = e(w_1, w_2)e(\sigma_1, F(m))$.

It follows from the proof of security given in [36], that the above signature scheme is unforgeable against a chosen message attack assuming the computational co-Diffie-Hellman problem is hard in $(\mathbb{G}_1, \mathbb{G}_2)$.

B   Proof of Theorem 8

Proof. We assume that an adversary $\mathcal{A}$ breaking the invisibility of the CUS scheme exists. Let **forge** be the event that $\mathcal{A}$ submits a convert or confirm/disavow query (m, σ) where σ is a valid signature on m which was not obtained through a sign query on m. In a successful attack by $\mathcal{A}$, either **forge** or ¬**forge** will occur. In the following we will construct algorithms $\mathcal{B}_1$ and $\mathcal{B}_2$ which will break the strong unforgeability of the scheme if **forge** occurs, and the decisional linear assumption if ¬**forge** occurs and $\mathcal{A}$ is successful, respectively.

Firstly assume that the event **forge** happens. $\mathcal{B}_1$ runs an unforgeability experiment, receives the input (par, pk, vk), and forwards (par, pk) as input to $\mathcal{A}$. While running, $\mathcal{A}$ can ask sign, convert and confirm/disavow queries. $\mathcal{B}_1$ responds to these queries as follows. If $\mathcal{A}$ makes a sign query, $\mathcal{B}_1$ forwards this queries to his own signing oracle, and returns the obtained signature to $\mathcal{A}$. If $\mathcal{A}$ makes a convert or confirm/disavow query (m, σ), $\mathcal{B}_1$ first checks if σ was returned as a response to a sign query on m. If this is not the case, $\mathcal{B}_1$ checks if (m, σ) is valid (using vk), and if so, returns (m, σ) as a forgery and halts. Otherwise, $\mathcal{B}_1$ either returns $tk_\sigma \leftarrow \text{Convert}(par, vk, m, \sigma)$ or $\perp$, or interacts with $\mathcal{A}$ running Confirm or Disavow, depending on the query type and the validity of (m, σ).

At some point, $\mathcal{A}$ outputs a challenge message m^*. As in the invisibility experiment, $\mathcal{B}_1$ flips a random coin $b \leftarrow \{0, 1\}$ and returns a random $\sigma^* \leftarrow \mathcal{S}$ if $b = 0$. Otherwise, $\mathcal{B}_1$ returns σ^* obtained by submitting m^* to his own signing oracle. After receiving σ^*, $\mathcal{A}$ can ask additional sign, convert and confirm/disavow queries which $\mathcal{B}_1$ answers as above. If **forge** happens, it is clear that $\mathcal{B}_1$ succeeds in winning in the unforgeability experiment.

Now assume that `forge` does not happen. $\mathcal{B}_2$ will attempt to solve the decisional linear assumption i.e. $\mathcal{B}_2$ receives $\mathbb{P} = (e, \mathbb{G}_1, \mathbb{G}_2, \mathbb{G}_T, p, \psi)$ and elements $u, v, u^x, v^y, h, h^z \in \mathbb{G}_2$. $\mathcal{B}_2$'s goal is to decide if $z = x + y$. Firstly, $\mathcal{B}_2$ picks a hash function family $\mathcal{H} = \{H_k : \{0,1\}^* \to \mathbb{Z}_p\}$ and an element $g_2 \leftarrow \mathbb{G}_2$, and sets $g_1 \leftarrow \psi(g_2)$ and $par \leftarrow (\mathbb{P}, g_1, g_2, \mathcal{H})$. $\mathcal{B}_2$ then generates a public key by choosing $\alpha \leftarrow \mathbb{Z}_p$ and $w_2 \leftarrow \mathbb{G}_2$, and setting $w_1 \leftarrow g_1^\alpha$, $v_1 \leftarrow u$, $v_2 \leftarrow v$ and $h_{pk} \leftarrow \mathbb{G}_1$. Furthermore, $\mathcal{B}_2$ picks a hash key $k \in \mathcal{K}$ and $d_0, \ldots, d_n \leftarrow \mathbb{Z}_p$, and sets $u_i \leftarrow h^{d_i}$ for $1 \leq i \leq n$, $pk \leftarrow (k, w_1, w_2, v_1, v_2, h_{pk}, u_0, \ldots, u_n)$ and $sk = w_2^\alpha$. Lastly, $\mathcal{B}_2$ runs $\mathcal{A}$ with input (par, pk).

While running, $\mathcal{A}$ can ask sign, convert and confirm/disavow queries which are answered as follows.

- *Sign*: Given a message m, $\mathcal{B}_2$ returns $\sigma = (\psi(v_1)^a, \psi(v_2)^b, \psi(w_2^\alpha F(M)^{a+b}), s) \leftarrow \texttt{Sign}(par, sk, m)$ but remembers the random choices $a, b \leftarrow \mathbb{Z}_p$ and stores (m, σ, a, b).
- *Convert*: Given (m, σ), $\mathcal{B}_2$ checks if σ was returned as a response to a sign query m. If this is not the case, $\mathcal{B}_2$ returns $\perp$ (note that this response is correct when `forge` does not happen). Otherwise, $\mathcal{B}_2$ recalls the random choices a, b used to construct σ, and returns $tk_\sigma = (g_1^a, g_1^b)$.
- *Confirm/Disavow*: Given (m, σ), $\mathcal{B}_2$ simulates the confirm protocol if σ was returned as a response to a sign query on m, but simulates the disavow protocol otherwise. Note that the employed proof systems by Cramer *et al.* [12] can be simulated by rewinding the adversary (see the full version [35] for more details). Furthermore, note that if `forge` does not happen, the confirm protocol will only be simulated for valid signatures, and the disavow protocol only simulated for invalid signatures.

At some stage, $\mathcal{A}$ outputs a challenge message m^*. $\mathcal{B}_2$ constructs a challenge signature by picking $s^* \leftarrow \mathbb{Z}_p$ and computing $t^* \leftarrow H_k(\psi(u^x) || \psi(v^y) || m^*)$, $M^* \leftarrow g_1^{s^*} h_{pk}^{t^*}$ and $\sigma^* \leftarrow (\psi(u^x), \psi(v^y), \psi(w_2^\alpha (h^z)^{d_0 + \sum_{i=1}^n d_i M_i^*}), s^*)$, where (u^x, v^y, h^z) are the elements received in the decisional linear problem. Note that if z is random, then σ^* will be a random element in $\mathbb{G}_1^3 \times \mathbb{Z}_p$, whereas if $z = x + y$, σ^* will be a valid signature on m^* since $(h^z)^{d_0 + \sum_{i=1}^n d_i M_i^*} = (h^{d_0 + \sum_{i=1}^n d_i M_i^*})^{x+y} = (u_0 \prod_{i=1}^n u_i^{M_i^*})^{x+y} = F(M^*)^{x+y}$.

$\mathcal{B}_2$ returns σ^* to $\mathcal{A}$ who can then ask additional sign, convert and confirm/disavow queries, but is not allowed to query σ^* to the convert or confirm/disavow oracle. $\mathcal{B}_2$ answers these queries as above. Eventually, $\mathcal{A}$ outputs a bit b which $\mathcal{B}_2$ forwards as his own solution to the decisional linear problem.

$\mathcal{B}_2$'s simulation of the invisibility experiment for $\mathcal{A}$ is perfect and it is clear that $\mathcal{B}_2$ will solve the decisional linear problem if $\mathcal{A}$ breaks the invisibility of the scheme. $\square$

Certificateless KEM and Hybrid Signcryption Schemes Revisited*

S. Sharmila Deva Selvi, S. Sree Vivek, and C. Pandu Rangan

Theoretical Computer Science Lab,
Department of Computer Science and Engineering,
Indian Institute of Technology Madras, India
{sharmila,svivek,prangan}@cse.iitm.ac.in

Abstract. Often authentication and confidentiality are required as simultaneous key requirements in many cryptographic applications. The cryptographic primitive called signcryption effectively implements the same and while most of the public key based systems are appropriate for small messages, hybrid encryption (KEM-DEM) provides an efficient and practical way to securely communicate very large messages. The concept of certificateless hybrid signcryption has evolved by combining the ideas of signcryption based on tag-KEM and certificateless cryptography. Recently, Lippold et al. [14] proposed a certificateless KEM in the standard model and the first certificateless hybrid signcryption scheme was proposed by Fagen Li et al. [16]. In this paper, we show that [14] is not Type-I CCA secure and [16] is existentially forgeable. We also propose an improved certificateless hybrid signcryption scheme and formally prove the security of the improved scheme against both adaptive chosen ciphertext attack and existential forgery in the appropriate security model for certificateless hybrid signcryption.

Keywords: Certificateless Cryptography, Signcryption, Cryptanalysis, Hybrid Signcryption, Tag-KEM, Bilinear Pairing, Provable Security, Random Oracle Model.

1 Introduction

Certificateless cryptography (CLC) was introduced by Al-Riyami at al. [1] to reduce the trust level of KGC (The trusted third party in CLC is the Key Generation Center, abbreviated as KGC) and thus to find an effective remedy to the key escrow problem in identity based cryptography (IBC). This can be achieved by splitting the private key into two parts; one is generated by the KGC and is known as the partial private key, other one is a user selected secret value. Any cryptographic operations can be done only when both these private key components are available. In CLC, the public key is consists of the identity of

---

* Work supported by Project No. CSE/05-06/076/DITX/CPAN on Protocols for Secure Communication and Computation sponsored by Department of Information Technology, Government of India.

J. Kwak et al. (Eds.): ISPEC 2010, LNCS 6047, pp. 294–307, 2010.

the user and the key derived from the secret value of the corresponding user. The main challenge in building a CLC is to build a system that can resist two types of attacks namely Type-I and Type-II attacks (described later in the paper).

In public key encryption schemes the messages are limited in their length or they should belong to a specific group. Key encapsulation mechanism (KEM) encrypts a key that is used in a symmetric data encapsulation mechanism (DEM) which increases the efficiency over public key encryption. This technique is called as *hybrid encryption*. The definitions and formal treatment of KEM/DEM can be found in [10] and [22]. All the Certificateless Key Encapsulation Mechanism (CL-KEM) schemes [6], [15] till date are generic constructions, i.e. they combine a public key based encryption scheme and an identity based KEM and thus they are very in-efficient. Lippold et al. [14] proposed the first direct construction for a CCA secure CL-KEM in the standard model.

Confidentiality and authenticity of messages are required for secure and authentic message transmission over an insecure channel like internet. Signcryption is the cryptographic primitive that offers both these properties with a very low cost when compared to encrypting and signing a message independently. Zheng [25] introduced the concept of signcryption in 1997 and many signcryption schemes were proposed till date [18,9,7,17,5,8,4,21], to name a few. Baek et al. in [3] gave the formal security model for signcryption and proved the security of [25] in that model. There are two different ways to construct signcryption schemes, one is public key signcryption and other is hybrid signcryption. In a public key signcryption scheme both encryption and signature are in public key setting. A few examples for this type of construct are schemes by An et al. [2], Malone-Mao [19] and Dodis et al.[12]. In a Hybrid signcryption scheme, the signature is in public key setting and encryption is in symmetric key setting, here an one-time secret key which is used in the symmetric key encryption of the message is encrypted by a public key encryption algorithm. The formal security model for a hybrid signcryption scheme was given by Dent [11] and Bjørstad [23].

Our Contribution: Our contribution in this paper is three fold. First, we show that the CL-KEM in [14] is not CCA secure. To the best of our knowledge, there exists only one certificateless hybrid signcryption scheme (CLSC-TKEM) by Fagen Li et al. [16]. We show that the concrete scheme proposed in [16] is existentially forgeable in the security model considered by the authors. Finally, we propose an improved certificateless hybrid signcryption scheme and prove its security in the random oracle model. We have used the same security model of Fagen Li et al. to prove our scheme.

2   Preliminaries

2.1   Certificateless Signcryption Tag-KEM (CLSC-TKEM)

A generic Certificateless Signcryption Tag-KEM scheme consists of the following seven probabilistic polynomial time algorithms:

- **Setup** (κ). Given a security parameter κ, the Key Generation Center (KGC) generates the public parameters *params* and master secret key *msk* of the system.
- **Extract Partial Private Key** (ID_A). Given an identity $ID_A \in_R \{0,1\}^*$ of a user A as input, the KGC computes the corresponding partial private key D_A and gives it to A in a secure way.
- **Generate User Key** (ID_A). Given an identity ID_A as input, this algorithm outputs a secret value x_A and a public key PK_A. This algorithm is executed by the user A to obtain his secret value which is used to generate his full private key and the corresponding public key which is published without certification.
- **Set Private Key** (D_A, x_A). The input to this algorithm are the partial private key D_A and the secret value x_A of a user A. This algorithm is executed by the user A to generate his full private key S_A.
- **Sym** $(ID_A, PK_A, S_A, ID_B, PK_B)$. This is a symmetric key generation algorithm which takes the sender's identity ID_A, public key PK_A, private key S_A, the receiver's identity ID_B and public key PK_B as input. It is executed by the sender A in order to obtain the symmetric key K and an internal state information ω, which is not known to B.
- **Encap** (ω, τ). This is the key encapsulation algorithm which takes a state information ω corresponding to K, an arbitrary tag τ, the sender's identity ID_A, public key PK_A and private key S_A as input. This algorithm is executed by the sender A in order to obtain the encapsulation ψ. The values τ and ψ are sent to B.
- **Decap** $(\psi, \tau, ID_A, PK_A, ID_B, PK_B, S_B)$. In order to obtain the key K encapsulated in ψ, the receiver B runs this algorithm. The input to this algorithm are the encapsulation ψ, a tag τ, the sender's identity ID_A, public key PK_A, the receiver's identity ID_B, public key PK_B and private key S_B. The output of this algorithm is a key K or *invalid* with respect to the validity of ψ.

The following consistency constraint must be satisfied: If $(K, \omega) = Sym(ID_A, PK_A, S_A, ID_B, PK_B)$ and $\psi = Encap(\omega, \tau)$, then $K = Decap(\psi, \tau, ID_A, PK_A, ID_B, PK_B, S_B)$.

2.2   Security Model for CLSC-TKEM

The security notions for certificateless signcryption scheme was first formalized by Barbosa et al. in [4]. A CLSC scheme should satisfy indistinguishability against adaptive chosen ciphertext and identity attacks and existential unforgeability against adaptive chosen message and identity attacks. We describe below the security models to prove the *confidentiality* and *unforgeability* of a CLSC-TKEM scheme. These are the strongest security notions for this problem.

Confidentiality. To prove the confidentiality of CLSC-TKEM scheme, we consider two games "IND-CLSC-TKEM-CCA2-I" and "IND-CLSC-TKEM-CCA2-II". A Type-I adversary $\mathcal{A}_I$ interacts with the challenger $\mathcal{C}$ in the IND-CLSC-TKEM-CCA2-I game and a Type-II adversary $\mathcal{A}_{II}$ interacts with the challenger

$\mathcal{C}$ in the IND-CLSC-TKEM-CCA2-II game. A CLSC-TKEM scheme is indistinguishable against adaptive chosen ciphertext attacks (IND-CLSC-TKEM-CCA2), if no polynomially bounded adversaries $\mathcal{A}_I$ and $\mathcal{A}_{II}$ have non-negligible advantage in both IND-CLSC-TKEM-CCA2-I and IND-CLSC-TKEM-CCA2-II games between $\mathcal{C}$ and $\mathcal{A}_I$, $\mathcal{A}_{II}$ respectively:

IND-CLSC-TKEM-CCA2-I: The following is the interactive game between $\mathcal{C}$ and $\mathcal{A}_I$.

Setup: The challenger $\mathcal{C}$ runs this algorithm to generate the master public and private keys, *params* and *msk* respectively. $\mathcal{C}$ gives *params* to $\mathcal{A}_I$ and keeps the master private key *msk* secret from $\mathcal{A}_I$.

Phase 1: $\mathcal{A}_I$ performs a series of queries in an adaptive fashion in this phase. The queries allowed are given below:

  – *Extract Partial Private Key queries:* $\mathcal{A}$ chooses an identity ID_i and gives it to $\mathcal{C}$. $\mathcal{C}$ computes the corresponding partial private key D_i and sends it to $\mathcal{A}_I$.

  – *Extract Private Key queries:* $\mathcal{A}_I$ produces an identity ID_i and requests the corresponding full private key. If ID_i's public key has not been replaced then $\mathcal{C}$ responds with the full private key S_i. If $\mathcal{A}_I$ has already replaced ID_i's public key, then $\mathcal{C}$ does not provide the corresponding private key to $\mathcal{A}_I$.

  – *Request Public Key queries:* $\mathcal{A}_I$ produces an identity ID_i to $\mathcal{C}$ and requests ID_i's public key. $\mathcal{C}$ responds by returning the public key PK_i for the user ID_i. (First by choosing a secret value if necessary).

  – *Replace Public Key queries:* $\mathcal{A}_I$ can repeatedly replace the public key PK_i corresponding to the user identity ID_i with any value PK_i' of $\mathcal{A}_I$'s choice. The current value of the user's public key is used by $\mathcal{C}$ in any computations or responses to $\mathcal{A}_I$'s queries.

  – *Symmetric Key Generation queries:* $\mathcal{A}_I$ produces a sender's identity ID_A, public key PK_A, the receiver's identity ID_B and public key PK_B to $\mathcal{C}$. The private key of the sender S_A is obtained from the corresponding list maintained by $\mathcal{C}$. $\mathcal{C}$ computes the symmetric key K and an internal state information ω, stores and keeps ω secret from the view of $\mathcal{A}_I$ and sends the symmetric key K to $\mathcal{A}_I$. It is to be noted that $\mathcal{C}$ may not be aware of the corresponding private key if the public key of ID_A is replaced. In this case $\mathcal{A}_I$ provides the private key of ID_A to $\mathcal{C}$.

  – *Key Encapsulation queries:* $\mathcal{A}_I$ produces an arbitrary tag τ, the sender's identity ID_A and public key PK_A, The private key of the sender S_A is known to $\mathcal{C}$. $\mathcal{C}$ checks whether a corresponding ω value is stored previously. If ω exists then $\mathcal{C}$ computes the encapsulation ψ with ω and τ and deletes ω, else returns *invalid*.

  – *Key Decapsulation queries:* $\mathcal{A}_I$ produces an encapsulation ψ, a tag τ, the sender's identity ID_A, public key PK_A, the receiver's identity ID_B and public key PK_B. The private key of the receiver S_B is obtained from the corresponding list maintained by $\mathcal{C}$. $\mathcal{C}$ returns the key K or *invalid* with respect to the validity of ψ. It is to be noted that $\mathcal{C}$ may not be aware of the corresponding private key if the public key of ID_B is replaced. In this case $\mathcal{A}_I$ provides the private key of ID_B to $\mathcal{C}$.

Challenge: At the end of *Phase 1* (which is decided by $\mathcal{A}_I$), $\mathcal{A}_I$ sends to $\mathcal{C}$, a sender identity ID_{A^*} and a receiver identity ID_{B^*} on which $\mathcal{A}_I$ wishes to be challenged. Here, the private key of the receiver ID_{B^*} was not queried in **Phase 1**. Now, $\mathcal{C}$ computes $\langle K_1, \omega^* \rangle$ using $Sym(ID_A, PK_A, S_A, ID_B, PK_B)$ and chooses $K_0 \in_R \mathcal{K}$, where $\mathcal{K}$ is the key space of the CLSC-TKEM scheme. Now $\mathcal{C}$ chooses a bit $\delta \in_R \{0,1\}$ and sends K_δ to $\mathcal{A}_I$. When $\mathcal{A}_I$ receives K_δ, it generates an arbitrary tag τ^* and sends it to $\mathcal{C}$. $\mathcal{C}$ computes the challenge encapsulation ψ^* with ω^* and τ^* and sends ψ^* to $\mathcal{A}_I$.

Phase 2: $\mathcal{A}_I$ can perform polynomially bounded number of queries adaptively again as in *Phase 1* but it cannot make a partial private key extraction query on ID_{B^*} or cannot query for the decapsulation of ψ^*. If the public key of ID_{B^*} is replaced after the **Challenge**, $\mathcal{A}_I$ can ask for the decapsulation of ψ^*.

Guess: $\mathcal{A}_I$ outputs a bit δ' and wins the game if $\delta' = \delta$.

The advantage of $\mathcal{A}_I$ is defined as $Adv^{IND-CLSC-TKEM-CCA2-I}(\mathcal{A}_I) = |2Pr[\delta' = \delta] - 1|$, where $Pr[\delta' = \delta]$ denotes the probability that $\delta' = \delta$.

IND-CLSC-TKEM-CCA2-II: The following is the interactive game between $\mathcal{C}$ and $\mathcal{A}_{II}$.

Setup: The challenger $\mathcal{C}$ runs this algorithm to generate the master public and private keys, *params* and *msk* respectively. $\mathcal{C}$ gives both *params* and *msk* to $\mathcal{A}_{II}$.

Phase 1: $\mathcal{A}_{II}$ performs a series of queries in an adaptive fashion in this phase. The queries allowed are similar to that of the IND-CLSC-TKEM-CCA2-I game except that *Extract Partial Private Key queries:* is excluded because $\mathcal{A}_{II}$ can generate it on need basis as it knows *msk*.

Challenge: At the end of *Phase 1* (which is decided by $\mathcal{A}_{II}$), $\mathcal{A}_{II}$ sends to $\mathcal{C}$, a sender identity ID_{A^*} and a receiver identity ID_{B^*} on which $\mathcal{A}_{II}$ wishes to be challenged. Here, the full private key of the receiver ID_{B^*} was not queried in **Phase 1**. Now, $\mathcal{C}$ computes $\langle K_1, \omega^* \rangle$ using $Sym(ID_A, PK_A, S_A, ID_B, PK_B)$ and chooses $K_0 \in_R \mathcal{K}$, where $\mathcal{K}$ is the key space of the CLSC-TKEM scheme. Now $\mathcal{C}$ chooses a bit $\delta \in_R \{0,1\}$ and sends K_δ to $\mathcal{A}_{II}$. When $\mathcal{A}_{II}$ receives K_δ, it generates an arbitrary tag τ^* and sends it to $\mathcal{C}$. $\mathcal{C}$ computes the challenge encapsulation ψ^* with ω^* and τ^* and sends ψ^* to $\mathcal{A}_{II}$.

Phase 2: $\mathcal{A}_{II}$ can perform polynomially bounded number of queries adaptively again as in *Phase 1* but it cannot make a partial private key extraction query on ID_{B^*} or cannot query for the decapsulation of ψ^*. If the public key of ID_{B^*} is replaced after the **Challenge**, $\mathcal{A}_I$ can ask for the decapsulation of ψ^*.

Guess: $\mathcal{A}_{II}$ outputs a bit δ' and wins the game if $\delta' = \delta$.

The advantage of $\mathcal{A}_{II}$ is defined as $Adv^{IND-CLSC-TKEM-CCA2-II}(\mathcal{A}_{II}) = |2Pr[\delta' = \delta] - 1|$, where $Pr[\delta' = \delta]$ denotes the probability that $\delta' = \delta$.

Existential Unforgeability. To prove the existential unforgeability of CLSC-TKEM scheme, we consider two games "EUF-CLSC-TKEM-CMA-I" and "EUF-CLSC-TKEM-CMA-II". A Type-I forger $\mathcal{F}_I$ interacts with the challenger $\mathcal{C}$ in the EUF-CLSC-TKEM-CMA-I game and a Type-II forger $\mathcal{F}_{II}$ interacts with $\mathcal{C}$ in the EUF-CLSC-TKEM-CMA-II game. A CLSC-TKEM scheme is existentially unforgeable against adaptive chosen message attack (EUF-CLSC-TKEM-CMA), if no polynomially bounded forgers $\mathcal{F}_I$ and $\mathcal{F}_{II}$ have non-negligible advantage in both EUF-CLSC-TKEM-CMA-I and EUF-CLSC-TKEM-CMA-II games between $\mathcal{C}$ and $\mathcal{F}_I$, $\mathcal{F}_{II}$ respectively:

EUF-CLSC-TKEM-CMA-I: The following is the interactive game between $\mathcal{C}$ and $\mathcal{F}_I$:

Setup: The challenger $\mathcal{C}$ runs this algorithm to generate the master public and private keys, *params* and *msk* respectively. $\mathcal{C}$ gives *params* to $\mathcal{F}_I$ and keeps the master private key *msk* secret from $\mathcal{F}_I$.

Training Phase: $\mathcal{F}_I$ performs a series of polynomially bounded number of queries in an adaptive fashion in this phase. The queries allowed are identical to the queries allowed in **Phase 1** of IND-CLSC-TKEM-CCA2-I game.

Forgery: At the end of the *Training Phase* (which is decided by $\mathcal{F}_I$), $\mathcal{F}_I$ sends to $\mathcal{C}$ an encapsulation $\langle \tau^*, \psi^*, ID_{A^*}, ID_{B^*} \rangle$, where ID_{A^*} is the sender identity and ID_{B^*} is the receiver identity. It is to be noted that the partial private key of the sender ID_{A^*} should not be queried and the public key of ID_{A^*} should not be replaced during the **Training Phase** simultaneously. In addition ψ^* should not be the response for any key encapsulation queries by $\mathcal{F}_I$ during the *Training Phase*.

$\mathcal{F}_I$ wins the game if the output of ***Decap***$(\psi^*, \tau^*, ID_{A^*}, PK_{A^*}, ID_{B^*}, PK_{B^*}, S_{B^*})$ is not *invalid*. The advantage of $\mathcal{F}_I$ is defined as the probability with which it wins the EUF-CLSC-TKEM-CMA-I game.

EUF-CLSC-TKEM-CMA-II: The following is the interactive game between $\mathcal{C}$ and $\mathcal{F}_{II}$:

Setup: The challenger $\mathcal{C}$ runs this algorithm to generate the master public and private keys, *params* and *msk* respectively. $\mathcal{C}$ gives both *params* and *msk* to $\mathcal{F}_{II}$.

Training Phase: $\mathcal{F}_{II}$ performs a series of polynomially bounded number of queries in an adaptive fashion in this phase. The queries allowed are identical to the queries allowed in **Phase 1** of IND-CLSC-TKEM-CCA2-II game.

Forgery: At the end of the *Training Phase* (which is decided by $\mathcal{F}_{II}$), $\mathcal{F}_{II}$ sends to $\mathcal{C}$ an encapsulation $\langle \tau^*, \psi^*, ID_{A^*}, ID_{B^*} \rangle$, where ID_{A^*} is the sender identity and ID_{B^*} is the receiver identity. It is to be noted that $\mathcal{F}_{II}$ should not query the secret value x_{A^*} of the sender ID_{A^*} and should not replace the public key of ID_{A^*} during the **Training Phase**. In addition ψ^* should not be the response for any key encapsulation queries by $\mathcal{F}_{II}$ during the *Training Phase*.

$\mathcal{F}_{II}$ wins the game if the output of $\boldsymbol{Decap}(\psi^*, \tau^*, ID_{A^*}, PK_{A^*}, ID_{B^*}, PK_{B^*}, S_{B^*})$ is not *invalid*. The advantage of $\mathcal{F}_{II}$ is defined as the probability with which it wins the EUF-CLSC-TKEM-CMA-II game.

Note: For details on bilinear pairing, Computation Diffie-Hellman Problem (CDH) and Computational Bilinear Diffie-Hellman Problem (CBDH) we refer to [13].

3   Review and Attack of Lippold et al.'s CL-KEM

In this section, we review the CL-KEM scheme of Lippold et al., presented in [14]. We show that the scheme in [14] is not CCA secure.

3.1   Review of the Scheme

This scheme has the following five algorithms.

1. **Setup:** Given a security parameter κ, the KGC performs the following to setup the system:
   - Chooses two groups $\mathbb{G}_1$ and $\mathbb{G}_2$ of prime order p, a bilinear map $\hat{e} : \mathbb{G}_1 \times \mathbb{G}_1 \rightarrow \mathbb{G}_2$, a random generator $g \in \mathbb{G}_1$ and a suitable Water's hash function H, as described in [24].
   - Chooses $u_1, u_2, \alpha \in \mathbb{G}_1$ and computes $z = \hat{e}(g, \alpha)$.
   - The public parameters of the system are $params = \langle \kappa, \mathbb{G}_1, \mathbb{G}_2, p, g, H, u_1, u_2, z \rangle$ and α is the master secret key.
2. **Identity-Based Key Derivation:** Given the master secret key α and the identity $ID \in {0, 1}^n$, the KGC generates an ID-Based private key corresponding to the given identity as follows:
   - Chooses $s \in_R \mathbb{Z}_p^*$ and returns $sk_{ID} = (\alpha H(ID)^s, g^s)$.
3. **User Key Generation:** This algorithm is executed by the user with identity ID, in order to generate his user secret value and the certificateless public key.
   - The user chooses a secret value $x_{ID} \in_R \mathbb{Z}_p^*$.
   - Computes the certificateless public key $\beta_{ID} = z^{x_{ID}}$ and returns $\langle x_{ID}, \beta_{ID} \rangle$.
4. **Encapsulation:** Given the public key β_{ID} of a user with identity ID and a message M, the sender generates an encryption key K and the corresponding encapsulation C as follows:
   - Chooses $r \in_R \mathbb{Z}_p^*$, computes $c_1 = g^r$, $c_2 = H(ID)^r$ and $t = TCR(c_1)$, where TCR is a Target Collision Resistant hash function.
   - Computes $c_3 = (u_1^t u_2)^r$ and $K = \beta_{ID}^r = (z^x)^r \in \mathbb{G}_2$.
   - Sets $C = \langle c_1, c_2, c_3 \rangle \in \mathbb{G}_1^3$.
   - Returns (K, C). (Note that K is the key that is used in a symmetric data encapsulation mechanism (DEM) for the encryption of the message and is not a part of the ciphertext.)

5. **Decapsulation:** Given the secret keys $d_1 = \alpha H(ID)^s$, $d_2 = g^s$ and x_{ID}, and an encapsulation $C = \langle c_1, c_2, c_3 \rangle$, the receiver of the ciphertext executes this algorithm to recover the key K from C as follows:

   - Chooses $r_1, r_2 \in_R \mathbb{Z}_p^*$ and computes $t = TCR(c_1)$.
   - Computes $K = \left(\dfrac{\hat{e}(c_1, d_1(u_1^t u_2)^{r_1} H(ID)^{r_2})}{\hat{e}(c_2, d_2 g^{r_2}) \hat{e}(g^{r_1}, c_3)} \right)^{x_{ID}}$
   - Returns the key K for data decapsulation.

3.2   Attack of Lippold et al.'s CL-KEM

In this section, we show that the CL-KEM by Lippold et al. [14] does not provide confidentiality. During the confidentiality game for Type-I adversary, the adversary is allowed to replace the public key of the receiver. The following attack is possible due to this liberalized constraint on the adversary.

   - Let ID^* be the target identity on which the adversary wishes to be challenged.
   - The adversary chooses $x' \in_R \mathbb{Z}_p^*$.
   - Replaces the public key of ID^* as $\beta'_{ID^*} = \hat{e}(g,g)^{x'}$.
   - The adversary submits ID^* to the challenger as the challenge identity.

Upon receiving the challenge identity ID^*, the challenger generates the challenge encapsulation C^*, the encapsulation key K^* and sends it to the adversary. On receiving $C^* = \langle c_1^*, c_2^*, c_3^* \rangle$ and K^* from the challenger, the Type-I adversary computes the key K' from C^* as follows and distinguishes C^*:

$$K' = \hat{e}(g^{x'}, c_1) = \hat{e}(g^{x'}, g^r) = \hat{e}(g, g)^{x'r} = (\beta'_{ID^*})^r$$

Now, K' is the key corresponding to the encapsulation C^* generated by the challenger. The adversary compares K' with K^*, and returns $b' = 1$ if they are identical, $b' = 0$ otherwise.

4   Review and Attack of Fagen Li et al.'s CLSC-TKEM

In this section we review the CLSC-TKEM scheme of Fagen Li et al, presented in [16]. We also show that the concrete schemes in [16] is existentially forgeable and the definition of the generic scheme is insufficient. We do not review the generic construct in our paper.

4.1   Review of the Scheme

This scheme has the following seven algorithms.

1. **Setup:** Given κ the security parameter, the KGC chooses two groups $\mathbb{G}_1$ and $\mathbb{G}_2$ of prime order q, a bilinear map $\hat{e} : \mathbb{G}_1 \times \mathbb{G}_1 \to \mathbb{G}_2$ and a generator $P \in_R \mathbb{G}_1$. It then chooses a master private key $s \in_R \mathbb{Z}_q^*$, sets a system-wide public key $P_{pub} = sP$ and chooses four cryptographic hash functions defined by $H_1 : \{0,1\}^* \to \mathbb{G}_1$, $H_2 : \{0,1\}^* \to \{0,1\}^n$, $H_3 : \{0,1\}^* \to \mathbb{G}_1$ and $H_4 : \{0,1\}^* \to \mathbb{G}_1$. Here n is the key length of a DEM. The public parameters $Params = \langle \mathbb{G}_1, \mathbb{G}_2, P, \hat{e}, H_1, H_2, H_3, H_4, P_{pub} \rangle$.

2. **Partial Private Key Extract:** Given an identity $ID_A \in \{0,1\}^*$, the KGC does the following to extract the partial private key corresponding to ID_A:
   - Computes $Q_A = H_1(ID_A) \in \mathbb{G}_1$ and the partial private key $D_A = sQ_A$.
3. **Generate User Key:** A user with identity ID_A chooses $x_A \in_R \mathbb{Z}_q^*$ and sets the public key $PK_A = x_A P$.
4. **Set Private Key:** The full private key of the user A is set to be $S_A = (x_A, D_A)$.
5. **Sym** $(ID_A, PK_A, S_A, ID_B, PK_B)$. Given the sender's identity ID_A, public key PK_A, private key S_A, the receiver's identity ID_B and public key PK_B as input, the algorithm produces the symmetric key K as follows:
   - The sender A chooses $r \in_R \mathbb{Z}_q^*$, computes $U = rP$ and $T = \hat{e}(P_{pub}, Q_B)^r$,
   - Computes $K = H_2(U, T, r(PK_B), ID_B, PK_B)$,
   - Outputs K and a set $\omega = \langle r, U, ID_A, PK_A, S_A, ID_B, PK_B \rangle$
6. **Encap** (ω, τ). Given a state information ω and an arbitrary tag τ, the sender A obtains the encapsulation ψ by performing the following:
   - Computes $H = H_3(U, \tau, ID_A, PK_A)$, $H' = H_4(U, \tau, ID_A, PK_A)$ and $W = D_A + rH + x_A H'$.
   - Outputs $\psi = \langle U, W \rangle$.
7. **Decap** $(\psi, \tau, ID_A, PK_A, ID_B, PK_B, S_B)$. Given the encapsulation ψ, a tag τ, the sender's identity ID_A, public key PK_A, the receiver's identity ID_B, public key PK_B and private key S_B the key K is computed by the receiver B as follows:
   - Computes $H = H_3(U, \tau, ID_A, PK_A)$ and $H' = H_4(U, \tau, ID_A, PK_A)$.
   - If $\hat{e}(P_{pub}, Q_A)\hat{e}(U, H)\hat{e}(PK_A, H') \stackrel{?}{=} \hat{e}(P, W)$, computes the value $T = \hat{e}(D_B, U)$ and outputs $K = H_2(U, T, x_B U, ID_B, PK_B)$, otherwise outputs *invalid*.

4.2   Attack of Fagen Li et al.'s CLSC-TKEM

We show in subsection 4.2.1 that the CLSC-TKEM by Fagen Li et al. [16] is existentially forgeable in the security model considered by them and in subsection 4.2.2 we show that the definition of the generic scheme is not sufficient.

4.2.1 Attack on Unforgeability: Fagen Li et al. [16] have claimed that their scheme is existentially unforgeable against both Type-I and Type-II attacks. We show that the scheme does not resist both Type-I and Type-II attacks. It is to be noted that, in the unforgeability games, EUF-CLSC-TKEM-CMA-I and EUF-CLSC-TKEM-CMA-II the corresponding forgers $\mathcal{F}_I$ and $\mathcal{F}_{II}$ have access to the full private key of the receiver B, also, $\mathcal{F}_I$ is not allowed to extract the partial private keys of the sender A and $\mathcal{F}_{II}$ is not allowed to extract the user secret key or replace the sender A's public key. These constraints are maintained in order to ensure insider security.

Attack by Type-I forger $\mathcal{F}_I$: During the EUF-CLSC-TKEM-CMA-I game, the forger $\mathcal{F}_I$ interacts with the challenger $\mathcal{C}$ during the **Training Phase**. $\mathcal{F}_I$ has access to the various oracles offered by $\mathcal{C}$ in addition to it, $\mathcal{F}_I$ has access to the full private key of the receiver too.

- During the **Training Phase** $\mathcal{F}_I$ queries $\mathcal{C}$ for an encapsulation with ID_A as sender and ID_B as receiver with an arbitrary tag τ.
- Here, the private key of ID_A is not queried by $\mathcal{F}_I$ and the corresponding public key is not replaced.
- $\mathcal{C}$ responds with $\psi = \langle U, W \rangle$.

Now, $\mathcal{F}_I$ obtains a forged encapsulation from the encapsulation ψ received during the **Training Phase** for the same tag τ, by performing the following steps:

- Let ID_{B^*} be a user whose full private key S_{B^*} is known to $\mathcal{F}_I$.
- $\mathcal{F}_I$ computes a new key $K' = H_2(U, T', x_{B^*}U, ID_{B^*}, PK_{B^*})$, where $T' = \hat{e}(D_{B^*}, U)$.
- Now, $\psi^* = \langle U, W \rangle$ is a valid encapsulation of the key K' from the sender ID_A to a new receiver ID_{B^*}.

The correctness of the attack can be easily verified because $\boldsymbol{Decap}$ $(\psi^*, \tau, ID_A, PK_A, ID_{B^*}, PK_{B^*}, S_{B^*})$ passes the verification and yields a different key K' as follows.

- Compute $H = H_3(U, \tau, ID_A, PK_A)$ and $H' = H_4(U, \tau, ID_A, PK_A)$. It is to be noted that the computation of H and H' will yield the same value for both ciphertexts ψ and ψ^* because both the computations do not use the receiver identity and public key. Also, the value of U is same in both the ciphertexts.
- The validity check $\hat{e}(P_{pub}, Q_A)\hat{e}(U, H)\hat{e}(PK_A, H') \stackrel{?}{=} \hat{e}(P, W)$ also holds because this verification is also dependent on the sender's identity and public key alone and no receiver component is used explicitly or implicitly.

The value $T^* = \hat{e}(D_{B^*}, U)$ is computed and $K' = H_2(U, T', x_{B^*}U, ID_{B^*}, PK_{B^*})$ is output as the key. Thus ψ^* is a valid forgery with respect to the new key K'.

Attack by Type-II forger $\mathcal{F}_{II}$: The attack by Type-II forger is identical to that of the attack by the Type-I forger $\mathcal{F}_I$ because as mentioned above a Type-II forger $\mathcal{F}_{II}$ also has access to the full private key of the receiver B. The forgery can be done in a similar way as described in ***Attack by Type-I forger*** $\mathcal{F}_I$ because the attack does not involve the user secret value of the sender A, which is not available to the forger $\mathcal{F}_{II}$.

4.2.2 Weakness of the Generic Scheme:
We also point out that the same weakness holds for the generic Certificateless Hybrid Signcryption scheme proposed in [16]. The binding of, the receiver to the signature component and the sender to the encryption component (i.e. the key K which can only be reconstructed by the receiver) of the encapsulation ψ should be emphasized in the generic construct. Since such bindings are missing in the generic scheme, attacks are possible.

5 Improved CLSC-TKEM Scheme (ICLSC-TKEM)

In the preceding section we saw that the CLSC-TKEM scheme proposed by Fagen Li et al. does not withstand chosen message attack. The weakness of the scheme was due to the lack of binding between the receiver identity and the signature generated by the sender. This is the reason, for an encapsulation ψ to act as a valid encapsulation for different keys K_i (for $i = 1$ to n, where n is the number of forged keys) from a single sender to n different receivers. This weakness can be eliminated by making the following changes in the **Sym, Encap** and **Decap** algorithms in Fagen Li et al's [16] scheme.

Remark 1: *It is to be noted that, in the literature, **Generate User Key** algorithm is usually split into two namely: **Set User Secret Value** and **Set Public Key**. In this paper we use the terminology by Fagen Li et al. [16] which clubs both the aforementioned algorithms together but in the proofs we have considered them as two separate oracles.*

Sym $(ID_A, PK_A, S_A, ID_B, PK_B)$. Given the sender's identity ID_A, public key PK_A, private key S_A, the receiver's identity ID_B and public key PK_B as input, the algorithm produces the symmetric key K as follows:

- The sender A chooses $r \in_R Z_q^*$, computes $U = rP$, $T = \hat{e}(P_{pub}, Q_B)^r$ and $K = H_2(U, T, r(PK_B), ID_B, PK_B)$,
- Outputs K and the intermediate information $\omega = (r, U, T, ID_A, PK_A, S_A, ID_B, PK_B)$

Encap (ω, τ). Given a state information ω and an arbitrary tag τ, the sender A obtains the encapsulation ψ by performing the following:

- Computes $H = H_3(U, \tau, T, ID_A, PK_A, ID_B, PK_B)$, $H' = H_4(U, \tau, T, ID_A, PK_A, ID_B, PK_B)$ and $W = D_A + rH + x_A H'$.
- Output $\psi = \langle U, W \rangle$

Remark 2: *Now, it is not possible for $\mathcal{F}_I$ and $\mathcal{F}_{II}$ to generate different forged keys from a sender ID_A, whose secret key is not known to $\mathcal{F}_I$ and $\mathcal{F}_{II}$ because the identity ID_B and the public key PK_B of the receiver is bound to the signature part of the encapsulation ψ which makes it unalterable.*

Decap $(\psi, \tau, ID_A, PK_A, ID_B, PK_B, S_B)$. Given the encapsulation ψ, a tag τ, the sender's identity ID_A, public key PK_A, the receiver's identity ID_B, public key PK_B and private key S_B the key K is computed as follows:

- Computes the value $T = \hat{e}(D_B, U)$, $H = H_3(U, \tau, T, ID_A, PK_A, ID_B, PK_B)$ and $H' = H_4(U, \tau, T, ID_A, PK_A, ID_B, PK_B)$.
- If $\hat{e}(P_{pub}, Q_A)\hat{e}(U, H)\hat{e}(PK_A, H') \stackrel{?}{=} \hat{e}(P, W)$ and outputs $K = H_2(U, T, x_B U, ID_B, PK_B)$, otherwise outputs *invalid*.

6   Security of the Improved CLSC-TKEM Scheme

Proof of Security of ICLSC-TKEM: The security of the improved CLSC-TKEM follows from the theorems in this section. The formal and rigorous proofs for these theorems will be found in the full version of the paper [20].

Theorem 1. *If an IND-ICLSC-TKEM-CCA2-I adversary $\mathcal{A}_I$ has an advantage ϵ against the IND-ICLSC-TKEM-CCA2-I security of the ICLSC-TKEM scheme, asking q_{H_i} ($i = 1, 2, 3, 4$) hash queries to random oracles $\mathcal{O}_{H_i}$ ($i = 1, 2, 3, 4$), q_{ppk} partial private key extract queries and q_{fpk} private key extract queries, then there exist an algorithm $\mathcal{C}$ that solves the CBDH problem with the following advantage*

$$\epsilon' \geq \epsilon \left(1 - \frac{q_{ppk}}{q_{H_1}}\right) \left(1 - \frac{q_{fpk}}{q_{H_1}}\right) \left(\frac{1}{q_{H_1} - (q_{ppk} + q_{fpk})}\right) \left(\frac{1}{q_{H_2}}\right)$$

Theorem 2. *If an IND-ICLSC-TKEM-CCA2-II adversary $\mathcal{A}_{II}$ has an advantage ϵ against the IND-ICLSC-TKEM-CCA2-II security of the ICLSC-TKEM scheme, asking q_{H_i} ($i = 1, 2, 3, 4$) hash queries to random oracles $\mathcal{O}_{H_i}$ ($i = 1, 2, 3, 4$), q_{fpk} full private key extract queries and q_{rpk} replace public key queries, then there exist an algorithm $\mathcal{C}$ that solves the CDH problem with the following advantage*

$$\epsilon' \geq \epsilon \left(1 - \frac{q_{fpk}}{q_{H_1}}\right) \left(1 - \frac{q_{rpk}}{q_{H_1}}\right) \left(\frac{1}{q_{H_1} - (q_{fpk} + q_{rpk})}\right) \left(\frac{1}{q_{H_2}}\right)$$

Theorem 3. *If there exists a forger $\mathcal{F}_I$ with an advantage ϵ against the EUF-ICLSC-TKEM-CMA-I security of the ICLSC-TKEM scheme, asking q_{H_i} ($i = 1, 2, 3, 4$) hash queries to random oracles $\mathcal{O}_{H_i}$ ($i = 1, 2, 3, 4$), q_{ppk} partial private key extract queries and q_{fpk} full private key extract queries, then there exist an algorithm $\mathcal{C}$ that solves the CDH problem with an advantage*

$$\epsilon' \geq \left(\epsilon - \frac{1}{2^{\kappa-1}}\right) \left(1 - \frac{q_{ppk}}{q_{H_1}}\right) \left(1 - \frac{q_{fpk}}{q_{H_1}}\right) \left(\frac{1}{q_{H_1} - (q_{ppk} + q_{fpk})}\right)$$

Theorem 4. *If there exists a forger $\mathcal{F}_I$ with an advantage ϵ against the EUF-ICLSC-TKEM-CMA-I security of the ICLSC-TKEM scheme, asking q_{H_i} ($i = 1, 2, 3, 4$) hash queries to random oracles $\mathcal{O}_{H_i}$ ($i = 1, 2, 3, 4$), q_{fpk} full private key extract queries and q_{rpk} replace public key queries, then there exist an algorithm $\mathcal{C}$ that solves the CDH problem with an advantage*

$$\epsilon' \geq \left(\epsilon - \frac{1}{2^{\kappa-1}}\right) \left(1 - \frac{q_{fpk}}{q_{H_1}}\right) \left(1 - \frac{q_{rpk}}{q_{H_1}}\right) \left(\frac{1}{q_{H_1} - (q_{fpk} + q_{rpk})}\right)$$

7   Conclusion

In this paper, we have showed that the only existing CL-KEM [14] proved in the standard model is not Type-I CCA secure and the only existing certificateless hybrid signcryption scheme of Fagen Li et al.'s [16] is existentially forgeable with respect to both Type-I and Type-II forgers. We have also proposed an improved certificateless hybrid signcryption scheme with the proper binding, that provides adequate security to the scheme. We have proved the improved certificateless hybrid signcryption scheme in the random oracle model.

References

1. Al-Riyami, S.S., Paterson, K.G.: Certificateless public key cryptography. In: Laih, C.-S. (ed.) ASIACRYPT 2003. LNCS, vol. 2894, pp. 452–473. Springer, Heidelberg (2003)
2. An, J.H., Dodis, Y., Rabin, T.: On the security of joint signature and encryption. In: Knudsen, L.R. (ed.) EUROCRYPT 2002. LNCS, vol. 2332, pp. 83–107. Springer, Heidelberg (2002)
3. Baek, J., Steinfeld, R., Zheng, Y.: Formal proofs for the security of signcryption. In: Naccache, D., Paillier, P. (eds.) PKC 2002. LNCS, vol. 2274, pp. 80–98. Springer, Heidelberg (2002)
4. Barbosa, M., Farshim, P.: Certificateless signcryption. In: ACM Symposium on Information, Computer and Communications Security - ASIACCS 2008, pp. 369–372. ACM, New York (2008)
5. Barreto, P.S.L.M., Libert, B., McCullagh, N., Quisquater, J.-J.: Efficient and provably-secure identity-based signatures and signcryption from bilinear maps. In: Roy, B. (ed.) ASIACRYPT 2005. LNCS, vol. 3788, pp. 515–532. Springer, Heidelberg (2005)
6. Bentahar, K., Farshim, P., Malone-Lee, J., Smart, N.P.: Generic constructions of identity-based and certificateless kems. Journal of Cryptology 21(2), 178–199 (2008)
7. Boyen, X.: Multipurpose identity-based signcryption. In: Boneh, D. (ed.) CRYPTO 2003. LNCS, vol. 2729, pp. 383–399. Springer, Heidelberg (2003)
8. Chen, L., Malone-Lee, J.: Improved identity-based signcryption. In: Vaudenay, S. (ed.) PKC 2005. LNCS, vol. 3386, pp. 362–379. Springer, Heidelberg (2005)
9. Chow, S.S.M., Yiu, S.-M., Hui, L.C.K., Chow, K.P.: Efficient forward and provably secure id-based signcryption scheme with public verifiability and public ciphertext authenticity. In: Lim, J.-I., Lee, D.-H. (eds.) ICISC 2003. LNCS, vol. 2971, pp. 352–369. Springer, Heidelberg (2004)
10. Cramer, R., Shoup, V.: Ronald Cramer and Victor Shoup. Design and analysis of practical public-key encryption schemes secure against adaptive chosen ciphertext attack. SIAM Journal on Computing 33(1), 167–226 (2003)
11. Dent, A.W.: Hybrid signcryption schemes with insider security. In: Boyd, C., González Nieto, J.M. (eds.) ACISP 2005. LNCS, vol. 3574, pp. 253–266. Springer, Heidelberg (2005)
12. Dodis, Y., Freedman, M.J., Jarecki, S., Walfish, S.: Versatile padding schemes for joint signature and encryption. In: ACM Conference on Computer and Communications Security - CCS 2004, pp. 344–353. ACM, New York (2004)
13. Dutta, R., Barua, R., Sarkar, P.: Pairing-based cryptographic protocols: A survey. Cryptology ePrint Archive, Report 2004/064 (2004), http://eprint.iacr.org/
14. Nieto, J.G., Lippold, G., Boyd, C.: Efficient certificateless kem in the standard model. Cryptology ePrint Archive, Report 2009/451 (Extended abstract of the paper accepted in ICISC-09) (2009), http://eprint.iacr.org/

15. Huang, Q., Wong, D.S.: Generic certificateless key encapsulation mechanism. In: Pieprzyk, J., Ghodosi, H., Dawson, E. (eds.) ACISP 2007. LNCS, vol. 4586, pp. 215–229. Springer, Heidelberg (2007)
16. Li, F., Shirase, M., Takagi, T.: Certificateless hybrid signcryption. In: Bao, F., Li, H., Wang, G. (eds.) ISPEC 2009. LNCS, vol. 5451, pp. 112–123. Springer, Heidelberg (2009)
17. Libert, B., Quisquater, J.-J.: Efficient signcryption with key privacy from gap diffie-hellman groups. In: Bao, F., Deng, R., Zhou, J. (eds.) PKC 2004. LNCS, vol. 2947, pp. 187–200. Springer, Heidelberg (2004)
18. Libert, B., Quisquater, J.-J.: A new identity based signcryption scheme from pairings. In: IEEE Information Theory Workshop, pp. 155–158 (2003)
19. Malone-Lee, J., Mao, W.: Two birds one stone: Signcryption using RSA. In: Joye, M. (ed.) CT-RSA 2003. LNCS, vol. 2612, pp. 211–225. Springer, Heidelberg (2003)
20. Selvi, S.S.D., Vivek, S.S., Pandu Rangan, C.: Breaking and re-building a certificateless hybrid signcryption scheme. Cryptology ePrint Archive, Report 2009/462 (2009), http://eprint.iacr.org/
21. Selvi, S.S.D., Vivek, S.S., Shukla, D., Rangan Chandrasekaran, P.: Efficient and provably secure certificateless multi-receiver signcryption. In: Baek, J., Bao, F., Chen, K., Lai, X. (eds.) ProvSec 2008. LNCS, vol. 5324, pp. 52–67. Springer, Heidelberg (2008)
22. Shoup, V.: Oaep reconsidered. In: Kilian, J. (ed.) CRYPTO 2001. LNCS, vol. 2139, pp. 239–259. Springer, Heidelberg (2001)
23. BjØrstad, T.E.: Provable security of signcryption. Masters Thesis, Norwegian University of Technology and Science (2005), http://www.nwo.no/tor/pdf/mscthesis.pdf
24. Waters, B.: Efficient identity-based encryption without random oracles. In: Cramer, R. (ed.) EUROCRYPT 2005. LNCS, vol. 3494, pp. 114–127. Springer, Heidelberg (2005)
25. Zheng, Y.: Digital signcryption or how to achieve cost (Signature & encryption) << cost(Signature) + cost(Encryption). In: Kaliski Jr., B.S. (ed.) CRYPTO 1997. LNCS, vol. 1294, pp. 165–179. Springer, Heidelberg (1997)

A Deniable Group Key Establishment Protocol in the Standard Model*

Yazhe Zhang, Kunpeng Wang, and Bao Li

State Key Laboratory of Information Security
Graduate University of Chinese Academy of Sciences, Beijing 100049, China
{yzzhang,kpwang,lb}@is.ac.cn

Abstract. We propose a deniable group key establishment protocol in the standard model. In a deniable group key establishment protocol, the transcript of the protocol session can not be used to prove the involvement of the participant in the protocol session. In other words, the participant can deny that she has joined in the protocol session which she has actually joined in. We figure out that the deniable group key establishment protocol should has the group deniable authentication characteristic, which implies authentication in the protocol execution and deniability after the protocol execution. We give a new definition of the group key establishment deniability in this paper. It is an extension of the definition given by Jens-Matthias Bohli and Rainer Steinwandt. We construct our deniable group key establishment protocol by using a variant of Schnorr's zero-knowledge identification scheme and Burmester's group key establishment protocol.

Keywords: group key establishment, group deniable authentication, deniability, standard model.

1 Introduction

Group key establishment(GKE) protocols allow $n \geq 2$ participants to establish a secret key for the encrypted communication. For the purpose of self-protection, we sometimes wish to deny that we have ever joined in some GKE session before. Formally, the protocol transcript can not be used to prove the involvement of us in the protocol by someone else, possibly by one or several other participants. We call GKE protocols with this characteristic deniable group key establishment(DGKE) protocols. Here we introduce the *group key establishment deniability* characteristic which is proposed by J-M. Bohli and R. Steinwandt[7]. Assuming that we run a key establishment protocol among a group of participants $\mathcal{U} = \{U_1, U_2, \cdots, U_l\}$, *deniability* means that the transcript of some key establishment communication is not able to prove that some participant $U_i \in \mathcal{U}$

---

* Supported by the National Natural Science Foundation of China (No.60673073 and No.60970153) and the National Basic Research Program of China(973 project) (No.2007CB311201).

has been involved in this key establishment session. More specifically, any subset participants of $\mathcal{P} \subset \mathcal{U}$ is not able to output a transcript to prove that some protocol participant $U_a \in \mathcal{U} \backslash \mathcal{P}$ has been involved in this key establishment session. We figure out that the GKE protocol should also be an authenticated protocol. The participant in GKE should authenticate herself to the other participants in the protocol execution. But she could deny the involvement after the protocol execution. So the deniability characteristic in GKE contains two seemingly contrary characteristics: authentication in the execution and deniability after the execution. We call it group deniable authentication.

The concept of *plausible deniability* in two party's case has been widely adopted in the key exchange protocols, in particular, in IKEv2 [17] and JFK [2]. Krawczyk [27] has proposed a variety of SIGMA protocols which satisfy some plausible partial deniability assuming key-aware derivation. Mao and Paterson[28] have analyzed several different degrees of plausible deniability and have proposed key establishment protocols achieving deniability by using identity-based techniques. Boyd, Mao and Paterson[9] have discussed how to achieve deniable authentication for the internet key exchange by using a construction method of Canetti and Krawczyk[15]. New problems occur in the GKE situation, insider attacks, conspiracy attacks etc.([24][11][12][13]). Bohli and Steinwandt[7] have given a definition of deniability in the group key establishment framework and a concrete deniable key establishment protocol in the Random Oracle model.

Organization. In section 2, we present the security model and the deniability model we adopted. The security model is based on Bresson, Chevassut, Pointcheval and Quisquater [10]. The deniability model is based on Bohli and Steinwandt[7]. Also we figure out that a DGKE protocol should have two seemingly contrary characteristics: authentication in the execution and deniability after the execution. Then we propose a new deniability definition for the group deniable authentication characteristic. The new definition is an extension of the original deniability definition of Bohli and Steinwandt[7]. In section 3, we propose our deniable group key establishment protocol along with the key secrecy proof and the deniability proof. All the proofs are in the standard model.

2 Group Key Establishment: Modeling Security and Modeling Deniability

2.1 Modeling Security of the Group Key Establishment Protocol

Our security model is based on Bresson's GKE model [10], which has been widely used to analyze the security of group key establishment protocols. It explicitly defined notions of security for both passive and active adversaries.

Protocol Participants. We assume for simplicity that a polynomial-size set $\mathcal{U} = \{U_1, U_2, \cdots, U_l\}$ of players who want to participate in a group key establishment protocol Γ. Each protocol participant $U \in \mathcal{U}$ is able to execute a polynomial number of protocol instances Π_U^s in parallel. We define a symbol **pid** to denote the group of instances that want to establish a secret key.

Long-Live Keys. We let LL_u to denote the long-live key pair (PK_i/SK_i) that each participant $U \in \mathcal{U}$ holds. In the initialization phase, a trusted LL-key generator $\mathcal{G}(1^k)$ generates the LL-key LL_u for each participant U and assigns it to U.

Session IDS. We let **sid** to denote the unique session identifier of a protocol execution. Each participant should get the same **sid** when a protocol execution is accepted.

Session Keys. We let **sk** to denote the secret key which is established by a protocol execution. Each participant should get the same **sk** when a protocol execution is accepted. The session key **sk** should be semantically secure to the outside adversary.

Communication network. The network over which the participants communicate is a broadcast network and arbitrary point-to-point communication among the participants is available.

Accepting. When an instance Π_U^s has enough information to compute the session key **sk**, it accepts and computes the **sk** and the **sid**.

Adversary model. The adversary can completely control all the communication over the network. She may monitor, delay, suppress, modify or insert messages at will. We model the adversary's behavior by the following *oracles*:

- **Send**(U_i, s_i, M). This oracle query sends the message M to the instance $\Pi_i^{s_i}$ and returns the reply generated by this instance.
- **Reveal**(U_i, s_i). This oracle query returns the session key $\mathbf{sk}_i^{s_i}$ to the adversary.
- **Corrupt**(U_i). This oracle query returns the long-live secret key SK_i of U_i to the adversary.
- **Test**(U_i, s_i). This oracle query is allowed only once at any time during the adversary's execution. On this query, a random bit b is generated. If b equals to 1, the **Test** oracle outputs the session key $\mathbf{sk}_i^{s_i}$; if b equals to 0, the **Test** oracle outputs an uniformly chosen random session key. The adversary guesses a bit b'. If b equals to b', we say that the adversary win in the **Test** oracle query.

Partnering. Partnering is defined via **sid** and **pid**. It is defined as follows:

Definition 1. *Two instances* $\Pi_i^{s_i}, \Pi_j^{s_j}$ *are partnered if* $\mathbf{sid}_i^{s_i} = \mathbf{sid}_j^{s_j}$ *and* $\mathbf{pid}_i^{s_i} = \mathbf{pid}_j^{s_j}$.

Freshness. Freshness is used to denote that the **Test** oracle must be queried only on those clean instances, who hold a key which is not known to the adversary. An instance $\Pi_i^{s_i}$ is called *fresh* if neither of the following two conditions hold:

- For some $U_j \in \mathbf{pid}_i^{s_i}$, a **Corrupt**$(U_j)$ query has been executed before.
- A **Reveal**(U_j, s_j) query has been executed for some accepted instance $\Pi_j^{s_j}$ with $U_j \in \mathbf{pid}_i^{s_i}$.

Key Secrecy. We define the event **Succ** indicating that the adversary $\mathcal{A}$ queries the **Test** oracle on a fresh instance $\Pi_i^{s_i}$, and $\mathcal{A}$ wins in this **Test** query.

For any PPT (probabilistic polynomial time) adversary $\mathcal{A}$, the advantage of $\mathcal{A}$ in attacking protocol Γ is defined as

$$Adv_{\mathcal{A}} := |2 \cdot \Pr[\textbf{Succ}] - 1| \; .$$

Definition 2. *We call a group key establishment protocol Γ ε-secure if for any PPT adversary $\mathcal{A}$, there exists such inequation $\mathrm{Adv}_{\mathcal{A}} \leq \varepsilon$. If ε is negligible, we claim that this group key establishment protocol is a secure group key establishment protocol.*

2.2   Modeling Deniability of the Group Key Establishment Protocol

Deniability of the group key establishment. It implies two meanings when saying that a group key establishment protocol is deniable. The first one is the authentication in the execution characteristic. In the protocol execution, a participant should authenticate herself to all the other participants. In other words, the participant who is running beyond this protocol should ascertain about with whom she is communicating. No one can personate someone else in an acceptable protocol execution. The second one is the deniability after the execution characteristic. It guarantees that the participants of the deniable group key establishment session are able to deny that they have ever joined in this session. Bohli has given a definition of the group deniability [7]. But his definition only concentrated on the deniability after the execution characteristic. We figure out that a deniable group key establishment protocol should have both of the two characteristics. We call it group deniable authentication. We propose a new definition for the deniability of the group key establishment protocol which formally defines the group deniable authentication characteristic.

Assuming that there exists an attacker $\mathcal{A}$ who wants to break the group deniable authentication characteristic of the DGKE protocol which executes among a group of participants $\mathcal{P} = \{U_1, U_2, \ldots, U_n\}$, deniability of the DGKE is formally defined by using two games between the attacker and a hypothetical *challenger*. The *challenger* can simulate the protocol execution by using two algorithms Sim and Sim^*.

First we define the **REAL** game:

1. The *challenger* generates a group of key pairs $\{(PK_i, SK_i)\}$ by running the key generation algorithm $\mathcal{G}(1^k)$.
2. The attacker $\mathcal{A}$ is invoked with the input of all the public keys $\{PK_i\}$. $\mathcal{A}$ can query two oracles:

   - A **Corrupt** oracle that takes an input of U_i and returns SK_i.
   - A **Challenge** oracle that takes no input. If $\mathcal{A}$ makes a **Challenge** query, the *challenger* invokes a simulator Sim with the inputs of all the public keys $\{PK_i\}$. Sim has the access to the **Send** oracle. Sim simulates an execution of the group key establishment protocol by querying the **Send**

oracle. This simulation is actually a real protocol execution. In the end of this execution, the **Challenge** oracle returns all the simulation of the protocol execution communication transcript to $\mathcal{A}$.

$\mathcal{A}$ terminates and outputs a bitstring x.

The **FAKE** game is defined as:

1. The *challenger* generates a group of key pairs $\{(PK_i, SK_i)\}$ by running the key generation algorithm $\mathcal{G}(1^k)$. The *challenger* also generates and maintains an empty MemoList.
2. The attacker $\mathcal{A}$ is invoked with the input of all the public keys $\{PK_i\}$. $\mathcal{A}$ can query two oracles:

   - A **Corrupt** oracle that takes an input of U_i and returns SK_i. If $\mathcal{A}$ makes a **Corrupt** query to U_i, the oracle returns SK_i to $\mathcal{A}$ and adds SK_i to the MemoList.
   - A **Challenge** oracle. If $\mathcal{A}$ makes a **Challenge** query, the *challenger* invokes Sim^* with all the public keys $\{PK_i\}$ and the MemoList to simulate an execution of the group key establishment protocol. Sim^* can not query the **Send** oracle. This simulation can not be a real protocol execution except that all the U_i have been corrupted before. It may only look like a real protocol execution. In the end of this execution, the **Challenge** oracle returns all the simulation of the protocol execution communication transcript to $\mathcal{A}$.

$\mathcal{A}$ terminates and outputs a bitstring x.

Definition 3. (Deniability for the group key establishment) *We say that a group key establishment protocol is deniable if*

1. *(Authentication in the execution) In the execution of the protocol, a principal $U_a \in \mathcal{P}$ unforgeably authenticates herself to all the others participants.*
2. *(Deniability after the execution) For all the polynomial-time attacker $\mathcal{A}$, there exists a protocol simulator Sim^* such that for all the polynomial time algorithms Dist the advantage:*

$$|Pr[Dist(x) = 1|\mathcal{A} \quad plays \quad \textbf{REAL}] - Pr[Dist(x) = 1|\mathcal{A} \quad plays \quad \textbf{FAKE}]|$$

is negligible as a function of the security parameter.

3   A Deniable Group Key Establishment Protocol

In this section, we propose a deniable group key establishment protocol in the standard model. The protocol is based on Burmester and Desmedt's group key establishment protocol [14] and Schnorr's zero-knowledge identification scheme [31].

3.1   Protocol Description and Design Rationale

The proposed protocol is summarized in Table 1. In our protocol, all the protocol instances perform an identical role, which means they do analogous computations. So we can concentrate on one instance $\Pi_i^{s_i}$ that is initialized with $\text{pid}_i^{s_i} = \{\Pi_1^{s_1}, \Pi_2^{s_2}, \ldots, \Pi_n^{s_n}\}$. For the sake of readability, we omit the upper index s_i in the protocol description for instance $\Pi_i^{s_i}$. We give a simple description of the protocol from the view of one instance Π_i of participant U_i in Table 1. The meanings of the symbols are presented bellow:

- G is a cyclic group of prime order q with a generator g such that the Decisional Diffie-Hellman assumption holds in G.
- $H(\cdot) : \{0,1\}^* \rightarrow \{0,1\}^t$ denotes a target collision-free hash function.
- $F(\cdot) : \{0,1\}^* \rightarrow \{0,1\}^k$ denotes a pseudorandom function ensemble.
- $\xleftarrow{R}$ denotes a random choice with uniform distribution.
- $\|$ denotes a simple conjoin of two bitstrings.
- The indices are to be understood mod n, i.e., $y_n = y_0$ and $y_{n+1} = y_1$.

Table 1. A deniable group key establishment protocol

	Protocol for instance Π_i of principal U_i
Round 1: Compute	$r_i \xleftarrow{R} \mathbb{Z}_q,\, r_i' \xleftarrow{R} \mathbb{Z}_q,\, y_i = g^{r_i},\, z_i = g^{r_i'}$
Broadcast	$M_i^1 = (y_i, z_i, U_i)$
Round 2: Compute	$X_i = (y_{i+1}/y_{i-1})^{r_i}$
	$\text{sid}_i = H(\text{pid}_i\|y_1\|\cdots\|y_n\|z_1\|\cdots\|z_n)$
Broadcast	$M_i^2 = (X_i, \text{sid}_i, U_i)$
Round 3: Compute	$\sigma_i = (y_{i-1})^{n r_i} \cdot X_i^{n-1} \cdot X_{i+1}^{n-2} \cdots X_{i+n-2}$
Session key	$\text{sk}_i = F_{\sigma_i}(\text{sid}_i\|1)$
	$c_i = F_{\sigma_i}(\text{sid}_i\|2)(\text{mod } q)$
	$d_i = r_i' - c_i \alpha_i (\text{mod } q)$
Broadcast	$M_i^3 = (d_i, U_i)$
Verify	$g^{d_j}(PK_j)^{c_i} = z_j$ for all $j \in \{1,\ldots,n\} \setminus \{i\}$

The initialization phase. The key generation algorithm $\mathcal{G}(1^k)$ generates a (PK_i/SK_i) key pair (g^{α_i}/α_i) with $\alpha_i \in \mathbb{Z}_q$ for each U_i. Then it delivers $SK_i = \alpha_i$ to U_i over a secure channel and broadcasts all the $\{PK_i = g^{\alpha_i}\}$.

Round 1. Each instance Π_i uniformly chooses two random values $r_i \xleftarrow{R} \mathbb{Z}_q$, $r_i' \xleftarrow{R} \mathbb{Z}_q$ as its secret number. Then it computes $y_i = g^{r_i}, z_i = g^{r_i'}$, and broadcasts $M_i^1 = (y_i, z_i, U_i)$.

Round 2. After having received all the $M_j^1(j \neq i)$ messages, instance Π_i computes $X_i = (y_{i+1}/y_{i-1})^{r_i}$ and the session identifier
$\mathrm{sid}_i = H(\mathrm{pid}_i||y_1||\cdots||y_n||z_1||\cdots||z_n)$. Then Π_i broadcasts $M_i^2 = (X_i, \mathrm{sid}_i, U_i)$.

Round 3. After having received all the $M_j^2(j \neq i)$ messages, instance Π_i checks if $\mathrm{sid}_j = \mathrm{sid}_i$ for all the other instances $\Pi_j(j \neq i)$. If so, it computes $\sigma_i = (y_{i-1})^{nr_i} \cdot X_i^{n-1} \cdot X_{i+1}^{n-2} \cdots X_{i+n-2}$, the session key $\mathrm{sk}_i = F_{\sigma_i}(\mathrm{sid}_i||1)$, $c_i = F_{\sigma_i}(\mathrm{sid}_i||2)(\mathrm{mod}\ q)$, and $d_i = r_i' - c_i\alpha_i(\mathrm{mod}\ q)$. Then Π_i broadcasts $M_i^3 = (d_i, U_i)$. Otherwise, it rejects.

The verification phase. After having received all the $M_j^3(j \neq i)$ messages, Π_i verifies if all the equations $g^{d_j}(PK_j)^{c_i} = z_j$ are satisfied for all the other instances $\Pi_j(j \neq i)$. If all the equations are satisfied, Π_i accepts with sk_i as its session key and sid_i as its session identifier. Otherwise it rejects.

The correctness of the protocol is straightforward. One can easily check that after a correct execution of the protocol, all the participants will accept with the same session key **sk**, the same session identifier **sid** and the same partners **pid**.

3.2   Deniability Analysis

Lemma 1. *The protocol described in Table 1 is a deniable group key establishment protocol in the sense of Def. 3.*

We need to prove the authentication in the execution characteristic and the deniability after the execution characteristic for the proof of Lemma 1.

3.2.1   Authentication in the Execution

Lemma 2. *Supposing that the Decisional Diffie-Hellman assumption holds in $G = <g>$, then with message M_a^3, a participant $U_a \in \mathcal{P}$ unforgeably authenticates herself to all the other participants in the protocol execution.*

Proof. Suppose that there exists an adversary $\mathcal{A}$ who wants to break Lemma 2 and let Adv_{DDH} denote the negligible probability to break the DDH assumption in G.

Except that $\mathcal{A}$ has corrupted all the others participants, σ_i is a random value with uniform distribution in G. The proof is analogous to the proof of proposition 1 (the reader can find proposition 1 in section 3.3). So c_i is a random value with uniform distribution in $\{0,1\}^k$ with $F(\cdot)$ being a pseudorandom function. In U_a's view, with message M_a^3, this authentication scheme is identical with the authentication protocol proposed by Schnorr [31]. It is actually a proof of knowledge in the sense of Feige [19]. So $\mathcal{A}$ is not able to give such a proof for a participant U_a except that $\mathcal{A}$ has made a **Corrupt** query to U_a before. Analogous to proposition 1 we have

$$\mathrm{Pr}[\textbf{Forge}] \leq n \cdot Adv_{DDH} \ . \qquad \square$$

3.2.2   Deniability after the Execution

Proof. We need to construct a protocol simulator Sim^* as described in Definition 3 and define the **FAKE** game for the proof. Supposing that there exists an algorithm Sim as described in the **REAL** game, we can use Sim as a black-box to construct Sim^* required in the **FAKE** game.

In the **FAKE** game, the *challenger* first generates a group of key pairs $\{(PK_i, SK_i)\}$ by running the key generation algorithm $\mathcal{G}(1^k)$. The *challenger* also generates and maintains an empty MemoList. The *challenger* claims that it is a **REAL** game and invokes $\mathcal{A}$ to attack it. $\mathcal{A}$ is invoked with the input of all the public keys $\{PK_i\}$ and can query two oracles **Corrupt** and **Challenge**.

If $\mathcal{A}$ makes a **Corrupt**(U_i) query, the *challenger* returns SK_i to $\mathcal{A}$ and records SK_i in the MemoList.

If $\mathcal{A}$ makes a **Challenge** query, the *challenger* invokes Sim^* to simulate an execution of the protocol. Sim^* simulates the **Send** oracle and invokes Sim with $\{PK_i\}$ and the simulated **Send** oracle to simulate the execution.

In the beginning, Sim^* first chooses all the $r_i \xleftarrow{R} \mathbb{Z}_q$ and computes all the y_i, c_i ahead of schedule for all the participants. Then Sim^* records all the r_i, y_i, c_i in the MemoList.

If Sim makes a **Send**(U_i, s_i, M_i^0) query, Sim^* checks the MemoList to find y_i. Once Sim^* needs to choose r_i' for the computation of z_i, it first checks the MemoList to see if SK_i is in it. If the answer is "yes", Sim^* chooses $r_i' \xleftarrow{R} \mathbb{Z}_q$, and computes $z_i = g^{r_i'}$ honestly; if the answer is "no", Sim^* first chooses $d_i \xleftarrow{R} \mathbb{Z}_q$, records d_i in the MemoList and computes $z_i = g^{d_i}(PK_i)^{c_j}$. Then Sim^* returns the value $M_i^1 = (y_i, z_i, U_i)$ to Sim.

If Sim makes a **Send**(U_i, s_i, M_i^1) query, Sim^* computes all the $X_i = \left(\frac{y_{i+1}}{y_{i-1}}\right)^{r_i}$, $\text{sid}_i = H(\text{pid}_i||y_1||\cdots||y_n||z_1||\cdots||z_n)$. Then Sim^* returns the value $M_i^2 = (X_i, \text{sid}_i, U_i)$ to Sim.

If Sim makes a **Send**(U_i, s_i, M_i^2) query, Sim^* computes sk_i honestly and checks the MemoList to find c_i. Once Sim^* needs to compute d_i, it first checks the MemoList to see if SK_i is in it. If "yes", Sim^* computes d_i from $d_i = r_i' - c_i\alpha_i(\text{mod } q)$ honestly; if "no", Sim^* checks the MemoList to find the value d_i. Then Sim^* returns the value $M_i^3 = (d_i, U_i)$ to Sim. Now we can see that all the values d_j that Sim^* returned will always pass the verification $(g^{d_j}(PK_j)^{c_i} = z_j)$ no matter U_j is corrupted or not. So in Sim's view, this game will be identical with a real protocol execution.

Once Sim outputs a transcript, Sim^* uses it as its own output. Because Sim was used with an indistinguishable simulation of the instances it interacted with, the output of Sim in this game (which is used as the output of Sim^*) must be indistinguishable from Sim's output in the **REAL** game. So there exists no polynomial time algorithm Dist that can distinguish which game $\mathcal{A}$ played with non-negligible probability. □

3.3   Security Analysis

Lemma 3. *Supposing that the DDH assumption holds in $G =< g >$, the protocol described in Table 1 is a secure group key establishment in the sense of Def. 2.*

Proof. Let $\mathcal{A}$ be an adversary who is allowed at most q_s queries to the **Send** oracle and at most q_r queries to the **Reveal** oracle. Moreover, let Adv_{DDH}, $Adv_{\mathcal{F}}$ be the by assumption negligible probabilities to break the DDH assumption and to distinguish a pseudorandom function ensemble from an uniform function ensemble.

Let **Forge** be the event that the adversary succeeds in forging the message of Round 3 M_a^3 for an uncorrupted participant U_a such that it is accepted by an instance of an honest user U_j. Lemma 2 guarantees that **Forge** only occurs with negligible probability.

$$\Pr[\mathbf{Forge}] \leq n \cdot Adv_{DDH} \ .$$

Let **Repeat** be the event that an instance chooses a r_i that was used before by any other instance for computing $y_i = g^{r_i}$ in round 1. There are at most q_s used oracles that may have chosen a nonce r_i and thus **Repeat** can only happen with a probability

$$\Pr[\mathbf{Repeat}] \leq \frac{(q_s)^2}{2 \cdot q} \ .$$

Let $\Pr[Succ]$ be the success probability for adversary $\mathcal{A}$ to win in the **Test** oracle query. We take the protocol execution as a game between a simulator Sim and an adversary $\mathcal{A}$. We construct a sequence of games with slightly modified protocols $\Gamma_0, \Gamma_1, \ldots$ from the original protocol Γ and bound the difference of the success probabilities for $\mathcal{A}$ to win in the **Test** query between each two adjacent games. In the end, we will be able to derive the desired negligible upper bound on $\Pr[Succ]$. Let $Succ_{\Gamma_i}$ denote the probability for $\mathcal{A}$ to win in the **Test** query in protocol Γ_i.

Game Γ_0: In Γ_0 Sim simulates the instances and the oracles faithfully. This simulation is exactly the same as a real protocol execution. There is no difference for the adversary to win in game Γ_0 or in a real protocol execution. So we have

$$Succ_{\Gamma_0} = \Pr[Succ] \ .$$

Game Γ_1: In Γ_1 the simulator stops the simulation as soon as one of the events **Forge** or **Repeat** occurs. So we have

$$|Succ_{\Gamma_1} - Succ_{\Gamma_0}| \leq \Pr[\mathbf{Forge}] + \Pr[\mathbf{Repeat}] \ .$$

Game Γ_2: Γ_2 differs from Γ_1 in the simulation of the **Send** oracle. On a **Send**(U_i, s_i, M_j^1) query, which takes the input of the broadcast message of round 1 and then executes round 2 to compute M_i^2, the simulator checks if all the instances in $\text{pid}_i^{s_i}$ are uncorrupted and all the messages M_j^1 were unmodified delivered to $\Pi_i^{s_i}$. If so, the simulator chooses two random values $\omega_i \xleftarrow{R} \mathbb{Z}_q, \omega_i' \xleftarrow{R} \mathbb{Z}_q$ and computes $X_i = g^{\omega_i}/g^{\omega_i'}$ instead of computing it from $X_i = (y_{i+1}/y_{i-1})^{r_i}$.

Also on a **Send**(U_i, s_i, M_j^2) query, which takes the input of the broadcast message of round 2 and executes round 3 to compute M_j^3. The simulator checks if all the instances in $\text{pid}_i^{s_i}$ are uncorrupted and all the messages M_j^2 were unmodified delivered to $\Pi_i^{s_i}$. If so, the simulator chooses $\sigma_i \xleftarrow{R} \mathbb{G}_q$ instead of computing it from $\sigma_i = (y_{i-1})^{nr_i} \cdot X_i^{n-1} \cdot X_{i+1}^{n-2} \cdots X_{i+n-2}$.

Proposition 1. *An adversary $\mathcal{A}$ who can distinguish Γ_2 and Γ_1 can be used to break the DDH assumption. And we have the probability inequation:*

$$|Succ_{\Gamma_2} - Succ_{\Gamma_1}| \leq n \cdot Adv_{DDH} .$$

n is the number of principals that has been involved in the protocol.

The core of the group key establishment we used is an adaptation of the protocol by M. Burmester and Y. Desmedt in [14]. They gave a simple proof of the key secrecy of their protocol based on the DDH assumption. But they claimed that n is even in their proof. We will give a new proof in the last part of this paper. The new proof is an extension of the original proof in [14] such that n could be either even or odd. The new proof is based on the DDH assumption too.

Game Γ_3: Γ_3 differs from Γ_2 in the simulation of the **Send** oracle. On a **Send**(U_i, s_i, M_j^2) query, which takes the input of the broadcast message of round 2 and executes round 3 to compute M_j^3. The simulator checks if all the instances in $\text{pid}_i^{s_i}$ are uncorrupted and all the messages M_j^2 were unmodified delivered to $\Pi_i^{s_i}$. If so, The simulator chooses $\text{sk}_i \xleftarrow{R} \{0,1\}^k$, $c_i^* \xleftarrow{R} \{0,1\}^k, c_i = c_i^*(\text{mod } q)$ instead of computing it from $\text{sk}_i = F_{\sigma_i}(\text{sid}_i\|1)$ and $c_i = F_{\sigma_i}(\text{sid}_i\|2)(\text{mod } q)$. Note that now the index σ_i is already a random value, so the probability that $\mathcal{A}$ guesses it correctly is negligible. And we have

Proposition 2. *An adversary $\mathcal{A}$ who can distinguish Γ_3 and Γ_2 can be used to distinguish a pseudorandom fucntion ensemble from an uniform function ensemble. And we have the probability inequation:*

$$|Succ_{\Gamma_3} - Succ_{\Gamma_2}| \leq min\{q_s, q_r\} \cdot Adv^F .$$

Proof. Note that if the adversary has not made any **Reveal** query, there will be no difference between Γ_2 and Γ_3 in the adversary's view. If the adversary has made a **Reveal** query, σ_i is already an uniformly chosen value in Γ_2. The adversary knows nothing about it. According to the definition of the pseudorandom function ensemble, we have the proposition 2. □

Now that the session key sk_i is a random value which is independent of any other value in the protocol execution. The adversary's success probability in the **Test** query is only $1/2$.

Putting all these inequations together we get:

$$\Pr[Succ] = Succ_{\Gamma_0} \leq \frac{1}{2} + \frac{(q_s)^2}{2 \cdot q} + 2n \cdot Adv_{DDH} + min\{q_s, q_r\} \cdot Adv^F \ .$$

So

$$\begin{aligned} Adv_\mathcal{A} &= |2 \cdot \Pr[Succ] - 1| \\ &= \frac{(q_s)^2}{q} + 4n \cdot Adv_{DDH} + 2 \cdot min\{q_s, q_r\} \cdot Adv^F \ . \end{aligned}$$

is negligible. Proof completes. $\square$

4 Conclusion

This research proposes an efficient deniable group key establishment protocol in the standard model. We figure out that the DGKE protocol should have two characteristic: authentication in the execution and deniability after the execution. We call it group deniable authentication. We use a transformed Schnorr's zero-knowledge identification scheme to provide this group deniable authentication characteristic. And we use the pseudorandom function ensemble to achieve the semantic secrecy of the agreed session key. We hope that the work we do is helpful for the research of analyzing the various security demands of group key establishment protocols.

The Proof of Proposition 1

Proof. We construct a sequences of modified protocols from $\Gamma_{1,0}$ to $\Gamma_{1,n+1}$ and bound the difference of the success probabilities for $\mathcal{A}$ to win in the **Test** query between each two adjacent games. $\Gamma_{1,0}$ is exactly the same as Γ_1. $\Gamma_{1,n+1}$ is exactly the same as Γ_2. The proof is as follows.

In $\Gamma_{1,1}$, everything is the same as in $\Gamma_{1,0}$ except that on the **Send**(U_1, s_i, M_j^1) and **Send**(U_2, s_i, M_j^1) queries, which deliver the broadcast message of round 1 to $\Pi_1^{s_i}$ and $\Pi_2^{s_i}$ and then execute round 2 for the computation of M_1^2 and M_2^2. The simulator checks if all the instances in $pid_i^{s_i}$ are uncorrupted and all the messages M_j^1 were unmodified delivered to $\Pi_1^{s_i}$ and $\Pi_2^{s_i}$. If so, it computes X_1 and X_2 from $X_1 = \frac{g^{\omega_{1,2}}}{g^{r_n r_1}}, X_2 = \frac{g^{r_3 r_2}}{g^{\omega_{1,2}}}$ but not from $X_1 = \frac{g^{r_2 r_1}}{g^{r_n r_1}}, X_2 = \frac{g^{r_3 r_2}}{g^{r_1 r_2}}$. $\omega_{1,2}$ is a random value uniformly chosen from $\mathbb{Z}_q$.

In $\Gamma_{1,2}$, everything is the same as in $\Gamma_{1,1}$ except that on the **Send**(U_2, s_i, M_j^1) and **Send**(U_3, s_i, M_j^1) queries, which deliver the broadcast message of round 1 to $\Pi_2^{s_i}$ and $\Pi_3^{s_i}$ and then execute round 2 for the computation of M_2^2 and M_3^2. The simulator checks if all the instances in $pid_i^{s_i}$ are uncorrupted and all the messages M_j^1 were unmodified delivered to $\Pi_2^{s_i}$ and $\Pi_3^{s_i}$. If so, it computes X_2 and X_3 from $X_2 = \frac{g^{\omega_{2,3}}}{g^{\omega_{1,2}}}, X_3 = \frac{g^{r_3 r_4}}{g^{\omega_{2,3}}}$ but not from $X_2 = \frac{g^{r_3 r_2}}{g^{\omega_{1,2}}}, X_3 = \frac{g^{r_4 r_3}}{g^{r_2 r_3}}$. $\omega_{1,2}, \omega_{2,3}$ are random values uniformly chosen from $\mathbb{Z}_q$.

We continue the modification analogously till we have modified the protocol to $\Gamma_{1,n}$.

We list the distribution of the protocol transcript $\mathbf{T}$ and the resulting session key $\mathbf{sk}$ as follows:

$\Gamma_{1,1}$:

$$\left\{ \begin{array}{c} r'_1, \ldots, r'_n \overset{R}{\leftarrow} \mathbb{Z}_q; z_1 = g^{r'_1}, \ldots, z_n = g^{r'_n} \\ \omega_{1,2}, r_1, \ldots, r_n \overset{R}{\leftarrow} \mathbb{Z}_q; y_1 = g^{r_1}, \ldots, y_n = g^{r_n} \\ X_1 = \frac{g^{\omega_{1,2}}}{g^{r_n r_1}}, X_2 = \frac{g^{r_3 r_2}}{g^{\omega_{1,2}}}, \ldots, X_n = \frac{g^{r_1 r_n}}{g^{r_{n-1} r_n}} \\ \mathrm{sid}_i = H(\mathrm{pid}_i || y_1 || \cdots || y_n || z_1 || \cdots || z_n) \\ \sigma_i = (y_{i-1})^{n r_i} \cdot (X_i)^{n-1} \cdots X_{i+n-2} \\ d_i = r'_i - (F_{\sigma_i}(\mathrm{sid}_i || 2) \cdot \alpha_i)(\bmod q) \\ \mathbf{T} = (y_1, \ldots, y_n, z_1, \ldots, z_n, X_1, \ldots, X_n, \mathrm{sid}_1, \ldots, \mathrm{sid}_n, d_1, \ldots, d_n) \\ \mathbf{sk} = F_{\sigma_i}(\mathrm{sid}_i || 1) \end{array} \right\} : (\mathbf{T}, \mathbf{sk})$$

.

.

$\Gamma_{1,n}$:

$$\left\{ \begin{array}{c} r'_1, \ldots, r'_n \overset{R}{\leftarrow} \mathbb{Z}_q; z_1 = g^{r'_1}, \ldots, z_n = g^{r'_n} \\ \omega_{1,2}, \ldots, \omega_{n,1}, r_1, \ldots, r_n \overset{R}{\leftarrow} \mathbb{Z}_q; y_1 = g^{r_1}, \ldots, y_n = g^{r_n} \\ X_1 = \frac{g^{\omega_{1,2}}}{g^{\omega_{n,1}}}, X_2 = \frac{g^{\omega_{2,3}}}{g^{\omega_{1,2}}}, \ldots, X_n = \frac{g^{\omega_{n,1}}}{g^{\omega_{n-1,n}}} \\ \mathrm{sid}_i = H(\mathrm{pid}_i || y_1 || \cdots || y_n || z_1 || \cdots || z_n) \\ \sigma_i = (y_{i-1})^{n r_i} \cdot (X_i)^{n-1} \cdots X_{i+n-2} \\ d_i = r'_i - (F_{\sigma_i}(\mathrm{sid}_i || 2) \cdot \alpha_i)(\bmod q) \\ \mathbf{T} = (y_1, \ldots, y_n, z_1, \ldots, z_n, X_1, \ldots, X_n, \mathrm{sid}_1, \ldots, \mathrm{sid}_n, d_1, \ldots, d_n) \\ \mathbf{sk} = F_{\sigma_i}(\mathrm{sid}_i || 1) \end{array} \right\} : (\mathbf{T}, \mathbf{sk})$$

For any PPT adversary $\mathcal{A}$ who can distinguish $\Gamma_{1,i}$ and $\Gamma_{1,i+1}, (0 \leq i \leq n-1)$, we can construct a PPT algorithm $\mathcal{D}$ that can break the DDH assumption. Given a DDH triple (g^a, g^b, Z), we construct $\mathcal{D}$ as follows:

$\mathcal{D}$ simulates the protocol Γ^* as follows and invokes $\mathcal{A}$ to attack Γ^*. Note that if the triple (g^a, g^b, Z) is a DDH triple, Γ^* is identical to $\Gamma_{1,i}$; if the triple (g^a, g^b, Z) is not a DDH triple, Γ^* is identical to $\Gamma_{1,i+1}$. So $\mathcal{D}$ can use $\mathcal{A}$'s outputs to determine its own output. If $\mathcal{A}$ outputs that Γ^* is $\Gamma_{1,i}$, $\mathcal{D}$ outputs that the triple (g^a, g^b, Z) is a DDH triple; else $\mathcal{D}$ outputs that the triple (g^a, g^b, Z) is not a DDH triple.

Γ^*:

$$\left\{\begin{array}{c} r'_1, \ldots, r'_n \stackrel{R}{\leftarrow} \mathbb{Z}_q; z_1 = g^{r'_1}, \ldots, z_n = g^{r'_n} \\ \omega_{1,2}, \ldots, \omega_{i,i+1}, r_1, \ldots, r_n \stackrel{R}{\leftarrow} \mathbb{Z}_q; \\ y_1 = g^{r_1}, \ldots, y_{i+1} = g^a, y_{i+2} = g^b, y_{i+3} = g^{r_{i+3}}, \ldots, y_n = g^{r_n} \\ X_1 = \frac{g^{\omega_{1,2}}}{g^{r_n r_1}}, \ldots, X_{i+1} = \frac{Z}{g^{\omega_{i,i+1}}}, X_{i+2} = \frac{g^{r_{i+2} r_{i+3}}}{Z}, \ldots, X_n = \frac{g^{r_1 r_n}}{g^{r_{n-1} r_n}} \\ \mathrm{sid}_i = H(\mathrm{pid}_i||y_1|| \cdots ||y_n||z_1|| \cdots ||z_n) \\ \sigma_i = (y_{i-1})^{nr_i} \cdot (X_i)^{n-1} \cdots X_{i+n-2} \\ d_i = r'_i - (F_{\sigma_i}(\mathrm{sid}_i||2) \cdot \alpha_i)(\mathrm{mod}\ q) \\ T = (y_1, \ldots, y_n, z_1, \ldots, z_n, X_1, \ldots, X_n, \mathrm{sid}_1, \ldots, \mathrm{sid}_n, d_1, \ldots, d_n) \\ \mathrm{sk} = F_{\sigma_i}(\mathrm{sid}_i||1) \end{array}\right\} : (\mathbf{T}, \mathbf{sk})$$

So for any PPT adversary $\mathcal{A}$, we have the probability that $\mathcal{A}$ win the **Test** query in $\Gamma_{1,i}$ and $\Gamma_{1,i+1}$ satisfy:

$$|Succ_{\Gamma_{1,i}} - Succ_{\Gamma_{1,i+1}}| \leq Adv_{DDH} .$$

And we have:

$$|Succ_{\Gamma_{1,0}} - Succ_{\Gamma_{1,n}}| \leq n \cdot Adv_{DDH} .$$

In protocol $\Gamma_{1,n}$, the values $\omega_{1,2}, \ldots, \omega_{n,1}$ are constrained by **T** according to the following n equations

$$log_g X_1 = \omega_{1,2} - \omega_{n,1} \tag{1}$$

$$\cdot$$
$$\cdot$$
$$\cdot$$

$$log_g X_n = \omega_{n,1} - \omega_{n-1,n} \tag{n}$$

Of which only $n - 1$ of these are linearly independent. Futhermore, σ_i may be expressed as $g^{\omega_{1,2}+\omega_{2,3}+\cdots+\omega_{n,1}}$; equivalently, we have

$$log_g \sigma_i = \omega_{1,2} + \omega_{2,3} + \cdots + \omega_{n,1} \tag{n+1}$$

Since equation $(n+1)$ is linearly independent from the set of the equations $(1), \ldots, (n)$ above, the value of σ_i is independent of **T**. So we can change $\Gamma_{1,n}$ to $\Gamma_{1,n+1}$ as follows. The only differences between $\Gamma_{1,n}$ and $\Gamma_{1,n+1}$ is that, on a **Send**(U_i, s_i, M_j^2) query, the simulator chooses $\sigma_i \stackrel{R}{\leftarrow} \mathbb{G}_q$, but does not compute it from $\sigma_i = g^{\omega_{1,2}+\omega_{2,3}+\cdots+\omega_{n,1}}$. There will be no PPT adversary that can distinguish $\Gamma_{1,n}$ and $\Gamma_{1,n+1}$, and we have

$$Succ_{\Gamma_{1,n}} = Succ_{\Gamma_{1,n+1}}$$

The transcript $\mathbf{T}$ and the resulting session key $\mathbf{sk}$ is denote as follows:
$\Gamma_{1,n+1}$:

$$
\left\{
\begin{array}{c}
r'_1, \ldots, r'_n \xleftarrow{R} \mathbb{Z}_q; z_1 = g^{r'_1}, \ldots, z_n = g^{r'_n} \\
\omega_{1,2}, \ldots, \omega_{n,1}, r_1, \ldots, r_n \xleftarrow{R} \mathbb{Z}_q; y_1 = g^{r_1}, \ldots, y_n = g^{r_n} \\
X_1 = \frac{g^{\omega_{1,2}}}{g^{\omega_{n,1}}}, X_2 = \frac{g^{\omega_{2,3}}}{g^{\omega_{1,2}}}, \ldots, X_n = \frac{g^{\omega_{n,1}}}{g^{\omega_{n-1,n}}} \\
\mathrm{sid}_i = H(\mathrm{pid}_i \| y_1 \| \cdots \| y_n \| z_1 \| \cdots \| z_n) \\
\sigma_i \xleftarrow{R} \mathbb{G}_q \\
d_i = r'_i - (F_{\sigma_i}(\mathrm{sid}_i \| 2) \cdot \alpha_i)(\mathrm{mod}\ q) \\
\mathbf{T} = (y_1, \ldots, y_n, z_1, \ldots, z_n, X_1, \ldots, X_n, \mathrm{sid}_1, \ldots, \mathrm{sid}_n, d_1, \ldots, d_n) \\
\mathbf{sk} = F_{\sigma_i}(\mathrm{sid}_i \| 1)
\end{array}
\right\} : (\mathbf{T}, \mathbf{sk})
$$

Note that $\Gamma_{1,n+1}$ is exactly the same as Γ_2. Putting all these equations together, we can get:

$$
|Succ_{\Gamma_1} - Succ_{\Gamma_2}| = |Succ_{\Gamma_{1,0}} - Succ_{\Gamma_{1,n+1}}| \leq n \cdot Adv_{DDH} \ . \qquad \square
$$

References

1. Abdalla, M., Pointcheval, D.: Interactive Diffie-Hellman Assumptions With Applications to Password-Based Authentication. In: S. Patrick, A., Yung, M. (eds.) FC 2005. LNCS, vol. 3570, pp. 341–356. Springer, Heidelberg (2005)
2. Aiello, W., Bellovin, S.M., Blaze, M., Canetti, M., Ioannidis, J., Keromytis, A.D., Reingold, O.: Just Fast Keying: Key Agreement In A Hostile Internet. ACM Transactions on Information and System Security 7(2), 1–30 (2004)
3. Bellare, M., Rogaway, P.: Entity Authentication and Key Distribution. In: Stinson, D.R. (ed.) CRYPTO 1993. LNCS, vol. 1440, pp. 232–249. Springer, Heidelberg (1999)
4. Bellare, M., Rogaway, P.: Provably-Secure Session Key Distribution: the Three Party Case. In: STOC 1995 (1995)
5. Bellare, M., Canetti, R., Krawczyk, H.: A Modular Approach to the Design and Analysis of Authentication and Key Exchange Protocols. In: STOC 1998 (1998)
6. Bellare, M., Pointcheval, D., Rogaway, P.: Authenticated Key Exchange Secure Against Dictionary Attacks. In: Preneel, B. (ed.) EUROCRYPT 2000. LNCS, vol. 1807, pp. 139–155. Springer, Heidelberg (2000)
7. Bohli, J.-M., Steinwandt, R.: Deniable Group Key Agreement. In: Nguyên, P.Q. (ed.) VIETCRYPT 2006. LNCS, vol. 4341, pp. 298–311. Springer, Heidelberg (2006)
8. Bohli, J.-M.: A framework for robust group key agreement. In: Gavrilova, M.L., Gervasi, O., Kumar, V., Tan, C.J.K., Taniar, D., Laganá, A., Mun, Y., Choo, H. (eds.) ICCSA 2006. LNCS, vol. 3982, pp. 355–364. Springer, Heidelberg (2006)
9. Boyd, C., Mao, W., Paterson, K.G.: Deniable Authenticated Key Establishment for Internet Protocols. In: Christianson, B., Crispo, B., Malcolm, J.A., Roe, M. (eds.) Security Protocols 2003. LNCS, vol. 3364, pp. 255–271. Springer, Heidelberg (2005)
10. Bresson, E., Chevassut, O., Pointcheval, D., Quisquater, J.-J.: Provably Athenticated Group Diffie-Hellman Key Exchange. In: Proc. of 8th Annual ACM Conference on Computer and Communications Security, pp. 255–264. ACM Press, New York (2001)

11. Bresson, E., Manulis, M., Schwenk, J.: On Security Models and Compilers for Group Key Exchange Protocols. In: Miyaji, A., Kikuchi, H., Rannenberg, K. (eds.) IWSEC 2007. LNCS, vol. 4752, pp. 292–307. Springer, Heidelberg (2007)
12. Bresson, E., Manulis, M.: Malicious Participants in Group Key Exchange: Key Control and Contributiveness in the Shadow of Trust. In: Xiao, B., Yang, L.T., Ma, J., Muller-Schloer, C., Hua, Y. (eds.) ATC 2007. LNCS, vol. 4610, pp. 395–409. Springer, Heidelberg (2007)
13. Bresson, E., Manulis, M.: Contributory group key exchange in the presence of malicious participants. IET Inf. Sec. 2(3), 85–93 (2008)
14. Burmester, M., Desmedt, Y.: A Secure and Efficient Conference Key Distribution System. In: De Santis, A. (ed.) EUROCRYPT 1994. LNCS, vol. 950, pp. 275–286. Springer, Heidelberg (1995)
15. Canetti, R., Krawczyk, H.: Analysis of Key-Exchange Protocols and Their Use for Building Secure Channels. In: Pfitzmann, B. (ed.) EUROCRYPT 2001. LNCS, vol. 2045, pp. 453–474. Springer, Heidelberg (2001)
16. Cao, T., Lin, D., Xue, R.: An Efficient ID-Based Deniable Authentication Protocol from Pairings. In: 19th International Conference on Advanced Information Networking and Applications (AINA 2005), vol. 1 (AINA papers), pp. 388–391. IEEE, Los Alamitos (2005)
17. Kaufman, C. (ed.): Internet Key Exchange (IKEv2) Protocol. Network Working Group Request for Comments: 4306 (December 2005), http://www.ietf.org/rfc/rfc4306.txt
18. Diffie, W., Hellman, M.: New Directions in Cryptography. IEEE Transactions on Information Theory 22, 644–654 (1976)
19. Feige, U., Fiat, A., Shamir, A.: Zero-Knowledge Proofs of Identity. In: Proceeding of STOC 1987, pp. 210–217 (1987); J. Cryptology 1, 77–95 (1988)
20. Ghodosi, H., Pieprzyk, J.: Multi-Party Computation with Omnipresent Adversary. In: Jarecki, S., Tsudik, G. (eds.) PKC 2009. LNCS, vol. 5443, pp. 180–195. Springer, Heidelberg (2009)
21. Goldreich, D.: Foundations of Cryptography: Basic Tools. Cambridge University Press, Cambridge (2001)
22. Goyal, V., Mohassel, P., Smith, A.: Efficient Two Party and Multi Party Computation Against Covert Adversaries. In: Smart, N.P. (ed.) EUROCRYPT 2008. LNCS, vol. 4965, pp. 289–306. Springer, Heidelberg (2008)
23. Kanukurthi, B., Reyzin, L.: Key Agreement from Close Secrets over Unsecured Channels. In: Joux, A. (ed.) EUROCRYPT 2009. LNCS, vol. 5479, pp. 206–223. Springer, Heidelberg (2009)
24. Katz, J., Shin, J.S.: Modeling insider attacks on group key-exchange protocols. In: 12th ACM Conference on Computer and Communications Security, pp. 180–189. ACM Press, New York (2005)
25. Katz, J., Yung, M.: Scalable Protocols for Authenticated Group Key Exchange. In: Boneh, D. (ed.) CRYPTO 2003. LNCS, vol. 2729, pp. 110–125. Springer, Heidelberg (2003)
26. Kim, H.J., Lee, S.U., Lee, D.H.: Constant-Round Authenticated Group Key Exchange for Dynamic Groups. In: Lee, P.J. (ed.) ASIACRYPT 2004. LNCS, vol. 3329, pp. 245–259. Springer, Heidelberg (2004)
27. Krawczyk, H.: SIGMA: The 'SIGn-and-MAc' Approach to Authenticated Diffie-Hellman and Its Use in the IKE Protocols. In: Boneh, D. (ed.) CRYPTO 2003. LNCS, vol. 2729, pp. 400–425. Springer, Heidelberg (2003)

28. Mao, W., Paterson, K.G.: On The Plausible Deniability Feature of Internet Protocols, http://isg.rhul.ac.uk/~kp/IKE.ps
29. Qian, H., Cao, Z., Wang, L., Xue, Q.: Efficient Noninteractive Deniable Authentication Protocols. In: The Fifth International Conference on Computer and Information Technology (CIT 2005), pp. 673–679. IEEE, Los Alamitos (2005)
30. Safavi-Naini, R., Jiang, S.: Non-interactive conference key distribution and its applications. In: ASIACCS, pp. 271–282. ACM, New York (2008)
31. Schnorr, C.-P.: Efficient Identification and Signatures for Smart Cards. In: Brassard, G. (ed.) CRYPTO 1989. LNCS, vol. 435, pp. 239–252. Springer, Heidelberg (1990)

Threshold Password-Based Authenticated Group Key Exchange in Gateway-Oriented Setting

Hui Li[1,2], Chuan-Kun Wu[1], and Lingbo Wei[3]

[1] State Key Laboratory Of Information Security, Institute of Software,
Chinese Academy of Sciences, Beijing 100190, China
[2] Graduate University of Chinese Academy of Sciences, Beijing 100049, China
[3] School of Electronics and Information Engineering, Beihang University,
Beijing 100191, China
{lihui,ckwu}@is.iscas.ac.cn, weilib@hotmail.com

Abstract. In this paper, we extend Abdalla et al. 's work in Asiacrypt 2005 to group-based setting. Our goal is to allow a group of users to establish a shared session key with a gateway under the assistance of an authentication server, while the server has no information about this session key and the gateway has no information about any password. Distinct to ordinary password-based group key exchange protocols, different shares of a groupwise password are assigned to group users respectively in our protocol. Each share is also a human-memorable password. According to our protocol, a group of at least k (a predefined threshold) users is authorized to establish a key with gateway. Additionally, the new protocol is proven secure in random-oracle model.

1 Introduction

Password-based authenticated key exchange (PAKE) protocol allows two entities to establish a secret session key and authenticate each other with a pre-shared human-memorable password. The first influential such work is the encrypted key exchanged protocol proposed by Bellovin and and Merritt [8]. Thereafter, a series of works about PAKE protocol are proposed [15,20,27]. However, the above works, do not provide formal security analysis. The early formal security model for PAKE is studied in [6,9] in random-oracle model. And then some PAKE protocols proved secure in standard model are proposed [14,16,12,13]. If two entities do not share a password at the beginning, a three-party password-based authenticated key exchange (three-party PAKE) protocol [25,17,11,26] is then necessary, where an authentication server involves and each client shares its password with the server. The first provably-secure three-party PAKE protocol is proposed by Abdalla et al. [3]. With the fast development of group-oriented applications, the research on password-based authenticated group key exchange (PAGKE) protocols obtains more and more attention [10,1,5,28]. Most existing PAGKE protocols assume that the group users have pre-shared a password (named groupwise password). However the risk of disclosing the groupwise password increases with the growth of the number of members in the group. Since

J. Kwak et al. (Eds.): ISPEC 2010, LNCS 6047, pp. 324–340, 2010.

the password is of low entropy, any password-based authenticated (group) key exchange protocol is susceptible to the dictionary attack. One is on-line dictionary attack, where the adversary embeds his guessing password in an interactive process, then verifies whether the guessing password is correct by checking the received responses. The other is off-line dictionary attack, where the adversary observes all the message flows exchanged during the executions of protocol, collects the redundancy about the password and then determines that which password makes sense.

When referring to the threshold setting in the password-based authenticated key exchange protocol, as far as we know, two early works have been given by MacKenzie et al. [18,19] and by DiRaimondo and Gennaro [22,23]. Their ideas are to split a password into several pieces, each of which is stored by an authentication server. Therefore, only a corruption of at least k (a threshold value) servers, the password is revealed. In [2], Abdalla et al. propose a new communication model for PAKE protocol, named gateway-oriented PAKE protocol. It allows that a session key is established between an user and a gateway with the assistance of an authentication server who has no information about the session key. The threshold version of gateway-oriented PAKE also splits the password into pieces to store in several authentication servers respectively. Recently, they improve this work by strengthening security model and adding anonymous feature [4].

Contributions. Consider the following scenario: a classified file is stored in a file server which locates behind the company gateway. To access the file, someone outside the company should launch a successful authentication with a correct password between himself and the gateway/authentication server. However the file is so sensitive that the password is divided into several pieces which are shared among a group of members. Only at least k members together have the privilege to access the classified file. In this paper, to solve the above issue, we pursue the line of the work in [2], and extend their work into group setting, where a group of users are allowed to establish a session key with the gateway under the assistance of an authentication server who has no information about the session key. Meanwhile, a threshold feature is added in a distinct way from the previous protocols. We require only at least k users are admitted to run the protocol successfully, i.e. a groupwise password is divided into several shares (these shares are also seemed as human-memorable passwords), each of which is assigned to a group user and a collusion of at least k users can recover the password. The motivation of this setting includes two points. One is that some practical applications, such as sensitive applications (e.g. corporation e-banking account) may ensure that there have been enough (legal) users participating in before providing services. The other is that the risk of leaking a groupwise password reduces after applying threshold technique among users (note that compromising an user are much easier than compromising the authentication server). Additionally, since users have different password shares, the deletion of users becomes easy in our protocol. At the end, the new protocol is proven secure in random-oracle model.

The rest of paper is organized as follows. Sect. 2 introduces some preliminary knowledge, including Lagrange interpolation, zero-knowledge proof of discrete logarithm and three cryptographic assumptions. Security model is described in Sect. 3. The detail of our protocol is given in Sect. 4. Then corresponding security results are proved in Sect. 5 and Sect. 6 is the conclusion of our paper.

2   Preliminaries

Lagrange Interpolating Polynomial. A Lagrange interpolating polynomial $f(x)$ is the polynomial of degree $k-1$ that passes through the k points $(x_1, f(x_1))$, $\cdots, (x_k, f(x_k))$. Then any point on this polynomial is given by $(x, f(x))$ such that:

$$f(x) = \sum_{i \in I} f(x_i) \lambda_{i,I}(x)$$

$$\lambda_{i,I}(x) = \prod_{j \in I, j \neq i} \frac{x - x_j}{x_i - x_j}.$$

where $I = \{1, 2, \cdots, k\}$.

Non-interactive Zero-Knowledge Proof of Discrete Logarithm. Let $\mathbb{G}$ be a group of a large prime order with generator g. Given $h = g^r \in \mathbb{G}$, a prover wants to prove that he knows the value of r without revealing this exponent. Denoted by $\Pi = NIZKPDL(m; g, h)$, the detailed zero-knowledge proof system due to Schnorr [24] is as follows (m is the message that is sent along with the proof Π, thus the proof can be seemed as a special signature of knowledge):

Let $h = g^r \in \mathbb{G}$ be given.

- The prover chooses $t \in \mathbb{Z}_q^*$ at random, computes $w = g^t$. He then computes $c = \mathcal{H}(m, g, h, w)$ where $\mathcal{H}$ is a hash function : $\{0, 1\}^* \to \mathbb{Z}_q^*$. Finally, he computes $z = t + rc \pmod{q}$ and sends to the verifier message m and the proof $\Pi = (c, z)$.
- Upon receiving m and $\Pi = (c, z)$, the verifier checks whether the following equality holds:

$$c = \mathcal{H}(m, g, h, g^z / h^c)$$

This scheme has been proved secure in random-oracle model, using forking lemma [21].

Compuatational Diffie-Hellman (CDH) Assumption. Let $\mathbb{G}_2$ be a cyclic group of prime order q with a generator g ($|g| = l$). The CDH assumption states that given inputs $(U = g^u, V = g^v)$ where $u, v \in_R \mathbb{Z}_q$, it is computationally hard to compute $W = g^{uv}$. For an attacker to break CDH assumption, we denote its advantage by $Succ_{\mathbb{G}_2}^{cdh}(l)$.

Inverse Computational Diffie-Hellman (ICDH) Assumption. Let $\mathbb{G}_2$ be a cyclic group of prime order q with a generator g ($|g| = l$). The ICDH assumption states that given input $(V = g^v)$ where $v \in_R \mathbb{Z}_q$, it is computationally hard to to compute $W = g^{1/v}$. For an attacker to break ICDH assumption, we denote its advantage by $Succ_{\mathbb{G}_2}^{icdh}(l)$.

Decisional Diffie-Hellman (DDH) Assumption. Let $\mathbb{G}_2$ be a cyclic group of prime order q with a generator g ($|g| = l$). The DDH assumption states that the distributions (g^u, g^v, g^{uv}) and (g^u, g^v, g^w) are computationally indistinguishable when $u, v, w \in_R \mathbb{Z}_q$. For an attacker to break DDH assumption, we denote its advantage by $Adv_{\mathbb{G}_2}^{ddh}(l)$.

3 Security Model

In our protocol, there are three kinds of roles: one is group user, another is the gateway GW and the other is the authentication server Svr. We stress that the channel between GW and Svr is private, which means that the adversary cannot intercept/modify the messages transferred between them. Thus we consider the security threat between users and the gateway. A formal security model which is suitable to our protocol is defined below:

Users, Gateway, Instances. Let $\mathcal{U} = \{U_1, \cdots, U_n\}$ denote a group of users. In setup phase, an authentication server assigns a groupwise password pw to user group $\mathcal{U}$, where each user U_i holds a (human-memorable) share pw_i of pw. pw_i is named user password of user U_i. During an execution of the protocol, each user U_i communicates with the gateway GW, and only a subgroup of at least k (a threshold value) users can successfully execute the protocol. To model concurrent executions of the protocol within one party (i.e. U_i, GW), we assume that there exists several instances within this party, each of which is modeled as an interactive probabilistic polynomial time machine. An instance $U_i^{t_i}$ of U_i (named user instance) is invoked by a "start" message for initialization of the protocol or an incoming message from gateway, while an instance GW^t of GW (named gateway instance) is invoked by an incoming message from users (since the channel between the gateway and the authentication server is private, the authentication server can be seemed as a part of gateway in our security model). A session is an execution of the protocol by an instance. We say an instance accepts only if it has computed the final session key.

Partnering. To describe a session, two notions are necessary: session identifier Sid and partner identifier Pid. The session identifier Sid is used to identify an unique session, which is usually defined as a concatenation of exchanged message flows (in our paper, it is the concatenation of exchanged messages between users and the gateway). The partner identifer Pid is the set of the identities of all the users and gateway that participate in that session. Note that Pid of an instance $U_i^{t_i}$ (resp. GW^t) includes U_i (resp. GW) itself. We say two instances are partnered if these two instances have both the same session identifer and the same partner identifer.

Adversarial Model. A probabilistic-polynomial-time adversary $\mathcal{M}$ is allowed to make the following queries:

- Execute($\{U_i^{t_i}\}_{i \in I}$, GW^t): This query is responded with the message flows that exchanged among $\{U_i^{t_i}\}_{i \in I}$ and GW^t during a certain session (I is the index set of users that involves in the session).
- Send($U_i^{t_i}$, m): This query is responded with the outgoing message that $U_i^{t_i}$ generates according to the description of the protocol, upon receiving the incoming message m (m may be "start" for initiation of the protocol).
- Send(GW^t, m): This query is responded with the outgoing message that GW^t generates according to the description of the protocol, upon receiving the incoming message m.
- Corrupt(U_i): $\mathcal{M}$ is given the user password pw_i (the share of groupwise password) held by user U_i.
- RevealKey($U_i^{t_i}$) (resp. RevealKey(GW^t)): $\mathcal{M}$ is given the session key held by $U_i^{t_i}$ (resp. GW^t). This query is asked under the condition that $U_i^{t_i}$ (resp. GW^t) accepts.
- Test($U_i^{t_i}$) (resp. Test(GW^t)): This query models the semantic security of the session key. This query is asked only once under the condition that $U_i^{t_i}$ (resp. GW^t) is fresh. The session owned by $U_i^{t_i}$ (resp. GW^t) is therefore called test session. To respond the query, a coin b is flipped, then $\mathcal{M}$ is given the real session key sk that $U_i^{t_i}$ (resp. GW^t) holds if $b = 1$ or a random string of the same length if $b = 0$. After Test query has been asked, $\mathcal{M}$ is still allowed to make the above queries as he wishes, but the test session should be guaranteed fresh.

Instance Freshness. An instance $U_i^{t_i}$ (resp. GW^t) is said fresh, if $U_i^{t_i}$ (resp. GW^t) has accepted and none of the following events occurs:

1. Either $U_i^{t_i}$ (resp. GW^t) or one of its partnered instances has been asked RevealKey query;
2. There is a Corrupt(U_j) query prior to Send(Ω, m) query, where Ω is $U_i^{t_i}$ (resp. GW^t) or one of its partnered instances, and U_j is a partner of $U_i^{t_i}$ (resp. GW^t).
3. Assume that U_i (resp. users communicating with GW^t) belongs to user group $\mathcal{U}$. There are at least k (the threshold value) corrupted users in $\mathcal{U}$.

In one word, it is guaranteed that the adversary cannot obtain the session key in a trivial way.
Now we give the definition of **AKE Security**.

Definition 1. *(AKE Security) Let P denote group key exchange protocol, $\mathcal{M}$ denote the adversary who has the capability to make the above queries and outputs a guessing coin b' then. The advantage of adversary $\mathcal{M}$ is computed as:*

$$Adv_P^{ake}(\mathcal{M}) = |2Pr[b' = b] - 1|$$

Key Privacy. The server Svr is a special entity in our protocol. It knows the groupwise password (but it does not necessarily store the user passwords as we can see later). Thus an honest-but-curious server is more dangerous than outside adversaries. Our goal is to make the session key established between users and the gateway unknown to the server. To capture honest-but-curious server, the corresponding security model for key privacy is similar to that for AKE security with two additional exceptions:

1. Once $\text{Test}(U_i^{t_i})$ (resp. $\text{Test}(GW^t)$) is asked, then $U_i^{t_i}$ (resp. GW^t) should be invoked by an Execute query, i.e. it cannot be invoked by a Send query.
2. $\text{Corrupt}(Svr)$ query is allowed to query, which is responded with the group-wise password of user group $\mathcal{U}$ and master keys of Svr.

The advantage of the adversary against key privacy is denoted by $Adv_P^{ake-kp}(\mathcal{M})$.

4   Our TPAGKE Protocol

In this section, we describe our new threshold gateway-oriented password-based authenticated group key exchange protocol. The notations are first defined below:

$\|x\|$	the bit length of an element x, or the size of a set x.
l	a security parameter.
q	a large prime with $\|q\| = l$.
p	a small prime with $\|p\| \ll l$.
$\mathbb{G}_1, \mathbb{G}_2$	$\mathbb{G}_1$ is a cyclic group of order p, $\mathbb{G}_2$ is a cyclic group of order q.
g, h, h_1, h_2	g is a generator of group $\mathbb{G}_1$, h, h_1, h_2 are generators of group $\mathbb{G}_2$.
$\mathbb{G}$	$\mathbb{G} = \mathbb{G}_1 \cdot \mathbb{G}_2$ (assume that the operations in $\mathbb{G}_1, \mathbb{G}_2$ are the same).
$\mathcal{D}$	a password space, we assume $\mathcal{D} = \mathbb{Z}_p$ in our paper ($\|p\|$ is small enough such that $pw \in \mathcal{D}$ is a human-memorable password).
$\mathcal{H}$	a hash function $\{0,1\}^* \to \mathbb{Z}_q^*$ ($\mathcal{H}$ is used in the zero-knowledge proof).
$\mathcal{H}_1$	a hash function $\{0,1\}^* \to \mathbb{G}$.
$\mathcal{G}$	a hash function $\{0,1\}^* \to \{0,1\}^l$.
$\mathcal{U}$	an user group, users in $\mathcal{U}$ are indexed from 1.
U_i	an user, i is its index in the user group.

Note 1: As in our protocol, not only a mapping from password space to $\mathbb{Z}_p$ is required, but also a mapping from $\mathbb{Z}_p$ to password space is necessary for password assignment in setup phase. For simplicity, we assume that the password space $\mathcal{D}$ is equal to $\mathbb{Z}_p$ ($\|p\|$ is small enough).

In our protocol, a set I of users ($\{U_i\}_{i \in I} \subseteq \mathcal{U}$) interact with the gateway, we require that the size of I is at least k, otherwise the protocol cannot be executed successfully. The detailed description of our threshold gateway-oriented password-based authenticated group key exchange protocol (TPAGKE) is as follows (keep in mind that the channel between the gateway and the server is private):

- **Setup.** For a given user group $\mathcal{U}$, Password Generation Center (PGC) chooses a random groupwise password $pw \in \mathbb{Z}_p^*$, and a password generation function, which is a $(k-1)$-degree polynomial: $f(x) = \sum_{i=0}^{k-1} a_i x^i \pmod{p}$, where

$a_i \in \mathbb{Z}_p^*, a_0 = pw$. For each user U_i ($i \geq 1$), PGC computes the password share $pw_i = f(i)$ and assigns pw_i to U_i in a secure way. Remark that pw_i is also a human-memorable password and named user password. Then PGC passes the groupwise password pw to authentication server Svr. Svr stores the groupwise password pw without maintaining the list of users' passwords. Moreover Svr stores the secret keys s_1, s_2 such that $h_1 = h^{s_1}, h_2 = h^{s_2}$. The system public parameters are $(l, p, q, \mathbb{G}, \mathbb{G}_1, \mathbb{G}_2, g, h, h_1, h_2, \mathcal{H}, \mathcal{H}_1, \mathcal{G})$, the master keys of the server are (s_1, s_2). Furthermore, there is a black list stored in the gateway. The black list is initialized empty, and the data in it is of form $(i, \mathcal{U})$, which means U_i in group $\mathcal{U}$ is blocked.

- **Key Exchange.** (see Figure. 1) When $\{U_i\}_{i \in I}$ participate in a session ($|I| \geq k$), then the following steps are executed. Assuming that all participating users know the set I at the beginning, since it is practical by letting users broadcast their indices first.

  - (**Users**) Each user U_i ($i \in I$) sends $((i, \mathcal{U}), \text{"hello"})$ message to gateway GW.

  - (**Gateway**) Upon receiving the messages $\{(i, \mathcal{U}), \text{"hello"}\}_{i \in I}$, gateway GW determines the set I, and checks whether there exists U_j ($j \in I$) in the black list. If such U_j exists, GW broadcasts an error message "U_j is blocked" and aborts. Otherwise it picks $R \in \mathbb{G}_2$ at random, then sends back R to users.

  - (**Users**) If receiving an error message, honest users abort. Otherwise if receiving R from gateway, each user U_i ($i \in I$) computes a Lagrange coefficient $\lambda_{i,I}(0) = \prod\limits_{k \in I, k \neq i} \frac{k}{k-i}$. Then he randomly picks $x_i \in \mathbb{Z}_q^*$ and computes $A_i = h_1^{x_i}, B_i = g^{pw_i} \mathcal{H}_1^{\lambda_{i,I}^{-1}(0)}(i, R, h^{x_i})$, where $\lambda_{i,I}^{-1}(0) \cdot \lambda_{i,I}(0) = 1 \pmod{pq}$. Next U_i sends $(i, \mathcal{U}, A_i, B_i)$ to GW.

  - (**Gateway**) Upon receiving the messages $\{(i, \mathcal{U}, A_i, B_i)\}_{i \in I}$, GW computes $B = \prod\limits_{i \in I} B_i^{\lambda_{i,I}(0)}$ and sends $(I, \mathcal{U}, R, B, \{A_i\}_{i \in I})$ to the authentication server.

  - (**Authentication Server**) Upon receiving the messages $(I, \mathcal{U}, R, B, \{A_i\}_{i \in I})$, Svr computes $A = \prod\limits_{i \in I} \mathcal{H}_1(i, R, (A_i)^{1/s_1})$ and verifies whether $B/g^{pw} = A$ (pw is the groupwise password for $\mathcal{U}$) holds. If it does not hold, Svr sends "error" to GW and aborts. Otherwise, Svr computes $\{C_i = A_i^{s_2/s_1}\}_{i \in I}$ and $C_0 = \prod\limits_{i \in I} C_i^{\lambda_{i,I}(0)}$. Then Svr chooses an index set J such that $J \cap I = \phi, |J| = |I| - 1$. For each $j \in J$, Svr computes $C_j = \prod\limits_{i \in I} C_i^{\lambda_{i,I}(j)}$, where the Lagrange coefficient $\lambda_{i,I}(j) = \prod\limits_{k \in I, k \neq i} \frac{k-j}{k-i}$. Next Svr sends the message $(J, C_0, \{C_j\}_{j \in J})$ to GW.

  - (**Gateway**) When GW receives "error" from Svr, it aborts. Otherwise when receiving $(J, C_0, \{C_j\}_{j \in J})$, GW randomly picks $y \in \mathbb{Z}_q^*$ and computes $Y = h_2^y, C_0' = C_0^y, \{C_j' = C_j^y\}_{j \in J}$. Next, GW generates a zero-knowledge proof $\Pi = NIZKPDL(\{C_j'\}_{j \in \{0\} \cup J}; h_2, Y)$. Next GW

computes the session key $sk_g = \mathcal{G}(\{U_i\}_{i\in I}, GW, R, \{A_i, B_i\}_{i\in I}, Y, C_0')$ and broadcasts $(J, Y, \{C_j'\}_{j\in J}, \Pi)$ to users.

- **(Users)** Upon receiving message $(J, Y, \{C_j'\}_{j\in J}, \Pi)$ from GW, Each user U_i computes $C_i' = Y^{x_i}$. Using Lagrange interpolation on $|I|$ points $\{(i, C_i'), \{(j, C_j')\}_{j\in J}\}$, U_i obtains $C_0' = \prod_{k\in J_i} (C_k')^{\lambda_{k,J_i}(0)}$, where $J_i = \{i\} \cup J$ and $\lambda_{k,J_i}(0) = \prod_{j\in J_i, j\neq k} \frac{j}{j-k}$. Then U_i verifies whether Π is a valid proof. If it is not, U_i aborts. Otherwise the session key $sk_i = \mathcal{G}(\{U_i\}_{i\in I}, GW, R, \{A_i, B_i\}_{i\in I}, Y, C_0')$ is computed.

- **New User Registration.** When a new user U intends to join a member group $\mathcal{U}$, then PGC assigns an unused index j for user U, looks for the corresponding password generation function $f(x)$ for user group $\mathcal{U}$, and distributes $pw_j = f(j)$ to U as his password share.

- **User Deletion.** In order to delete user U_i from the user group $\mathcal{U}$ (e.g. a corruption of U_i has been detected), then $(i, \mathcal{U})$ is added into the black list in GW. We can see that the deletion operation does not influence the remaining valid users and the server.

5   Security Results

In this section, we prove that our protocol achieves AKE security and key privacy in random-oracle model. First, we present the following theorem.

Theorem 1. *(AKE Security) Let P denote our TPAGKE protocol, $\mathcal{M}$ denote a probabilistic-polynomial-time adversary. After making all possible queries defined in Sect. 3, The advantage of $\mathcal{M}$ against AKE security of P is:*

$$Adv_P^{ake}(\mathcal{M}) \leq \frac{q_\mathcal{H}^2 + (n+1)(q_s + q_e)^2}{q-1} + \frac{q_{\mathcal{H}_1}^2}{pq} + \frac{q_\mathcal{G}^2}{2^l} + \frac{2q_s}{N} + 4|I| \cdot q_\mathcal{H} Succ_{\mathbb{G}_2}^{cdh}(l)$$
$$+ 2q_{\mathcal{H}_1} Succ_{\mathbb{G}_2}^{icdh}(l) + 4(|I|+1)(q_\mathcal{H} + q_\mathcal{G})Succ_{\mathbb{G}_2}^{cdh}(l)$$

where n is the total number of users in the user group, q_s, q_e are the numbers of sessions invoked by Send, Execute queries respectively, $q_\mathcal{H}, q_{\mathcal{H}_1}, q_\mathcal{G}$ are the numbers of hash queries to oracles $\mathcal{H}, \mathcal{H}_1, \mathcal{G}$ respectively, N is the size of dictionary $\mathcal{D}$ (i.e. $N = p$, since $\mathcal{D} = \mathbb{Z}_p$), I is the largest subgroup of users in a session during the attack.

Proof. We define a simulator $\mathcal{S}$ who simulates a sequence of games $\mathbf{G_i}$, $i = 0, 1, \cdots, 7$. $\mathbf{S_i}$ denotes the event that $\mathcal{M}$ successfully breaks AKE-security property of P in game $\mathbf{G_i}$ by outputting guessing bit b' which is identical to the bit b randomly chosen in answering Test query.

Game $\mathbf{G_0}$: This game is identical to the real game, and played between $\mathcal{S}$ and $\mathcal{M}$ in random oracle model. Thus we have:

$$Adv_P^{ake}(\mathcal{M}) = |2Pr[S_0] - 1|$$

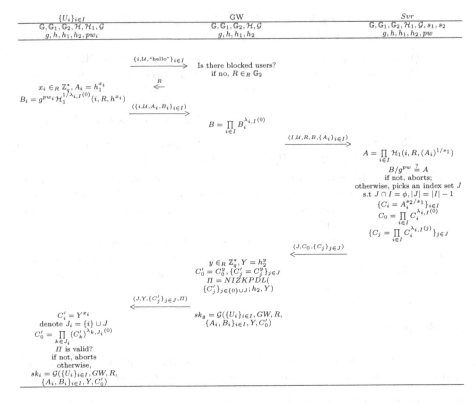

Fig. 1. Our TPAGKE protocol (the channel between GW and Svr is private)

Game G_1: In this game, $\mathcal{S}$ simulates the hash oracles $\mathcal{H}, \mathcal{H}_1, \mathcal{G}$ as usual by maintaining hash lists $\Lambda_{\mathcal{H}}, \Lambda_{\mathcal{H}_1}, \Lambda_{\mathcal{G}}$. In addition, two more private hash functions are maintained: $\mathcal{H}' : \{0,1\}^* \to \mathbb{Z}_q^*$ and $\mathcal{G}' : \{0,1\}^* \to \{0,1\}^l$, which are used in later games. However, $\mathcal{S}$ cancels the game if some collisions appear on the output of hash oracles $\mathcal{H}, \mathcal{H}_1$ and $\mathcal{G}$. Following birthday paradox, the probability of such bad event is at most $q_{\mathcal{H}}^2/2(q-1) + q_{\mathcal{H}_1}^2/2pq + q_{\mathcal{G}}^2/2^{l+1}$. Thus we have:

$$|\Pr[S_1] - \Pr[S_0]| \leq \frac{q_{\mathcal{H}}^2}{2(q-1)} + \frac{q_{\mathcal{H}_1}^2}{2pq} + \frac{q_{\mathcal{G}}^2}{2^{l+1}}$$

Game G_2: In this game, $\mathcal{S}$ aborts the game if x_i is used by U_i's instances in two different sessions or R is used by gateway's instances in two different sessions. Since there are at most $q_s + q_e$ sessions invoked by $\mathcal{M}$, thus we have:

$$|\Pr[S_2] - \Pr[S_1]| \leq \frac{n(q_s + q_e)^2}{2(q-1)} + \frac{(q_s + q_e)^2}{2q} \leq \frac{(n+1)(q_s + q_e)^2}{2(q-1)}$$

Game G_3: In this game, $\mathcal{S}$ aborts the game if the following event occurs: assume that an user instance $U_i^{t_i}$ outputs an outgoing message $(i, \mathcal{U}, A_i, B_i)$ when it is invoked by an Execute query or a Send query, adversary $\mathcal{M}$ asks an appropriate hash query $\mathcal{H}_1(i, R, (A_i)^{1/s_1})$, where s_1 is one of the master keys, i.e. $h^{s_1} = h_1$ and R is the value previously outputted by the gateway during the same session. Next, we briefly prove that the probability of such event is negligible.

If such event occurs, then an attacker against ICDH assumption can be constructed. $\mathcal{S}$ is given $\mathbb{G}_2, h, V(= h^b)$ and intends to compute $V' = h^{1/b}$. Then $\mathcal{S}$ sets $h_1 = V, h_2 = V^s$, where s is randomly selected by $\mathcal{S}$. Next, he picks a group $\mathbb{G}_1$ of prime p and a group $\mathbb{G} = \mathbb{G}_1 \cdot \mathbb{G}_2$, initializes an user group $\mathcal{U} = \{U_1, \cdots, U_n\}$ and all necessary passwords (including groupwise password and user passwords), answers all the queries for adversary $\mathcal{M}$ as follows:

- Execute($\{U_i^{t_i}\}_{i \in I}, GW^t$): $\{U_i^{t_i}\}_{i \in I}$ first generate $fl_0 = \{i, \mathcal{U}, \text{"hello"}\}_{i \in I}$ and GW generates a random value $fl_1 = R$. Then for each $U_i^{t_i}$, $\mathcal{S}$ picks $x_i \in_R \mathbb{Z}_q^*, B_i \in_R \mathbb{G}$, then computes $A_i = h^{x_i}$. Denote messages $\{i, \mathcal{U}, A_i, B_i\}_{i \in I}$ by fl_2. For GW^t, $\mathcal{S}$ picks $y \in \mathbb{Z}_q^*$ and computes $Y = V^{sy}$. Then $\mathcal{S}$ chooses a set J such that $J \cap I = \phi, |J| = |I| - 1$ and computes $\{C_j' = \prod_{i \in I} (A_i^{sy})^{\lambda_{i,I}(j)}\}_{j \in J}$ and $C_0' = \prod_{i \in I} (A_i^{sy})^{\lambda_{i,I}(0)}$. Next $\mathcal{S}$ simulates the zero-knowledge proof $\Pi = NIZKPDL(\{C_j'\}_{j \in \{0\} \cup J}; h_2, Y)$ with the knowledge y. Denote message $(J, Y, \{C_j'\}_{j \in J}, \Pi)$ by fl_3. All user instances $\{U_i^{t_i}\}_{i \in I}$ and gateway instance GW^t compute the session key as $sk = \mathcal{G}(\{U_i\}_{i \in I}, GW, R, \{A_i, B_i\}_{i \in I}, Y, C_0')$. $\mathcal{S}$ returns fl_0, fl_1, fl_2, fl_3 to adversary $\mathcal{M}$.
- Send($U_i^{t_i}$, "start"): $\mathcal{S}$ returns $(i, \mathcal{U}, \text{"hello"})$ to $\mathcal{M}$.
- Send($GW^t, \{i, \mathcal{U}, \text{"hello"}\}_{i \in I}$): $\mathcal{S}$ returns a random value $R \in \mathbb{G}$ to $\mathcal{M}$.
- Send($U_i^{t_i}, R$): $\mathcal{S}$ picks $x_i \in_R \mathbb{Z}_q^*, B_i \in_R \mathbb{G}$, then computes $A_i = h^{x_i}$. $\mathcal{S}$ returns $(i, \mathcal{U}, A_i, B_i)$ to $\mathcal{M}$.
- Send($GW^t, \{i, \mathcal{U}, A_i, B_i\}_{i \in I}$): $\mathcal{S}$ answers this query exactly according to the description of the protocol, since $C_i = A_i^s$ can be computed on his own.
- Send($U_i^{t_i}, (J, Y, \{C_j'\}_{j \in J}, \Pi)$): $\mathcal{S}$ exactly follows the description of the protocol.
- RevealKey($U_i^{t_i}$), RevealKey(GW^t) and Corrupt(U_i) are answered in a straight way.

The above simulation is indistinguishable to game $\mathbf{G_2}$ unless $\mathcal{M}$ asks an appropriate query $\mathcal{H}_1(i, R, A_i^{1/b})$ with A_i generated by an user instance. If such event occurs, $\mathcal{S}$ randomly picks $(i, R, Q, *)$ from hash list $\Lambda_{\mathcal{H}_1}$ and computes Q^{1/x_i}. With a non-negligible probability of $\frac{1}{q_{\mathcal{H}_1}}$, the value Q^{1/x_i} equals to $h^{1/b}$, which implies that ICDH assumption is solved. Thus we have:

$$|\Pr[\mathbf{S_3}] - \Pr[\mathbf{S_2}]| \leq q_{\mathcal{H}_1} Succ_{\mathbb{G}_2}^{icdh}(l)$$

Game $\mathbf{G_4}$: In this game, We show that the success probability of $\mathcal{M}$ is negligible when the test session is invoked by an Execute query. To do so, $\mathcal{S}$ modifies the way of deriving the session keys of instances which are invoked by Execute queries.

$\mathcal{S}$ is given a tuple $< h, U(= h^a), V(= h^b) >$ where h is a generator of group $\mathcal{G}_2$ of prime order q, the goal of $\mathcal{S}$ is to compute $W = CDH(U, V) = h^{ab}$. Then $\mathcal{S}$ picks two additional generators $h_1 = h^{s_1}, h_2 = h^{s_2}$ of $\mathbb{G}_2$ with s_1, s_2 known to $\mathcal{S}$, a group $\mathbb{G}_1$ of small prime order p. Hence a group $\mathbb{G} = \mathbb{G}_1 \cdot \mathbb{G}_2$ is obtained. Next he initializes an user group $\mathcal{U} = \{U_1, \cdots, U_n\}$ and all necessary passwords, and simulates Execute queries for adversary $\mathcal{M}$ as follows ($\mathcal{S}$ simulates Send queries similarly to game $\mathbf{G_3}$):

- Execute($\{U_i^{t_i}\}_{i \in I}, GW^t$): Instances $\{U_i^{t_i}\}_{i \in I}$ generate $fl_0 = \{i, \mathcal{U}, \text{``hello''}\}_{i \in I}$ to start protocol and GW returns back a random value $fl_1 = R$. Then for each $U_i^{t_i}$, $\mathcal{S}$ picks $x_i \in_R \mathbb{Z}_q^*, B_i \in_R \mathbb{G}$, then computes $A_i = U^{s_1 x_i}$. Let fl_2 denote message $\{i, \mathcal{U}, A_i, B_i\}_{i \in I}$. For GW^t, $\mathcal{S}$ picks $y \in \mathbb{Z}_q^*$ and computes $Y = V^{s_2 y}$. Next, $\mathcal{S}$ chooses a set J such that $J \cap I = \phi, |J| = |I| - 1$ and randomly chooses $|J|$ elements $\{C_j'\}_{j \in J}$ from $\mathbb{G}_2$. Then $\mathcal{S}$ simulates the zero-knowledge proof $\Pi = (c, z) = NIZKPDL(\{C_j'\}_{j \in J}; h_2, Y)$ without knowledge $\log_{h_2} Y$, where hash oracle $\mathcal{H}$ (used in zero-knowledge proof) is replaced with the private hash oracle $\mathcal{H}'$. Let fl_3 denote message $(J, Y, \{C_j'\}_{j \in J}, \Pi)$. All user instances $\{U_i^{t_i}\}_{i \in I}$ and gateway instance GW^t compute the session key $sk = \mathcal{G}'(\{U_i\}_{i \in I}, GW, R, \{A_i, B_i\}_{i \in I}, Y)$, where $\mathcal{G}'$ is another private hash oracle. $\mathcal{S}$ returns fl_0, fl_1, fl_2, fl_3 to $\mathcal{S}$. The transcript of this session is denoted by $T = (\{U_i\}_{i \in I}, GW, R, \{A_i, B_i\}_{i \in I}, J, Y, \{C_j'\}_{j \in J}, \Pi)$.

This game is indistinguishable to game $\mathbf{G_3}$, unless that adversary $\mathcal{M}$ makes $\mathcal{G}(\{U_i\}_{i \in I}, GW, R, \{A_i, B_i\}_{i \in I}, Y, C_0')$ query or $\mathcal{H}(C_0' || \{C_j'\}_{j \in J}, h_2, Y, h_2^z / Y^c)$ query, where C_0' is obtained in either of the following ways:

1. For an index $i \in I$, C_0' is obtained by Lagrange interpolation on $|I|$ points: $\{(j, C_j')\}_{j \in J}$, and $(i, (CDH(U, V))^{s_2 x_i y})$;
2. C_0' is obtained by Lagrange interpolation on $|I|$ points: $\{(i, (CDH(U, V))^{s_2 x_i y})\}_{i \in I}$.

If either of the above events occurs, it is obviously to see that h^{ab} can be computed with non-negligible probability and CDH assumption is therefore solved. Thus we have:

$$|\Pr[\mathbf{S_4}] - \Pr[\mathbf{S_3}]| \leq (|I| + 1)(q_{\mathcal{H}} + q_{\mathcal{G}}) Succ_{\mathbb{G}_2}^{cdh}(l)$$

Game $\mathbf{G_5}$: In this game, we consider passive attacks via honest Send queries, where adversary $\mathcal{M}$ honestly forwards the messages it received from the instance oracles. $\mathcal{S}$ simulates these honest Send queries as the same way of simulating Execute queries in game $\mathbf{G_4}$. Thus, we have:

$$|\Pr[\mathbf{S_5}] - \Pr[\mathbf{S_4}]| \leq (|I| + 1)(q_{\mathcal{H}} + q_{\mathcal{G}}) Succ_{\mathbb{G}_2}^{cdh}(l)$$

Game $\mathbf{G_6}$: In this game, we consider the case that given a transcript $(\{U_i\}_{i \in I}, GW, R, \{A_i, B_i\}_{i \in I}, J, Y, \{C_j'\}_{j \in J}, \Pi)$, the component $(J, Y, \{C_j'\}_{j \in J}, \Pi)$ is generated by gateway instance, but there exists at least a component $(i, \{A_i, B_i\})$

which is not generated by the user instance. In such case, S aborts the simulation. Thus this game is distinguishable from game $\mathbf{G_5}$ with the probability of event that adversary $\mathcal{M}$ correctly guesses user password of U_i or the corresponding groupwise password, and sends an appropriate message $\{i, \mathcal{U}, A_i, B_i\}$ on behalf of U_i. We denote such event by **Guess_withGW**. Thus we have:

$$|\mathrm{Pr}[\mathbf{S_6}] - \mathrm{Pr}[\mathbf{S_5}]| \leq \mathrm{Pr}[\mathbf{Guess\_withGW_6}]$$

Game $\mathbf{G_7}$: In this game, we consider the case that given a transcript $(\{U_i\}_{i \in I},$ $GW, R, \{A_i, B_i\}_{i \in I}, J, Y, \{C'_j\}_{j \in J}, \Pi)$, the component $\{i, \mathcal{U}, A_i, B_i\}_{i \in I}$ is generated by user instances but $(J, Y, \{C'_j\}_{j \in J}, \Pi)$ is not generated by gateway instance. In such case, S modifies the simulation as follow: When an user instance $U_i^{t_i}$ receives an incoming message $(J, Y, \{C'_j\}_{j \in J}, \Pi)$ which is generated by $\mathcal{M}$, then S aborts. Therefore, game $\mathbf{G_7}$ is indistinguishable to $\mathbf{G_6}$ except that $\mathcal{M}$ successfully forges a message $(J, Y, \{C'_j\}_{j \in J}, \Pi)$ for at least one instance $U_i^{t_i}$. We denote this event by **Forgery**. The probability of event **Forgery** is analyzed in **Lemma 1** (see appendix A), and it is at most $|I| \cdot q_{\mathcal{H}} Succ_{\mathbb{G}_2}^{cdh}(l)$. Thus we have:

$$|\mathrm{Pr}[\mathbf{S_7}] - \mathrm{Pr}[\mathbf{S_6}]| \leq |I| \cdot q_{\mathcal{H}} Succ_{\mathbb{G}_2}^{cdh}(l)$$
$$|\mathrm{Pr}[\mathbf{Guess\_withGW_7}] - \mathrm{Pr}[\mathbf{Guess\_withGW_6}]| \leq |I| \cdot q_{\mathcal{H}} Succ_{\mathbb{G}_2}^{cdh}(l)$$

By now, it is easy to see that $\mathrm{Pr}[\mathbf{S_7}] = 1/2$. Moreover, all passwords are not used during the simulation, which implies the passwords can be chosen until the end of the simulation. Thus $\mathrm{Pr}[\mathbf{Guess\_withGW_7}] = q_s/N$, where N is the size of the dictionary $\mathcal{D}$. Combining all above (in)equalities, **Theorem 1** is proved. ∎

Next, we discuss key privacy against honest-but-curious authentication server.

Theorem 2. *(Key Privacy against Authentication Server) Let P denote our TPAGKE protocol, Svr is a honest-but-curious server. After making all allowable queries, The advantage of Svr against key privacy of protocol P is:*

$$Adv_P^{ake-kp}(Svr) \leq 2Adv_{\mathbb{G}_2}^{ddh}(l) + negl(l)$$

where $negl(\cdot)$ is a negligible function.

Proof. Since the probability that the collisions appear in hash queries and random values x_i or R is reused in different session by the same user or gateway has been proved to be $negl(l)$ in Theorem 1, the following proof is based on the condition that the collisions during hash queries and reusing of x_i or R have been totally excluded. From an efficient honest-but-curious server who has broken key-privacy security of P, a distinguisher S against DDH assumption is constructed. Two experiments are as follows:

Experiment 1: Assume that S is given a tuple $(h, U = h^a, V = h^b, W = h^{ab})$ where h is a generator of group $\mathbb{G}_2$ of prime order q. Then S chooses a group $\mathbb{G}_1$

of small prime order p with generator g. Password space $\mathcal{D}$ is set to be $\mathbb{Z}_p$. Then $\mathcal{S}$ prepares an user group $\mathcal{U} = \{U_1, \cdots, U_n\}$ and all necessary passwords (including the groupwise password and user passwords). Two additional generators $h_1 = h^{s_1}, h_2 = h^{s_2}$ of $\mathbb{G}_2$ are picked. Three hash oracles $\mathcal{H}_1, \mathcal{H}, \mathcal{G}$ are maintained as usual.

- Execute($\{U_i^{t_i}\}_{i \in I}, GW^t$): Instances $\{U_i^{t_i}\}_{i \in I}$ generate $fl_0 = \{i, \mathcal{U}, \text{``hello''}\}_{i \in I}$ to start protocol and GW returns back a random value $fl_1 = R$. Then for each $U_i^{t_i}$, $\mathcal{S}$ picks $x_i \in \mathbb{Z}_q^*$ and computes $A_i = U^{s_1 x_i}, B_i = \mathcal{H}_1^{\lambda_{i,I}^{-1}(0)}(i, R, U^{x_i})$, where $\lambda_{i,I}(0)$ is the corresponding Lagrange coefficient. Let fl_2 denote message $\{i, \mathcal{U}, A_i, B_i\}_{i \in I}$. For GW^t, $\mathcal{S}$ picks $y \in \mathbb{Z}_q^*$ and computes $Y = V^{s_2 y}, C_0' = \prod_{i \in I} W^{s_2 y x_i \lambda_{i,I}(0)}$. Next, $\mathcal{S}$ chooses a set J such that $J \cap I = \phi, |J| = |I| - 1$ and respectively computes $|J|$ elements $\{C_j'\}_{j \in J}$ according to the description of protocol P. Then $\mathcal{S}$ simulates the zero-knowledge proof $\Pi = NIZKPDL(C_0' || \{C_j'\}_{j \in J}; h_2, Y)$ without knowing $\log_{h_2} Y$. Let fl_3 denote the message $(J, Y, \{C_j'\}_{j \in J}, \Pi)$. All user instances $\{U_i^{t_i}\}_{i \in I}$ and gateway instance GW^t computes the session $sk = \mathcal{G}(\{U_i\}_{i \in I}, GW, R, \{A_i, B_i\}_{i \in I}, Y, C_0')$. $\mathcal{S}$ returns fl_0, fl_1, fl_2, fl_3 to adversary $\mathcal{M}$.
- Send queries: All Send queries are simulated by exactly following the description of protocol P.
- RevealKey($U_i^{t_i}$), RevealKey(GW^t),Corrupt(U_i) and Corrupt(Svr) are answered in a straight way.

Experiment 2: This experiment is identical to **Experiment 1**, except that $\mathcal{S}$ is given a tuple $(h, U = h^a, V = h^b, W = h^c)$, where c is independent to a, b. Then $\mathcal{S}$ simulates all Execute and Send queries with this tuple, using the same trick of **Experiment 1**.

We denote W_i as the event that Svr wins the game in **Experiment i**. We have:

$$Adv_P^{ake-kp}(Svr) = |2\Pr[W_1] - 1|$$
$$|\Pr[W_2] - \Pr[W_1]| \le Adv_{\mathbb{G}_2}^{ddh}(l)$$

Form information-theoretical view, it is deduced that $\Pr[W_2] = \frac{1}{2}$. Thus **Theorem 2.** is easily proved. ∎

6   Conclusion

In this paper, we propose a threshold gateway-oriented password-based authenticated group key exchange protocol, which extends the previous work to a group setting. Additionally, threshold feather is added in the new protocol, where only at least of t (the threshold value) users together can successfully execute the protocol. Therefore our protocol may be practical for some sensitive applications. Meanwhile, the risk of leaking groupwise password reduces since the groupwise password has been split into pieces, each of which is also a human-memorable password and assigned to users respectively. The new protocol is proven secure in random-oracle model.

References

1. Abdalla, M., Bresson, E., Chevassut, O., Pointcheval, D.: Password-based Group Key Exchange in a Constant Number of Rounds. In: Yung, M., Dodis, Y., Kiayias, A., Malkin, T.G. (eds.) PKC 2006. LNCS, vol. 3958, pp. 427–442. Springer, Heidelberg (2006)
2. Abdalla, M., Chevassut, O., Fouque, P.A., Pointcheval, D.: A Simple Threshold Authenticated Key Exchange from Short Secrets. In: Roy, B. (ed.) ASIACRYPT 2005. LNCS, vol. 3788, pp. 566–584. Springer, Heidelberg (2005)
3. Abdalla, M., Fouque, P.A., Pointcheval, D.: Password-based authenticated key exchange in the three-party setting. IET Information Security 153(1), 27–39 (2005)
4. Abdalla, M., Izabachene, M., Pointcheval, D.: Anonymous and Transparent Gateway-based Password-Authenticated Key Exchange. In: Franklin, M.K., Hui, L.C.K., Wong, D.S. (eds.) CANS 2008. LNCS, vol. 5339, pp. 133–148. Springer, Heidelberg (2008)
5. Abdalla, M., Pointcheval, D.: A Scalable Password-based Group Key Exchange Protocol in the Standard Model. In: Lai, X., Chen, K. (eds.) ASIACRYPT 2006. LNCS, vol. 4284, pp. 332–347. Springer, Heidelberg (2006)
6. Bellare, M., Pointcheval, D., Rogaway, P.: Authenticated Key Exchange Secure against Dictionary Attacks. In: Preneel, B. (ed.) EUROCRYPT 2000. LNCS, vol. 1807, pp. 139–155. Springer, Heidelberg (2000)
7. Bellare, M., Palacio, A.: The Knowledge-of-Exponent Assumptions and 3-round Zero-Knowledge Protocols. In: Franklin, M. (ed.) CRYPTO 2004. LNCS, vol. 3152, pp. 273–289. Springer, Heidelberg (2004)
8. Bellovin, S.M., Merritt, M.: Augmented Encrypted Key Exchange: A Password-Based Protocol Secure Against Dictionary Attacks and Password File Compromise. In: Proceedings of the 1st ACM Conference on Computer and Communication Security, pp. 244–250. ACM, New York (1993)
9. Boyko, V., MacKenzie, P., Patel, S.: Provably Secure Password-Authenticated Key Exchange Using Diffie-Hellman. In: Preneel, B. (ed.) EUROCRYPT 2000. LNCS, vol. 1807, pp. 156–171. Springer, Heidelberg (2000)
10. Bresson, E., Chevassut, O., Pointcheval, D.: Group Diffie-Hellman Key Exchange secure against dictionary attacks. In: Zheng, Y. (ed.) ASIACRYPT 2002. LNCS, vol. 2501, pp. 497–514. Springer, Heidelberg (2002)
11. Byun, J.W., Jeong, I.R., Lee, D.H., Park, C.-S.: Password-Authenticated Key Exchange between Clients with Different Passwords. In: Deng, R.H., Qing, S., Bao, F., Zhou, J. (eds.) ICICS 2002. LNCS, vol. 2513, pp. 134–146. Springer, Heidelberg (2002)
12. Gennaro, R., Lindell, Y.: A framework for password-based authenticated key exchange. ACM Transactions on Information and System Security (TISSEC) 9(2), 181–234 (2006)
13. Gennaro, R.: Faster and Shorter Password-Authenticated Key Exchange. In: Canetti, R. (ed.) TCC 2008. LNCS, vol. 4948, pp. 589–606. Springer, Heidelberg (2008)

14. Goldreich, O., Lindell, Y.: Session Key Generation using Human Passwords Only. In: Kilian, J. (ed.) CRYPTO 2001. LNCS, vol. 2139, pp. 408–432. Springer, Heidelberg (2001)
15. Jablon, D.P.: Strong Password-Only Authenticated Key Exchange. ACM SIGCOMM Computer Communication Review 26(5), 5–26 (1996)
16. Katz, J., Ostrovsky, R., Yung, M.: Practical Password-Authenticated Key Exchange Provably Secure under Standard Assumptions. In: Pfitzmann, B. (ed.) EUROCRYPT 2001. LNCS, vol. 2045, pp. 475–494. Springer, Heidelberg (2001)
17. Lin, C.L., Sun, H.M., Hwang, T.: Three-party encrypted key exchange: attacks and a solution. ACM SIGOPS Operating System Review 34(4), 12–20 (2000)
18. MacKenzie, P., Shrimpton, T., Jakobsson, M.: Threshold password-authenticated key exchange. In: Yung, M. (ed.) CRYPTO 2002. LNCS, vol. 2442, pp. 18–22. Springer, Heidelberg (2002)
19. MacKenzie, P., Shrimpton, T., Jakobsson, M.: Threshold password-authenticated key exchange. Journal of Cryptology, LNCS 19(1), 27–66 (2006)
20. Patel, S.: Number Theoretic Attacks on Secure Password Schemes. In: Proceedings of the 1997 IEEE Symposium on Security and Privacy, pp. 236–247 (1997)
21. Pointcheval, D., Stern, J.: Security Arguments for Digital Signatures and Blind Signatures. Journal of Cryptology, LNCS 13, 361–396 (2000)
22. Raimondo, M.D., Gennaro, R.: Provably secure threshold password-authenticated key exchange. In: Biham, E. (ed.) EUROCRYPT 2003. LNCS, vol. 2656, pp. 507–523. Springer, Heidelberg (2003)
23. Di Raimondo, M., Gennaro, R.: Provably secure threshold password-authenticated key exchange. Journal of Computer and System Sciences 72(6), 978–1001 (2006)
24. Schnorr, C.P.: Efficient identification and signatures for smart cards. In: Quisquater, J.-J., Vandewalle, J. (eds.) EUROCRYPT 1989. LNCS, vol. 434, pp. 688–689. Springer, Heidelberg (1990)
25. Steiner, M., Tsudik, G., Waidner, M.: Refinement and Extension of Encrypted Key Exchange. ACM SIGOPS Operating System Review 29(3), 22–30 (1995)
26. Sun, H.M., Chen, B.C., Hwang, T.: Secure key agreement protocols for three-party against guessing attacks. The Journal of Systems and Software 75, 63–68 (2005)
27. Wu, T.: The Secure Remote Password Protocol. In: Proceedings of the 1998 Internet Society Symposium on Network and Distributed System Security (NDSS 1998), pp. 97–111 (1998)
28. Wu, S.H., Zhu, Y.F.: Constant-Round Password-Based Authenticated Key Exchange Protocol for Dynamic Groups. In: Tsudik, G. (ed.) FC 2008. LNCS, vol. 5143, pp. 69–82. Springer, Heidelberg (2008)

Appendix A

Lemma 1. *If event **Forgery** defined in game **G_7** in **Theorem 1** occurs, then CDH assumption can be solved with the advantage $Succ_{\mathbb{G}_2}^{cdh}(l)$:*

$$Succ_{\mathbb{G}_2}^{cdh}(l) \geq \frac{1}{|I| \cdot q_{\mathcal{H}}} \Pr[\textbf{Forgery}]$$

where I is the largest subgroup of users in a session during the attack.

Proof. Simulator $\mathcal{S}$ is given $\mathbb{G}_2, h, U = h^u, V = h^v$ and intends to compute $W = h^{uv}$. Then $\mathcal{S}$ sets $h_1 = h^s, h_2 = V$, where s is randomly selected by $\mathcal{S}$, then he picks a group $\mathbb{G}_1$ with small prime order p. Cyclic group $\mathbb{G}$ represents $\mathbb{G}_1 \cdot \mathbb{G}_2$. $\mathcal{S}$ next prepares an user group $\mathcal{U} = \{U_1, \cdots, U_n\}$ and all necessary passwords, simulates the game as follows:

- Execute($\{U_i^{t_i}\}_{i \in I}, GW^t$): Instances $\{U_i^{t_i}\}_{i \in I}$ generate $fl_0 = \{i, \mathcal{U}, \text{"hello"}\}_{i \in I}$ to start protocol and GW returns back a random value $fl_1 = R$. Then for each $U_i^{t_i}$, $\mathcal{S}$ picks $x_i \in_R \mathbb{Z}_q^*, B_i \in_R \mathbb{G}$, and computes $A_i = U^{x_i}$. Let fl_2 denote $\{i, \mathcal{U}, A_i, B_i\}_{i \in I}$. For GW^t, $\mathcal{S}$ picks $y \in \mathbb{Z}_q^*$ and computes $Y = V^y$. Next, $\mathcal{S}$ chooses a set J such that $J \cap I = \phi, |J| = |I| - 1$ and and randomly chooses $|J|$ elements $\{C_j'\}_{j \in J}$ from $\mathbb{G}_2$. Then $\mathcal{S}$ simulates the zero-knowledge proof $\Pi = NIZKPDL(\{C_j'\}_{j \in J}; h_2, Y)$ with the knowledge y, where hash oracle $\mathcal{H}$ is replaced with the private hash oracle $\mathcal{H}'$. Let fl_3 denote $(J, Y, \{C_j'\}_{j \in J}, \Pi)$. All user instances $\{U_i^{t_i}\}_{i \in I}$ and gateway instance GW^t compute the session $sk = \mathcal{G}'(\{U_i\}_{i \in I}, GW, R, \{A_i, B_i\}_{i \in I}, Y)$ ($\mathcal{G}'$ is another private hash oracle). $\mathcal{S}$ returns fl_0, fl_1, fl_2, fl_3 to $\mathcal{M}$.
- Send($U_i^{t_i}$, "start"): $\mathcal{S}$ returns $(i, \mathcal{U}, \text{"hello"})$ to $\mathcal{M}$.
- Send($GW^t, \{i, \mathcal{U}, \text{"hello"}\}_{i \in I}$): $\mathcal{S}$ returns a random value $R \in \mathbb{G}$ to $\mathcal{M}$.
- Send($U_i^{t_i}, R$): $\mathcal{S}$ picks $x_i \in_R \mathbb{Z}_q^*, B_i \in_R \mathbb{G}$, then computes $A_i = U^{x_i}$. $\mathcal{S}$ returns $(i, \mathcal{U}, A_i, B_i)$ as the answer.
- Send($GW^t, \{i, \mathcal{U}, A_i, B_i\}_{i \in I}$): The process is divided into two cases:
    1. If $\{i, \mathcal{U}, A_i, B_i\}_{i \in I}$ is generated by user instances: $\mathcal{S}$ first verifies whether $\{i, \mathcal{U}, A_i, B_i\}_{i \in I}$ is valid by following the description of the protocol, then picks $y \in \mathbb{Z}_q^*$ and computes $Y = V^y$. Next, $\mathcal{S}$ chooses a set J such that $J \cap I = \phi, |J| = |I| - 1$ and and randomly chooses $|J|$ elements $\{C_j'\}_{j \in J}$ from $\mathbb{G}_2$. $\mathcal{S}$ next simulates the zero-knowledge proof $\Pi = NIZKPDL(\{C_j'\}_{j \in J}; h_2, Y)$ with the knowledge y, where hash oracle $\mathcal{H}$ is replaced with the private hash oracle $\mathcal{H}'$. The session key is set as $\mathcal{G}'(\{U_i\}_{i \in I}, GW, R, \{A_i, B_i\}_{i \in I}, Y)$.
    2. If there exists a component $(i, \{A_i, B_i\})$ is not generated by the user instance: $\mathcal{S}$ aborts (as the same in previous game).
- Send($U_i^{t_i}, (J, Y, \{C_j'\}_{j \in J}, \Pi)$): If the message $(J, Y, \{C_j'\}_{j \in J}, \Pi)$ is generated by the gateway instance, $\mathcal{S}$ verifies Π via using the private hash oracle $\mathcal{H}'$. If verification does not succeed, $\mathcal{S}$ aborts, else if verification succeeds, $\mathcal{S}$ sets the session key of $U_i^{t_i}$ as $\mathcal{G}'(\{U_i\}_{i \in I}, GW, R, \{A_i, B_i\}_{i \in I}, Y)$. Otherwise if $(J, Y, \{C_j'\}_{j \in J}, \Pi)$ is not generated by the gateway instance, $\mathcal{S}$ aborts.
- RevealKey($U_i^{t_i}$), RevealKey(GW^t) and Corrupt(U_i) are answered in a straight way.

Consider the event **Forgery**, i.e. $\mathcal{M}$ forges a valid message $(J, Y, \{C_j'\}_{j \in J}, \Pi)$ where $\Pi = (c, z)$. According to zero-knowledge proof of discrete logarithm scheme, we note that $z = t + cy$, where $c = \mathcal{H}(\{C_j'\}_{j \in \{0\} \cup J}, h_2, Y, g^t), y = \log_{h_2} Y$. Following forking lemma [21], by rewinding the simulation to the point that $\mathcal{M}$ asks $\mathcal{H}(\{C_j'\}_{j \in \{0\} \cup J}, h_2, Y, g^t)$ query, at this point, $\mathcal{S}$ answers the query with a different value (denoted by c'). Then another successful proof is forged with a non-negligible probability: $z' = t + c'y$. Therefore $\mathcal{S}$ obtains $y = (z - z')/(c - c')$. Furthermore, since $\mathcal{M}$ forges a valid proof for user instances, e.g. $U_i^{t_i}$, then he has to obtain an appropriate C_0', where C_0' is computed by interpolating on $|I|$ points $\{(j, C_j')\}_{j \in \{0\} \cup J}$. Otherwise $\mathcal{H}(\{C_j'\}_{j \in \{0\} \cup J}, h_2, Y, g^t)$ query cannot be asked appropriately by $\mathcal{M}$. To do so, $\mathcal{M}$ has to compute $C_i' = Y^{x_i u/s}$, where x_i is previously chosen by $\mathcal{S}$ for $U_i^{t_i}$. $\mathcal{S}$ then outputs a pair of values $(P = Y^{x_i/s}, C_i')$. Keep in mind that P and C_i' satisfies $C_i' = P^u$. Note that $U = h^u$. According to KEA-1 assumption [7], there exists an algorithm to extract $y' = \log_h P = vyx_i/s$. Finally $\mathcal{S}$ obtains $v = y's/(yx_i)$. and CDH problem is therefore solved in a trivial way. Thus Lemma 1 is proved.   ∎

Binary Image Steganographic Techniques Classification Based on Multi-class Steganalysis

Kang Leng Chiew[1,2] and Josef Pieprzyk[2]

[1] Faculty of Computer Science and Information Technology
Universiti Malaysia Sarawak
93050 Kota Samarahan, Malaysia
klchiew@fit.unimas.my
[2] Department of Computing, Macquarie University
NSW 2109, Australia
josef@science.mq.edu.au

Abstract. In this paper, we propose a new multi-class steganalysis for binary image. The proposed method can identify the type of steganographic technique used by examining on the given binary image. In addition, our proposed method is also capable of differentiating an image with hidden message from the one without hidden message. In order to do that, we will extract some features from the binary image. The feature extraction method used is a combination of the method extended from our previous work and some new methods proposed in this paper. Based on the extracted feature sets, we construct our multi-class steganalysis from the SVM classifier. We also present the empirical works to demonstrate that the proposed method can effectively identify five different types of steganography.

Keywords: Multi-class steganalysis, steganography, co-occurrence matrix, run length, SVM.

1   Introduction

Digital data hiding techniques have received considerable attention from the research community. Many data hiding techniques have been proposed for a variety of digital applications including steganographic and watermarking applications. Steganography considers methods and techniques that can be used to create covert communication channels for unobtrusive transmission for military purposes. Watermarking, on the other hand, can be used for variety of purposes that include document authentication (by inserting an appropriate digital signature), annotation, file duplication management and ownership protection.

There are two basic operations involved in steganography, namely, embedding a secret message and its extraction. During the embedding operation, the secret message is inserted into the medium by altering some portion of it. The extraction operation allows to recover the secret message from the medium. There are many kinds of multimedia that can be used in steganography. By far the

J. Kwak et al. (Eds.): ISPEC 2010, LNCS 6047, pp. 341–358, 2010.
© Springer-Verlag Berlin Heidelberg 2010

most common medium is image. The main reason for this is large redundancy of images that allows easy embedding of messages [14]. The input image used in the embedding operation is called a cover image and the generated output image (with a secret message embedded in it) is called a stego image. Ideally, both images (cover and stego) should look as two identical copies or in other words, the stego image should be difficult to tell apart from the cover image by an unsuspected user.

A list of possible choices for cover images include: binary (black and white) images, grayscale images and color images. For example, Tseng and Pan [23] have developed a steganography that embeds secret message in binary image and the work by Liang et al. [12] also uses binary image in their steganography. The OutGuess [19] and F5 [25] are examples of steganography that apply grayscale and color images. A more recent steganography developed by Yang (see [27]) is using color image.

Because of the invasive nature of steganography, it leaves detectable traces within stego image characteristic. This allows adversary to use steganalysis techniques to reveal that secret communication is taking place. In general, there are two types of steganalysis. One is targeted steganalysis and the other is blind steganalysis.

Targeted steganalysis is designed specifically to attack one particular embedding algorithm. For example, the works developed in [1], [9], [11] and [8] are considered as targeted steganalysis. Targeted steganalysis may produce more accurate results, but it normally fails if the embedding algorithm differs from the target one.

Blind steganalysis can be considered as a universal technique which can detect different types of steganography. Because blind steganalysis can detect a wider class of steganographic techniques, it is generally less accurate compared to targeted steganalysis. However, blind steganalysis is capable of detecting a new steganographic technique where there is no targeted steganalysis available yet. In order words, blind steganalysis is an irreplaceable detection tool if the embedding algorithm is unknown or secret. Some successful blind steganalysis include feature-based steganalysis developed in [7]. Other blind steganalysis are those developed in [22] and [13] by Shi et al. and Liu et al., respectively.

In general, blind steganalysis can be considered as two-class classification. This means given an image, the steganalysis should be able to decide which class (cover or stego) the image belong to. Furthermore, it is also possible to extend some of the blind steganalysis to form a multi-class steganalysis. Practically, multi-class steganalysis is similar to blind steganalysis. However, instead of classifying two classes, multi-class steganalysis is capable of classifying more classes. Namely, the additional classes come from different type of stego images produced by different embedding techniques. Hence, the task of multi-class steganalysis is to identify which embedding algorithm has been applied to produce the given stego image (correspondingly if no embedding is performed on the given image, it should be classified as cover image).

In [17], Pevný and Fridrich have extended their previous blind steganalysis developed in [7] to form the multi-class steganalysis. Their multi-class steganalysis is capable of classifying the embedding algorithms based on the given JPEG stego images. Rodriguez and Peterson [20] studied a different multi-class steganalysis for JPEG images. In [20], the extracted features are based on wavelet decomposition and support vector machine (SVM) is employed as the classifier. The most recent work is the technique developed by Dong et al. in [6]. The main contribution of this multi-class steganalysis is the ability to carry out the classification in two different image domains, namely the frequency domain (e.g. JPEG images) and spatial domain (e.g. BMP images). Other multi-class steganalysis can be found in [18], [21] and [24] and they are all developed to cater JPEG image steganography.

It is worthy of note that the above mentioned multi-class steganalysis techniques are for images with at least 8 bits per pixel intensity. This means that the images can be grayscale, color or true color images. It is not clear how the existing multi-class steganalysis can be generalized for binary images (i.e. black and white images). Unlike grayscale and color images, binary images have a rather modest statistical nature. This has imposed great difficulty to apply the existing multi-class steganalysis on binary images. To our best knowledge, there is no multi-class steganalysis proposed for binary images in the literature.

In this paper, we propose a multi-class steganalysis for binary images. The work in this paper is based on the extension of our previously developed blind steganalysis for binary images in [4]. The main contribution of this paper is three fold. First, we incorporate additional new features to our existing feature sets. Second, the concept of cover image estimation is incorporated to enhance the features sensitivity. Third, a new multi-class steganalysis technique is developed. Consequently, we are able to assign a given image to its appropriate class. This will provide valuable trace to steganalysts (e.g. forensic examiners) towards the goal of hidden message extraction.

The remainder of the paper is as follow. In the next section, we give a brief description of the steganographic techniques. The method of analysis we apply is given in Section 3. The construction of multi-class classifier is discussed in Section 4. Section 5 presents the experimental results of the analysis. Section 6 concludes the paper.

2   Comparison of the Steganography Techniques under Analysis

There are five different types of steganography that will be analyzed in this paper. We will describe these steganographic techniques with a special attention put on their embedding algorithm.

As noted in [23] and [3], these steganographic techniques are actually extended from the technique developed in [16]. Without loss of generality, we will describe the technique given in [16] as an example for the sake of presentation clarity.

As noted before, a steganography involves two basic operations which are embedding and extraction operation. The embedding operation in [16] starts by partitioning a given image into non-overlap blocks of size $m \times n$. The payload for each non-overlap block is r bits. The message bits are segmented into streams of r bits and embedded by modifying some pixels in the blocks (noted that a pixel in the binary image has only one bit, hence only this bit of pixel will be modified). The modification of some pixels is governed by certain criteria which are computed through bitwise exclusive-or and pairwise multiplication operation between the non-overlap block, random binary (denoted as κ) and secret matrix (denoted as ω). Both the κ and ω are $m \times n$ matrices and served as the stegokey.

During the extraction operation, the parameters like m, n and r need to be communicated correctly between the sender and receiver in order to construct the right size of non-overlap blocks and right number of r bits per stream. In addition, the right stegokey (κ and ω) is needed to successfully extract the secret message. After that, the receiver can derive the message bits by using the inverse of the criteria used in the embedding operation.

In fact, the steganography in [23] is an improved version of the steganography developed initially in [16]. The improvement is mainly on controlling the visual quality of the produced stego image where only boundary pixels are allowed to be flipped. On the other hand, we are not able to include the enhanced steganography proposed by Chang et al. [3] as the authors did not give details about the enhancement. The extraction operation for Tseng and Pan [23] and Chang et al. [3] steganographic techniques are similar to that of Pan et al. [16] technique.

It is interesting to mention that for example, the techniques developed in [16] can embed as many as $\lfloor \log_2(mn+1) \rfloor$ message bits but only need to alter 2 pixels at most to accommodate this. As opposed to a conventional technique where 1 pixel alteration can only accommodate at most 1 message bit. Furthermore, adjusting m and n will result in changing the payload and affecting the security level as well. This gives flexibility to balance between payload and security level.

The steganography developed in [12] is considered as the boundary-based steganography. This type of steganography will hide a message along the edges where white pixels meet the black ones and these pixels are known as boundary pixels. To obtain higher imperceptibility, the locations of pixels used for embedding are permuted and distributed over the whole image. The permutation is controlled by pseudorandom number generator whose seed is a secret shared by the sender and the receiver.

However, not all boundary pixels are suitable to carry the message bits because embedding a bit into an arbitrary boundary pixel may convert it into a non-boundary one. This will jeopardize the operation of extraction and the recovery of hidden message is impossible. Because of this technical difficulties, some improvement is developed by adding restrictions on the selection of boundary pixels for embedding. A currently evaluated boundary pixel is considered to be eligible for embedding if the following two conditions are satisfied:

(i) Among the four neighboring pixels, there exist at least two unmarked neighboring pixels and they must be two different pixel values in total.

(ii) For each marked neighboring pixel (if any), its four neighboring pixels must also satisfy the first criterion.

A pixel is said to be *marked* if it has been already evaluated or in other words, it is assigned a (pseudorandom) index with a smaller value than the current index. In contrast, a pixel is said to be *unmarked* if it is evaluated after the current pixel. Once the boundary pixel is found eligible, the message bit will be embedded to the pixel by overwriting its value if the message bit does not match the value otherwise the pixel will be left intact. The same procedure is applied to embed all other bits of the message.

The last steganography under our analysis is the technique developed by Wu and Liu in [26]. This technique also starts by partitioning a given image into blocks. In order to avoid synchronization problem between embedding and extraction, this technique will embed a fixed number of message bits within a block. Given in their implementation details, the authors opt to embed 1 message bit per block. The embedding algorithm is based on the odd-even relationship of the number of black pixels within a block. In other words, the total number of black pixels within a block is kept as odd number when a message bit of 1s is embedded. Whereas, the total number of black pixels is kept as even number for a message bit of 0s. Clearly, when this odd-even relationship holds for the message bit that is intended to be embedded then no flipping is required. Otherwise, some pixels are required to be flipped.

Like any other embedding techniques, the most important part is the selection of pixels for flipping. An efficient selection approach can ensure minimum distortion. That is why we can see in [26], Wu and Liu introduced a flippability scoring system in order to select pixels for flipping. The score for each pixel is computed by examining the pixel and its immediate neighbors (e.g. neighbors within a 3×3 block). In fact the flippability score is produced by a decision module based on the input of two measurements. Namely, the first measurement is the smoothness which computes the total number of transitions in horizontal, vertical and the two diagonal directions. The second measurement is the connectivity which computes the total number of black and white clusters formed within a block. These measurements are all computed within a 3×3 block.

All these steganographic techniques are developed to embed secret message in binary image.

3   Proposed Steganalysis

As the ultimate goal for steganalysis is to extract the full hidden message. This task, however, may be very difficult to achieve. Thus, we may start with more realistic and modest goal such as identifying the type of steganographic technique used for the embedding. As a result, we want to proceed and improve our existing technique so that we can identify which embedding algorithm has been employed.

In order to do that, we will propose a multi-class steganalysis. Multi-class steganalysis can be viewed as a supervised machine learning problem where we would like to classify which class (multiple classes, i.e. cover, stego type-1, type-2, $\cdots$, type-n) a given image belongs to. Our analysis includes two stages, namely, feature extraction and data classification. First stage is crucial and we show how to construct the existing features combined with new features in this section. The second stage uses the Support Vector Machine (SVM) [5] to construct our multi-class classifier. We will describe in detail the multi-class classifier in Section 4.

3.1   Increasing Gray Level via Pixel Difference

Observe that the number of gray levels is not sufficient for an analysis of black and white images, where the number of gray levels is drastically reduced (note that in grayscale and color images, the number of gray levels is larger which is at less 256). To fix this technical difficulty, we propose a solution that allows us to create more gray levels and consequently more meaningful statistics. Our approach is to use pixel difference.

Pixel difference is the difference between a pixel and its neighboring pixels. Given a pixel $p(x, y)$ of an image, with $x \in [1, X]$ and $y \in [1, Y]$, where X and Y are the image width and height, respectively. The vertical difference for the pixel $p(x, y)$ in the vertical direction (further on, we call it simply pixel difference) is defined as follows:

$$p_v(x', y') = p(x, y + 1) - p(x, y), \tag{1}$$

where $x' \in [1, X - 1]$ and $y' \in [1, Y - 1]$. Pixel difference for horizontal, main diagonal and minor diagonal direction are defined in similar way. Figure 1 illustrates pixel difference in the vertical direction.

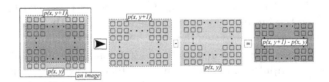

Fig. 1. Pixel difference in vertical direction

It is easy to observe and has been confirmed by experiments that the introduction of pixel difference has increased (almost doubled) the number of gray levels. To illustrate the point, consider a grayscale image with the number of gray levels equal to 256. After introduction of pixel difference the range of gray levels becomes $[-255, +255]$. The same doubling effect happens for binary images. This effect is a desired property to fix the technical difficulty mentioned before.

For this purpose, we incorporated the pixel difference developed in [13]. Their features are defined as below:

$$p_c^{n+1}(x, y) = p^n(x, y+1) - p^n(x, y),$$
$$p_r^{n+1}(x, y) = p^n(x+1, y) - p^n(x, y), \tag{2}$$
$$p^1(x, y) = |p_r^1(x, y)| + |p_c^1(x, y)|, \tag{3}$$
$$p^2(x, y) = p_r^1(x, y) - p_r^1(x-1, y) + p_c^1(x, y) - p_c^1(x, y-1), \tag{4}$$

where $n = 0, 1, 2$ and $|\cdot|$ represents absolute value. $p_c^1(x, y)$ and $p_r^1(x, y)$ can be considered as pixel difference for vertical and horizontal direction, respectively. $p^1(x, y)$ and $p^2(x, y)$ are the respective higher order total difference. $p^0(x, y)$ is a special case and is actually the given binary image.

In addition, we have further defined the pixel difference an order higher as follows:

$$p_c^3(x, y) = p^2(x, y+1) - p^2(x, y),$$
$$p_r^3(x, y) = p^2(x+1, y) - p^2(x, y), \tag{5}$$

and we named them simply as third order pixel difference. We would like to stress that all the statistical features we use in our analysis are based on this third order pixel difference and can be summarized in the following two stages:

1. In the first stage we use the third order pixel difference to increase the number of gray levels. Note that $p^2(x, y)$ in Equation (4) is obtained by summing the pixel differences computed in horizontal and vertical directions. Note also the doubling effects of gray levels on the pixel difference are increased from [0, 1] for $p(x, y)$ to [-4, 4] for $p^2(x, y)$. This is not hard to verify. For example, consider the minimum and maximum of gray levels for p_r^1 is -1 and +1, respectively. The same is applied to p_c^1. Hence, we can obtain the minimum and maximum gray level for $p^2(x, y)$. The minimum is obtained when the neighboring differences for both p_r^1 and p_c^1 (right components) in Equation (4) are -2, which will produce $p^2(x, y) = -4$. Whereas the maximum is obtained when the neighboring differences for both p_r^1 and p_c^1 are 2, which will produce $p^2(x, y) = 4$. Finally, using the same concept for the third order pixel difference, we can increase the number of gray levels to 17 (i.e. [-8, 8]).
2. In the second stage we proceed with the computed third order pixel difference to extract each of the specific feature set. In other words, certain feature set (the feature sets will be discussed in Subsection 3.2 and 3.3) is extracted on top of this third order pixel difference.

3.2   Gray Level Run Length Matrix

The first feature set we try to extract is based on the gray level run length (GLRL). The length is measured by the number of consecutive pixels for a given gray level g and a direction θ. Note that $0 \leq g \leq G - 1$ and G is the total number of gray levels and θ, where $0° \leq \theta \leq 180°$, indicates the direction. The sequence of pixels (at a gray level) is characterized by its length (run length) and its frequency count (also called run length value) that tells us how many times the run has occurred in the image. Thus our feature is a GLRL matrix that fully characterizes different gray runs in the two dimensions: the gray level g and the run length ℓ. The general GLRL matrix is defined as follows:

$$r(g, \ell|\theta) = \# \{(x, y) \mid p(x, y) = p(x + s, y + t) = g;$$
$$p(x + u, y + v) \neq g;$$
$$0 \leq s < u \quad \& \quad 0 \leq t < v; \qquad u = \ell \cos(\theta) \quad \& \quad v = \ell \sin(\theta);$$
$$0 \leq g \leq G - 1 \quad \& \quad 1 \leq \ell \leq L \quad \& \quad 0° \leq \theta \leq 180°\} \qquad (6)$$

where $\#$ denotes the number of element and $p(x, y)$ is the pixel intensity (gray level) at position x, y. G is the total gray levels and L is the maximum run length.

For our practical implementation, we simply concatenate $p_c^3(x, y)$ with $p_r^3(x, y)$ and substitute $p(x, y)$ in Equation (6). In addition, we also observed that it is significant to use only two directions for θ, which is $0°$ and $90°$. Therefore, the extracted GLRL matrices from the third order pixel difference can be considered as a higher order statistical features.

3.3   Gray Level Co-occurrence Matrix

In this paper, we have replaced Gray Level Gap Length (GLGL) matrix which has been proposed in our previous work with Gray Level Co-occurrence matrix (GLCM). From the empirical studies, we have found that GLCM can perform better in multi-class classification compared to GLGL. GLCM can be considered as an approach of capturing the inter-pixel relationship. More precisely, the elements in GLCM matrix represent the relative frequencies of two pixels (with gray level g_1 and g_2, respectively) separated by a distance, d. GLCM can be defined as follows:

$$o(g_1, g_2, d|\theta) = \# \{(x, y) \mid p(x, y) = g_1;$$
$$p(x + u, y + v) = g_2;$$
$$u = d \cos(\theta) \quad \& \quad v = d \sin(\theta);$$
$$0 \leq g_1, g_2 \leq G - 1 \quad \& \quad 1 \leq d \leq D \quad \& \quad 0° \leq \theta \leq 180°\} \qquad (7)$$

where $\#$ denotes the number of element and $p(x, y)$ is the pixel intensity (gray level) at position x, y. G is the total gray levels and D is the maximum distance between two pixels.

In our implementation, we substitute $p(x, y)$ in Equation (7) with $p_c^3(x, y)$, $p_r^3(x, y)$ and $|p_c^3(x, y)| + |p_r^3(x, y)|$. To avoid confusion, we name the resultants as $o_1(g_1, g_2, d|\theta)$, $o_2(g_1, g_2, d|\theta)$ and $o_3(g_1, g_2, d|\theta)$, respectively. Thus, we can obtain four GLCM matrices from each of the $o_1(g_1, g_2, d|\theta)$, $o_2(g_1, g_2, d|\theta)$ and $o_3(g_1, g_2, d|\theta)$. Namely, each matrix is come from one direction for a total of four directions ($0°$, $45°$, $90°$ and $135°$). We set the distance, d to 1.

3.4   Cover Image Estimation

Cover image estimation is a process of eliminating embedding artifacts[1] in a given image with the objective of getting a near "clean image". Cover image estimation was first proposed by Fridrich in [7] and was known as image calibration. For brevity, consider the following proposition:

Let I_c and I_s represent the cover image and stego image, respectively. If $\sum |I_c - I_c'| < \sum |I_s - I_s'|$, then

$$\phi(I_c) - \phi(I_c') < \phi(I_s) - \phi(I_s') \tag{8}$$

where I_c' and I_s' are the estimated cover images and $I - I'$ is the pixel-wise difference between two same resolution images. $|\cdot|$ represents absolute value and $\phi()$ indicates feature extraction function.

From this proposition, the feature sets extracted from the feature differences (e.g. $\phi(I_s) - \phi(I_s')$) can be considered as the differences caused by the embedding operation as long as the relationship holds. This is desired because we want to have feature sets that are sensitive to the embedding artifacts and invariant to the content of the image.

Hence, we choose image filtering approach to achieve cover image estimation. There are several alternative image filters and from our empirical studies, we found that Gaussian filter produces the best results. In order to use this filter, there are three parameters we need to determine. These parameters include standard deviation of Gaussian distribution (σ), distances for horizontal and vertical directions (d_h and d_v, respectively). We have determined $\sigma = 0.6, d_h = 3$ and $d_v = 3$ from trial and error which give us the optimum solution.

3.5   Final Feature Sets

It is too computational expensive to use all elements in GLRL and GLCM matrix as the feature elements. Therefore, we propose to simplify by transforming the two-dimensional of GLRL and GLCM matrix to one-dimensional histogram.

$$h_g^{GLRL} = \sum_{\ell=1}^{L} r(g, \ell | \theta), \quad 0 \le g \le G - 1, \tag{9}$$

where $\theta = 0°$ and $90°$, and the rest of notations are the same as in Equation (6). In addition, we observe that within a GLRL matrix, there are some high concentration of frequencies near the short runs which may be important. Hence, we propose to extract the first four short runs as a single histogram, $h_g^{sr^\alpha}$.

$$h_g^{sr^\alpha} = r(g, \alpha | \theta), \quad 0 \le g \le G - 1, \tag{10}$$

where $\theta = 0°$ and $90°$ and $\alpha = 1, 2, 3, 4$ are the selected short runs.

---

[1] Embedding artifact refers to any alteration or mark introduced during embedding.

Whereas for the one-dimensional histogram of GLCM matrix, $h_g^{GLCM_\eta}$, it can be obtained in the similar way as in Equation (9), which is defined as follows:

$$h_g^{GLCM_\eta} = \frac{\sum_{g_1=0}^{G-1} o_\eta(g_1, g, d|\theta) + \sum_{g_2=0}^{G-1} o_\eta(g, g_2, d|\theta)}{2}, \quad 0 \le g \le G-1, (11)$$

where $\eta = 1, 2, 3$ and $\theta = 0°, 45°, 90°$ and $135°$. $d = 1$ and the rest of notations are the same as in Equation (7).

As we noted before, multi-class steganalysis can be considered as multi-class classification, so the extracted feature sets must be sensitive to embedding alteration. This is to say the feature values should be very distinctive. The larger the difference across different classes, the better the features. Hence, we apply characteristic function, CF on each of the above histogram to achieve better discrimination. Characteristic function can be computed by using discrete Fourier transform as shown in Equation (12).

$$CF_k = \sum_{n=0}^{N-1} h_n e^{-\frac{2\pi i}{N} kn}, \quad 0 \le k \le N-1, \tag{12}$$

where N is the length of vector, i is the imaginary unit and $e^{-\frac{2\pi i}{N}}$ is a N-th root of unity.

For each of the characteristic function (one for each histogram), we compute mean, variance, kurtosis and skewness. Except for the characteristic function of the four $h_g^{GLCM_\eta}$ histograms (i.e. for the four directions) shown in Equation (11), we compute the average of these characteristic functions. Based on the averaged characteristic function, we compute its mean, variance, kurtosis and skewness.

In addition, we also include another four statistics for each of the computed GLCM matrix as discussed in Subsection 3.3. These four statistics can be defined as follow:

$$contrast = \sum_{g_1} \sum_{g_2} |g_1 - g_2|^2 o(g_1, g_2), \tag{13}$$

$$energy = \sum_{g_1} \sum_{g_2} o(g_1, g_2)^2, \tag{14}$$

$$homogeneity = \sum_{g_1} \sum_{g_2} \frac{o(g_1, g_2)}{1 + |g_1 - g_2|}, \tag{15}$$

$$correlation = \sum_{g_1} \sum_{g_2} \frac{(g_1 - \mu_{g_1})(g_2 - \mu_{g_2}) o(g_1, g_2)}{\sigma_{g_1} \sigma_{g_2}}, \tag{16}$$

where μ_{g_1} and μ_{g_2} are the means of $o(g_1, g_2)$, whereas σ_{g_1} and σ_{g_2} are the standard deviations of $o(g_1, g_2)$.

All together, we form 100-dimensional feature space and are summarized in Table 1.

Table 1. Respective feature sets and the total number of dimensions for each set

	Direction, θ	Number of Matrix	CF	Mean, Variance, Kurtosis and Skewness	Total
h_g^{GLRL}	2	1	applied	4	8 dimensions
$h_g^{sr^{\alpha}}$	2	4	applied	4	32 dimensions
$h_g^{GLCM_\eta}$	4 (averaged to 1)	3	applied	4	12 dimensions
contrast	4	3	-	-	12 dimensions
energy	4	3	-	-	12 dimensions
homogeneity	4	3	-	-	12 dimensions
correlation	4	3	-	-	12 dimensions

4 Multi-class Classification

As we have stated in Section 3, the second stage of our proposed steganalysis is the multi-class classification. We have chosen Support Vector Machine (SVM) as our multi-class classifier. We will start this section by explaining in general the terminology of the two-class SVM classification. After that, we will show how to generalize the two-class classification to multi-class classification using SVM.

SVM can be considered as a classification technique that has the ability to learn from a sample. More precisely, we can train the SVM to recognize and assign the labels (i.e. classes) based on the given collection of data (i.e. features). For example, we train the SVM to differentiate cover image (*class-1*) from stego image (*class-2*) by examining the extracted features from many instances of cover images and stego images. To illustrate the point, let interpret the above example by using the illustration shown in Figure 2. The X and Y axis represent two different features. Cover images and stego images are represented by circles and stars, respectively. Given an unknown image (represented by a square) the SVM is required to predict which class it belongs to.

In this example, it is fairly easy as we can notice that the two different classes (i.e. cover and stego) formed two distinct clusters (can be separated by a line). Hence, what the SVM does is by finding the separating line and determines which cluster the unknown image falls. Finding the right separating line is crucial and this is what the training is meant for. In practice, the features dimensionality are higher and we need a separating plane instead of line which is known as separating hyperplane.

As we can see, the goal of SVM is to find the separating hyperplane that can effectively separate classes. In order to do that, the SVM will try to maximize the margin of the separating hyperplane during the training. Obtaining this maximum-margin hyperplane will optimize the SVM's ability to predict the right class of the unknown object (e.g. image).

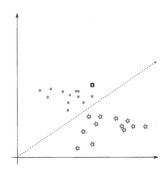

Fig. 2. Two-class SVM classification

However, there are often existed non-separable dataset which cannot be separated by straight separating line or flat plane. The solution to this difficulty is to use kernel function. The kernel function can be considered as a mathematical routine that projects the features from a low-dimensional space to a higher dimensional space. It should also be noted that the choice of kernel function will affect the classification accuracy as well. For further reading of SVM, readers are referred to [15].

Although the nature of SVM is for two-class classification, it is not hard to generalize the SVM to handle multi-class classification. There are several approaches can be used, they are *one-against-one*, *one-against-all* and *all-together* to name a few. According to the recommendations given in [10], the approach using one-against-one provides the best and efficient classifications.

Hence, we will discuss only the approach one-against-one here as we will be using this approach. For other approaches and the details of comparison, readers are referred to [10].

For the multi-class SVM which is based on the one-against-one approach, $K(K-1)/2$ number of two-class SVMs are constructed. Each of these SVM classifiers is assigned to classify a non-overlapping pair of classes (which means there are no two pairs with the same combination of classes). After all the two-class classifications have been completed, majority voting strategy is employed to decide which final class the object belongs to.

Consider the following example. Suppose we have *class-1*, *class-2* and *class-3*. Then we can construct 3 two-class SVMs, namely *SVM-a* classifying *class-1* and *-2*, *SVM-b* classifying *class-1* and *-3* and *SVM-c* classifying *class-2* and *-3*.

Table 2. Example of Majority Voting Strategy for Multi-class SVM

	class-1	*class-2*	*class-3*
SVM-a	0	1	0
SVM-b	1	0	0
SVM-c	0	1	0
Total Votes	1	**2**	0

Assume given an image, each of the two-class SVM classification result can be obtained and is tabulated in Table 2. From the table, the given image can be identified as belonging to *class-2* because we have the highest number of vote (as bolded) in the *class-2* column.

5   Experimental Results

5.1   Experiment Setup

In order to cover wider range of images, we have constructed three sets of image database. The first set of image database consists of 659 binary images as the cover image. The images are all textual documents with white color background and black color foreground. The resolution of the images are all 200 dpi. The second set of image database also consists of 659 binary images as the cover image. These images has the same properties as the first set of image database. However, we have added some graphics (i.e. cartoons, clipart and random shapes) with randomly position in each textual document. In the third set of image database, we have constructed 1338 binary images from a grayscale images using Irfanview version 4.10 freeware . These images are actually converted from natural images. The resolution of these images are set to 72 dpi.

Overall we have constructed 2656 cover images and these image databases can be summarized in Table 3. For brevity, we will name the first, second and third set of image database as textual database, mixture database and scene database, respectively.

Table 3. Summary of Image Databases

Database	Total Images	Resolution	Image Type
Textual	659	200 dpi	Textual
Mixture	659	200 dpi	Textual with Graphic
Scene	1338	72 dpi	Scene

As discussed in Section 2, we have used five different steganographic techniques to generate different types (classes) of stego images. Due to the different embedding algorithm in each technique, the steganographic capacity produced also varies significantly. Hence, in order to obtain a fair comparison we opt to use *absolute steganographic capacity* which can be measured as bits per pixel (bpp). Since binary image only has one bit per pixel, we can think bpp as the average bit per image. For example, 0.01bpp embedding means for every 100 pixels only 1 pixel is used to carry the message bits. 0.01bpp is considerably small which also means less distortion caused on the image. This also implies that the produced stego image is relatively secure and harder for a steganalysis to detect.

In order to verify the effectiveness of our proposed multi-class steganalysis, we have constructed the stego images with the capacity of 0.003bpp, 0.006bpp

Table 4. Summary of Stego Image Databases

Database	Total Images	Steganography	0.003bpp	0.006bpp	0.01bpp	Total Images
Textual	659	5	1	1	1	9885
Mixture	659	5	1	1	1	9885
Scene	1338	5	-	-	1	6690

Table 5. Confusion Matrix of the Multi-Class Steganalysis for the Textual Database

	Classified as					
	WL (%)	LWZ (%)	CTL (%)	TP (%)	PCT (%)	Cover (%)
Cover	0.00	0.00	0.00	0.00	0.00	**100.00**
PCT (0.003bpp)	0.00	0.00	0.77	0.00	**99.23**	0.00
TP (0.003bpp)	0.00	0.00	0.00	**100.00**	0.00	0.00
CTL (0.003bpp)	0.00	0.00	**100.00**	0.00	0.00	0.00
LWZ (0.003bpp)	0.00	**99.23**	0.77	0.00	0.00	0.00
WL (0.003bpp)	**96.15**	0.77	0.77	1.54	0.00	0.77
PCT (0.006bpp)	0.00	0.00	0.00	0.00	**100.00**	0.00
TP (0.006bpp)	0.00	0.00	0.00	**100.00**	0.00	0.00
CTL (0.006bpp)	0.00	0.00	**100.00**	0.00	0.00	0.00
LWZ (0.006bpp)	0.00	**99.23**	0.77	0.00	0.00	0.00
WL (0.006bpp)	**98.46**	0.00	0.77	0.77	0.00	0.00
PCT (0.01bpp)	0.00	0.00	0.00	0.00	**100.00**	0.00
TP (0.01bpp)	0.77	0.00	0.00	**99.23**	0.00	0.00
CTL (0.01bpp)	0.00	0.00	**100.00**	0.00	0.00	0.00
LWZ (0.01bpp)	0.00	**100.00**	0.00	0.00	0.00	0.00
WL (0.01bpp)	**99.23**	0.00	0.77	0.00	0.00	0.00

and 0.01bpp for each of the instances of steganography. This means that we have used relatively huge stego image databases of 26460 images in total (as summarized in Table 4).

We will extract the feature sets for each image from all the image databases mentioned above using the feature extraction methods proposed in Section 3. These feature sets will serve as the input for the multi-class SVM. As elaborated in Section 4 we will use the approach one-against-one to construct our multi-class steganalysis. We use the SVM implemented in [2] for our multi-class steganalysis. We follow the recommendations given in [10] to use RBF as the kernel function and the optimum parameters for the SVMs were determined through grid-search tool from [2]. We dedicate 80 percent of each image databases to train the classifiers and the remaining 20 percent for the testing.

Table 6. Confusion Matrix of the Multi-Class Steganalysis for the Mixture Database

| | Classified as | | | | | |
	WL (%)	LWZ (%)	CTL (%)	TP (%)	PCT (%)	Cover (%)
Cover	0.00	0.77	0.00	0.00	0.00	**99.23**
PCT (0.003bpp)	0.00	0.00	2.31	0.77	**96.92**	0.00
TP (0.003bpp)	2.31	1.54	0.00	**96.15**	0.00	0.00
CTL (0.003bpp)	0.00	0.77	**92.31**	0.77	6.15	0.00
LWZ (0.003bpp)	1.54	**96.15**	0.77	1.54	0.00	0.00
WL (0.003bpp)	**96.92**	1.54	0.77	0.77	0.00	0.00
PCT (0.006bpp)	0.00	0.00	2.31	0.00	**97.69**	0.00
TP (0.006bpp)	0.00	0.77	0.00	**99.23**	0.00	0.00
CTL (0.006bpp)	0.00	0.00	**99.23**	0.00	0.77	0.00
LWZ (0.006bpp)	0.00	**99.23**	0.00	0.00	0.77	0.00
WL (0.006bpp)	**98.46**	0.00	0.00	0.00	0.77	0.77
PCT (0.01bpp)	0.00	0.00	1.54	0.00	**98.46**	0.00
TP (0.01bpp)	0.00	0.00	0.00	**100.00**	0.00	0.00
CTL (0.01bpp)	0.00	0.00	**99.23**	0.00	0.77	0.00
LWZ (0.01bpp)	0.00	**99.23**	0.00	0.00	0.77	0.00
WL (0.01bpp)	**99.23**	0.00	0.00	0.00	0.77	0.00

5.2   Results Comparison

To ease the presentation, we will abbreviate the five steganography as PCT, TP, CTL, LWZ and WL for [16], [23], [3], [12] and [26], respectively. Our multi-class steganalysis classification results will be displayed in the table format called confusion matrix. In the confusion matrix, the first column consists of the classes which include one cover image class and five different classes of stego image (i.e. each class of the stego image is produced by each of the five steganographic techniques discussed before). The value within the bracket beside each class indicates the embedded capacity. As for the cover image class, there is no embedding and we can consider the embedded capacity as zero (0.0bpp). Whereas the first row of the confusion matrix indicates which class a given image has been classified to.

We have separated to three confusion matrices for each of the three image databases as in Table 5, Table 6 and Table 7, respectively. To better illustrate the results, we have typeset the desired results to bold. In other words, the right classification results are aligned along the diagonal elements within each confusion matrix.

From the confusion matrices, we can clearly see that the multi-class steganalysis gives very promising results. Especially in Table 5, the detections are nearly perfect. The results obtained for the mixture image database (Table 6) are also very accurate although slightly less than the results obtained in Table 5. The results obtained for the scene image database (Table 7) appeared to be the least

Table 7. Confusion Matrix of the Multi-Class Steganalysis for the Scene Database

| | Classified as | | | | | |
	WL (%)	LWZ (%)	CTL (%)	TP (%)	PCT (%)	Cover (%)
Cover	2.26	5.26	1.88	8.65	0.38	**81.58**
PCT (0.01bpp)	0.76	0.38	4.51	0.00	**93.99**	0.38
TP (0.01bpp)	11.65	3.01	0.38	**80.08**	0.00	4.89
CTL (0.01bpp)	1.13	1.50	**89.10**	0.00	3.76	4.51
LWZ (0.01bpp)	1.88	**91.35**	0.38	2.26	0.38	3.76
WL (0.01bpp)	**85.34**	2.26	0.38	10.90	0.38	0.75

accurate among the others. However, the reliability of the detection is still very good and all the detection results show at least 80% of the accuracy. From our observation, we notice that the type of cover images used will affect our detection accuracy. Which means it is relatively easier to detect images with textual contents than images with natural scenes. This observation is also supported by the detection accuracy orders (where the results in Table 5 are the best, followed by the results in Table 6 and lastly the results in Table 7).

We attribute this phenomenon to the fact that the textual content in an image has sort of periodic patterns which are more uniform and consistent. However, for an image with scene content, there are less fix patterns and may look like more random.

In addition, it is also worthwhile to mention that the longer the secret message is embedded, the more distortion it will cause in the image. Hence, it is relatively easier to detect stego image with embedded longer message (higher bpp) than shorter message (lower bpp). This can be justified by comparing the rows with 0.01bpp to the rows with 0.003bpp in the confusion matrices.

6   Conclusion

We have successfully proposed a multi-class steganalysis for binary image. Our proposed new 60-dimensional feature sets used in combination with existing 40-dimensional feature sets extended from our previous work can effectively and accurately classify a given image to its appropriate class. Namely, one class of cover image and five classes of stego image produced by five different steganographic techniques. In addition, we have employed the concept of cover image estimation which has improved the classification as well. Experimental results also showed that our proposed method can detect low embedded capacity. Furthermore, the experimental results showed that the detection accuracy of at least 92% can be achieved in detecting the textual or mixture of textual and graphic images. However, the accuracy is slightly decreased to 80% in detecting natural scene binary images.

Acknowledgments. Kang Leng Chiew has been supported by SLAI Scholarship (Ministry of Higher Education Malaysia) and HDR Project Support Funds (Macquarie University). Josef Pieprzyk has been supported by Australian Research Council grant DP0987734.

References

1. Böhme, R., Westfeld, A.: Breaking cauchy model-based jpeg steganography with first order statistics. In: Samarati, P., Ryan, P.Y.A., Gollmann, D., Molva, R. (eds.) ESORICS 2004. LNCS, vol. 3193, pp. 125–140. Springer, Heidelberg (2004)
2. Chang, C.-C., Lin, C.-J.: LIBSVM: a library for support vector machines (2001), Software available at http://www.csie.ntu.edu.tw/~cjlin/libsvm
3. Chang, C.-C., Tseng, C.-S., Lin, C.-C.: Hiding data in binary images. In: Deng, R.H., Bao, F., Pang, H., Zhou, J. (eds.) ISPEC 2005. LNCS, vol. 3439, pp. 338–349. Springer, Heidelberg (2005)
4. Chiew, K.L., Pieprzyk, J.: A countermeasure for binary image steganography. In: International Conference on Availability, Reliability and Security (2010)
5. Cortes, C., Vapnik, V.: Support-vector networks. Machine Learning 20(3), 273–297 (1995)
6. Dong, J., Wang, W., Tan, T.: Multi-class blind steganalysis based on image run-length analysis. In: Ho, A.T.S., Shi, Y.Q., Kim, H.J., Barni, M. (eds.) Digital Watermarking. LNCS, vol. 5703, pp. 199–210. Springer, Heidelberg (2009)
7. Fridrich, J.: Feature-based steganalysis for JPEG images and its implications for future design of steganographic schemes. In: Fridrich, J. (ed.) IH 2004. LNCS, vol. 3200, pp. 67–81. Springer, Heidelberg (2004)
8. Fridrich, J., Goljan, M., Soukal, D., Holotyak, T.: Forensic steganalysis: determining the stego key in spatial domain steganography. In: Proceedings of the SPIE on Security and Watermarking of Multimedia Contents VII, vol. 5681, pp. 631–642 (2005)
9. He, J., Huang, J.: Steganalysis of stochastic modulation steganography. Science in China Series F: Information Sciences 49(3), 273–285 (2006)
10. Hsu, C.-W., Lin, C.-J.: A comparison of methods for multiclass support vector machines. IEEE Transactions on Neural Networks 13, 415–425 (2002)
11. Jiang, M., Wu, X., Wong, E., Memon, A.: Steganalysis of boundary-based steganography using autoregressive model of digital boundaries. In: IEEE International Conference on Multimedia and Expo, vol. 2, pp. 883–886 (2004)
12. Liang, G.-l., Wang, S.-z., Zhang, X.-p.: Steganography in binary image by checking data-carrying eligibility of boundary pixels. Journal of Shanghai University (English Edition) 11(3), 272–277 (2007)
13. Liu, Z., Ping, L., Chen, J., Wang, J., Pan, X.: Steganalysis based on differential statistics. In: Pointcheval, D., Mu, Y., Chen, K. (eds.) CANS 2006. LNCS, vol. 4301, pp. 224–240. Springer, Heidelberg (2006)
14. Morkel, T., Eloff, J.H.P., Olivier, M.S.: Using image steganography for decryptor distribution. In: Meersman, R., Tari, Z., Herrero, P. (eds.) OTM 2006 Workshops. LNCS, vol. 4277, pp. 322–330. Springer, Heidelberg (2006)
15. Noble, W.S.: What is a support vector machine? Nature biotechnology 24(12) (2006)
16. Pan, H.-K., Chen, Y.-Y., Tseng, Y.-C.: A secure data hiding scheme for two-color images. In: 5th IEEE Symposium on Computers and Communications, pp. 750–755 (2000)

17. Pevný, T., Fridrich, J.: Multi-class blind steganalysis for jpeg images. In: Proceedings of the SPIE on Security and Watermarking of Multimedia Contents VIII, vol. 6072(1), pp. 257–269 (2006)
18. Pevny, T., Fridrich, J.: Merging markov and DCT features for multi-class jpeg steganalysis. In: Proceedings of the SPIE on Security and Watermarking of Multimedia Contents IX, vol. 6505(1), pp. 1–13 (2007)
19. Provos, N.: Defending against statistical steganalysis. In: Proceedings of the 10th conference on USENIX Security Symposium, vol. 10, pp. 323–335 (2001)
20. Rodriguez, B., Peterson, G.L.: Detecting steganography using multi-class classification. In: IFIP International Conference on Digital Forensics, vol. 242, pp. 193–204 (2007)
21. Savoldi, A., Gubian, P.: Blind multi-class steganalysis system using wavelet statistics. In: 3rd International Conference on Intelligent Information Hiding and Multimedia Signal Processing, vol. 2, pp. 93–96 (2007)
22. Shi, Y.Q., Chen, C., Chen, W.: A markov process based approach to effective attacking jpeg steganography. In: Camenisch, J.L., Collberg, C.S., Johnson, N.F., Sallee, P. (eds.) IH 2006. LNCS, vol. 4437, pp. 249–264. Springer, Heidelberg (2007)
23. Tseng, Y.-C., Pan, H.-K.: Secure and invisible data hiding in 2-color images. In: Twentieth Annual Joint Conference of the IEEE Computer and Communications Societies, vol. 2, pp. 887–896 (2001)
24. Wang, P., Liu, F., Wang, G., Sun, Y., Gong, D.: Multi-class steganalysis for Jpeg stego algorithms. In: 15th IEEE International Conference on Image Processing, pp. 2076–2079 (2008)
25. Westfeld, A.: F5-A steganographic algorithm. In: Moskowitz, I.S. (ed.) IH 2001. LNCS, vol. 2137, pp. 289–302. Springer, Heidelberg (2001)
26. Wu, M., Liu, B.: Data hiding in binary image for authentication and annotation. IEEE transactions on multimedia 6(4), 528–538 (2004)
27. Yang, C.-Y.: Color image steganography based on module substitutions. In: 3rd IEEE International Conference on Intelligent Information Hiding and Multimedia Signal Processing, vol. 2, pp. 118–121 (2007)

Game Theoretic Resistance to Denial of Service Attacks Using Hidden Difficulty Puzzles

Harikrishna Narasimhan[1,*], Venkatanathan Varadarajan[1,*],
and C. Pandu Rangan[2,**]

[1] Department of Computer Science and Engineering,
College of Engineering, Guindy, Anna University, Chennai, India
{nhari88,venk1989}@gmail.com
[2] Department of Computer Science and Engineering,
Indian Institute of Technology Madras, Chennai, India
prangan@iitm.ac.in

Abstract. Denial of Service (DoS) vulnerabilities are one of the major concerns in today's internet. Client-puzzles offer a good mechanism to defend servers against DoS attacks. In this paper, we introduce the notion of hidden puzzle difficulty, where the attacker cannot determine the difficulty of the puzzle without expending a minimal amount of computational resource. We propose three concrete puzzles that satisfy this requirement. Using game theory, we show that a defense mechanism is more effective when it uses a hidden difficulty puzzle. Based on the concept of Nash equilibrium, we develop suitable defense mechanisms that are better than the existing ones.

Keywords: Denial of Service (DoS) Attack, Proof of Work, Hidden Difficulty Puzzle, Infinitely Repeated Game, Nash Equilibrium.

1 Introduction

Denial of Service (DoS) vulnerabilities are one of the major concerns in today's internet. The aim of a DoS attack is to make a network service unavailable to its legitimate users. A denial of service attack may either be a brute force attack, where the attacker generates spurious network traffic to exhaust server resources or a semantic attack, where the attacker exploits the vulnerabilities of the protocol used [15].

Proofs of work or client-puzzles offer a good mechanism for a server to counterbalance computational expenditure when subjected to a denial of service attack. On receiving a request, the server generates a puzzle of appropriate difficulty and sends it to the client. When a response is received, the server verifies the solution and provides the requested service only if the solution is correct. This

---

* Work supported by IITM Summer Fellowship Programme May-July 2009.
** This author was partially supported by Indo-Australian Project on Protecting Critical Information Infrastructure from DoS attacks, CSE/08-09/102/DSTX/SVRA-IAP.

J. Kwak et al. (Eds.): ISPEC 2010, LNCS 6047, pp. 359–376, 2010.

approach was first proposed by Dwork and Naor [4] to control junk mails. Over the years, lot of research has gone into this area and different client-puzzles have been proposed [13,8,2,18,19,6,16,20,17].

A challenge in the client-puzzle approach is deciding on the difficulty of the puzzle to be sent. One approach suggested by Feng et al. [6] is to adjust the puzzle difficulty proportional to the current load on the server. Juels and Brainard [8] suggested that the difficulty of the puzzle be scaled uniformly for all clients according to the severity of the attack on the server. In both these approaches, the quality of service to legitimate users is not considered. Alternatively, the server can generate puzzles of varying difficulties based on a probability distribution. Such an approach based on game theory can be seen in [3,5].

Though there have been several works that formally analyze denial of service attacks using game theory [3,11,5,9,10,14,1], only a few of them analyze the client-puzzle approach [3,5,10]. Bencsath et al. [3] modeled the client-puzzle approach as a single-shot strategic game and identified the server's optimal strategy. Fallah [5], on the other hand, used an infinitely repeated game to come up with puzzle-based defense mechanisms. He also proposed extensions to tackle distributed attacks. Recently, Jun-Jie [10] applied game theory to puzzle auctions.

Game theoretic defense mechanisms against DoS attacks focus on *fine tuning the parameters* of the system in such a way that the server is not overloaded by the attacker. Our work builds on the game theoretic model and defense mechanisms proposed by Fallah.

Our Contribution. In addition to the basic properties of a good puzzle [15], we introduce the following requirement: *the difficulty of the puzzle should not be determined by the attacker without expending a minimal amount of computational effort.* We propose three concrete puzzles that satisfy this requirement. Using game theory, we show that defense mechanisms are more effective when the puzzle difficulty is hidden from the attacker.

The rest of the paper is organized as follows: Section 2 contains an example of a hidden difficulty puzzle (HDP). In Section 3, we show using game theory that a defense mechanism is more effective when it uses HDPs. In Section 4, we develop defense mechanisms based on Nash equilibrium. New puzzles are described in Section 5 and we conclude the paper in Section 6.

2   Hidden Difficulty Puzzle (HDP)

The difficulty of a client puzzle is said to be hidden if it cannot be determined by an attacker without expending a minimal amount of computational effort. We first introduce a modified version of the hash-reversal puzzle [8], which satisfies this requirement. The puzzle generation and verification are detailed in Fig. 1.

A preimage X is generated by hashing a server secret S, a server nonce N_s and a session parameter M together. The server nonce is used to check whether the puzzle is recent and the session parameter allows the server to be stateless [15]. The preimage is again hashed to obtain Y and some of the first k bits of X are

Client	Defender
$\xrightarrow{\quad Request \quad}$	$X = H(S, N_s, M)$
	$Y = H(X)$
$\xleftarrow{(X',Y), N_s}$	$X' = X \oplus (I_1, I_2, ..., I_{k-1}, 1, 0_{k+1}, ..., 0_n)$
Find rp such that	$\xrightarrow{\quad rp, N_s \quad}$ $X = H(S, N_s, M)$
$H(rp) = Y$	$H(rp) \overset{?}{=} H(X)$

Fig. 1. Hidden Difficulty Puzzle 1. Here, H is a cryptographic hash function and I is a binary number chosen uniformly at random.

randomly inverted. Let X' be the resultant binary string. The puzzle consisting of X' and Y is sent to the client along with the server nonce.

Note that k determines the difficulty of the puzzle and is unknown to the client. In order to solve the puzzle he would have to carry out an exhaustive search and arrive at the solution after testing up to 2^k possible preimages. The solution to the puzzle along with the received nonce is sent back to the defender. The defender recomputes the preimage X and verifies the solution.

Here, puzzle generation takes 2 hash computations, while the verification takes 3 hash computations. Further, the client needs to compute an average of $\frac{(2^k+1)}{2}$ hashes to solve the puzzle.

Assume the defender uses two instances of the described hidden difficulty puzzle, P_1 and P_2 with difficulty levels k_1 and k_2 respectively. On receiving a puzzle, the attacker does not know whether it is P_1 or P_2. Any solution to P_1 would have the k_1^{th} bit inverted, while any solution to P_2 will have the k_2^{th} bit inverted. Clearly, the solution spaces of the two puzzles do not overlap. To solve the puzzle, the attacker could first test possible preimages for one of the puzzles and if it is not solved, test preimages for the other. He could also try out preimages for both puzzles simultaneously. In any case, the attacker would know the puzzle difficulty only after putting in the effort required to solve one of the puzzles. Clearly, the attacker cannot determine the puzzle difficulty without minimal resource expenditure.

3   Game Theoretic Analysis of HDP

We shall now see how a hidden difficulty puzzle can make a defense mechanism more effective. We assume the network consists of a server, a set of legitimate clients/users and an attacker. The attacker seeks to mount a denial of service attack on the client-server protocol by overloading the computational resources of the server. The client-puzzle approach is used as a defense mechanism against the attack. The interaction between the attacker and the defender during a denial of service attack is viewed as a two-player game. We use the same notations as in [5] to model the game.

Rational Attacker. Our primary assumption is that the attacker is rational. The objective of the attacker is to maximize the resource expenditure of the defender with minimum computational effort. This is reasonable from the point of view of the proof of work paradigm, where a rational attacker is the **strongest** attacker. On the other hand, if the attacker is not rational and takes non-optimal decisions, it would be in the interest of the defender.

3.1   Model

Consider a game between an attacker and a defender. We categorize the puzzles used by the defender as either easy or difficult. A puzzle is easy if the time taken to solve it is lesser than the time taken by the defender to provide the requested service and is difficult if the time taken to solve the puzzle is greater than the service time. Assume that the defender uses an easy puzzle P_1 and a difficult puzzle P_2 to defend himself. (We later show in Section 4.1 that two puzzles are sufficient for an effective defense mechanism.)

Let T be a reference time period. Let α_m be the fraction of the time T that the defender spends in providing the service, α_{PP} be the fraction of T he takes to produce a puzzle and α_{VP} be the fraction of T he takes to verify it. Let α_{SP_1} be the fraction of T that the attacker is expected to spend to solve P_1 and let α_{SP_2} be the fraction of T to solve P_2. As mentioned earlier, the defender chooses the puzzles P_1 and P_2 such that $\alpha_{SP_1} < \alpha_m < \alpha_{SP_2}$.

Attacker Actions. On receiving a puzzle, the attacker may choose from one among the following actions: (i) correctly answer the puzzle (CA), (ii) randomly answer the puzzle (RA) and (iii) try to answer the puzzle, but give up if it is too hard (TA). In the case of TA, the attacker gives a correct answer if the puzzle is solved and a random answer if he gives up. Note that TA is relevant only when the puzzle difficulty is hidden. If the attacker knows the difficulty of the puzzle on receiving it, he can immediately decide on whether to answer it correctly or randomly.

Attacker Payoff. Let u_2 denote the payoff of the attacker. Attacker's action is profitable if the defender expends computational resource, else it is a loss when he himself incurs an expenditure. Let P_i, $i = 1, 2$, be the puzzle received by the attacker. If he chooses CA, he incurs a cost α_{SP_i} in solving the puzzle, while the defender expends resources in generating and verifying the puzzle and providing the requested service. His payoff is therefore

$$u_2(P_i; CA) = \alpha_{PP} + \alpha_{VP} + \alpha_m - \alpha_{SP_i}.$$

If the attacker chooses RA, the attacker incurs no cost, while the defender incurs a cost in generating and verifying the puzzle.

$$u_2(P_i; RA) = \alpha_{PP} + \alpha_{VP}.$$

If the attacker's response is TA, his payoff depends on when he gives up.

Try and Answer. When the attacker receives puzzle P_1, he is better off answering it correctly, rather than answering it randomly. This is because $u_2(P_1; CA) > u_2(P_1; RA)$ (as $\alpha_{SP_1} < \alpha_m$). On the other hand, when he receives P_2, $u_2(P_2; CA) < u_2(P_2; RA)$ (as $\alpha_{SP_2} > \alpha_m$) and hence, RA would be a better choice than CA. A decision on RA and CA can be made only if the puzzle difficulty is known. In the case of HDPs, the attacker is sure that the puzzle is not P_1 only when he fails to solve it after expending α_{SP_1} amount of resource. Hence, when the attacker chooses TA, he puts in the (minimal) effort required to solve P_1 and gives up when he realizes the puzzle is P_2. If the puzzle sent is P_1, the attacker would solve it with the minimal effort and give the correct answer, while if it is P_2, he would give up and send a random answer. His payoff for the action TA is given by

$$u_2(P_1; TA) = \alpha_{PP} + \alpha_{VP} + \alpha_m - \alpha_{SP_1} \text{ and}$$

$$u_2(P_2; TA) = \alpha_{PP} + \alpha_{VP} - \alpha_{SP_1}.$$

3.2 Analysis of Attacker Payoff

Let $0 < p < 1$ be the probability with which the attacker receives puzzle P_1. ($1-p$ is the probability with which he receives P_2.) We denote the corresponding mixed strategy of the defender as α_1. If the difficulty of the puzzle is hidden, the expected payoff of the attacker for his actions is given by

$$U_2(\alpha_1; CA) = \alpha_{PP} + \alpha_{VP} + \alpha_m - p\alpha_{SP_1} - (1-p)\alpha_{SP_2}, \tag{1}$$

$$U_2(\alpha_1; RA) = \alpha_{PP} + \alpha_{VP} \text{ and} \tag{2}$$

$$U_2(\alpha_1; TA) = \alpha_{PP} + \alpha_{VP} + p\alpha_m - \alpha_{SP_1}. \tag{3}$$

The attacker's choice is influenced by the probability p and the values of α_{SP_1} and α_{SP_2}. The attacker would prefer RA over TA only if $p < \frac{\alpha_{SP_1}}{\alpha_m} = p_t$. He would prefer RA over CA when $p < \frac{\alpha_{SP_2} - \alpha_{SP_1}}{\alpha_{SP_2} - \alpha_m} = p_c$. From the payoffs, it is evident that the action CA is more beneficial than TA when $\alpha_{SP_2} - \alpha_{SP_1} < \alpha_m$.

On the other hand, if the difficulty of the puzzle is known to the attacker, he would choose CA if the puzzle is P_1 and RA if it is P_2 [5]. We represent the corresponding strategy as (CA, RA) and his expected payoff is

$$U_2(\alpha_1; (CA, RA)) = \alpha_{PP} + \alpha_{VP} + p(\alpha_m - \alpha_{SP_1}). \tag{4}$$

We now show that **the attacker receives lower payoff when HDPs are used.** Consider each of the attacker's actions:

(i) **RA**. The attacker chooses RA when (a) $\alpha_{SP_2} - \alpha_{SP_1} < \alpha_m$ and $p < p_t$ or (b) $\alpha_{SP_2} - \alpha_{SP_1} > \alpha_m$ and $p < p_c$. From (2) and (4), for $0 < p < 1$,

$$U_2(\alpha_1; RA) < U_2(\alpha_1; (CA, RA)). \tag{5}$$

(ii) **TA**. The attacker chooses TA when $\alpha_{SP_2} - \alpha_{SP_1} < \alpha_m$ and $p > p_t$. From (3) and (4), for $0 < p < 1$,

$$U_2(\alpha_1; TA) < U_2(\alpha_1; (CA, RA)). \tag{6}$$

(iii) **CA**. The attacker chooses CA when $\alpha_{SP_2} - \alpha_{SP_1} > \alpha_m$ and $p > p_c$. From (1) and (4), as $\alpha_{SP_2} < \alpha_m$ and $0 < p < 1$,

$$U_2(\alpha_1; CA) < U_2(\alpha_1; (CA, RA)). \tag{7}$$

In all three cases, the attacker is benefited less when the puzzle difficulty is hidden than when it is known to him.

Effectiveness. We define the effectiveness of a defense mechanism using proof of work as *the difference between the amount of work done by the attacker and the amount of work done by the defender.* Clearly, a defense mechanism would be more effective when it uses a HDP.

4   Defense Mechanisms

We propose two defense mechanisms against DoS attacks based on the concept of Nash equilibrium. Hidden difficulty puzzles are used in both the defense mechanisms. As in [5], the Nash equilibrium is used in a prescriptive way, where the defender selects and takes part in a specific equilibrium profile and the best thing for the attacker to do is to conform to his equilibrium strategy. Initially, we assume that the attack takes place from a single machine and later propose an extension to handle distributed attacks.

4.1   Strategic Game

The attacker is unaware of the difficulty of a puzzle when he receives it and the defender is unaware of the attacker's response when he sends the puzzle. We therefore model the interaction between an attacker and defender during a denial of service attack as a strategic game.

Defender's Actions. We assume the defender uses n puzzles P_1, P_2, ..., P_n such that $\alpha_{SP_1} < ... < \alpha_{SP_k} < \alpha_m < \alpha_{SP_{k+1}} < ... < \alpha_{SP_n}$, where α_{SP_i} is the cost incurred by an attacker in solving puzzle P_i. The generation and verification costs are same for all puzzles and equal to α_{PP} and α_{VP} respectively. (This assumption is reasonable as generation and verification time for a good client-puzzle is negligible [15].)

Defender's Payoff. The defender seeks to maximize the effectiveness of the defense mechanism and minimize the cost to a legitimate user. We introduce a balance factor $0 < \eta < 1$ that allows him to strike a balance between the two. His payoff is therefore given by $u_1 = (1-\eta)(\text{effectiveness})+\eta(-\text{legitimate user cost})$.

Table 1. Cost incurred by the players and the legitimate user when action profile a is chosen. Here $1 \leq l \leq n$, $1 \leq i \leq k$ and $k+1 \leq j \leq n$.

a	$\psi_1(a)$	$\psi_2(a)$	$\psi_u(a)$
$(P_l; RA)$	$\alpha_{PP} + \alpha_{VP}$	0	α_{SP_l}
$(P_i; TA)$	$\alpha_{PP} + \alpha_{VP} + \alpha_m$	α_{SP_i}	α_{SP_i}
$(P_j; TA)$	$\alpha_{PP} + \alpha_{VP}$	α_{SP_k}	α_{SP_j}
$(P_l; CA)$	$\alpha_{PP} + \alpha_{VP} + \alpha_m$	α_{SP_l}	α_{SP_l}

Let $\psi_1(a)$ and $\psi_2(a)$ be the cost incurred by the defender and attacker, respectively, when the action profile a is chosen. Let $\psi_u(a)$ be the corresponding cost to a legitimate user. Hence,

$$u_1(a) = (1 - \eta)(-\psi_1(a) + \psi_2(a)) + \eta(-\psi_u(a)).$$

The costs incurred by the players and the legitimate user for the various action profiles are tabulated in Table 1.

A legitimate user always solves the given puzzle and incurs a cost α_{SP_i} for a puzzle P_i. Here, it is assumed that the attacker and a legitimate user take equal time to solve a puzzle. The model can be easily extended to distributed attacks, where the computational power of the attacker is considered much higher than that of a legitimate user [12].

For the puzzles P_1, P_2, ... and P_k, the attacker is better off giving the correct answer, while for puzzles P_{k+1}, ... and P_n, the attacker is better off giving a random answer. When the puzzle difficulty is unknown, the attacker may choose to try and answer (TA), where the maximum effort he puts in is the effort required to solve P_k. If the puzzle is solved with a maximum resource expenditure of α_{SP_k}, he sends a correct answer. Otherwise, he gives up and sends a random answer.

Proposition 1. *In the strategic game of the client-puzzle approach, the best response of the defender to the attacker's action TA is the puzzle P_k or the puzzle P_{k+1} or a lottery over both.*

The proof for proposition 1 is available in the full version of this paper [12]. For all other propositions stated in this section, the proofs have been given in Appendix A.

Let P_1 and P_2 be the two puzzles corresponding to proposition 1.

Analysis of Defender Payoff. Let us consider the defender's mixed strategy α_1, where he chooses P_1 with probability $0 < p < 1$ and P_2 with probability $1 - p$. A legitimate user would always incur a cost $\psi_u = p\alpha_{SP_1} + (1 - p)\alpha_{SP_2}$. If the puzzle difficulty is hidden, the attacker would choose an action $a_2 \in \{RA, TA, CA\}$. The defender's payoff would then be

$$u_1(\alpha_1; a_2) = (1 - \eta)(-u_2(\alpha_1; a_2)) + \eta(-\psi_u).$$

As discussed earlier, the attacker would choose $a_2 = (CA; RA)$ [5] if the puzzle difficulty is not hidden and the corresponding payoff to the defender would be

$$u_1(\alpha_1; (CA; RA)) = (1 - \eta)(-u_2(\alpha_1; (CA; RA))) + \eta(-\psi_u).$$

For the same value of η, it is seen from (5), (6) and (7) that $u_1(\alpha_1; a_2) > u_1(\alpha_1; (CA; RA))$ for all $a_2 \in \{RA, TA, CA\}$. Hence, **the defender receives higher payoff while using HDPs.**

Nash Equilibrium. We now analyze the existence of Nash equilibria in the game of the client-puzzle approach. One possible Nash equilibrium is where the attacker chooses the action TA. The conditions for such an equilibrium are given in the following proposition.

Proposition 2. *In the strategic game of the client-puzzle approach, for $0 < \eta < \frac{1}{2}$, a Nash equilibrium of the form $(p \circ P_1 \oplus (1 - p) \circ P_2; TA)^1$, $0 < p < 1$, exists if $\eta = \frac{\alpha_m}{\alpha_m + \alpha_{SP_2} - \alpha_{SP_1}}$, $\alpha_{SP_2} - \alpha_{SP_1} > \alpha_m$ and $p > \frac{\alpha_{SP_1}}{\alpha_m}$.*

We now construct a defense mechanism against a DoS attack by prescribing the Nash equilibrium given in proposition 2. A Nash equilibrium allows us to predict the behavior of a rational attacker during a DoS attack, but does not prevent the flooding attack from being successful.

Mitigating DoS Attack. Let N be the maximum number of requests that an attacker can send in time T. It is assumed that the defender has a resource r_p for puzzle generation and verification and another resource r_m for providing the requested service [5]. As per the property of a good client puzzle, the generation and verification time must be negligible. In fact, the verification time can be minimized by using a table lookup [19]. Hence, it is reasonable to assume that r_p is not exhausted in an attack, i.e., $N(\alpha_{PP} + \alpha_{VP}) < 1$. On the other hand, the attack is successful when r_m is exhausted before all requests are serviced. If β is the probability with which the attacker solves a given puzzle, $N\beta$ is the expected number of attack requests for which the defender would provide service. When $N\beta\alpha_m > 1$, the defender is overwhelmed and the attack is successful. In order to mitigate an attack, we need to ensure that

$$N\beta\alpha_m \leq 1 \text{ or } \beta \leq \frac{1}{N\alpha_m}.$$

In the prescribed Nash equilibrium, $\beta = p$ and the following condition must hold for an attack to be unsuccessful: $\frac{\alpha_{SP_1}}{\alpha_m} < p < \frac{1}{N\alpha_m}$. Note that this is possible only if $\alpha_{SP_1} < \frac{1}{N}$.

The probability p is chosen such that the defender can provide service for all attack requests. It has to be remembered that even legitimate requests need to be serviced during an attack. Hence, out of the total number of requests that

---

[1] The notation $p_1 \circ a_1 \oplus p_2 \circ a_2 \oplus ... \oplus p_n \circ a_n$ denotes a lottery over the set of actions $\{a_1, a_2, ..., a_n\}$, where $p_1 + p_2 + ... + p_n = 1$.

the defender can service, we take $\frac{1}{\alpha_m}$ as the number of requests allocated to the defense mechanism, while the rest are for the legitimate users.

We propose a defense mechanism based on the prescribed Nash equilibrium. (We call it the **strategic game defense mechanism**.) The idea is to fine tune the various parameters such that the conditions for the equilibrium are satisfied.

1. For a desirable balance factor η, $0 < \eta < \frac{1}{2}$, choose two puzzles P_1 and P_2 such that

$$\alpha_{SP_1} < \frac{1}{N} < \alpha_m < \alpha_{SP_2}, \ \alpha_{SP_2} - \alpha_{SP_1} > \alpha_m \ and$$

$$\eta = \frac{\alpha_m}{\alpha_m + \alpha_{SP_2} - \alpha_{SP_1}}.$$

2. Choose a value for p such that

$$\frac{\alpha_{SP_1}}{\alpha_m} < p < \frac{1}{N\alpha_m}.$$

3. On receiving a request, generate a random variable $\mathbf{x}$ such that $Pr(\mathbf{x}=0) = p$ and $Pr(\mathbf{x}=1) = 1 - p$. If $\mathbf{x}=0$, send puzzle P_1. Otherwise, send puzzle P_2.

The other possible Nash equilibria in the strategic game have been discussed in the full version of this paper [12].

4.2   Infinitely Repeated Game

During a denial of service attack, the attacker repeatedly sends requests to the defender. Since the game is played repeatedly, this scenario can be modeled as a repeated game. Also, the probability of arrival of a request is non-zero at any point in time and hence, the game is infinitely repeated [5].

Threat of Punishment. In repeated games, the payoff of a player is not only influenced by his decision in the current game, but is also influenced by his decisions in all periods of the game. A player would therefore be willing to take sub-optimal decisions for the current game if it would give him a higher payoff in the long run. Deviation of a player from a desired strategy profile can be prevented if he is threatened with sufficient punishment in the future. Therefore, Nash equilibria with high payoffs can be achieved in an infinitely repeated game if a player is patient enough to see long term benefits over short term gains.

Minmax Payoff. The minmax payoff of a player is the minimum payoff that he can guarantee himself in a game, even when the opponents play in the most undesirable manner. The minmax payoff of player i in a strategic game is given by

$$v_i^* = \min_{\alpha_{-i} \in \Delta(A_{-i})} \max_{a_i \in A_i} u_i(a_i, \alpha_{-i}),$$

where $\Delta(X)$ is the set of probability distributions over X, A_i is the set of permitted actions for player i and u_i is his payoff function.

Nash Equilibrium. Consider a two-player infinitely repeated game. Let v_1^* be the minmax payoff of player 1 and v_2^* be the minmax payoff of player 2. Let the mixed strategy profile resulting in v_1^* and v_2^* be $M^1 = (M_1^1; M_2^1)$ and $M^2 = (M_1^2; M_2^2)$ respectively. Here, M_1^2 is player 1's minmax strategy against player 2 and M_2^1 is player 2's minmax strategy against player 1.

Let $(\alpha_1; \alpha_2)$ be a strategy profile such that $v_1 = u_1(\alpha_1; \alpha_2) > v_1^*$ and $v_2 = u_2(\alpha_1; \alpha_2) > v_2^*$. Fudenberg and Maskin [7] show that an equilibrium where each player i receives an average payoff of v_i is possible through threat of punishment. The following repeated game strategy for player i is a Nash equilibrium.

(A) Play α_i each period as long as $(\alpha_1; \alpha_2)$ was played last period. After any deviation from phase (A), switch to phase (B).

(B) Play M_i^j, $j \neq i$, τ times (say) and then start phase (A) again. If there are any deviations while in phase (B), restart phase (B).

A description of their theorem along with the calculation of τ has been detailed in the full version of the paper [12].

Interpretation. A possible equilibrium in the game of the client-puzzle approach consists of two phases:

Normal Phase (A). The defender and attacker choose a strategy profile, where each of them receive a payoff greater than the minmax payoff. Note that the strategy played may not be the optimal choice of the players in the given period. However, if either of them deviate, the game switches to the punishment phase (B).

Punishment Phase (B). In this phase, each player chooses a minmax strategy against the other player. This phase remains for τ periods, after which the game switches to the normal phase. Again, the minmax strategy may not be the optimal strategy of a player in the current period. But, any deviation from this strategy would restart the phase.

Any deviation in the normal phase is deterred by the threat of switching to the punishment phase. Similarly, a deviation from the punishment phase is deterred by the threat of prolonged punishment. Note that the **punishment period** τ must be sufficiently long for the equilibrium to exist.

The following propositions identify some minmax strategies in the game of the client-puzzle approach.

Proposition 3. *In the game of the client-puzzle approach, when $\alpha_{SP_2} - \alpha_{SP_1} < \alpha_m$, one of the defender's minmax strategy against the attacker is*

$$p_1 \circ P_1 \oplus (1 - p_1) \circ P_2,$$

where $p_1 = \frac{\alpha_{SP_2} - \alpha_m}{\alpha_{SP_2} - \alpha_{SP_1}}$.

Proposition 4. *In the game of the client-puzzle approach, when $\alpha_{SP_2} - \alpha_{SP_1} < \alpha_m$ and $0 < \eta < \frac{1}{2}$, the attacker's minmax strategy against the defender is*

$$p_2 \circ CA \oplus (1 - p_2) \circ RA,$$

where $p_2 = \frac{\eta}{1-\eta}$.

Punishment Phase Strategies. During the punishment phase, the defender chooses the mixed strategy $p_1 \circ P_1 \oplus (1 - p_1) \circ P_2$, while the attacker chooses the mixed strategy $p_2 \circ CA \oplus (1 - p_2) \circ RA$. It can be shown that the corresponding strategy profile is a Nash equilibrium, where both the players receive their minmax payoff. This means that each player's strategy in the punishment phase is the best response to the opponent's strategy. Clearly, deviations in the punishment phase are not profitable.

Normal Phase Strategies. The following strategy profile is chosen during the normal phase:

$$(p \circ P_1 \oplus (1 - p) \circ P_2; TA),$$

where $0 < p < 1$. For a Nash equilibrium, this profile must give each player a payoff greater than his minmax payoff. This is possible when

$$\frac{\alpha_{SP_1}}{\alpha_m} < p < \frac{\alpha_{SP_1} - \eta(\alpha_{SP_2} - \alpha_m + \alpha_{SP_1})}{\alpha_m - \eta(\alpha_{SP_2} + \alpha_m - \alpha_{SP_1})}.$$

It can shown that the defender receives higher payoff in the Nash equilibrium of the repeated game than in the Nash equilibrium of the single-shot strategic game described in Section 4.1.

Mitigating DoS Attack. As seen in the previous defense mechanism, the existence of a Nash equilibrium does not necessarily prevent flooding. In the **normal phase**, flooding is prevented if

$$N\alpha_m p < 1 \text{ or } p < \frac{1}{N\alpha_m}.$$

In the **punishment phase**, even if the attacker chooses to answer all the puzzles correctly, his average resource expenditure would be $p_1 \alpha_{SP_1} + (1 - p_1)\alpha_{SP_2} = \alpha_m$. Since he cannot overload the defender, flooding is not possible in this phase.

The defense mechanism based on the described Nash equilibrium is given below. (We call it the **repeated game defense mechanism**.)

1. For a desirable balance factor η, $0 < \eta < \frac{1}{2}$, choose two puzzles P_1 and P_2 such that $\alpha_{SP_1} < \frac{1}{N} < \alpha_m < \alpha_{SP_2}$ and $\alpha_{SP_2} - \alpha_{SP_1} < \alpha_m$.
2. Choose a value for p such that

$$\frac{\alpha_{SP_1}}{\alpha_m} < p < min\left(\frac{1}{N\alpha_m}, \frac{\alpha_{SP_1} - \eta(\alpha_{SP_2} - \alpha_m + \alpha_{SP_1})}{\alpha_m - \eta(\alpha_{SP_2} + \alpha_m - \alpha_{SP_1})}\right)$$

   and determine the value of p_1 according to

$$p_1 = \frac{\alpha_{SP_2} - \alpha_m}{\alpha_{SP_2} - \alpha_{SP_1}}.$$

3. Determine an appropriate value for τ.
4. Phase (A) and phase (B) of the defense mechanism have been described in Fig. 2, where $\mathbf{x}$ and $\mathbf{y}$ are random variables and $\phi(msg)$ is the phase corresponding to the puzzle whose solution has been received.

Here, we have considered only one possible minmax strategy profile in the defense mechanism. The other strategy profiles have been analyzed in [12].

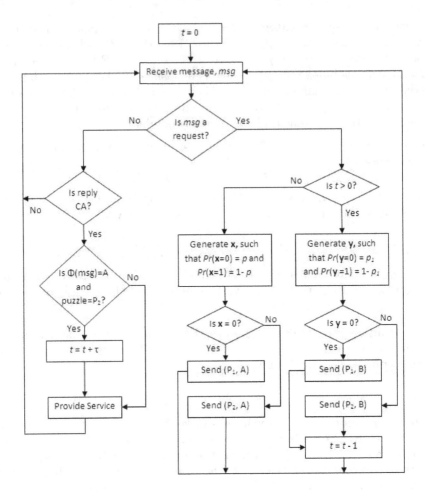

Fig. 2. Closed-Loop Defense Mechanism

4.3   Comparison with Previous Work

We now compare the proposed HDP-based defense mechanisms with the corresponding defense mechanisms proposed by Fallah [5], where puzzle difficulties are known to the attacker. Previously, while analyzing the payoffs of the attacker and defender, we did not consider the existence of a Nash equilibrium in the game. We now present an analysis of the attacker and defender payoffs under the equilibrium conditions given by the various defense mechanisms.

For the sake of convenience, the HDP-based strategic game defense mechanism shall be referred to as $HDM1$, while the HDP-based repeated game defense mechanism shall be referred to as $HDM2$. The corresponding puzzle-based defense mechanisms in [5] would be referred to as $PDM1$ and $PDM2$ respectively.

Proposition 5. *The expected equilibrium payoff of an attacker in HDM1 is lower than that in PDM1, while the expected equilibrium payoff of the defender is the same in both defense mechanisms.*

Note that the equilibrium conditions are different in the two defense mechanisms. As a consequence, the defender's expected payoff does not change when HDPs are used. However, the attacker is benefited less in $HDM1$ making it more effective than $PDM1$.

Proposition 6. *The minmax payoff of the defender in HDM2 is higher than that in PDM2, while the minmax payoff of the attacker is the same in both defense mechanisms.*

Since the minmax payoff is a lower bound on the defender's payoff, the defender is better off in HDM2. Moreover, in $PDM2$, only P_2 puzzles are used by the defender in the punishment phase. Whereas, in $HDM2$, the defender's minmax strategy against the attacker is a lottery over P_1 and P_2. Clearly, **a legitimate user is hurt less in the punishment phase of HDM2 as he has a chance of receiving P_1**.

5 Client-Puzzles

The requirements of a puzzle in our defense mechanisms are given below.

1. **Hidden Difficulty:** The difficulty of the puzzle should not be determined without a minimal number of computations.
2. **High Puzzle Resolution:** The granularity of puzzle difficulty must be high. This allows us to fine tune the parameters of the defense mechanisms.
3. **Partial Solution:** Submission of partial solutions should be possible without increasing the verification time. This requirement allows the defender to determine whether the attacker chose RA or TA.

We now introduce two new puzzles that conform to these requirements.

Puzzle 2: The puzzle is described in Fig. 3. Here, the client can submit a partial solution by giving the correct answer for the first part ($rp1$) of the puzzle and a random answer for the second part ($rp2$). It takes 4 hash computations for generating a puzzle and a maximum of 6 hash computations for verifying the puzzle solution. When $l = 1$, the average number of hash computations required to solve the puzzle is $\frac{(2^k+1) + (D+1)}{2}$. Thus, the difficulty of the puzzle can be varied exponential by adjusting k and linearly by adjusting D. Also, the client is not aware of the difficulty of the puzzle when he receives it.

Puzzle 3: Fig. 4 contains the puzzle description. When $l = 1$, the average number of hash computations required to solve this puzzle is $\frac{(D_a+1) + (D_b+1)}{2}$ and hence, the difficulty varies linearly with D_a and D_b. The production of the puzzle requires 4 hash computations and the verification requires a maximum of 6 hash computations. Even here, the puzzle difficulty is hidden from the client.

Client	Defender
	Request $\longrightarrow$ $\quad X = H(S_1, N_s, M)$
	$Y = H(X)$
	$a = H(S_2, N_s, M) \bmod D + l$
	$X' = X - a$
	$Z = H(X')$
$(X'', Y, Z), N_s \longleftarrow$ $\quad X'' = X' \oplus (I_1, ..., I_{k-1}, 1, 0_{k+1}, ..., 0_n)$	
Find $rp1$ such that	
$\quad H(rp1) = Z$.	
Find a' such that	
$\quad H(rp2) = Y$,	
where $rp2 = rp1 + a'$. $rp1, rp2, N_s \longrightarrow$	$X = H(S_1, N_s, M)$
	$a = H(S_2, N_s, M) \bmod D + l$
	$H(rp1) \overset{?}{=} H(X - a)$
	$H(rp2) \overset{?}{=} H(X)$

Fig. 3. Hidden Difficulty Puzzle 2. Here, S_1 and S_2 are server secrets, N_s is a server nonce, M is a session parameter, D and k are difficulty parameters, l is a constant and I is a binary number chosen uniformly at random.

Client	Defender
	Request $\longrightarrow$ $\quad X = H(S_1, N_s, M)$
	$Y = H(X)$
	$a = H(S_2, N_s, M) \bmod D_a + l$
	$X' = X - a$
	$Z = H(X')$
$(X'', Y, Z), N_s \longleftarrow$ $\quad X'' = X' - b$	
Find b' such that	
$\quad H(rp1) = Z$,	
where $rp1 = X'' + b'$.	
Find a' such that	
$\quad H(rp2) = Y$,	
where $rp2 = rp1 + a'$. $rp1, rp2, N_s \longrightarrow$	$X = H(S_1, N_s, M)$
	$a = H(S_2, N_s, M) \bmod D_a + l$
	$H(rp1) \overset{?}{=} H(X - a)$
	$H(rp2) \overset{?}{=} H(X)$

Fig. 4. Hidden Difficulty Puzzle 3. Here, b is a value chosen uniformly at random from $\{1, ..., D_b\}$.

6 Conclusions

In this paper, we have given emphasis on hiding the difficulty of client-puzzles from a denial of service attacker. We have constructed three concrete puzzles that satisfy this requirement. Using game theory, we have developed defense mechanisms that make use of such puzzles and have shown that they are more effective than the existing ones. Future direction of work would be to incorporate the proposed defense mechanisms in the Internet Key Exchange (IKE) protocol and to estimate its effectiveness in real-time.

References

1. Agah, A., Das, S.K.: Preventing dos attacks in wireless sensor networks: A repeated game theory approach. International Journal of Network Security 5(2), 145–153 (2007)
2. Aura, T., Nikander, P., Leiwo, J.: DOS-resistant authentication with client puzzles. In: Christianson, B., Crispo, B., Malcolm, J.A., Roe, M. (eds.) Security Protocols 2000. LNCS, vol. 2133, pp. 170–177. Springer, Heidelberg (2001)
3. Bencsath, B., Vajda, I., Buttyan, L.: A game based analysis of the client puzzle approach to defend against dos attacks. In: Proceedings of the 2003 International Conference on Software, Telecommunications and Computer Networks, pp. 763–767 (2003)
4. Dwork, C., Naor, M.: Pricing via processing or combatting junk mail. In: Brickell, E.F. (ed.) CRYPTO 1992. LNCS, vol. 740, pp. 139–147. Springer, Heidelberg (1993)
5. Fallah, M.: A puzzle-based defense strategy against flooding attacks using game theory. IEEE Transactions on Dependable and Secure Computing 99(2), 5555
6. Feng, W., Kaiser, E., Luu, A.: Design and implementation of network puzzles. In: INFOCOM 2005. 24th Annual Joint Conference of the IEEE Computer and Communications Societies. Proceedings IEEE, March 2005, vol. 4, pp. 2372–2382 (2005)
7. Fudenberg, D., Maskin, E.: The folk theorem in repeated games with discounting or with incomplete information. Econometrica 54(3), 533–554 (1986)
8. Juels, A., Brainard, J.: Client puzzles: A cryptographic countermeasure against connection depletion attacks. In: Proceedings of NDSS 1999 (Networks and Distributed Security Systems), pp. 151–165 (1999)
9. Komathy, K., Narayanasamy, P.: Secure data forwarding against denial of service attack using trust based evolutionary game. In: Vehicular Technology Conference, VTC Spring 2008., pp. 31–35. IEEE, Los Alamitos (2008)
10. Lv, J.-J.: A game theoretic defending model with puzzle controller for distributed dos attack prevention. In: 2008 International Conference on Machine Learning and Cybernetics, July 2008, vol. 2, pp. 1064–1069 (2008)
11. Mahimkar, A., Shmatikov, V.: Game-based analysis of denial-of-service prevention protocols. In: CSFW 2005: Proceedings of the 18th IEEE workshop on Computer Security Foundations, pp. 287–301. IEEE Computer Society, Washington (2005)
12. Narasimhan, H., Varadarajan, V., Pandu Rangan, C.: Game theoretic resistance to denial of service attacks using hidden difficulty puzzles. Cryptology ePrint Archive, Report 2009/350 (2009), http://eprint.iacr.org/

13. Rivest, R.L., Shamir, A., Wagner, D.A.: Time-lock puzzles and timed-release crypto. Technical report, Cambridge, MA, USA (1996)
14. Sagduyu, Y.E., Ephremides, A.: A game-theoretic analysis of denial of service attacks in wireless random access. Wireless Networks 15(5), 651–666 (2009)
15. Smith, J.: Denial of Service: Prevention, Modelling and Detection. PhD thesis, Queensland University of Technology, Brisbane, QLD 4001 Australia (June 2007)
16. Tritilanunt, S., Boyd, C., Foo, E., Nieto, J.G.: Toward non-parallelizable cryptographic puzzles. In: Bao, F., Ling, S., Okamoto, T., Wang, H., Xing, C. (eds.) CANS 2007. LNCS, vol. 4856, pp. 247–264. Springer, Heidelberg (2007)
17. Tsang, P.P., Smith, S.W.: Combating spam and denial-of-service attacks with trusted puzzle solvers. In: Chen, L., Mu, Y., Susilo, W. (eds.) ISPEC 2008. LNCS, vol. 4991, pp. 188–202. Springer, Heidelberg (2008)
18. Wang, X.F., Reiter, M.K.: Defending against denial-of-service attacks with puzzle auctions. In: SP 2003: Proceedings of the 2003 IEEE Symposium on Security and Privacy, p. 78. IEEE Computer Society, Washington (2003)
19. Waters, B., Juels, A., Alex Halderman, J., Felten, E.W.: New client puzzle outsourcing techniques for dos resistance. In: CCS 2004: Proceedings of the 11th ACM conference on Computer and Communications Security, pp. 246–256. ACM, New York (2004)
20. Zhang, R., Hanaoka, G., Imai, H.: A generic construction of useful client puzzles. In: ASIACCS 2009: Proceedings of the 4th International Symposium on Information, Computer, and Communications Security, pp. 70–79. ACM, New York (2009)

A   Proof of Propositions

A.1   Proposition 2

Proof. Let us prove the existence of a Nash equilibrium, where the defender uses a mixed strategy $\alpha_1 = p \circ P_1 \oplus (1-p) \circ P_2$, where $0 < p < 1$ and the attacker uses the pure strategy TA. The profile $(\alpha_1; TA)$ is a Nash equilibrium if

$$u_1(P_1; TA) = u_1(P_2; TA), \tag{8}$$

$$u_2(\alpha_1; TA) > u_2(\alpha_1; RA) \text{ and} \tag{9}$$

$$u_2(\alpha_1; TA) > u_2(\alpha_1; CA). \tag{10}$$

Equation (8) is satisfied when

$$\eta = \frac{\alpha_m}{\alpha_m + \alpha_{SP_2} - \alpha_{SP_1}}, \tag{11}$$

(9) is satisfied when $p > \frac{\alpha_{SP_1}}{\alpha_m}$ and (10) is satisfied when

$$\alpha_{SP_2} - \alpha_{SP_1} > \alpha_m. \tag{12}$$

From (11) and (12), it can be easily seen that the maximum value that η can take is less than $\frac{1}{2}$. Hence, $0 < \eta < \frac{1}{2}$.

A.2   Proposition 3

Proof. Let $\alpha_1 = p_1 \circ P_1 \oplus (1 - p_1) \circ P_2, 0 < p_1 < 1$, be the defender's minmax strategy against the attacker. By our assumption, $\alpha_{SP_2} - \alpha_{SP_1} < \alpha_m$. Clearly, the attacker would prefer CA over TA. Therefore, the attacker's minmax payoff is $max(U_2(\alpha_1; CA), U_2(\alpha_1; RA))$, where U_i is the expected payoff of player i for $i = 1, 2$. Note that $U_2(\alpha_1; CA) > U_2(\alpha_1; RA)$ when $\alpha_{PP} + \alpha_{VP} + \alpha_m - p_1\alpha_{SP_1} - (1 - p_1)\alpha_{SP_2} > \alpha_{PP} + \alpha_{VP}$ or $p_1 > \frac{\alpha_{SP_2} - \alpha_m}{\alpha_{SP_2} - \alpha_{SP_1}}$. Higher the value of p_1 above $\frac{\alpha_{SP_2} - \alpha_m}{\alpha_{SP_2} - \alpha_{SP_1}}$, higher is the attacker's payoff. If $p_1 \leq \frac{\alpha_{SP_2} - \alpha_m}{\alpha_{SP_2} - \alpha_{SP_1}}$, the attacker's payoff is minimum and equal to $\alpha_{PP} + \alpha_{VP}$. This is the attacker's minmax payoff and hence, the attacker is minmaxed when the defender chooses the mixed strategy $p_1 \circ P_1 \oplus (1 - p_1) \circ P_2$, where $p_1 = \frac{\alpha_{SP_2} - \alpha_m}{\alpha_{SP_2} - \alpha_{SP_1}}$.

A.3   Proposition 4

Proof. Let the attacker's minmax strategy against the defender be $\alpha_2 = q_1 \circ RA \oplus q_2 \circ CA \oplus q_3 \circ TA$, where $q_1 + q_2 + q_3 = 1$. By our assumption, $\alpha_{SP_2} - \alpha_{SP_1} < \alpha_m$. When the attacker chooses CA, the defender would receive equal or lower payoff than when the attacker chooses TA. Hence, the attacker's minmax strategy against the defender should assign non-zero probabilities to CA and RA and zero probability to TA, i.e, $q_1 = p_2$, $q_2 = 1 - p_2$ and $q_3 = 0$, where $0 < p_2 < 1$. When $0 < \eta < \frac{1}{2}$, the defender's best response for the attacker's pure strategy RA is P_1 and that for CA is P_2. For the attacker's mixed strategy α_2, the defender's best response is P_1 only if $U_1(P_1; \alpha_2) > U_1(P_2; \alpha_2)$. This is possible when $p_2((1 - \eta)\alpha_{SP_1}) - \eta\alpha_{SP_2} > p_2((1 - \eta)\alpha_{SP_2}) - \eta\alpha_{SP_2}$ or $p_2 < \frac{\eta}{1 - \eta}$. The lower the value of p_2 below $\frac{\eta}{1 - \eta}$, higher is the defender's payoff. Similarly, if $p_2 > \frac{\eta}{1 - \eta}$, the defender would prefer P_2 over P_1 and his payoff increases as p_2 increases. Clearly, the defender is minmaxed when $U_1(P_1; \alpha_2) = U_1(P_2; \alpha_2)$ or $p_2 = \frac{\eta}{1 - \eta}$.

A.4   Proposition 5

Proof. Let α^1 be the equilibrium strategy profile used in HDM1. Under equilibrium conditions, the expected payoff of the defender is $U_1(\alpha^1) = (1 - \eta)(-\alpha_{PP} - \alpha_{VP} - \alpha_m + \alpha_{SP_1}) - \eta\alpha_{SP_1}$. The attacker, on the other hand, receives an average payoff of

$$U_2(\alpha^1) = \alpha_{PP} + \alpha_{VP} + p\alpha_m - \alpha_{SP_1}. \tag{13}$$

In the case of PDM1 [5], the strategy profile $\alpha^2 = (p \circ P_1 \oplus (1 - p) \circ P_2;$ $(CA, RA))$ corresponds to an equilibrium when $\alpha_{SP_1} < \alpha_m < \alpha_{SP_2}, \alpha_{VP} < \alpha_m - \alpha_{SP_1}, \alpha_{VP} < \alpha_{SP_2} - \alpha_m$ and $\eta = \frac{\alpha_m - \alpha_{SP_1}}{\alpha_m - 2\alpha_{SP_1} + \alpha_{SP_2}}$, where $0 < \eta < \frac{1}{2}$ and $0 < p < 1$. Under the equilibrium conditions, the expected payoff for the defender is $U_1(\alpha^2) = (1 - \eta)(-\alpha_{PP} - \alpha_{VP} - \alpha_m + \alpha_{SP_1}) - \eta\alpha_{SP_1}$ and that for the attacker is

$$U_2(\alpha^2) = \alpha_{PP} + \alpha_{VP} + p(\alpha_m - \alpha_{SP_1}). \tag{14}$$

Note that we are looking at two games with different equilibrium conditions. For a given value of $0 < \eta < \frac{1}{2}$, we choose the same values for α_{PP}, α_{VP}, α_{SP_1} and p and different values for α_{SP_2} in the two games such that equilibrium conditions are satisfied. Clearly, $U_1(\alpha^1) = U_1(\alpha^2)$, while from (13) and (14), for $0 < p < 1$,

$$U_2(\alpha^1) < U_2(\alpha^2).$$

Thus, the expected payoff for the defender is same in both the defense mechanisms, while the attacker's expected payoff is lower in HDM1.

A.5   Proposition 6

Proof. In PDM2, the minmax strategy profile in the infinitely repeated game is $(P_2; RA)$ [5]. The corresponding minmax payoff for the defender is

$$U_1(P_2; RA) = (1 - \eta)(-\alpha_{PP} - \alpha_{VP}) - \eta\alpha_{SP_2} \tag{15}$$

and that for the attacker is $U_2(P_2; RA) = \alpha_{PP} + \alpha_{VP}$. In the case of HDM2, the minmax strategy profile is $(\alpha_1; \alpha_2)$, where $\alpha_1 = p_1 \circ P_1 \oplus (1 - p_1) \circ P_2$ and $\alpha_2 = p_2 \circ CA \oplus (1 - p_2) \circ RA$. The defender's minmax payoff in HDM2 is given by $U_1(\alpha_1; \alpha_2) = p_1(p_2u_1(P_1; CA) + (1 - p_2)u_1(P_1; RA)) + (1 - p_1)(p_2u_1(P_2; CA) + (1 - p_2)u_1(P_2; RA))$, which reduces to

$$U_1(\alpha_1; \alpha_2) = (1 - \eta)(-\alpha_{PP} - \alpha_{VP}) - \eta\alpha_m. \tag{16}$$

Similarly, the attacker's minmax payoff in HDM2 is given by $U_2(\alpha_1; \alpha_2) = p_1(p_2u_2(P_1; CA) + (1 - p_2)u_2(P_1; RA)) + (1 - p_1)(p_2u_2(P_2; CA) + (1 - p_2)u_2(P_2; RA)) = \alpha_{PP} + \alpha_{VP}$. It is clear that the attacker's minmax payoff is same in both defense mechanisms. For a given value of $0 < \eta < \frac{1}{2}$, choosing same values for α_{PP}, α_{VP} and α_{SP_1} in equations (15) and (16) and different values for α_{SP_2} satisfying the corresponding equilibrium criteria, we have

$$U_1(\alpha_1; \alpha_2) > U_1(P_2; RA)$$

and $U_2(\alpha_1; \alpha_2) = U_2(P_2; RA)$. Thus, the defender's minmax payoff is higher in HDM2 when compared to PDM2, while the attacker's minmax payoff is same in both the defense mechanisms.

Attacking and Improving on Lee and Chiu's Authentication Scheme Using Smart Cards*

Youngsook Lee[1],[**], Hyungkyu Yang[2], and Dongho Won[3],[***]

[1] Department of Cyber Investigation Police, Howon University, Korea
ysooklee@howon.ac.kr
[2] Department of Computer and Media Information, Kangnam University, Korea
hkyang@kangnam.ac.kr
[3] Department of Computer Engineering, Sungkyunkwan University, Korea
dhwon@security.re.kr

Abstract. This paper discusses the security of Lee and Chiu's remote user authentication scheme making use of smart cards. We first figure out that Lee and Chiu's scheme does not achieve two-factor security. If an attacker steals some user's smart card and extracts the information stored in the smart card, he/she can easily find out the user's password. We show this by mounting an off-line dictionary attack on the scheme. In addition, we showed what really is causing the problem and how to fix it and proposed the scheme which improves on Lee and Chiu's scheme.

Keywords: distributed system; authentication scheme; smart card; two-factor security; off-line dictionary attack.

1 Introduction

In a typical password-based authentication scheme using smart cards [4, 17, 8, 15, 5, 9, 19], remote users are authenticated using their smart card as an identification token; the smart card takes as input a password from a user, recovers a unique identifier from the user-given password, creates a login message using the identifier, and then sends the login message to the server who then checks the validity of the login request before allowing access to any services or resources. This way, the administrative overhead of the server is greatly reduced and the remote user is allowed to remember only his password to log on. Besides just creating and sending login messages, smart cards support mutual authentication where a challenge-response interaction between the card and the server takes place to verify each other's identity. Mutual authentication is a critical requirement in most real-world applications where one's private information should not be released to anyone until mutual confidence is established [1].

The experience has shown that the design of secure authentication schemes is not an easy task to do, especially in the presence of an active adversary; there

---

* This work was supported by Howon University in 2010.
** The first author.
*** Corresponding author.

J. Kwak et al. (Eds.): ISPEC 2010, LNCS 6047, pp. 377–385, 2010.
© Springer-Verlag Berlin Heidelberg 2010

is a long history of schemes for this domain being proposed and subsequently broken by some attacks (e.g., [6, 2, 3, 13, 7, 19, 18, 11]). Therefore, authentication schemes must be subjected to the strictest scrutiny possible before they can be deployed into an untrusted, open network, which might be controlled by an adversary.

To analyze the security of remote user authentication schemes using smart cards, we need to consider the capabilities of the adversary. First, we assume that the adversary has complete control of every aspect of all communications between the server and the remote user. That is, he/she may read, modify, insert, delete, replay and delay any messages in the communication channel. Second, he/she may try to steal a user's smart card and extract the information in the smart card by monitoring the power consumption of the smart card [10, 14]. Third, he/she may try to find out a user's password. Clearly, if both (1) the user's smart card was stolen and (2) the user's password was exposed, then there is no way to prevent the adversary from impersonating the user. However, a remote user authentication scheme should be secure if only one of (1) and (2) is the case. So the best we can do is to guarantee the security of the scheme when either the user's smart card or its password is stolen, but not both. This security property is called two-factor security [20].

In 2003, Wu and Chieu [16] proposed a simple remote user authentication scheme. Wu and Chieu's scheme exhibits various merits: (1) it does not require the server to maintain a password table for verifying the legitimacy of login users; (2) it allows users to choose and change their passwords according to their liking and hence gives more user convenience; and (3) it is more secure in terms of the security property since the protocol based on having both properties of the discrete logarithm problem and only a few hash function operations. However, Lee and Chiu [12] have pointed out that Wu and Chieu's scheme is vulnerable to a user impersonation attack, in which the attacker who does not know some user's password is able to impersonated the legitimate user to the server. To fix this security problem, Lee and Chiu have presented a modified scheme of Wu and Chieu's scheme, and have claimed, among others, that their modified scheme achieves the property of the strong authentication. However, in Lee and Chiu's scheme, if an attacker steals some user's smart card and extracts the information stored in the smart card, he/she can violate its fundamental goal of two-factor security. We show this by mounting an off-line dictionary attack on Lee and Chiu's scheme. Besides discussing the security flaw on Lee and Chiu's scheme, we also figure out what has gone wrong with the scheme and how to fix it and proposed the enhanced version of Lee and Chiu's scheme.

The remainder of this paper is organized as follows. We begin by reviewing Lee and Chiu's remote user authentication scheme in Section 2. Then in Section 3, we present security weaknesses in Lee and Chiu's authentication scheme. We continue in Section 4 with the description of our proposed scheme which improves on Lee and Chiu's scheme and analyze the security of the proposed scheme. Finally, we conclude this work in Section 5.

2   Review of Lee and Chiu's Authentication Scheme

Lee and Chiu [12] have recently presented an improved version of Wu and Chieu's [16] scheme. Besides preventing a user impersonation attack, Lee and Chiu's scheme intends to preserve the property of the strong authentication between an authentication server and a remote user. We begin by describing the top level structure of the scheme. The scheme consists of two phases: registration phase and authentication phase. The registration phase is performed only once per user when a new user registers itself with the remote server. The authentication phase is carried out whenever a user wants to gain access to the server.

Before the registration phase is performed for the first time, the server S decides on the following system parameters: a one-way hash function h, a cryptographic key x, a large number p, and a generator g of $\mathbb{Z}_p^*$. The key x is kept secret by the server. A high level depiction of the scheme is given in Fig. 1, where dashed lines indicate a secure channel, and a more detailed description follows:

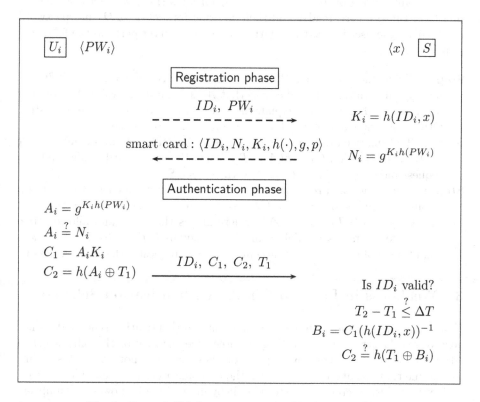

Fig. 1. Lee and Chiu's remote user authentication scheme

2.1   Registration Phase

This is the phase where a new registration of a user takes place. The registration proceeds as follows:

Step 1. A user U_i, who wants to register with the server S, chooses its password PW_i at will and submits a registration request $\langle ID_i, PW_i \rangle$ to the remote server S via a secure channel.

Step 2. When the server S receives the request, it first computes

$$K_i = h(ID_i, x) \quad \text{and} \quad N_i = g^{K_i h(PW_i)} \bmod p$$

and then issues a smart card containing $\langle ID_i, N_i, K_i, h(\cdot), g, p \rangle$ to the user U_i.

2.2   Authentication Phase

This phase constitutes the core of the scheme and is performed whenever some user U_i wants to log on to the server S. U_i initiates this phase by inserting its smart card into a card reader and then entering its identity ID_i and password PW_i. Given the user input, the smart card and the server perform the following steps:

Step 1. Using the user-given PW_i, the smart card computes $A_i = g^{K_i h(PW_i)} \bmod p$. Then the smart card checks that A_i is equal to the value N_i stored in its smart card. If they are equal, the smart card proceeds to the next step. Otherwise, the smart card aborts the authentication phase.

Step 2. The smart card generates the current timestamp T_1 and computes $C_1 = A_i K_i \bmod p$ and $C_2 = h(A_i \oplus T_1)$. Then the smart card sends the login request message $\langle ID_i, C_1, C_2, T_1 \rangle$ to the server S.

Step 3. When the login request arrives, S first acquires the current timestamp T_2 and computes $B_i = C_1(h(ID_i, x))^{-1} \bmod p$. Then S verifies that: (1) ID_i is valid, (2) $T_2 - T_1 \leq \Delta T$, where ΔT is the maximum allowed time interval for transmission delay, and (3) C_2 equals $h(T_1 \oplus B_i)$. If all of these conditions hold, the server S accepts the login request; otherwise, rejects it.

3   Weakness in Lee and Chiu's Authentication Scheme

Unfortunately, Lee and Chiu's [12] remote user authentication scheme does not acheive two-factor security which guarantees the security of the scheme when either the user's smart card or its password is stolen, but not both. To see this, we assume that the attacker has stolen the U_i's smart card or gained access to it and extracted the secret values stored in it by monitoring its power consumption [10, 14]. Then the following description represents our off-line dictionary attack mounted by the attacker U_a against U_i's password. The attacker U_a now guesses possible passwords and checks them for correctness.

1. As preliminary step, the attacker U_a obtains the values N_i and K_i stored in the U_i's smart card.
2. First, U_a makes a guess PW_i' for PW_i and computes $A_i' = g^{K_i h(PW_i')}$ by using K_i.
3. U_a then verifies the correctness of PW_i' by checking the equality $A_i' = N_i$. Notice that if PW_i' and PW_i are equal, then $A_i' = N_i$ ought to be satisfied.
4. U_a repeats steps (2) and (3) until a correct password is found.

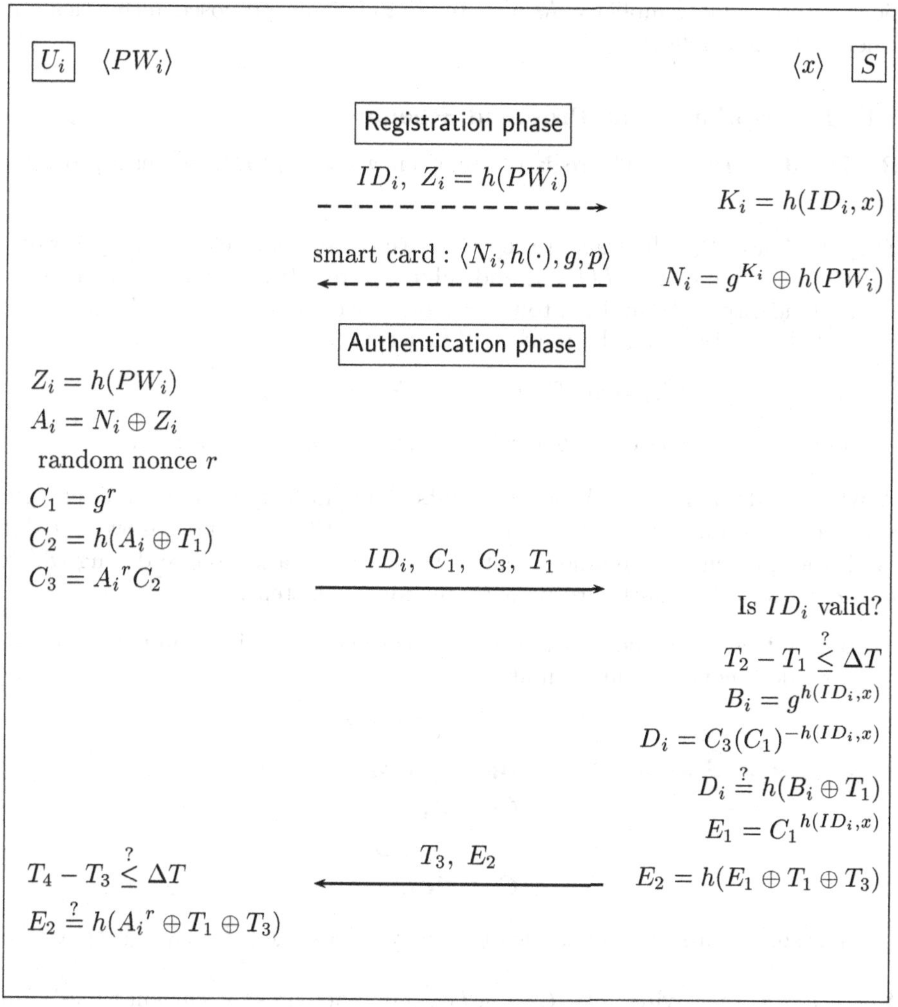

$\boxed{U_i}$ $\langle PW_i \rangle$ $\qquad\qquad\qquad\qquad\qquad\qquad\qquad \langle x \rangle$ $\boxed{S}$

$\boxed{\text{Registration phase}}$

$ID_i,\ Z_i = h(PW_i)$
$\text{- - - - - - - - - - - - - } \rightarrow$ $\qquad K_i = h(ID_i, x)$

$\text{smart card}: \langle N_i, h(\cdot), g, p \rangle$
$\leftarrow \text{- - - - - - - - - - - - -}$ $\qquad N_i = g^{K_i} \oplus h(PW_i)$

$\boxed{\text{Authentication phase}}$

$Z_i = h(PW_i)$
$A_i = N_i \oplus Z_i$
random nonce r
$C_1 = g^r$
$C_2 = h(A_i \oplus T_1)$ $\qquad ID_i,\ C_1,\ C_3,\ T_1$
$C_3 = A_i{}^r C_2$ $\qquad \xrightarrow{\hspace{3cm}}$

$\qquad\qquad\qquad\qquad\qquad\qquad$ Is ID_i valid?
$\qquad\qquad\qquad\qquad\qquad\qquad T_2 - T_1 \overset{?}{\leq} \Delta T$
$\qquad\qquad\qquad\qquad\qquad\qquad B_i = g^{h(ID_i, x)}$
$\qquad\qquad\qquad\qquad\qquad\qquad D_i = C_3 (C_1)^{-h(ID_i, x)}$
$\qquad\qquad\qquad\qquad\qquad\qquad D_i \overset{?}{=} h(B_i \oplus T_1)$
$\qquad\qquad\qquad\qquad\qquad\qquad E_1 = C_1{}^{h(ID_i, x)}$
$T_4 - T_3 \overset{?}{\leq} \Delta T$ $\qquad \overset{T_3,\ E_2}{\xleftarrow{\hspace{3cm}}}$ $\qquad E_2 = h(E_1 \oplus T_1 \oplus T_3)$
$E_2 \overset{?}{=} h(A_i{}^r \oplus T_1 \oplus T_3)$

Fig. 2. Our proposed remote user authentication scheme

4   Security Enhancement

In this section we propose a password-based authentication scheme which improves on Lee and Chiu's scheme. As mentioned earlier, our scheme enhances over Lee and Chiu's [12] remote user authentication scheme in three ways: (1) it does not store the hashed server's secret key in the smart cards, (2) it provides mutual authentication between a remote users and an authentication server, and (3) it can provide two-factor security in which the security of the scheme is achieved when either the user's smart card or its password is stolen, but not both. The system parameters $\langle h, x, g, p \rangle$ in our scheme are the same as in Lee and Chiu's scheme. In describing the protocol, we will omit 'mod p' from expressions for notational simplicity. As depicted in Fig. 2, our proposed authentication scheme works as follows.

4.1   Description of the Proposed Scheme

Registration Phase. The registration of a new user U_i to the server S proceeds as follows:

Step 1. A user U_i, who wants to register with the server S, chooses its password PW_i, computes $Z_i = h(PW_i)$ and submits a registration request, consisting of its identity ID_i and Z_i, to the remote server S via a secure channel.

Step 2. Upon receiving the request, S first computes

$$K_i = h(ID_i, x) \quad \text{and} \quad N_i = g^{K_i} \oplus h(PW_i)$$

and issues a smart card containing $\langle N_i, h(\cdot), g, p \rangle$ to the user U_i.

Authentication Phase. When U_i wants to log in to the server, it inserts its smart card into a card reader and enters its identity ID_i and password PW_i. With the user input, the scheme enters the authentication phase during which the server and the smart card perform the following steps:

Step 1. Given PW_i, the smart card obtains the current timestamp T_1, chooses a random nonce r and computes

$$\begin{aligned} Z_i &= h(PW_i), \\ A_i &= N_i \oplus Z_i, \\ C_1 &= g^r, \\ C_2 &= h(A_i \oplus T_1), \\ C_3 &= A_i{}^r C_2. \end{aligned}$$

The smart card then sends the login request message $\langle ID_i, C_1, C_3, T_1 \rangle$ to the server S.

Step 2. After receiving $\langle ID_i, C_1, C_3, T_1 \rangle$, S first acquires the current timestamp T_2 and computes $B_i = g^{h(ID_i, x)}$ and $D_i = C_3(C_1)^{-h(ID_i, x)}$. Then S verifies that: (1) ID_i is valid, (2) $T_2 - T_1 \leq \Delta T$, where ΔT is the maximum allowed time interval for transmission delay, and (3) D_i equals $h(B_i \oplus T_1)$. If one of these conditions is untrue, S rejects the login request. Otherwise, S generates a new timestamp T_3, computes $E_1 = C_1{}^{h(ID_i, x)}$ and $E_2 = h(E_1 \oplus T_1 \oplus T_3)$, and sends the response message $\langle T_3, E_2 \rangle$ to U_i.

Step 3. Upon receipt of the response $\langle T_3, E_2 \rangle$, user U_i obtains a new timestamp T_4 and checks that: (1) $T_4 - T_3 \leq \Delta T$ and (2) E_2 is equal to $h(A_i{}^r \oplus T_1 \oplus T_3)$. If both of these conditions hold, U_i believes the responding party as the authentic server. Otherwise, U_i aborts its login attempt.

4.2   Security Analysis

The vulnerability of Lee and Chiu's scheme to achieving two-factor security is due to the following fact: to find out the password of the user, it suffices to obtain the information stored in its smart card. More concretely, the problem with the scheme is that anyone who knows the values of N_i and K_i is able to learn the password PW_i of U_i. But, our proposed scheme effectively defeats this kind of attack mentioned above. Even if the attacker obtains the information (i.e., N_i) stored in the smart card, he/she can no longer find out the password of the user U_i. In the proposed protocol, the only information related to passwords is $N_i(= g^{K_i} \oplus h(PW_i))$, but because K_i is the secret information that the server only knows, this value does not help the attacker to verify directly the correctness of guessed passwords. Thus, off-line guessing attacks would be unsuccessful against the proposed protocol.

Besides guaranteeing two-factor security, our scheme achieves its main security goal of authenticating between a remote individual and the server. To do this, we support mutual authentication by sending the server S's response of the user U_i's login request. This adding, server-to-user authentication, allows the user who received the sever's response message $\langle T_3, E_2 \rangle$ to believe the responding party as the authentic server by checking the equality $E_2 \overset{?}{=} h(A_i^r \oplus T_1 \oplus T_3)$.

Finally, our scheme can resist two impersonation attacks, a server impersonation attack and a user impersonation attack. Although the attacker obtains the information (i.e., N_i) stored in the smart card, he/she can no longer forge a valid response message $\langle E_2, T_3 \rangle$ or a valid login request message $\langle ID_i, C_1, C_3, T_1 \rangle$. Forging a response message is impossible because computing $E_2 = h(E_1 \oplus T_1 \oplus T_3)$ requires the knowledge of $E_1 = C_1^{h(ID_i, x)}$ which in turn needs the server's secret value x. Forging a login request message is also infeasible. This is because no one can compute $C_3(= A_i^r C_2)$ without knowing $A_i(= N_i \oplus h(PW_i))$ or equivalently knowing $g^{h(ID_i, x)}$. Clearly, computing A_i requires either the server's secret value x or U_i's password PW_i. But since the attacker knows neither x nor PW_i, he/she cannot compute A_i. Therefore, this kind of attacks will no longer be applied against our revised scheme.

5   Conclusion

We have analyzed the security of the smart card based user authentication scheme proposed by Lee and Chiu [12]. Our security analysis uncovered that

Lee and Chiu 's scheme does not achieve its main security goal of the two-factor security. To demonstrate this, we have shown that the scheme is vulnerable to an off-line dictionary attack in which an attacker, who has obtained the secret values stored in the user's smart card, can easily find out its password. Besides reporting the security problem, we showed what really is causing the problem and how to fix it and proposed the scheme which improves on Lee and Chiu's scheme.

References

1. Anti-Phishing Working Group, http://www.antiphishing.org
2. Bird, R., Gopal, I., Herzberg, A., Janson, P.A., Kutten, S., Molva, R., Yung, M.: Systematic design of a family of attack-resistant authentication protocols. IEEE Journal on Selected Areas in Communications 11(5), 679–693 (1993)
3. Carlsen, U.: Cryptographic protocol flaws: know your enemy. In: Proceedings of the 7th IEEE Computer Security Foundations Workshop, pp. 192–200 (1994)
4. Chang, C.-C., Wu, T.-C.: Remote password authentication with smart cards. IEE Proceedings E-Computers and Digital Techniques 138(3), 165–168 (1991)
5. Chien, H.-Y., Jan, J.-K., Tseng, Y.-M.: An efficient and practical solution to remote authentication: smart card. Computers & Security 21(4), 372–375 (2002)
6. Diffie, W., van Oorschot, P.C., Wiener, M.J.: Authentication and authenticated key exchange. Designs, Codes and Cryptography 2(2), 107–125 (1992)
7. Hsu, C.-L.: Security of Chien et al.'s remote user authentication scheme using smart cards. Computer Standards and Interfaces 26(3), 167–169 (2004)
8. Hwang, M.-S., Li, L.-H.: A new remote user authentication scheme using smart cards. IEEE Transaction on Consumer Electronics 46(1), 28–30 (2000)
9. Hwang, M.-S., Li, L.-H., Tang, Y.-L.: A simple remote user authentication. Mathematical and Computer Modelling 36, 103–107 (2002)
10. Kocher, P., Jaffe, J., Jun, B.: Differential power analysis. In: Wiener, M. (ed.) CRYPTO 1999. LNCS, vol. 1666, pp. 388–397. Springer, Heidelberg (1999)
11. Ku, W.-C., Chang, S.-T., Chiang, M.-H.: Weaknesses of a remote user authentication scheme using smart cards for multi-server architecture. IEICE Transactions on Commmunications E88-B(8), 3451–3454 (2005)
12. Lee, N.-Y., Chiu, Y.-C.: Improved remote authentication scheme with smart card. Computer Standards & Interfaces 27, 177–180 (2005)
13. Lowe, G.: An attack on the Needham-Schroeder public-key authentication protocol. Information Processing Letters 56(3), 131–133 (1995)
14. Messerges, T.-S., Dabbish, E.-A., Sloan, R.-H.: Examining smart card security under the threat of power analysis attacks. IEEE Transaction on Computers 51(5), 541–552 (2002)
15. Sun, H.-M.: An efficient remote user authentication scheme using smart cards. IEEE Transaction on Consumer Electronics 46(4), 958–961 (2000)
16. Wu, S.T., Chieu, B.: A user friendly remote authentication scheme with smart cards. Computer & Security 22(6), 547–550 (2003)
17. Yang, W.-H., Shieh, S.-P.: Password authentication schemes with smart card. Computers & Security 18(8), 727–733 (1999)

18. Yoon, E.-J., Kim, W.-H., Yoo, K.-Y.: Security enhancement for password authentication schemes with smart cards. In: Katsikas, S.K., López, J., Pernul, G. (eds.) TrustBus 2005. LNCS, vol. 3592, pp. 90–99. Springer, Heidelberg (2005)
19. Yoon, E.-J., Ryu, E.-K., Yoo, K.-Y.: An improvement of Hwang-Lee-Tang's simple remote user authentication scheme. Computers & Security 24(1), 50–56 (2005)
20. Tian, X., Zhu, R.W., Wong, D.: Improved Efficient Remote User Authentication Schemes. International Journal of Network Security 4(2), 149–154 (2007)

Protection Profile for Secure E-Voting Systems*

Kwangwoo Lee, Yunho Lee, Dongho Won, and Seungjoo Kim**

Information Security Group,
School of Information and Communication Engineering, Sungkyunkwan University,
300 Cheoncheon-dong, Jangan-gu, Suwon, Gyeonggi-do, 440-746, Korea
{kwlee,younori,dhwon,skim}@security.re.kr

Abstract. In this paper, we propose a protection profile for e-voting systems. Currently, there are three protection profiles for e-voting systems, BSI-PP-0031 in Germany, PP-CIVIS in France, and IEEE P1583 in USA. Although these protection profiles consider the overall security requirements for e-voting systems, they did not consider the voter verifiable audit trail. The voter verifiable audit trail allows voters to verify that their votes were captured correctly. Moreover, it provides a means to audit the stored electronic results, and to detect possible election fraud. Today, several voter verifiable audit trail e-voting systems already exist in the market, and used in public elections. However, a protection profile does not reflect this situation. Therefore, it is required that a protection profile for e-voting systems should consider the voter verifiability. To accomplish this, we propose a protection profile considering the voter verifiability with the existing protection profiles, and then discuss voter verifiability issues related to the electoral process. The proposed protection profile can be used to increase reliability of the entire e-voting process and tabulation result.

Keywords: e-voting system, common criteria, evaluation, protection profile, verifiability, voter verifiable audit trail.

1 Introduction

Currently, many countries such as Korea and Estonia consider or intend to introduce e-voting systems to replace existing plain paper based voting system. U.S., UK, Brazil, India, Swiss, etc. already adopt the e-voting system in public election. E-voting systems may include optical scan systems, direct-record electronic (DRE) systems, and internet voting systems. E-voting systems have many advantages such as accurate and fast tabulation of votes, low cost, and improved accessibility than the existing voting system. According to these advantages, a number of electronic voting systems have been developed during the past two decades. In particular, the DRE systems are widely used in these days. Many countries try to adopt these types of machine in their election. Despite of these advantages, however, there are lots of researches about vulnerabilities and security requirements of e-voting systems in the

---

* This work was supported by the University IT Research Center Project funded by the Korea Ministry of Information and Communication.
** Corresponding author.

J. Kwak et al. (Eds.): ISPEC 2010, LNCS 6047, pp. 386–397, 2010.

literature [1, 2]. Since the Florida election in 2000, e-voting systems have caused several technical accidents such as power supply failure or unrecorded vote. Therefore, many experts still express their concerns about the voting machines' trustworthiness. To overcome these problems, many countries are trying to evaluate the e-voting system using the CC (common criteria). In the evaluation process, it is important to have well-defined security evaluation criteria, i.e., protection profile, because it can reduce risks and make voter to trust the election result.

Currently, there are three protection profiles for e-voting systems, BSI-PP-0031 in Germany [9], PP-CIVIS in France [10], and IEEE P1583 in USA [11]. Although these protection profiles consider the overall security requirements of e-voting systems, they did not consider the voter verifiable audit trail. The voter verifiable audit trail allows voters to verify that their votes were captured correctly. Moreover, it provides a means to audit the stored electronic results, and to detect possible election fraud. Today, several voter verifiable audit trail e-voting systems already exist in the market, and used in public elections. However, none of the existing protection profiles reflect this situation. Therefore, it is required that a protection profile for e-voting systems should consider the voter verifiability. To accomplish this, in this paper, we propose a protection profile for e-voting systems and compare our protection profile to the existing protection profiles. The proposed protection profile can be used to increase reliability of the entire e-voting process and tabulation result.

The rest of this paper is organized as follows. In Section 2, we briefly describe the e-voting system and protection profile according to common criteria. We review the existing e-voting system protection profiles in Section 3. In Section 4, we propose a protection profile for e-voting system. To do this, we present the target of evaluation (TOE) and describe security environment, security objectives and derive security requirements of the e-voting systems. In Section 5, we analyze our protection profile. Finally, we summarize and conclude in Section 6.

2   Overview of E-Voting and Protection Profile

2.1   General Electoral Process

Various e-voting systems and protocols have been proposed during the past two decades. However, the fundamental electoral process is almost similar to each other. The main principle of e-voting is that it must be as similar to regular voting as possible and compliant with election legislation and principles [4]. The general e-voting system should include below actors [5]:

Voter: Voter has the right for voting, and he votes in the election.

Registration Authority: Registration authorities register eligible voters before the election day. These authorities ensure that only registered voters can vote and they vote only once on the election day. Registration authorities may be registrar, authenticator, authorizer, ballot distributor and/or key generator.

Tallying Authority: The tallying authorities collect the cast votes and tally the results of the election. Tallying authorities may be counter, collector, or tallier.

388   K. Lee et al.

E-voting system should also involve below four phases [5]:

Registration: Voters register themselves to registration authorities and the list of eligible voters is compiled before the election day.
Authentication and Authorization: On the election day registered voters request ballot or voting privilege from the registration authorities. Registration authorities check the credentials of those attempting to vote and only allow those who are eligible and registered before.
Voting: Voter casts his vote.
Tallying: The tallying authorities count the votes and announce the election results.

Fig.1 illustrates the general process of e-voting and its actors.

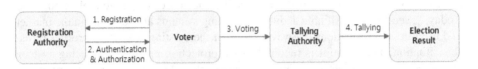

Fig. 1. The general process of e-voting and its actors

2.2 General Security Requirements of an E-Voting System

E-voting system should provide the same level of security as existing plain paper based voting system. According to [3, 13], we summarize the previous security requirements of an e-voting system as follows:

Table 1. General security requirements of e-voting system [3]

Security requirements	Description
Completeness	All valid votes are counted correctly.
Soundness	The dishonest voter cannot disrupt the voting.
Privacy	All votes must be secret.
Eligibility	No one who isn't allowed to vote can vote .
Unreusability	No voter can vote twice.
Fairness	Noting must affect the voting.
Verifiability	No one can falsify the result of the voting.

Therefore, e-voting must be uniform and secret, only eligible persons must be allowed to vote, every voter should be able to cast only one vote, a voter must not be able to prove in favor of whom he/she voted. The collecting of votes must be secure, reliable and accountable. From a technical point of view the e-voting system must be as simple as possible as well as transparent so that a wide range of specialists would be able to audit it. The e-voting system must be reusable in a way that developing a new system for the next voting is not needed [5]. Among these security requirements, verifiability can be ensured by two points of view. E-voting system should provide the verifiability by voters whether casting and counting ballots are performed correctly or not. Verifiable e-voting involves the following two distinct checks [6]:

Individual verifiability: A voter should be able to satisfy him/herself that the voted ballot has been captured correctly (cast-as-intended)

Universal verifiability: Anyone should be able to satisfy him/herself that the voted ballot is counted correctly (counted-as-cast)

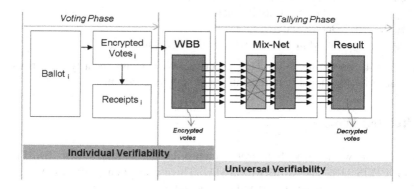

Fig. 2. Individual verifiability and Universal verifiability

Fig. 2 shows two kinds of verifiability of e-voting system. The universal verifiability can be satisfied by using various methods such as secure mix-network. However, the individual verifiability, it is not straightforward to verify without voter verifiable receipts, because no one can believe e-voting systems [12]. Therefore, the voter verifiable receipts should be issued for trustworthy e-voting system. In this paper, we believe that voter verifiable receipts are prerequisite for voter's trust in electronic machine based election.

2.3 Overview of Common Criteria and Protection Profile

The ISO/IEC 15408 permits comparability between the results of independent security evaluations. The ISO/IEC 15408 does so by providing a common set of requirements for the security functionality of IT products and for assurance measures applied to these IT products during a security evaluation. These IT products may be implemented in hardware, firmware or software. The evaluation process establishes a level of confidence that the security functionality of these IT products and the assurance measure applied to these IT products meet these requirements. The evaluation results may help consumers to determine whether these IT products fulfill their security needs [7].

The protection profile is a document that expresses an implementation-independent set of security requirements for an IT product or system that meets consumers' specific need [7]. Thus, through the protection profile, consumers can request an appropriate system and developers can design demanded system. Because the evaluation of an IT products or systems begins with verification whether the product or system reflects the claimed protection profile accurately, the protection profile is a basis of the evaluation. In general, the protection profile consists of 7 subsections; PP introduction, Conformance Claims, Security Problem Definition, Security Objectives,

Extended Components Definition (optional), and Security Requirements. The security requirements section is the key section of the protection profile, since it includes requirements of potential consumer and specifies security functions of the system. The followings are steps to develop IT security requirements [8].

Step 1. Define TOE and TOE boundary
Step 2. Define Security Problems
Step 3. Derive Security Objectives
Step 4. Select or refine Security Requirements using CC part 2

In Section 4, we define TOE, TOE security environment, security objectives, and finally security functional requirements for the e-voting systems.

3 Related Works

In this section, we describe three protection profiles for e-voting system, BSI-PP-0031 [9], PP-CIVIS [10], and IEEE P1583 [11]. Three protection profiles have different EAL (evaluation assurance level) and CC version with each other.

The BSI-PP-0031 has been developed using CC v2.3 and it requires EAL3+ evaluation process. This protection profile describes the election system criteria using digital election pen. However, BSI-PP-0031 does not evaluate the voter verifiability. Therefore, even though voting machine can be evaluated, voters cannot trust the election result. Only one system was evaluated so far, and used at Hamburg election in Germany, 2008. However, the system is not need any more since voters did not put their trust on it. The PP-CIVIS has been developed under CC v3.0 and it requires EAL2+ evaluation process. Unlike the BSI-PP0031, it deals with the security requirements of DRE (Direct-Recording Electronics) machine. This protection profile was evaluated and was listed in the common criteria portal website. However, it also does not provide any proof of its honesty. At last, IEEE P1583 presents the protection profile, the definition of the minimum security requirements that must be implemented for the secure e-voting machine in order to ensure compliance with 2002 FEC (Federal Election Commission Guidelines), the IEEE P1583 draft standard for the evaluation of voting equipment and HAVA (Help America Vote Act) [11]. As similar with other protection profiles, it does not evaluate the voter verifiability.

Table 2. Comparisons between the existing protection profiles of e-voting systems

Protection Profile	BSI-PP-0031	PP-CIVIS	IEEE P1583
EAL	EAL3+	EAL2+	EAL2
CC version	CC v2.3	CC v3.0	CC v2.3
Voter verifiability	Not provided	Not provided	Not provided
TOE boundary	Digital pen election system	DRE machine	DRE machine
Feature	This PP uses an electric digital pen to record a vote	Only this PP is listed in common criteria portal website	Voter cannot verify his/her vote

As mentioned above, previous protection profiles consider the overall security requirements of e-voting system. But they did not consider the verifiability. The voter verifiable audit trail allows voters to verify that their votes were captured correctly. Moreover, it provides a means to audit the stored electronic results, and to detect possible election fraud. Therefore, voting machines must provide the voter verifiable audit trail. However, current protection profiles do not reflect this situation. Therefore, it is required that a protection profile for e-voting systems should consider the voter verifiability. To accomplish this, we propose a protection profile for e-voting systems in the next section.

4 Proposed E-Voting System and Protection Profile

In this section, we describe the proposed e-voting system and protection profile.

4.1 Protection Profile Introduction

The TOE can be a system or a product and consists of software, hardware and firmware. In this paper, the TOE is the security system and its security functions. Important information of TOE is audit record of voting and security parameters of e-voting system. Fig. 3 represents the TOE.

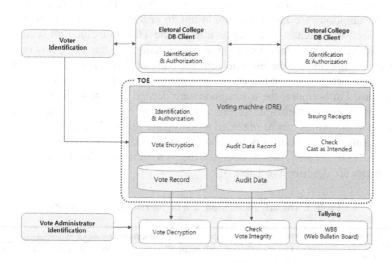

Fig. 3. The TOE

The TOE is normally installed in voting station and operated by the voting card issued by electoral college database. Before voting, database has to check duplicate. We assume that this check process has done in secure way.

The voting card has unique serial number and voter progresses voting with voting card issued by database. All processing steps are displayed on screen to voter. After voting, e-voting system issues receipts for each voter to verify his/her vote. Voter can verify the vote result by comparing the WBB (web-bulletin board) and receipts.

4.2 Security Problem Definition

The TOE security environment defines the IT environment in which the TOE is intended to be used. The TOE security environment consists of three subsections, threats, assumptions, and organizational security policies. Because the security functional requirements are based on threats, assumptions, and the organizational security policies, the analysis of TOE security environments is the most important. In order to deduce the threats, we analyze the vulnerabilities of the e-voting systems. To achieve this, we have searched the Internet sites that provide materials of the vulnerabilities [1, 14], the paper for vulnerability from related conferences and workshops [2, 15, 16, 17], and the news articles for vulnerabilities [18, 19, 20].

The threats include all potential threats and this is the key point on how to design robust security system, because assessment of threats is a first step to determine the security functional requirements. A description of threats shall include all threats to the assets against which specific protection within the TOE or its environment is required. A threat shall be described in terms of an identified threat agent, the attack, and the asset that is the subject of the attack. Threat agents should be described by addressing aspects such as expertise, available resources, and motivation. Attacks should be described by addressing aspects such as attack methods, any vulnerabilities exploited, and opportunity. In this protection profile, we assume that attacker has high performance and can destroy the e-voting system to obtain vulnerabilities of the system, because e-voting system has to secure against high performance attacker.

The Assumptions are necessary conditions in order to guarantee completeness of the TOE security. Because it is impossible for the TOE to include all security functions and there can be numerous possible environments for the TOE, it is natural that the TOE is supported by the environment for additional security functions and environment is characterized and specialized for the TOE. These are described in the assumptions. Furthermore, the assumptions are needed to reinforce physical and personal security requirements those are not managed by common criteria. In other words, the assumptions can be regarded as axiomatic for the TOE evaluation.

The organizational security policies define rules and policies of organization, supporting the TOE security, which operates the TOE. The security problem definitions for this paper are described in Table 3.

Table 3. Threats, assumption, and organization security policy

Item	Description
T.Malfunction	Users can cause malfunction like re-installation, and/or initialization of e-voting system.
T.Unexpected Events	E-voting can loss audit record by unexpected events like hardware, software and/or storage devices fault.
T.Unauthorized System Modification	Unauthorized modification of the system, affecting operational capabilities, can be occurred.
T.Audit Record Alteration	Alteration of voting system audit record can be occurred.
T.Voting Record Alteration	Alteration of the recording of vote can be occurred.
T.Recording Prevention	Prevention of recording can be occurred.
T.Unauthorized voting	Duplicate or fraudulent vote can be occurred.
T.System DataAlteration	Alteration of system data can be occurred.

Table 3. *(continued)*

T.Voting Data Exposure	Authorized or otherwise access can expose selection of voter.
T.New Vulnerability	Attacker can use new vulnerabilities not reported to gain access to e-voting system.
T.Recording Failure	Because of storage limitation, audit data may fail to be record.
T.TSF data tampering	Attacker can modify TSF data in unauthorized way to avoid record or cause misusage.
T.Bypass	Attacker can bypass the TOE security functions.
TE.Management	Administrator can threat the TOE security by insecure management, configuration, and operation.
TE.Delivery	The TOE can be harmed in delivery process.
A.Physical	It is assumed that appropriate physical security is provided for the TOE and protects from unauthorized physical access by outsider.
A.Secure Installation and Operation	It is assumed that operating system of TOE is installed and managed in secure way.
A.Trusted Administrator	It is assumed that administrator are non-hostile, well trained and follow all administrator guidance.
A.Network	It is assumed that network service for TOE is based on secure communication protocols to ensure the identification and authentic of authorized system.
A.Connect	It is assumed that all connections to peripheral devices reside within the controlled access facilities.
A.Timestamp	It is assumed that TOE environment provides secure timestamp fulfill RFC 1305.
P.Audit	TOE must audit every auditable event and keep the audit record secure. This audit record is protected from unauthorized access.
P.Secure Managmenet	Authorized administrator must manage the TOE, audit log and so on forth in secure way.
P.Manager	Management rights must be given administrator authorized by election officials.
P.Alert	TOE activity must be monitored and an auditable or visual notification must be provided to an authorized administrator.
P.Alert Report	Documented procedures must be implemented for responding to and reporting violations of the TOE.
P.Authorized User	A voter must be authorized before voting.
P.Contingency Plan	A documented plan to maintain continuity of operation in an emergency or disaster must be given.
P.Data Authentication	Voting data must be authorized to verity its integrity.
P.Recover	The TOE must be capable of being restored to a secure state without losing any fatal data.
P.Test	The TOE and its associated documentation must demonstrate that it is an accurate implementation of a voting system.

4.3 Security Objectives

The security objectives derived from the security environment and describe abstract security functions which reinforce all assumptions, threats, and organizational security policies. Each element of the security environment must be mapped to one or more security objectives. If not, it is hard to ensure that entire system includes the TOE is completely secure. The security objectives are divided into two folds; the one is the security objectives for the TOE and the other is the security objectives for the operational environment. The security objectives for the operational environment are also derived from the security problems and not countered completely by the TOE and/or organizational security policies, but countered by additional non-technical/procedural measures. The security objectives for this paper are described in Table 4.

Table 4. The Security Objectives for the TOE

Security Objectives	Description
O.Voter Authentication	An individual that has been determined to be a registered voter and is authorized to vote in the current election.
O.Encryption	The TOE must encrypt election data that is transmitted over a public network to protect against unauthorized access or modification.
O.Alert	The TOE must sound an alarm when a violation to a security policy has occurred.
O.Install	The TOE is delivered, installed, managed and operated in a manner that maintains security objectives.
O.Vote Validation	The TOE must ensure that votes recorded are verified by the voters as their intended vote prior to recording the vote.
O.Restore	The TOE must be capable of being restored to a secure state without losing the results of previously entered CVRs in the event of a disruption to normal operation.
O.Duplicate	The TOE must prevent duplicate.
O.Self Protection	The TOE must protect itself against attempts by unauthorized users to bypass, deactivate, or tamper with TOE security functions.
O.Test	The TOE must support testing of its security functions.
O.Audit	The TOE must provide a means to record readable audit record of security related events, with accurate dates, time, and events. Furthermore, the TOE must provide variable manners to refer audit record.
O.Update	The TOE must keep secure against new vulnerabilities.
O.Manage	The TOE must provide manners that maintain the TOE secure to administrator.
O.Identification and Authentication	The TOE must every user before any action.
O.TSF Data Protection	The TOE must protect TSF data from unauthorized exposure, alteration, and deletion.
O.Vote Verification	The TOE must provide manner for every voter to verity their intended vote.
OE.Contingency Plan	A contingency plan and associated procedure for emergency situations must be in effect.
OE.Event Reporting	Procedures for responding to and reporting security violations of the TOE security policy must be implemented.
OE.Integrity	The TOE must prevent unauthorized modification of election data during creation, storage and transmission.
OE.Policy Documentation	Security policies for the TOE must be documented and distributed to all personnel responsible for implementation.
OE.Physical	Appropriate physical security must be provided for the TOE.
OE.Trusted Administrator	Authorized administrator must be trained as to establishment and maintenance of security policies in practice.
OE.Management	The TOE must be managed in way that maintains security policies.
OE.Access Point	Every transmission between user and database must pass through the TOE.
OE.Timestamp	The TOE environment must provide secure timestamp fulfill RFC 1305.

4.4 Security Requirements

Each security functional requirement must be related to one or more security objectives. These requirements are defined in CC part 2, and protection profile author just chooses and uses appropriate requirements. In addition, if the requirements defined in CC part 2 are not sufficient to demonstrate the security objectives, then, the protection profile author can refine and reinforce conditions in detail to established requirements. The security functional requirements for this paper are described in Table 5.

Table 5. The Security Functional Requirements

Class	Components	
	FAU_GEN.1	Audit data generation
	FAU_GEN.2	User identification association
	FAU_SAA.1	Potential violation analysis
Security Audit	FAU_SAR.1	Audit review
	FAU_SAR.2	Restricted audit review
	FAU_SAR.3	Selectable audit review
	FAU_STG.1	Protected audit trail storage
	FCS_CKM.1	Cryptographic key generation
Cryptographic Support	FCS_CKM.2	Cryptographic key distribution
	FCS_CKM.3	Cryptographic key access
	FCS_CKM.4	Cryptographic key destruction
	FCS_COP.1	Cryptographic operation
	FDP_ACC.1	Subset access control
	FDP_ACF.1	Security attribute based access control
	FDP_DAU.1	Basic data authentication
	FDP_DAU.2	Data authentication with identity of guarantor
User Data Protection	FDP_ITT.1	Basic internal transfer protection
	FDP_RIP.1	Subset residual information protection
	FDP_RIP.2	Full residual information protection
	FDP_SDI.1	Stored data integrity monitoring
	FDP_UIT.1	Data exchange integrity
	FIA_ATD.1	User attribute definition
Identification & Authentication	FIA_SOS.1	Verification of secrets
	FIA_UAU.1	Timing of authentication
	FIA_UID.2	User identification before any action
	FMT_MOF.1	Management of security functions behavior
	FMT_MSA.1	Management of security attributes
Security Management	FMT_MSA.2	Secure security attributes
	FMT_MSA.3	Static attribute initialization
	FMT_SMR.1	Security roles
	FMT_SMR.2	Restrictions on security roles
Privacy	FPR_ANO.2	Anonymity without soliciting information
	FPR_PSE.1	Pseudonymity
	FPT_AMT.1	Abstract machine testing
	FPT_FLS.1	Failure with preservation of secure state
Protection of the TSF	FPT_PHP.1	Passive detection of physical attack
	FPT_RCV.1	Manual recovery
	FPT_STM.1	Reliable time stamp
	FPT_TST.1	TST testing
Fault Tolerance	FRU_RSA.2	Minimum and maximum quotas
Trusted Path/Channel	FTP_ITC.1	Inter-TSF trusted channel

Our protection profile adopts EAL 4+ level in common criteria. Because e-voting system is a critical information system and the result of attack can cause terrible confusion in society, we extend security assurance requirements to reinforce verification of implementation e-voting system. Extended requirements are ADV_IMP.2, ATE_DPT.3, AVA_VAN.4.

5 Comparison

In this section, we compare our protection profile to the existing protection profiles. BSI-PP-0031, PP-CIVIS, and IEEE P1583 consider the overall security requirements of e-voting system. However, the BSI-PP-0031 is aimed for the specific system which uses the digital pen, and the PP-CIVIS does not describe enough threats to the TOE assets. Moreover, they did not consider the voter verifiable audit trail. On the other hand, proposed protection profile overcomes these drawbacks. It considers the voter verifiability issues in the electoral process. In order to assure the highest level of security, we describe threats more precisely by referencing previous security analysis of e-voting systems and reduce the number of assumptions and OSPs as possible. Table 6 shows the differences between the existing and proposed PP of e-voting systems.

Table 6. Comparisons between the existing and proposed PP of e-voting systems

PP	BSI-PP-0031	PP-CIVIS	IEEE P1583	The Proposed PP
EAL	EAL3+	EAL2+	EAL2	EAL4+
CC Ver.	CC v2.3	CC v3.0	CC v2.3	CC v3.1
TOE Boundary	digital pen, docking station, firmware, software	DRE machine (hardware, software)	DRE machine (hardware, software)	DRE machine (hardware, software)
No. of T^1.	7	1	13	15
No. of A^2.	17	5	8	7
No. of P^3.	4	22	21	10
$VVAT^4$	X	X	X	O

^{1}: Threat, ^{2}:Assumption, ^{3}:OSP(Organization Security Policy), ^{4}: Voter Verifiable Audit Trail
X : Not provided, O : Provided

6 Conclusion

With increasing attention of e-government, the importance of secure e-voting system increases rapidly. However, many of voters cannot believe the black-box e-voting machines. Therefore, it is required that a protection profile for e-voting systems should consider the voter verifiability. To accomplish this, in this paper, we proposed a protection profile of an e-voting system for evaluation against CC and then discuss voter verifiability issues related to the electoral process. The proposed protection profile can be used to increase reliability of an entire e-voting process and tabulation result. Furthermore, these results can be used by both developers and consumers to evaluate the e-voting systems.

References

1. Mercuri, R.: A Better Ballot Box? IEEE Spectrum Online, 46–50 (October 2002)
2. Kohno, T., Stubblefield, A., Rubin, A.D., Wallach, D.: Analysis of an Electronic Voting System. In: Proceedings IEEE Symposium on Security and Privacy, Oakland, California, May 2004, pp. 27–42. IEEE Computer Society Press, Los Alamitos (2004)

3. Fujioka, Okamoto, T., Ohta, K.: A Practical Secret Voting Scheme for Large Scale Elections. In: Zheng, Y., Seberry, J. (eds.) AUSCRYPT 1992. LNCS, vol. 718, pp. 244–251. Springer, Heidelberg (1993)

4. Maaten, E.: Towards remote e-voting: Estonian case. In: Electronic Voting in Europe Proceedings of the 1st International Workshop on Electronic Voting, pp. 83–100 (2004)

5. Cetinkaya, O., Cetinkaya, D.: Verification and Validation Issues in Electronic Voting. The Electronic Journal of e-Government 5(2), 117–126 (2007)

6. Neff, A.C., Adler, J.: Verifiable e-Voting: Indisputable Electronic Elections at Polling Places. VoteHere Inc. (2003), http://votehere.com/vhti/documentation/VH_VHTi_WhitePaper.pdf

7. CCMB, Common Criteria for Information Technology Security Evaluation, version 3.1, CCMB-2006-09-004 (2006)

8. Oksana, S.: A Protection Profile and Its Content. In: SIBCON 2005 Proceeding, pp. 60–64 (2005)

9. Volkamer, M., Vogt, R.: Digitales wahlstift-system. Common Criteria Protection Profile BSI-PP-0031. Bundesamt für Sicherheit in der Informationstechnik (2006)

10. Secretariat general de la defense nationale, Protection Profile: Machine a voter, PP-CIVIS (2006), http://www.commoncriteriaportal.org/files/ppfiles/pp0604.pdf

11. IEEE P1583 SCC 38, IEEE P1583TM/D5.0 Draft standard for the Evaluation of Voting Equipment (2005)

12. Lee, Y., Lee, K., Kim, S., Won, D.: Efficient Voter Verifiable E-Voting Schemes with Cryptographic Receipts. In: Proc. of IAVoSS Workshop On Trustworthy Election (WOTE 2006), Cambridge, United Kingdom, pp. 145–152 (2006)

13. Sako, K., Kilian, J.: Reciept-free Mix-Type Voting Scheme. In: Guillou, L.C., Quisquater, J.-J. (eds.) EUROCRYPT 1995. LNCS, vol. 921, pp. 393–403. Springer, Heidelberg (1995)

14. Rubin, A.: Avi Rubin's e-voting page, http://avirubin.com/vote/

15. VSRW 2006 Threat Analyses for Voting System Categories (2006), http://vote.cs.gwu.edu/vsrw2006/

16. WOTE 2001 Workshop on Trustworthy Elections, http://www.vote.caltech.edu/wote01/

17. FEE2005 Workshop Frontiers in Electronic Elections, http://www.win.tue.nl/~berry/fee2005/program.html

18. Poulsenm, K.: E-Voting security debate comes home, http://www.securityfocus.com/news/2197

19. Morphy, E.: Study: Hackers Could Change E-Voting Machine Results, http://www.technewsworld.com/story/58572.html

20. McCullagh, D.: E-voting hobbled by security concerns, http://news.cnet.com/E-voting-hobbled-by-security-concerns/2100-1028_3-5889705.html

Author Index